Fourth Edition

Hands-On Ethical Hacking and Network Defense

MICHAEL T. SIMPSON
NICHOLAS D. ANTILL
ROBERT S. WILSON

٠٠ Cengage

Australia • Brazil • Canada • Mexico • Singapore • United Kingdom • United States

Hands-On Ethical Hacking and Network Defense, **Fourth Edition**

Michael T. Simpson, Nicholas D. Antill, and Robert S. Wilson

SVP, Higher Education Product Management: Erin Joyner

VP, Product Management, Learning Experiences: Thais Alencar

Product Director: Mark Santee

Product Manager: Natalie Onderdonk

Product Assistant: Ethan Wheel

Learning Designer: Natalie Onderdonk

Content Manager: Michele Stulga

Digital Delivery Quality Partner: Jim Vaughey

Technical Editor: Danielle Shaw

Developmental Editor: Lisa Ruffolo

VP, Product Marketing: Jason Sakos

Director, Product Marketing: Danaë April

Portfolio Marketing Manager: Mackenzie Paine

IP Analyst: Ann Hoffman

IP Project Manager: Ilakkiya Jayagopi, Lumina Datamatics

Production Service: Straive

Sr Designer: Erin Griffin

Cover Image Source: Rudchenko Liliia/ Shutterstock.com

For product information and technology assistance, contact us at **Cengage Customer & Sales Support, 1-800-354-9706 or support.cengage.com.**

For permission to use material from this text or product, submit all requests online at **www.copyright.com.**

Library of Congress Control Number: 2022930454

ISBN: 978-0-357-50975-3

Loose-leaf Edition:
ISBN: 978-0-357-50976-0

Cengage
200 Pier 4 Boulevard
Boston, MA 02210
USA

Cengage is a leading provider of customized learning solutions with employees residing in nearly 40 different countries and sales in more than 125 countries around the world. Find your local representative at **www.cengage.com**

To learn more about Cengage platforms and services, register or access your online learning solution, or purchase materials for your course, visit **www.cengage.com.**

Notice to the Reader

Publisher does not warrant or guarantee any of the products described herein or perform any independent analysis in connection with any of the product information contained herein. Publisher does not assume, and expressly disclaims, any obligation to obtain and include information other than that provided to it by the manufacturer. The reader is expressly warned to consider and adopt all safety precautions that might be indicated by the activities described herein and to avoid all potential hazards. By following the instructions contained herein, the reader willingly assumes all risks in connection with such instructions. The publisher makes no representations or warranties of any kind, including but not limited to, the warranties of fitness for particular purpose or merchantability, nor are any such representations implied with respect to the material set forth herein, and the publisher takes no responsibility with respect to such material. The publisher shall not be liable for any special, consequential, or exemplary damages resulting, in whole or part, from the readers' use of, or reliance upon, this material.

Printed at CLDPC, USA, 05-22

BRIEF CONTENTS

TABLE OF CONTENTS

INTRODUCTION

The need for security professionals who understand how attackers compromise networks is growing each day. You can't read the news without seeing an article on ransomware or personal information being stolen from unprotected databases. Since the first edition of *Hands-On Ethical Hacking and Network Defense* was published, the United States has created an organization with the sole purpose of countering cyber threats and attacks. Both public and private companies rely on skilled professionals to conduct test attacks on their networks as a way to discover vulnerabilities before attackers do. "Ethical hacker" is one term used to describe these professionals; others are "security tester" or "penetration tester."

This course isn't intended to provide comprehensive training in security testing or penetration testing. It does, however, introduce security testing to those who are new to the field. This course is intended for novices who have a thorough grounding in computer and networking basics but want to learn how to protect networks by using an attacker's knowledge to compromise network security. By understanding what tools and methods a hacker uses to break into a network, security testers can protect systems from these attacks.

The purpose of this course is to guide you toward becoming a skilled security tester. This profession requires creativity and critical thinking, which are sometimes difficult skills to learn in an academic environment. However, with an open mind and a willingness to learn, you can think outside the box and learn to ask more questions than this course or your instructor poses. Being able to dig past the surface to solve a problem takes patience and the willingness to admit that sometimes there's no simple answer.

Conducting a security test involves more than running exploits against a system and informing your client of existing vulnerabilities. Isn't it possible that you neglected to test for some areas that might be vulnerable to attacks? Haphazard approaches undermine the security profession and expose companies to theft. The goal of this course is to offer a more structured approach to conducting a security test and to introduce novices to professional certifications available in this growing field.

INTENDED AUDIENCE

Although people with a wide range of backgrounds can take this course, it's intended for those with a Security+ and Network+ certification or equivalent. A networking background is necessary so that you understand how computers operate in a networked environment and can work with a network administrator when needed. In addition, readers must know how to use a computer from the command line and how to use popular operating systems, such as Windows and Kali Linux.

This course can be used at any educational level, from technical high schools and community colleges to graduate students. Current professionals in the public and private sectors can also use this course.

NEW TO THIS EDITION

This fourth edition of *Hands-On Ethical Hacking and Network Defense* includes:

- Updated discussions and examples of new hacking tools
- Updated discussion of recent vulnerabilities and exploits
- Updated Internet of Things (IoT) security section and updated discussion of embedded devices
- Updated section regarding web application hacking, security, and web-hacking tools
- Additional in-depth review questions that require research and reporting on key security topics
- A new **Final Project** module where you create a penetration testing report by testing a lab of virtual machines for vulnerabilities using some of the tools and methodologies discussed in the course

MODULE DESCRIPTIONS

Following is a summary of the topics covered in each module of this course:

- **Module 1,** "Ethical Hacking Overview," defines what an ethical hacker can and can't do legally. This module also describes the roles of security and penetration testers and reviews certifications that are current at the time of publication.
- **Module 2,** "TCP/IP Concepts Review," describes the layers of the TCP/IP protocol stack and important ports and reviews IP addressing along with binary, octal, and hexadecimal numbering systems.
- **Module 3,** "Network and Computer Attacks," defines types of malicious software, explains methods for protecting against malware attacks, and discusses types of network attacks and physical security.
- **Module 4,** "Footprinting and Social Engineering," explores using web tools for footprinting and methods of gathering competitive intelligence. It also describes DNS zone transfers and social engineering methods.
- **Module 5,** "Port Scanning," explains the types of port scans and describes how to use port-scanning tools, how to conduct ping sweeps, and how to use shell scripting to automate security tasks.
- **Module 6,** "Enumeration," describes steps and tools for enumerating operating systems, such as Windows and UNIX/Linux.
- **Module 7,** "Programming for Security Professionals," gives you an overview of programming concepts as they relate to network and computer security.
- **Module 8,** "Desktop and Server OS Vulnerabilities," discusses vulnerabilities in Windows and Linux and explains best practices for hardening computers and servers running these operating systems.
- **Module 9,** "Embedded Operating Systems: The Hidden Threat," explains what embedded operating systems are and where they're used and describes known vulnerabilities and best practices for protecting embedded operating systems.
- **Module 10,** "Hacking Web Servers," explains web applications and their vulnerabilities and describes the tools used to attack web servers.
- **Module 11,** "Hacking Wireless Networks," gives you an overview of wireless technology and IEEE wireless standards. This module also covers wireless authentication, wardriving, and wireless hacking tools and countermeasures.
- **Module 12,** "Cryptography," summarizes the history and principles of cryptography, explains encryption algorithms and public key infrastructure components, and offers examples of different attacks on cryptosystems.
- **Module 13,** "Network Protection Systems," covers a variety of devices used to protect networks, such as routers, firewalls, and intrusion detection and prevention systems.
- **Module 14,** "Hands-On Ethical Hacking Final Project," guides you through the process of creating a penetration testing report document by using some of the tools and methodologies discussed in the course to test a lab of virtual machines for vulnerabilities.

- **Appendix A,** "Legal Resources," lists state laws affecting network security and provides applicable excerpts from the Computer Fraud and Abuse Act.
- **Appendix B,** "Resources," lists additional reference books and important URLs referenced throughout the modules.

FEATURES

To help you understand computer and network security, this course includes many features designed to enhance your learning experience:

- *Module objectives*—Each module begins with a detailed list of the concepts to master. This list gives you a quick reference to the module's contents and serves as a useful study aid.
- *Figures and tables*—Numerous screenshots show you how to use security tools, including command-line tools, and how to create programs. In addition, a variety of diagrams aid you in visualizing important concepts. Tables present information in an organized, easy-to-grasp manner.
- *Hands-on activities*—One of the best ways to reinforce learning about network security and security testing is to practice using the many tools security testers use. Hands-on activities are interspersed throughout each module to give you practice in applying what you have learned.
- *Notes*—Notes draw your attention to helpful material related to the subject being covered. In addition, notes with the title "Security Bytes" offer real-world examples related to security topics in each module.
- *Tips*—Tips offer extra information on resources and how to solve problems.
- *Caution*—Caution icons warn you about potential mistakes or problems and explain how to avoid them.
- *Module summary*—Each module ends with a summary of the concepts introduced in the module. These summaries are a helpful way to review the material covered in each module.
- *Key terms*—All terms in the module introduced with bold text are gathered together in the key terms list at the end of the module. This useful reference encourages a more thorough understanding of the module's key concepts. A full definition of each key term is provided in the Glossary.
- *Review questions*—The end-of-module assessment begins with review questions that reinforce the main concepts and techniques covered in each module. Answering these questions helps ensure that you have mastered important topics.
- *Case projects*—Each module closes with one or more case projects that help you evaluate and apply the material you have learned. To complete these projects, you must draw on real-world common sense as well as your knowledge of the technical topics covered to that point in the course. Your goal for each project is to come up with answers to problems similar to those you'll face as a working security tester. To help you with this goal, many case projects are based on a hypothetical company typical of companies hiring security consultants.

MINDTAP

MindTap for *Hands-On Ethical Hacking and Network Defense* is an online learning solution designed to help you master the skills needed in today's workforce. Research shows employers need critical thinkers, troubleshooters, and creative problem-solvers to stay relevant in our fast-paced, technology-driven world. MindTap helps you achieve this with assignments and activities that provide hands-on practice, real-life relevance, and mastery of difficult concepts. Students are guided through assignments that progress from basic knowledge and understanding to more challenging problems. MindTap activities and assignments are tied to learning objectives. MindTap features include the following:

- *Live Virtual Machine labs* allow you to practice, explore, and try different solutions in a safe sandbox environment. Each module provides you with an opportunity to complete an in-depth project hosted in a live virtual machine environment. You implement the skills and knowledge gained in the module through real design and configuration scenarios in a private cloud created with OpenStack.
- *The Adaptive Test Prep (ATP)* app is designed to help you quickly review and assess your understanding of key IT concepts. Test yourself multiple times to track your progress and improvement by filtering results by correct answers, by all questions answered, or only by incorrect answers to show where additional study help is needed.
- *Security for Life* assignments encourage you to stay current with what's happening in the IT field.
- *Pre- and Post-Quizzes* assess your understanding of key concepts at the beginning and end of the course.
- *Reflection* activities encourage classroom and online discussion of key issues covered in the modules.

Instructors, MindTap is designed around learning objectives and provides analytics and reporting so you can easily see where the class stands in terms of progress, engagement, and completion rates. Use the content and learning path as is or pick and choose how your materials will integrate with the learning path. You control what the students see and when they see it. Visit https://www.cengage.com/mindtap/ to learn more.

INSTRUCTOR RESOURCES

Instructors, please visit cengage.com and sign in to access instructor-specific resources, which include the instructor manual, solutions manual, PowerPoint presentations, and figure files.

- **Instructor manual.** The instructor manual that accompanies this course provides additional instructional material to assist in class preparation, including suggestions for classroom activities, discussion topics, and additional projects.
- **Solutions and Answer Guide.** Answers to the review questions, scenario-based practice questions, performance-based questions, case projects, and reflection activities are provided.
- **PowerPoint presentations.** This course comes with Microsoft PowerPoint slides for each module. These are included as a teaching aid for classroom presentation, to make available to students on the network for module review, or to be printed for classroom distribution. Instructors, please feel at liberty to add your own slides for additional topics you introduce to the class.
- **Figure files.** All of the figures in the course are reproduced on the Instructor Resource Site. Similar to the PowerPoint presentations, these are included as a teaching aid for classroom presentation, to make available to students for review, or to be printed for classroom distribution.

LAB REQUIREMENTS

The hands-on activities in this course help you apply what you have learned about conducting security or penetration tests. The following are the minimum system requirements for completing all activities:

- Computers that boot to Windows 10 or later.
- Access to the Internet, with each computer configured to receive IP configuration information from a router running DHCP
- Kali Linux for hands-on activities. This could be a live bootable version of Kali Linux on a USB, a Kali Linux Virtual Machine, or a computer with a full Kali Linux operating system installation.

Operating Systems and Hardware

The Windows activities in this course were designed for Windows 10 but should also run on Windows 11. Computers should meet the following minimum requirements:

- If you plan to run Kali Linux from a USB flash drive, you need a PC with BIOS that supports booting from a USB drive and an 8 GB USB flash drive with a minimum 15 MB/second read and write speed
- Video card with 512 MB video RAM
- 80 GB hard drive
- 1.5 GHz 32-bit or 64-bit processor
- 8 GB system RAM
- Wireless card for some optional wireless activities
- Mouse or another pointing device and a keyboard

Security-Testing Tools

This course includes hands-on activities that involve using many security tools. You can download these tools as freeware, shareware, or free home and educational versions. Because website addresses change frequently, use a search engine to find tools if the URL listed in an activity is no longer valid.

In addition, you use Microsoft Office Word (or other word-processing software) and need to have email software installed on your computer.

ABOUT THE AUTHORS

Michael T. Simpson is president/senior consultant of MTS Consulting, Inc., specializing in network security and network design. Mike's certifications include CEH, CISSP, Security+, OSSTMM Professional Security Tester (OPST), OSSTMM Professional Security Analyst (OPSA), MCSE, MCDBA, MCSD, MCT, and OCP. He has authored or co-authored eight books and has more than 30 years of industry experience, including 20 years with the Department of Defense (DoD), where he designed and configured computer networks and served as an Oracle database administrator, UNIX administrator, and information systems security officer (ISSO).

Nicholas D. Antill is a seasoned information security professional with over 10 years of specialized cybersecurity experience. Nicholas specializes in penetration testing, proactive security controls, and network defense. He holds many industry certifications, including the OSCP, GWAPT, GPEN, GCIH, CISA, CISSP, and GCFE. Nicholas currently manages the ethical hacking program at a large U.S. financial institution. He started his career at a small grocery chain in Pittsburgh, Pennsylvania, where he developed a fascination with network attack and defense techniques. He worked in support of both the U.S. Department of Justice and the U.S. Department of Defense before returning to the private sector.

Robert S. Wilson is the Cybersecurity Curriculum Coordinator and a cybersecurity instructor for Willis College (Canada's oldest career college). Rob created Willis College's Software Development and Cybersecurity Analyst (CSA) programs. Willis College's CSA program is currently being used by the Canadian military to train cyber operator recruits. Rob has a Computer Science degree from the University of Waterloo, holds numerous certifications from CompTIA, Microsoft, and Cisco, and has over 40 years of experience in the computing field. Rob has expertise in many areas including real-time programming and embedded systems development (having worked for a company that has software on Mars), database development and administration, network and domain administration, penetration testing, and cybersecurity.

ACKNOWLEDGMENTS

Creating the fourth edition of *Hands-On Ethical Hacking and Network Defense* was a group effort. I couldn't have completed my contributions without the invaluable assistance of the following people.

First, I would like to thank Sam Mozner, Senior National Account Manager from Cengage Canada. Who knew that a simple query to Sam about the availability of Cengage content would lead to me creating Cengage content? I wouldn't have had the opportunity to pen the fourth edition of this book if Sam hadn't suggested me as an author to his coworkers. Writing this book has been immensely exciting and satisfying. I look forward to the next book.

Second, I would like to thank all my students past and present. It's true that I gave a lot of myself in the classroom to guide you in your education and help you achieve your next career, but many of you have also given back to me. Those of you that I have kept in touch with and continued to mentor in your careers have provided me with invaluable insight into the real-world happenings in our field. Thank you for keeping me connected and current.

Next, I would like to thank the team from Cengage that worked with me and guided me throughout this edition of the book. Michele Stulga, Cengage Content Manager: Thank you, Michele, for guiding and coordinating this ship and keeping it on course, and for keeping me; the captain of the ship, aware of objects on the horizon. Lisa Ruffolo, my editor: Thank you, Lisa, for making me seem smarter. Your skill in the English language is unmatched and I hope you will be my editor on my next project so that I continue to seem smarter. Danielle Klahr, former Associate Product Manager and now Product Marketing Manager: Thank you, Danielle, for helping me learn the ways of Cengage authorship and for continuing to support me even after moving into your marketing position. Natalie Onderdonk, Learning Designer and now Product Manager: Natalie, I appreciate your expertise in designing learning content and how you passed that knowledge on to me. I look forward to your guidance as Product Manager for my next book.

Thank you to the copyeditors who used their observational skills to point out errors, omissions, and anomalies in each module before it was committed to print. I am very impressed with your abilities to find needles in haystacks.

Thank you to the many reviewers who read each module of the book and provided valuable feedback. Your suggestions greatly improved each module. Your time and efforts were truly appreciated.

Thank you to reviewers Shawn Brown, Elizabethtown Community and Technical College; Jenelle Davis, Colorado Christian University; Mike Saylor, Collin College; and Ping Wang, Robert Morris University.

And finally, thank you to the previous authors upon whose shoulders I stood to complete this fourth edition, Michael T. Simpson and Nicholas D. Antill. Thank you, gentlemen, for going before me and blazing the trail.

DEDICATION

This book is dedicated to my grandson, Harrison Begrande. Some of my fondest memories are of Harrison and me sitting in the shower of the lawn sprinkler on hot summer days, playing with cars, Legos, and action figures. If I could freeze a moment in time and live in it forever, I would choose one of those moments. In my lifetime the growth of technology has been astounding. I wonder what new technological marvels will be created in Harry's lifetime?

KALI LINUX

Kali Linux is used throughout this course for many of the hands-on activities. To run Kali Linux, you have the following options:

- Install Kali Linux as a virtual machine with free virtualization software, such as VMware Server or VirtualBox. The advantage of using a virtual machine is that it enables you to run Kali and Windows at the same time.
- Install Kali Linux on a USB flash drive with at least 8 GB storage capacity. With this method, you can move your personalized Linux system and run it on any system. You can also save files and reports on this drive.

- Install Kali Linux in a dual-boot arrangement with Windows. Dual-boot installations can vary depending on the hardware and require some complex steps if BitLocker or other disk encryption is used. Dual-boot installation isn't explained in this course, but you can find plenty of information online.
- Install Kali Linux directly on computer hardware as the only operating system. If you do this, make sure not to overwrite any existing operating system.

CREATING A BOOTABLE USB FLASH DRIVE

To install Kali Linux on a USB flash drive, you need a drive with a capacity of at least 8 GB. Note that the speed of some flash drives isn't adequate for running a live Linux OS. Performance improvements can be substantial if you use a flash drive with faster read and write speeds. For the best results, a flash drive with a minimum of 15 MB/second read and write speed is recommended. You can check websites, such as https://usb.userbenchmark.com, for performance benchmarks to help you choose a suitable drive within your budget.

After you find the proper flash drive, you'll find up-to-date USB installation instructions on the Kali Linux website (https://www.kali.org/docs/usb/). The website provides installation instructions for those using Windows, Linux, or macOS. These instructions walk you through downloading Kali Linux to booting into Kali Linux for the first time. You must make sure your Kali Linux software is up to date, so run the `apt-get update` and `apt-get upgrade` commands, which check the Kali Linux repositories for updates.

INSTALLING NEW SOFTWARE

Because Kali is a Debian-based Linux distribution, thousands of free programs are available that you can download and install with just a few commands. These programs, which are specific to an OS version, are stored on Internet archives called repositories. To install new software, you can use the command `apt-get install` *packagename* (replacing *packagename* with the name of the software package you want to install). If you don't know the software package name, use a search engine to look it up.

COMMUNITY SUPPORT FOR KALI LINUX

To find the most recent Kali Linux updates and online forums for help in solving problems, visit www.kali.org. This website is a good place to start if you want to learn more about Kali Linux.

ETHICAL HACKING OVERVIEW

After reading this module and completing the exercises, you will be able to:

1. Describe the role of an ethical hacker
2. Explain what you can do legally as an ethical hacker
3. Describe what you can't do as an ethical hacker

The term "ethical hacker" might seem like an oxymoron—like an ethical pickpocket or ethical embezzler. In this module, you learn that ethical hackers are employed or contracted by companies to do what illegal hackers do: break in. Why? Companies need to know what, if any, parts of their security infrastructure are vulnerable to attack. To protect a company's network, many security professionals recognize that knowing what tools the cyber attackers use and how they think helps to better protect (harden) a network's security.

Remember the old adage: You're only as secure as your weakest link. Cyber attackers spend a lot of time and energy trying to find weak links. This course provides the tools you need to protect a network and shares some approaches an ethical hacker—also called a "security tester" or a "penetration tester"—might use to discover vulnerabilities in a network. The course is by no means a definitive study of ethical hacking. Rather, it gives you an overview of a security tester's role and includes activities to help you develop the skills you need to protect a network from attack. This course helps you understand how to protect a network when you discover the methods the bad actors (hackers) or the good actors (ethical hackers, also known as white hat hackers) use to break into a network. It also helps you select the most appropriate tools to make your job easier.

As a security professional, you will need to understand what laws can affect you when performing your job as a security tester, especially if you use the testing methods outlined in this course. Another topic covered in the text, understanding the importance of having a contractual agreement with a client before performing any aspects of a security test, might help you avoid breaking the law.

INTRODUCTION TO ETHICAL HACKING

Companies sometimes hire ethical hackers to conduct penetration tests. In a penetration test, an ethical hacker attempts to break into a company's network or applications to find weak links. In a vulnerability assessment, the tester attempts to enumerate all the vulnerabilities found in an application or on a system. Often, a vulnerability assessment is done first to identify targets for penetration testing. In a security test, testers do more than attempt to break in; they also analyze a company's security policy and procedures and report any vulnerabilities to management. Security testing, in other words, takes penetration testing to a higher level. As Peter Herzog states in the *Open Source Security*

Testing Methodology Manual, "[Security testing] relies on a combination of creativeness, expansion [of] knowledge bases of best practices, legal issues, and client industry regulations as well as known threats and the breadth of the target organization's security presence (or point of risk)."

These are only some of the issues security testers must examine. In doing so, they alert companies to areas that need to be monitored or secured. As a security tester, you can't make a network impenetrable. The only way to do that with certainty is to unplug the network cable. When you discover vulnerabilities ("holes") in a network, you can correct them. This process might entail tasks such as updating an operating system (OS), eliminating unnecessary applications or services, or installing a vendor's latest security patch.

If your job is a penetration tester, you simply report your findings to the company. It's up to the company to make the final decision on how to use the information you have supplied. However, as a security tester, you might also be required to offer solutions for securing or protecting the network. The modules in this course are written with the assumption that you're working toward becoming a network security professional in charge of protecting a corporate network, so the emphasis is on using a security tester's skills to secure or protect a network.

In this course, you learn how to find vulnerabilities in a network and correct them. A security tester's job is to document all vulnerabilities and alert management and information technology (IT) staff of areas that need special attention.

The Role of Security and Penetration Testers

A hacker accesses a computer system or network without the authorization of the systems owner. By doing so, a hacker is breaking the law and can go to prison. Those who break into systems to steal or destroy data are often referred to as crackers; hackers might only want to prove how vulnerable a system is by accessing the computer or network without destroying any data. For the purpose of this course, no distinction is made between the terms "hackers" and "crackers." The U.S. Department of Justice labels all illegal access to computer or network systems as "hacking," and this course follows that usage.

An ethical hacker is a person who performs most of the same activities a hacker does but with the permission of the owner or company. This distinction is important and can mean the difference between being charged with a crime and not being charged. Ethical hackers are usually contracted to perform penetration tests or security tests. Companies realize that intruders might attempt to access their network resources and are willing to pay for someone to discover these vulnerabilities first. Companies would rather pay a "good hacker" to discover problems in their current network configuration than have a "bad hacker" discover these vulnerabilities. Bad hackers spend many hours scanning systems over the Internet, looking for openings or vulnerable systems.

Some hackers are skillful computer experts, but others are younger, inexperienced people who experienced hackers refer to as script kiddies or packet monkeys. These derogatory terms refer to people who copy code or use tools created by knowledgeable programmers without understanding how they work. Many experienced penetration testers can write programs or scripts in Python, Ruby, Perl, or C to carry out attacks. (A script is a set of instructions that runs in sequence to perform tasks on a computer system.) You have a chance to write a script in one of these languages in a later module.

A person who hacks computer systems for political or social reasons is called a hacktivist. For several years, the hacktivist group known as Anonymous wreaked havoc on federal government computer systems as well as those in the private sector. The group once threatened to release the names of Ku Klux Klan (KKK) members after hacking the organization's Twitter account. This type of hacking is called "hacktivism."

Nation-states are now engaging in cyber hacking attacks with greater frequency and sophistication. The infamous SolarWinds supply chain attack that compromised government agencies and even cybersecurity companies was a nation-state cyber attack perpetrated by Russia.

An Internet search on IT job recruiter sites for "penetration tester" produces hundreds of job announcements, many from Fortune 500 companies looking for experienced applicants. A typical ad might include the following requirements:

- Perform vulnerability, attack, and penetration assessments in Internet, intranet, and wireless environments.
- Perform discovery and scanning for open ports and services.
- Apply appropriate exploits to gain access and expand access as necessary.
- Participate in activities involving application penetration testing and application source code review.
- Interact with the client as required throughout the engagement.
- Produce reports documenting discoveries during the engagement.
- Debrief with the client at the conclusion of each engagement.

- Participate in research and provide recommendations for continuous improvement.
- Participate in knowledge sharing.
- Demonstrate a good understanding of current country, state, and city cyber laws.

Penetration testers and security testers usually have a laptop computer configured with multiple OSs and hacking tools. This course uses Windows, Kali Linux, and other Linux tools needed to conduct actual network and web application attacks. Learning how to install an OS isn't covered in this book, but you can find resources on this topic easily. The most recent versions of Kali Linux can be found at www.kali.org. The procedure for installing security tools varies, depending on the tool and the OS.

Activity 1-1: Determining the Corporate Need for IT Security Professionals

Time Required: 10 minutes

Objective: Examine corporations looking to employ IT security professionals.

Description: Many companies are eager to employ or contract security testers for their corporate networks. In this activity, you search the Internet for job postings, using the keywords "IT Security," and read some job descriptions to determine the IT skills (as well as any non-IT skills) most companies want an applicant to possess.

1. Start your web browser, and go to **indeed.com**.
2. In the What search box, type **IT Security**. In the Where search box, enter the name of a major city near you, and then press **Enter**.
3. Note the number of jobs. Select three to five job postings, and read the job description in each posting.
4. When you're finished, exit your web browser.

SECURITY BYTES

The urgent cybersecurity needs of organizations has created a labor shortage for qualified security professionals. In response, a company called Synack developed a "crowdsourced" model to provide ethical hacking services. Synack created a software platform that offers automated ways for companies to discover security flaws; then it turns those vulnerabilities over to penetration testers—basically, ethical hackers who use their skills for good. These ethical hackers are freelancers hired online on a job-by-job basis. If you choose to become an ethical hacker, you will find many employment opportunities and enjoy long-term job security.[1]

Penetration-Testing Methodologies

Ethical hackers who perform penetration tests use one of these models:

- White box model
- Black box model
- Gray box model

In the white box model, the tester is told what network topology and technology the company is using and is given permission to interview IT personnel and company employees. For example, the company might print a network diagram showing all the company's routers, switches, firewalls, and intrusion detection systems (IDSs; see Figure 1-1) or give the tester a floor plan detailing the location of computer systems and the OSs running on these systems (see Figure 1-2).

This background information makes the penetration tester's job easier than it is with using the black box model. In the black box model, management doesn't divulge to staff that penetration testing is being conducted, nor does it give the tester any diagrams or describe what technologies the company is using. This model puts the burden on the tester to find this information by using techniques you learn throughout this course. This model also helps management see whether the company's security personnel can detect an attack.

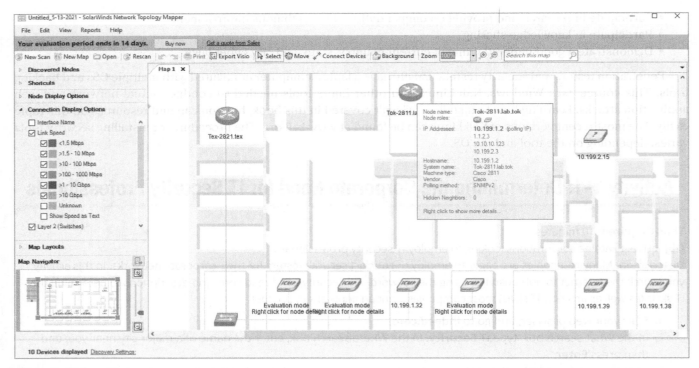

Figure 1-1   Network diagram

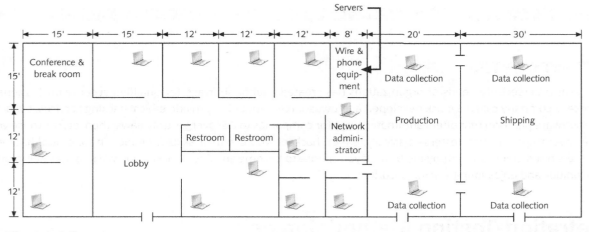

Figure 1-2   Sample floor plan

The **gray box model** is a hybrid of the white and black box models. In this model, the company gives the tester only partial information. For example, the tester might acquire information about which OSs are used but not receive any network diagrams.

SECURITY BYTES

Hospitals often check the intake procedures medical staff perform by having interns and nurses pose as "potential patients." In one psychiatric hospital, intake staff was told in advance that some people presenting as patients would actually be doctors or nurses. Surprisingly, the number of patients admitted that month was unusually low, even though none of the patients were interns or nurses, indicating the intake staff altered its behavior because of the advance notice. In the same vein, if a company knows that it's being monitored to assess the security of its systems, employees might behave more vigilantly and adhere to existing procedures. Many companies don't want this false sense of security; they want to see how personnel operate without forewarning that someone might attempt to attack their network.

Certification Programs for Network Security Personnel

As most IT professionals are aware, professional certification is available in just about every area of network security. The following sections cover several applicable certifications. Whether you're a security professional, computer programmer, database administrator, or network specialist, professional organizations offer enough certifications and exams to keep you busy for the rest of your career. You should have already earned, at minimum, CompTIA Security+ certification or have equivalent knowledge, which assumes networking competence at the CompTIA Network+ level of knowledge, a prerequisite for the Security+ certification. For more details, visit the CompTIA website (www.comptia.org).

CompTIA PenTest+

The PenTest+ certification (www.comptia.org) is an advanced certification that verifies successful candidates have the knowledge and skills required to plan and scope an assessment, understand legal and compliance requirements, perform vulnerability scanning and penetration testing, analyze data, and effectively report and communicate results. The following domains (subject areas) are covered by the certification exam:

- Planning and scoping
- Information gathering
- Vulnerability identification
- Attacks and exploits
- Penetration testing tools
- Reporting and communication

Offensive Security Certified Professional

The Offensive Security Certified Professional (OSCP; www.offensive-security.com) is an advanced certification that requires students to demonstrate hands-on abilities to earn their certificates. It covers network and application exploits and gives students experience in developing rudimentary buffer overflows, writing scripts to collect and manipulate data, and trying exploits on vulnerable systems.

Certified Ethical Hacker

The International Council of Electronic Commerce Consultants (EC-Council) has developed a certification designation called Certified Ethical Hacker (CEH; www.eccouncil.org). Currently, the multiple-choice CEH exam is based on 22 domains the tester must be familiar with. Knowledge requirements change periodically, so if you're interested in taking this exam, visit the EC-Council website for the most up-to-date information. The 22 domains tested in the CEH exam are as follows:

- Ethics and legal issues
- Footprinting
- Scanning
- Enumeration
- System hacking
- Trojans and backdoors
- Sniffers
- Denial of service
- Social engineering
- Session hijacking
- Hacking web servers
- Web application vulnerabilities
- Web-based password-cracking techniques
- Structured Query Language (SQL) injection
- Hacking wireless networks
- Viruses and worms
- Physical security
- Hacking Linux
- IDSs, firewalls, and honeypots

- Buffer overflows
- Cryptography
- Penetration-testing methodologies

As you can see, you must be familiar with a vast amount of information to pass this exam. Although you do need a general knowledge of these 22 domains for the exam, in the workplace, you'll most likely be placed on a team that conducts penetration tests. This team, called a red team in the industry, is composed of people with varied skills who perform the tests. For example, a red team might include a programming expert who can perform SQL injections or other programming vulnerability testing. The team might also include a network expert who's familiar with port vulnerabilities and IDS, router, or firewall vulnerabilities. It's unlikely that one person will perform all tests. However, passing the exam requires general knowledge of all the domains listed.

Open Source Security Testing Methodology Manual Professional Security Tester

The OSSTMM Professional Security Tester (OPST) certification is designated by the Institute for Security and Open Methodologies (ISECOM; www.isecom.org), a nonprofit organization that provides security training and certification programs for security professionals. The OPST certification uses the Open Source Security Testing Methodology Manual (OSSTMM), written by Peter Herzog, as its standardized methodology. You'll use many of its methodologies throughout this course. Because the manual is updated periodically, you should check the ISECOM site regularly to download the most current version.

The exam covers some of the following topics:

- *Professional*—Rules of engagement (defining your conduct as a security tester)
- *Enumeration*—Internet packet types, denial-of-service testing
- *Assessments*—Network surveying, controls, competitive intelligence scouting
- *Application*—Password cracking, containment measures
- *Verification*—Problem solving, security testing

The exam requires testers to answer multiple-choice questions and successfully conduct security testing on an attack network. This practical-application portion of the exam ensures that testers can apply their knowledge to a real-world setting.

Certified Information Systems Security Professional

The Certified Information Systems Security Professional (CISSP) certification for security professionals is issued by the International Information Systems Security Certification Consortium (ISC²; www.isc2.org). Even though the CISSP certification isn't geared toward the technical IT professional, it has become one of the standards for many security professionals. The exam doesn't require testers to have technical knowledge in IT; it tests security-related managerial skills. CISSPs are usually more concerned with policies and procedures than the actual tools for conducting security tests or penetration tests, so they don't need the skills of a technical IT professional. ISC² requires exam takers to have five years of experience before taking the five-hour exam, so don't rush into this certification until you've been in the industry a while. The exam covers questions from the following 10 domains:

- Security and risk management
- Asset security (protecting security of assets)
- Security engineering (engineering and management of security)
- Communication and network security (designing and protecting network security)
- Identity and access management (controlling access and managing identity)
- Security assessment and testing (designing, performing, and analyzing security testing)
- Security operations (foundational concepts, investigations, incident management, and disaster recovery)
- Software development security (understanding, applying, and enforcing software security)

SANS Institute

The SysAdmin, Audit, Network, Security (SANS) Institute (www.sans.org) offers training and IT security certifications through Global Information Assurance Certification (GIAC, www.giac.org). Two related certifications in ethical hacking are the GIAC Certified Penetration Tester (GPEN) and the GIAC Certified Web Application Tester (GWAPT).

In addition to its well-respected certification, SANS offers its training courses through an accredited university, SANS Technology Institute. Alongside its training and degree programs, SANS disseminates research documents on computer and network security worldwide at no cost. One of its most popular documents is the Top 25 Software Errors list, which describes the most common network exploits and suggests ways of correcting vulnerabilities. This list offers a wealth of information for penetration testers or security professionals, and you examine it in Activity 1-2.

Which Certification Is Best?

Deciding which certification exam to take can be difficult. Both penetration testers and security testers need technical skills to perform their duties effectively. They must also have a good understanding of networks and the role of management in an organization, skills in writing and verbal communication, and a desire to continue learning. Any certification, if it encourages you to read and study more, is worth working toward. Being certified gives you a hiring advantage over someone who is not. If you have certifications in the area an employer is looking for, your resume will often go to the top of the prospects pile. The danger of certification exams is that some participants simply memorize terminology and don't have a good grasp of the subject matter or complex concepts, much like students who have managed to pass a final exam by cramming but then forget most of the information after taking the test. Use the time you spend studying for a certification exam wisely, discovering areas in which you might need improvement instead of memorizing answers to questions.

By learning the material in this course, you can acquire the skills you need to become a competent IT security professional and pass exams covering ethical hacking, penetration-testing methods, and network topologies and technologies. Regardless of the exam you take, however, the most critical point to remember is that laws govern what you can or cannot do as an ethical hacker, a security tester, or a penetration tester. Following the laws and behaving ethically are more important than passing an exam.

Be sure to visit websites for the organizations conducting certification testing because exam requirements change as rapidly as technology does. For example, several years ago, the CISSP exam had no questions on the Internet of Things (IoT), but now the exam covers this topic.

NOTE

Be aware that websites change often. You might have to dig around to find the information you're looking for. Think of this activity as practice for being a skilled security tester.

Activity 1-2: Examining the Top 25 Most Dangerous Software Flaws

Time Required: 15 minutes

Objective: Examine the SANS list of the most common network exploits.

Description: As fast as IT security professionals attempt to correct network vulnerabilities, someone creates new exploits, and network security professionals must keep up to date on these exploits. In this activity, you examine some current exploits used to attack networks. Don't worry—you won't have to memorize your findings. This activity simply gives you an introduction to the world of network security.

1. Start your web browser, and go to **www.sans.org**.
2. Under Resources, click the **Top 25 Programming Errors** link. (Because websites change frequently, you might have to search to find this link.)
3. Read the contents of the Top 25 list. (This document changes often to reflect the many new exploits created daily.) The Top 25 list is also known as the Top 25 Most Dangerous Software Errors. Links in the list explain the scoring system and framework used to rank these errors.
4. Investigate the first few flaws by clicking the **CWE-#** link. For each flaw, note the description, applicable platform, and consequences.
5. When you're finished, exit your web browser.

WHAT YOU CAN DO LEGALLY

Because laws involving computer technology change as rapidly as technology itself, you must keep abreast of what's happening in your area of the world. What's legal in Des Moines might not be legal in Indianapolis, for example. Finding out what's legal in your state or country can be just as difficult as performing penetration tests, however. Many state officials aren't aware of the legalities surrounding computer technology. This confusion also makes it difficult to prosecute wrongdoers in computer crimes. The average citizen on a jury doesn't want to send a person to jail for doing something the state prosecutor hasn't clearly defined as illegal.

As a security tester, you must be aware of what you're allowed to do and what you should not or cannot do. For example, some security testers know how to pick a deadbolt lock, so a locked door wouldn't deter them from gaining physical access to a server. However, testers must be knowledgeable about the laws for possessing lockpicks before venturing out to a corporate site with tools in hand. In fact, laws vary from state to state and country to country. In some states, the mere possession of lockpicking tools constitutes a crime, whereas other states allow possession as long as a crime hasn't been committed. In one state, you might be charged with a misdemeanor for possessing these tools; in another state, you might be charged with a felony.

 TIP   The Open Organisation of Lockpickers (TOOOL) is worth a look if you are considering adding this skill to your arsenal. Their website, https://toool.us/laws.html, makes it easy for you to check the laws in each state before your pack your suitcase with your lockpicking tools.

Laws of the Land

As with lockpicking tools, having hacking tools on your computer or mobile device might be illegal. You could contact local law enforcement agencies or research online about the laws for your state or country before installing hacking tools on your devices. You can see how complex this issue gets as you travel from state to state or country to country. New York City might have one law for installing hacking tools, and a quick drive over the George Washington Bridge brings you to a different law in New Jersey. Table A-1, in Appendix A, compares Vermont's computer crime statutes to New York's to demonstrate the variety of verbiage the legal community uses.

Laws are written to protect society, but often the written words are open to interpretation, which is why courts and judges are necessary. In Hawaii, for example, the state must prove that the person charged with committing a crime on a computer had the "intent to commit a crime." So just scanning a network isn't a crime in Hawaii. Also, the state has the even more difficult task of having to prove that the computer used in committing a crime had been used by only one person—the one alleged to have committed the crime. If the person charged with the crime claims that more than one person had access to the computer used to gather evidence of wrongdoing, the state can't use that computer as evidence.

What do these laws have to do with a network security professional using penetration-testing tools? Laws for having hacking tools that allow you to view a company's network infrastructure aren't as clearly defined as laws for possession of lockpicking tools because laws haven't been able to keep up with the speed of technological advances. In some states, running a program that gives an attacker an overview and a detailed description of a company's network infrastructure isn't seen as a threat.

As another example of how laws can vary, is taking photos of a bank's exterior and interior legal? Security personnel at a bank in Hawaii say you would be asked to stop taking photos and leave the premises. An FBI spokesperson put it in simple terms: You can be asked to stop taking photos if you're on private property. Taking photos across the street from the bank with a zoom lens is legal, but if you use the photos to commit a crime in the future, an attorney would tell you the charges against you might be more serious. Because of the fear of terrorism, in certain parts of the United States and many parts of Europe, taking photos of bridges, train stations, and other public areas is illegal.

The point of mentioning all these laws and regulations is to make sure you're aware of the dangers of being a security tester or a student learning hacking techniques. Table 1-1 lists a small fraction of the cases prosecuted in the past few years; in these cases, many people have been sentenced to prison for hacking. Most attacks involved more than scanning a business, but the cases show that the government is serious about punishment for cybercrimes.

Table 1-1   Overview of recent hacking cases

State and year	Description
Kansas, 2021	A resident of Ellsworth County, Kansas, was charged with one count of tampering with a public water system and one count of reckless damage to a protected computer during unauthorized access. The indictment alleged that a former employee knowingly accessed the Ellsworth County Rural Water District's protected computer system without authorization. During this unauthorized access, the accused allegedly performed activities that shut down the processes at the facility, which affected cleaning and disinfecting procedures, with the intention of harming the public drinking water system. If found guilty, the accused faces up to 25 years in prison and a fine of up to $500,000 for illegally accessing the protected computer and tampering with the water system.
California, 2021	A former employee of an IT consulting firm accessed the server of a company in Carlsbad, California, and deleted more than 1,200 of the company's 1,500 Microsoft user accounts. The employee was apparently retaliating for being fired. The attack affected most of the Carlsbad company's employees so that they could not access email or other network services, effectively shutting down the company for days and causing continuous IT problems for three months. The former contractor was sentenced in federal court to two years in prison and ordered to pay the company more than $560,000.
Nevada, 2021	A Russian national offered $1 million to an employee of Tesla's electric battery plant in Nevada in a scheme to have the insider introduce malicious software into the company's computer network. The malware attack was designed to extract data from the company's network and then demand a ransom for its return. The ransomware case is considered unusual because it involves face-to-face bribery rather than anonymous hacking via the Internet. Such an attack typically carries a penalty of up to five years in prison and a $250,000 fine.
Atlanta, 2021	A Cypriot national hacked into major websites as a teenager and threatened that he would release stolen user information unless the websites paid a ransom. The hacker identified vulnerable websites, including those for sports news and online games, and then stole personally identifiable information from user and customer databases. He became the first Cypriot national extradited from Cyprus to the United States, and paid nearly $600,000 in restitution to his victims. In addition, he has been sentenced to federal prison for at least three years.
New Jersey, 2021	While employed at a data analytics and risk assessment firm based in New Jersey, a resident of Moorefield, Nebraska, obtained confidential information that belonged to the firm— including names, passwords, email addresses, and telephone numbers of clients—and then attempted to sell the information. Nearly two years after his arrest, the hacker was sentenced to three years of supervised release and ordered to pay restitution of more than $290,000.
Florida, 2021	A Florida high school conducted online voting to select a homecoming queen but found out that an assistant principal in the school district manipulated the vote electronically. She accessed a network database storing confidential student information—including grades, medical history, and credentials—and then used the credentials to cast ballots in favor of her daughter. The pair were arrested and charged with fraudulently accessing confidential student information. The daughter was expelled from the high school, and her mother was suspended from her job as they awaited sentencing.

Some of the most infamous cases are hacks carried out by students, such as the recent attack on Miami-Dade schools. Many hackers use software to crack passwords of online accounts. This act, performed by many security professionals when given permission to do so by a network's owner, is a federal offense when done without permission and can add substantial prison time to a hacker's sentence.

SECURITY BYTES

HackerOne is a security platform that connects hackers with organizations needing security vulnerability assessments.[2] The hackers are ethical hackers who use their devious skills for good. HackerOne pays the ethical hackers a so-called bug bounty according to the criticality of the bugs they find. A handful of HackerOne hackers have become millionaires as a result of the bug bounty payments.

Is Port Scanning Legal?

Port scanning is a common activity in penetration testing. Testers use port scanning to detect computing devices on a network and itemize the services they offer. For example, if a scan detects that a computer at the IP address 192.168.1.100 has port 443 open for connections, the machine is probably a web server and could later be targeted for web server penetration tests.

Some states consider port scanning as noninvasive or nondestructive in nature and deem it legal. This isn't always the case, however, so you must be prudent before you start using penetration-testing tools. Some companies have filed criminal charges against hackers for scanning their systems, but judges ruled that no damage was done to the networks, so the charges were dismissed. It's just a matter of time before a business will claim that its network is also private property, and it should have the right to say that scanning is not allowed.

Because the federal government currently doesn't see these infringements as a violation of the U.S. Constitution, each state is allowed to address these issues separately. However, a company could bring up similar charges against you if you decide to practice using the tools you learn in this course. Even if you're found innocent in your state, the legal costs could be damaging to your business or personal finances. Therefore, you must research your state laws before using what you learn, even if you're using the tools for the benefit of others, not criminal activity. As of this writing, you can check www.ncsl.org/research/telecommunications-and-information-technology/computer-hacking-and-unauthorized-access-laws.aspx for each state's laws on unauthorized access and hacking. (If this URL doesn't work, go to the home page at www.ncsl.org and do a search.) Spending time at this site is certainly preferable to spending time in court or prison.

> **TIP**   When traveling outside the United States, be aware of the cyber laws of the country you're visiting. For example, driving a car equipped with an antenna designed to identify wireless access points is a crime in Germany.

You should also read your ISP contract, specifically the section titled "Acceptable Use Policy" or something similar. Most people glance at and accept the terms of their contract. Figure 1-3 is an excerpt from an actual ISP contract. Notice that section (c) might create some problems if you run scanning software that slows down network access or prevents users from accessing network components.

Acceptable Use Policy

(a)   PacInfo Net makes no restriction on usage provided that such usage is legal under the laws and regulations of the State of Hawaii and the United States of America and does not adversely affect PacInfo Net customers. Customer is responsible for obtaining and adhering to the Acceptable Use Policies of any network accessed through PacInfo Net services.

(b)   PacInfo Net reserves the right without notice to disconnect an account that is the source of spamming, abusive, or malicious activities. There will be no refund when an account is terminated for these causes. Moreover, there will be a billing rate of $125 per hour charged to such accounts to cover staff time spent repairing subsequent damage.

(c)   Customers are forbidden from using techniques designed to cause damage to or deny access by legitimate users of computers or network components connected to the Internet. PacInfo Net reserves the right to disconnect a customer site that is the source of such activities without notice.

Figure 1-3   Sample acceptable use policy

Another ISP responded to an email about the use of scanning software with the following message:

Any use of the Service that disturbs the normal use of the system by HOL or by other HOL customers or consumes excessive amounts of memory or CPU cycles for long periods of time may result in termination pursuant to Section 1 of this Agreement. Users are strictly prohibited from any activity that compromises the security of HOL's facilities. Users may not run IRC "bots" or any other scripts or programs not provided by HOL.

Regards,
Customer Support
Hawaii Online

The statement prohibiting the use of Internet Relay Chat (IRC) bots or any other scripts or programs not provided by the ISP might be the most important for penetration testers. An IRC bot is a program that sends automatic responses to users, giving the appearance of a person on the other side of a connection. For example, a bot can welcome new users joining a chat session, even though a person isn't actually present to welcome them. Even if you have no intentions of creating a bot, the "any other scripts or programs" clause should still raise an eyebrow.

Another consideration when performing port scans is whether your computer is connected to your business network by a virtual private network (VPN). Many people work from home using a VPN to connect to their work network. If you run a port scanner while your VPN is connected, you may end up scanning work computers, which could be problematic.

Table A-1 in Appendix A shows which legal statutes to look at before you begin your journey. The statutes listed in the table might have changed since the writing of this book, so keep up with your state laws before trying penetration-testing tools. In Activity 1-3, you research the laws of your state or country, using Table A-1 as a guide.

Activity 1-3: Identifying Computer Statutes in Your State or Country

Time Required: 30 minutes

Objective: Learn what laws might prohibit you from conducting a network penetration test in your state or country.

Description: For this activity, you use Internet search engines to gather information on computer crime in your state or country (or a location selected by your instructor). You have been hired by ExecuTech, a security consulting company, to gather information on any new statutes or laws that might affect the security testers it employs. Write a one-page memo to Liang Choi, director of security and operations, listing applicable statutes or laws and offering recommendations to management. For example, you might note in your memo that conducting a denial-of-service attack on a company's network is illegal because your state's penal code prohibits this type of attack unless authorized by the owner.

Federal Laws

You should also be aware of applicable federal laws when conducting your first security test (see Table 1-2). Federal computer crime laws are becoming more specific about cybercrimes and intellectual property issues. In fact, the government has a branch of computer crime called computer hacking and intellectual property (CHIP).

Table 1-2 Federal computer crime laws

Federal law	Description
The No Electronic Theft Act (P.L. 105–147)	Extends the reach of criminal copyright law to specifically include electronic means as one method for committing the crime (17U S. C. § 501 (a) (1)). The act also expands the scope of the criminal conduct covered under this crime, allowing for prosecutions without showing that the distributor of the copyrighted material profited from the activity.
The Economic Espionage Act (EEA)	The EEA offers trade secret protection to both businesses and the government. The significance of information to society, and the problems that are attached to protecting this information, make the EEA an important step in how the law can provide protection from computer crime.

(continues)

Table 1-2 Federal computer crime laws *(continued)*

Federal law	Description
The Computer Fraud and Abuse Act (CFAA). Title 18, Crimes and Criminal Procedure. Part I: Crimes, Chapter 47, Fraud and False Statements, Sec. 1030: Fraud and related activity in connection with computers	This law makes it a federal crime to access classified information or financial information without authorization.
The Identity Theft and Assumption Deterrence Act (ITADA) [18 U.S.C. Section 1028(a)(7)]	This act criminalizes identity theft and allows courts to assess the losses suffered by individual consumers. While the CFAA covers certain aspects of identity theft, the ITADA addresses restitution and relief for the victims.
Electronic Communication Privacy Act. Title 18, Crimes and Criminal Procedure. Part I: Crimes, Chapter 119, Wire and Electronic Communications Interception and Interception of Oral Communications, Sec. 2510: Definitions and Sec. 2511: Interception and disclosure of wire, oral, or electronic communications prohibited	These laws make it illegal to intercept any communication, regardless of how it was transmitted.
U.S. PATRIOT Act, Sec. 217. Interception of Computer Trespasser Communications	This act largely seeks to amend previous privacy and surveillance laws and fund government surveillance programs. It also specifies ways for the government to monitor individuals and allows victims of cybercrimes to monitor the activity of trespassers on their systems.
Homeland Security Act of 2002, H.R. 5710, Sec. 225: Cyber Security Enhancement Act of 2002	This amendment to the Homeland Security Act of 2002 specifies sentencing guidelines for certain types of computer crimes.
The Computer Fraud and Abuse Act. Title 18, Crimes and Criminal Procedure, Sec. 1029: Fraud and related activity in connection with access devices	This law makes it a federal offense to manufacture, program, use, or possess any device or software that can be used for unauthorized use of telecommunications services.
Stored Wire and Electronic Communications and Transactional Records Act. Title 18, Crimes and Criminal Procedure. Part I: Crimes, Chapter 121, Stored Wire and Electronic Communications and Transactional Records Act, Sec. 2701: Unlawful access to stored communications (a) Offense. Except as provided in subsection of this section whoever (1) intentionally accesses without authorization a facility through which an electronic communication service is provided; or (2) intentionally exceeds an authorization to access that facility; Sec. 2702: Disclosure of contents	This law defines unauthorized access to computers that store classified information.

SECURITY BYTES

Even though you might think you're following the requirements set forth by the client who hired you to perform a security test, don't assume that management will be happy with your results. One tester was reprimanded by a manager who was upset that security testing revealed logon names and passwords. The manager believed that the tester shouldn't know this information and considered stopping the security testing. A nondisclosure agreement (NDA) should be in place to assure clients that testers will not reveal or use any information they find. An NDA could be sufficient to allay management fears about password discovery. Rules of engagement should also indicate whether discovering and reading logon credentials is allowed or disallowed.

Activity 1-4: Examining Federal and International Computer Crime Laws

Time Required: 30 minutes
Objective: Increase your understanding of U.S. federal and international laws related to computer crime.
Description: For this activity, use Internet search engines to gather information on U.S. Code, Title 18, Sec. 1030, which covers fraud and related activity in connection with computers. Also, research the Convention on Cybercrime (the Budapest Convention). Write a summary explaining how these laws can affect ethical hackers and security testers.

WHAT YOU CANNOT DO LEGALLY

After reviewing the state, federal, and international laws on computer crime, you can see that accessing a computer without permission, destroying data, and copying information without the owner's permission are illegal. It doesn't take a law degree to understand that certain actions are illegal, such as installing viruses on a network, denying users access to network resources. As a security tester, you must be careful that your actions don't prevent the client's employees from doing their jobs. If you run a program that uses network resources to the extent that a user is denied access to them, you have violated federal law. For example, denial-of-service (DoS) attacks, covered in a later module, should not be initiated on your client's networks.

Get it in Writing

As discussed, you can cause a DoS attack inadvertently by running certain hacking programs on a client's network. This possibility makes your job difficult, especially if you're conducting security tests as an independent contractor hired by a company instead of working as an employee of a large security company that has a legal team to draw up a contract with the client. Employees of a security company are protected under the company's contract with the client.

For the purposes of this discussion, assume you're an independent contractor who needs guidance in creating a written contract. Some contractors think written contracts undermine their relationships with clients. However, consulting an attorney and signing a written contract are good business. Consultants who haven't received payment from the client usually vote yes on the contract question. Similarly, users often aren't convinced of the importance of backing up important documents until their computers crash. Don't wait until you're in court to wish you had something in writing.

If you want additional information, you can consult books on working as an independent contractor, such as *Getting Started in Consulting* (Alan Weiss, 2019, ISBN 978-111-954215-5) and *The Consulting Bible: Everything You Need to Know to Create and Expand a Seven-Figure Consulting Practice* (Alan Weiss, 2011, ISBN 978-0-470-92808-0). The Internet is also a helpful resource for finding free contract templates that can be modified to fit your business situation. The modifications you make might create more problems than having no contract at all, however, so having an attorney read your contract before it's signed is a good investment of your time and money.

Are you concerned? Good. Most books or courses on ethical hacking gloss over this topic, yet it's the most important part of the profession. If your client gives you a contract drawn up by the company's legal department, consulting a lawyer can save you time and money. Attempting to understand a contract written by attorneys representing the company's best interests warrants an attorney on your side looking out for your best interests. The complexity of law is too much for most non-legal professionals to understand. Keeping up with computer technology is difficult enough. Both fields are changing constantly, but law is even more complex, as it changes from state to state.

SECURITY BYTES

The job of an ethical hacker is fairly new, and cybersecurity laws are changing constantly. Even if a company hires you to test its network for vulnerabilities, be careful that you aren't breaking any laws in your state or country. If you're worried that one of your tests might slow the network because of excessive bandwidth use, your concern should signal a red flag. The company might consider suing you for lost time or monies caused by this delay. Documentation spelling out the rules of engagement and scope of the tests should cover this situation. You should not burden systems being actively used by clients unless doing so has been approved by the client and documented in your penetration testing agreement.

Ethical Hacking in a Nutshell

After reading all the dos and don'ts, you might be considering a different profession. Before switching careers, however, take a look at the skills a security tester needs to help determine whether you have what it takes to do this job:

- *Knowledge of network and computer technology*—As a security tester, you must have a good understanding of networking concepts. You should spend time learning and reviewing TCP/IP and routing concepts and be able to read network diagrams. If you don't have experience working with networks, start now. Being a security tester is impossible without a high level of expertise in this area. You should also have a good understanding of computer technologies and OSs. Read as much as you can on OSs in use today, paying particular attention to Linux and Windows because most security testing is done on these popular systems.
- *Ability to communicate with management and IT personnel*—Security testers need to be good listeners and must be able to communicate verbally and in writing with management and IT personnel. Explaining your findings to CEOs might be difficult, especially if they don't have a technical background. Your reports should be clear and succinct and offer constructive feedback and recommendations.
- *An understanding of the laws that apply to your location*—As a security tester, you must be aware of what you can and can't do legally. Gathering this information can be difficult when working with global companies, as laws can vary widely in other countries.
- *Ability to apply the necessary tools to perform your tasks*—Security testers must have a good understanding of tools for conducting security tests. More important, you must be able to think outside the box by discovering, creating, and modifying tools when current tools don't meet your needs.

SECURITY BYTES

If being liked by others is important to you, you might want to consider a profession other than security testing. If you're good at your job, many IT employees resent your discovering vulnerabilities in their systems. In fact, it's one of the only professions in which the better you do your job, the more enemies you make.

SUMMARY

- Many companies hire ethical hackers to perform penetration tests. The purpose of a penetration test is to discover vulnerabilities in a network. A security test is typically done by a team of people with varied skills, sometimes referred to as a "red team," and goes further to recommend solutions for addressing vulnerabilities.
- Penetration tests are usually conducted using one of three models: white box model, black box model, or gray box model. The model the tester uses is based on the amount of information the client is willing to supply. In some tests, the client doesn't want the tester to access any of the company's information. In other words, the client is saying, "Find out what you can about my company without my help."
- Security testers can earn certifications from multiple sources. The most popular certifications are CEH, CISSP, and OCSP. Each certification requires taking an exam and covers different areas the tester must master. Because test requirements change periodically, visit the certification company's website to verify exam requirements.
- As a security tester or penetration tester, you must be aware of what you're allowed or not allowed to do by law. Start by researching local laws before conducting any security testing.
- Your ISP might have an acceptable use policy in the contract you signed. It could limit your ability to use many of the tools available to security testers. Running scripts or programs not authorized by the ISP can result in termination of services.
- State and federal laws pertaining to computer crime should be understood before conducting a security test. Federal laws are applicable for all states, whereas state laws can vary. Being aware of the laws that apply is imperative.
- Get it in writing. As an independent contractor, you must have the client sign a written contract allowing you to conduct penetration testing before you begin. You should also have an attorney read the contract, especially if you or the company representative made any modifications.
- You need to understand the tools available to conduct security tests. Learning how to use them should be a focused and methodical process.

Key Terms

black box model
Certified Ethical Hacker (CEH)
Certified Information Systems
  Security Professional (CISSP)
cracker
ethical hacker
Global Information Assurance
  Certification (GIAC)
gray box model
hacker

hacktivist
Institute for Security and Open
  Methodologies (ISECOM)
Offensive Security Certified
  Professional (OCSP)
Open Source Security
  Testing Methodology Manual
  (OSSTMM)
OSSTMM Professional Security
  Tester (OPST)

packet monkey
penetration test
PenTest+
red team
script kiddy
security test
SysAdmin, Audit, Network, Security
  (SANS) Institute
vulnerability assessment
white box model

Review Questions

1. The U.S. Department of Justice defines a hacker as which of the following?
   a. A person who accesses a computer or network without the owner's permission
   b. A penetration tester
   c. A person who uses phone services without payment
   d. A person who accesses a computer or network system with the owner's permission

2. A penetration tester is which of the following?
   a. A person who breaks into a computer or network without permission from the owner
   b. A person who uses telephone services without payment
   c. A security professional hired to break into a network to discover vulnerabilities
   d. A hacker who breaks into a system without permission but doesn't delete or destroy files

3. Some experienced hackers refer to inexperienced hackers who copy or use prewritten scripts or programs as which of the following? (Choose all that apply.)
   a. Script monkeys
   b. Packet kiddies
   c. Packet monkeys
   d. Script kiddies

4. What three models do penetration or security testers use to conduct tests?

5. A team composed of people with varied skills who attempt to penetrate a network is called which of the following?
   a. Green team
   b. Blue team
   c. Black team
   d. Red team

6. How can you find out which computer crime laws are applicable in your state? (Choose all that apply.)
   a. Contact your local law enforcement agencies.
   b. Contact your ISP provider.
   c. Contact your local computer store vendor.
   d. Research online for the laws in your area.

7. What portion of your ISP contract might affect your ability to conduct a penetration test over the Internet?
   a. Scanning policy
   b. Port access policy
   c. Acceptable use policy
   d. Warranty policy

8. If you run a program in New York City that uses network resources to the extent that a user is denied access to them, what type of law have you violated?
   a. City
   b. State
   c. Local
   d. Federal

9. Which federal law prohibits unauthorized access of classified information?
   a. Computer Fraud and Abuse Act, Title 18
   b. Electronic Communication Privacy Act
   c. Stored Wire and Electronic Communications and Transactional Records Act
   d. Fifth Amendment

10. Which federal law prohibits intercepting any communication, regardless of how it was transmitted?
    a. Computer Fraud and Abuse Act, Title 18
    b. Electronic Communication Privacy Act
    c. Stored Wire and Electronic Communications and Transactional Records Act
    d. Fourth Amendment

11. Which federal law amended Chapter 119 of Title 18, U.S. Code?
    a. Computer Fraud and Abuse Act, Title 18
    b. Electronic Communication Privacy Act
    c. Stored Wire and Electronic Communications and Transactional Records Act
    d. U.S. PATRIOT Act, Sec. 217: Interception of Computer Trespasser Communications

12. What is the Budapest Convention?
    a. A hacking convention held in Europe
    b. The first international treaty seeking to address Internet and computer crime
    c. International rules governing penetration testing
    d. A European treaty governing the protection of personal information

13. What organization offers the CEH certification exam?
    a. ISC²
    b. EC-Council
    c. CompTIA
    d. GIAC

14. What organization offers the PenTest+ certification exam?
    a. ISC²
    b. CompTIA
    c. SANS Institute
    d. GIAC

15. What is an OSCP?
    a. Open Security Consultant Professional
    b. Offensive Security Certified Professional
    c. Official Security Computer Programmer
    d. OSSTMM Security Certified Professional

16. As a security tester, what should you do before installing hacking software on your computer? (Choose all that apply.)
    a. Check with local law enforcement agencies.
    b. Contact your hardware vendor.
    c. Contact your ISP.
    d. Research online for the laws in your area.

17. Before using hacking software over the Internet, you should contact which of the following? (Choose all that apply.)
    a. Your ISP
    b. Your vendor
    c. Local law enforcement authorities to check for compliance
    d. The FBI

18. Which organization issues the Top 25 list of software errors?
    a. SANS Institute
    b. ISECOM
    c. EC-Council
    d. OPST

19. A written contract isn't necessary when a friend recommends a client. True or False?

20. A security tester should have which of the following attributes? (Choose all that apply.)
    a. Good listening skills
    b. Knowledge of networking and computer technology
    c. Good verbal and written communication skills
    d. An interest in securing networks and computer systems

Case Projects

Case Project 1-1: Determining Legal Requirements for Penetration Testing

Time Required: 45 minutes

Objective: Increase your understanding of state and federal laws related to computer crime.

Description: Alexander Rocco Corporation, a large real estate management company in Maui, Hawaii, has contracted your computer consulting company to perform a penetration test on its computer network. The company owns property that houses a five-star hotel, golf courses, tennis courts, and restaurants. Claudia Mae, the vice president, is your only contact at the company. To avoid undermining the tests you're conducting, you won't be introduced to any IT staff or employees. Claudia wants to determine what you can find out about the company's network infrastructure, network topology, and any discovered vulnerabilities, without any assistance from her or company personnel.

Based on this information, write a report outlining the steps you should take before beginning penetration tests of the Alexander Rocco Corporation. Research the laws applying to the state where the company is located, and be sure to reference any federal laws that might apply to what you have been asked to do.

Case Project 1-2: Researching Hacktivists at Work

Time Required: 45 minutes

Objective: Consider the legal and ethical concerns surrounding hacktivism.

Description: A 2021 *U.S. News & World Report* article discusses how a new wave of hacktivism is adding a twist to cybersecurity woes. At a time when U.S agencies and companies are fighting off hacking campaigns originating in Russia and China, activist hackers looking to make a political point are reemerging.

The government's response shows that officials regard the return of hacktivism with alarm. An acting U.S. Attorney was quoted as saying, "Wrapping oneself in an allegedly altruistic motive does not remove the criminal stench from such intrusion, theft, and fraud."

A counterintelligence strategy released in 2020 stated, "ideologically motivated entities such as hacktivists, leaktivists, and public disclosure organizations, are now viewed as 'significant threats', alongside five countries, three terrorist groups, and transnational criminal organizations."

Previous waves of hacktivism, notably by the collective known as Anonymous in the early 2010s, have largely faded away due to law enforcement pressure. Now a new generation of youthful hackers, angry about how the cybersecurity world operates and upset about the role of tech companies in spreading propaganda, is joining the fray.

Research hacktivism, and write a one-page paper that answers the following questions:

- Is hacktivism an effective political tool?
- Did any of the hacktivists you researched go too far?
- Can hacktivism ever be justified?

References

1. Fazzini, Katy, "Why Some of the World's Top Cybersecurity Hackers Are Being Paid Millions to Use Their Powers for Good," CNBC Disruptor 50, May 18, 2019, accessed April 15, 2021, www.cnbc.com/2019/05/17/cybersecurity-hackers-are-paid-millions-to-use-their-powers-for-good.html.
2. Winder, Davey, "These Hackers Have Made $100 Million and Could Earn $1 Billion by 2025," Forbes.com, May 29, 2020, accessed April 15, 2021, https://www.forbes.com/sites/daveywinder/2020/05/29/these-incredible-100-million-hackers-could-make-1-billion-by-2025-hackerone-bounty-millionaires/?sh=6df3ff5677b8.

TCP/IP CONCEPTS REVIEW

After reading this module and completing the exercises, you will be able to:

1. Explain the TCP/IP protocol stack
2. Explain the basic concepts of IP addressing
3. Compare the binary, octal, and hexadecimal numbering systems

Almost everything you do as a network security analyst or security tester depends on your understanding of networking concepts and knowledge of Transmission Control Protocol/Internet Protocol (TCP/IP). It's assumed you already understand networking concepts and TCP/IP and are CompTIA Network+ certified or have equivalent knowledge. This module, however, serves as a review of how these topics relate to IT security and security testers. In the activities and case projects, you apply your knowledge of TCP/IP and networking concepts to security-testing techniques.

Most of the tools both cyber attackers and security testers use run over IP, which is a standard networking protocol. However, IP version 4 (IPv4), still the most widely used version, was developed without security functions in mind, so professionals need the knowledge and skills to tighten security holes resulting from the use of IP.

In this module, you examine the TCP/IP protocol stack and IP addressing. You also review the binary, octal, and hexadecimal numbering systems and the ports associated with services that run over TCP/IP.

OVERVIEW OF TCP/IP

For computers to communicate with one another over the Internet or across an office, they must speak the same language. This language is referred to as a protocol, and the most widely used is Transmission Control Protocol/Internet Protocol (TCP/IP). No matter what medium connects workstations on a network—copper wires, fiber-optic cables, or a wireless setup—the same protocol must be running on all computers if communication is going to function correctly.

You've probably already studied TCP/IP, but a review is helpful to make sure you have a thorough understanding. TCP/IP is more than simply the combination of two protocols (TCP and IP). It's usually referred to as the TCP/IP stack, which contains four distinct layers (see Figure 2-1). The Network layer is concerned with physically moving bits across a medium (whether the medium is copper wire, fiber-optic cables, or wireless), and the Internet layer is responsible for routing packets by using IP addresses. The Transport layer is concerned with controlling the flow of data, sequencing packets for reassembly, and encapsulating the segment with a TCP or User Datagram Protocol (UDP) header. The Application layer is where applications and protocols, such as HTTPS and SSH, operate.

This module discusses only the Application, Transport, and Internet layers, covered in the following sections, because security testing doesn't usually involve getting down to the Network layer's hardware level. However, some computer attacks use physical hardware, such as a keylogger.

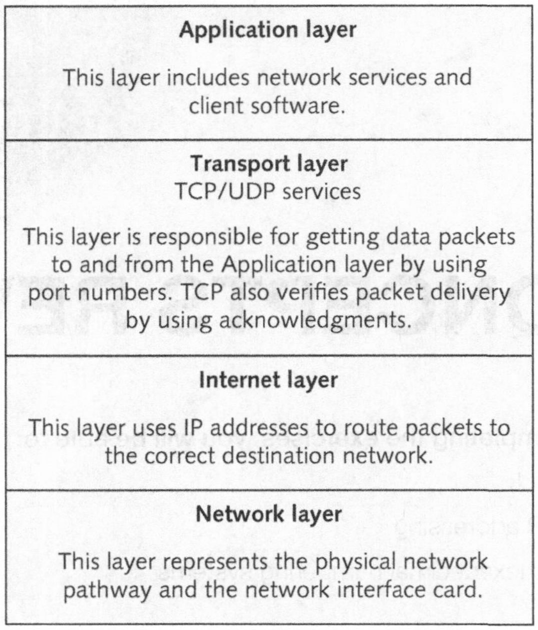

```
┌─────────────────────────────────────────────┐
│             Application layer                 │
│                                               │
│     This layer includes network services      │
│            and client software.               │
├─────────────────────────────────────────────┤
│             Transport layer                   │
│              TCP/UDP services                 │
│                                               │
│   This layer is responsible for getting data  │
│   packets to and from the Application layer    │
│   by using port numbers. TCP also verifies     │
│   packet delivery by using acknowledgments.    │
├─────────────────────────────────────────────┤
│              Internet layer                   │
│                                               │
│    This layer uses IP addresses to route       │
│   packets to the correct destination network.  │
├─────────────────────────────────────────────┤
│              Network layer                    │
│                                               │
│   This layer represents the physical network   │
│    pathway and the network interface card.     │
└─────────────────────────────────────────────┘
```

Figure 2-1   The TCP/IP protocol stack

The Application Layer

The Application-layer protocols are the front end to the lower-layer protocols in the TCP/IP stack. In other words, this layer is what you can see and touch. Table 2-1 lists some of the main applications and protocols running at this layer.

Table 2-1   Application-layer programs

Application	Description
Hypertext Transfer Protocol Secure (HTTPS)	The primary protocol used to communicate over the web (see RFC 2818 at www.ietf.org for details)
File Transfer Protocol (FTP)	Allows different operating systems (OSs) to transfer files between one another
Simple Mail Transfer Protocol (SMTP)	The main protocol for transmitting email messages across the Internet
Simple Network Management Protocol (SNMP)	Primarily used to monitor devices on a network, such as monitoring a router's state remotely
Secure Shell (SSH)	Enables users to securely log on to a remote server and issue commands interactively
Internet Relay Chat (IRC)	Enables multiple users to communicate over the Internet in discussion forums
Telnet	Enables users to insecurely log on to a remote server and issue commands interactively

The Transport Layer

The Transport layer is where data is encapsulated into segments. A segment can use TCP or UDP as its method for connecting to and forwarding data to a destination host (or node). TCP is a **connection-oriented protocol**, meaning the sender doesn't send any data to the destination node until the destination node acknowledges that it's listening to the sender. In other words, a connection is established before data is sent. For example, if Computer A wants to send data to Computer B, it sends Computer B a SYN packet first. A SYN (short for synchronize) packet is a query to the receiver, much like asking "Hello, Computer B. Are you there?" Computer B sends back an acknowledgment called a SYN-ACK packet, which is like replying "Yes, I'm here. Go ahead and send." Finally, Computer A sends an ACK (short for acknowledgment) packet to Computer B in response to the SYN-ACK. This process, called a three-way handshake, involves the following steps:

1. Host A sends a TCP packet with the SYN flag set (i.e., a SYN packet) to Host B.
2. After receiving the packet, Host B sends Host A its own SYN packet with an ACK flag (a SYN-ACK packet) set.
3. In response to the SYN-ACK packet from Host B, Host A sends Host B a TCP packet with the ACK flag set (an ACK packet).

TCP Segment Headers

As a security professional, you should know the critical components of a TCP header: TCP flags, the initial sequence number, and source and destination port numbers. Figure 2-2 shows a diagram of the TCP header.

16-bit	32-bit
Source Port	Destination Port
Sequence Number	
Acknowledgment Number (ACK)	
Offset Reserved U A P R S F	Window
Checksum	Urgent Pointer
Options and Padding	

Figure 2-2 TCP header diagram

Attackers leverage knowledge of TCP header components. You need to understand these components before learning how they can be abused. Only then can you check whether your network has vulnerabilities in these areas. Remember, to protect a network, you need to know the basic methods of hacking into networks.

TCP Flags

Each TCP flag occupies 1 bit of the TCP segment and can be set to 0 (off) or 1 (on). These are the six flags of a TCP segment:

- *SYN flag*—The synchronize flag signifies the beginning of a session.
- *ACK flag*—The acknowledgment flag acknowledges a connection and is sent by a host after receiving a SYN-ACK packet.
- *PSH flag*—The push flag is used to deliver data directly to an application. Data isn't buffered; it's sent immediately.
- *URG flag*—This flag is used to signify urgent data.
- *RST flag*—The reset flag resets or drops a connection.
- *FIN flag*—The finish flag signifies that the connection is finished.

Initial Sequence Number

The initial sequence number (ISN) is a 32-bit number that tracks packets received by a node and allows reassembling large packets that have been broken up into smaller packets. Steps 1 and 2 of the three-way handshake send an ISN. That is, the ISN from the sending node is sent with the SYN packet, and the ISN from the receiving node is sent back to the sending node with the SYN-ACK packet. An ISN can be quite a large number because 2^{32} allows a range of numbers from zero to more than four billion.

SECURITY BYTES

A TCP header's ISN might not seem important to network security professionals who aren't familiar with penetration testing or hacking techniques. In fact, most people ignore many of these fundamental concepts. However, numerous network attacks have used **network session hijacking**, an attack that relies on guessing the ISNs of TCP packets. One of the most famous is Kevin Mitnick's attack on a Japanese corporation—referred to as a "TCP sequence prediction attack." Understanding TCP flags and the basic elements of a TCP packet can go a long way toward understanding how an attacker thinks—and how you should think. To become a better security professional, try to discover vulnerabilities or weaknesses as you study the basics. Too many network security professionals wait for attackers to discover vulnerabilities in a network instead of beating them at their own game.

Activity 2-1: Viewing RFC-793

Time Required: 30 minutes

Objective: Examine the details of components of a TCP segment and explore how to use Request for Comments (RFC) documents.

Description: The amount of information available to an IT security professional can be overwhelming. To protect an organization's resources (or "assets," as they're commonly called), you're expected to have skills in many areas. To gain the necessary skills, you should know where to look for technical information that helps you better understand a particular technology. Want to know how the Domain Name System (DNS) works? Want a better understanding of Dynamic Host Configuration Protocol (DHCP)? Reading the RFCs on these topics can answer any questions you might have. In this activity, you examine the details of a TCP segment and get an overview of some TCP header components. You don't have to memorize your findings. This activity is merely an introduction to the wonderful world of RFCs.

1. Start your web browser and go to **www.ietf.org**.
2. On the Internet Engineering Task Force home page, choose **RFCs** from the **INTERNET STANDARDS** menu. (If time permits, you might want to navigate to other selections for information on useful topics.)
3. Read the instructions on the RFCs page, click the **RFC Search Page** link, type **793** in the RFC number text box, and then click **Search**. Click **ASCII** or **PDF** under Files to view the RFC. Note the title page of this RFC.
4. Scroll down the document and read the table of contents to get an overview of this document's information. Read Sections 2.6, 2.7, and 2.8 to get a better idea of how TCP works. (Note that Section 2.6 discusses reliable communication.)
5. Scroll down to Section 3.1, "Header Format." The diagram might not be what you're used to seeing in computer documentation, but it's typical of what you find in an RFC. The numbers at the top make it easier for you to see the position of each bit. For example, the upper 0, 1, 2, and 3 show you that there is a total of 32 bits (0 to 31) across this segment. Note that the source port and destination port fields are 16 bits long, and both the ISN and the acknowledgment number are 32 bits long.
6. Read Section 3.1 and note the use of the binary numbering system. This information should help solidify your knowledge of binary and hexadecimal numbering.
7. Scroll down to Section 3.4, "Establishing a connection," and skim the description of a three-way handshake. The author clarifies the process and adds a little humor about why an ACK doesn't occupy sequence number space. Many RFC authors have a knack for explaining complex material in an easy-to-understand manner.
8. Scroll through the rest of the document to get an overview of what's covered. You can read the entire document later, if you like. When you're finished, exit your web browser.

TCP Ports

A TCP packet has two 16-bit fields containing the source and destination port numbers. A **port** is the logical, not physical, component of a TCP connection and can be assigned to a process that requires network connectivity. For example, the HTTPS service uses port 443 by default. Understanding ports is important so that you know how to stop or disable services that aren't being used on your network. The more services you have running on a server, the more ports are open for a potential attack. In other words, securing a house with 1000 open doorways is more difficult than securing a house with only 10 open doorways.

SECURITY BYTES

The most difficult part of a network security professional's job is balancing system security with ease of use and availability for users. Closing all ports and stopping all services would certainly make your network more secure, but your users couldn't connect to the Internet, send or receive email, or access any network resources. So your job is to allow users to work in a secure network environment without preventing them from using services such as email and web browsing. This task isn't easy, as you'll learn throughout this course.

A possible 65,535 TCP and UDP port numbers are available, but the good news is that only 1023 are considered well-known ports. To see the list of well-known ports, visit the Internet Assigned Numbers Authority (IANA) at www.iana.org. The website probably provides more information than you need, but navigating the site gives you practice in searching for information. A successful security professional knows how to be persistent in looking for answers by using a structured methodology.

 TIP You can access the page about well-known ports by entering www.iana.org/assignments/port-numbers as the URL, but you bypass the IANA home page, which has more information and access to the IANA Whois service. You can review this service while browsing the IANA page.

You don't need to memorize the 1023 well-known ports. However, you should memorize the following TCP ports and the services they represent. Much of what you do as a security professional and penetration tester relies heavily on understanding this information.

- *Ports 20 and 21 (File Transfer Protocol)*—FTP has been around as long as the Internet. It was the standard for moving and copying large files and is still used today, although to a lesser extent because of the popularity of HTTP. FTP uses port 20 for data transfer and port 21 for control. FTP requires entering a logon name and password and is more secure than Trivial File Transfer Protocol (TFTP; covered later in this list). FTP does not use encryption, so data in transit can be intercepted and understood. Secure File Transfer Protocol (SFTP) uses Secure Shell (SSH; covered later in this list) to make FTP secure by providing encryption and authentication. Figure 2-3 shows an FTP program called FileZilla being used to connect to a U.S. Census Bureau FTP site.
- *Port 22 (Secure Shell)*—Secure Shell (SSH) uses encryption and authentication to create a secure channel over an unsecure network. SSH is used to secure logons, file transfers, and port forwarding. FTP is unsecure, but you can make it secure using an SSH channel. FTP using SSH is known as SFTP.
- *Port 25 (Simple Mail Transfer Protocol)*—Email servers listen on this port. If you attempt to send email to a remote user, your workstation connects to port 25 on a mail server.
- *Port 53 (Domain Name System)*—If a server on your network uses DNS, it's using port 53. Most networks require a DNS server so that users can connect to websites with URLs instead of IP addresses. When a user enters a URL, such as www.google.com, the DNS server resolves the name to an IP address. The DNS server might be internal to the company, or each computer might be configured to point to the IP address of a DNS server that's serviced by the company's ISP.
- *Port 69 (Trivial File Transfer Protocol)*—Many network engineers use the TFTP service to transfer router and backup router configurations.
- *Port 80 (Hypertext Transfer Protocol)*—Most certification exams have a question about port 80 being used for HTTP. Port 80 is used when you connect to a web server. HTTP is not secure, so most web servers use HTTPS (port 443).
- *Port 143 (IMAP)*—Email clients use this port to retrieve email messages from a mail server over a TCP/IP connection.

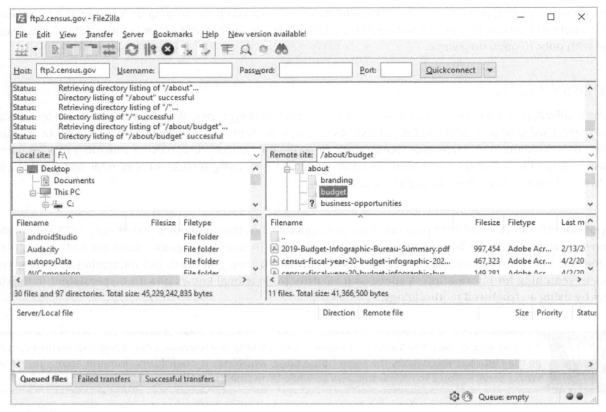

Figure 2-3   Connecting to an FTP site

- *Port 443 (Secure Hypertext Transfer Protocol)*—Port 443, like port 80, is used when you connect to a web server. However, 443 typically is reserved for secure connections.
- *Port 993 (IMAPS)*—IMAP over SSL/TLS uses port 993. Connections using this port are secured, so it is preferred over the unsecured version IMAP, which uses port 143.

SECURITY BYTES

Often technical personnel who aren't familiar with security techniques think that restricting access to ports on a router or firewall can protect a network from attack. This is easier said than done. After all, if a firewall prevents any traffic from entering or exiting a network on ports 80 and 443, you have indeed closed vulnerable ports to access from hackers. However, you have also closed the door to Internet access for your users, which probably isn't acceptable in your organization. The tricky (and almost impossible) part for security personnel is attempting to keep out attackers while allowing authorized users to work and use the Internet. As you progress through this course, you'll see that as long as users can connect to the Internet through an open port, attackers can get in. It's that simple. If a user can get out, an attacker can get in.

- *Port 110 (Post Office Protocol 3)*—To retrieve email from a mail server, one option is to access port 110 using Post Office Protocol 3 (POP3). An enhanced email retrieving protocol, IMAP4, is also available and is covered later in this list. POP3 is still around, however, and is one of the most common email retrieval systems.
- *Port 119 (Network News Transfer Protocol)*—This port is used to connect to a news server for use with newsgroups.
- *Port 135 (Remote Procedure Call)*—This port, used by Microsoft RPC, is critical for the operation of Microsoft Exchange Server and Active Directory, available in Windows 2000 Server and later.
- *Port 139 (NetBIOS)*—This port is used by the Microsoft NetBIOS Session Service to share resources.
- *Port 143 (Internet Message Access Protocol 4)*—IMAP4 uses this port to retrieve email.

Activity 2-2: Creating a Mail Server Using VirtualBox

Time Required: 45 minutes

Objective: Create a mail server in VirtualBox for use in Activities 2-3 and 2-4.

Description: Activities 2-3 and 2-4 ask you to use the `telnet` command to access various ports of a mail server. In this activity, you create a mail server virtual machine using Oracle VirtualBox, a free virtualization product that can run on many OSs.

Installing VirtualBox and a Mail Server

1. Use a web browser to go to **www.virtualbox.org/wiki/Downloads** to download and install VirtualBox (see Figure 2-4).

Figure 2-4   Downloading VirtualBox

2. Click the download link for your operating system, such as **Windows hosts** for Windows systems. Run the executable file you download, and follow the steps to install VirtualBox. If you need more guidance, look for a link to the installation documentation in the left pane of the download webpage.

NOTE

You need storage for the virtual machines you create, so if the default installation location is almost full, change the location to a drive with more space.

3. After a successful installation, the VirtualBox Manager window opens (see Figure 2-5).

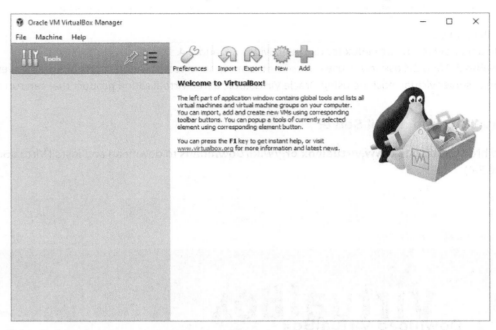

Figure 2-5 VirtualBox Manager window

4. Go to **www.axigen.com/mail-server/download**, scroll down to the Virtual Appliances section, and then click the **DOWNLOAD** button for Axigen 10.3.3 VMWare/VirtualBox Image. Downloading the Axigen file may take some time. The latest version number of the Axigen VMWare/VirtualBox Image may have changed. Select the most recent version.

5. Extract the virtual appliance (a file with an .ova extension) from the zip file you downloaded.

6. In VirtualBox, click **File** on the menu bar, and then click **Import Appliance**. Navigate to the folder containing the .ova file you extracted, click the .ova file, and then click the **Open** button to import Axigen into VirtualBox. Complete any additional steps that VirtualBox directs you to perform.

Setting Up the Mail Server

1. In the left pane of the VirtualBox Manager window, click the Axigen appliance, such as **Axigen-CentOS-VM**, click **Start** on the toolbar, and then click **Normal Start**.

2. After the Axigen appliance starts, a window resembling Figure 2-6 opens. Note the URL displayed for accessing the WebAdmin interface.

3. Follow the prompts to open your web browser, go to the WebAdmin URL you noted in Step 2, accept the license agreement, and then set your admin password. Use a secure and memorable password.

4. On the Your license page, choose the free license, and then click **CONTINUE** to run all the services listed.

5. Create an email domain named **cyber.com**, and then click **CONTINUE** to display the WebAdmin Dashboard (see Figure 2-7).

NOTE

Axigen provides online resources for installing and performing an initial configuration. You can find these resources on the following webpages:

www.axigen.com/documentation/performing-the-initial-configuration-onboarding-p65437723

www.axigen.com/documentation/deploying-running-axigen-in-vmware-virtualbox-p58327042

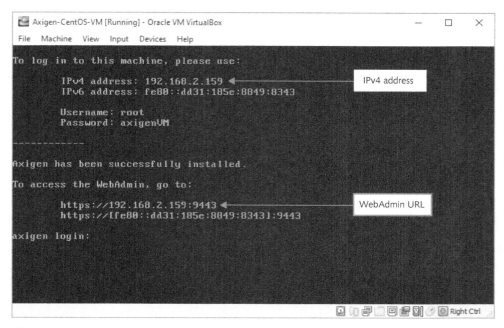

Figure 2-6   Axigen WebAdmin URL

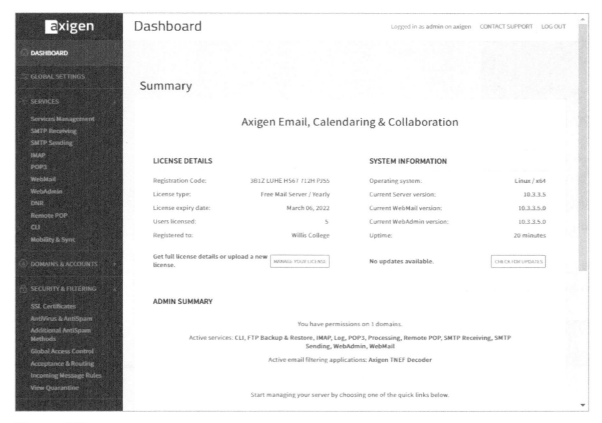

Figure 2-7   WebAdmin Dashboard

6. In the left pane of the Dashboard window, click **Acceptance & Routing**. Scroll down and click to uncheck the **Activate Greylisting** check box to disable Greylisting. Click the **SAVE CONFIGURATION** button to save this change.

 **CAUTION**   If Greylisting is not disabled, the Axigen server will reject unauthenticated emails, and Activity 2-3 will not work.

7. In the left pane of the Dashboard window, click **Services Management** to display a list of running services. Click the arrow button to start each service except for Instant Messaging Proxy and Reporting (see Figure 2-8).

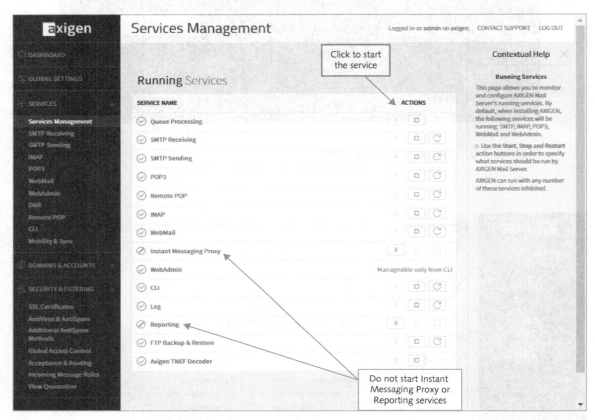

Figure 2-8   Services Management window

8. In the left pane of the Services Management window, click **SMTP Receiving** to make sure SMTP receiving listeners are enabled (see Figure 2-9).

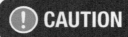 **CAUTION**   Enable all listeners; otherwise, Activity 2-3 will not work.

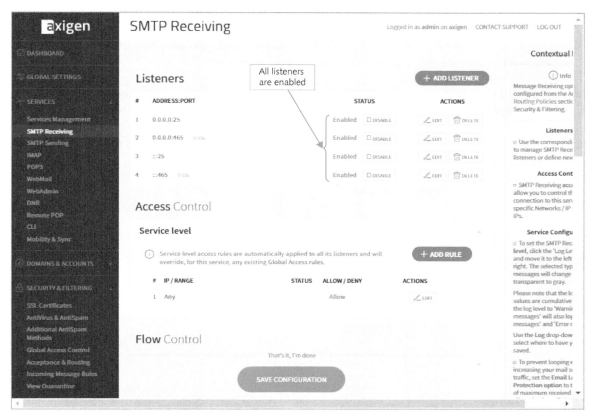

Figure 2-9   SMTP Receiving window

9. In the left pane of the SMTP Receiving window, click **DOMAINS & ACCOUNTS**, and then click **Manage Accounts** to add accounts to the Axigen server so that you have email addresses to use for Activities 2-3 and 2-4. Click the **ADD ACCOUNT** button, complete the requested information, and then click **QUICK ADD**.

Activity 2-3: Connecting to Port 25 (SMTP)

Time Required: 30 minutes

Objective: Use the `telnet` command to access port 25 on your mail server, log on, and send an email message to a recipient. Your mail server is the Axigen server you set up in the Activity 2-2. You may try using the `telnet` command on another mail server (such as one in your classroom or your ISP's mail server) if firewall rules prevent you from connecting.

Description: As an IT security professional, you should be aware of the ports used in a network infrastructure. A good way to test whether a service is running on a server is to use the `telnet` command to access the port using that service. For example, the SMTP service uses port 25. In this activity, you use the Telnet service to access the Axigen mail server from your Windows computer.

NOTE

If you can't connect to a mail server with the commands in Activities 2-3 and 2-4, you should still read through the steps and examine the figures to give you an idea of what a successful Telnet connection looks like.

NOTE

The following steps include generic placeholder text such as *LocalDomainName*. When performing the step, substitute the placeholders with specific text, such as an actual domain name.

1. Telnet is disabled by default in most Windows installations, so you'll most likely need to enable it. Open Control Panel and click **Programs**. In the Programs and Features section, click **Turn Windows features on or off**. In the Windows Features dialog box, scroll down and click the **Telnet Client** check box (see Figure 2-10). You can select other services you want to enable at this time, too. When you're finished, click **OK**, and then close the Windows Features dialog box and Control Panel.

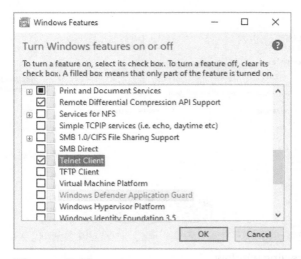

Figure 2-10   Enabling Telnet

2. To open a Command Prompt window in Windows 10, right-click the **Start** button, and then click **Command Prompt**.

3. Type **telnet** *RemoteMailServer* **25** (replacing *RemoteMailServer* with the IP address for the Axigen email server you set up in Activity 2-2). Press **Enter**. You must enter the port number of the service you're attempting to connect to. In this case, you use port 25 for SMTP. At the prompt shown in Figure 2-11, type **helo** *LocalDomainName* and press **Enter**. Replace *LocalDomainName* with a real domain name. The mail server accepts almost anything you enter after the `helo` command as valid, but you should use the cyber.com domain you created when you configured Axigen.

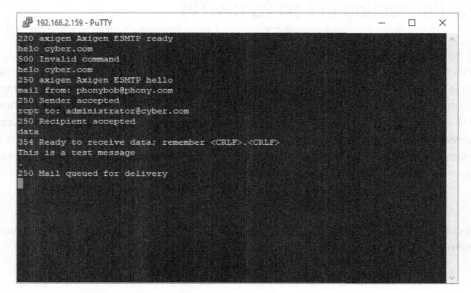

Figure 2-11   Using Telnet to send email

4. Type **mail from:** *YourMailAccount* and press **Enter**. Replace *YourMailAccount* with your email address, which is displayed in the recipient's From field. Figure 2-11 shows a phony email address, which is how someone can spoof an email. You should receive a "250 OK" message.

5. Type **rcpt to:** *RecipientMailAccount* and press **Enter**. Replace *RecipientMailAccount* with a valid email address, such as your own address, to send a message to yourself for the next activity. The email isn't actually sent unless the *RecipientMailAccount* is valid. You should receive a "Recipient OK" message.

6. Type **data** and press **Enter**. Type your message, press **Enter**, and then type **.** (a single period), and press **Enter** to end your message. You should receive a message saying that your email was queued.

 TIP   If you make a typo, you have to reenter your commands. Pressing Backspace or using the arrow keys doesn't edit the commands.

7. Type **quit** and press **Enter** to end the Telnet session. You can leave the Command Prompt window open for the next activity.

Activity 2-4: Connecting to Port 110 (POP3)

Time Required: 30 minutes

Objective: Use the `telnet` command to access port 110 on your mail server, log on, and retrieve an email message that has been sent to your email account.

Description: The POP3 service uses port 110. In this activity, you use the `telnet` command to access your mail server from your Windows computer and retrieve an email message that has been sent to your mailbox.

1. Open a Command Prompt window, if necessary.

2. Type **telnet** *RemoteMailServer* **110** (replacing *RemoteMailServer* with the IP address for the Axigen email server) and press **Enter**. You receive an +OK message, indicating you can log on.

 **CAUTION**   If you cannot connect to the remote mail server through port 110 in Step 2, a firewall might be preventing your connection. If you are using the Axigen mail server, you can log on to the Axigen server in VirtualBox and perform Steps 2–11 in this activity on the Axigen server from its command line.

3. Type **user** *YourMailAccount* (replacing *YourMailAccount* with a valid mail account name) and press **Enter** to enter the user command for logging on to your account (see Figure 2-12).

```
[root@axigen ~]# telnet 192.168.2.159 110
Trying 192.168.2.159...
Connected to 192.168.2.159.
Escape character is '^]'.
+OK AXIGEN POP3 server on axigen ready <139906144548608.1314369297@axigen>
user administrator@cyber.com
+OK administrator@cyber.com needs a password
```

Figure 2-12   Logging on to an email server

4. Type **pass** *YourPassword* (replacing *YourPassword* with a valid password) and press **Enter** to enter your password.

5. Type **list** and press **Enter** to list all the messages in your mailbox, including the number of messages, as shown in Figure 2-13.

```
+OK administrator@cyber.com has 4 messages (4161 octets)
list
+OK Scan listing follows
1 566
2 2468
3 566
4 561
.
_
```

Figure 2-13   Viewing email messages in a mailbox

6. Type **retr 4** and press **Enter** to retrieve message number 4 (see Figure 2-14).

```
+OK administrator@cyber.com has 4 messages (4161 octets)
list
+OK Scan listing follows
1 566
2 2468
3 566
4 561
.
retr 4
+OK 561 bytes
Return-Path: <phonybob@phony.com>
Received: from cyber.com (192.168.2.98) by axigen (Axigen) with SMTP id 120518;
 Tue, 23 Mar 2021 13:34:04 +0000
Message-ID: <1616506480326161188@axigen>
Received-SPF: none (phony.com: phonybob@phony.com does not designate permitted
 sender hosts) client-ip=192.168.2.98; envelope-from=phonybob@phony.com;
 mechanism=default; identity=mailfrom; receiver=axigen;
X-AXIGEN-SPF-Result: No records
X-AXIGEN-DK-Result: No records
DomainKey-Status: no signature
X-AXIGEN-DKIM-Result: No records
DKIM-Status: no signature
.
```

Figure 2-14   Retrieving an email message

7. Type **quit** and press **Enter**. This command deletes any messages marked for deletion, logs you out of the mail server, and ends the Telnet session.
8. Open another Command Prompt window, type **netstat**, and press **Enter** to view open ports on your Windows computer. Figure 2-15 shows the result of running netstat while multiple ports are open.

Figure 2-15   Using the netstat command to view open ports

9. If the results show no active ports open, try typing **netstat   -a** and pressing **Enter**. This command lists all connections and listening ports on your system (see Figure 2-16). Notice the many TCP and UDP ports listed.

Figure 2-16   Using netstat with the –a option

10. Minimize the Command Prompt window, and open a web browser.
11. Connect to **google.com**. Maximize the Command Prompt window, type **netstat** again, and press **Enter**. Notice the new entry indicating that port 443 (HTTPS) has a connection.
12. Close the Command Prompt window and any other open windows.

User Datagram Protocol

User Datagram Protocol (UDP) is a fast but unreliable delivery protocol that operates on the Transport layer. Imagine trying to compete in the mail courier business and touting that your service is fast but unreliable. It would probably be difficult to sell. However, UDP is a widely used protocol on the Internet because of its speed. It doesn't need to verify whether the receiver is listening or ready to accept the packets. The sender doesn't care—it just sends, even if the receiver isn't ready to accept the packet. See why it's faster? Some applications that use UDP have built-in utilities to warn recipients of undeliverable messages, but UDP doesn't. In other words, it depends on the higher layers of the TCP/IP stack to handle these problems. Think of UDP as someone announcing over a loudspeaker that school will be closed that afternoon. Some lucky students will hear the message, and some won't. This type of delivery protocol is referred to as **connectionless**.

The Internet Layer

The Internet layer of the TCP/IP stack is responsible for routing a packet to a destination address. Routing is done by using a logical address, called an IP address. Like UDP, IP addressing packet delivery is connectionless.

Internet Control Message Protocol

Internet Control Message Protocol (ICMP) is used to send messages related to network operations. For example, if a packet can't reach its destination, you might see the "Destination Unreachable" error.

ICMP makes it possible for network professionals to troubleshoot network connectivity problems (with the ping command) and track the route a packet traverses from a source IP address to a destination IP address (with the traceroute command). Security professionals can use ICMP type codes (see Table 2-2) to block ICMP packets from entering or leaving a network. For example, a router can be configured to not allow an ICMP packet with the type code 8 to enter a network. Try pinging www.microsoft.com and see what happens. Microsoft doesn't allow its IP address to be pinged, which is the type code 8 (Echo).

Table 2-2   ICMP type codes

ICMP type code	Description
0	Echo Reply
3	Destination Unreachable
4	Source Quench
5	Redirect
6	Alternate Host Address
8	Echo
9	Router Advertisement
10	Router Solicitation
11	Time Exceeded
12	Parameter Problem
13	Timestamp
14	Timestamp Reply
15	Information Request
16	Information Reply
17	Address Mask Request
18	Address Mask Reply
19	Reserved (for Security)
20–29	Reserved (for Robustness Experiment)
30	Traceroute
31	Datagram Conversion Error
32	Mobile Host Redirect
33	IPv6 Where-Are-You
34	IPv6 I-Am-Here
35	Mobile Registration Request
36	Mobile Registration Reply
37	Domain Name Request
38	Domain Name Reply
39	Skip
40	Photuris
41–255	Reserved

 TIP   For a more detailed description of ICMP, see RFC 792.

IP ADDRESSING

An IPv4 address consists of 4 bytes divided into two components: a network address and a host address. Based on the starting decimal number of the first byte, you can classify IP addresses as Class A, Class B, or Class C, as shown in Table 2-3.

Table 2-3   TCP/IP address classes

Address class	Range	Address bytes	Number of networks	Host bytes	Number of hosts
Class A	1–126	1	126	3	16,777,214
Class B	128–191	2	16,128	2	65,534
Class C	192–223	3	2,097,152	1	254

Using Table 2-3, you can determine, for example, that a user with the IP address 193.1.2.3 has a Class C address, and a user with the IP address 9.1.2.3 has a Class A address. An IP address is composed of 4 bytes. A byte is equal to 8 bits. Eight bits can also be called an octet, so you sometimes see an IP address defined as four octets instead of 4 bytes. The following list describes each address class:

- *Class A*—The first byte of a Class A address is reserved for the network address, making the last 3 bytes available to assign to host computers. Because a Class A address has a three-octet host address, Class A networks can support more than 16 million hosts. The number of Class A addresses is limited, so these addresses are reserved for large corporations and governments. Class A addresses have the format *network.node.node.node*.
- *Class B*—These addresses are divided evenly between a two-octet network address and a two-octet host address, allowing more than 65,000 hosts per Class B network address. Large organizations and ISPs are often assigned Class B addresses, which have the format *network.network.node.node*.
- *Class C*—These addresses have a three-octet network address and a one-octet host address, resulting in more than two million Class C addresses. Each address supports up to 254 hosts. These addresses, usually available for small businesses and home use, have the format *network.network.network.node*.

SECURITY BYTES

The 127 address missing from Table 2-3 is used for loopback and testing. It's not a valid IP address that can be assigned to a network device. Class D and Class E addresses are reserved for multicast and experimental addressing and aren't covered in this module.

Subnetting allows a network administrator to divide these networks into smaller segments. The use of subnets is important for both performance and security purposes. In addition to a unique network address, each network must be assigned a subnet mask, which helps distinguish the network address bits from the host address bits.

Consider the following example.

The IP address 128.214.018.016 represented in binary is

```
10000000.11010110.00010010.00010000
```

If you define a subnet mask of 255.255.255.0, it's expressed in binary as

```
11111111.11111111.11111111.00000000
```

The subnet part of the IP address is

```
10000000.11010110.00010010
```

The host address is

```
00010000
```

You can determine which subnet the IP address belongs in by performing a bitwise AND operation on the IP address and the subnet mask. This calculation is vertically for each column. With the AND operation, if both bits are 1, the resulting value is 1. Otherwise, the resulting value is 0.

```
10000000.11010110.00010010.00010000 AND
11111111.11111111.11111111.00000000 =
10000000.11010110.00010010.00000000
```

This calculation results in the subnet of 128.215.018.0, meaning that the original IP address 128.214.018.016, with a subnet mask of 255.255.255.0, belongs in the subnet 128.214.018.0.

An understanding of these concepts is important for a security professional, but you can find many free subnetting calculators on the Internet.

CIDR Notation

IPv4 allows for roughly 4.3 billion unique IP addresses. That sounds like a lot of addresses. However, with a growing number of Internet-connected devices, almost all of the world's IPv4 addresses are in use. The long-term solution is IPv6 addressing. One short-term fix was CIDR (Classless Inter-Domain Routing), which was developed in 1993 and helped prolong the life of IPv4 by allowing for more efficient IP-assignment space.

Here is an example of a subnet in CIDR notation: 192.168.1.0/24. In CIDR, the number following the "/" is the prefix. A subnet using a CIDR prefix of 24 is analogous to a Class C subnet. The CIDR prefix /16 is the default subnet mask for Class B addresses, and the CIDR prefix /8 is the default subnet mask for Class A addresses. CIDR optimizes the way IP space was assigned, or allocated, by allowing engineers more options to rightsize assignments. By assigning a /23 containing 512 addresses to an organization that requires 400 IP addresses, CIDR conserves more than 65,000 addresses (almost an entire Class B) that would have been required under a classful assignment. A list of important CIDR prefixes is found in Table 2-4. A full listing of CIDR address options can be found through an Internet search.

Table 2-4   CIDR addressing

CIDR prefix	# Class C equivalent	Number of usable hosts
/27	1/8th of a Class C	30 hosts
/26	1/4th of a Class C	62 hosts
/25	1/2 of a Class C	126 hosts
/24	1 Class C	254 hosts
/23	2 Class C	510 hosts
/22	4 Class C	1022 hosts
/21	8 Class C	2046 hosts
/20	16 Class C	4094 hosts
/19	32 Class C	8190 hosts
/18	64 Class C	16,382 hosts
/17	128 Class C	32,766 hosts
/16	1 Class B	65,534 hosts
/15	2 Class B	131,070 hosts
/14	4 Class B	262,142 hosts
/13	8 Class B	524,286 hosts
/12	16 Class B	1,048,574 hosts
/11	32 Class B	2,097,150 hosts
/10	64 Class B	4,194,302 hosts
/9	128 Class B	8,388,606 hosts
/8	1 Class A	16,777,214 hosts

Planning IP Address Assignments

When companies assign IP addresses, they must give a unique IP address to each network segment that's separated by a router. For example, a company has been issued two IP addresses: 193.145.85.0 and 193.145.86.0 (or 193.145.85.0/24 and 193.154.86.0/24 in CIDR notation). Looking at the first byte of each address, the company determines that both are Class C addresses. With a default subnet mask of 255.255.255.0, 254 host addresses can be assigned to each segment. You use the formula $2^x - 2$ for this calculation, with x representing the number of unmasked bits. For this example, x equals 8 because there are 8 bits in the fourth octet:

$2^8 - 2 = 254$

You must subtract 2 in the formula because the network portion and host portion of an IP address can't contain all 1s or all 0s. Remember, you can't assign a network user the IP address 192.168.8.0 if you used the 255.255.255.0 mask. Also, you can't give a user an address of 192.168.8.255 because it would produce all 1s in the host portion of an IP address; this address is reserved as a broadcast address to all nodes on the segment 192.168.8.0.

To access entities and services on other networks, each computer must also have the IP address of its gateway. Before sending a packet to another computer, the TCP/IP Internet layer uses the sending computer's subnet mask to determine the destination computer's network address. If this address is different from the sending computer's network address, the sending computer relays the packet to the IP address specified in the gateway parameter. The gateway computer then forwards the packet to its next destination. In this way, the packet eventually reaches the destination computer.

For example, if a Linux server has the IP address 192.168.8.2 and the subnet mask 255.255.255.0, and a user has a computer with the IP address 192.168.9.200 and the subnet mask 255.255.255.0, the company must configure a default gateway address. The default gateway sends the message to a router, which routes it to the different network segment. If the default gateway isn't configured on the user's computer, and this user attempts to use the ping command to contact the server, the user receives the "Destination Unreachable" message (see Table 2-2). The user's computer can't connect to the other host—a Linux server located on a different network segment—because there's no router to help it. The router's job is to take packets destined for a computer on a different network segment from the sending computer and send them on their way.

Security professionals must understand these basic network concepts before attempting to conduct a penetration test on a network, especially one that's been subnetted. In a subnetted network, it might be easy to mistake a broadcast address as a valid host address, a major blunder that could cause a denial-of-service attack after thousands of packets are sent to all hosts on a network instead of to the one host you were trying to reach. Just be sure to verify the IP address you're sending packets to before pressing Enter.

IPv6 Addressing

As a security professional, you should spend some time reviewing the IP addressing system Internet Protocol version 6 (IPv6). As mentioned, IPv4 wasn't designed with security in mind, and many current network vulnerabilities are caused by this oversight. This section gives you some basics of IPv6, but reading RFC 2460 (www.ietf.org/rfc/rfc2460.txt) is recommended for more details.

IPv6 was developed to increase the IP address space and provide additional security. Instead of the 4 bytes used in IPv4, IPv6 uses 16 bytes, or a 128-bit address, so 2^{128} addresses are available—about 2000 IP addresses for every square foot on the planet. You might think this many IP addresses aren't necessary, but they'll be needed to support the Internet of Things (IoT). Many new products—such as toasters, microwaves, refrigerators, and TVs—can be accessible via the Internet and need IP addresses.

Here's an example of an IPv6 number: 1111:0cb7:75a2:0110:1234:3a2e:1113:7777. If it looks odd to you, a review of hexadecimal numbers might refresh your memory. The colons separate each group of four hexadecimal numbers. The good news is that being an effective security tester doesn't require being an expert at translating or memorizing these long numbers.

As a security tester, you should be aware that all newer OSs are configured to enable IPv6, but some router-filtering devices, firewalls, and intrusion detection systems (IDSs) are not. This makes it possible for hackers to bypass these security systems using IPv6. You can find numerous articles online that discuss the weaknesses with IPv4, IPv6, and the protocols that support them. Cyber attackers spend hours reading these types of articles. Security testers should, too.

Activity 2-5: Working with IP Addresses and Subnet Masks

Time Required: 30 minutes

Objective: Apply your knowledge of IP addresses and subnet masks to answer a series of networking questions.

Description: As a security professional, you need to understand IP addresses, classes, and subnet masks for many useful purposes. One such purpose is to identify what network includes a particular device.

1. Identify the classes of the following IP addresses: 10.20.0.1, 172.16.42.42, and 192.168.255.255
2. What is the CIDR notation equivalent of the 192.168.1.0 255.255.255.0 network?

3. Given the IP address 192.168.1.128 and subnet mask 255.255.255.128, what are the subnet part of the address and the host part of the address?
4. Computer A has an IP address of 192.168.1.10 and a subnet mask of 255.255.255.128. Computer B has an IP address of 192.168.1.200 and a subnet mask of 255.255.255.128. Are Computer A and Computer B on the same subnet?
5. How many hosts can be on a subnet with a subnet mask of 255.255.255.128?
6. How many bits are in an IPv6 address?

OVERVIEW OF NUMBERING SYSTEMS

Your knowledge of numbering systems comes into play as a security professional. The following sections offer a quick review of the binary, octal, and hexadecimal numbering systems.

Reviewing the Binary Numbering System

You learned base-10 math in elementary school, although you might not have realized it at the time. When you see the number 3742, for example, you recognize it as "three thousand seven hundred and forty-two." By placing each number in a column, as shown in the following lines, you can see that each number has a different value and magnitude. This numbering system uses 10 as its base and goes from right to left, multiplying the base number in each column by an exponent, starting from zero. Valid numbers in base 10 are 0 through 9. That is, each column can contain any number from 0 to 9.

```
1000     100     10      1
10³      10²     10¹     10⁰
3        7       4       2
```

As you can see, you get 3742 by multiplying 2 by 1, 4 by 10, 7 by 100, and 3 by 1000, and then adding all these values. The binary numbering system, on the other hand, uses 2 as its base. Each binary digit (bit) is represented by a 1 or 0. Bits are usually grouped by eight because a byte contains 8 bits. Computer engineers chose this numbering system because logic chips make binary decisions based on true or false, on or off, and similar conditions. With 8 bits, a programmer can represent 256 different colors for a video card, for example. (Two to the power of eight, or 2^8, equals 256.) Therefore, black can be represented by 00000000, white by 11111111, and so on.

Another example of using binary numbering can be seen in file permissions for users: r (read), w (write), and x (execute). A 1 represents having the permission, and a 0 removes the permission. Therefore, 111 (rwx) means all permissions apply, and 101 (r-x) means the user can read and execute the file but not write to it. (The - symbol indicates that the permission isn't granted.) Those familiar with Unix will recognize this numbering system. Unix allows using the decimal equivalent of binary numbers, so for the binary 111, you enter the decimal number 7. For the binary 101, you enter the decimal number 5. Confused? You'll be a binary expert in a few minutes, so hang in there.

To simplify the concept of binary numbers, think of a room with two light switches, and consider how many different combinations of positions you could use for the switches. For example, both switches could be off, Switch 1 could be off and Switch 2 could be on, and so forth. Here's a binary representation of these switch positions:

```
0     0     (off, off)
0     1     (off, on)
1     0     (on, off)
1     1     (on, on)
```

The two switches have four possible occurrences, or 2^x power; x represents the number of switches (bits) available. For the light switches, x equals 2.

Examples of Determining Binary Values

Now that you've been introduced to the basic concepts, you can see how bits are used to notate binary numbers. First, however, you must learn and memorize the columns for binary numbers, just as you did for base 10 numbering:

```
128    64    32    16    8    4    2    1
```

From right to left, these numbers represent increasing powers of two. Using the preceding columns, try to determine the value of the binary number 01000001:

128	64	32	16	8	4	2	1
2^7	2^6	2^5	2^4	2^3	2^2	2^1	2^0
0	1	0	0	0	0	0	1

The byte in the preceding example represents the decimal number 65. You calculate this value by adding each column containing a 1 (64 + 1). Now try another example with the binary number 11000001:

128	64	32	16	8	4	2	1
2^7	2^6	2^5	2^4	2^3	2^2	2^1	2^0
1	1	0	0	0	0	0	1

To convert the binary number to decimal (base 10), add the columns containing 1s:

```
128 + 64 + 1 = 193
```

Adding the values in these columns can be tedious, but you can learn some tricks of the trade to help you translate binary to decimal quickly. However, make sure to memorize each binary column before working through the remaining examples in this chapter.

Understanding Nibbles

Psychologists have found that people have difficulty memorizing numbers of seven digits or more. This difficulty is why phone numbers have only seven digits and a dash follows the first three numbers; the dash gives your brain a chance to pause before moving on to the next four numbers.

Likewise, binary numbers are easier to read when they are separated by a space. For example, 1111 1010 is easier to read than 11111010. If you need to convert a binary number written as 11111010, you should visualize it as 1111 1010. In other words, you break the byte into two nibbles (sometimes spelled "nybbles"). A nibble is half a byte, or 4 bits. The 4 bits on the left are called the high-order nibble, and the 4 bits on the right are the low-order nibble.

The following examples show how to convert a low-order nibble to a decimal number. Note the pattern at work in the binary numbers as you go through the examples:

```
0000 = 0
0001 = 1
0010 = 2
0011 = 3
0100 = 4
0101 = 5
0110 = 6
0111 = 7
1000 = 8
1001 = 9
1010 = 10
1011 = 11
1100 = 12
1101 = 13
1110 = 14
1111 = 15
```

The largest decimal number you can represent with four low-order bits is 15. You should memorize these numbers if you can, especially the ones that have convenient memory aids. For example, 1010 is equal to the decimal number 10. Just remember the phrase "It's 10, silly, 10!" 1011 is just as easy: "Not 10, but 11." You can make up your own tricks, but you can always simply add the columns if you forget.

You can also practice converting decimal numbers into binary numbers by using license plate numbers. For example, if a license plate number ends with 742, you should visualize 0111, 0100, 0010. (You can eliminate the leading zeros after a few days of practice.) When you get comfortable with the low-order nibble and can identify a sequence of 4 bits quickly, you can move to the high-order side.

For example, what does the binary number 1010 1010 equal in decimal? On the low-order side, you can quickly convert 1010 to the decimal number 10. The high-order side is also 10, but it's 10 times 16, or 160. Next, add the low-order side of 10 to the high-order side of 160 to get the answer, 170. You can always add the columns if you're confused:

```
128 + 32 = 160
```

Any value in the high-order nibble is multiplied by the number 16. For example, the binary number 0010 0000 is equal to 32. You can multiply the nibble value of 2 by 16, but in this case, it's easier to recognize the 1 in the 32 column, which makes the answer 32.

You should memorize the following high-order nibble values, which will help you with subnetting. As you may recall from subnetting basics, 128, 192, 224, and so on are used as subnet masks.

```
1000 = 128
1100 = 192
1110 = 224
1111 = 240
```

If you recognize 1111 0000 as 240, the binary number 1111 1000 should be easy to calculate as 248. By the same token, the binary number 1111 1111 is equal to the decimal 255, or 240 + 15, the largest number you can represent with 8 bits.

NOTE

To help you convert numbers correctly, note that all odd numbers have the low-order bit turned on. For example, 1001 can't be an even number, such as 10 or 8, because the low-order bit is turned on. You can also guess that the number is larger than 8 because the 8 column bit is turned on. Similarly, you can identify 0101 as converting to a decimal number lower than 8 because the 8 column isn't turned on and identify it as an odd number because the low-order bit is on.

NOTE

You can use other easy ways to memorize and break down binary numbers. For example, 1010 is 10, and 0101 converts to half of 10: 5. The two numbers are mirror images of each other in binary, and one number is half of the other in decimal. In the same way, 1110 equals 14 and 0111 is 7. In the high-order nibble, 1110 equals 224, and 0111 in the high-order nibble equals 112 (half of 224). This trick helps you convert binary numbers quickly. For example, the binary number 0101 1010 equals 90. In this number, the high-order nibble converts to 80 because 1010 equals 160. The low-order nibble converts to 10, and quick addition gives you the final answer of 90.

Reviewing the Octal Numbering System

An octal number is a base-8 number, so it's written by using these eight values: 0, 1, 2, 3, 4, 5, 6, and 7. Because you're a binary expert now, it's easy to see how binary converts to octal. An octal digit can be represented with only 3 bits because the largest digit in octal is 7. The number 7 is written as 00000111, or 111 if you drop the leading zeros. The binary equivalent of the octal number 5 is then 101.

To see how this concept relates to network security, take a look at Unix permissions again. Octal numbering is used to express the following permissions on a directory or file: owner permissions, group permissions, and other permissions. Setting the permission (rwxrwxrwx) for a directory means that the owner of the directory, members of a group, and everyone else (other) have read, write, and execute permissions for this directory.

Because each category has three unique permissions, and because each permission can be expressed as true or false (on or off), 3 bits are used. You don't need all 8 bits because 3 bits (rwx) are enough. Recall from binary numbering that 0 is counted as a number, so with 3 bits, there are eight possible occurrences: 000, 001, 010, 011, 100, 101, 110, and 111. Using octal numbering, 001 indicates that the execute (x) permission is granted, 010 indicates that the write (w) permission is granted but not read and execute, and so on. The octal number 7 indicates all 1s (111), or 1 + 2 + 4. So, in Unix and Linux systems, 777 (in binary, 111 111 111) indicates that the owner, group, and other have all permissions (rwx) to a file or directory.

Figure 2-17 shows a listing of files with permission settings. The names of the files and directory describe what their permission settings mean.

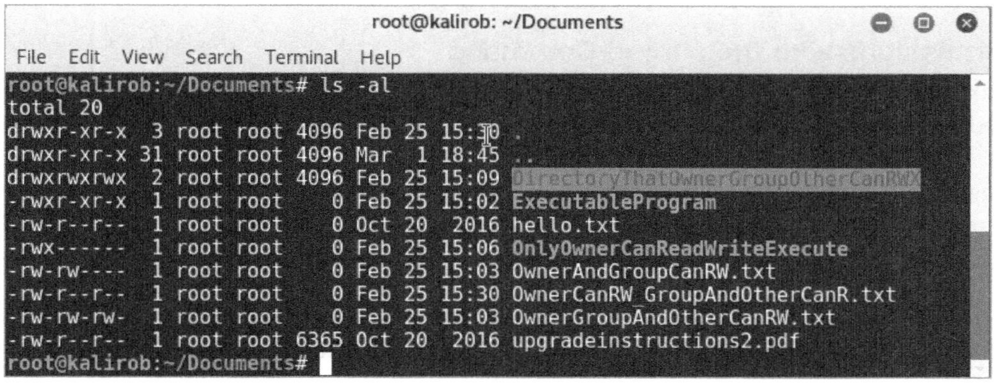

Figure 2-17   File listing with permission settings

Table 2-5 explains the permissions in detail.

Table 2-5   File permissions

Filename	Permissions	Owner	Group	Other	Description
DirectoryThatOwnerGroupOtherCanRWX	drwxrwxrwx	rwx	rwx	rwx	Directory with full permissions for owner, group, and other
ExecutableProgram	rwxr-xr-x	rwx	r-x	r-x	Executable program that owner has full permissions over—group and other can execute
hello.txt	rw-r—r--	rw-	r--	r--	A nonexecutable file that owner can read and write—group and other can only read
OnlyOwnerCanReadWriteExecute	rwx------	rwx	---	---	Owner can read, write, and execute—group and other have no permissions
OwnerAndGroupCanRW.txt	rw-rw----	rw-	rw-	---	Owner and group can read and write—other has no permissions

(continues)

Table 2-5   File permissions *(continued)*

Filename	Permissions	Owner	Group	Other	Description
OwnerCanRW_GroupAndOtherCanR.txt	rw-r—r--	rw-	r--	r--	Owner can read and write—group and other can only read
OwnerGroupAndOtherCanRW.txt	rw-rw-rw-	rw-	rw-	rw-	Owner, group, and other can read and write—nobody can execute

Changing Permissions with the chmod Command

In Unix and Linux systems, the chmod command allows you to alter the permissions of files and directories. This is useful if you need to provide more or less permissions to a file or directory for security purposes.

You can use chmod to change permissions in two main ways. One way is to provide the permissions as an octal number. For example, to change the permissions of the file hello.txt so that the owner, group, and other members have full read, write, and execute permissions, enter the following command:

```
chmod 777 hello.txt
```

Remember that 7 octal in binary is 111, which means the r, w, and x bits are all enabled, giving read, write, and execute permissions. The first 7 in 777 gives the owner full rwx permissions, the second 7 gives the group full rwx permissions, and the final 7 gives other full rwx permissions.

If you want to change permissions so that other users have no permission at all for the file hello.txt, use the following command:

```
chmod 770 hello.txt
```

If you want to change permissions so that the owner has read and write permissions, the group has read permissions, and other has execute permissions, use the following command:

```
chmod 641 hello.txt
```

Keep in mind that the chmod 641 hello.txt command completely changes all the permissions you set with chmod 770 hello.txt.

Besides providing a full three-digit octal permission number, chmod allows you to target specific permission sets (owner, group, or other) and turn individual read, write, or execute permissions on or off. To do this, you need to specify who you are setting permissions for, what change are you making (adding or removing the permission), and which permission you are setting. You may find this targeted approach more convenient.

The "who" values you can use are the following:

u: User, meaning the owner of the file

g: Group, meaning members of the group the file belongs to

o: Others, meaning people not governed by the u and g permissions

a: All, meaning all of the above

The "what" values you can use are the following:

− Minus sign to remove the permission

+ Plus sign to grant the permission

= Equals sign to set a permission and remove others.

The "which" values you can use are the following:

r: Read permission

w: Write permission

x: Execute permission

For example, if you want to change the permissions for the file hello.txt so that the other users could have read permissions again, use the following command:

```
chmod o+r hello.txt
```

To take away execution permission from group members, use following command:

```
chmod g-x hello.txt
```

Reviewing the Hexadecimal Numbering System

A hexadecimal (or hex for short) number is written with two characters, each representing a nibble. Hexadecimal is a base-16 numbering system, so its valid numbers range from 0 to 15. Like base 2 (binary), hex uses exponents that begin with 0 and increase from right to left:

```
4096        256         16          1
16³         16²         16¹         16⁰
A           0           C           1
```

Fortunately, in hex, you have to memorize only the final two columns: 1 and 16. As you can see from the preceding example, the value contains alphabetic characters—valid hex numbers range from 0 to 15, and hex solves the problem of expressing two-digit numbers in a single slot by using letters. For example, A represents the number 10, B stands for 11, C is 12, D is 13, E is 14, and F is 15.

Hex numbers are sometimes expressed with "0×" in front of them. For example, 0x10 equals decimal number 16. As with decimal and binary numbers, you multiply the value in each column by the value of the column to determine hex numbers. In the previous example, you simply multiply 1 by 16 to get 16. To convert a hex number to binary, you write each nibble from left to right. For example, 0×10 is 0001 0000 in binary, and 0×24 is 0010 0100. As a security professional, sometimes you need to review output from software that displays values in hexadecimal numbers. For example, the tcpdump tool uses hexadecimal numbers in much of its output, especially if the systems being analyzed use IPv6. As explained, all IPv6 addresses are in hexadecimal notation.

SECURITY BYTES

Could knowing hexadecimal save your life if you were trapped on Mars? *Spoiler alert:* It worked for Matt Damon's character, astronaut Mark Watney, in the 2015 movie *The Martian.* Watney needed a way to communicate with NASA that made use of cards positioned around a circle and a camera that rotated 360 degrees. However, the 26-character alphabet created problems with the camera angles. He needed a smaller alphabet. Fortunately, hexadecimal has only 16 characters. Writing the hexadecimal characters he got from an ASCII table, which contains 255 characters, he could communicate with NASA. For example, the letter A in ASCII is equivalent to 41 in hex. Many free ASCII-to-hex converters are available online. You can use them to enter a two-digit hex number and get the ASCII letter equivalent. (There's one at www.rapidtables.com/convert/number/ascii-to-hex.htm. Try writing the word HELP! in hex. Don't forget the exclamation point.)

Reviewing the Base-64 Numbering System

Base 64 has a number of uses, both legitimate and illegitimate. A common use for base 64 is for the encoding and transportation of binary files sent through email. All you need to know right now is that attackers can use base 64 in many ways to obfuscate their actions.

Base-64 character mappings are shown in Table 2-6.

To represent 0 to 63 characters, you need only 6 bits, or 26. So the binary representation of the letter A is 000000, B is 000001, C is 000010, and so on. Z is represented as 011001. Just remember that the high-order bit is the 32 column, not the 128 column, as with 8 bits. The lowest number you can represent with 6 bits is 000000 (0), and the highest number is 111111 (63). To convert a base-64 number to its decimal equivalent, simply break the sequence into groups of four characters and represent each character by using 6 bits (24 bits = 6 × 4).

Table 2-6 Base-64 character mappings

Character or symbol	Representation in base 64
Uppercase A to Z	0–25
Lowercase a to z	26–51
Numerals 0 to 9	52–61
+ and / symbols	62, 63

As an example, here is how to convert the base-64 string SGFwcHkgQmlydGh-kYXk= into its decimal equivalent. In this example, the first four characters—S, G, F, and w—are written as three 8-bit numbers (24 bits = 3 × 8).

1. Convert the decimal value of each letter to binary:

   S = 18 decimal, binary 010010

   G = 6 decimal, binary 000110

   F = 5 decimal, binary 000101

   w = 48 decimal, binary 110000

2. Rewrite the four binary groups into three groups of 8 bits. For example, starting with the lower-order bit of the binary equivalent of "w," writing from right to left produces [01]110000. The bracketed binary numbers represent the first two lower-order bits from the F binary equivalent, 1 and 0:

   01001000 01100001 01110000

3. Convert the binary into its decimal equivalent:

   01001000 = 72 ASCII H

   01100001 = 97 ASCII a

   01110000 = 112 ASCII p

Repeat Steps 1 to 3 for the next four base-64 numbers, cHkg, until each letter's base-64 number is converted. (You use one or two equal signs when 3 bytes [24 bits] aren't needed to represent the integer.) What does the base-64 string convert to? Your answer should be "Happy Birthday."

Base-64 decoders are available for free online. As a security professional, you don't need to know how to convert base-64 code manually, but it's important to see how numbering systems are used in practical applications, not just academic exercises.

Activity 2-6: Working with Binary and Octal Numbering

Time Required: 30 minutes

Objective: Apply your skills in binary and octal numbering to configuring *nix directory and file permissions.

Description: As a security professional, you need to understand different numbering systems. For example, if you work with routers, you might have to create access control lists (ACLs) that filter inbound and outbound network traffic, and most ACLs require understanding binary numbering. Similarly, if you're hardening a Linux system, your understanding of binary helps you create the correct umask and permissions. Unix uses base-8 (octal) numbering for creating directory and file permissions. You don't need to do this activity on a computer; you can simply use a pencil and paper.

1. Write the octal equivalents for the following binary numbers: 100, 111, 101, 011, and 010.
2. Write how to express *nix owner permissions of r-x in binary. (Remember that the - symbol means the permission isn't granted.) What's the octal representation of the binary number you calculated? (The range of numbers expressed in octal is 0 to 7. Because *nix has three sets of permissions, three sets of 3 binary bits logically represent all possible permissions.)

3. In binary and octal numbering, how do you express granting read, write, and execute permissions to the owner of a file and no permissions to anyone else?

4. In binary and octal numbering, how do you express granting read, write, and execute permissions to the owner of a file; read and write permissions to group; and read permission to other?

5. In Unix, a file can be created by using a umask, which enables you to modify the default permissions for a file or directory. For example, a directory has the default permission of octal 777. If a Unix administrator creates a directory with a umask of octal 020, what effect does this setting have on the directory? *Hint:* To calculate the solution, you can subtract the octal umask value from the octal default permissions.

6. The default permission for a file on a Unix system is octal 666. If a file is created with a umask of octal 022, what are the effective permissions? Calculate your results.

MODULE SUMMARY

- TCP/IP is the most widely used protocol for communication over the Internet. The TCP/IP stack consists of four layers that perform different functions: Network, Application, Transport, and Internet.
- The Application-layer protocols are the front end to the lower-layer protocols. Examples of protocols operating at this layer are HTTP, SMTP, Telnet, and SNMP.
- The Transport layer is responsible for encapsulating data into segments and uses UDP or TCP headers for managing the transmission of data. TCP is a connection-oriented protocol. UDP is a connectionless protocol. TCP provides guaranteed delivery of data packets but is slower than UDP, which does not guarantee delivery.
- The critical components of TCP segment headers are TCP flags, the ISN, and source and destination port numbers.
- TCP ports identify the services running on a system. Port numbers from 1 to 1023 are considered well-known ports. A total of 65,535 port numbers are available.
- The Internet layer is responsible for routing a packet to a destination address. IP addresses as well as ICMP messages are used in this layer. IP, like UDP, is a connectionless protocol. ICMP is used to send messages related to network operations.
- A type code identifies the ICMP message type and can be used to filter out network traffic.
- IP addresses consist of 4 bytes, also called octets, which are divided into two components: a network address and a host address. Three classes of addresses are used on the Internet: A, B, and C.
- IPv6 addresses consist of 16 bytes and are written in hexadecimal notation.
- Digital devices use the binary numbering system mainly because logic chips make binary decisions based on true or false, on or off, yes or no settings. Binary numbers are represented by 0 or 1.
- The octal numbering system (base 8) uses numbers from 0 to 7. It uses only 3 bits of the binary numbering system because the highest number in base 8 is the number 7, which can be written with 3 binary bits: 111.
- Unix and Linux systems use the octal numbering system to express file and directory permission settings. You can use the chmod command to adjust permission settings.
- Hexadecimal is a base-16 numbering system that uses numbers from 0 to 15. After 9, the numbers 10, 11, 12, 13, 14, and 15 are represented as A, B, C, D, E, and F.
- Base64 is a numbering system that uses numbers from 0 to 63. Numbers 0–61 are represented with alphanumeric characters; 62 and 63 are symbols.

Key Terms

ACK
connection-oriented protocol
connectionless

initial sequence number (ISN)
Internet Assigned Numbers
   Authority (IANA)

Internet Control Message Protocol
   (ICMP)
network session hijacking

port   SYN-ACK   Transmission Control Protocol/
protocol   TCP flag   Internet Protocol (TCP/IP)
SYN   three-way handshake   User Datagram Protocol (UDP)

Review Questions

1. The `netstat` command indicates that POP3 is in use on a remote server. Which port is the remote server most likely using?
   a. Port 25
   b. Port 110
   c. Port 143
   d. Port 80

2. On a Windows computer, what command can you enter to show all open ports being used?
   a. `netstat`
   b. `ipconfig`
   c. `ifconfig`
   d. `nbtstat`

3. What does the command `chmod u+x script.sh` do?

4. Which protocol offers guaranteed delivery and is connection oriented?
   a. UDP
   b. IP
   c. TCP
   d. TFTP

5. TCP communication can be likened to which of the following?
   a. Announcement over a loudspeaker
   b. Bullhorn at a sporting event
   c. Driving on a highway
   d. Phone conversation

6. Which of the following protocols is connectionless? (Choose all that apply.)
   a. UDP
   b. IP
   c. TCP
   d. SPX

7. Which command verifies the existence of a node on a network?
   a. `ping`
   b. `ipconfig`
   c. `netstat`
   d. `nbtstat`

8. What numbering system is used to express IPv6 addresses?
   a. Binary
   b. Octal
   c. Hexadecimal
   d. Decimal

9. List the three components of the TCP/IP three-way handshake.

10. What protocol is used for reporting or informational purposes?
    a. IGMP
    b. TCP
    c. ICMP
    d. IP

11. List the six flags of a TCP packet.

12. How many hosts can a CIDR /24 network have?

13. What port, other than port 110, is used to retrieve email?
    a. Port 25
    b. Port 143
    c. Port 80
    d. Port 135

14. What port does DNS use?
    a. Port 80
    b. Port 69
    c. Port 25
    d. Port 53

15. Given an IP address of 192.168.1.17 and a subnet mask of 255.255.255.192, what are the subnet part of the address and the host part of the address?

16. Which of the following is *not* a valid octal number?
    a. 5555
    b. 4567
    c. 3482
    d. 7770

17. The ISN is set at which step of the TCP three-way handshake?
    a. 1, 2, 3
    b. 1, 3
    c. 1
    d. 1 and 2

18. A `ping` command initially uses which ICMP type code?
    a. Type 0
    b. Type 8
    c. Type 14
    d. Type 13

19. What class is the IP address 172.16.0.1?

   a. Class A

   b. Class B

   c. Class C

   d. Class D

20. What's the hexadecimal equivalent of the binary number 1111 1111?

   a. FF

   b. 255

   c. EE

   d. DD

Case Projects

Case Project 2-1: Determining the Services Running on a Network

Time Required: 30 minutes

Objective: Write a memo summarizing port numbers and services run on most networks. Discuss well-known ports and describe the most commonly used ports: 25, 53, 80, 110, 143, 443, and 993.

Description: Alexander Rocco Corporation has multiple OSs running in its many branch offices. Before conducting a penetration test to determine the network's vulnerabilities, you must analyze the services currently running on the network. Leilani Kaikea, a member of your security team experienced in programming and database design but weak in networking concepts, wants to be briefed on network topology issues at Alexander Rocco Corporation.

Write a memo to Leilani summarizing port numbers and services that run on most networks. The memo should discuss the concepts of well-known ports and give a brief description of the most commonly used ports: 25, 53, 80, 110, 143, 443, and 993.

Case Project 2-2: Investigating Possible Email Fraud

Time Required: 30 minutes

Objective: Write a memo to the vice president outlining the steps an employee might have taken to create an email message that appears to come from another employee's account.

Description: A vice president at Alexander Rocco Corporation says he received a hostile email message from an employee in the Maui office. Human Resources has informed him that the message's contents are grounds for termination, but the vice president wonders whether the employee actually sent the message. When confronted, the employee claims he didn't send the message and doesn't understand why the message shows his return address.

Write a memo to the vice president outlining the steps an employee might have taken to create an email message that appears to come from another employee's account. Be sure to include some SMTP commands the culprit might have used.

NETWORK AND COMPUTER ATTACKS

After reading this module and completing the exercises, you will be able to:

1 Describe the different types of malicious software and what damage they can do

2 Describe methods of protecting against malware attacks

3 Describe the types of network attacks

4 Identify physical security attacks and vulnerabilities

As an IT security professional, you need to be aware of the ways an intruder can attack your network. Attacks include unauthorized attempts to access network resources or systems, attempts to destroy or corrupt information, and attempts to prevent authorized users from accessing resources. You must have a good understanding of both network security and computer security. Network security involves protecting the network infrastructure as well as stand-alone systems. Therefore, computer security is necessary to protect computers and laptops that aren't part of a network infrastructure but still contain important or confidential information. Protective measures include examining physical security (down to checking door locks) and assessing the risks associated with a lack of physical security.

This module gives you a strong foundation on what attackers are doing. Just as law enforcement personnel must be aware of the methods criminals use, you must know what computer attackers are up to. How can a denial-of-service attack be used to shut down a company? How can worms and viruses be introduced into a company's corporate database? How can a laptop be removed from your office with little risk of the intruder being caught or stopped? This module gives you an overview of attack methods and protective measures. To understand the importance of physical security, you also learn that a skilled attacker can pick a lock in seconds.

MALICIOUS SOFTWARE (MALWARE)

Typically, network attacks are initiated to steal data that can be used or sold for financial gain or to carry out a sociopolitical agenda. Network attacks tend to focus on organizations and their interconnected desktop and server computers, but personal devices (such as mobile phones and other Internet-connected devices) are also targets of attacks and malware exploits.

Malware is malicious software, such as a virus, worm, or Trojan program, introduced into a network to help attackers accomplish their goals. The lines between these categories of malware are blurring, with advanced malware now having rich target-dependent functionality that covers multiple categories. The tables in this module show malware that spans multiple categories. Previously, the main goal of malware was to destroy or corrupt data or to shut down a network or computer system. Today, more often than not, the goal is to make money. Scores of cybercrime organizations have warehouses full of programmers who do nothing but write malware with signatures unknown to antivirus programs. Malware was once targeted specifically at Windows, Linux, and other traditional operating systems. Now, it is written to target tablets, smartphones, and other Internet-connected devices. The following sections cover different types of malware that attackers use.

SECURITY BYTES

Security professionals have determined that a highly sophisticated group of cybercriminals were behind the SolarWinds attack of 2020. Called Silverfish, this group used server resources belonging to another cybercrime organization known as EvilCorp. Experts have not officially identified the nation involved in the Silverfish group, but indications point to Russia. When you learn how to use a security tool, remember that the cybercriminals are learning how to use it, too. Because of this, organizations need ethical hackers who know how to use security tools to defend against cybercriminal attacks.

Viruses

A **virus** is a program that attaches itself to a file or another program, often sent via email. The key word is "attaches." A virus doesn't stand on its own, so it can't replicate itself or operate without the presence of a host. A virus attaches itself to a host file or program (such as Microsoft Word), just as the flu attaches itself to a host organism, and then performs whatever the creator designed it to do.

Figure 3-1 shows an example of a phishing message that contains a link to a fake website. The sender of a phishing email uses social engineering to lure a user into following the link to the fake website. When the user follows the link, the fake website tries to steal the victim's logon credentials and credit card information while downloading malicious code to the victim's computer.

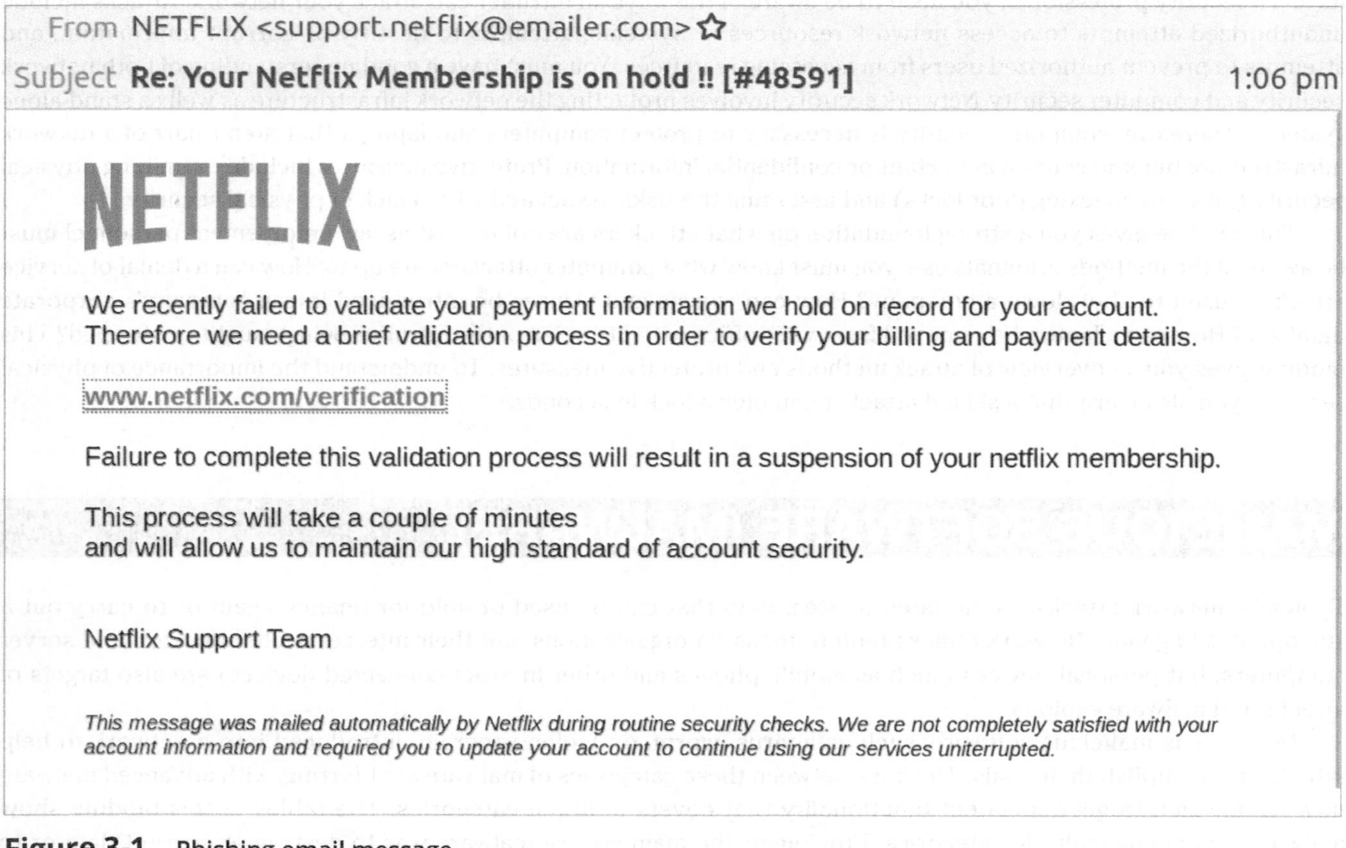

From NETFLIX <support.netflix@emailer.com> ☆

Subject **Re: Your Netflix Membership is on hold !! [#48591]**   1:06 pm

NETFLIX

We recently failed to validate your payment information we hold on record for your account.
Therefore we need a brief validation process in order to verify your billing and payment details.

www.netflix.com/verification

Failure to complete this validation process will result in a suspension of your netflix membership.

This process will take a couple of minutes
and will allow us to maintain our high standard of account security.

Netflix Support Team

This message was mailed automatically by Netflix during routine security checks. We are not completely satisfied with your account information and required you to update your account to continue using our services uninterrupted.

Figure 3-1   Phishing email message

Ransomware, a type of virus that locks a target system until a ransom is paid, is a growing trend in viruses. Over the years, ransomware creators have become more sophisticated. Now, it is common to find a ransomware virus that captures credentials to cloud storage and prevents users from accessing those accounts in addition to files on their local devices.

The bad news about viruses is that there's no foolproof method of preventing them from attaching themselves to computers, no matter how skilled you are as a security professional. Many antivirus software packages are available, but none can guarantee protection because new viruses are created constantly. Antivirus software compares signatures (hashes or code patterns) and common malicious programmatic behaviors (heuristic analysis) of known viruses against every file on a computer; if there's a match, the software warns you that the program or file is infected. These signatures are kept in a virus signature file that the antivirus software maintains. If the virus isn't known, however, the antivirus software doesn't detect a match. Therefore, updating virus signature files regularly is crucial. Many antivirus software packages offer automatic updates. For example, with Symantec Endpoint Protection (SEP), administrators can configure a server that handles pushing antivirus updates to client computers in an organization.

Besides using antivirus software to combat malware, security professionals use network security devices and sandboxing. Network security devices can monitor entire networks and intercept malware before it reaches users. Sandboxing allows users to run programs in a secure, isolated operating area that prevents malicious files from being written to the hard drive. Sandboxing is often used by security professionals to safely test whether a file has malware.

Table 3-1 shows some common viruses that have plagued computer systems. As of the time of this writing, thousands of viruses and variants are being created each day. Listing all known viruses would take up this entire book.

Table 3-1   Common computer viruses

Virus	Description
Ryuk	The Ryuk ransomware virus was responsible for more than one-third of all ransomware attacks in 2020. Ryuk is used in attacks targeting companies, hospitals, and government municipalities. Ryuk encrypts critical files and typically demands a multimillion-dollar ransom.
FormBook	FormBook is a malware family of data stealers and form grabbers. It attempts to steal the contents of the Windows Clipboard, log what you type on the keyboard, and steal data while you browse the web. It is sold as "malware-as-a-service" on hacking forums. Hackers can purchase a subscription and use the FormBook tool. FormBook is usually distributed through spam email containing malicious attachments.
CryptoLocker	CryptoLocker is less prevalent now, but is considered the father of many ransomware viruses. CryptoLocker has become a term referring to families of ransomware viruses. In 2016, it was estimated to have infected more than 250,000 computers. This malware locks the user's files in an encrypted container and requires the victim to pay ransom for their decryption. Like most malware, it is delivered through an email message that is designed to trick users into clicking a malicious link or attachment. Once a machine is infected, victims have a set amount of time to pay the ransom if they want to retrieve their files.
MalumPOS	Malware has targeted devices responsible for processing payments, referred to as POS (point of sale) systems. The MalumPOS virus was used in mid-2015 to attack POS devices at hotel chains. This virus was programmed to find, intercept, copy, and exfiltrate payment card information (e.g., credit/debit card numbers and other information stored on the magnetic strip of a credit card). POS attacks were rare in 2020, but a new strain seems to target personally identifying information only instead of full payment card information.
Carbanak	This virus is spread via phishing emails that almost always target financial institutions. These phishing emails contain a Word document and a malicious .cpl file. (Keep this in mind for the upcoming base-64 decoding exercise.) When it first accesses a system, the malware runs a number of checks to ensure it can gain the proper privileges to further its attack. When proper privileges are obtained or verified, the malware opens a backdoor to a few remote servers under the control of an unknown (to this point) malicious actor. This malware has been used to facilitate fraudulent transactions in financial institutions' funds transfer systems and ATM machines.

(continues)

Table 3-1 Common computer viruses *(continued)*

Virus	Description
Gumblar	First detected in March 2009, this malware spread by mass-hacking hundreds of thousands of websites, which then exploited visiting browsers via Adobe PDF and Flash vulnerabilities. It has made a resurgence in 2020, crashing thousands of blogs and websites that use WordPress, Drupal, Joomla, and other PHP-based constructs. The malware steals FTP credentials and uses them to further compromise websites that the victim maintains. It also hijacks Google searches and blocks access to antivirus update sites to prevent removal. Recent variations install a backdoor that attempts to connect to a botnet.
Gpcode or PGPCoder	This ransomware virus was detected in 2008 and was still active in 2020. Although not widespread, it is unique because it uses practically unbreakable 1024-bit asymmetric key encryption to hide a user's documents on the computer and hold them for ransom until the victim pays for the encryption key.

The following warning was returned to a user with a file called Price.cpl attached to the email message. The email provider rejected sending the message because the attachment was recognized as a potential virus.

```
This message was created automatically by mail delivery software. A message that you
sent could not be delivered to one or more of its recipients. This is a permanent
error. The following address (es) failed:
```

```
CustomerService@MSIGroupInc.com
```

```
        This message has been rejected because it has a potentially executable attachment
        "Price.cpl"
```

```
        This form of attachment has been used by recent viruses or other malware. If you
        meant to send this file then please package it up as a zip file and resend it.
```

[Message header deleted for brevity]

```
boundary="--------sghsfzfldbjbzqmztbdx"--------
```

```
sghsfzfldbj bzqmztbdx
```

```
Content-Type: text/html; charset="us-ascii"
```

```
Content-Transfer-Encoding: 7bit
```

```
<html><body>
```

```
:))
```

```
<br>
```

```
</body></html>
```

```
--------sghsfzfldbjbzqmztbdx
```

```
Content-Type: application/octet-stream; name="Price.cpl"
```

```
Content-Transfer-Encoding: base64
```

```
Content-Disposition: attachment; filename="Price.cpl"
```

```
TVqQAAMAAAAEAAAA//8AALgAAAAAAAAQAAAAAAAAAAAAAAAAAAAAAAAAAAAAAAAAAAAAAAAAAAAg
AAAAA4fug4AtAnNIbgBTM0hVGhpcyBwcm9ncmFtIGNhbm5vdCBiZSBydW4gaW4gRE9TIG1vZGUuDQ0KJAAAAAAA
ABQRQAATAEDAA+kgUEAAAAAAAAAOAADiELAQUMAAwAAACAAAAAAAAQBUAAAAQAAAAIAAAAAAEAAQAAAAgAABA
AAAAAAAA
```

[Several pages of code cut for brevity]

This cryptic code has been encoded in base 64. Recall that base 2 (binary), base 8 (octal), and base 16 (hexadecimal) are common numbering systems that computers use. Base 64 is another one you should know. Running a base-64 decoder on the Price.cpl code reveals the following suspicious programming code:

```
This program cannot be run in DOS mode.
user32.dll CloseHandle() CreateFileAb GetWindowsDirectory WriteFile
```

```
strcat kernel32.dll Shell Execute shell32 KERNEL32.DLL USER32.DLL
GetProcAddress LoadLibrary ExitProcess Virtual FreeMessageBox
```

This code shows something suspicious happening in an attachment. The first line, "This program cannot be run in DOS mode," identifies the text that follows as a program, which alerts you that the email attachment contains a hidden computer program. In the third line, a shell being executed adds to the suspicious nature of the Price. cpl attachment. A shell is an executable piece of programming code that creates an interface to an OS for issuing system commands and shouldn't appear in an email attachment. References to User32.dll and especially Kernel32. dll should also raise a red flag because dynamic link library (DLL) files are executables. In addition, Kernel32.dll is responsible for memory management and I/O operations, so a reference to this file in an email attachment should raise more than a red flag; it should raise your blood pressure. You can see that the email provider's rejection of this email message was valid.

Activity 3-1: Identifying New Computer Viruses and Worms

Time Required: 30 minutes

Objective: Examine some current computer virus threats.

Description: As a security professional, you must keep abreast of the many new viruses and worms that might attack networks and computers. If one computer is compromised, all computers in your network could be compromised. Many firewalls don't detect malware attached to an executable program or a macro virus (covered later in this section), so security professionals need to train users on the dangers of installing software, including games and graphics, on a computer. Remember, a firewall doesn't examine packets internal to the network, so malware can spread internally in an organization regardless of how effective the firewall is. A good place to learn about new threats is the Internet.

1. Start your web browser and go to **en.wikipedia.org**.
2. On the home page, type **Ryuk (ransomware)** in the search box on the top right, and then click the magnifying glass. What is the probable country of origin of this malware?
3. Give a brief description of Ryuk ransomware and ways to protect yourself from it.
4. Next, go to **www.mcafee.com/enterprise/en-ca/threat-center.html**.
5. Scroll down until you see the latest cybersecurity threats list.
6. List the five most recent viruses or worms displayed on this page.
7. Select one of the viruses or worms you listed in Step 6. Summarize the overview of this piece of malware. What countries are most affected by it? List and briefly describe some of the techniques used by this malware to infect systems. Are there any solutions for protecting systems from this virus? If so, what are they?
8. Leave your web browser open for the next activity.

SECURITY BYTES

Security professionals have many resources for finding information on current vulnerabilities or possible network attacks. You can visit many excellent websites to learn about OS and application vulnerabilities. One site that should be bookmarked in any security professional's web browser is the Mitre Corporation's Common Vulnerabilities and Exposures site at cve.mitre.org. Other helpful sites are www.packetstormsecurity.com, www.exploit-db.com, www.securityfocus.com, Microsoft Security Bulletins (https://docs.microsoft.com/en-us/security-updates/securitybulletins/securitybulletins), www .kb.cert.org/vuls, and, of course, www.google.com.

By identifying all the vulnerabilities associated with a customer's OSs and applications, you can determine which type of attack to use on a network when conducting a security test. You might also discover a vulnerability associated with a different OS that could be used to compromise your client's OS. Remember to think outside the box. Security testing is more than memorizing tools and rules; it relies heavily on creativity and imagination.

> **NOTE**
>
> One difficulty in writing about network security is the varying terminology that professionals use. Security professionals will sometimes use the terms "vulnerability" and "exposure" interchangeably. The Open Source Security Testing Methodology Manual (OSSTMM) attempts to solve this problem, but until all professional organizations adopt one standard, ambiguity will prevail.

Macro Viruses

A macro virus is a virus coded as a macro in programs that support a macro programming language, such as Visual Basic for Applications (VBA). For example, you can write a macro, which is basically a list of commands, in Microsoft Word that highlights a document's contents (Ctrl+A), copies the selected data (Ctrl+C), and then pastes the information into a different part of the document (Ctrl+V). Macro viruses can be coded to carry out a number of malicious actions, such as deleting important files, stealing passwords and web browser history, or allowing remote access to the device. These commands can be set to run automatically as soon as a file is opened.

Macro viruses have been around for decades. Microsoft Office apps such as Word, Excel, and Outlook automatically take measures to counteract macro viruses and prevent them from executing. The fact that productivity software diligently guards against macro viruses underscores that they are still a clear and present danger. A macro virus that first attacked Apple Mac computers in 2017 by injecting lethal code into the OS is still infecting the Mac user community today. The most infamous macro virus is Melissa, which appeared in 1999. It was initiated after a user opened an infected document; the virus then sent an email message to the first 50 contacts it located in the infected computer's address book.

A macro virus is an example of a Trojan horse attack and serves as a specific example of how a malicious payload can be delivered to an unsuspecting target.

In the past, viruses were created by programmers who found the challenge of creating a destructive program rewarding. Today, even nonprogrammers can create viruses easily. In fact, anyone with Internet access can find many websites to learn how to create a virus step by step. This easy access adds to the problems you must deal with as a security professional. It's helpful to put yourself in computer criminals' frame of mind and, like an FBI profiler, try to understand how they think. A good place to start is visiting websites of virus creators and seeing what they have to say. For example, a Google search for "Macro Virus Tutorial" directs you to many websites.

The following excerpt was taken from http://web.textfiles.com/virus/mactut.txt and precedes instructions on how to create and use a macro virus with the intent of clearing the author of responsibility for misuse. Although the text was written in the mid-1990s, it still accurately reflects the "pirate" mindset of some malware creators. If you were to surf the dark areas of the web in search of malware and hacking tools, you would find similar comments from other rogues tagging their wares. Hackers and malicious code creators don't do their work only for the money; they also enjoy being the first to breach a vulnerability and thereby achieve prestige and bragging rights.

LEGALESE

I SHALL NOT BE HELD RESPONSIBLE FOR ANY DAMAGE CREATED BE IT DIRECT OR INDIRECT USE OF THE PUBLICISED MATERIAL. THIS DOCUMENT IS COPYRIGHT 1996 TO ME, DARK NIGHT OF VBB. HEREWITH I GRANT ANYBODY LICENSE TO REDISTRIBUTE THIS DOCUMENT AS LONG AS IT IS KEPT IN WHOLE AND MY COPYRIGHT NOTICE IS NOT REMOVED. SO IF I FIND ANY LAMERS WHO JUST TAKE THE CODE PUBLISHED HERE AND SAY IT IS THEIR OWN I WILL SEE THAT THEY'LL BE PUNISHED. (BELIEVE IT OR NOT:-))!!!

INTRODUCTION

MANY OF YOU MAY BE WONDERING RIGHT NOW WHO I AM AND WHO VBB IS. COME ON LAMERS! GET ALIVE. VBB IS ONE OF THE COOLEST VIRUS GROUPS AROUND. YOU CAN'T TELL ME YOU'VE NEVER HEARD OF US. WELL, OK I'LL ADMIT IT. WE'RE NOT THAT POPULAR YET, BUT THAT'LL COME. SO FOR NOW HERE'S MY CONTRIBUTION TO THE GROUP AS THE LEADER. WELCOME TO THE MACROVIRUS WRITING TUTORIAL PART 1! ENJOY! !

THE TOOLS

FIRST OF ALL YOU'LL NEED MS WORD 6.0 OR UP (DUH), THEN YOU MAY WANT TO GET VBB'S MACRO DISASSEMBLER BY AURODREPH SO THAT YOU CAN STUDY ENCRYPTED MACROS. ALSO YOU SHOULD MAKE BACK-UPS OF YOUR NORMAL. DOT TEMPLATE IN YOUR WINWORD6\TEMPLATE\DIRECTORY, AS THIS IS THE

DOCUMENT COMMONLY INFECTED BY MACRO VIRII. SO WATCH OUT. ALSO I RECOMMEND TO HAVE AT LEAST
A SMALL KNOWLEDGE OF WORD BASIC, SO THAT YOU KIND A KNOW WHAT'S GOING ON. WELL, THAT'S IT.
YOU'VE MADE IT THIS FAR. IT'S NOW TIME TO GET INTO THE MACRO VIRUS GENERALS. . . .

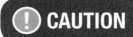 **CAUTION**   Connecting to sites that offer hacking tools or information on creating viruses can be dangerous.
Many of these sites contain Trojan programs and viruses that might compromise your computer.

The rest of the document was deleted because of space constraints. However, you can see that finding information
on creating a macro virus is all too easy.

Activity 3-2: Identifying Macro Viruses

Time Required: 30 minutes

Objective: Examine current macro viruses that pose threats to users.

Description: While macro viruses have been around for a long time, they still remain a viable and potent threat to computers.
You should be aware of new macro virus trends. In this activity, you review some uses of macro viruses and then find out
how to create them.

1. Start your web browser, if necessary, and go to **www.virusbulletin.com/virusbulletin/2014/07/vba-not-dead**.
2. The chart in the article shows a major drop in macro virus activity from 2001 to 2006. Speculate as to why macro
   virus usage has increased since 2012.
3. How are Word documents and Excel spreadsheets designed to trick users into running macros?
4. List some of the recent malware that has used macro viruses. (See the "Final Payload" section.)
5. Use Google to search for **how to create a macro virus**. Did you locate any sites or videos with instructions on
   creating a macro virus?
6. Read or watch the tutorial you discovered in Step 5. Does creating a macro virus seem difficult or easy?
7. Leave your web browser open for the next activity.

Worms

A worm is a program that replicates and propagates itself without having to attach itself to a host (unlike a virus,
which needs to attach itself to a host). Self-propagation allows the malware to "crawl" the network and attempt to
infect other devices that it finds. It is called a worm because of this "crawling" behavior. The most infamous worms are
Stuxnet (covered in Activity 3-3), Code Red, and Conficker. Theoretically, a worm that replicates itself multiple times
to every user it infects can infect every computer in the world over a short period. This result is unlikely, but as with
many pyramid schemes, you can see how a worm can propagate throughout an entire network and even across the
Internet. Online banking, shopping, and other forms of e-commerce have to contend with the threat worms pose to
their infrastructure of computers and servers and to the computers and mobile devices used by their clients.

Table 3-2 describes some of the most infamous worms that have cost businesses billions of dollars as a result of
lost productivity caused by computer downtime and time spent recovering lost data, reinstalling programs and operating systems, and hiring or contracting IT personnel.

Trojans

The most insidious attacks against networks and computers worldwide take place via Trojan programs. Trojans
disguise themselves as useful programs and can install a backdoor or rootkit on a computer. Backdoors or rootkits
are programs that give attackers a means of regaining access to the attacked computer later. A rootkit is created after
an attack and usually hides itself in the OS tools, so it's almost impossible to detect. Back Orifice is a good example of

Table 3-2 Common computer worms

Worm	Description
WannaCry	WannaCry is a ransomware cryptoworm that began its attack in 2017. It targeted vulnerabilities in the Microsoft Windows file-sharing protocol server message block (SMB), which allowed it to spread from system to system. Once on a system, it would then release its ransomware attack. Within a day, WannaCry had infected more than 230,000 computers in about 150 countries.
Flame (also called KyWiper)	Often touted as the most complex malware ever created, Flame was discovered in May 2012. It used advanced techniques to infect both local and remote computers. Its capabilities included microphone/webcam spying, keystroke logging, and screen capturing.
Stuxnet	In 2010, this malicious code was found on the industrial control systems (ICSs) in a nuclear production facility in Iran. Believed to have been delivered via USB drive, the worm may have used newly discovered Windows exploits to propagate itself, according to later analysis. Once the malware spread to a system that was running specific control software, the malware took control of the attached uranium refinement equipment, causing centrifuges to spin erratically and then fail. This is analogous to making a washing machine spin so fast that the motor burns out.
Duqu	Detected in October of 2011, Duqu had design features similar to Stuxnet but with a different objective. Instead of causing damage to uranium refinement equipment, its goal was to steal data from users. This malware targeted government agencies in Europe and the Middle East, where the majority of infections occurred.
Storm	Detected in January 2007, this worm spread through automatically generated email messages. It is estimated that this botnet Trojan program and its variants infected millions of systems.
Waledac	This email worm harvests and forwards passwords and spreads itself in an email attachment called eCard.exe. It has many variants that can be controlled remotely. A recent variant used a geographic IP address lookup to customize the email message so that it looked like a Reuters news story about a dirty bomb that exploded in a city near the victim.
Conficker	Detected in late 2008, this botnet worm and its variants propagated through the Internet by using a Microsoft network service vulnerability. It updates itself dynamically but can be detected remotely with a standard port scanner, such as Nmap, and a special Conficker signature plug-in.
Slammer	Detected in 2003, this worm was purported to have shut down more than 13,000 ATMs of one of the largest banks in America by infecting database servers located on the same network.

Activity 3-3: Analyzing the Stuxnet Worm

Time Required: 15 minutes

Objective: Examine the Stuxnet worm.

Description: The Stuxnet worm damaged physical equipment at the Iranian nuclear facilities it infected. As a security professional, you should be aware of past attacks, because history often repeats itself.

1. Start your web browser, if necessary, and go to **www.google.com**.
2. Type **Stuxnet Dossier** in the search box, and then press **Enter**.
3. What vulnerability did the worm use to propagate itself?
4. Did the worm seem to target specific countries?
5. Did the worm target specific systems? If so, how?
6. Leave your web browser open for the next activity.

a Trojan that has been popular over the past decade. It allows attackers to take full control of the attacked computer, similar to the way Windows Remote Desktop functions, except that Back Orifice works without the user's knowledge. The program has been around since 1999, but it's now marketed as an administrative tool rather than a hacking tool. Table 3-3 lists some ports that Trojan programs use.

Table 3-3   Trojan programs and ports

Trojan program	TCP ports used
Agobot, Backdoor.Hacarmy.C, Linux.Backdoor.Kaitenh, Backdoor.Clt, Backdoor.IRC.Flood.E, Backdoor.Spigot.C, Backdoor.IrcContact, Backdoor.DarkFtp, Backdoor.Slackbot.B	6667
Backdoor.Danton	6969
Backdoor.Nemog.C	4661, 4242, 8080, 4646, 6565, and 3306
Backdoor.Rtkit.B	445
Backdoor.Systsec, Backdoor.Zincite.A	1034
Emotet	20, 22, 80, 443, 7080 and 50000
Trickbot	447, 8082
W32.Beagle.Y@mm	1234
W32.Korgo.A	13, 2041, and 3067
W32.Mytob.MX@mm	7000

The programmer who wrote Backdoor.Slackbot.B, for example, can control a computer by using Internet Relay Chat (IRC), which is on port 6667. A good software or hardware firewall would most likely identify traffic that's using unfamiliar ports, but Trojans that use common ports, such as TCP port 80 (HTTP) or UDP port 53 (DNS), are more difficult to detect. Also, many home users and small businesses don't manage which ports are open or closed on their firewalls.

SECURITY BYTES

Many software firewall products for home users do a good job of recognizing port-scanning programs or detecting connection attempts from a computer via a questionable port, such as port 6667. However, many of these firewalls prompt users to allow or disallow this traffic. The problem is that users who aren't aware of these Trojans simply click Allow when warned about suspicious activity on a port. Also, many Trojans use standard ports to conduct their exploits, which makes it difficult for average users to distinguish between suspicious activity and normal Internet traffic. You should educate network users about these basic concepts if no corporate firewall or corporate policy establishes rules and restrictions to combat Trojans.

Spyware

If you search the web using the keyword "spyware," you'll be bombarded with hundreds of links. Some tout spyware removal, but others install spyware on a computer when the user clicks the Yes button in a dialog box asking whether the computer should be checked for spyware (see Figure 3-2). When you click the Yes button, the spyware installation begins.

A spyware program sends information from the infected computer to the person who initiated the spyware program on your computer. This information could be confidential financial data, passwords, PINs—just about any data stored on your computer. You need to make sure users understand that this information collection is possible and that spyware programs can register each keystroke entered. It's that simple. This type of technology not only exists but is prevalent. It can be used to record and send everything a user enters to an unknown person located halfway around the world. Tell users they shouldn't assume that physical security measures, such as locked doors, are enough to keep all intruders out.

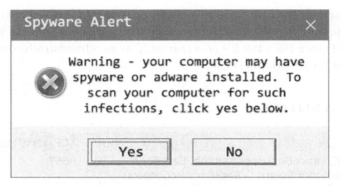

Figure 3-2   Spyware initiation program

Activity 3-4: Identifying Spyware

Time Required: 30 minutes

Objective: Examine prevalent spyware programs.

Description: Network security professionals know that spyware is one of the worst types of malicious attacks on corporate networks. Spyware can be installed on any computer through various means; the most common approach is installing spyware automatically after a user clicks a hyperlink or runs a program without verifying its authenticity. You should be aware of any new spyware programs as well as software that can remove spyware from a computer.

1. Start your web browser, if necessary, and go to **www.google.com**. Type **spyware** in the search box, and then press **Enter**.
2. List some of your search results.
3. Write a description of spyware based on one of the sites you listed in Step 2.
4. In your web browser, go to **us-cert.cisa.gov**.
5. On the home page, enter **spyware** in the search box, and then press **Enter**.
6. Click the **Recognizing and Avoiding Spyware** link. Read the Security Tip article and write a brief description outlining the "How do you know?," "How can you prevent?," and "How do you remove?" sections of the article.
7. Leave your web browser open for the next activity.

Adware

The difference between spyware and adware is a fine line. Both programs can be installed without users being aware of their presence. Adware, however, sometimes displays a banner that notifies users of its presence. Adware's main purpose is to determine a user's purchasing habits so that web browsers can display advertisements tailored to the user. The gathering of your purchasing habits is a security and privacy violation, and this information is likely being sent back to the hackers that deployed the adware.

SECURITY BYTES

Network security begins with each user understanding how vulnerable a computer is to attack. However, being aware of malware's presence, just as you're aware of unscrupulous telemarketers who call you during dinnertime, can better equip you to make valid decisions. If someone offers to sell you property in Tahiti for $99.95 over the phone and asks for your credit card number, you'd refuse. Computer users should be just as skeptical when prompted to click an OK button or install a free computer game.

PROTECTING AGAINST MALWARE ATTACKS

Protecting an organization from malware attacks is difficult because new viruses, worms, and Trojans appear daily. Fortunately, antivirus software can detect many malware programs. For example, Figure 3-3 shows Malwarebytes antivirus software detecting a potentially unwanted program. Educating users about these types of attacks and other attacks, covered later in this section, is also important. After all, users can't be patched. Antivirus programs can mitigate some risks associated with malware, but users who aren't trained thoroughly can open holes into a network that no technology can protect against.

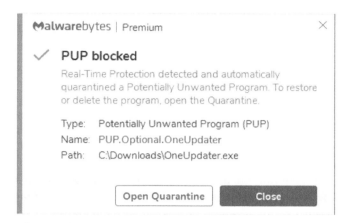

Figure 3-3 Detecting a virus

Antivirus protection must be deployed on user computers, but it should also be deployed on servers (such as email servers) to eliminate malware before it reaches user computers. Hardware solutions can also detect and remove malware for entire networks, such as Unified Threat Management (UTM) devices.

Educating Your Users

No matter how hard you try to protect a network from malware being introduced, it's nearly impossible to prevent infection. It is, however, possible to minimize the damage and the frequency with which computers become infected.

An important nontechnical consideration is conducting structured training of all employees and management. In fact, many U.S. government agencies make security awareness programs mandatory, and many private-sector companies follow their example. A simple but effective method of educating users is emailing monthly security updates to all employees to inform them of the most recent viruses, spyware, and adware detected on the Internet. In addition to structured training, some organizations are now actively phishing their employees and sending them to training content if they click a link they should not click.

To help prevent malicious code from being introduced into corporate networks, many organizations look to application white-listing as a last line of defense. Application whitelisting comes in a few forms, but ultimately it allows only approved programs to run on a computer. For example, programs such as Winword.exe, Excel.exe, and Safari.exe would be whitelisted. All programs not on the white list would be prevented from executing on the user's computer, including a malicious program attached to a phishing email with a link a user clicks.

Another recommendation you should make to a client is to update virus signature files as soon as they're available from the vendor. Most antivirus software updates the signature file automatically or prompts the user to do so. An organization cannot depend on employee vigilance to protect its systems, so centralizing all antivirus updates from a corporate server is prudent.

To counter the introduction of spyware and adware into a corporate network, you should invest in an antivirus product. While many antivirus packages don't fully address the problem of spyware and adware, it is an important first step. As of this writing, two popular spyware and adware removal programs are HitmanPro and Malwarebytes

Anti-Malware (MBAM). Other websites offer similar programs, but remember to use caution when downloading any programs from unknown websites.

Email is the primary way that malware enters an organization. Training employees on safe email practices and how to recognize and avoid phishing messages is essential. A phishing message is an email message a hacker sends that disguises itself as legitimate email. Phishing messages usually include malware attachments or embedded links that download malware if the user clicks the links.

You can also help protect a network by installing a firewall. Many of the top antivirus vendors offer software firewalls for home and small-business users who don't have a hardware firewall or an intrusion detection system (IDS) installed. Companies using firewalls can follow the vendor's configuration instructions. For example, the W32/Sobig.F worm uses UDP port 8998 to contact the attacker's server. By blocking all outbound traffic on this port, you can prevent this attack from occurring. Many services are also started by default on a computer, though they don't need to be. For example, the average home user or small-business owner doesn't typically use Telnet. This service shouldn't be active on most computers because it's vulnerable to many outside attacks.

Avoiding Fear Tactics

You'd be surprised how many users don't know that clicking an icon in an email message can activate a virus or Trojan or allow another person to access their computers from a remote location. Consequently, some security professionals use fear tactics to scare users into complying with security measures. Their approach is to tell users that if they don't take a particular action, their computer systems will be attacked by every malcontent who has access to the Internet. This method is sometimes used to generate business for security testers and, in this context, is not only unethical but also against the OSSTMM's Rules of Engagement. The rule states: "The use of fear, uncertainty, and doubt may not be used in the sales or marketing presentations, websites, supporting materials, reports, or discussion of security testing for the purpose of selling or providing security tests. This includes but is not limited to crime facts, criminal or hacker profiling, and statistics."

Your approach to users or potential customers should promote awareness rather than instill fear. You should point out to users how important it is not to install programs—especially those not approved by the company—on their devices because of the possibility of introducing malware. Users should be aware of potential threats, not terrified by them.

In addition, when training users, be sure to build on the knowledge they already have. For example, some users are familiar with Windows Remote Assistance or other remote control programs, such as TeamViewer and VNC. Users' experience with these programs makes the job of explaining how an intruder can take control of their computers easier because they already know the technology is available.

INTRUDER ATTACKS ON NETWORKS AND COMPUTERS

An **attack** is defined as any attempt by an unauthorized person to access, damage, or use network resources or computer systems. Typically, an attack happens when a weakness or **vulnerability** is exploited. An **exploit** is a specially crafted string of data intended to take advantage of a vulnerability. **Network security** is concerned with the security of computers or devices that are part of a network infrastructure. **Computer security** is defined as securing a stand-alone computing device that's not part of a network infrastructure. The FBI, CIA, and Interpol warn that computer crime is the fastest-growing type of crime worldwide. After all, attacking a corporate network from the comfort of home is much easier than breaking into a business at 3:00 a.m. Speaking on the subject of the difficulty of prosecuting computer criminals, FBI agent Arnold Aanui, Jr., from the Honolulu FBI Cybercrime Division, stated in an interview: "Even if the FBI tracks down the computer used in a crime, if more than one person has access to that computer, the FBI can't arrest the alleged perpetrator because any one of the users might have committed the crime." Unless the laws change so that the punishment for committing these crimes becomes more of a deterrent, security professionals will be busy for many years.

In an affluent neighborhood in Hawaii, the FBI stormed into a quiet residential home with warrants in hand, prepared to arrest the occupant and confiscate his desktop computer, which was alleged to contain records of drug transactions and other incriminating evidence. While FBI personnel were cautiously entering the front of the house, they heard a gunshot from a rear bedroom. When they entered the room, they saw a man seated on the bed and a 12-gauge shotgun leaned against a closed door. He had just emptied a round into the computer, destroying the hard drives so thoroughly that the data couldn't be recovered. The FBI agents could have tried sending the disks to a lab that specialized in data recovery from hard disks but decided not to because they believed they had enough evidence from other sources.

Denial-of-Service Attacks

As the name implies, a denial-of-service (DoS) attack prevents legitimate users from accessing network resources. In a DoS attack, attackers aren't attempting to access the information on a remote computer. However, they might be using the attack to cripple the network.

As a security tester, you don't usually install a virus or worm on a customer's computer as part of your testing. Similarly, you should know how a DoS attack can take place and attempt to protect a company from it, but conducting the attack yourself isn't wise. Doing so would be like a safety consultant blowing up a refinery after being hired to look for safety hazards. You simply need to explain how the attack could be carried out.

An old but useful example of a DoS attack is the Ping of Death attack. This attack causes the victim computer to freeze and malfunction. It is not as common as it was during the late 1990s. The attacker creates an ICMP packet larger than the maximum-allowed 65,535 bytes. The large packet is fragmented into smaller packets and reassembled at its destination. The user's system at the destination point can't handle the reassembled oversized packet, thereby causing the system to crash or freeze. This is also an example of a buffer overflow attack, which is discussed later in this module.

Distributed Denial-of-Service Attacks

A distributed denial-of-service (DDoS) attack is launched against a host from multiple servers or workstations. In a DDoS attack, a network could be flooded with billions of packets; typically, each participant in the attack sends only a few of the total number of packets. If one server bombards an attacked server with hundreds or even thousands of packets, available network bandwidth could drop to the point that legitimate users notice a performance degradation. Now imagine 1000 servers or even 10,000 distributed servers involved, with each server sending several thousand IP packets to the attacked server. There you have it: a DDoS attack.

Keep in mind that participants in the attack often aren't aware their computers are taking part in the attack. They, too, have been attacked by the culprit. In fact, in one DDoS attack, a company was flooded with IP packets from thousands of Internet routers and web servers belonging to Yahoo.com.

A Dark DDoS attack is a smoke screen to distract network defenders while another stealthier and likely more damaging attack is occurring. By focusing network defenders on a sustained "noisy" DDoS attack, the attacker can carry out a fraudulent transaction or exfiltration of data that might have been caught if the defenders had not focused on the DDoS.

Security professionals will be studying one of the world's most widespread DDoS attacks for years. Estonia, in Northern Europe, fell victim to a DDoS attack in 2007 that shut down government websites, banks, and other financial institutions. The malicious traffic came from all over the world, including the United States and Canada. DDoS attacks are difficult to stop because owners of the compromised computers, referred to as zombies, are unaware that their systems are sending malicious packets to a victim thousands of miles away. These compromised computers are usually part of a botnet (a network of "robot" computers) following instructions from a central location or system. For more information, search for "Estonia DDoS."

Buffer Overflow Attacks

A number of buffer overflow attacks on different OSs have taken place over the years. In a **buffer overflow attack**, an attacker finds a vulnerability in poorly written code that doesn't check for a defined amount of memory space use. If a program defines a variable size of 64 bytes (the total amount of memory the variable is supposed to use), and the program writes data over the 64-byte mark without triggering an error or preventing this occurrence, you have a buffer overflow. For example, the QEMU virtualization software reserved a buffer of 512 bytes to receive data from a virtual drive, but a researcher found a way to send more than 512 bytes and take control of the VM host from inside a virtual machine. Basically, the attacker writes code that overflows the buffer, which is possible because the program accepts unvalidated user input. The trick is to not fill the overflowed memory with meaningless data, but to fill it with executable program code. That way, the OS runs the code, and the attacker's program does something harmful. Usually, the code elevates the attacker's permissions to an administrator's level or creates a service that allows an attacker to remotely access the target system. Table 3-4 describes some current buffer overflow vulnerabilities.

Table 3-4   Buffer overflow vulnerabilities

Buffer overflow	Description
Cisco ASA Internet Key Exchange	Cisco Security Advisory for CVE-2016-1287 (https://tools.cisco.com/security/center/content/CiscoSecurityAdvisory/cisco-sa-20160210-asa-ike) discusses a serious buffer overflow vulnerability in the Cisco ASA product line. Attackers could send a specially crafted packet to the affected device, allowing them to gain full administrative privileges. This attack could be carried out from anywhere on the Internet if ASAs are used on a company's perimeter.
GHOST	This vulnerability made headlines across the globe when it was discovered by security researchers at Qualys (https://community.qualys.com/blogs/laws-of-vulnerabilities/2015/01/27/the-ghost-vulnerability). Under the right conditions, GHOST could be exploited to gain administrative access to a remote system with no credentials. The vulnerability resulted from a weakness with the "glibc" library, a central component of Linux operating systems.
PAN-OS	In 2020, Palo Alto Networks released a fix for a buffer overflow vulnerability in its PAN-OS operating system found in many of its next-generation firewalls. A remote, unauthenticated attacker could use this vulnerability to disrupt system processes or to execute code.
StageFright Android Overflow Vulnerability	Buffer overflows not only affect traditional operating systems but mobile devices as well. This vulnerability, CVE-2015-1538, was found in Android's media playback libraries. Researchers found that a special MMS (Multimedia Messaging Service) message sent to a target Android device could cause an overflow, which allows for remote code execution without any user interaction.
VPN Product	In 2020, the NSA alerted administrators about buffer overflow vulnerabilities in three popular VPN products, namely Pulse Secure, Palo Alto GlobalProtect, and Fortinet FortiGate. The vulnerability allowed for arbitrary file downloads and remote code execution on some of these products.
Windows Server Service	Microsoft Security Bulletin MS08-067 (https://docs.microsoft.com/en-us/security-updates/securitybulletins/2008/ms08-067) discusses this buffer overflow vulnerability, which makes it possible for attackers to run arbitrary code placed in memory. This vulnerability allowed the infamous Conficker worm to spread.

In defense of programmers, most are not adequately trained to write programs with computer security in mind. In the past, programs were written for ease of use and to create efficient executable code that ran quickly and used as few computer resources as possible. Today, the trend is to make sure programmers are aware of how their code might be vulnerable to attack, but checking for security vulnerabilities as a standard practice still isn't widespread. A branch of cybersecurity called DevSecOps addresses the need for programmers to develop code with security in mind. Many educational institutions offer courses on writing programs while taking security into consideration.

Independent and sponsored initiatives, such as Open Web Application Security Project (OWASP) and Building Security In Maturity Model (BSIMM), are encouraging secure development and helping organizations build better software. At Microsoft, programmers are now rewarded for writing code that doesn't show up later as a vulnerability in the system. In Activity 3-5, you examine some software with vulnerabilities caused by overlooking the security factor in the program design.

Activity 3-5: Researching Software Vulnerabilities

Time Required: 30 minutes

Objective: Examine some vulnerabilities released by the U.S. Computer Emergency Readiness Team (US-CERT).

Description: As a security professional conducting a security test on a customer's network, you need to investigate any vulnerabilities that might be exploited. After discovering vulnerabilities that might affect a client's network, you must document your findings and make recommendations to correct the problem. In this activity, you examine vulnerabilities reported by US-CERT and learn what solutions or recommendations you might give to customers.

1. Start your web browser, if necessary, and go to **www.us-cert.gov/ncas**.
2. Scroll down and click the **View Bulletins** link, and then click the most recent bulletin.
3. Investigate the first few vulnerabilities. Pick one and use the links in the "Source & Patch Info" column to answer the following questions: What recommendations would you give to someone whose system had been exploited because of this vulnerability? Can anything be done to prevent exploitation of this vulnerability?
4. Exit your web browser.

Activity 3-5 gives you insight into software vulnerabilities used to exploit an OS or software running on an OS. Usually, the main purpose of a buffer overflow attack is to insert code into the overwritten area of memory that elevates the attacker's permissions or gives an attack remote access to a machine.

Eavesdropping

An attacker can listen to unencrypted network communications to intercept confidential information or gather credentials that can be used to extend the attack. Eavesdropping can be accomplished with sniffing tools designed to capture copies of packets being sent across a network (e.g., tcpdump and Wireshark). Later, these captured packets, typically stored in a .pcap file, can be reconstructed and scoured for data and credentials. Useful tools for viewing .pcap files include RSA's NetWitness Investigator and CapAnalysis. To defend against the threat of eavesdropping, network equipment and applications should be forced to communicate only over encrypted protocols and use valid, trusted certificates.

Man-in-the-Middle Attacks

One step beyond eavesdropping is a man-in-the-middle attack. Attackers can inject themselves between two parties or systems communicating with one another to manipulate messages being passed back and forth.

Network Session Hijacking

Network session hijacking enables an attacker to join a TCP session and make both parties think he or she is the other party. This is a complex attack beyond the scope of this book.

ADDRESSING PHYSICAL SECURITY

Protecting a network from attacks is not always a software issue. You should have some basic skills in protecting a network from physical attacks as well. No matter how effective your firewall is, you must secure servers and computers from an attack from within the organization. In fact, there's a higher chance that an attacker who breaks into the network is from inside the company rather than outside.

SECURITY BYTES

On a military base in Hawaii, a pickup truck parked in front of an office building, and the driver entered the building and walked into an empty office. He disconnected a computer from the network, carried it out of the office, placed it in the truck's flatbed, and drove off, never to be seen again. When upper management questioned the staff, employees said they remembered seeing someone walking out of the building with the computer but assumed he was a help desk employee. Physical security is only as strong as the weakest link. All employees need to be aware of what's happening in their work environment. For example, if they notice a stranger sitting in front of a computer downloading files, they should contact security and then confront the person. Employees should be vigilant and not depend on security personnel alone to pay attention.

Keyloggers

Keyloggers are hardware devices or software that can be used to capture keystrokes on a computer. If you are conducting a security test on a system and need to obtain passwords, keyloggers can be a helpful tool. Of course, you should have written permission from the client before using software or hardware keyloggers. Software keyloggers behave like viruses or Trojans. A hardware keylogger is a small device—often smaller than an inch long. It can usually be installed in less than 30 seconds.

Keyloggers can be used by organizations and people who want to monitor the activity of users on their computer systems. Law enforcement and forensic experts also use keyloggers for the same monitoring purpose.

Most hardware keyloggers are small devices that connect to a USB port in a keyboard and a USB port on the back of a computer. These keyloggers store the keystrokes of users internally, so the keylogging device often has to be extracted to examine the contents. Many keyloggers have built-in Wi-Fi so that you can retrieve the stored keystrokes remotely without having to remove the device. Some Wi-Fi keyboards even have built-in Wi-Fi keyloggers.

Some common hardware keyloggers are KeyGrabber and KeyGhost. Once installed, KeyGrabber automatically starts to record keystrokes. To enter playback mode, users can enter a key combination to enable a hidden flash drive. In this flash drive, users can find LOG.TXT, which contains a log regarding every keystroke entered since the device was installed. Figure 3-4 shows a Wi-Fi USB device and a keyboard and the smartphone app that can read their stored keystrokes.

Figure 3-4   Wi-Fi USB keylogger, keylogger keyboard, and keylogger phone app

Attackers can also use keylogger devices. An unscrupulous employee can connect a keylogger to a manager's computer and retrieve confidential information later. Installing this device does require access to the computer, which might pose a problem if the manager's office is locked. If the attacker uses a Wi-Fi-capable keylogger, keystroke information can be retrieved remotely, eliminating the need to gain access to the manager's office in the future. Recall that keyloggers are also available as software (spyware) loaded on a computer, and retrieved information can be emailed or transferred to a remote location.

When doing random visual tests of computers in your organization, keep an eye out for any suspicious hardware attached to the keyboard cable that wasn't installed by security personnel. This check is a simple way to monitor for keyloggers (or even computer systems) that the company didn't install.

Behind Locked Doors

As a security professional, you should be aware of the types of locks used to secure a company's assets. If an intruder gets physical access to a server—whether it's running Linux, Windows, or another OS—it doesn't matter how good your firewall or IDS is. Encryption or public key infrastructure (PKI) enforcements don't help in this situation, either. If intruders can sit in front of your server, they can hack it. Simply put, *lock up your server*.

In the same way that terrorists can learn how to create a bomb by doing Internet research, attackers can find countless articles about lockpicking. One website, "Lockpicking-by Deviant Ollam" (http://deviating.net/lockpicking/), discusses the vulnerabilities of a variety of locks and has videos to show lockpicking techniques. In just a few days of practice, the average person can learn how to pick a typical American home lock in less than five minutes. Those who have more time on their hands, such as hackers, can learn to pick a deadbolt lock in under 30 seconds. If you're responsible for protecting a network infrastructure that has night-shift workers, don't assume that locked doors or cabinets can keep out unscrupulous employees with time on their hands. Typically, fewer employees are around during nonstandard business hours, which makes it easier for them to get into areas to which they might not normally have access. Your server room should have the best lock your company can afford. Take the time to look into locks that organizations such as the Department of Defense use, where protecting resources might be a life-or-death situation. Spending $5000 to $10,000 on a lock isn't unheard of in these organizations.

SECURITY BYTES

Some legitimate websites offer tools and manuals on lockpicking for police or security professionals. They often require you to complete a form, but it could be worth your while if you plan to become a security professional. For example, if you're conducting a security test on an organization that has a locked server room and you want to gain access, knowing how to pick a lock could be beneficial. Remember, however, that you must get written permission from management before conducting this level of testing.

When ordering lockpicking tools, be aware that many states or countries consider the mere possession of these tools a crime. Remember that possession of certain hacking tools is also illegal.

Rotary locks that require pushing in a sequence of numbered bars are more difficult to crack than deadbolt locks. However, neither lock type keeps a record of who has entered the locked room, so some businesses require using card access for better security. With this method, a card is scanned, and access is given to the cardholder while documenting the time of entry. This method also makes it possible for one card to allow access to several doors without having to issue multiple keys or having users memorize different combinations.

Biometric security devices that read fingerprints or retinal scans are also used to restrict access to secure areas. Biometric devices can complement traditional physical locks and provide a second authentication factor, or they can be used on their own without a traditional physical lock. Traditional locks with numbered combinations are vulnerable to someone sharing the password with an unauthorized person. Biometric devices avoid this vulnerability.

SECURITY BYTES

Biometric security devices are useful options for access authentication but are not without faults. Some biometric scanners can be tricked, allowing unauthorized users access to secure resources, though improvements in biometric technology have reduced that possibility. Some smartphones come with a biometric fingerprint lock or a facial recognition feature that can be used authenticate access to the phone. These security features have been easily circumvented in the past. In one instance, a photograph was used to trick facial recognition. Biometrics should be used with another authorization method, such as a passcode, to provide multifactor authentication, which is more secure.

MODULE SUMMARY

- Security professionals must be aware of attacks that can take place on network infrastructures, computers, mobile phones, and other Internet-capable devices.
- Network and computer attacks can be perpetrated by insiders as well as outside attackers.
- Malicious software (malware)—such as viruses, worms, and Trojans—can attack a network or computer. A virus attaches itself to a host. A worm can replicate and propagate itself without attaching itself to a host. A Trojan disguises itself as a useful program or application and can install a backdoor or rootkit on a computer.
- Users can install spyware programs inadvertently, thinking they're installing software to protect their computers. Spyware can record information from a user's computer and send it to the attacker.
- Security professionals can minimize the damage and likelihood of an infection by following best practices and implementing technical and nontechnical measures.
- Adware programs can also be installed without users' knowledge. They're used to discern users' buying patterns for the purpose of sending web advertisements tailored to their buying habits.
- A denial-of-service (DoS) attack prevents authorized users from accessing network resources. The attack is usually accomplished through excessive use of bandwidth, memory, and CPU cycles.
- A distributed denial-of-service (DDoS) is an attack on a host from multiple servers or computers.
- The main purpose of buffer overflows is to insert executable code into an area of memory that elevates the attacker's permissions to the level of an administrator or allows an attacker remote access to the target system.
- In a Ping of Death attack, the attacker crafts an ICMP packet to be larger than the maximum 65,535 bytes, which causes the recipient system to crash or freeze. Most systems today aren't affected by this exploit.
- In network session hijacking, the attacker joins a TCP session and makes both parties think he or she is the other party.
- Keyloggers make it possible to monitor what's being entered on a computer system. They can be installed on a keyboard connector easily and store information internally. Security personnel should conduct random checks of computer hardware to detect these devices.
- Physical security is everyone's responsibility. All desktop systems and servers must be physically secured.

Key Terms

adware	exploit	shell
attack	keylogger	spyware
backdoor	macro virus	Trojan program
botnet	malware	virus
buffer overflow attack	network security	virus signature file
computer security	Ping of Death attack	vulnerability
denial-of-service (DoS) attack	ransomware	white-listing
distributed denial-of-service	rootkit	worm
(DDoS) attack	sandboxing	zombie

Review Questions

1. What is the main purpose of malware?
   a. Financial gain or destruction
   b. Learning passwords
   c. Discovering open ports
   d. Identifying an operating system

2. A computer _____ relies on a host to propagate throughout a network.
   a. worm
   b. virus
   c. program
   d. sniffer

3. An exploit that attacks computer systems by inserting executable code in areas of memory because of poorly written code is called which of the following?
   a. Buffer overflow
   b. Trojan program
   c. Virus
   d. Worm

4. Which of the following exploits might hide its destructive payload in a legitimate application or game?
   a. Trojan
   b. Macro virus
   c. Worm
   d. Buffer overflow

5. Antivirus software is one of the main points of defense against malware and network attacks. Perform research to discover five of the best "free" antivirus solutions. In a few paragraphs, describe your findings and choose which antivirus software you think is the best and explain why.

6. Which of the following doesn't attach itself to a host but can replicate itself?
   a. Worm
   b. Virus
   c. Trojan
   d. Buffer overflow

7. Which of the following is an example of a macro programming language?
   a. C++
   b. Shell
   c. Basic
   d. Visual Basic for Applications

8. One annoying attribute of adware is to determine a user's purchasing habits and then show pop-up ads featuring items the user might want to buy. Social media platforms, search engines, and e-commerce sites do the same thing. Research the interaction between social media platforms, search engines, and e-commerce sites and how they track users and display targeted ads. In a few paragraphs, describe what you have discovered, and discuss whether you think this is helpful or harmful.

9. Viruses, worms, Trojans, adware, and spyware are five types of malware. Choose one type, and research online the latest piece of malware in that family, how it is affecting businesses and individuals, how it is being delivered to victims, and what is being done to counteract it. In a few paragraphs, describe your findings.

10. A software or hardware component that records each keystroke a user enters is called which of the following?
    a. Key sniffer
    b. Keylogger
    c. Trojan
    d. Buffer overflow

11. Email is the most common way that malware enters organizations. Research some of the latest and cleverest email malware campaigns. In a few paragraphs, describe your findings, and suggest ways to counteract this threat.

12. The Ping of Death is an exploit that sends multiple ICMP packets to a host faster than the host can handle. True or false?
    a. True
    b. False

13. What type of network attack relies on multiple servers participating in an attack on one host system?
    a. Trojan attack
    b. Buffer overflow
    c. Denial-of-service attack
    d. Distributed denial-of-service attack

14. What exploit is used to elevate an attacker's permissions by inserting executable code in the computer's memory?
    a. Trojan
    b. Buffer overflow
    c. Ping of Death
    d. Buffer variance

15. What component can be used to reduce the risk of a Trojan or rootkit sending information from an attacked computer to a remote host?
    a. Base-64 decoder
    b. Keylogger
    c. Telnet
    d. Firewall

16. To reduce the risk of a virus attack on a network, you should do which of the following?
    a. Use antivirus software.
    b. Educate users about opening attachments from suspicious email.
    c. Keep virus signature files current.
    d. All of the above

17. What is the primary way that malware enters an organization?
    a. USB sticks
    b. Email
    c. Buffer overflows
    d. Backdoors

18. An exploit that leaves an attacker with another way to compromise a network later is called which of the following? (Choose all that apply.)
    a. Rootkit
    b. Worm
    c. Backroot
    d. Backdoor

19. Which of the following is a good place to begin your search for vulnerabilities in Microsoft products?
    a. Hacking websites
    b. Microsoft Security Bulletins
    c. Newsgroup references to vulnerabilities
    d. User manuals

20. Four common operating systems are Microsoft Windows, Linux, Android OS, and Apple iOS. Research online to discover current vulnerabilities and exploits that are affecting or attacking each of these operating systems. Usually exploits are specific to a certain operating system. Can you find any single exploit that is capable of attacking two or more of these operating systems? In a few paragraphs, discuss your findings.

Case Projects

Case Project 3-1: Determining Vulnerabilities for a Database Server

Time Required: 60 minutes

Objective: Research known vulnerabilities in a common database server.

Description: You have interviewed Ms. Erin Roye, an IT staff member, after conducting your initial security testing of the Alexander Rocco Corporation. She informs you that the company is running an older version of Oracle's database, Oracle 10g, for its personnel database. You decide to research whether Oracle 10g has any known vulnerabilities that you can include in your report to Ms. Roye. You don't know whether Ms. Roye has installed any patches or software fixes; you simply want to create a report with general information.

Based on this information, write a memo to Ms. Roye describing any CVEs (common vulnerabilities and exposures) or CAN (candidate) documents you found related to Oracle 10g. (*Hint:* A search of the CVE website sponsored by US-CERT, https:// cve.mitre.org/, can save you a lot of time.) If you do find vulnerabilities, your memo should include recommendations and be written in a way that doesn't generate fear or uncertainty but encourages prudent decision making.

Case Project 3-2: Investigating Possible Vulnerabilities of Microsoft IIS

Time Required: 60 minutes

Objective: Research known vulnerabilities in a common web server.

Description: Carrell Jackson, the web developer for Alexander Rocco Corporation, has informed you that the company uses Microsoft IIS for its website. He's proud of the direction the website is taking and says it has more than 1000 hits per week. Customers can reserve hotel rooms, schedule tee times for golf courses, and make reservations at any of the facility's many restaurants. Customers can enter their credit card information and receive confirmations via email.

Based on this information, write a memo to Mr. Jackson listing any technical cybersecurity alerts or known vulnerabilities of IIS. If you find vulnerabilities, your memo should include recommendations and be written in a way that doesn't generate fear or uncertainty but encourages prudent decision making. The website cve.mitre.org is one location you can research IIS vulnerabilities. Using the Search CVE List feature with the keyword IIS will reveal new and past vulnerabilities.

FOOTPRINTING AND SOCIAL ENGINEERING

After reading this module and completing the exercises, you will be able to:

1. Use web tools for footprinting
2. Conduct competitive intelligence
3. Describe DNS zone transfers
4. Identify the types of social engineering

In this module, you learn how to use tools readily available on the Internet to find out how a company's network is designed. You also learn the skills needed to conduct competitive intelligence and how to use these skills for information gathering. Before you conduct a security test on a network, you need to perform most, if not all, of the footprinting tasks covered in this module.

This module also explains the tactics of attackers who use social engineering to get information from a company's key employees. In addition, you examine some of the less glamorous methods attackers use—such as looking through garbage cans, wastepaper baskets, and dumpsters for old computer manuals, discarded media, and other materials—to find information that can enable them to break into a network.

USING WEB TOOLS FOR FOOTPRINTING

In movies, before thieves rob a bank or steal jewelry, they "case the joint" by taking pictures and getting floor plans. Movie thieves are usually lucky enough to get schematics of alarm systems and air-conditioning/ventilation systems, too. At least, that's how Hollywood portrays thieves. Any FBI agent would tell you that most real-life thieves aren't that lucky. However, the smart ones who don't get caught are meticulous and cautious. Many attackers do case the joint to look over the location, find weaknesses in the security system, and determine what types of locks and alarm systems are being used. They try to gather as much information as possible before committing a crime.

As a security tester, you, too, must find out as much as you can about the organization that hired you to test its network security. That way, you can advise management of any problem areas. In computer jargon, the process of finding information on a company's network is called footprinting. You might also hear the term "reconnaissance," and you should be familiar with both terms.

An important concept is that footprinting is passive, or nonintrusive; in other words, you aren't accessing information illegally or gathering unauthorized information with false credentials. With passive reconnaissance, you are not even engaging with the remote systems, but rather attempting to glean information about your target from other sources. Passive activities are likely to go unnoticed.

Active reconnaissance, on the other hand, means you are actually prodding the target network in ways that might seem suspicious to network defenders. This includes activities such as port scans, DNS zone transfers, and interacting with a target's web server. With active footprinting techniques, you are likely to be noticed and your actions logged.

The security tester (or attacker) tries to discover as much as possible about the organization and its network using both passive and active techniques. Almost all of the tools available for footprinting are free and open source. These tools are often referred to as Open Source Intelligence (OSINT) tools. The term OSINT refers to the characteristics of the tools being used, and to a methodology for gathering information from readily available public sources (like the Internet). Table 4-1 lists some footprinting tools; many are available in the latest version of Kali Linux.

> **NOTE**
>
> Many command-line utilities included for Linux systems aren't part of a Windows environment. For example, the `dig`, `netcat`, and `wget` commands don't work from a Windows 10 command prompt, but you can usually download Windows versions from the websites listed in Table 4-1. Security testers should spend time learning to use these command-line tools on a Linux system.

Table 4-1   Summary of reconnaissance tools

Tool	Function
`dig` (Command available on all *nix systems; can be downloaded for Windows platforms from www.isc.org/downloads/bind. `dig` is contained in the BIND download, so download BIND.)	Perform DNS zone transfers; replaces the `nslookup` command.
Domain Dossier (https://centralops.net/co/domaindossier.aspx)	This web tool is useful in gathering IP and domain information (including whois, DNS, and traceroute).
FOCA (www.elevenpaths.com/labstools/foca/index.html)	Extract metadata from documents on websites to reveal the document creator's network logon and email address, information on IP addresses of internal devices, and more.
Google (www.google.com) and Google Hacking Database (GHDB), also called Google Dorks	Uncover files, systems, sites, and other information about a target using advanced operators and specially crafted queries. Some of these queries can be found at the GHDB (www.exploit-db.com/google-hacking-database).
Google Groups (https://groups.google.com)	Search for email addresses in technical or nontechnical newsgroup postings.
Maltego (www.maltego.com)	Discover relevant files, email addresses, and other important information with this powerful graphic user interface (GUI) tool.
`netcat` (command available on all *nix systems; can be downloaded for Windows platforms from https://nmap.org/ncat)	Read and write data to ports over a network.
Netcraft Site Report (https://sitereport.netcraft.com)	Uncover the underlying technologies that a website operates on.
OSINT Framework (https://osintframework.com)	A collection of OSINT tools presented in an interactive web-based mind map that organizes the information visually. You can expand nodes to find collections of tools suited for the task you want to accomplish.
Recon-ng (https://github.com/lanmaster53/recon-ng)	Automate footprinting with this powerful, advanced framework using search engines, social media, and many other sources.
SpiderFoot (www.spiderfoot.net)	A tool with a graphical user interface (GUI) that queries more than 100 OSINT sources to grab intelligence on email addresses names, IP addresses, domain names, web servers, and more.
Spyse (https://spyse.com)	Spyse is a cybersecurity search engine. You can use it to search entire domains or individual systems for vulnerabilities, IPs, DNS records, domains, and more. Spyse claims to be "the most complete Internet assets registry for every cybersecurity professional."

Tool	Function
TheHarvester (https://github.com/laramies/theHarvester)	Used for finding email addresses, subdomains, IPs, URLs, employee names, and more. This is a command line only tool.
WayBackMachine (https://archive.org/web)	Search through previous versions of the website to uncover historical information about a target.
wget (command available on all *nix systems; can be downloaded for Windows platforms from http://gnuwin32.sourceforge.net/packages/wget.htm)	Retrieve HTTP, HTTPS, and FTP files over the Internet.
White Pages (www.whitepages.com)	Conduct reverse phone number lookups and retrieve address information.
Whois (https://whois.domaintools.com or www.arin.net)	Gather IP and domain information.
Zed Attack Proxy (https://owasp.org/www-project-zap)	This is a useful website analysis tool that can crawl through remote websites and even produce a list of vulnerabilities for a remote website.

In this module, you use the Domain Dossier and whois.domaintools.com utilities to retrieve information about a company's web presence, and see how DNS zone transfers can be used to determine computers' IP address ranges and hostnames.

SECURITY BYTES

Each year, Department of Defense (DoD) employees are required to complete security awareness training that emphasizes the dangers of terrorists and spies being able to collect unclassified information. This information can be found in newspapers, websites, and TV and radio news programs, but it can also be gathered from Facebook, LinkedIn, and Twitter. By combining small pieces of information, terrorists can create a fairly detailed picture of the DoD's activities. The DoD wants its employees to realize that discussing seemingly inconsequential information might be more dangerous than imagined. This information, when combined with information from other sources, can be damaging to national security.

For example, a sailor in the U.S. Navy meets a friend in a restaurant and mentions that he'll be gone for six months. At the same restaurant, a civilian working for the DoD mentions to a friend over lunch that she has to work overtime ordering supplies. As you can see, terrorists could easily pick up both pieces of information by listening in on conversations. This example might sound far-fetched, but it's a major method of gathering intelligence. The point is that you, too, need to pay attention to all information that's available, whether it's on a website, in email headers, or in an employee's statement in an interview. Unfortunately, attackers check webpages and newsgroups, examine IP addresses of companies, read job listings, and look for postings from IT personnel asking questions about OSs or firewall configurations. Remember that after gathering a piece of information, you should continue to dig to see what else potential attackers could discover.

CONDUCTING COMPETITIVE INTELLIGENCE

If you want to open a piano studio to compete against another studio that has been in your neighborhood for many years, getting as much information as possible about your competitor is wise. How could you know the studio was successful without being privy to its bank statements? First, many businesses fail after the first year, so the studio being around for years is a testament to the owner doing something right. Second, you can simply park your car across the street from the studio and count the students entering to get a good idea of the number of clients. You can easily find out the cost of lessons by calling the studio or looking for ads in social media, flyers, websites, billboards, and so on. Numerous resources are available to help you discover as much as is legally possible about your competition. Business people have been doing this for years. This information gathering, called competitive intelligence, is also done on an even higher level through technology. As a security professional, you should be able to explain to your clients the methods competitors use to gather information. To limit the amount of information a company makes public, you need a good understanding of what a competitor would do to discover confidential information.

SECURITY BYTES

Just because you can find information about a company and its employees doesn't mean you should divulge it. For example, suppose that during security testing, you discover an employee is visiting a dating service website or questionable newsgroups. As long as this activity doesn't jeopardize the company in any way, you're not obligated to inform the company. Depending on the laws of your country or state, privacy issues might affect your decision on how to handle this situation. Security professionals and company officials can be sued for releasing confidential information of this nature.

Analyzing a Company's Website

Attacks often begin by gathering information from a company's website, because webpages are an easy way for attackers to discover critical information about an organization. Websites are often referred to as web applications. Web applications are programs that run on a web server, and a website is one such program.

Many tools are available for this type of information gathering. One example, Zed Attack Proxy (ZAP), is a powerful tool for Linux, macOS, and Windows that can be downloaded free (www.zaproxy.org). ZAP is an HTTP proxy that processes HTTP requests between the browser and the user.

The figures in this section are intended to show one tool you can use to gather information about a company's website and discover any existing vulnerabilities. More important than the specific tool is that you understand the process a security tester uses when beginning a security test.

Note that you should perform ZAP scans on a website only when you have permission to do so. Scanning a website for vulnerabilities is an attack, and performing this scan without authorization can lead to trouble. You can download a virtual box appliance called Metasploitable2 and use it as a target to scan (https://sourceforge.net/projects/metasploitable/files/Metasploitable2). In fact, this is what was done to capture the ZAP figures in this module.

ZAP requires having Java installed (downloaded from www.java.com). Figure 4-1 shows the main window of ZAP.

Figure 4-1   ZAP main window

To use ZAP to harvest information from a website or web application, you must change settings on the browser used to access the website. ZAP has a feature called Launch Browser on its Quick Start tab that edits the configuration of a web browser to direct traffic through the ZAP proxy. This allows the ZAP tool to intercept and manipulate traffic sent between your web browser and the target web server.

To use the Launch Browser feature, select the Quick Start tab, choose the browser you want to use from the drop-down menu next to the Launch Browser button, and then click the Launch Browser button. Figure 4-2 shows the Launch Browser feature with Firefox selected as the browser.

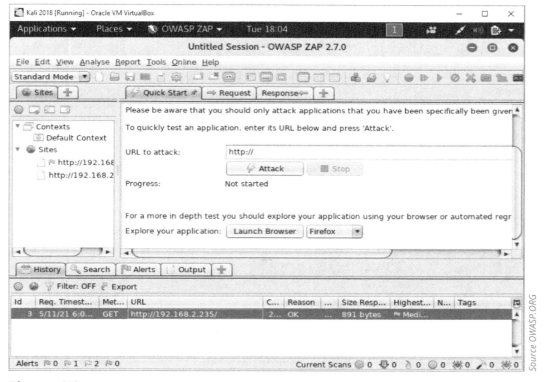

Figure 4-2   ZAP Launch Browser

After the browser is configured, you (or an attacker) can use it within ZAP to navigate to the target site. Figure 4-3 shows the target site in Firefox. In this case, an IP address was used to specify the website, not a URL.

Figure 4-3   Target website open in ZAP-launched browser

In ZAP, the target website is now listed on the History tab in the lower pane and in the Sites list in the left pane. You can right-click the site in either location, point to Attack on the shortcut menu, and then click Spider. See Figure 4-4. In the pop-up window that opens when you select Spider, click the Start Scan button to begin spidering.

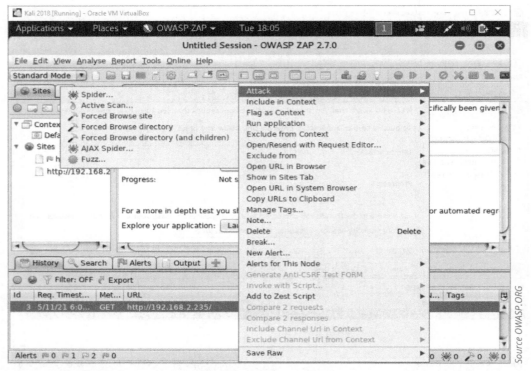

Figure 4-4   Executing a spider (crawl) of targeted website

Spidering (or **crawling**) is an automated way to discover pages of a website by following links. Within a matter of seconds, the paths to webpages on the "spidered" site, including filenames, are displayed on the URLs tab. Spidering is not an attack, but an exploration of a website for content. It is a quieter, friendlier way to analyze a website. See Figure 4-5.

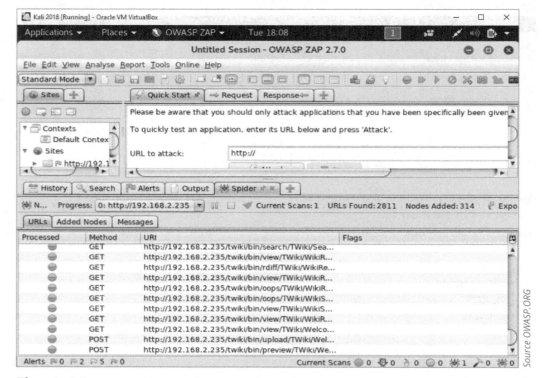

Figure 4-5   Displaying filenames of content on a website

After the site has been spidered, you can actively scan the site using the ZAP Attack feature. An attack is an active scan that first spiders the website, and then sends the web server a series of requests designed to identify vulnerabilities. Once complete, ZAP displays the vulnerabilities on the Alerts tab. You can export the vulnerability information to an HTML report format. Figure 4-6 shows a sample HTML report, with a summary of findings on the top and details about medium-risk vulnerabilities on the bottom.

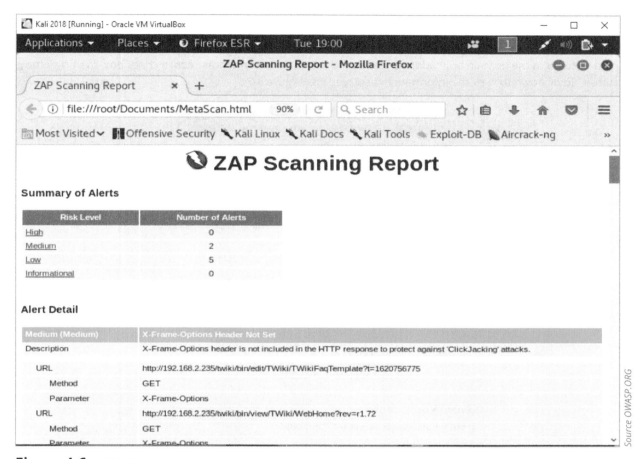

Figure 4-6 ZAP Scanning Report

As you can see, an attack scan allows you to test areas of the site that might have problems. Any vulnerabilities of the website are indicated in the Risk Level column as either High, Medium, Low, or Informational. In Figure 4-6, the risk levels are flagged as Low and Medium.

Gathering competitive intelligence through scans of this type is time consuming, and the more you find out, the deeper you want to dig. Set a reasonable duration for this phase of your investigation so you do not spend too much time on scanning. On the other hand, you don't want to rush your information gathering, because much of what you learn can be used for further testing and investigation.

Using Other Footprinting Tools

The Whois utility is a common web tool for gathering IP address and domain information. With only a company's web address, you can discover a tremendous amount of information. Unfortunately, attackers can also use this information. Often companies don't realize they're publishing information on the web that computer criminals can use. The Whois utility gives you information on a company's IP addresses and any other domains the company might be part of. In Activity 4-1, you practice using the Domain Dossier and whois.domaintools.com Whois functions.

Activity 4-1: Using Footprinting Tools

Time Required: 30 minutes

Objective: Learn how to use footprinting tools (also known as passive reconnaissance tools), specifically the Domain Dossier and whois.domaintools.com Whois function.

Description: Security testers need to know how to use tools for gathering information about networks. With the Whois function, you can discover which network configuration factors might be used in attacking a network.

1. Start your web browser and go to **https://centralops.net/co/domaindossier.aspx**.
2. Type **mit.edu** in the domain or IP address text box, check the **domain whois record** check box, then click the **go** button. Scroll down to view the information displayed (see Figure 4-7).

Source: centralops.net

Figure 4-7   Viewing information with the Domain Dossier Whois utility

Your result may not match exactly what is shown in Figure 4-7. Many domains are reducing the amount of information revealed to help improve security. Notice in the figure the line that reads "Read about reduced Whois data due to the GDPR." The GDPR is the General Data Protection Regulation, a set of European Union (EU) laws governing the protection of personal information. Any country wanting to do business with the EU must comply with these protection regulations.

3. Note the IP addresses and name servers listed.

4. Enter several other organization's domain names in the domain or IP address text box and repeat Steps 2 and 3. Some organizations are discreet about what is listed in their domain records. For example, when describing an administrative contact, showing only a job title is more secure than listing an actual name, as you'll soon discover.

5. Open a new tab in your web browser and go to **https://whois.domaintools.com**.

6. Perform steps 2 through 4 again but using the search function of the **whois.domaintools.com** website. How do the results compare to Domain Dossier?

7. Leave your web browser open for the next activity.

Using Email Addresses

After seeing the information you can gather with the commands covered in this module, you might wonder what else you can do. Knowing a user's email address can help you dig even further. Based on an email account listed in DNS output, you might discover that the company's email address format is first-name initial followed by last name and the @companyname.com sequence. You can find other employee email accounts by acquiring a company phone directory or searching the Internet for any @companyname.com references. Groups.google.com is the perfect tool for this job. In Activity 4-2, you use it to find company email addresses.

Keep in mind that your goal is to learn what attackers can discover via email. As an ethical security tester, you would use that information only to secure systems.

Activity 4-2: Identifying Company Email Accounts

Time Required: 30 minutes

Objective: Determine email addresses for company employees.

Description: Knowing the email addresses of employees can help you discover security vulnerabilities and gather competitive intelligence data. For example, you might discover that an employee has joined a newsgroup using his or her company email account and shared proprietary information about the company. IT employees, when posting technical questions to a newsgroup, might reveal detailed information about the company's firewall or IDS, or a marketing director might mention a new ad campaign strategy the company is considering.

1. Start your web browser, if necessary, and go to **https://groups.google.com**.

2. In the search bar, select **All groups and messages** in the first field, type **@microsoft.com** in the second field, and then press **Enter**. This method is a fast and easy way to find email accounts of people posting questions to the Microsoft domain.

3. Scroll down the list of items and look for postings from employees who work at different companies. (*Hint:* Choose entries containing "Re:" in the listing. They're usually responses to questions sent by employees.) The list will vary, but it should give you an idea of the danger in using a company's email address when posting questions to forums or newsgroups.

4. In a new query, type **@cisco.com** and press **Enter**. Now you can find out who's posting questions to the security company Cisco. Most likely, the postings are from users of Cisco's products. Can you see how an attacker could use this information?

5. Scroll through the list and look for questions from employees of the security company and customers wanting advice. Could attackers use this information for malicious purposes? If so, how?

6. Did you find any information that could be useful to a security tester? How old are many of the returned links?

7. To view more recent postings, modify your query to include **"2020"** and **"2021"**. (Include the quotation marks around search terms to make sure the search results don't include phone numbers or addresses containing these numbers.)

NOTE

In Activity 4-2, you did not search for complete email addresses. However, if you know a user's email address, you can enter it in the groups.google.com search page and perform a targeted search for email messages involving that user. In Case Project 4-1, you have a chance to search on a specific email address. If you were conducting a live security test, you would search for email accounts of IT staff and other key personnel.

Using HTTP Basics

Recall that HTTP operates on port 80, and HTTPS (the secure version of HTTP) operates on port 443. Both versions use HTTP commands (also known as methods) to interact with web servers. A security tester can pull information from a web server using HTTP commands. You've probably seen HTTP client error codes before, such as 404 Not Found. A basic understanding of HTTP can be beneficial to security testers, and you don't have to know too many codes to extract information from a web server. If you know the return codes a web server generates, you can determine what OS is used on the computer where you're conducting a security test. Table 4-2 lists common HTTP client errors, and Table 4-3 lists HTTP server errors that might occur.

Table 4-2 HTTP client errors

Error	Description
400 Bad Request	Request not understood by server
401 Unauthorized	Request requires authentication
402 Payment Required	Reserved for future use
403 Forbidden	Server understands the request but refuses to comply
404 Not Found	Unable to match request
405 Method Not Allowed (Note: Methods are covered later in this module.)	Request not allowed for the resource
406 Not Acceptable	Resource doesn't accept the request
407 Proxy Authentication Required	Client must authenticate with proxy
408 Request Timeout	Request not made by client in allotted time
409 Conflict	Request couldn't be completed because of an inconsistency
410 Gone	Resource is no longer available
411 Length Required	Content length not defined
412 Precondition Failed	Request header fields evaluated as false
413 Request Entity Too Large	Request is larger than server is able to process
414 Request-URI (uniform resource identifier) Too Long	Request-URI is longer than the server is willing to accept

Table 4-3 HTTP server errors

Error	Description
500 Internal Server Error	Request couldn't be fulfilled by the server
501 Not Implemented	Server doesn't support the request
502 Bad Gateway	Server received invalid response from the upstream server
503 Service Unavailable	Server is unavailable because of maintenance or overload
504 Gateway Timeout	Server didn't receive a timely response
505 HTTP Version Not Supported	HTTP version not supported by the server

In addition, you need to understand some of the available HTTP methods, shown in Table 4-4. You don't have to be fluent in using HTTP methods, but you need to be well versed enough to use the most basic HTTP method: `GET / HTTP/1.1`.

Table 4-4   HTTP methods

Method	Description
GET	Retrieves data by URI
HEAD	Same as the GET method, but retrieves only the header information of an HTML document, not the document body
OPTIONS	Requests information on available options
TRACE	Starts a remote Application-layer loopback of the request message
CONNECT	Used with a proxy that can dynamically switch to a tunnel connection, such as Secure Sockets Layer (SSL) or Transport Layer Security (TLS)
DELETE	Requests that the origin server delete the identified resource
PUT	Requests that the entity be stored under the Request-URI
POST	Allows data to be posted (i.e., sent to a web server)

 TIP   For a more detailed definition of HTTP methods, see RFC 2616.

If you know HTTP methods, you can send a request to a web server and, from the generated output, determine what OS the web server is using. You can also find other information that could be used in an attack, such as known vulnerabilities of operating systems and other software. After you determine which OS version a company is running, you can search for any exploits that might be used against that network's systems.

Activity 4-3: Using HTTP Methods

Time Required: 30 minutes

Objective: Determine web server information by using HTTP methods.

Description: Armed with the information gathered from a company web server by using basic HTTP methods, a security tester can discover system vulnerabilities and use this information for further testing. For example, querying a web server might reveal that the server is running the Linux OS and using Apache software. In this activity, you use the `nc` (netcat) command to connect to port 80 and then use HTTP methods. Most web servers use port 443. Those using port 80 are vulnerable, so finding servers using port 80 and using netcat to probe them is a valid penetration testing activity.

1. Start a computer that is running Kali Linux. Log on and then open a command shell by clicking the **Terminal** icon on the panel taskbar. At the command prompt, type **nc www.google.com 80** and press **Enter**. (Port 80 is the HTTP port.)

 TIP   A computer running Kali Linux could be a physical computer where you have installed Kali Linux, a virtual machine running Kali Linux that you have created, or a live bootable USB stick installation of Kali Linux. If you need help, search the Internet for instructions on how to accomplish these Kali Linux computer options.

2. On the next line, type **OPTIONS / HTTP/1.1** and press **Enter**. (Note the spaces around the slash character between the words OPTIONS and HTTP.)

3. On the next line, type **HOST:127.0.0.1** and press **Enter** twice. After several seconds, you see the screen shown in Figure 4-8.

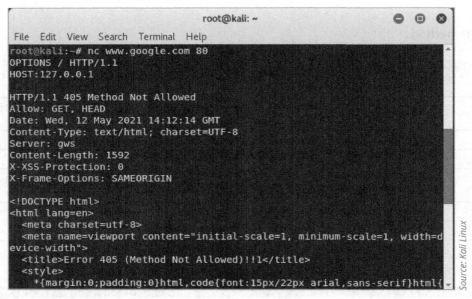

Figure 4-8   Using the OPTIONS HTTP method

Although the OPTIONS / HTTP/1.1 method was not allowed, the response tells you what options are allowed. It's not surprising that Google would disallow commands that might reveal vulnerabilities to hackers.

4. What information generated from the `nc` command might be useful to a security tester? What other options are available when accessing this web server? (Use Figure 4-8 to answer the question if the command doesn't work when you try it.)

5. Type **nc www.google.com 80** and press **Enter** again.

6. On the next line, type **HEAD / HTTP/1.0** and press **Enter** twice to retrieve header information. Your screen should look similar to Figure 4-9. Note the additional information the HEAD method produced, such as indicating that the connection has been closed and specifying the content length (0 bytes).

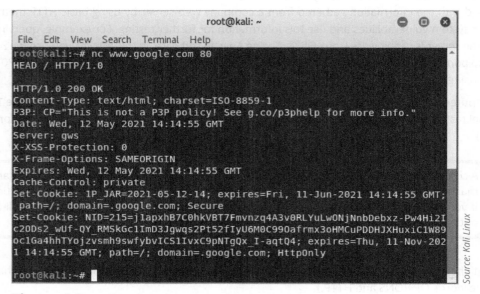

Figure 4-9   Using the HEAD HTTP method

7. On the terminal command line, type **wget www.google.com** and press **Enter**. This command downloads the index page (starting page) of the www.google.com website and stores the HTML code for that page locally on your computer. You can open the resulting file in an editor to examine it. Your screen should look similar to Figure 4-10.

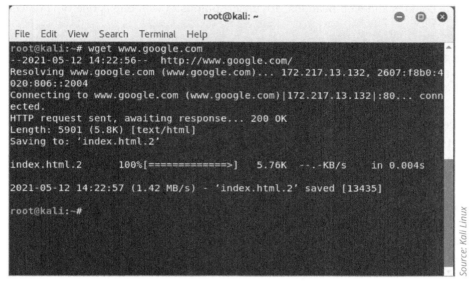

Figure 4-10   Using the WGET HTTP method

8. Close the Terminal shell and log off Linux for the next activity.

 TIP   To see additional parameters for the `nc` command, you can type `nc -h` at the command prompt (see Figure 4-11).

Figure 4-11   netcat parameters

Using Other Methods to Gather Information

So far, you have learned several methods for gathering information from company websites and email addresses. With only a URL, you can determine which web server and OS a company is using and learn the names of IT personnel, for example. You need to be aware of other methods attackers use to gather information about a company. Some of these methods, such as using cookies and web beacons, are unscrupulous. A web bug is one type of web beacon.

Detecting Cookies and Web Bugs

A cookie is a text file generated by a web server and stored on a user's browser. The information in this file is sent to the web server when the user returns to the website. For example, a returning customer can be shown a customized webpage when he or she revisits an online store's website. Some cookies can cause security issues because unscrupulous people might store personal information in cookies that can be used to attack a computer or server. Other cookies store sensitive information (such as user credentials) unencrypted.

A web bug is a 1-pixel × 1-pixel image file referenced in an <IMG> tag, and it usually works with a cookie. It is one type of web beacon, a hidden graphic or piece of code embedded in a webpage to track user activity and harvest user information. The purpose of a web bug is similar to that of spyware and adware: to collect information about the person visiting the website, such as an IP address, when the web bug was viewed, and the type of browser used to view the page. All this information can be useful to hackers. Web bugs are not from the same website as the webpage creator. They come from third-party companies specializing in data collection. Because web bugs are a type of standard image file, usually a GIF, they can't be blocked by a browser or rejected by a user. Also, web bugs usually match the color of the webpage's background, which renders them invisible.

Another form of web beacon embeds JavaScript code into the webpages of a website. That JavaScript code returns tracking information to a data-gathering organization. This type of web beacon is also hidden from the user because it is part of the background code of a webpage and is not visible.

If you don't have a tool for detecting web bugs or JavaScript web beacons, one way to find them is by examining the webpage's source code to find a file in an tag loading from a web server different from other image files on the page. Using a different server might indicate that the image file is a web bug. Also look for pieces of JavaScript that seem to be collecting and sending data to known data-harvesting organizations. Another way to detect web beacons is to check the network connections on a machine (perhaps using netstat) or capture network traffic (perhaps using Wireshark) and see if data is being sent to known data-harvesting organizations. In Activity 4-5, you research the topic of web beacons. As you do, you will likely discover who these "data-harvesting organizations" are. Security professionals need to be aware of cookies and web beacons to keep these information-gathering tools off company computers.

Activity 4-4: Discovering Cookies in Webpages

Time Required: 30 minutes

Objective: Determine whether cookies are present in webpages.

Description: Many companies include cookies in their webpages to gather information about visitors to their websites. This information might be used for competitive intelligence or to determine visitors' buying habits, for example. Security testers should know how to verify whether a webpage contains cookies.

1. Boot your computer into Windows, and start the Microsoft Edge web browser. If you have been using this browser in Windows, cookies are probably loaded on your computer already, so you can analyze them as well as the new cookies you create in this activity by visiting a new site.
2. Click the **Settings and more** button (...) in the upper-right corner of the Edge window, and then click **Settings**.
3. On the Settings page, click the **Cookies and site permission** link in the left pane, and then click **Manage and delete cookies and site data** in the right pane.
4. On the Cookies and site data page, click the **See all cookies and site data** link. A list of cookies is displayed, as shown in the Figure 4-12. The listed cookies depend upon websites you have already visited with this browser.

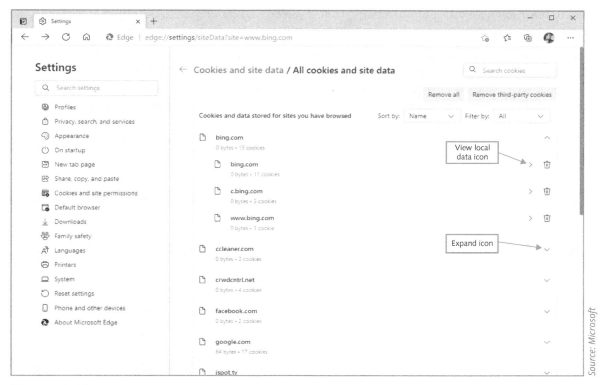

Figure 4-12   Edge browser cookies and site data

5. Click the **expand** icon (a down arrow) to the right of a listed website to open a list of specific cookie groups. Click the **View local data** icon (a right arrow) for a site to display the specific cookies stored for the group. In the list of specific cookies, click the **expand** icon to see the data stored in a cookie. Clicking the trash can icon allows you to delete individual cookies or all cookies for a website. See Figure 4-13.

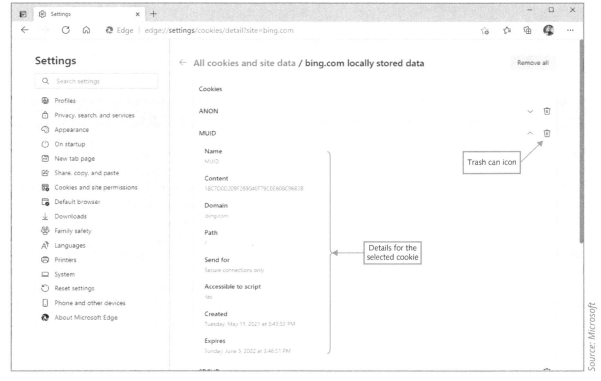

Figure 4-13   Edge browser cookies locally stored data

Check to see if you have cookies from Amazon.com. If you do, you can choose to clear them, or choose a website you haven't visited before and use that for the cookie-checking exercise in the next step.

6. Open a new tab and go to **www.amazon.com** (or a website of your choice). Search for **shoes**.
7. Return to the tab with the All cookies and site data information (navigate back if you clicked deeper), refresh the page, and then expand the amazon.com entry. Are cookies created for more than only the amazon.com domain? Open the cookies information for amazon.com until you display the data contained in the actual cookies. Do any of the cookies have personal information in them?
8. If time permits, visit some sites that require signing in with an account name and password. See whether these sites create any cookies with personal information.

Activity 4-5: Examining Web Beacons and Privacy

Time Required: 60 minutes
Objective: Gain an understanding of data collection with web beacons.
Description: Web beacons are considered more invasive than cookies. As a security professional, you should understand how companies use them to gather information on users who visit websites.

1. Start your web browser in Windows, if necessary, and go to **https://en.wikipedia.org/wiki/web_beacon**.
2. Read the entire article, making note of the methods used and the organizations and applications that use these methods.
3. Perform a web search using the term **web beacons** combined with the names of various social media and search engine companies, such as **web beacons google**. Read some of the information contained in your query results and make note of your findings.
4. Write a one-page report on your discoveries. Your report should include your opinion regarding the hidden tracking methods you've discovered, as well as a description of your findings. Present this report to members of your class, or to a family member.

USING DOMAIN NAME SYSTEM ZONE TRANSFERS

Another way to gather information when footprinting a network is through the Domain Name System (DNS). As you know from learning basic networking concepts, DNS is the network component responsible for resolving hostnames to IP addresses and vice versa. People would much rather memorize a URL than an IP address. Unfortunately, using URLs comes at a high price. DNS is a major area of potential vulnerability for network attacks.

Without going into too much detail, DNS uses name servers to resolve names. After you determine what name server a company is using, you can attempt to transfer all the records for which the DNS server is responsible. This process, called a zone transfer, can be done with the dig command. (If you are familiar with the nslookup command, dig is now the recommended command.) To determine a company's primary DNS server, you can look for a DNS server containing a Start of Authority (SOA) record. An SOA record shows for which zones or IP addresses the DNS server is responsible. After you determine the primary DNS server, you can perform another zone transfer to see all host computers on the company network. In other words, the zone transfer gives you an organization's network diagram. You can use this information to attack other servers or computers that are part of the network infrastructure.

Activity 4-6: Identifying IP Addresses by Using Zone Transfers (Optional)

Time Required: 30 minutes

Objective: Perform a zone transfer on a DNS server.

Description: When footprinting a network, you need to find the IP addresses and hostnames of all servers, computers, and other nodes connected to the network. With commands such as `dig`, you can perform zone transfers of DNS records. You can then use this information to create network diagrams and establish a good picture of how the network is organized. For example, you can see how many hosts are on the network and how many subnets have been created.

NOTE

In this example, zonetransfer.me is used to demonstrate conducting a zone transfer so that you can see what kind of information can be gathered from a zone transfer. At the time of this writing, the zone transfer with zonetransfer.me worked. However, many organizations are tightening security and no longer allow zone transfers, but you should still know the steps for performing one.

1. Log on to Kali Linux and open a Terminal shell. (Your Kali Linux installation could be a physical computer, a virtual machine, or a Kali Linux live bootable USB stick.) At the command prompt, type **dig NS zonetransfer.me** and press **Enter**. A screen similar to Figure 4-14 appears.

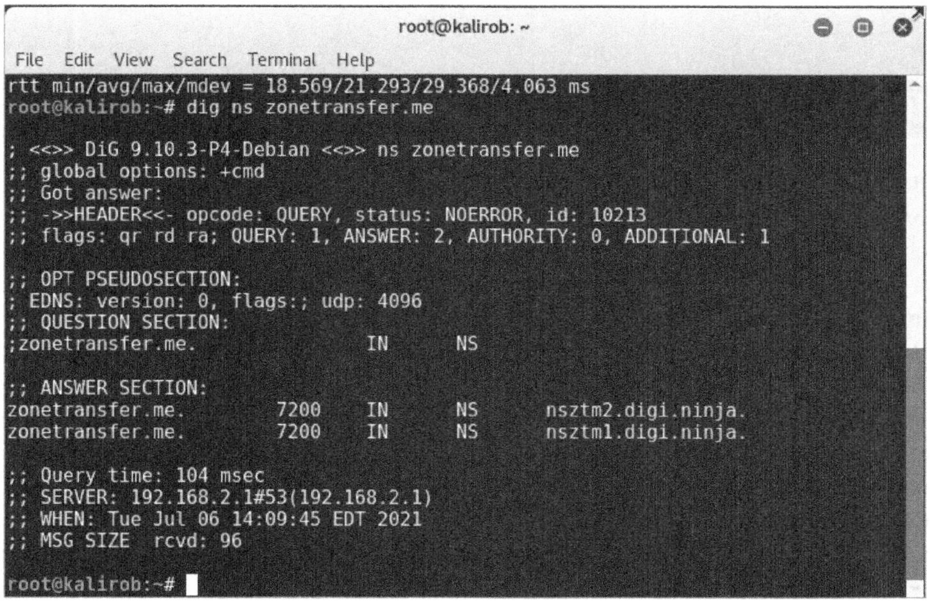

```
                              root@kalirob: ~
File  Edit  View  Search  Terminal  Help
rtt min/avg/max/mdev = 18.569/21.293/29.368/4.063 ms
root@kalirob:~# dig ns zonetransfer.me

; <<>> DiG 9.10.3-P4-Debian <<>> ns zonetransfer.me
;; global options: +cmd
;; Got answer:
;; ->>HEADER<<- opcode: QUERY, status: NOERROR, id: 10213
;; flags: qr rd ra; QUERY: 1, ANSWER: 2, AUTHORITY: 0, ADDITIONAL: 1

;; OPT PSEUDOSECTION:
; EDNS: version: 0, flags:; udp: 4096
;; QUESTION SECTION:
;zonetransfer.me.                IN       NS

;; ANSWER SECTION:
zonetransfer.me.        7200    IN       NS       nsztm2.digi.ninja.
zonetransfer.me.        7200    IN       NS       nsztm1.digi.ninja.

;; Query time: 104 msec
;; SERVER: 192.168.2.1#53(192.168.2.1)
;; WHEN: Tue Jul 06 14:09:45 EDT 2021
;; MSG SIZE  rcvd: 96

root@kalirob:~#
```

Source: Kali Linux

Figure 4-14   Using the dig command

Two name servers, indicated by "NS," are listed: nsztm1.digi.ninja and nsztm2.digi.ninja. (This information might change by the time you perform this activity. If so, ask your instructor for guidelines.) You can see the information that was available to a hacker during zone transfers. If a DNS administrator configured DNS correctly, the following commands shouldn't work. Incorrect DNS configurations leave systems vulnerable to attacks.

2. To perform a zone transfer on the nsztm1.digi.ninja DNS server, type **dig axfr @nsztm1.digi.ninja zonetransfer. me** and press **Enter**. The nsztm1.digi.ninja server is the one for which you're attempting the zone transfer, and the second zonetransfer.me statement is the domain where the server is located. After a short wait, a few records appear.

3. Do the transfer again, but this time use the | less parameter by typing **dig axfr @nsztm1.digi.ninja zonetransfer.me | less** and pressing **Enter**.

4. Press **Enter** or **Spacebar** to view additional records, and then press **q** to quit. Close the Terminal shell and log off Linux.

NOTE

As a security tester, you should always be aware that an attack might be successful one day and unsuccessful another day. So, if an attack works, copy all files and data obtained in the hack to a hard disk or thumb drive as quickly as possible. In the example in Activity 4-6, the security tester would have already obtained the necessary information and saved it to the company's server. It would not matter if DNS were properly reconfigured after the zone transfer took place. Game over!

The tools you've just learned about aren't the only way to collect information. Sometimes information about a company is gathered using nontechnical skills. In fact, the best hackers aren't necessarily the most technically adept people. Instead, they possess a more insidious—and often underestimated—skill called social engineering, discussed in the following section.

INTRODUCTION TO SOCIAL ENGINEERING

You can gather intelligence without using hacking tools, or intelligence-gathering software. One nontechnical method of collecting information is called social engineering. Social engineering uses the art of deception to extract valuable information from well-meaning people who are trying to be helpful. The best defense against social engineering is user training because the object being hacked for information is a person and not a computer. Training users so they are aware of social engineering tactics is your best defense.

The art of social engineering has been around much longer than computers.

Social engineering uses knowledge of human nature to gather information from people. In computer attacks, the information is usually a password to a network or other information an attacker could use to compromise a network. A salesperson, for example, can gather personal information about customers, such as income, hobbies, social life, and music preferences, by asking the customer the right questions. The salesperson uses communication skills to connect to customers and craft a message that persuades customers to buy a product or service. Social engineers might use similar persuasion tactics along with intimidation, coercion, extortion, and even blackmail to gather the information they need. Social engineers are probably the biggest security threat to networks and the most difficult to protect against.

You have probably heard the saying "Why try to crack a password when you can simply ask for it?" Many attackers do just that: They ask users for passwords and other credentials. Unfortunately, many users give attackers everything they need to break into a network. Most people who have worked at a help desk or in network support know this to be true. Even if a company policy states that passwords must not be given to anyone, users often think this policy doesn't apply to IT personnel and recite their passwords out loud when an IT technician is seated in front of their computers. IT personnel don't want to know a user's password. They especially don't want a user to say it aloud or type it in email messages. Yet users often don't consider their company passwords private, so they don't guard them as carefully as they might for personal passwords or PINs. Users might not think that the data they store on their company's computers would be of interest to an attacker. Social engineers know how to put these types of users at ease. The following is an example of a typical social-engineering tactic.

First, the social engineer poses as "Mike," a name he found after performing a zone transfer and examining the company's DNS server. Mike might not be the current IT point of contact (POC), but it doesn't matter. Depending on the company's size, users often don't know everyone on the IT staff. The social engineer then places a call for Taisha, an employee name he found from the zone transfer information and several company webpages that show the format of email addresses. To acquire the phone number, he calls the company's main switchboard and asks for Taisha. Then he says he wants to leave a message for Taisha and asks to be directed to her voicemail. "Taisha's in the office now," replies the friendly receptionist. "Would you like me to connect you to her?" The social engineer says, "Darn, my other line is ringing. I misplaced her extension. Can you please give it to me, and I'll call her back in a few minutes? I really have to get that call."

In this exchange, the social engineer's tactic is to create a sense of urgency yet remain cordial. The tactic usually works because most receptionists don't see a problem with connecting a caller to an employee or providing an employee's direct number or extension. After all, the caller knows Taisha's name and seems to know her. "Extension 4100," the receptionist says. "Thanks! Gotta go," the social engineer replies.

After 30 minutes or so, the social engineer calls the company again. "Hello. Extension 4101, please," he asks. The receptionist connects him, and a man answers "Dillon Bayard, Accounting." "Sorry, Dillon. Mike here. I was calling Taisha, but I guess I got your extension by mistake. Taisha was having a problem connecting to the Internet, so we're checking IP address information. We just fixed her system. Are you also having a problem?" Dillon says, "It looks like only the Accounting Department is having a problem with the VLAN config." Mike then asks, "Still running Windows 7?" Dillon answers no, but tells Mike which operating system he's using. Dillon probably feels as though he knows Mike, even though he doesn't.

Another way to find out how the IT staff operates is for Mike to pose as Dillon and call with a question or problem he's having. Mike would then learn how the help desk person handles the call. Does the help desk issue a help ticket? Does Dillon have to give any information to the caller other than his name and phone number? Many help desk offices require assigning a unique number to the help call until the problem is solved.

The social engineer used Taisha's name to give his call more credibility. Also, because he had gathered information about the operating system through other means, he took advantage of that knowledge, as shown by his Windows version question. Mike might try to get what he wants from Dillon, or he might decide to attempt the final attack with Taisha. If he calls her, he can talk about Dillon as though they're old friends. What he wants is Dillon's or Taisha's password. He might try the following ploy: "Dillon, there's a good chance we'll have to shut down Accounting's network connectivity for an hour or so. I could reduce this time for your system to five minutes if I could work on the issue from here. Only problem is I need your password. I already have your logon account as dbayard@gmail-info.com. Is that correct?" Chances are good that Dillon will give his password to Mike over the phone.

Not all social engineering takes place on the phone, but it's probably the most common method because it's anonymous and allows a social engineer to carry out multiple attacks in the same organization. This method can be more difficult if one or two employees hear different stories from the same person. However, a well-dressed person carrying a clipboard can also be successful in gathering information from employees. This approach requires more courage because the social engineer has to face the people from whom he's attempting to gather information.

Social engineers study human behavior. They learn to recognize personality traits, such as shyness or insecurity, and how to read body language: slouched shoulders, avoidance of eye contact, nervous fidgeting, and so on. If the ploy is conducted over the phone, the person's tone of voice can give clues to the social engineer, who uses the clues to identify the most vulnerable person in an organization. The social engineer then takes advantage of the employee's traits to extract information.

SECURITY BYTES

A security professional's most difficult job is preventing social engineers from gathering crucial information from company employees. No matter how thorough a security policy is or how much money is spent on firewalls and intrusion detection systems (IDSs), employees are still the weakest link in an organization. Attackers know this vulnerability and use it. Employees must be trained and tested periodically on security practices. Just as fire drills help prepare people to evacuate during a fire, random security drills can improve a company's security practices. For example, randomly selecting and testing employees each month to see whether they give their passwords to someone inside or outside the organization can help to raise awareness and compliance with security practices.

Social engineers use many techniques in their attempts to gain information from unsuspecting people, including the following:

- *Urgency*—"I need the information now or the world will come to an end!" For example, a social engineer might tell a user he needs the information quickly or the network will be down for a long time, thus creating a false sense of urgency.
- *Quid pro quo*—"I can make your life better if you give me the information I need." The social engineer might promise users faster Internet access, for example, if they help by supplying information.
- *Status quo*—"Everyone else is doing it, so you should, too." By using the names of other employees, a social engineer can easily convince others to reveal their passwords.
- *Kindness*—This tactic is probably the most dangerous weapon social engineers wield. People want to help those who are kind to them. The saying "It's easier to catch flies with honey than with vinegar" also applies to social engineering.
- *Position*—Convincing an employee that you're in a position of authority in the company can be a powerful means of gaining information. This is especially true in the military, where rank has its privileges. Social engineers can claim that a high-ranking officer is asking for the information, so it's imperative to give it as quickly as possible.

SECURITY BYTES

As a security tester, you should never use social-engineering tactics unless the person who hired you gives you permission in writing. You should also confirm on which employees you're allowed to perform social-engineering tests and document the tests you conduct. Your documentation should include the responses you received, and all test results should, of course, be confidential.

Training users not to give outsiders any information about OSs must be part of security training. Employees should also be taught to confirm the identity of the person asking questions. They should routinely ask the person for a company phone number to call back instead of trusting a stranger on the other end of the phone line. Making employees aware that most hacking is done through social engineering, not programming skills, can increase their vigilance against attackers.

The Art of Shoulder Surfing

Another method social engineers use to gain access to information is **shoulder surfing**. A shoulder surfer is skilled at reading what users enter on their keyboards, especially logon names and passwords. Shoulder surfers also use this skill to read PINs entered on ATM keypads, or passcode numbers used to open doors with keypad locks. Keypad number theft is easier than computer shoulder surfing because a keypad has fewer characters to memorize than a computer keyboard.

SECURITY BYTES

A common tactic of shoulder surfers is using smartphone cameras to take photos of unaware shoppers' credit cards in supermarkets and stores. With this technique, they can capture the credit card number and expiration date. Combining this technique with observing the shopper entering a PIN increases the risk of identity theft.

Many keyboard users don't follow the traditional fingering technique taught in typing classes. Instead, they hunt and peck with two or three fingers. However, shoulder surfers train themselves to memorize key positions on a standard keyboard. A standard keyboard could be a physical or virtual keyboard on a computer or mobile device. Armed with this knowledge, shoulder surfers can determine which keys are pressed by noticing the location on the keyboard, not which finger the typist is using.

Shoulder surfers also know the popular letter substitutions most people use when creating passwords: $ for s, @ for a, 1 for i, 0 for o, and so forth. Many users think p@$$w0rd is difficult to guess, but it's not for a skilled shoulder surfer. In addition, many users are required to use passwords containing special characters, and often they type these passwords more slowly to make sure they enter the correct characters. Slower typing makes a shoulder surfer's job easier.

SECURITY BYTES

With so many people taking their mobile devices to airports, commercial airlines warn customers to be aware of shoulder surfers. In the tight confines of an airplane, someone could easily observe the keys pressed and read the data on a screen. Products that prevent off-axis viewing of screens, such as screen overlays or a security lens, are recommended for travelers. Many employees conduct business on airplanes, and shoulder surfers can use the information they gather to compromise computer systems at the company.

To help prevent shoulder-surfing attacks, you must educate users to not type logon names and passwords when someone is standing directly behind them—or even standing nearby. You should also caution users about typing passwords when someone nearby is talking on a cell phone because of the wide availability of camera phones. To further reduce the risk of shoulder surfing, make sure all display screens face away from the door or the cubicle entryway. Warn your users to change their passwords immediately if they suspect someone might have observed them entering their passwords.

The Art of Dumpster Diving

Another method social engineers use to gain access to information is dumpster diving. Although not a glamorous form of gathering information, examining trash can yield information attackers can use. For example, discarded computer documentation can indicate what OS is being used. If the instructions are for Windows Server 2016, chances are the new system is a more recent Windows OS, such as Windows Server 2019. Sometimes network administrators write notes in documentation or even jot down passwords, and social engineers can make use of this information.

Company phone directories are another source of information. A dumpster diver who finds a directory listing company employees can use this information to pose as an employee for the purpose of gathering information. Company calendars with meeting schedules, employee vacation schedules, and so on can be used to gain access to offices that won't be occupied for a specified time period. Trash can be worth its weight in gold for the dumpster diver who knows what to do with it. Here are some other items that can be useful to dumpster divers:

- Financial reports
- Interoffice memos
- Discarded digital media
- Company organizational charts showing managers' names
- Resumes of employees
- Company policies or systems and procedures manuals
- Professional journals or magazines
- Utility bills
- Solicitation notices from outside vendors
- Regional manager reports
- Quality assurance reports
- Risk management reports
- Minutes of meetings
- Federal, state, or city reports
- Employee charge card receipts

Dumpster diving can produce a tremendous amount of information, so users must be educated on how to dispose of trash properly. Drives containing company information should be formatted with "disk-cleaning" software that writes binary 0s on all portions of the disks. This formatting should be done at least seven times to ensure that all previous data is unreadable. Old computer manuals should be discarded offsite so that dumpster divers can't associate the manuals with the company. Before disposal, all these items should be placed in a locked room with adequate physical, administrative, and technical safeguards. All documents should be shredded, even if the information seems innocuous. Social engineers know how to pull together information from different sources. Putting a puzzle together from many small pieces makes it possible for attackers to break into a network.

The Art of Piggybacking

Sometimes security testers need to enter part of a building that's restricted to authorized personnel. In this case, a tester or an attacker uses a technique called piggybacking. Piggybacking is trailing closely behind an employee who has access to an area without the employee realizing you didn't use a PIN or a security badge to enter the area. Those skilled in piggybacking watch authorized personnel enter secure areas and wait for the opportune time to join them quickly at the security entrance. They count on human nature and the desire of others to be polite and hold open a secured door. This ploy usually works, especially if the piggybacker has both hands full and seems to be struggling to remove an access card from a purse or pants pocket. Some piggybackers wear a fake badge around their necks or pretend to scan a security card across a card reader. If they're detected, they might say their card has been giving them problems and use their social-engineering skills to convince the security guard to let them through.

A good preventive measure against piggybacking is using turnstiles at areas where piggybacking can occur. However, the best preventive measure is to train personnel to notify security when they notice a stranger in a restricted area. Employees must feel a vested interest in area security and should not rely on security personnel. Employees should be taught not to hold secured doors open for anyone, even people they know. Educate your users to get in the habit of making sure all employees use their access cards to enter a restricted area and to report any suspicious or unknown people to security.

SECURITY BYTES

A well-dressed security tester walked into a hospital with a laptop and sat down in the waiting area next to the nurses' station. He was able to access passwords and logon information on his laptop and collected data for more than a week without being questioned by security or hospital personnel. In fact, the security tester felt as though he was invisible. Doctors, nurses, administrators, and other hospital personnel never questioned the presence of the stranger in their midst, even though he had covered most of the waiting room table with legal pads and his laptop. After the security test was completed, it was determined that everyone thought the stranger was working for someone else in the area. No one felt responsible for finding out who the stranger was and why he was there.

Phishing

Almost everyone with an email address has received a phishing email at some point. "Update your account details" is a typical subject line. The message is usually framed as an urgent request to visit a website to make sure you're not locked out of an account, such as your online banking service. The website is a fake, but if you're tricked into giving out your personal account data, the money you lose is real. Figure 4-15 shows an actual phishing email purportedly from PayPal. One clue that the email isn't legitimate is that the recipient is addressed by the generic "Hi Customer" instead of their name. Spelling, grammar, and formatting mistakes are also telltale signs of phishing emails.

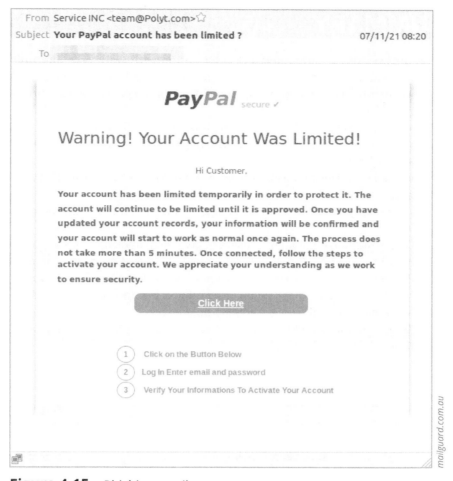

Figure 4-15   Phishing email message

A practice potentially more dangerous to companies is spear phishing, another attack carried out by email that combines social engineering with exploiting vulnerabilities. Attackers have used spear phishing to steal millions of dollars. Unlike phishing, this attack is directed at specific people in an organization and uses social engineering based on previous reconnaissance data to hook victims. A spear phishing email might appear to come from a sender the recipient knows and mention topics of mutual interest. The goal is to entice victims into opening an attachment or clicking a link; this action installs the "spear phished" malware, which can have devastating effects on an organization's network.

Some security consulting companies incorporate spear phishing attacks as part of their testing, using tools that can inject shell code into Adobe PDF files. One example of these tools is Metasploit, which is included in Kali Linux. Email authentication technologies—such as Sender Policy Framework, DomainKeys Identified Mail, S/MIME, and PGP—as well as security awareness training for users and constant vigilance help reduce the threat of phishing and spear phishing.

MODULE SUMMARY

- Footprinting is the process of gathering network information with web tools and utilities. Web tools for gathering information about a network infrastructure include Whois, OSINT Framework, and Google.
- Corporate information can be gathered by using competitive intelligence gained through observation and web tools.
- IP addresses and domain names can be found by using tools such as Domain Dossier and the `dig` command.
- Security testers must be aware of how cookies and web bugs can be used to retrieve information and access data without a user's knowledge.
- Zone transfers can be used to retrieve information about a network's topology and view all the network's host computers and domains.
- Social engineering is the ability to use an understanding of human nature to extract information from unsuspecting people.
- Social engineers use many methods to convince users to give them information, such as creating a false sense of urgency, pretending to have a position of authority, being kind and friendly, offering something in return for complying with the request, or giving the impression that everyone else has complied with the request.
- Educating company personnel about social-engineering attacks is important, but random testing can also be done to ensure that employees are following company policies.
- Attackers use techniques such as shoulder surfing, dumpster diving, piggybacking, and phishing to gather confidential information.

Key Terms

competitive intelligence	phishing	spidering (or crawling)
cookie	piggybacking	web beacon
dumpster diving	shoulder surfing	web bug
footprinting	social engineering	zone transfer
Open Source Intelligence (OSINT)	spear phishing	

Review Questions

1. Which of the following is a fast and easy way to gather information about a company? (Choose all that apply.)
   a. Conduct port scanning.
   b. Perform a zone transfer of the company's DNS server.
   c. View the company's website.
   d. Look for company ads in publications.

2. To find information about the key IT personnel responsible for a company's domain, you might use which of the following tools? (Choose all that apply.)
   a. Whois
   b. Whatis
   c. Domain Dossier
   d. Nbtstat

3. _____ is one of the components most vulnerable to network attacks.
   a. TCP/IP
   b. WINS
   c. DHCP
   d. DNS

4. Which of the following contains host records for a domain?
   a. DNS
   b. WINS
   c. Linux server
   d. UNIX web clients

5. Which of the following is a good website for gathering information on a domain?
   a. www.google.com
   b. whois.domaintools.com at https://centralops.net/co/
   c. www.arin.net
   d. All of the above

6. A cookie can store information about a website's visitors. True or False?

7. Which of the following enables you to view all host computers on a network?
   a. SOA
   b. ipconfig
   c. Zone transfers
   d. HTTP HEAD method

8. What command-line tool can be used to harvest DNS information?
   a. `dns-get`
   b. `dug`
   c. `dig`
   d. `axfer`

9. Which of the following is one method of gathering information about the operating systems a company is using?
   a. Search the web for email addresses of IT employees.
   b. Connect via Telnet to the company's web server.
   c. Ping the URL and analyze ICMP messages.
   d. Use the ipconfig /os command.

10. To determine a company's primary DNS server, you can look for a DNS server containing which of the following?
    a. Cname record
    b. Host record
    c. PTR record
    d. SOA record

11. When conducting competitive intelligence, which of the following is a good way to determine the size of a company's IT support staff?
    a. Review job postings on websites such as www .indeed.com.
    b. Use the nslookup command.
    c. Perform a zone transfer of the company's DNS server.
    d. Use the host -t command.

12. Open your web browser and go to https:// osintframework.com/. Explore the framework by expanding nodes to discover different tools. Choose two tools. In four paragraphs describe what these two tools can do, how to use them, and how they would be useful in footprinting.

13. Which of the following tools can assist you in finding general information about an organization and its employees? (Choose all that apply.)
    a. www.google.com
    b. https://groups.google.com
    c. netcat
    d. nmap

14. What is the first method a security tester should attempt to find a password for a computer on the network?
    a. Use a scanning tool.
    b. Install a sniffer on the network.
    c. Ask the user.
    d. Install a password-cracking program.

15. Many social engineers begin gathering the information they need by using which of the following?
    a. Internet
    b. Phone
    c. Company intranet
    d. Email

16. Open a web browser and go to https://spyse. com. The free version has a daily lookup limit, so don't waste your lookups. You can start a free trial if you need more lookups. Search for the domain name of a major news organization of your choice as a target. In three paragraphs, discuss what basic information you have discovered and any security issues that are revealed, and then propose solutions for the security issues. In your discussion, include the organization's security rating, DNS information, and any email addresses you discover.

17. Chances are that your computer has cookies stored on it that you are unaware of. Open the web browser that you use most often and find the setting where cookies are stored. Check the contents of these cookies to see what kind of information is being recorded. If you are unsure how to find this information, perform an Internet search for how to find cookies for your specific browser. In two paragraphs, describe which websites are storing information on your computer and what they are storing.

18. Dumpster diving, though messy, is an effective way to gather intelligence on a targeted organization or individual. Dumpster dive your own trash to discover what actionable information you may have thrown away. You might be surprised at what personal information you (or other family members) have casually tossed out. In two paragraphs, describe what you have found (leaving out private details), and what steps you can take to correct this security flaw.

19. What social-engineering technique involves telling an employee that you're calling from the CEO's office and need certain information ASAP? (Choose all that apply.)
    a. Urgency
    b. Status quo
    c. Position of authority
    d. Quid pro quo

20. Before conducting a security test by using social-engineering tactics, what should you do?
    a. Set up an appointment.
    b. Document all findings.
    c. Get written permission from the person who hired you to conduct the security test.
    d. Get written permission from the department head.

Case Projects

Case Project 4-1: Gathering Security Intelligence from a Reluctant Administrator

Time Required: 30 minutes

Objective: Gather intelligence and create a security memo.

Description: Alexander Rocco Corporation has multiple OSs running in its many offices. Before conducting a security test to determine the vulnerabilities you need to correct, you want to determine whether any OSs are running that you're not aware of. The network administrator is resistant to giving you information after learning you are working to discover network security vulnerabilities. The administrator sees you as a threat. After several hours of interviews, you learn only that the network administrator's personal email address is vader2601@gmail.com, and an old Red Hat Enterprise Linux (RHEL) server is running on one of the company's systems. Based on this information, answer the following questions:

1. What tools might you use after learning the network administrator's email address?
2. What can you determine by entering the network administrator's email address into Google? What about entering only the handle vader2601?
3. Could the information you learned from Google be used to conduct vulnerability testing?

Write a memo to the IT manager, Jawad Safari, about the potential issues with running an old RHEL 5.8 server, and mention the importance of patch hygiene. Make sure your memo explains how you gathered this information and offers constructive feedback. Your memo shouldn't point a finger at any company employees; it should discuss problems on a general level.

Case Project 4-2: Testing DNS Security

Time Required: 30 minutes

Objective: Create a report outlining a plan to determine if any DNS servers are vulnerable to zone transfer attacks.

Description: You have just joined the IT department at the Alexander Rocco Corporation. You are trying to learn the configuration of the corporate network, including what DNS servers are in place and how they are configured. Other IT staff members are too busy to train you, so you decide to figure things out for yourself. You know better than to start scanning the network and checking for vulnerabilities without written authorization, so you are going to create a document that will outline what you would like to do and have it approved by your manager.

Create a two-page report to submit for your manager's approval. In this report, outline what tools you might use and how you would use them to discover what DNS servers you have on your network and whether any DNS servers you discover are vulnerable to zone transfer attacks.

PORT SCANNING

After reading this module and completing the exercises, you will be able to:

1 Describe port scanning and types of port scans

2 Describe port-scanning tools

3 Explain what ping sweeps are used for

4 Explain how shell scripting is used to automate security tasks

Port scanning, also referred to as service scanning, is the process of examining a range of IP addresses to determine what services are running on a network. Open ports on a computer can identify the services running on it. For example, HTTP uses port 80 to connect to a web service. Instead of pinging each IP address in a range of addresses and waiting for an ICMP Echo Reply (type 0) to see whether a computer can be reached, you can use scanning tools to simplify this procedure. After all, pinging several thousand IP addresses manually is time consuming.

Port-scanning tools can be complex, so you need to devote time to learning their strengths and weaknesses and understanding how and when you should use these tools. In this module, you look at port-scanning tools that enable you to identify services running on a network and use this knowledge to conduct a security test. In addition, you see how to use shell scripting to automate ping sweeps and other security-testing tasks.

INTRODUCTION TO PORT SCANNING

Recall that you can perform a zone transfer with the dig command to determine a network's IP addresses. Suppose the zone transfer indicates that a company is using a subnetted Class C address with 126 available host IP addresses. How do you verify whether all these addresses are being used by computers that are up and running? You use a port scanner to ping the range of IP addresses you discovered.

A more important question a security tester should ask is "What services are running on the computers that were identified?" **Port scanning** is a method of finding out which services a host computer offers. For example, if a server is hosting a website, is it likely that the server has port 443 and perhaps port 80 open? Are any of the services vulnerable to attacks or exploits? Are any services not being filtered by a firewall, thus making it possible to load a Trojan that can send information from the attacked computer? Which computer is most vulnerable to an attack? You already know how to search for known vulnerabilities using the Common Vulnerabilities and Exposures (https://cve.mitre.org) and US-CERT (www.us-cert.gov) websites. You can also use port-scanning tools that identify vulnerabilities—for example, Angry IP Scanner (angryip.org), a free port scanner with a GUI interface (see Figure 5-1). Using this tool, an attacker can quickly identify an open port and then launch an exploit to attack the system.

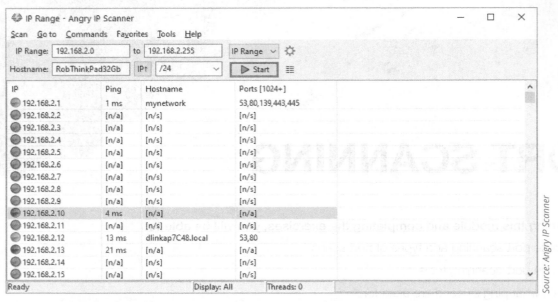

Figure 5-1   Angry IP port scanner interface

As a security tester, you need to know which ports attackers are going after so you can close and protect those ports. Security testers must scan all ports when doing a test, not just the well-known ports. Many programs use port numbers outside the range of well-known ports. For example, TeamViewer, a well-known PC remote control program, operates on ports 5938, 443, and 80. A hacker who discovers that port 5938 is open can check the information at the CVE website for a possible vulnerability in TeamViewer. After a hacker discovers an open service, finding a vulnerability or exploit is not difficult, especially when systems are out of date and unpatched.

SECURITY BYTES

Most security testers and hackers argue that port scanning is legal simply because it doesn't invade others privacy; it merely discovers whether the party being scanned is available. The typical analogy is a person walking down the street and turning the doorknob of every house along the way. If the door opens, the person notes that the door is open and proceeds to the next house. Of course, entering the house is a crime in most parts of the world, just as entering a computer or network system without the owner's permission is a crime. To date, no one has been convicted just for port scanning in the United States, although some laws call for prosecuting scanning if it causes damage or loss of more than $5000 (U.S. Code 18 1030).

Port scanning helps you answer questions about open ports and services by enabling you to scan thousands or even tens of thousands of IP addresses quickly. Many port-scanning tools produce reports of their findings, and some give you best-guess assessments of which OS is running on a system. Most, if not all, scanning programs report **open ports**, **closed ports**, and **filtered ports** in a matter of seconds. An open port allows access to applications and can be vulnerable to an attack. When a web server needs to communicate with applications or other computers, for example, port 443 is opened. A closed port doesn't allow entry or access to a service. For instance, if ports 443 and 80 are closed on a web server, users can't access websites. A port reported as filtered might indicate that a firewall is being used to allow specified traffic into or out of the network.

Types of Port Scans

Before delving into using port-scanning tools, look at the types of scans that can be used for port scanning:

- *SYN scan*—In a normal TCP session, a packet is sent to another computer with the SYN flag set. The receiving computer sends back a packet with the SYN/ACK flag set, indicating an acknowledgment. The sending computer then sends a packet with the ACK flag set. If the SYN packet is sent to a closed port, the computer responds with an RST/ACK (reset/acknowledgment) packet. If an attacker's computer receives a SYN/ACK packet, it responds quickly with an RST/ACK packet, closing the session. This is done so that a full TCP connection is never made and logged as a transaction. In this sense, it's "stealthy." After all, attackers don't want a transaction logged showing their connection to the attacked computer and listing their IP addresses.

- *Connect scan*—This type of scan relies on the attacked computer's OS, so it's riskier to use. A connect scan is similar to a SYN scan, except that it completes the three-way handshake. This means the attacked computer most likely logs the transaction or connection, indicating that a session took place. Therefore, unlike a SYN scan, a connect scan isn't stealthy and can be detected easily.

- *NULL scan*—In a NULL scan, all packet flags are turned off. A closed port responds to a NULL scan with an RST packet, so if no packet is received, the best guess is that the port is open. Windows, however, does not follow the standard and might respond in an unexpected way.

- *XMAS scan*—In this type of scan, the FIN, PSH, and URG flags are set. Closed ports respond to this type of packet with an RST packet. This scan can be used to determine which ports are open. For example, an attacker could send this packet to port 53 on a system and see whether an RST packet is returned. If not, the DNS port might be open. Again, Windows does not follow the standard and responds randomly to XMAS scans.

- *ACK scan*—Attackers typically use ACK scans to get past a firewall or other filtering device. A filtering device looks for the SYN packet, the first packet in the three-way handshake, that the ACK packet was part of. Remember this packet order: SYN, SYN/ACK, and ACK. If the attacked port returns an RST packet, the packet filter was fooled, or there's no packet-filtering device. In either case, the attacked port is considered to be "unfiltered."

- *FIN scan*—In this type of scan, a FIN packet is sent to the target computer. If the port is closed, it sends back an RST packet. When a three-way handshake ends, both parties send a FIN packet to end the connection.

- *UDP scan*—In this type of scan, a UDP packet is sent to the target computer. If the port sends back an ICMP "Port Unreachable" message, the port is closed. Again, not receiving that message might imply the port is open, but this isn't always true. A firewall or packet-filtering device could undermine your assumptions.

A computer that receives a SYN packet from a remote computer responds with a SYN/ACK packet if its port is open. In a three-way handshake, a SYN packet is sent from one computer, a SYN/ACK is sent from the receiving computer to the sender, and finally, the sender sends an ACK packet to the receiving computer. If a port is closed and receives a SYN packet, it sends back an RST/ACK packet. Determining whether a port is filtered is more complex. Many scanning tools, such as Nmap, use a best-guess approach. That is, if a UDP packet doesn't receive a response from the receiving port, many scanning tools report that the port is open.

SECURITY BYTES

In Canada, a man was found guilty of scanning a company's computers. The company prosecuted him for using microwatts of its electrical power to perform the scan. Doing so without the company's permission was considered a crime—petty, yes, but effective. To play it safe, always get permission from a company if you're going to perform an intensive scan on its network infrastructure. If your scan slows down a network's traffic, the company might argue that a low-level DoS attack, which is illegal, was performed.

USING PORT-SCANNING TOOLS

Hundreds of port-scanning tools are available for both hackers and security testers. Some are commercial, and some are freeware or open source. How do you decide which tool to use? Not all are accurate, so using more than one port-scanning tool is recommended. In addition, becoming familiar with a variety of tools is wise. Although you should practice often with a tool to gain proficiency in using it, don't fall into the trap of using one tool exclusively.

Nmap

Originally written for *Phrack* magazine in 1997 by Fyodor, Nmap has become one of the most popular port scanners and adds new features constantly, such as OS detection and fast multiple-probe ping scanning. Nmap also has a GUI front end called Zenmap that makes working with complex options easier. Nmap has been enhanced over the years because, like many other security tools, it's open source; if bugs are found, users can offer suggestions for correcting them.

Nmap is referred to often in this course because it's currently the standard port-scanning tool for security professionals. Regardless of the other port-scanning tools available, any security tester with a modicum of experience has worked with Nmap. As a beginning student, you can use it during every part of a security or penetration test but remember to build proficiency in a variety of tools.

SECURITY BYTES

As most security professionals will tell you, Hollywood seldom depicts attackers actually hacking into a system. Typically, they're using a GUI program, frantically clicking, or typing a decryption algorithm. One exception is *The Matrix Reloaded*. The female protagonist, Trinity, sits at a computer terminal and runs Nmap. She discovers that port 22 (SSH) is open, runs an SSHv1 CRC32 exploit (an actual bug in SSH) that allows her to change the root password to Z1ON0101, and then proceeds to shut down the grid. Moral of the story? Know your tools and exploits, and you might save the world.

You don't have to memorize how each flag is set when running a port scan with Nmap. In fact, just typing the command nmap 193.145.85.2 01 scans common ports on the computer with this IP address. However, port scanning can be an involved process. Some attackers want to be hidden from network devices or IDSs that recognize an inordinate number of pings or packets being sent to their networks, so they use stealth attacks and limit their scan speeds to make their activities more difficult to detect. In addition to these techniques, an attacker could target only a few ports instead of scanning all common ports. In the following activities, you become familiar with the basic Nmap commands and then learn some of the more complex options.

Activity 5-1: Getting to Know Nmap

Time Required: 30 minutes

Objective: Learn the basic commands and syntax of Nmap.

Description: In this activity, you use Nmap to perform quick scans of a network. You send a SYN packet to a host on the attack network your instructor has supplied. In this example, the attack network IP addresses are 136.142.35.137 to 136.142.35.140, but your attack range might be different. Make sure to follow the rules of engagement, and don't perform port scanning on any systems not included in the IP range your instructor gives you.

1. Boot your computer into Linux. Open a command shell by clicking the **Terminal** icon on the panel taskbar. Type **nmap -h | less** and press **Enter** to see all available Nmap commands. Your screen should look like Figure 5-2. You can scroll to review the command parameters.
2. After reviewing the parameters, write down three options that can be used with the Nmap command, and then press **q** to exit the help screen.
3. To send a SYN packet to an IP address in your attack range, type **nmap -sS -v 136.142.35.137** and press **Enter**. (Replace 136.142.35.137 with an attack network IP address your instructor supplied.) What are the results of your SYN scan?
4. Next, try sending a new SYN packet to a different IP address in your attack range. What are the results of this new scan? Do you see any differences? If so, list them.
5. Nmap can scan through a range of IP addresses, so entering one IP address at a time isn't necessary. To send a SYN packet to every IP address in your attack range, type **nmap -sS -v 136.142.35.137-140** and press **Enter**. (Replace 136.142.35.137-140 with the attack network IP address range your instructor supplied.)
6. To see the output in a format you can scroll, press the **Up Arrow** key, add the | **less** option to the end of the Nmap command, and press **Enter**. The command should look like this: nmap -sS -v 136.142.35.137-140 | less.
7. Next, add one more parameter to the Nmap command to determine which computers in your attack range have the SMTP service or HTTP service running. Using what you've learned so far in this activity, enter the command and note the output. (*Hint*: What ports do SMTP and HTTP use?) The command's output might vary, but what's important is learning how to build on the Nmap command. You can select specific ports in the Nmap command, so not all 65,000 ports must be scanned.
8. Leave the Terminal shell open for the next activity.

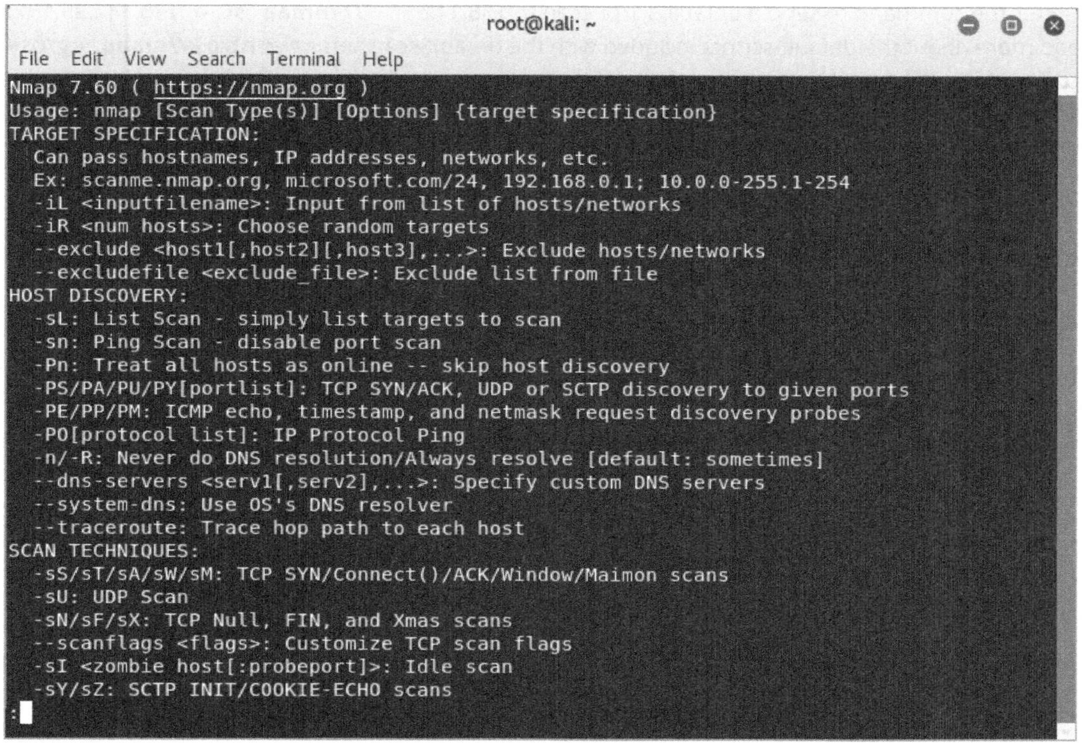

```
                              root@kali: ~                        ⊖ ▢ ✕
 File  Edit  View  Search  Terminal  Help
Nmap 7.60 ( https://nmap.org )
Usage: nmap [Scan Type(s)] [Options] {target specification}
TARGET SPECIFICATION:
  Can pass hostnames, IP addresses, networks, etc.
  Ex: scanme.nmap.org, microsoft.com/24, 192.168.0.1; 10.0.0-255.1-254
  -iL <inputfilename>: Input from list of hosts/networks
  -iR <num hosts>: Choose random targets
  --exclude <host1[,host2][,host3],...>: Exclude hosts/networks
  --excludefile <exclude_file>: Exclude list from file
HOST DISCOVERY:
  -sL: List Scan - simply list targets to scan
  -sn: Ping Scan - disable port scan
  -Pn: Treat all hosts as online -- skip host discovery
  -PS/PA/PU/PY[portlist]: TCP SYN/ACK, UDP or SCTP discovery to given ports
  -PE/PP/PM: ICMP echo, timestamp, and netmask request discovery probes
  -PO[protocol list]: IP Protocol Ping
  -n/-R: Never do DNS resolution/Always resolve [default: sometimes]
  --dns-servers <serv1[,serv2],...>: Specify custom DNS servers
  --system-dns: Use OS's DNS resolver
  --traceroute: Trace hop path to each host
SCAN TECHNIQUES:
  -sS/sT/sA/sW/sM: TCP SYN/Connect()/ACK/Window/Maimon scans
  -sU: UDP Scan
  -sN/sF/sX: TCP Null, FIN, and Xmas scans
  --scanflags <flags>: Customize TCP scan flags
  -sI <zombie host[:probeport]>: Idle scan
  -sY/sZ: SCTP INIT/COOKIE-ECHO scans
:
```

Figure 5-2   Nmap help screen

Source: Kali Linux

SECURITY BYTES

A security professional came to work one evening and noticed that the company's firewall had crashed because someone ran a port-scanning program on the network by using ACK packets. Many attackers use ACK scans to bypass packet-filtering devices (such as firewalls). In this case, the company's firewall was disabled because it was flooded with tens of thousands of ACK packets bombarding its routing tables. This ACK scan constituted a DoS attack on the network, so don't get complacent when running port scans on networks. Always get the network owner's written permission before doing a port scan.

Activity 5-2: Using Additional Nmap Commands

Time Required: 30 minutes

Objective: Perform more complex port-scanning attacks with Nmap.

Description: In this activity, you continue to use Nmap for port scanning on your attack network. You add to the parameters used in Activity 5-1 using Nmap scripts to discover more information about the remote host. You should practice these commands until they are second nature, but Fyodor developed a well-written help page (called a "man page" in UNIX/Linux circles) that you can use as a resource. You begin this activity by looking at this help page.

1. If a Terminal window isn't open, boot your computer into Kali Linux, open a Terminal shell, and at the command prompt, type **man nmap** and press **Enter**. You can see that this command produces more information than the `nmap -h` command. Don't be concerned about memorizing the manual; just know it's there when you need it.

2. Next, enter the command to send a default script scan to 136.142.35.137 (**nmap –sC –v 136.142.35.137**). You can read more about the default scripts included with the default scan setting at **https://nmap.org/nsedoc/categories/default.html**. What are the results of the script scan? What brand and version of HTTP server is running on ports 80 and 443?

3. Now, limit the scope so you scan only port 443 by using the –p flag (**nmap –p44 3 –v 136.142.35.137**). This makes the Nmap scan more targeted and less noticeable.

Nessus and OpenVAS (or Greenbone Security Assistant)

Security testers should also investigate Nessus. Nessus is a vulnerability assessment tool from Tenable that extends NMAP capabilities by analyzing open ports for specific version information and provides detailed vulnerability information on the corresponding service. A vulnerability assessment tool automates the process of scanning for IP addresses, open ports, and vulnerabilities. Vulnerability scanners have a database of known vulnerabilities and a database of security check plug-ins (scripts and logic) that are used to check for vulnerabilities. Nessus Professional is a product you purchase, but Tenable provides a free version called Nessus Essentials. Essentials has the same capabilities as Nessus Professional but limits the number of IP addresses you can scan. Nessus Essentials is useful for experimentation and learning. Figure 5-3 shows the results of a Nessus vulnerability scan.

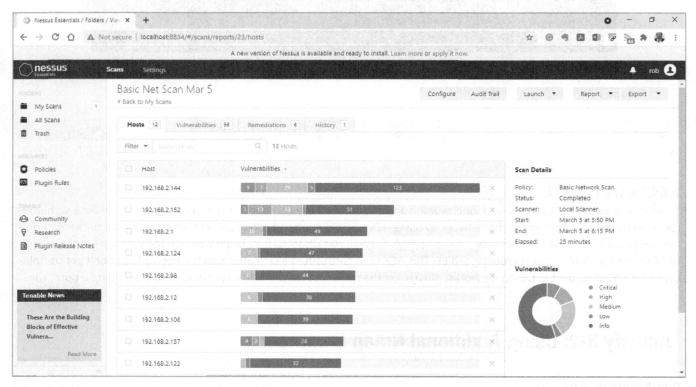

Figure 5-3   Nessus Essentials scanning results

Source: tenable.org

Nessus also has an open-source fork called OpenVAS, now branded as Greenbone Security Assistant. OpenVAS has no restrictions, so you can use it as a vulnerability assessment tool to scan any IP address you want.

OpenVAS can update security check plug-ins when they become available. An OpenVAS plug-in is a security test program (script) that can be selected from the client interface. The person who writes the plug-in decides whether to designate it as dangerous, and the author's judgment on what's considered dangerous might differ from yours. Therefore, leaving the Safe checks enabled in the policy is advisable. Figure 5-4 shows the home screen for the OpenVAS web interface.

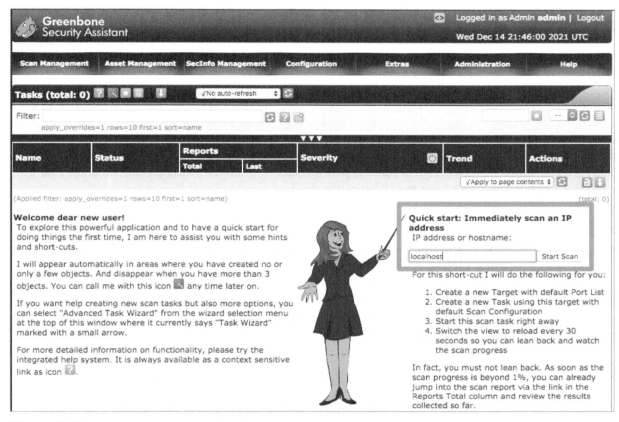

Figure 5-4 OpenVAS (Greenbone Security Assistant) home screen

Source: GNU General Public License

An OpenVAS scan isn't limited to determining which services are running on a port. OpenVAS plug-ins can also determine what vulnerabilities are associated with these services, as shown in Figure 5-5.

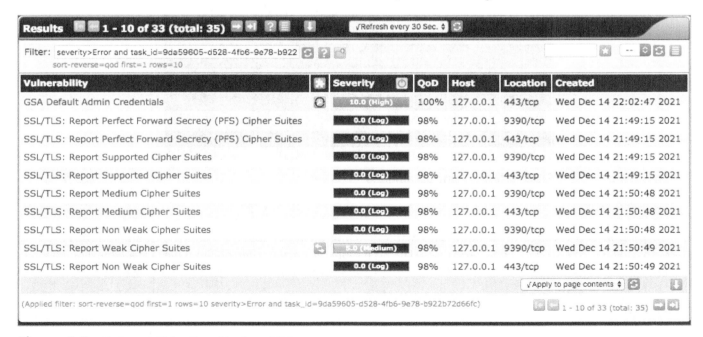

Figure 5-5 Vulnerabilities listed in OpenVAS

Source: GNU General Public License

CONDUCTING PING SWEEPS

Port scanners can also be used to conduct a ping sweep of a large network to identify which IP addresses belong to active hosts. In other words, to find out which hosts are "live," ping sweeps simply ping a range of IP addresses and see what type of response is returned. The problem with relying on ping sweeps to identify live hosts is that a computer might be shut down at the time of the sweep and indicate that the IP address doesn't belong to a live host. Another problem with ping sweeps is that many network administrators configure nodes to not respond to an ICMP Echo Request (type 8) with an ICMP Echo Reply (type 0). This response doesn't mean the computer isn't running; it just means it isn't replying to the attack computer. Add the possibility of a firewall filtering out ICMP traffic, and you have many reasons for using caution when running ping sweeps. You can use many tools to conduct a ping sweep of a network, and you learn about some in the following sections.

Fping

With the Fping tool (www.fping.org), you can ping multiple IP addresses simultaneously. Fping, included with Kali Linux, can accept a range of IP addresses entered at a command prompt, or you can create a file containing multiple IP addresses and use it as input for the Fping command. For example, the `fping -f ip_address.txt` command uses ip_address.txt, which contains a list of IP addresses, as its input file. The input file is usually created with a shell-scripting language so that you don't need to type the thousands of IP addresses needed for a ping sweep on a Class B network, for example. Figure 5-6 shows some parameters you can use with the Fping command.

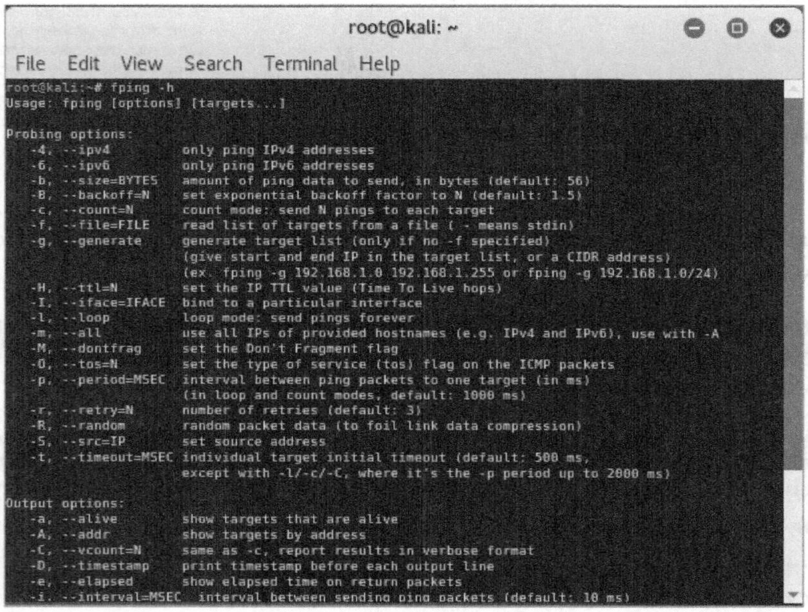

Figure 5-6   Fping parameters

Source: GNU Public License

To ping sweep a range of IP addresses without using an input file, you use the command `fping  -g BeginningIPAddress EndingIPAddress`. The `-g` parameter is used when no input file is available. For example, the `fping -g 192.168.185.1 192.168.185.5` command returns the results shown in Figure 5-7.

Hping3

You can also use the Hping3 tool to perform ping sweeps. However, many security testers use it to bypass filtering devices by injecting crafted or otherwise modified IP packets. This tool offers a wealth of features, and security testers should spend as much time as possible learning this advanced port-scanning tool. For a quick overview, use the

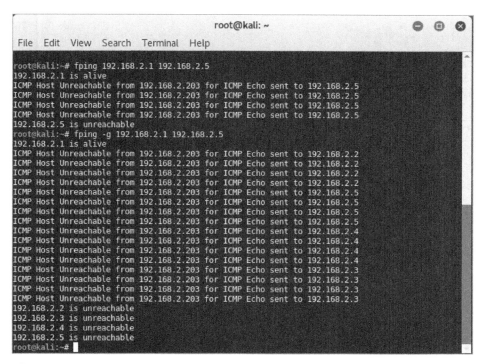

Figure 5-7   Results of fping commands

Source: GNU General Public License

`hping3 -help | less` command, and browse through the parameters you can use (see Figures 5-8, 5-9, and 5-10). As you can see, you can add many parameters to the `Hping3` command, enabling you to craft an IP packet for your purposes. When you craft an IP packet in Activity 5-4, you can refer to these figures when using the Hping3 tool.

Figure 5-8   Hping3 help page 1

Source: GNU General Public License

Figure 5-9   Hping3 help page 2

Source: GNU General Public License

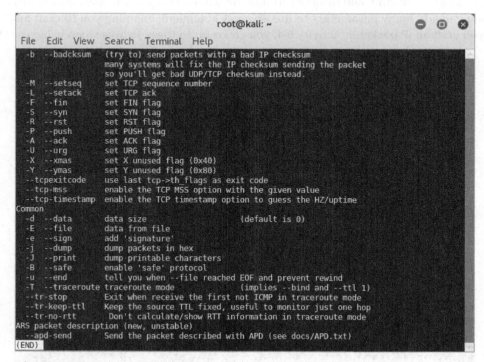

Figure 5-10   Hping3 help page 3

Source: GNU General Public License

SECURITY BYTES

If you decide to use ping sweeps, be careful not to include the broadcast address in the range of IP addresses. Including it by mistake might happen if subnetting is used in an organization. For example, if the IP network 193.145.85.0 is subnetted with the 255.255.255.192 subnet mask, four subnets are created: 193.145.85.0, 193.145.85.64, 193.145.85.128, and 193.145.85.192. The broadcast addresses for each subnet are 193.145.85.63, 193.145.85.127, 193.145.85.191, and 193.145.85.255. If a ping sweep is activated inadvertently on the range of hosts 193.145.85.65 to 193.145.85.127, an inordinate amount of traffic could flood the network because the broadcast address 193.145.85.127 is included. This error is more of a problem on a Class B address, but if you perform ping sweeps, make sure your client signs a written agreement authorizing the testing.

Crafting IP Packets

Packets contain source and destination IP addresses as well as information about the flags you learned earlier: SYN, ACK, FIN, and so on. You can create a packet with a specific flag set. For example, if you aren't satisfied with the response you get from the host computer after sending a SYN packet, you can create another packet with the FIN flag set. The SYN flag might have returned a "closed port" message, but a FIN packet sent to the same computer might return a "filtered port" message. You can craft any type of packet you like. Hping3 and Fping are helpful tools for crafting IP packets, and you work with both tools in Activity 5-3.

Activity 5-3: Crafting IP Packets with Fping and Hping3

Time Required: 30 minutes

Objective: Learn to craft IP packets with Fping and Hping3.

Description: In this activity, you see how security testers can craft IP packets to find out what services are running on a network. The more ways you know how to send a packet to an unsuspecting port on a computer and get a response, the better. If a computer doesn't respond to an ICMP packet sent to a particular port, it doesn't mean any packet sent to the same port will get the same response. You might need to send different packets to get the results you need for a thorough security test.

1. If necessary, boot your computer into Linux. Open a Terminal shell, and then type **fping -h** and press **Enter**.
2. To see the live computers in the attack range your instructor gave you, type **fping -g *BeginningIPaddress EndingIPaddress*** and press **Enter**. Note the results. (Be sure to use the beginning and ending IP addresses in your attack range.)
3. Next, type **hping3 -S *IPAddressAttackedComputer*** (substituting an IP address from your attack range) and press **Enter**. By using the -S parameter, you craft a TCP SYN packet.
4. Open another Terminal shell, and then type **tcpdump** and press **Enter**.
5. Arrange both shell windows next to each other so that you can observe what happens after entering the Hping3 command. In the shell that's not running Tcpdump, press **Ctrl+C** to return to the command prompt, type **hping3 -S *IPAddressAttackedComputer***, and press **Enter**. Watch the Tcpdump window fill with the traffic that's generated. To stop Tcpdump from capturing packets, press **Ctrl+C** in that shell window.
6. If time permits, consult the Hping3 help pages (refer to Figures 5-8, 5-9, and 5-10, if needed) and experiment with creating different types of packets. Note the differences in network traffic generated with the Tcpdump command. Security testers need to understand how slight variations in packets sent to an attacked computer can produce different results. For example, if a computer doesn't respond to a SYN packet, try sending an ACK packet. What happens when a FIN packet is sent? If you aren't having any success, try sending the same packets to different ports. Does this method change the response from the attacked computer?
7. When you're done, close both shells.

UNDERSTANDING SCRIPTING

Some tools might need to be modified to better suit your needs as a security tester. Creating a customized script—a program that automates a task that takes too much time to perform manually—can be a time-saving solution. As mentioned, Fping can use an input file to perform ping sweeps. Creating an input file manually with thousands of IP addresses isn't worth the time, however. Instead, most security testers rely on basic programming skills to write a script for creating an input file.

Scripting Basics

If you have worked with DOS batch programming, scripting will be familiar. If you're from a networking background and new to programming, however, start with the basics. A script or batch file is a text file containing multiple commands that are usually entered manually at the command prompt. If you use a set of commands repeatedly to perform the same task, this task might be a good candidate for a script. You can run the script by using just one command. The best way to learn how to create a script is by doing it, so you get an opportunity to practice writing one in Activity 5-4.

Activity 5-4: Creating an Executable Script

Time Required: 45 minutes

Objective: Learn to create, save, and run an executable script.

Description: Many hacking tools are written in scripting languages, such as VBScript or JavaScript. In this activity, you create a script that populates a file with a range of IP addresses. This type of file can be used as an input file for Nmap or Fping.

1. If necessary, boot your computer into Linux, and then open a Terminal shell. Type **vim Myshell** and press **Enter**.

2. Press **i** to enter insert mode. If this is your first time using the vim editor, use Table 5-1 as a reference. The name "vim" means "vImproved" as it builds on the functionality of the older text editor vi. If you've struggled with vi in the past, vim is easier to use. (For a more detailed description of this versatile editor, type **man vim** in a different Terminal shell and press **Enter**.)

Table 5-1   Summary of vim commands

vim command	Description
A	Appends text after the insertion point
I	Inserts text before the insertion point
Delete key	Overwrites the last character when in Insert mode
X	Deletes the current character
Dd	Deletes the current line
Dw	Deletes the current word
P	Replaces the previously deleted text
Wq	Writes changes and quits the edit session
ZZ	Exits vi and saves all changes

3. Type **#!/bin/sh** and press **Enter**. This line identifies the file you're writing as a script. You should enter a few lines of documentation in any scripts or programs you write because they help later with program modifications and maintenance. When a line is used for documentation purposes, it's preceded with a # character. Figure 5-11 shows examples of documentation comments added, but don't enter them for this activity.

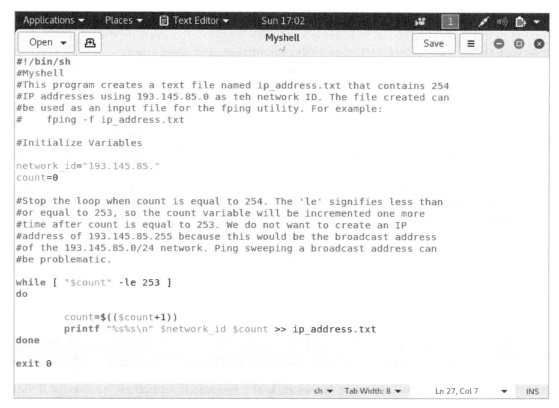

Figure 5-11   Shell script with comments

Source: Kali Linux gedit

 **CAUTION**   Make sure the slashes point in the correct direction (/). Windows users often make this mistake because they're used to typing backslashes (\). Also, be careful to only use spaces where instructed to do so and match uppercase and lowercase characters as shown. If you use spacing incorrectly, your script will not work correctly.

4. The second line is the name of the script you're creating. Type # **Myshell** and press **Enter**. If this script were used in a production setting, you would also enter the date and your name.

5. Read the documentation comments added in Figure 5-11 about the purpose of the script, but don't type them in your script. Your script should have only `#!/bin/sh` and `# Myshell` statements so far.

6. Type **network_id="193.145.85."** and press **Enter**. Be sure to include the quotation marks and the period after 85. (Because you aren't using this script on a live network, the address entered in this line doesn't matter.)

7. Type **count=0** and press **Enter**. This command initializes the count variable to zero, which is always wise because a variable shouldn't be used in a program without having a value set.

   Figure 5-11 shows more documentation comments added as an example, but skip entering them and move on to entering the program code. You need your script to add the number 1 to the 193.145.85. network ID and continue incrementing and adding numbers to the network ID until the IP address range 193.145.85.1 to 193.145.85.254 is written to a file named ip_address.txt. In programming, this repeated process is called looping. To avoid creating an endless loop, you need to add a condition in a while statement.

8. Type **while ["$count" -le 253]** and press **Enter**. Note the spaces inside the square brackets and pay close attention to the use of quotation marks and dollar signs.

9. Type **do** and press **Enter**. This statement is where the script performs its main task. The action takes place between the do statement and the done statement (added in Step 11). To increment the count variable by 1, type **count=$(($count+1))**, paying careful attention to the parentheses, and press **Enter**.

10. Type **printf "%s%s\n" $network_id $count >> ip_address.txt** and press **Enter**. This command uses the printf function to write data to a file. The **>>** characters add each IP address to the end of the ip_address.txt file.

11. Type **done** and press **Enter**, and then type **exit 0** and press **Enter**. Figure 5-11 shows the entire script. Save your hard work by pressing **Esc** and typing **:** (a colon). At the : prompt, type **wq** and press **Enter**.

12. Now that you've saved your script, you need to make it executable so that you can run it. At the command prompt, type **chmod +x Myshell** and press **Enter**.

13. To run your script, type **./Myshell** and press **Enter**. Because your script doesn't create any screen output, you need to examine the contents of the ip_address.txt file to see whether the script worked.

14. Type **cat ip_address.txt** and press **Enter**. How many IP addresses were created in the ip_address.txt file?

15. Close the shell. You can leave your system running for the end-of-module projects.

MODULE SUMMARY

- Port scanning, also referred to as service scanning, is the process of examining a range of IP addresses to determine what services are running on a system or network.
- Different port scans might elicit different information, so security testers need to be aware of the port scan types, such as SYN, ACK, FIN, and so on.
- A multitude of port-scanning tools are available. The most popular are Nmap, Nessus, and OpenVAS.
- Ping sweeps are used to determine which computers on a network are "live" (computers the attack computer can reach).
- Using scripts can help security professionals by automating time-consuming tasks.

Key Terms

closed ports	Nessus	ping sweep
filtered ports	Nmap	port scanning
Fping	open ports	
Hping3	OpenVAS	

Review Questions

1. Security testers and hackers use which of the following to determine the services running on a host and the vulnerabilities associated with these services?
   a. Zone transfers
   b. Zone scanning
   c. Encryption algorithms
   d. Port scanning

2. What is the most widely used port-scanning tool?
   a. Netcat   c. Nmap
   b. Netstat   d. Nslookup

3. Perform an Nmap scan of your home network. Write a one-page report outlining the services that you discovered. Were you surprised by anything you discovered?

4. Install Nessus Essentials and perform a basic network scan of your home network. Write a one-page report of your discoveries.

5. Which of the following Nmap commands sends a SYN packet to a computer with the IP address 193.145.85.210? (Choose all that apply.)
   a. nmap -sS 193.145.85.210
   b. nmap -v 193.145.85.210
   c. nmap -sA 193.145.85.210
   d. nmap -sF 193.145.85.210

6. Which flags are set on a packet sent with the nmap -sX 193.145.85.202 command? (Choose all that apply.)
   a. FIN   c. SYN
   b. PSH   d. URG

7. Port scanning is not illegal but must be performed in a controlled manner. The Open Source Security Testing Methodology Manual (OSSTMM) can be found online at https://isecom.org/research.html. Read "Chapter 2 -What you need to do" and in a one-page report, summarize the guidance it gives.

8. A closed port responds to a SYN packet with which of the following packets?
   a. FIN   c. SYN
   b. SYN-ACK   d. RST

9. Which parameter can be added to nmap to run a script scan with the default scripts?
   a. -sC   c. -p
   b. -oA   d. -rT

10. Security testers can use Hping3 to bypass filtering devices. True or false?

11. A FIN packet sent to a closed port responds with which of the following packets?
    a. FIN   c. RST
    b. SYN-ACK   d. SYN

12. A(n) _____ scan sends a packet with all flags set to NULL.
    a. NULL   c. SYN
    b. VOID   d. XMAS

13. Using your Nessus Essentials scan from question 4, write a one-page report describing one of the Common Vulnerabilities and Exposures (CVEs) that you discovered. In the report, include what operating systems this CVE affects, the details of the CVE, and what can be done to fix this vulnerability.

14. Port scanning provides the state for all but which of the following ports?
    a. Closed   c. Filtered
    b. Open   d. Buffered

15. A NULL scan requires setting the FIN, ACK, and URG flags. True or false?

16. Why does the fping -f 193.145.85.201 193.145.85.220 command cause an error?
    a. An incorrect parameter is used.
    b. The IP range should be indicated as 193.145.85.201-220.
    c. There's no such command.
    d. IP ranges aren't allowed with this command.

17. In basic network scanning, ICMP Echo Requests (type 8) are sent to host computers from the attacker, who waits for which type of packet to confirm that the host computer is live?
    a. ICMP SYN-ACK packet
    b. ICMP SYN packet
    c. ICMP Echo Reply (type 8)
    d. ICMP Echo Reply (type 0)

18. To bypass some ICMP-filtering devices on a network, an attacker might send which type of packets to scan the network for vulnerable services? (Choose all that apply.)
    a. PING packets
    b. SYN packets
    c. ACK packets
    d. Echo Request packets

19. Which of the following is a tool for creating a custom TCP/IP packet and sending it to a host computer?
    a. Tracert   c. Hping3
    b. Traceroute   d. Nmapping

20. Fping doesn't allow pinging multiple IP addresses simultaneously. True or false?

Case Projects

Case Project 5-1: Gathering Information on a Network's Active Services

Time Required: 30 minutes

Objective: Write a one-page memo to the IT manager explaining the tools you used to discover the services running on his network.

Description: After conducting a zone transfer and running security tools on the Alexander Rocco network, you're asked to write a memo to the IT manager, Jawad Safari, explaining which tools you used to determine the services running on his network. Mr. Safari is curious about how you gathered this information. You consult the Open Source Security Testing Methodology Manual (OSSTMM) and read Section C on port scanning and the "Internet Technology Security" section, particularly the material on identifying services, so that you can address his concerns.

Based on this information, write a one-page memo to Mr. Safari explaining the steps you took to find this information. Your memo should mention any information you found in the OSSTMM that relates to this stage of your testing.

Case Project 5-2: Finding Port-Scanning Tools

Time Required: 30 minutes

Objective: Write a one-page report to your manager describing some port-scanning tools that might be useful to your company.

Description: Alexander Rocco Corporation, which has hired you as a security tester, asked you to research any new tools that might help you perform your duties. It has been noted that some open-source tools your company is using lack simplicity and clarity or don't meet the company's expectations. Your manager, Gloria Petrelli, has asked you to research new or improved products on the market.

Based on this information, write a one-page report for Ms. Petrelli describing some port-scanning tools that might be useful to your company. The report should include available commercial tools and their costs.

ENUMERATION

After reading this module and completing the exercises, you will be able to:

1 Describe the enumeration step of security testing

2 Enumerate Windows OS targets and services

3 Enumerate *nix OS targets and services

Enumeration takes port scanning to the next level. Now that you know how to discover live systems on a network, the next steps are finding what resources are shared on the systems, discovering logon accounts and passwords, and gaining access to network resources. Enumeration involves connecting to a remote system, not just identifying that a system is present on a network. Hackers aren't satisfied with knowing that computer systems are running on a network; their goals are to find live systems and gain access to them. For security testers, enumeration is a more intrusive part of testing, and not having permission from the network's owner for this step could result in being charged with a criminal offense. Be sure you have a Rules of Engagement (ROE) and possibly a Statement of Work (SOW) in place to clearly define what actions you will be taking, and make sure to get written permission. During enumeration, you attempt to retrieve information and gain access to servers by using company employees' logon accounts. Knowledge of operating systems and how they store information can be helpful in these activities. Not knowing how Windows and Linux handle shares and file permissions can make accessing information and finding possible vulnerabilities more difficult. In this module, you learn some basics of various OSs and the tools for enumerating them. Some of these tools have been covered previously and some are new, but they make enumeration as easy as entering a single command or clicking a button.

INTRODUCTION TO ENUMERATION

In previous modules, you have seen how to perform a zone transfer, use the `dig` command, and discover what computers are live on a network. You have also seen how to use port scanning tools (such as Nmap) to discover devices and services on a network. The next step in security testing is enumeration, the process of extracting the following information from a network:

- Resources or shares on the network
- Network topology and architecture
- Usernames or groups assigned on the network
- Information about users and recent logon times

To determine what resources or shares are available on a network, security testers must use port scanning and footprinting first to determine what OS is used. If a network is running a Windows OS, for example, testers can use specific tools to view shares and possibly access resources. As mentioned, enumeration is more intrusive because you're not just identifying a resource; you're attempting to access it. Enumeration goes beyond passive scanning of a network to find open ports. For example, sometimes this process entails guessing passwords after determining a username. In Activity 6-1, you use NBTscan ("NBT" stands for NetBIOS over TCP/IP), a tool for enumerating Windows OSs that's part of the Kali Linux suite of security tools.

NOTE

In some activities in this module, you work with a partner so that one partner boots into Windows and the other boots into Linux. The reason for doing this is to have some Windows computers running in the classroom so that the enumeration tools you're working with can find systems to enumerate. NetBIOS doesn't run on Linux by default.

Activity 6-1: Using the NBTscan Tool

Time Required: 5 minutes

Objective: Learn how to use the NBTscan tool.

Description: In this activity, you work with a partner and use the NBTscan tool to find systems running NetBIOS.

1. Discuss with your partner to decide who will boot into Windows and who will boot into Kali Linux. If you are working alone, use two computers, real or virtual.

2. Open a terminal shell, then type **nbtscan -h | less** and press **Enter** to view the help page. Using this information, enter the NBTscan command to scan a range of IP addresses on your network and see whether any computers are identified. Can you identify your partner's Windows computer in the output? Figure 6-1 shows an example of output from the NBTscan command. Note the computers with NetBIOS names. The command also reveals the computers' MAC addresses.

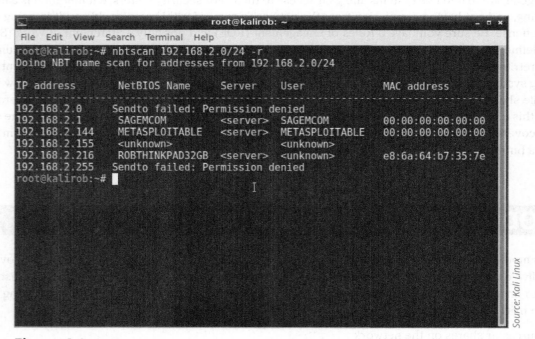

Figure 6-1   NBTscan finds computers running NetBIOS

Source: Kali Linux

3. Shut down Kali Linux and boot into Windows. If you are working with a partner, your partner should boot into Kali Linux and perform Steps 1 and 2.

4. If necessary, shut down Linux and boot into Windows for the next activity.

ENUMERATING WINDOWS OPERATING SYSTEMS

To understand how an attacker might gain access to resources or shares on a Windows network, in this section you take a brief look at Windows OSs as they relate to enumeration. By default, little information can be enumerated from Windows systems after Windows 7. Table 6-1 describes Windows OSs from Windows 95 to Windows Server 2019.

Table 6-1   Windows OS descriptions

Windows OS version	Description
Windows 95	The first Microsoft GUI product that doesn't rely on DOS, Windows 95 is the beginning of plug and play and the ActiveX standard used in all Windows versions today. A major enhancement is the Registry, a database storing information about the system's hardware and software. Previously, this information was stored in files. Windows 95 runs on stand-alone and networked computers and uses the FAT16 file system. Version OSR2 adds support for FAT32.
Windows 98 and Me	Compared to their predecessors, these versions have an improved file system (FAT32), new hardware support, and better backup and recovery tools. The enumeration process for Windows Me is the same as for Windows 98.
Windows NT 3.51 Server/ Workstation	These OSs were created with security and enhancement of network functionality in mind. They emphasize domains instead of workgroups and use the client/server model instead of peer-to-peer networks; the server is responsible for authenticating users and giving them access to network resources. The client/server model also allows for having many computers in a domain instead of the limited number of computers in a workgroup. NTFS replaces FAT16 and FAT32 because of the difficulty in incorporating security in the earlier file systems. NTFS includes file-level security features not possible in FAT.
Windows NT 4.0 Server/ Workstation	These upgrades to Windows NT 3.51 have improved GUIs and performance.
Windows 2000 Server/ Professional	In this upgrade to NT, Microsoft includes Active Directory (AD) for object storage. AD is more scalable than other available solutions for managing large networks. It uses Lightweight Directory Access Protocol (LDAP), which is still in use today. Also, this update includes the first version of Microsoft Management Console (MMC) and Encrypted File System (EFS). Enumeration of these OSs includes enumerating Active Directory.
Windows XP Professional	This OS includes Windows 2000 features, such as standards-based security, improved manageability, and the MMC. In addition, Windows XP has an improved user interface and better plug-and-play support. Security improvements in the kernel data structures make them read-only to prevent rogue applications from affecting the OS core, and Windows File Protection is added to prevent overwriting core system files. With Service Pack 2 (SP2), security is improved further with features such as Data Execution Prevention (DEP) and a firewall enabled by default. DEP fixes a security exposure caused by vulnerable running services that hackers often use for buffer overflow attacks, and the firewall makes it more difficult for hackers to exploit Windows service vulnerabilities and enumerate shares and services. In fact, enumeration of Windows XP SP2 and later systems can be difficult without modifying the configuration. Disabling the Windows Firewall is common in corporate networks, but this practice gives hackers additional attack surface. In these environments, the enumeration processes used for earlier Windows versions still work much the same way in Windows XP Professional.
Windows Server 2003	Windows Server 2003 includes improvements over Windows 2000 in some security areas, such as Internet Information Services (IIS), and comes in four editions. Generally, all editions include Remote Desktop, load balancing, VPN support, management services such as Windows Management Instrumentation (WMI), and .NET application services. The higher-end editions offer better support for PKI, certificate services, and Active Directory as well as enhancements to reliability, scalability, manageability, and security. Even with improvements in security and stability, enumeration techniques described for other Windows versions are effective with Windows Server 2003.

(continues)

Table 6-1   Windows OS descriptions *(continued)*

Windows OS version	Description
Windows Vista	Vista comes in several editions and is the first Windows version to introduce User Account Control (UAC) and built-in full drive encryption, called BitLocker (available in Vista Enterprise and Ultimate editions). UAC allows running Vista in nonprivileged mode to prevent unwanted code or user actions from damaging or controlling the computer (maliciously or inadvertently). However, UAC has been widely criticized because of its intrusive security prompts that force many users to disable it. In Windows 7, you can configure the frequency of these prompts. Also introduced in this release is Address Space Layout Randomization (ASLR), which makes exploitation of overflow-type vulnerabilities much more difficult. By default, Vista in a stand-alone environment can be difficult to enumerate without modifying its configuration.
Windows Server 2008	This OS features security options similar to Vista, including BitLocker drive encryption and UAC. Vista and Windows Server 2008 support Network Access Protection (NAP), which reduces the possibility of rogue systems being able to access network resources. Features, services, and roles in Windows Server 2008 can be fine-tuned to meet specific needs. A command-line version that requires fewer resources, called Server Core, is available for certain server roles. This version is designed to reduce maintenance, use of resources, and the "attack surface." Hyper-V, a full-featured virtualization product, is included with Windows Server 2008 and allows installing guest OSs, such as Linux and other Windows versions.
Windows 7	Windows 7 builds on the security advances made in Vista with the introduction of AppLocker, which allows for control over application execution. Including the Action Center in Windows 7 allows users to view potential configurations in one simple interface. Other improvements include refinements to the UAC feature and Windows Defender, which protect the system from known spyware.
Windows 8.1	Boasting "groundbreaking malware resistance," Windows 8.1 comes with features that make user-level infection much less dangerous by limiting the privileges of basic users. In addition, Windows 8.1 includes several heap integrity checks designed to make exploitation more difficult. Upgrades to Windows Defender make it a full anti-malware product. SmartScreen is extended to the OS to display an alert when an application is launched on a PC. For the first time, SecureBoot prevents execution of non-trusted boot content, preventing rootkits/bootkits.
Windows Server 2012	With this edition, Microsoft introduces Authentication Silos to prevent pass-the-hash attacks, a major weakness in all earlier versions of Windows servers. It also includes enhanced support for Domain Name System Security Extensions (DNSSEC), which relies on digital signatures to prove zone ownership.
Windows 10	Designed for use on tablets, gaming consoles, and traditional PCs, Windows 10 can be found in more places than ever. Numerous security enhancements were brought to Windows 10. One of the more progressive enhancements is that it only allows trusted apps by default through Device Guard. It also adds Credential Guard, which uses virtualization to protect access tokens from theft by attackers. Originally released in 2015, Windows 10 has improved through many feature and security enhancements. Windows 10 was supposed to be the last name change for Windows, but it is rumored that the next major release of Windows in 2021 will be called Windows 11.
Windows Server 2016	Windows Server 2016 features a number of security upgrades. The most important, Windows Containers, allows for application isolation to protect applications from one another. Windows Defender (malware protection) is now enabled by default. In this version, the option for telnet server is eliminated completely (telnet client is still available). A feature named Just Enough Administration (JEA) allows for more detailed access control settings on tasks.
Windows Server 2019	Windows Server 2019 was developed concurrently with Windows 10. It contains a number of new features and security measures including container services, storage spaces direct, storage migration services, storage replication, shielded virtual machines, and improved Windows Defender Advanced Threat Protection (ATP).

Many of the enumeration techniques that work with older Windows OSs still work with the newer versions.

NetBIOS Basics

Before learning how to enumerate Microsoft systems, you need to review the basics of how Network Basic Input/ Output System (NetBIOS) works. NetBIOS is a Windows programming interface that allows computers to communicate across a local area network (LAN). Most Windows OSs use NetBIOS to share files and printers. NetBIOS listens on UDP ports 137 (NetBIOS Name service) and 138 (NetBIOS Datagram service) and TCP port 139 (NetBIOS Session service). File and printer sharing in Windows also requires an upper-level service called Server Message Block (SMB), which runs on top of NetBIOS. In Windows 2000 and later, SMB listens on TCP port 445 and doesn't need to use NetBIOS over TCP/IP unless support for older Windows versions is required.

NOTE

Enumeration is a process of discovery. Using one enumeration tool may lead to a discovery that directs you to use another enumeration tool. For example, if you had used Nmap and learned that a device had UPD ports 137 and 138 and TCP port 139 (all the NetBIOS ports) open, you might then use a NetBIOS enumeration tool such as NBTscan to see what more you could discover about that device.

The computer names you assign to Windows systems are called NetBIOS names and have a limit of 16 characters; the last character is reserved for a hexadecimal number (00 to FF) that identifies the service running on the computer. Therefore, you can use only 15 characters for a computer name, and NetBIOS adds the last character automatically to identify the service that has registered with the OS. For example, if a computer is running the Server service, the OS stores this information in a NetBIOS table.

A NetBIOS name must be unique on a network. Table 6-2 lists the NetBIOS suffixes that correspond to the services, or resource types, running on a computer. You don't need to memorize all these suffixes but note that some identify the computer or server being enumerated as a stand-alone computer or domain controller. Hackers often exert more effort to attack computers identified as domain controllers because these systems store more information, including logon names for user accounts and network resources. You can perform an Internet search to find a more comprehensive list of NetBIOS suffixes.

Table 6-2   Important NetBIOS names and suffixes

NetBIOS name	Suffix	Description
<computer name>	00	The Workstation service registered the computer name (also called the NetBIOS name).
<computer name>	20	Registered by the Server service. A computer must have this service running to share printers or files.
<computer name>	22	Registered by the Microsoft Exchange Interchange service.
<computer name>	23	Registered by the Microsoft Exchange Store service. A store is where mailboxes and public folders are stored.
<computer name>	24	Registered by the Microsoft Exchange Directory service.
<computer name>	87	Signifies that Microsoft Exchange Message Transfer Agent (MTA) is running on this computer.
<domain name>	00	Indicates that Domain Name System (DNS) is running.
<domain name>	1C	Identifies the computer as a domain controller.
<iNet~Services>	1C	Indicates that IIS is running.
<IS~computer name>	00	Also indicates that IIS is running.

NetBIOS Null Sessions

Historically, one of the biggest vulnerabilities of NetBIOS systems is a null session, which is an unauthenticated connection to a Windows computer that uses no logon and password values. Many enumeration tools covered in this module establish a null session to gather information such as logon accounts, group membership, and file shares from an attacked computer. This vulnerability has been around for more than a decade and is still present in Windows XP. Null sessions have been disabled by default in Windows Server 2003, although administrators can enable them if they are needed for some reason. In Windows Vista and Server 2008, null sessions aren't available and can't be enabled, even by administrators. You might ask, "Why are we talking about these ancient operating systems? Who uses Windows XP anymore?" You would be surprised. If you as a penetration tester find an older operating system, you have just discovered a major security vulnerability as these operating systems are no longer supported and do not receive security updates. Your courses of action include upgrading the operating system, isolating the vulnerable ancient OS so it is not connected to any networks, or decommissioning the system.

NetBIOS Enumeration Tools

The `nbtstat` command is a powerful enumeration tool included with Windows. To display the NetBIOS table, you issue the `nbtstat-a IPaddress` command. (If you want to run Nbtstat locally, the command is `nbtstat-s`.) Figure 6-2 shows the entry LON-DC1. The 20 represents the Server service running on the LON-DC1 computer. The NetBIOS table also shows that ADATUM is a domain controller, as indicated by the 1C suffix.

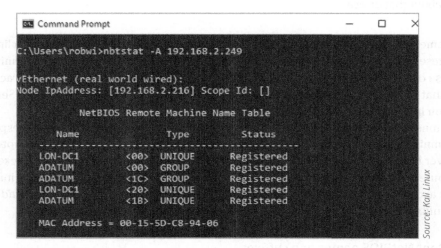

Figure 6-2 Using the Nbtstat command

Another built-in Windows tool is the `net view` command, which gives you a quick way to see whether there are any shared resources on a computer or server. To display the syntax for this command, type `net view ?`. Using the `net view` command, an attacker can view remote shares, as shown in Figure 6-3.

You can also use the IP address of computers you discovered with port-scanning tools. For example, Figure 6-4 shows the command used on a remote Windows 10 computer. A share name called wow is displayed. The next command an attacker could use against this computer is `\\robthinkpad32gb\wow` to explore the share drive and look for interesting files.

Although you can download or buy enumeration tools, you should learn how to take advantage of the tools available in Windows. A simple command-line utility can give you the name of a logged-on user, and a guess of that user's password can give you access to the system quickly. Many password-cracking programs can determine a password in a matter of seconds. A quick Internet search will reveal many free password-cracking programs you can try. However, security testers can often guess passwords without needing a special program because some users are careless when creating passwords. For example, many users, despite guidelines in company security policies, use simple passwords, such as "password" or "p@$$w0rd." Some systems also have default logon credentials that users often neglect to change, such as a username of "admin" with a password that is also "admin". You can find lists of default credentials for various devices on the Internet. Many password-cracking programs mentioned earlier can use brute force and attempt thousands of logons using dictionaries containing thousands of passwords. These dictionaries include well-known poor passwords (like password1234) and well-known default credentials.

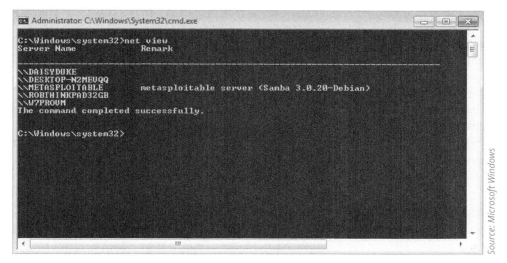

Figure 6-3   Using the net view command

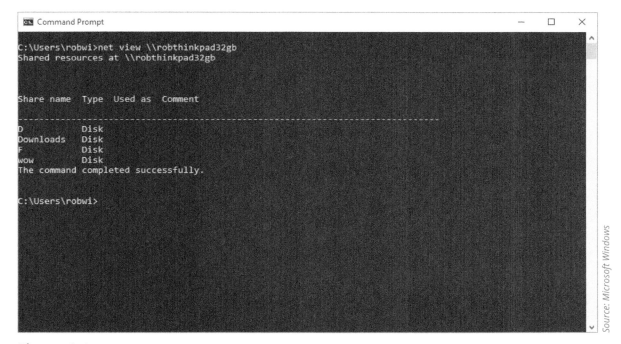

Figure 6-4   Using the net view command with a hostname

Activity 6-2: Using Built-in Windows NetBIOS Tools

Time Required: 30 minutes
Objective: Learn to use the Windows Nbtstat, Net view, and Net use commands.
Description: In this activity, you work with a partner to examine the Windows tools for viewing NetBIOS services and shares. (If you are working alone use two computers, real or virtual.) After using the Nbtstat command to discover a network computer or server that's sharing a resource, you use the Net view and Net use commands to enumerate these shared resources and possibly access them from your computer.

1. Start your computer and log on to Windows, if necessary.
2. Right-click **Start** and then click **File Explorer**. Click **This PC** in the left pane, double-click **Local Disk (C:)** (or other hard disk name), click the **Home** tab on the ribbon (if necessary), and then click **New Folder**. Type *YourFirstName* for the folder name and press **Enter**.

NOTE

YourFirstName is a placeholder used in the following commands; use your real first name instead. (If you create a folder called YourFirstName, that's okay; just remember the name of the folder.)

3. Right-click the folder you created, click **Give access to**, and then click **Specific people**. In the Network access dialog box, type **Everyone**, click **Add**, and then click **Share**. Click **Done** to close the Network access dialog box.

4. Open a command prompt window, and then type **ipconfig** and press **Enter**. Write down your IP address and give it to your partner.

NOTE

In the following steps, the IP address you found in Step 4 is represented by the variable *Partner'sIPaddress*. Instead of typing Partner'sIPaddress, type the IP address you shared with your partner when you see this variable in a command.

5. At the command prompt, type **net view \\Partner'sIPaddress** and press **Enter**. What does the command produce as output?

6. Type **net use ?** and press **Enter**. You use the `Net use` command to connect to a computer containing shared folders or files. Figure 6-5 shows the results of the command you entered.

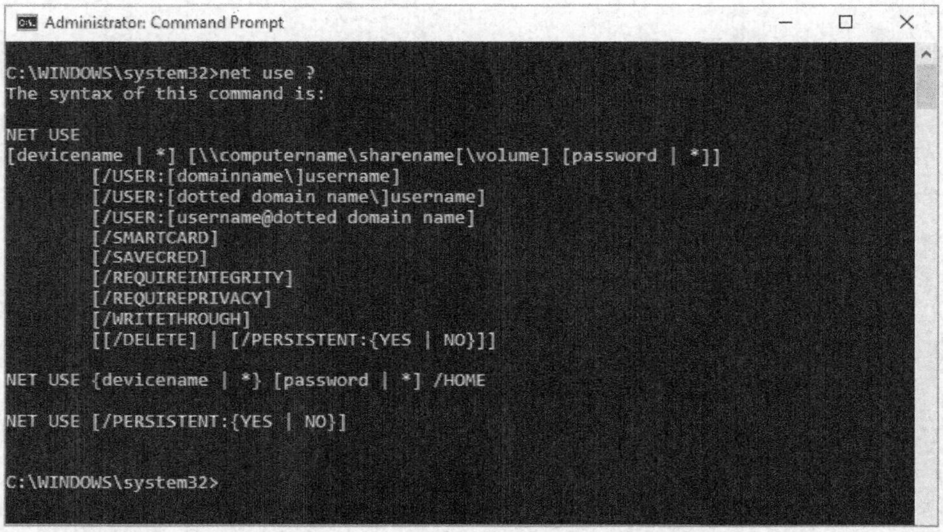

```
Administrator: Command Prompt                                      —   □   ×

C:\WINDOWS\system32>net use ?
The syntax of this command is:

NET USE
[devicename | *] [\\computername\sharename[\volume] [password | *]]
        [/USER:[domainname\]username]
        [/USER:[dotted domain name\]username]
        [/USER:[username@dotted domain name]
        [/SMARTCARD]
        [/SAVECRED]
        [/REQUIREINTEGRITY]
        [/REQUIREPRIVACY]
        [/WRITETHROUGH]
        [[/DELETE] | [/PERSISTENT:{YES | NO}]]

NET USE {devicename | *} [password | *] /HOME

NET USE [/PERSISTENT:{YES | NO}]


C:\WINDOWS\system32>
```
Source: Microsoft Windows

Figure 6-5   Viewing help for the net use command

7. Type **net use \\Partner'sIPaddress\YourFirstName** (replacing *Partner'sIPaddress* with the actual IP address you shared with your partner and *YourFirstName* with the name of the folder you created) and press **Enter**. What are the results of this command?

8. Type **nbtstat -a Partner'sIPaddress** and press **Enter**. What are the results of this command?

9. Close all open windows and decide which partner will boot with Kali Linux for the next activity.

Additional Enumeration Tools

As you have seen, several built-in Windows tools can assist you in enumerating NetBIOS systems. In the following activity, you examine some additional tools for this task. One of these tools is enum4linux, a tool for enumerating information from Windows and Samba systems. It is written in Perl and uses the Samba tools smbclient, rpclient, net, and nmblookup. Because enum4linux is written in Perl, you must run it on a system that supports Perl, such as Kali Linux.

Activity 6-3: Using Windows Enumeration Tools

Time Required: 30 minutes

Objective: Learn to use Windows network mapping and enumeration tools.

Description: In this activity, you explore and test some Windows enumeration tools included with Kali Linux. As in Activity 6-1, one partner has booted into Windows, and the other boots into Kali Linux. (If you are working alone use two computers, real or virtual.)

1. Boot your computer into Kali Linux.
2. Open a terminal window, then type **enum4linux –h** and press **Enter** to view the usage details for enum4linux.
3. Use the tool to enumerate your partner's Windows shares: Type **enum4linux -S *Partner'sIPaddress*** and press **Enter**. The results should be similar to what is shown in Figure 6-6.

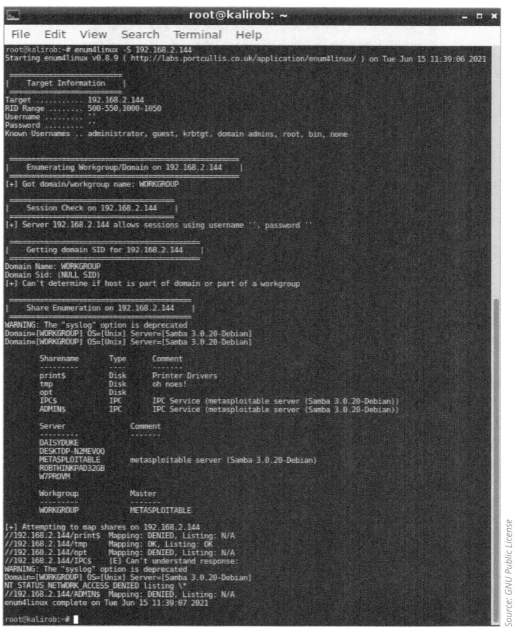

Figure 6-6   Results from enum4linux

If enum4linux fails to enumerate shares, it might be that Windows 10 has disabled guest access to list shares remotely by default. If you have an older version of Windows, you will probably see results. If Activity 6-2 worked, your partner's computer was probably added to the "HomeGroup." (Do a quick Internet search to understand more about Windows HomeGroup.) Modern versions of Windows hardly provide any information to enum4linux. This tool is more effective with older versions of Windows.

4. Click the **Applications** button and then click **01 - Information Gathering** to display other available tools (see Figure 6-7).

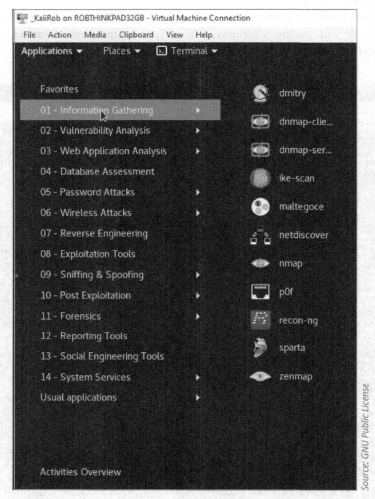

Figure 6-7   Kali information-gathering tools

5. Spend a few minutes exploring the functions of some of these tools. Don't hesitate to experiment or search the Internet for more information. Besides enum4linux and Nmap, are any other tools suited for enumerating Windows systems?

6. Switch computers with your partner, and the one who ran Windows previously should perform this activity. When you're finished, make sure both computers are booted into Kali Linux for the next activity.

DumpSec

DumpSec is a popular enumeration tool for Windows NT, 2000, and XP systems. It does not work well on newer versions of Windows. In your enumeration efforts you may come across older Windows NT, 2000, or XP systems where DumpSec can be useful. It is produced by Foundstone, Inc., and can be downloaded from www.systemtools.com/somarsoft/index.html. The information you can gather with this tool is astonishing. For example, after connecting to a Windows server, you can download—or, as it's called in DumpSec, "dump"—the following information:

- Permissions for shares
- Permissions for printers
- Permissions for the Registry
- Users in column or table format
- Policies (such as local, domain, and group policies)
- Rights
- Services

Hyena

Hyena, available at www.systemtools.com, is an excellent GUI tool for managing and securing Windows OSs. The interface is easy to use and gives security professionals a wealth of information. It is a paid-for tool but has a free trial you can experiment with.

You can use Hyena to look at the shares and user logon names for Windows servers and domain controllers. If any domains or workgroups are on the network, this tool displays them, too. Hyena can also display a graphical representation of the following areas, as shown in Figure 6-8:

- Microsoft Terminal Services
- Microsoft Windows network
- Web client network
- Users and groups

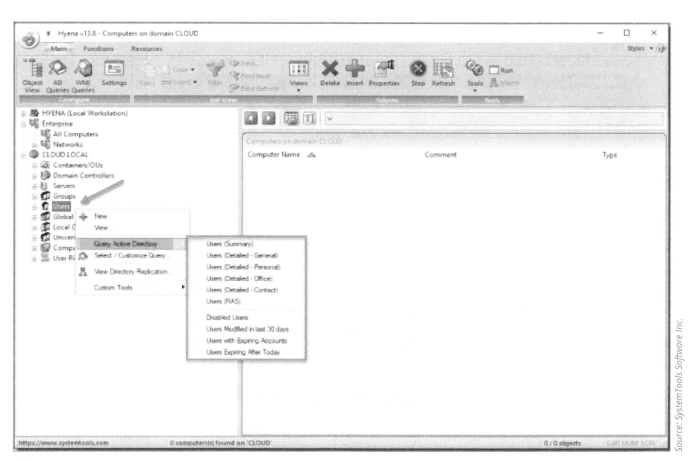

Figure 6-8   Hyena querying tool interface

Nessus and OpenVAS (aka Greenbone Security Assistant)

You may already be familiar with the OpenVAS, or Greenbone Security Assistant (GSA), and Nessus tools. GSA operates in client/server mode and is the open-source descendant of Nessus, a popular tool for identifying vulnerabilities. Nessus and OpenVAS are both compatible with, and easy to install on, Kali Linux. You can download the latest Nessus Essentials version for Windows, Linux, and macOS at www.tenable.com. Recall that Nessus Essentials has all the features of Nessus Professional, but is limited in the number of IP addresses you are allowed to scan. OpenVAS installation instructions for Kali Linux can be found at https://linuxhint.com/install-openvas-kali-linux. The installation process of OpenVAS often changes. You may have to perform an Internet search to find the latest guidance.

You can use Nessus or OpenVAS interchangeably for most purposes when enumerating systems. For example, Figure 6-9 shows OpenVAS reporting the details of an "SSH Brute Force Logins With Default Credentials" vulnerability. OpenVAS was able to log on through SSH using known default credentials, which is a security risk. The suggested solution is to "Change the password as soon as possible." OpenVAS has enumerated the target and discovered it is running the SSH service. The SSH service is vulnerable to attack.

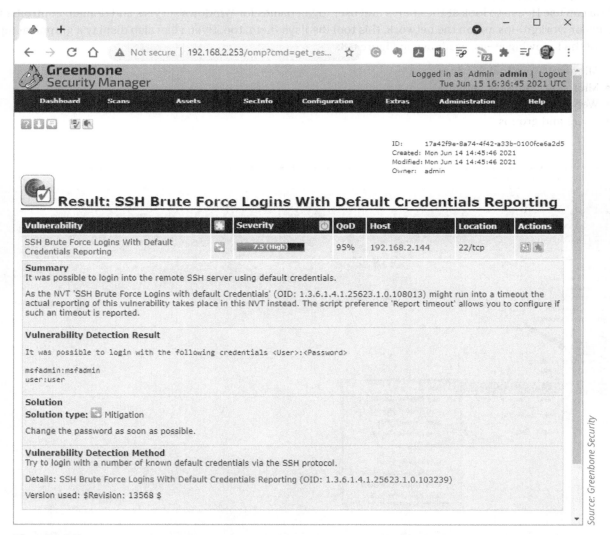

Source: Greenbone Security

Figure 6-9   OpenVAS enumerating a SSH Brute Force Logins With Default Credentials Vulnerability

The following figures show examples of how Nessus can be used. You should become familiar with Nessus because many public and private companies use it when conducting security testing. Nessus is easy to install and takes a few minutes to configure. This tool can come in handy when you need to enumerate different OSs on a large network.

Nessus is accessed using a web interface via port 8834. After you browse to the Nessus web interface and authenticate, the Scans page shown in Figure 6-10 opens. On this screen, you create, edit, and delete scans. If you click the New Scan button, you can select a scan template that is suitable for your goals.

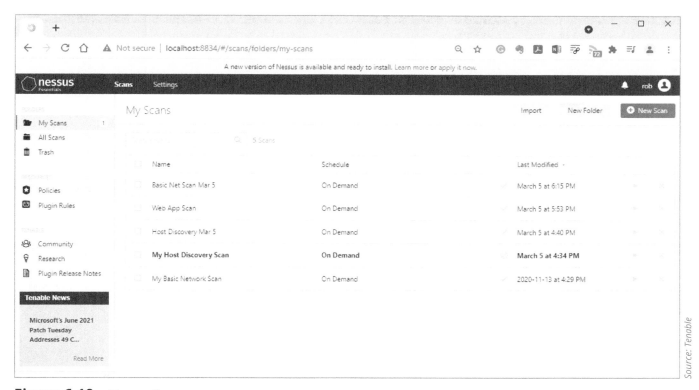

Figure 6-10   Nessus Scans page

The next several figures show Nessus in action. Figure 6-11 shows information Nessus has discovered using NetBIOS. This information includes computer names, running services (ports being listened on), and so forth. Nessus identifies the computer name as W7PROVM and the workgroup or domain name as WORKGROUP. This information could be useful for later attacks.

An additional Nessus scan to enumerate SMB shares has provided a list of folders that are accessible via SMB (see Figure 6-12). Folders that are accessible via SMB can be accessed remotely over the network. Hackers can use this information to launch attacks directed at each of these folders. As a penetration tester, you would take steps to protect these folders from hackers by making sure these SMB-accessible folders are secured with strong credentials, and that any unnecessary SBM shares are removed.

Nessus is also helpful in identifying the OS and service pack running on a computer. Figure 6-13 shows that the system with the IP address 192.168.2.250 is running Windows 7 Professional and has a few vulnerabilities. Windows 7 is no longer supported by Microsoft, so the presence of a Windows 7 machine on your network is a major security concern. Besides enumerating Windows OSs, Nessus can also enumerate Linux and Unix systems.

ENUMERATING *NIX OPERATING SYSTEM

Of the OSs covered in this module, UNIX is the oldest. Most computer vendors have developed their own flavors of this popular OS, but because of copyright restrictions, they can't use "UNIX" in their product names. (Only AT&T can use the name UNIX.) Other variations of UNIX include the following:

- Solaris (Sun Microsystems) and OpenSolaris
- HP-UX (Hewlett-Packard)

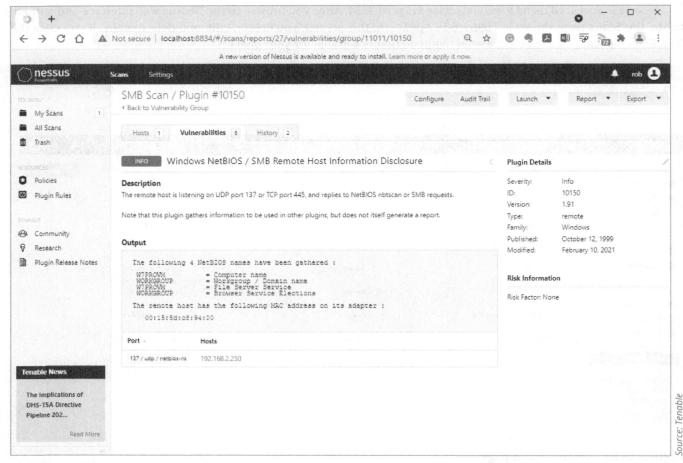

Figure 6-11 Nessus enumerates a NetBIOS system

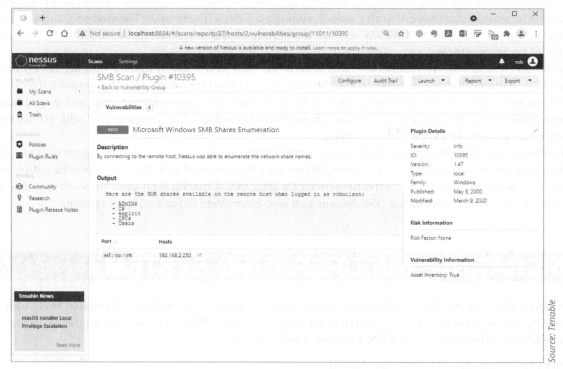

Figure 6-12 Enumerating shares using Nessus

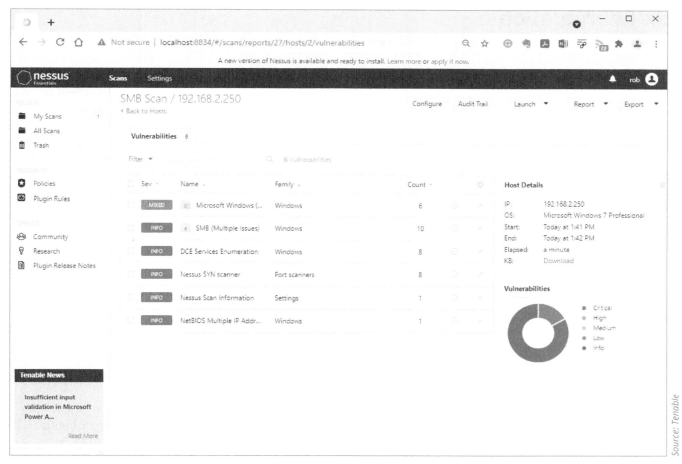

Figure 6-13   Nessus showing the operating system and vulnerabilities of 192.168.2.250

- Mac OS X and OpenDarwin, based on FreeBSD
- AIX (IBM)
- BSD UNIX (University of California at Berkley)
- FreeBSD (BSD-based UNIX, developed by contributors)
- OpenBSD (BSD-based UNIX, developed by contributors)
- NetBSD (BSD-based UNIX, developed by contributors)
- Linux, including the following distributions:
  - Ubuntu (Debian based, sponsored by Canonical)
  - Kali Linux (Debian based)
  - Red Hat Enterprise Linux (released commercially by Red Hat)
  - Fedora Linux (developed by contributors and sponsored by Red Hat)
  - Debian Linux (developed by contributors)
  - SUSE Linux (Micro Focus) and OpenSUSE
  - Mandriva Linux (distant commercial fork of 1990 Red Hat)
  - Slackware (oldest surviving Linux distribution)

As you can see, many organizations have a UNIX version. Linux, created by Linus Torvalds, is just that: a variation of UNIX originally designed for inexpensive Intel PCs. With all the UNIX variations available, it's no wonder that many computer professionals are using this OS. Recent versions of Linux are easier to install and configure and include GUIs and web browsers that make the software less complicated to use. With Grand Unified Bootloader (GRUB), you can have your desktop computer or laptop start in both Windows and Linux. Even novice computer users can install the latest version easily. Most Linux distributions have Live CD/DVD or USB stick versions that you can try without installing them on your hard drive. Variants of Linux can also be found running on devices such as smartphones, Apple computers, Internet of Things devices, and network security devices.

*nix Enumeration

An old but still popular network management service for network administrators is Simple Network Management Protocol (SNMP), which enables remote administration. The SNMP service can run on both Windows and *nix, though in this section, you focus on *nix. SNMP is useful for administrators who want to see system statistics, version numbers, and other detailed host information remotely. For this reason, it is also useful for hackers. By default, the SNMP service uses "public" as a credential for read-only access and "private" for read-write access. SNMPWalk is a tool useful in enumerating hosts running SNMP with the default configuration. (See Figure 6-14.) If attackers know the processor architecture (typically 32-bit or 64-bit) and the detailed version number of the remote operating system, they will have an easier time finding exploits that will be successful. The SNMP daemon (snmpd) listens on UDP port 161. SNMP often runs on network hardware such as routers, switches, and firewalls. These devices also have operating systems that may have vulnerabilities that can be exploited.

```
root@kali:~# snmpwalk -c public 192.168.56.110 -v1
iso.3.6.1.2.1.1.1.0 = STRING: "Vyatta VyOS 1.1.6"
iso.3.6.1.2.1.1.2.0 = OID: iso.3.6.1.4.1.30803
iso.3.6.1.2.1.1.3.0 = Timeticks: (1816453) 5:02:44.53
iso.3.6.1.2.1.1.4.0 = STRING: "root"
iso.3.6.1.2.1.1.5.0 = STRING: "vyos"
iso.3.6.1.2.1.1.6.0 = STRING: "Unknown"
iso.3.6.1.2.1.1.7.0 = INTEGER: 14
iso.3.6.1.2.1.1.8.0 = Timeticks: (14) 0:00:00.14
iso.3.6.1.2.1.1.9.1.2.1 = OID: iso.3.6.1.2.1.10.131
iso.3.6.1.2.1.1.9.1.2.2 = OID: iso.3.6.1.6.3.11.3.1.1
iso.3.6.1.2.1.1.9.1.2.3 = OID: iso.3.6.1.6.3.15.2.1.1
iso.3.6.1.2.1.1.9.1.2.4 = OID: iso.3.6.1.6.3.10.3.1.1
iso.3.6.1.2.1.1.9.1.2.5 = OID: iso.3.6.1.6.3.1
iso.3.6.1.2.1.1.9.1.2.6 = OID: iso.3.6.1.2.1.49
```

Source: GNU Open Source License

Figure 6-14   Using the SNMPWalk command

Nessus is also helpful in *nix enumeration. Figure 6-15 shows what Nessus found when scanning a Ubuntu 15.10 system.

Vulnerability scanners such as Nessus and OpenVAS are useful for enumerating *nix hosts, but simple tools like Nmap script scanning can also help an attacker gain information about remote *nix hosts. Figure 6-16 shows what Nmap found when scanning a Ubuntu 15.10 system.

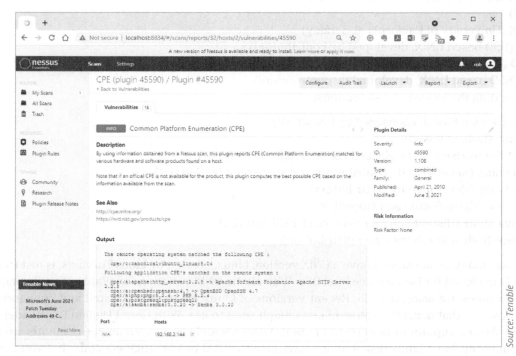

Source: Tenable

Figure 6-15   Nessus enumerates a Linux system

Figure 6-16 Nmap script scan enumerates a Linux system

An older but sometimes useful enumeration tool for both security testers and hackers is the Finger utility, which lets you use a single command to find out who's logged on to a *nix system. Finger is both a client and a server. The Finger daemon (fingerd) listens on TCP port 79.

Activity 6-4: Enumerating *nix Web Servers with Nmap

Time Required: 30 minutes
Objective: Learn to use the Nmap tool on local and remote *nix systems.
Description: In this activity, you use the Nmap command to enumerate your computer and see how this powerful command can gather information from a remote system. You'll also learn how to start and stop services on your local machine.

 **CAUTION** For this exercise, you enable a few services that could put your machine at risk if you don't take the proper precautions. If your Kali installation does not have root logon capability, you need to change your password by using the command `passwd root`. This will enable root logon.

1. If necessary, boot your computer into Kali Linux and log on.
2. Most Linux services are started from a series of scripts stored in the directory /etc/init.d/. You can view the contents of this folder with the following command: **ls /etc/init.d/.**

3. Start the ssh and samba services on your local host with the following commands: **/etc/init.d/ssh start** and **/etc/init.d/samba start.**
4. Use Nmap to run a scripted scan of the localhost (127.0.0.1). Figure 6-16 shows an example of an Nmap scripted scan. What results were returned? What version of SSH is your computer running? What version of Samba?
5. Are there any vulnerabilities associated with these versions of SSH or Samba?
6. Use the following commands to stop the services you enabled: **/etc/init.d/sshd stop** and **/etc/init.d/samba stop.** Shut down your Kali Linux computer.

MODULE SUMMARY

- Enumeration is the process of extracting usernames, passwords, and shared resources from a system.
- Enumeration can give an attacker insight into sensitive areas of a network, systems running old software, or even simple misconfigurations that the attacker can take advantage of.
- Enumerating Windows targets can be done with built-in Windows tools, such as the Nbtstat, Net view, and Net use commands, or with a variety of other utilities. Tools such as enum4linux can enumerate Windows from various versions of *nix. Newer versions of Windows are more difficult to enumerate because of advances in Windows security over time.
- Enumeration of *nix systems can be done with tools used for enumerating other OSs, such as Nessus and its open-source descendant, OpenVAS.
- SNMP can be used to enumerate both *nix and Windows hosts that are running the SNMP service/daemon with the default configuration.

Key Terms

enum4linux
enumeration

Network Basic Input/Output
  System (NetBIOS)
  null session

Simple Network Management
  Protocol (SNMP)

Review Questions

1. Which of the following testing processes is the most intrusive?
   a. Port scanning
   b. Enumeration
   c. Null scanning
   d. Numeration

2. Security testers conduct enumeration for which of the following reasons? (Choose all that apply.)
   a. Gaining access to shares and network resources
   b. Obtaining user logon names and group memberships
   c. Discovering services running on computers and servers
   d. Discovering open ports on computers and servers

3. Which of the following tools can be used to enumerate Windows systems? (Choose all that apply.)
   a. OpenVAS or Nessus
   b. Reddit
   c. DumpIt
   d. Hyena

4. Enumeration of Windows systems can be more difficult if port _____ is filtered.
   a. 110/UDP
   b. 443/UDP
   c. 80/TCP
   d. 139/TCP

5. Perform a Net view scan of your own computer. Write a brief report (three paragraphs) of your findings. Were you surprised by any of the shares you discovered? Describe the shares you discovered and why they are there.

6. The Net view command can be used to see whether a server has any shared resources. True or false?

7. To identify the NetBIOS names of systems on the 193.145.85.0 network, which of the following commands do you use?
   a. nbtscan 193.145.85.0/24
   b. nbtscan 193.145.85.0-255
   c. nbtstat 193.145.85.0/24
   d. netstat 193.145.85.0/24

8. Which of the following is a Windows command-line utility for seeing NetBIOS shares on a network?
   a. Net use
   b. Net user
   c. Net view
   d. Nbtuser

9. The Nbtstat command is used to enumerate *nix systems. True or false?

10. Not counting the reserved character at the end, a NetBIOS name can contain a maximum of _____ characters.
    a. 10
    b. 11
    c. 15
    d. 16

11. Which of the following commands connects to a computer containing shared files and folders?
    a. Net view
    b. Net use
    c. Netstat
    d. Nbtstat

12. Which port numbers indicate NetBIOS is in use on a remote target?
    a. 135 to 137
    b. 389 to 1023
    c. 135 to 139
    d. 110 and 115

13. Perform a Nessus scan of your own computer. Try a variety of scans to see what kind of information you can enumerate. Did you find any vulnerabilities? If so, research the solutions to those vulnerabilities and see if you can apply the fixes. Nessus may list solutions directly in its description or you may have to look up the CVEs at https://cve.mitre.org/cve/search_cve_list.html. List the information you enumerated, but do not list your vulnerabilities. (For security reasons, you do not want to share your vulnerabilities.)

14. Most NetBIOS enumeration tools connect to the target system by using which of the following?
    a. ICMP packets
    b. Default logons and blank passwords
    c. Null sessions
    d. Admin accounts

15. What is the best method of preventing NetBIOS attacks?
    a. Filtering certain ports at the firewall
    b. Telling users to create difficult-to-guess passwords
    c. Pausing the Workstation service
    d. Stopping the Workstation service

16. Which of the following is a commonly used UNIX enumeration tool?
    a. Netcat
    b. Nbtstat
    c. Netstat
    d. SNMPWalk

17. Which of the following commands should you use to determine whether there are any shared resources on a Windows computer with the IP address 193.145.85.202?
    a. netstat -c 193.145.85.202
    b. nbtscan -a 193.145.85.202
    c. nbtstat -a 193.145.85.202
    d. nbtstat -a \\193.145.85.202
       \\193.145.85.202

18. Log on to your Kali Linux instance. Use each of the Linux-based tools discussed in this module on the Kali Linux instance itself. List your findings. Were there any surprises? If so, what were they?

Case Projects

Case Project 6-1: Enumerating Systems on the Alexander Rocco Network

Time Required: 20 minutes

Objective: Create a report advising the IT manager what steps to take after you discover a security issue involving shared folders.

Description: After conducting enumeration of the Alexander Rocco network, you discover several Windows computers with shared folders for the Help Desk Department. You're concerned when you access one of the shared folders containing information for help desk personnel and find an Excel spreadsheet listing email addresses and passwords for all employees. Help desk employees use this shared folder to access the Excel spreadsheet if users call saying they have forgotten their passwords and need this information even when they're away from their offices.

Based on this information, write a one-page memo to the IT manager, Jawad Safari, describing the steps you would take after this discovery. The memo should also mention any information you find in the OSSTMM that relates to your discovery and offer recommendations.

Case Project 6-2: Researching enum4Linux on the Internet

Time Required: 20 minutes

Objective: Create a report explaining to your boss what the enum4linux tool is capable of, why you want to use the tool, and convincing him to allow you to use it.

Description: You are given permission to use your credentials to run some basic security checks on the Alexander Rocco domain. You don't have access to Nessus or OpenVAS, so you have to use other tools to enumerate the domain. After some research, you come across the enum4linux tool. To make sure your boss is okay with this tool, you need to tell him why you want to use enum4linux and what it's capable of.

Write a one-page memo on the enum4linux tool in which you describe the goal of your enumeration and the checks available in enum4linux. Your memo should persuade your boss into letting you use the tool for enumeration purposes.

PROGRAMMING FOR SECURITY PROFESSIONALS

After reading this chapter and completing the exercises, you will be able to:

1 Explain basic programming concepts

2 Write a simple C program

3 Explain how webpages are created with HTML

4 Describe and create basic Perl programs

5 Explain basic object-oriented programming concepts

6 Describe and create basic Python programs

As a security professional, you need to know how both hackers and security testers use computer programming. This module describes the basic skills of programming. You won't be an expert programmer after this module, but you'll have a clearer idea of how programs are written. Removing the mystique eliminates the fear many networking professionals experience when hearing the word "programming." Having a basic understanding of programming can also help you in developing custom security tools or modifying existing tools when you're conducting security tests. In fact, most position descriptions for professional security testers include a requirement for creating customized security tools. Just as a good carpenter knows how to modify a tool to fit a special job, security testers should know how to modify computer tools created for one purpose so that they can be used for other functions.

This module gives you a general overview of C, HTML, Perl, and Python. Becoming a programmer takes a lot of time and practice, but this module gives you an opportunity to examine some programs and practice writing a couple yourself.

INTRODUCTION TO COMPUTER PROGRAMMING

Just as book editors must understand the rules and syntax of the English language, computer programmers must understand the rules of programming languages and deal with syntax errors. A command's syntax must be exact, right down to the placement of semicolons and parentheses. One minor mistake and the program won't run correctly, or even worse, will produce unpredictable results. Being a programmer takes a keen eye and patience; keep in mind that errors aren't unusual the first time you try to create a program.

Unfortunately, most colleges don't teach programming with security in mind. Many current attacks on operating systems and applications are possible because of poor programming practices. Mary Ann Davidson, Oracle's chief security officer (CSO), speaks all over the world on this topic. She argues that software developers focus on "cool technology" and the latest programming languages. "They don't think like attackers," she stated to an audience filled with more than 1,000 information assurance professionals. "Nor is there a requirement for software developers to demonstrate proficiency in safe, secure programming as a condition of matriculation," she added.

Details on this issue are beyond the scope of this book, but if you decide to pursue programming or software engineering as a major, urge the college you're attending to cover secure programming. Oracle's CSO offered some suggestions to change the higher education system. She believes security should be part of every computer science class, "not just in a single class that students file and forget," and computer science textbooks should be written to emphasize secure programming techniques. Grades should be based in part on the "hackability" of code students submit for assignments, and students should be required to use automated tools to find vulnerabilities in their coding. Security must be integrated into any software engineering project from its inception, not after the fact. A new field in cybersecurity called SecDevOps attempts to adjust the mindset of programmers to develop code with security and IT operations in mind. The term SecDevOps stands for security, development, and operations. Developing code with security in mind and understanding IT operations result in more robust and exploit-resistant software. Instead of adding security by changing someone else's code to make it more secure, SecDevOps attempts to have the original developers "bake" security into code from the start.

This module intends to whet your appetite and give you an overview of programming. To begin, take a look at some programming fundamentals.

Programming Fundamentals

Manuals filled with a programming language's syntax and commands can take up a lot of space on your bookshelves, but you can learn some basics in any programming language without consulting manuals or online guides. In fact, you can begin writing programs with only some knowledge of programming fundamentals, which you can remember with the acronym BLT (as in bacon, lettuce, and tomato): branching, looping, and testing.

Branching, Looping, and Testing (BLT)

Most programming languages have a way to branch, loop, and test. For example, a function in a C program can branch to another **function** in the program, perform a task there, and then return to its starting point. A function is a mini program within the main program that carries out a task. For example, you can write a function that adds two numbers and then returns the answer to the function that called it. **Branching** takes you from one area of a program (a function) to another area. **Looping** is performing a task over and over. A loop usually completes after **testing** is conducted on a variable and returns a value of true or false. Although you don't need to worry about the syntax for now, examine the following program to see where it uses branching, looping, and testing:

```
#include <stdio.h>
main()
{
    int a = 1; // Variable initialized as integer, value 1
    if (a > 2) ; // Testing whether "a" is greater than 2
       printf ("a is greater than 2");
    else
       GetOut(); // Branching: calling a different function
  GetOut() // Do something interesting here
  {
       for (int a=1; a<11; a + + ) // Loop to display 10 times
       {
       printf("I'm in the GetOut() function") ;
       }
  }
}
```

There you have it: the BLT of computer programming. There's a lot more to learn in programming, but by knowing how to do these three actions, you can examine a program and understand its functionality.

A program contains different functions, or modules, that perform specific tasks. Say you're writing a program for making a BLT sandwich. The first step is to list the tasks in this process. In computer lingo, you're writing an **algorithm** (a recipe) to make a BLT sandwich. You keep an algorithm as simple as possible, but creating an algorithm is one of the most important programming skills to master.

Skipping a step in an algorithm can cause problems. For example, not rinsing the lettuce might result in a **bug** in your sandwich. Similarly, not reviewing your programs code carefully might result in having a bug in your program—an error that causes unpredictable results. Bugs are worse than syntax errors because a program can run successfully with a bug, but the output might be incorrect or inconsistent. Performing tasks in the incorrect order might also create havoc. For example, putting mayonnaise on the bread before toasting it can result in soggy toast. The following list is an example of an algorithm for making a BLT sandwich:

- Purchase the ingredients.
- Gather all the utensils needed for making the sandwich.
- Clean the tomatoes and lettuce.
- Slice the tomatoes and separate the lettuce leaves.
- Fry the bacon.
- Drain the bacon.
- Toast the bread.
- Put mayonnaise on the toast.
- Put the fried bacon, sliced tomato, and lettuce leaves on the toast.
- Join the two slices of toasted bread.

A programmer would then convert this algorithm into **pseudocode**. Pseudocode isn't a programming language; it's an English-like language you can use to help create the structure of your program. The following example is the pseudocode that addresses purchasing all the ingredients needed for a BLT sandwich before you write the programming code:

```
PurchaseIngredients Function
     Call GetCar Function
     Call DriveToStore Function
     Purchase Bacon, Bread, Tomatoes, Lettuce, and Mayonnaise at store
End PurchaseIngredients Function
```

After writing pseudocode, you can begin writing your program in the language of your choice. Are outlining an algorithm and writing pseudocode necessary for every computer program you write? No. If the program you're writing has very few lines of code, you can skip these steps, but for beginning programmers, these two steps are helpful.

Documentation

When writing any program, you must document your work. To do this, you add comments to the code that explain what you're doing. Documentation not only makes your program easier for someone else to modify; it also helps you remember what you were thinking when you wrote the program. The phrase "No comment" might be appropriate for politicians or Wall Street investors with inside trading information, but not for programmers.

Although documentation is important, many programmers find it time consuming and tedious. Often, they think their code is self-explanatory and easy enough for anyone to maintain and modify, so documenting their work isn't necessary. You'll soon discover, however, that without good documentation, you won't understand the lines of code you wrote three weeks ago, let alone expect a stranger to figure out your train of thought. For example, the following comments can help the next programmer understand why a new function was added to an existing program:

```
/* The following function was added to the program June 15, 2021 per a request from the
Marketing Department.

Reports generated by the sales() function were not giving the marketing folks information
about sales in Asia.

This new function uses data from text files from the offices in Tokyo and Hong Kong. -
Kendra Choi */
```

Software engineering companies don't retain programmers who don't document their work because they know that 80 percent of the cost of software projects is maintenance. They also know that an average of 10 bugs for every 1,000 lines of code is the industry standard. For example, Windows 10 is estimated to contain over 50 million lines of code, but Microsoft software engineers, partly because of strict documentation rules and Secure Software Development Lifecycle Practices, can limit bugs to fewer than the average. In general, the average number of bugs in Microsoft code is below the industry standard. With bugs being so prevalent in many programs, however, it's easy to see how attackers can discover vulnerabilities in software. Programmers can easily overlook problems in thousands of lines of code that might create a security hole attackers can exploit.

SECURITY BYTES

In July 2021, Microsoft issued an emergency patch for a critical bug dubbed PrintNightmare. The bug was accidentally disclosed by researchers. Using this vulnerability, hackers could install programs; view, change, and delete data; or create new accounts with full user rights remotely on all versions of Windows. The bug involved a vulnerability in the Windows Print Spooler, a part of Windows that manages printing. Windows 7 has reached the end of its life and is no longer actively supported by Microsoft, but the bug was severe enough that Microsoft also released a fix for Windows 7.

Activity 7-1: Writing Your First Algorithm

Time Required: 10 minutes

Objective: Learn to write an algorithm.

Description: Programmers must approach problem-solving in logical steps or tasks. Missing a step can have disastrous effects, so you should train yourself to think in a structured, logical way. A good way to test whether you can follow a step-by-step approach is by doing exercises that encourage you to think in this manner. For this activity, list at least seven steps for making scrambled eggs. When writing the steps, make sure you don't take anything for granted. Assume someone with no knowledge of cooking—or even of eggs—will try to follow your algorithm.

LEARNING THE C LANGUAGE

Many programming languages are available to security testers. You'll begin your journey with an introduction to one of the most popular programming languages: C, developed by Dennis Ritchie at Bell Laboratories in 1972. The C language is both powerful and concise. In fact, UNIX, which was first written in **assembly language**, was soon rewritten in C. Not many programmers want to write programs in binary (machine code) or machine language, so assembly language was developed. It uses a combination of hexadecimal numbers and expressions, such as mov, add, and sub, so writing programs in this language is easier than in machine language.

This module gives you a basic overview of the C language. At many colleges, an entire course is devoted to learning this language; others skip C and teach C++, an enhancement of the C language. Many security professionals and hackers still use C because of its power and cross-platform usability. However, security professionals also consider C to be one of the least secure programming languages due to its susceptibility to buffer overflows. It is therefore helpful for you to know the language to avoid its pitfalls.

A **compiler** is a program that converts a text-based program, called source code, into executable or binary code. Table 7-1 lists some available C compilers. Most C compilers can also create executable programs in C++. The Intel and Microsoft compilers must be purchased, but many other compilers are free and can be found with an Internet search. Online compilers don't require the programmer to have a compiler locally installed on their computer. These online compilers have webpages that accept code from the programmer and then compile it on the online compiler provider's servers using the appropriate compiler for the programming language being used. Online compilers are fine

Table 7-1   C language compilers

Compiler	Description
Intel compilers for Windows and Linux	Intel's C++ compiler is designed for developing applications for Windows servers, desktops, laptops, and mobile devices. The Intel Linux C++ compiler claims to optimize the speed of accessing information from a MySQL database, an open-source database program used by many corporations and e-commerce companies.
Microsoft Visual C++ Compiler	This compiler is widely used by programmers developing C and C++ applications for Windows platforms.
GNU C and C++ compilers (GCC)	These free compilers can be downloaded for Windows and *nix platforms. Most *nix systems include the GNU GCC compiler.

for experimentation and learning, but aren't practical for real-world programming. The security issues of uploading your code to a third-party server, and the slowness of compiling large projects make online compilers inappropriate and impractical for serious development.

NOTE

What's dangerous about C is that a beginner can make some big blunders. For example, a programmer can accidentally write to areas of memory that could cause the program to crash, or worse, give an attacker the ability to take control of the remote system. Usually, what's written is executable code that might give an attacker a backdoor into the system, escalate an attacker's privileges to that of an administrator, or simply crash the program. This type of attack is usually possible because the programmer didn't check users' input. For example, if users can enter 300 characters when prompted to enter their last names, an attacker can probably enter executable code at this point of the program. When you see the term "buffer overflow vulnerability," think "poor programming practices." Keep in mind that although C is easy to learn and use, errors in using it can result in system damage.

Anatomy of a C Program

Many veteran programmers can't think of the C language without remembering the "Hello, world!" program, the first program a C student learns:

```
/* The famous "Hello, world!" C program */
#include <stdio.h> /* Load the standard IO library. The library contains functions your C
program might need to call to perform various tasks. */
main()
{
    printf("Hello, world!\n\n") ;
}
```

That's it. You can write these lines of code in almost any text editor, such as Notepad if you're using Windows or the vim editor if you're using Linux. If you want more editing features than in Notepad or vim, you can install and use Notepad++ in Windows or use gedit in Linux. You can download Notepad++ from https://notepad-plus-plus.org/downloads/. The following sections explain each line of code in this program.

Many C programs use the /* and */ symbols to enclose long comments instead of using the // symbols for one-line comments. For example, you can type the /* symbols, add as many lines of comment text as needed, and then type the closing */ symbols. Forgetting to add the */ at the end of comment text can cause errors when compiling the program, so be careful.

The #include statement is used to load libraries that hold the commands and functions used in your program. In the Hello, world! example, the #include <stdio.h> statement loads the stdio.h library, which contains many C functions.

The parentheses in C mean you're dealing with a function. C programs must contain a `main()` function, but you can also add your own functions to a C program. Note that after the `main()` function, an open brace (the { symbol) is on a line by itself. Braces show where a block of code begins and ends. In the Hello, world! program, the closing brace indicates the end of the program. Forgetting to add a closing brace is a common mistake.

Inside the `main()` function, the program calls another function: `printf()`. When a function calls another function, it uses parameters, also known as arguments. Parameters are placed between opening and closing parentheses. In this example, the parameters `"Hello, world! \n\n"` are passed to the `printf()` function. The `printf()` function then displays (prints) the words "Hello, world!" onscreen, and the `\n\n` characters add two new lines after the Hello, world! display. Table 7-2 lists some special characters that can be used with the `printf()` function.

Table 7-2 Special characters for use with the `printf()` function

Character	Description
\n	New line
\t	Tab

Declaring Variables

A variable represents a numeric or string value. For example, you can solve `x + y = z` if you know two of the variable values. In programming, you can declare variables at the beginning of a program so that calculations can be carried out without user intervention. A variable might be defined as a character or characters, such as letters of the alphabet, or it can be assigned a numeric value, as in the expression `int x = 1`. Table 7-3 shows some variable types used in C.

Table 7-3 Variable types in C

Variable type	Description
Int	Use this variable type for an integer (positive or negative number).
Float	This variable type is for a real number that includes a decimal point, such as 1.299999.
Double	Use this variable type for a double-precision floating-point number.
Char	This variable type holds the value of a single letter.
String	This variable type holds the value of multiple characters or words.
Const	A constant variable is created to hold a value that doesn't change for the duration of your program. For example, you can create a constant variable called TAX and give it a specific value: const TAX =.085. If this variable is used in areas of the program that calculate total costs after adding an 8.5% tax, it's easier to change the constant value to a different number if the tax rate changes, instead of changing every occurrence of 8.5% to 8.6%.

If the `printf()` function contains values other than a quoted sentence, such as numbers, you need to use **conversion specifiers**. A conversion specifier tells the compiler how to convert the value in a function. For example, `printf("Your name is %s! ", name) ;` displays the following if you have assigned the value Sue to the `string` variable called `name`:

`Your name is Sue!`

Table 7-4 lists conversion specifiers for the `printf()` function.

In addition to conversion specifiers, programmers use operators to compare values, perform mathematical calculations, and the like. Most likely, programs you write will require calculating values based on mathematical operations, such as addition or subtraction. Table 7-5 describes mathematical operators used in C.

You might also need to test whether a condition is true or false when writing a C program. To do that, you need to understand how to use relational and logical operators, described in Table 7-6.

Using compound assignment operators as a shorthand method, you can perform more complex operations with fewer lines of code. For example, `TotalSalary +-5` is a shorter way of writing `TotalSalary = TotalSalary + 5`. Similarly, `TotalSalary -= 5` means the `TotalSalary` variable now contains the value `TotalSalary - 5`.

Table 7-4 Conversion specifiers in C

Specifier	Type
%c	Character
%d	Decimal number
%f	Floating decimal or double number
%s	Character string

Table 7-5   Mathematical operators in C

Operator	Description
+ (unary)	Doesn't change the value of the number. Unary operators use a single argument; binary operators use two arguments. Example: +(2).
- (unary)	Returns the negative value of a single number.
++ (unary)	Increments the unary value by 1. For example, if a is equal to 5, ++a changes the value to 6.
— (unary)	Decrements the unary value by 1. For example, if a is equal to 5, —a changes the value to 4.
+ (binary)	Addition. For example, a + b.
- (binary)	Subtraction. For example, a – b.
* (binary)	Multiplication. For example, a * b.
/ (binary)	Division. For example, a / b.
% (binary)	Modulus. For example, 10 % 3 is equal to 1 because 10 divided by 3 leaves a remainder of 1.

Table 7-6   Relational and logical operators in C

Operator	Description
==	Equal operator; compares the equality of two variables. In a == b, for example, the condition is true if variable a is equal to variable b.
! =	Not equal; the exclamation mark negates the equal sign. For example, the statement `if a != b` is read as "if a is not equal to b."
>	Greater than.
<	Less than.
>=	Greater than or equal to.
<=	Less than or equal to.
&&	AND operator; evaluates as true if both sides of the operator are true. For example, `if (( a > 5) && (b > 5)) printf ("Hello, world!");` prints only if both a and b are greater than 5.
| |	OR operator; evaluates as true if either side of the operator is true.
!	NOT operator; the statement `! (a == b)`, for example, evaluates as true if a isn't equal to b.

NOTE

Many beginning C programmers make the mistake of using a single equal sign (=) instead of the double equal sign (==) when attempting to test the value of a variable. A single equal sign (the assignment operator) is used to assign a value to a variable. For example, `a = 5` assigns the value 5 to the variable a. To test the value of variable a, you can use the statement `if (a == 5)`. If you mistakenly write the statement as `if (a = 5)`, the value 5 is assigned to the variable a, and then the statement is evaluated as true. This happens because any value not equal to zero is evaluated as true, and a zero value is evaluated as false.

Although this module covers only the most basic elements of a program, with what you have learned so far, you can write a C program that displays something onscreen. Security testers should gain additional programming skills so that they can develop tools for performing specific tasks, as you see in "Understanding Perl" and "Understanding Python" later in this module.

Branching, Looping, and Testing in C

Branching in C is as easy as placing a function in your program followed by a semicolon. The following C code does nothing, but it shows you how to begin writing a program that can be developed later. For example, in the following code, the `prompt();` statement (indicated by the semicolon at the end) at the beginning branches to go to the `prompt()` function:

```
main()
{
        prompt() ;    //Call function to prompt user with a question
        display();    //Call function to display graphics onscreen
        calculate();    //Call function to do complicated math
        cleanup();    //Call function to make all variables equal to
                      //zero
        prompt()
        {
        [code for prompt() function goes here]
        }
        display()
        {
        [code for display() function goes here]
        }
        [and so forth]
}
```

When the program runs, it branches to the prompt() function and then continues branching to the functions listed subsequently. By creating a program in this fashion, you can develop each function or module one at a time. You can also delegate writing other functions to people with more experience in certain areas. For example, you can have a math wizard write the calculate() function if math isn't your forte.

C has several methods for looping. The while loop is one way of having your program repeat an action a certain number of times. It checks whether a condition is true, and then continues looping until the condition becomes false. Look at the following example (with the important code bolded) and see whether you can understand what the program is doing:

```
main()
{
        int counter = 1; //Initialize (assign a value to)
                         //the counter variable
        while (counter <= 10) //Do what's inside the braces until false
        {
             printf("Counter is equal to %d\n", counter);
             ++counter; //Increment counter by 1;
        }
}
```

Figure 7-1 shows the output of this program. In this example, when the counter variable is greater than 10, the while loop stops processing, which causes printf() to display 10 lines of output before stopping.

A do loop performs an action first and then tests to see whether the action should continue to occur. In the following example, the do loop performs the print() function first, and then checks whether a condition is true:

```
main()
{
        int counter = 1; //Initialize counter variable
        do
        {
            printf("Counter is equal to %d\n", counter);
            ++counter; //Increment counter by 1
        } while (counter <= 10); //Do what's inside the braces until false
}
```

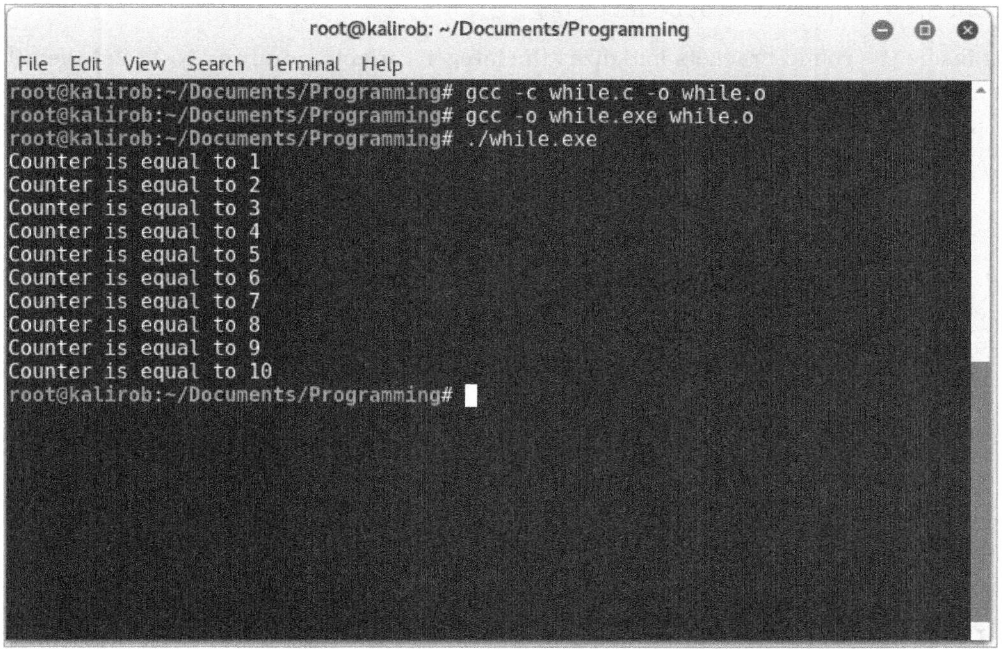

Source: Kali Linux

Figure 7-1 A `while` loop in action

NOTE

Which is better to use: the `while` loop or the `do` loop? It depends. The `while` loop might never execute if a condition isn't met. A `do` loop always executes at least once.

The last loop type in C is the `for` **loop**, one of C's most interesting pieces of code. A `for` loop starts with the keyword `for` followed by three items in starting and ending round brackets (also called parentheses). The first item inside the brackets initializes the variable that the `for` loop will use. The second item defines a test that if false, causes the `for` loop to exit. The final item defines an action to take if the test is true. After the `for` statement, you place any code you want to execute in starting and ending curly brackets (also called braces). The code inside the curly brackets will be executed for each iteration of the `for` loop. The code shown in Figure 7-2 has the following `for` loop:

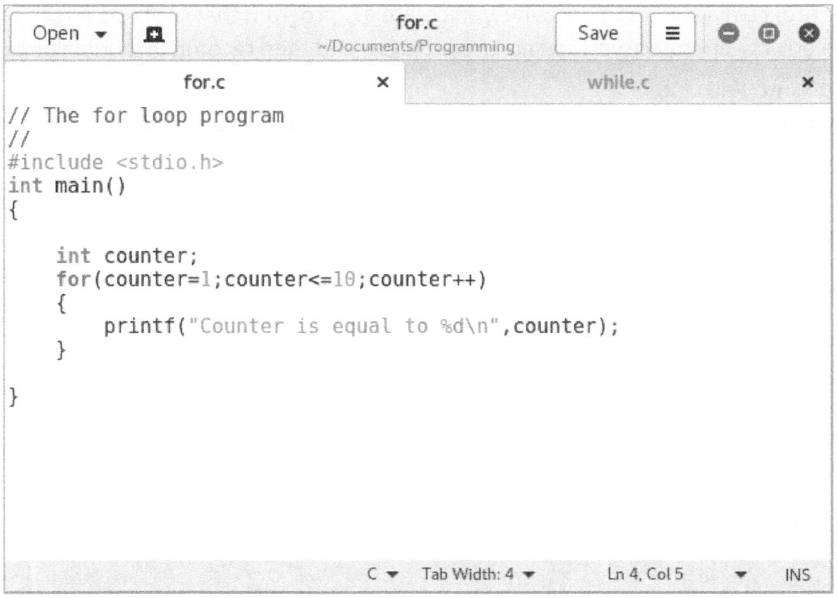

Source: Kali Linux

Figure 7-2 A for loop

```
for (counter=1;counter<=10;counter++);
```

The first part inside the round brackets initializes the integer variable `counter` to 1, and then the second part tests a condition. That condition directs the `for` loop to continue looping as long as the variable `counter` has a value equal to or less than 10. The last part of the `for` loop increments the variable `counter` by 1. Figure 7-2 shows an example of a `for` loop.

NOTE

The line of code `int main()` near the top of the program starts with `int` so that the function `main` defines a return type. If you leave out the `int`, the program will successfully compile, but the compiler will give you a warning message that it is assuming `int` for you since you did not explicitly declare it.

You might see some C programs with a `for` loop containing nothing but semicolons, as in the following example:

```
for (;;)
{
    printf("Wow!");
}
```

This code is a powerful, yet dangerous, implementation of the `for` loop. The `for (;;)` statement tells the compiler to keep doing what's in the brackets over and over and over. You can create an endless loop with this statement if you don't have a way to exit the block of code that's running. Usually, a programmer has a statement inside the block that performs a test on a variable, and then exits the block when a certain condition is met.

Activity 7-2: Learning to Use the GNU GCC Compiler

Time Required: 30 minutes

Objective: Learn how to use the GNU GCC compiler included with most *nix operating systems.

Description: In the past, programmers had to read through their code line by line before submitting the job to the mainframe CPU. The job included all the commands the CPU would execute. If a program was full of errors, the mainframe operator notified the programmer, who had to go through the code again and fix the errors. With today's compilers, you can write a program, compile it, and test it yourself. If the compiler finds errors, it usually indicates what they are so that you can correct the code and compile the program again. In this activity, you create a C program that contains errors and try to compile the program. After seeing the errors generated, you correct the program and then recompile it until you get it right.

1. Boot your computer into Kali Linux.
2. Open a terminal window and at the shell prompt, type **vim syntax.c** and press **Enter** to use the vim editor.
3. Type **i** to enter insert mode.
4. Type the following code, pressing **Enter** after each line:

```
#include <stdio.h>
int main()
{
  int age
  printf("Enter your age: ");
  scanf("%d", &age);
  if (age > 0)
  {
      printf("You are %d years old\n", age);
  }
}
```

5. Exit and save the file by pressing **Esc** and then pressing **:** (a colon). At the : prompt, type **wq** and press **Enter**.
6. To compile the program, type **gcc -o syntax syntax.c** and press **Enter**. This gcc command has its parameters ordered differently from what has been shown in previous examples. This way of executing gcc also works. The -o switch tells the compiler to create an output file called syntax. The compiler returns an error (or several errors) similar to the one in Figure 7-3. The error varies depending on the compiler version you use. In any event, you should be warned about a syntax error before printf(). The error will indicate the compiler was expecting something before printf() such as an equal sign, comma, or semicolon. In this case, the error occurred because no semicolon follows the int age statement.

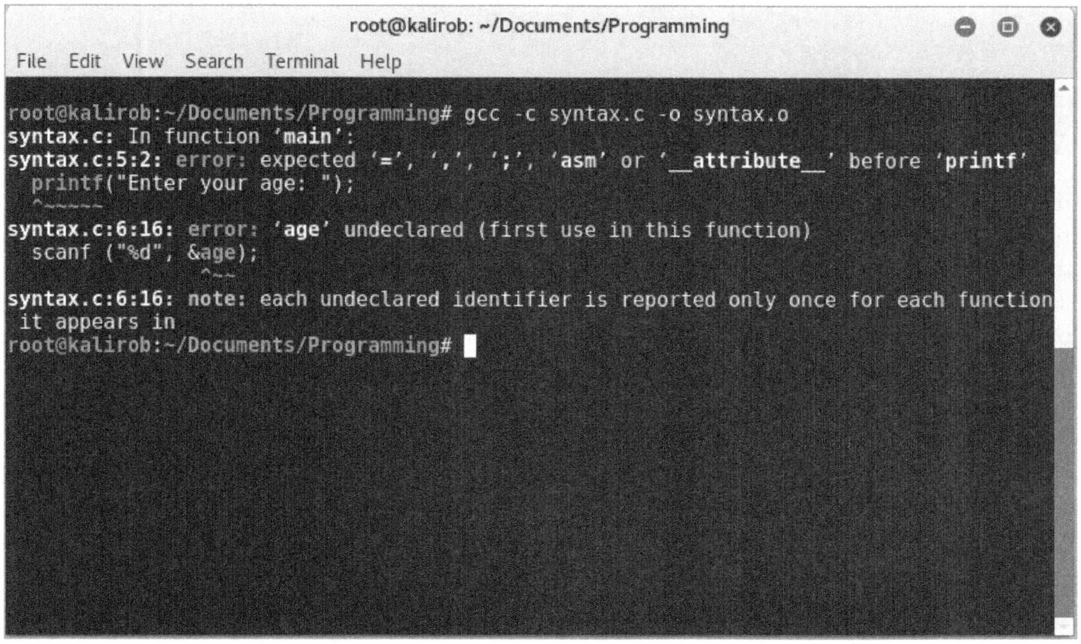

Figure 7-3   Example of a syntax error message

NOTE

If the source code you created contains no errors, a shell prompt is displayed.

NOTE

Sometimes you can correct an error easily by looking at the line number of the first error detected

7. To correct the missing semicolon error, you can use the vim editor again. Type **vim syntax.c** and press **Enter**. Type **a** to enter Append mode. Add a semicolon to the end of the line containing the variable declaration int age.
8. Save and exit the program.
9. Compile the program again by typing **gcc -o syntax syntax.c** and pressing **Enter**. (You can also use the Up Arrow key to return to previous commands.)
10. If you entered everything correctly, the shell prompt should be displayed. To run the program, type **./syntax** and press **Enter**.
11. Log off the Kali Linux session for the next activity.

NOTE

You should know how to use the vi editor (vim). Even though you might find vim primitive and awkward, it may be the only editor available in some circumstances. The gedit editor is more user friendly and uses color to highlight commands, variables, and other constructs. When coding, feel free to use gedit instead of vim, but do practice using vim as often as you can.

SECURITY BYTES

There are two schools of thought on how to handle syntax errors. Many programmers believe the compiler should check for errors in their code, so they spend little time reading and stepping through their programs looking for syntax or logic errors. They just compile a program and see what errors pop up. Others refuse to compile the program until they have examined the code thoroughly and are confident it's accurate and syntactically correct. For beginning programmers, examining the code carefully before compiling helps make you a better programmer. You'll increase your skills and develop the keen eye needed to spot a missing brace or semicolon.

UNDERSTANDING HTML BASICS

HTML is a markup language used mainly for indicating the formatting and layout of webpages, so HTML files don't contain the kind of programming code you see in a C program. As a security professional, you should understand basic HTML syntax because it's still the basis of web development. No matter what language is used to create a webpage, the webpage itself contains HTML statements, so knowing HTML is the foundation for learning other web languages.

Security professionals often need to examine webpages and recognize when something looks suspicious. You should understand the limitations of HTML, be able to read an HTML file, and have a basic understanding of what's happening. This section isn't going to make you a web developer, but it does introduce some HTML basics so that you have a foundation for exploring and learning other programming and scripting languages. The current version of HTML is HTML5. It offers significant improvements over earlier versions of HTML. For example, HTML5 natively supports rich media elements such as video and audio. Third-party media players (such as the now defunct Flash Player) were often problematic and proved to be security risks, but are no longer needed. HTML5's ability to natively support rich media has removed these concerns.

NOTE

Today, many websites use Extensible Markup Language (XML). Although this language isn't covered in this book, it's a good one to study if you want to specialize in web security. Learning additional web-development languages, such as Extensible HTML (XHTML; see www.w3c.org for more information), Perl, JavaScript, PHP, and Python can also enhance your skills as a security professional.

Creating a Webpage with HTML

You can create an HTML webpage in Notepad and then view it in a web browser. Because HTML is a markup language, not a programming language, it doesn't use branching, looping, or testing. The following is a simple example of HTML code:

```
<!-- This is how you add a comment to an HTML webpage -->
<html>
<head>
<title>Hello, world--again</title>
</head>
<body>
This is where you put page text, such as marketing copy for an e-commerce business.
</body>
</html>
```

The < and > symbols denote HTML tags, which act on the data they enclose. Notice that each tag has a matching closing tag that includes a forward slash (/). For example, the <html> tag has the closing tag </html>, and the `<head>`, `<title>`, and `<body>` tags have similar closing tags. Most HTML webpages contain these four tags. Table 7-7 describes some common formatting tags used in an HTML webpage.

Table 7-7   HTML formatting tags

Opening tag	Closing tag	Description
`<h1>`, `<h2>`, `<h3>`, `<h4>`, `<h5>`, and `<h6>`	`<h1>`, `<h2>`, `<h3>`, `</h4>`, `</h5>`, and `</h6>`	Formats text as different heading levels. Level 1 is the largest font size, and level 6 is the smallest.
`<p>`	`</p>`	Marks the beginning and end of a paragraph.
`<b>`	`</b>`	Formats enclosed text in bold.
`<i>`	`</i>`	Formats enclosed text in italics.

Other tags format tables, lists, and other elements, but Table 7-7 gives you a general overview of HTML tags. You can find many references online to learn more about creating HTML webpages. In Activity 7-3, you practice creating a webpage using Notepad as the editor.

Activity 7-3: Creating an HTML Webpage

Time Required: 30 minutes

Objective: Create an HTML webpage.

Description: As a security tester, you might be required to view webpages to check for possible web security issues. A basic knowledge of HTML can help you with this task. In this activity, you create a simple HTML webpage and then view it in your browser.

1. Start your computer in Windows. In Windows 10, right-click the **Start** button, click **Run**, type **notepad MyWeb.html**, and then press **Enter**. If you're prompted to create a new file, click **Yes**.

2. In the new Notepad document, type the following lines, pressing **Enter** after each line:

   <!-- This HTML webpage has many tags -->
   <html>
   <head>
   <title>HTML for Security Testers</title>
   </head>

3. Type the next two lines, pressing **Enter** *twice* after each line:

   `<body>`

   Security Tester Website

4. Type **<p>There are many good websites to visit for security testers. For vulnerabilities, click** and press **Enter**.

5. Type **<a href="https://cve.mitre.org/"><font color="red">here!</font> </a>** and press **Enter**.

6. Type **</p>** and press **Enter**.

7. Type **</body>** and press **Enter**. On the last line, type **</html>** to end your code.

8. Verify that you have typed everything correctly. Your file should look similar to Figure 7-4. When you're done, save the file.

9. To test whether you have created the webpage correctly, start File Explorer and navigate to the default location—typically, C:\Users*YourUserName*\Documents). Right-click the **MyWeb.html** file you created, point to **Open with**, and then click **Microsoft Edge**. If you entered the information correctly, your webpage should look like the one shown in Figure 7-5.

10. Click the **here!** hyperlink you created to check whether you're sent to the correct website. If not, make corrections to your HTML code.

11. When you're finished, exit your browser, but leave Windows running for the next activity.

Figure 7-4   HTML source code

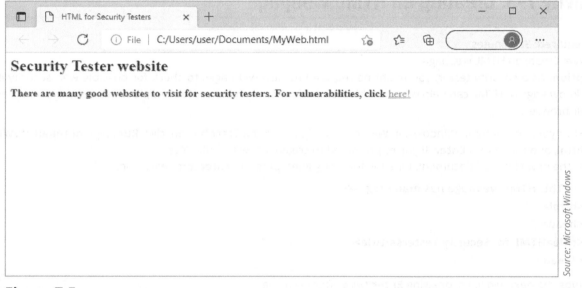

Figure 7-5   HTML webpage

UNDERSTANDING PERL

Many scripts and programs for security professionals are written in Practical Extraction and Report Language (Perl), a powerful scripting language. Perl and Python are two popular languages for security professionals; this module covers some basics of Perl. In this section, you see why this language is so popular, examine the syntax of the language, and practice writing Perl scripts. You also create a utility for examining the configuration of a Windows computer.

Background on Perl

Perl, developed by Larry Wall in 1987, can run on almost any platform, and *nix-based OSs invariably have Perl installed already. The Perl syntax is similar to C, so C programmers have few difficulties learning Perl. More than 20 versions of Perl have been released since its creation. Each new version is created and released to fix bugs, add new features, and address security concerns. Some updates involve large-scale revisions of the entire Perl system. Perl 5.34 is the current stable version, which was released in May 2021. For more details, visit https://en.wikipedia.org/wiki/Perl.

Hackers use Perl to create automated exploits and malicious bots, but system administrators and security professionals use it to perform repetitive tasks and conduct security monitoring. Before examining the Perl syntax, you write your first Perl script in Activity 7-4. As with any programming language, the best way to learn Perl is by using it.

Activity 7-4: Writing a Perl Script Using GVim

Time Required: 60 minutes
Objective: Write a Perl script using GVim.
Description: Security professionals and hackers alike use the Perl scripting language. Many hacking programs are written in Perl, so any skills you develop in this language will help you in your career. In previous activities, you used vim as a text editor. In this activity, you write a basic Perl script using the graphical version of vim, called GVim. Unlike vim, GVim lets you click to navigate instead of relying on keyboard commands.

1. Boot your computer into Kali Linux.
2. Open a terminal window, and then change the directory to the desktop using the **cd ~/Desktop** command.
3. Type **gvim first.pl** and press **Enter**.
4. Select the **Syntax** tab at the top of the GVim window and select **Automatic**. This enables syntax highlighting for your Perl project.
5. On the first line, type **# This is my first Perl script program** and press **Enter**.
6. Type **# I should always have documentation/comments in my scripts!** and press **Enter** twice.
7. Type **#This code displays "Hello security testers" to the screen** and press **Enter** twice to add another comment describing what the following code does.
8. Type **print "Hello security testers!\n\n";** and press **Enter**.
   Your script should look similar to Figure 7-6. Be careful not to miss a semicolon or quotation mark. Remember that programming requires a keen eye.

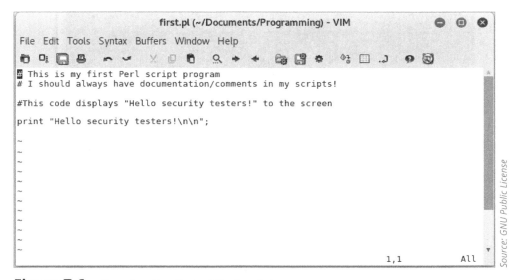

Figure 7-6   Creating the first.pl Perl script

9. Save the file.
10. At the command prompt, type **perl first.pl** and press **Enter**.
    If your code does not contain errors, your screen should look like Figure 7-7. If you receive error messages, read through your file and compare it with the lines of code in this activity's steps. Correct any errors and save the file again.
11. Close the command prompt window, and leave Windows running for the next activity.

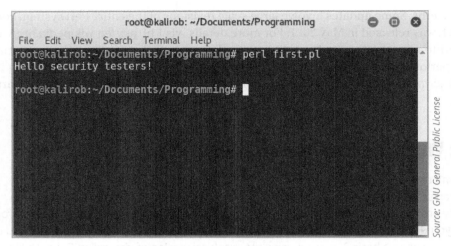

Figure 7-7   Running the first.pl Perl script

Understanding the Basics of Perl

Knowing how to get help quickly in any programming language is useful. The `perl -h` command gives you a list of parameters used with the `perl` command (see Figure 7-8).

```
root@kalirob:~/Documents/Programming# perl -h

Usage: perl [switches] [--] [programfile] [arguments]
  -0[octal]         specify record separator (\0, if no argument)
  -a                autosplit mode with -n or -p (splits $_ into @F)
  -C[number/list]   enables the listed Unicode features
  -c                check syntax only (runs BEGIN and CHECK blocks)
  -d[:debugger]     run program under debugger
  -D[number/list]   set debugging flags (argument is a bit mask or alphabets)
  -e program        one line of program (several -e's allowed, omit programfile)
  -E program        like -e, but enables all optional features
  -f                don't do $sitelib/sitecustomize.pl at startup
  -F/pattern/       split() pattern for -a switch (//'s are optional)
  -i[extension]     edit <> files in place (makes backup if extension supplied)
  -Idirectory       specify @INC/#include directory (several -I's allowed)
  -l[octal]         enable line ending processing, specifies line terminator
  -[mM][-]module    execute "use/no module..." before executing program
  -n                assume "while (<>) {... }" loop around program
  -p                assume loop like -n but print line also, like sed
  -s                enable rudimentary parsing for switches after programfile
  -S                look for programfile using PATH environment variable
  -t                enable tainting warnings
  -T                enable tainting checks
  -u                dump core after parsing program
  -U                allow unsafe operations
  -v                print version, patchlevel and license
  -V[:variable]     print configuration summary (or a single Config.pm variable)
  -w                enable many useful warnings
  -W                enable all warnings
  -x[directory]     ignore text before #!perl line (optionally cd to directory)
  -X                disable all warnings

Run 'perldoc perl' for more help with Perl.

root@kalirob:~/Documents/Programming#
```

Figure 7-8   Using the perl –h command

The website https://perldoc.perl.org/ is an excellent repository of Perl information. You can choose the version of Perl you are interested in and then look up information specific to that version, such as detailed command descriptions. The website also has tutorials and frequently asked questions (FAQs) you can access to learn more. See Figure 7-9.

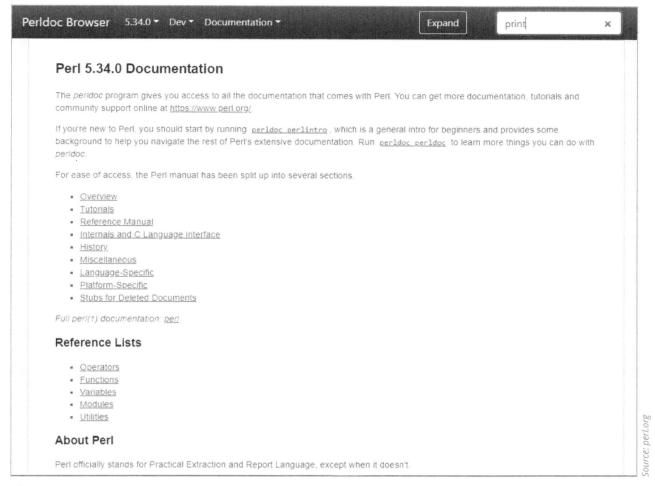

Figure 7-9   Online Perl reference website

Perl has a `printf` command for formatting complex variables. Table 7-8 shows how to use this command to format specific data. Note the similarities to C.

Table 7-8   Using `printf` to format output

Formatting character	Description	Input	Output
%c	Character	`printf '%c' , "d"`	d
%s	String	`printf '%s', "This is fun!"`	This is fun!
%d	Signed integer in decimal	`printf '%+d%d', 1, 1`	+1 1
%u	Unsigned integer in decimal	`printf '%u', 2`	2
%o	Unsigned integer in octal	`printf '%o' , 8`	10
%x	Unsigned integer in hexadecimal	`printf '%x', 10`	a
%e	Floating-point number in scientific notation	`printf '%e' , 10;`	1.000000e+001 (depending on the OS)
%f	Floating-point number in fixed decimal notation	`printf '%f' , 1;`	1.000000

Understanding the BLT of Perl

As you learned previously, all programming languages must have a way to branch, loop, and test. The following sections use code examples to show you how Perl handles these BLT functions. As you examine these examples, keep the following syntax rules in mind:

- The sub keyword is used before function names.
- Variables begin with the $ symbol.
- Comment lines begin with the # symbol.
- The & symbol indicates a function.

Except for these minor differences, Perl's syntax is much like the C syntax. This similarity is one of the reasons many security professionals with C programming experience choose Perl as a scripting language.

Branching in Perl

In a Perl program, to go from one function to another, you call the function by entering its name in your source code. In the following example, the &name_best_guitarist line branches the program to the sub name_best_guitarist function:

```
# Perl program illustrating the branching function
# Documentation is important
# Initialize variables
$first_name = "Jimi";
$last_name = "Hendrix";
&name_best_guitarist;
sub name_best_guitarist
{
    printf "%s %s %s", $first_name, $last_name, "was the best!";
}
```

Looping in Perl

Suppose you want to send an important message to everyone in your class by using the Net send command. Because you're sending the same message to multiple users, it's a repetitive task that requires looping. In Activity 7-5, you write a Perl script to do just that: Send a message to everyone in the class. As you learned in C, you have several choices for performing a loop. In this section, you learn about two of Perl's looping mechanisms: the for loop and the while loop.

The Perl for loop is identical to the C for loop:

```
for (variable assignment; test condition; increment variable)
{
    a task to do over and over
}
```

Substituting the variable $a, you have the following code:

```
for ($a = 1; $a <= 10; $a++)
{
    print "Hello, security testers!\n"
}
```

This loop prints the phrase 10 times. Next, try producing the same output using the while loop, which has the following syntax:

```
while (test condition)
{
    a task to do over and over
}
```

The following code produces the same output as the `for` loop:

```
$a = 1;
while ($a <= 10)
{
      print "Hello, security testers!\n";
      $a++
}
```

SECURITY BYTES

Chris Nandor, known for developing the Mac Classic version of Perl 5.8.0, became one of the first hackers to use a Perl script in an online election. Apparently, his Perl script added more than 40,000 votes for several Red Sox players during an online election in 1999 for the All-Stars game. Similarly, in 1993, an online election involving the Denver Broncos traced more than 70,000 votes coming from one IP address. The power of the loop!

Testing Conditions in Perl

Most programs must be able to test the value of a variable or condition. The two looping examples shown previously use the less than or equal to operator (<=). Other operators used for testing in Perl are similar to C operators. Table 7-9 lists the operators you can use in Perl.

Table 7-9   Perl operators

Operator	Function	Example
+	Addition	`$total = $sal + $commission`
–	Subtraction	`$profit = $gross sales – $cost of goods`
*	Multiplication	`$total = $cost * $quantity`
/	Division	`$GPA = $total_points / $number of classes`
%	Modulus	`$a % 10 = 1`
**	Exponent	`$total = $a**10`
Assignments		
=	Assignment	`$Last name = "Rivera"`
+=	Add, then assignment	`$a+ = 10;` shorthand for `$a=$a+10`
-=	Subtract, then assignment	`$a-=10;` shorthand for `$a=$a-10`
*=	Multiply, then assignment	`$a* = 10;` shorthand for `$a=$a*10`
/=	Divide, then assignment	`$a/ = 10;` shorthand for `$a=$a/10`
%=	Modulus, then assignment	`$a%=10;` shorthand for `$a=$a%10`
**=	Exponent and assignment	`$a**=2;` shorthand for `$a=$a**2`
++	Increment	`$a++;` increment `$a` by 1
—	Decrement	`$a--;` decrement `$a` by 1
Comparisons		
==	Equal to	`$a==1;` compare value of `$a` with 1
!=	Not equal to	`$a!=1;` `$a` is not equal to 1
>	Greater than	`$a>10`
<	Less than	`$a<10`
>=	Greater than or equal to	`$a>=10`
<=	Less than or equal to	`$a<=10`

Often you combine these operators with Perl conditionals, such as the following:

- if—Checks whether a condition is true. Example:

```
if ($age < 12) {
   print "You must be a know-it-all! ";
}
```

- else—Used when there's only one option to carry out if the condition is not true. Example:

```
if ($age) > 12 {
   print "You must be a know-it-all! ";
        }
else
{
   print "Sorry, but I don't know why the sky is blue.";
}
```

- elsif—Used when there are several conditionals to test. Example:

```
if ( ($age > 12) && ($age < 20) )
   {
        print "You must be a know-it-all!";
   }
elsif ($age > 39)
   {
        print "You must lie about your age!";
   }
   else
   {
        print "To be young...";
   }
```

- unless—Executes unless the condition is true. Example:

```
unless ($age == 100)
{
   print "Still enough time to get a bachelor's degree.";
}
```

The message is displayed until the $age variable is equal to 100. With some practice and lots of patience, these examples can give you a start at creating functional Perl scripts.

Activity 7-5: Writing a Perl Script for Security Testing

Time Required: 30 minutes

Objective: Write a Perl script that uses branching, looping, and testing components.

Description: Security professionals often need to automate or create tools to help them conduct security tests. In this activity, you write a Perl script that uses the notify-send command and a for loop to select IP numbers from the classroom range your instructor has provided. You can use the following reference for the Perl ping command: http://perldoc.perl.org/Net/Ping.html.

1. Write down the IP address range used in the class network.
2. Open a terminal window, type **apt-get install libnotify-bin**, and then press **Enter** to install the notification service you will use in this activity.

3. Change the directory to the desktop with **cd ~/Desktop**. To use the gedit editor to create your script, type **gedit ping.pl** and press **Enter**.
4. Type **# Program to ping workstations on your network** and press **Enter**.
5. Type **# If the ping is successful, a message is sent to the screen** and press **Enter**.
6. Type **# Program assumes a Class C address (w.x.y.z) where w.x.y is the network portion of the address** and press **Enter**.
7. Type **# Change the value of $class_IP below to reflect the network portion of your network** and press **Enter**.
8. Type **# The "z" octet will be incremented from 1 - 254 using a for loop** and press **Enter** twice.
9. Type **use diagnostics;** and press **Enter** twice.
10. Type **use Net::Ping; # Loads the net library** and press **Enter** twice.
11. Type **$p = Net::Ping->new(); # Creates a new ping object with default settings** and press **Enter** twice.
12. The next line initializes the variable you're using to hold your network ID. Type **$class_IP = "192.168.2"; # Network ID** (change the value in the quotation marks to reflect your topology) and press **Enter** twice.
    The next lines of code are the for loop, which increments the last octet of the network IP address to all available IP addresses in your class. The code inside the for loop should be indented for readability.
13. Type **for ($z=1; $z<255; $z++) {** and press **Enter**.
14. Press the **Tab** key to indent, type **$wkstation = "$class_IP.$z"; # Creates full IP address of host to be scanned**, and then press **Enter**.
15. Press the **Tab** key to indent, type **print "Looking for live systems to enumerate. Trying $wkstation \n"; # Displays target info**, and then press **Enter**.
16. Press the **Tab** key to indent, type **system("notify-send '$wkstation is ready to enumerate.'") if $p->ping($wkstation); # Sends message if ping is successful**, and then press **Enter**.
17. Type **}** and press **Enter** to end your program, which should look similar to Figure 7-10.

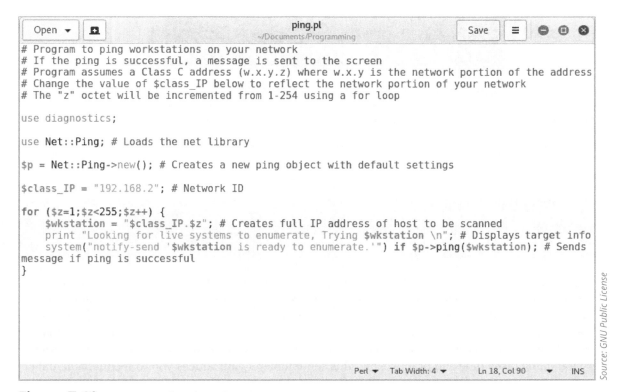

Figure 7-10   Creating the ping.pl Perl script

18. To improve this program's documentation, add comment lines to your code stating the author and date written and explaining any complex algorithms.
19. Go through each line of code and make sure the syntax is correct. Note that the $class_IP variable holds the network portion of your class's IP address range. After verifying the syntax and contents of the Perl script, save it and return to the terminal window.

20. Run your script by typing **perl ping.pl** and pressing **Enter**. If you have no errors, your program should begin pinging IP addresses, as shown in Figure 7-11. If a live address is found, you'll see a notification at the bottom of the screen.

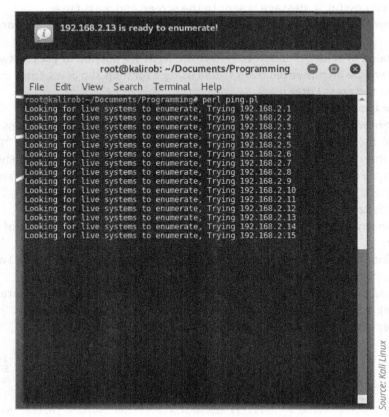

Figure 7-11   Running ping.pl on a live network

21. To terminate the Perl script, press **Ctrl+C**. Leave the command prompt window open for the next activity.

UNDERSTANDING OBJECT-ORIENTED PROGRAMMING CONCEPTS

Just when you think you're comfortable with a technology concept, something new comes along. Although the concept of object-oriented programming (OOP) isn't new to experienced programmers, it might not be familiar to those just learning how to write their first Perl script, for example. Perl 5.0 uses object-oriented programming concepts, and Perl 6.0 will be based solely on this model, so this section covers some basic object-oriented concepts as a foundation for writing another Perl script. This section is by no means a complete discussion of a complex concept. Learning object-oriented programming takes time and practice, and this section merely introduces you to the fundamental concepts.

Components of Object-Oriented Programming

The version of Perl you installed has additional functions that can make program calls to the Windows application programming interface (Win API). Programmers should know what functions are available in different OSs so that they can write programs that interact with these functions. For example, a C programmer knows that the Win API has the NodeName() function, which returns the NetBIOS computer name. To use this function, the programmer references it with `Win32::NodeName()`. The `::` separates the name of the **class**, `Win32`, from the member function, `NodeName()`. In object-oriented programming, classes are structures that hold pieces of data and functions. The following code example shows the `Employee` class in C++. Classes can be written in many object-oriented languages (e.g., Java, Object COBOL, and Perl). What's important is recognizing what a class looks like:

```
// This is a class called Employee created in C++
class Employee
{
    public:
            char firstname[25];
            char lastname[25];
            char PlaceOfBirth[30];
            [code continues]
};
void GetEmp()
{
    // Perform tasks to get employee info
    [program code goes here]
}
```

The structure created in this code can contain employee information as well as a function that performs a lookup. A function contained in a class is called a member function. As mentioned, to access a member function, you use the class name followed by two colons and the member function's name:

```
Employee::GetEmp()
```

The `Win32` class contains many functions you can call from your Perl script. Table 7-10 describes some commonly used Win32 API functions.

Table 7-10   Win32 API functions

Function	Description
`GetLastError()`	Returns the last error generated when a call was made to the Win32 API.
`OLELastError()`	Returns the last error generated by the object linking and embedding (OLE) API.
`BuildNumber()`	Returns the Perl build number.
`LoginName()`	Returns the username of the person running Perl.
`NodeName()`	Returns the NetBIOS computer name.
`DomainName()`	Returns the name of the domain the computer is a member of.
`FsType()`	Returns the name of the file system, such as NTFS or FAT.
`GetCwd()`	Returns the current active drive.
`SetCwd(newdir)`	Enables you to change to the drive designated by the `newdir` variable.
`GetOSName()`	Returns the OS name.
`FormatMessage(error)`	Converts the error message number into a descriptive string.
`Spawn(command, args, $pid)`	Starts a new process, using arguments supplied by the programmer and the process ID (`$pid`).
`LookupAccountSID(sys, sid, $acct, $domain, $type)`	Returns the account name, domain name, and security ID (SID) type.
`InitiateSystemShutdown(machine, message, timeout, forceclose, reboot)`	Shuts down a specified computer or server.

(continues)

Table 7-10   Win32 API functions *(continued)*

Function	Description
AbortSystemShutdown(machine)	Aborts the shutdown if it was done in error.
GetTickCount()	Returns the Win32 tick count (time elapsed since the system first started).
ExpandEnvironmentalStrings (envstring)	Returns the environmental variable strings specified in the envstring variable.
GetShortPathName(longpathname)	Returns the 8.3 version of the long pathname. In DOS and older Windows programs, filenames could be only eight characters, with a three-character extension.
GetNextAvailableDrive()	Returns the next available drive letter.
RegisterServer(libraryname)	Loads the DLL specified by libraryname and calls the DLLRegisterServer() function.
UnregisterServer(libraryname)	Loads the DLL specified by libraryname and calls the DLLUnregisterServer() function.
Sleep(time)	Pauses the number of milliseconds specified by the time variable.

Attackers and security professionals can use these functions to discover information about a remote computer. Although these functions aren't difficult to understand, becoming proficient at using them in a program takes time and discipline. For security professionals who need to know what attackers can do, gaining this skill is worth the time and effort.

In Activity 7-6, you create a Perl script that uses some of the Win32 API functions listed in Table 7-10. This script gives you the following information about the Windows computer you have been using for this module's activities:

- Logon name of the user
- Computer name
- File system
- Current directory
- OS name

Activity 7-6: Creating a Perl Script to Access the Win32 API

Time Required: 30 minutes

Objective: Install Perl on Windows and learn how to access the Win32 API from a Perl script.

Description: In this activity, you'll install ActivePerl on a Windows computer and write a basic Perl script, using the formatting functions you have already learned and the Win32 API functions in Table 7-10. Windows doesn't support Perl by default, so you have to download and install a Perl engine. If possible, work in groups of three to four students. Start your web browser and go to www.activestate.com/products/perl/.

1. The ActivePerl page displays a free version and a commercial version. Click the **DOWNLOAD** button for the **Download for free** version as shown in Figure 7-12. Clicking the DOWNLOAD button displays the download page. Scroll down and then click the **ActivePerl 5.28 for Windows** link to download Perl (see Figure 7-13). As newer versions of ActivePerl are available, the version number increases, so it may not be 5.28 when you download it.

2. After the file has been downloaded, locate and run the installation file. If necessary, respond to any security prompts.

3. In the welcome window of the ActivePerl Setup Wizard, click **Next**.

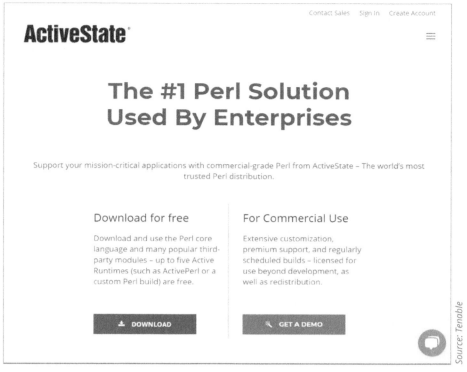

Figure 7-12   Downloading ActivePerl

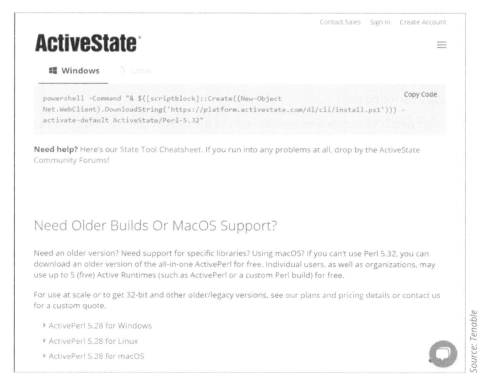

Figure 7-13   The download page for ActivePerl

4. Read the license agreement, verify that the **I accept the terms in the License Agreement** option button is selected, and then click **Next**.

5. If you need to change from the default location, enter the path to the new location. Click **Next**.

6. In the Ready to Install window, click **Install**. Click **Yes** to respond to the UAC prompt, if necessary. After several minutes, the program is installed.

7. In the last window, click **Finish**. Read the release notes, which are displayed in your web browser automatically.

   Next, you install a program called Notepad++ to use as an editor for your programming. Recall that Notepad++ is an improvement on the Windows Notepad program. Notepad++ is aware of programming constructs and displays your code with formatting that assists you while you are coding.

8. Go to **https://notepad-plus-plus.org/** and download and install the latest version. Download the 64-bit (x64) version of the installer.

9. To begin writing your Perl script, start the Notepad++ application. Save the file as **Win32.pl** in the C:\Perl64 directory.

10. In the new Notepad++ file, type **# Win32.pl** on the first line and press **Enter**.

11. Use what you've learned in this module to write comments for documenting the program. Be sure to enter the author's name, date, and a brief description of what the program does, such as the functions it accesses from the Win32 API.

12. After your lines of documentation, press **Enter** several times to create blank lines for separating your comments from the program code. Then type **use win32;** and press **Enter**. (*Note:* Don't forget the semicolon.)

13. You need five pieces of information (noted in the bulleted list before this activity) from the Win32 API. Attempt to write the code for getting this information, and then save the program. If you need assistance, use the following steps.

14. Type **$login = Win32::LoginName();** and press **Enter**. This line populates the `$login` variable with the information gathered from `LoginName()`.

15. Type the following lines to populate the other variables needed to complete the task, pressing **Enter** after each line:

```
$NetBIOS = Win32::NodeName();
$Filesystem = Win32::FsType();
$Directory = Win32::GetCwd();
$os_name = Win32::GetOSName();
```

16. The following variables need to be displayed onscreen. Type the lines of code as shown, pressing **Enter** after each line. When you're finished, your window should look similar to Figure 7-14.

```
print "$login\n";
print "$NetBIOS\n";
print "$Filesystem\n";
print "$Directory\n";
print "$os_name\n";
```

17. After typing all the code, save the program, run it, and debug any errors. Figure 7-15 shows the output. What's wrong with this report?

18. Spend time improving the report's formatting so that anyone reading the output could understand its meaning.

19. Meet with your group to discuss improvements that should be made to the script. Explain these improvements. What other information might be beneficial for a security professional to get from this report?

20. Select a spokesperson from your group to give a three- to five-minute presentation on the final script, and state why your program is the most marketable. After all the presentations, have the class choose a winner.

21. Close all open windows.

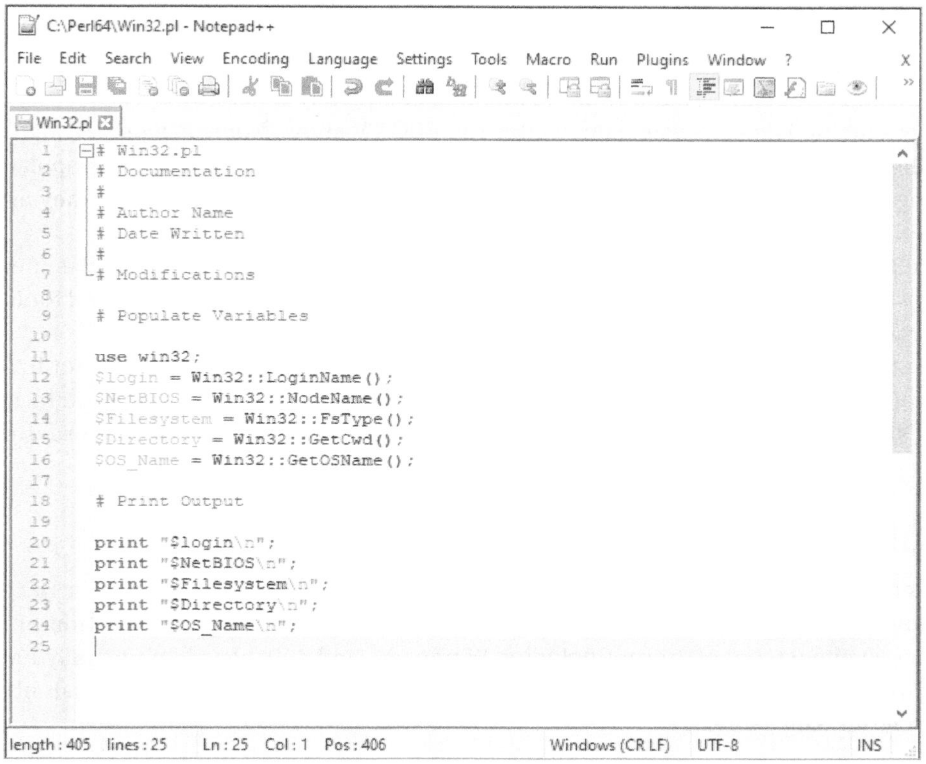

Source: Microsoft Windows

Figure 7-14 Using the Win32 API from a Perl script

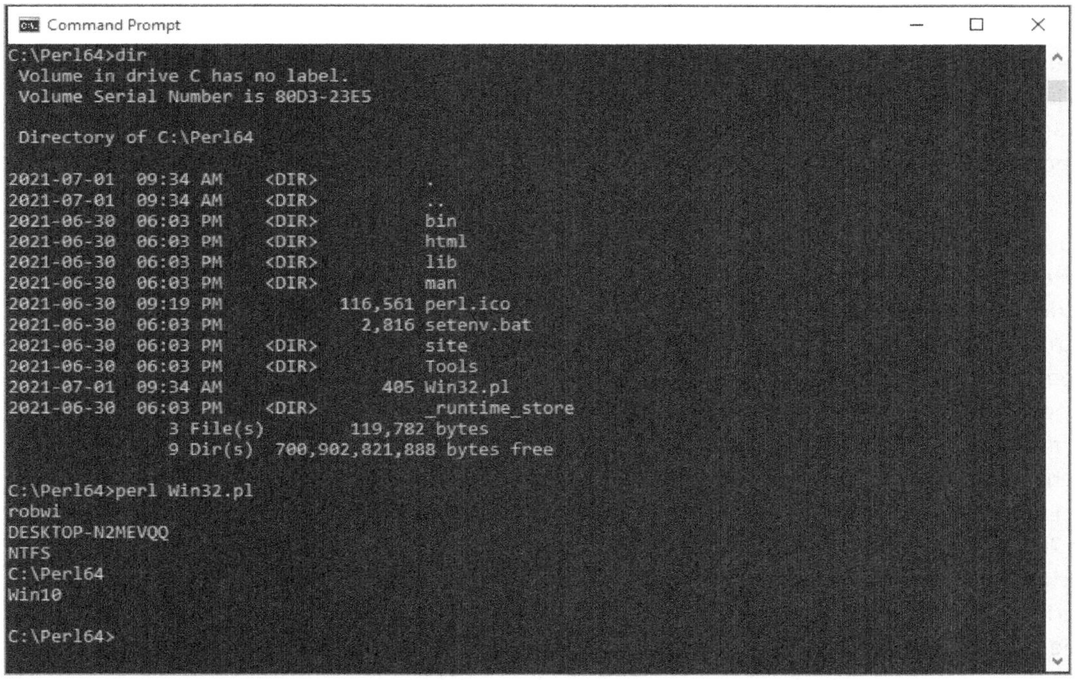

Source: Tenable

Figure 7-15 Running the Win32.pl Perl script

UNDERSTANDING PYTHON

As another famous Python once said, "And now for something completely different."

The Python programming language was named after the BBC TV show, *Monty Python's Flying Circus*. Python, like Perl, is a scripting language with some object-oriented features. As a scripting language, it is popular for creating small to medium-sized programs quickly. Scripting languages don't need to be compiled because they are interpreted, and this arguably makes them faster when creating, testing, and executing short programs.

Ethical hackers often create programs to help automate their activities, and Python is well-suited for this purpose. In fact, Python is growing in popularity in the ethical hacking community. Hacking libraries and tools written in Python are becoming widely available.

Python emphasizes code readability and uses indentation to define blocks of code (not brackets and braces like Perl or C). Using incorrect spacing can produce a syntax error in Python, so be sure to indent statements correctly and consistently. In this section, you will examine the syntax of Python and practice writing Python scripts.

Python Background

Guido van Rossum conceived of Python in the late 1980s and began its implementation in December 1989. He is Python's principal author and a continuing central figure in decisions regarding the direction of Python's development. Python can run on almost any platform (including Windows), and *nix-based OSs usually have Python already installed. Python 3.9 (released in October 2020) is a recent stable release. For more details, visit https://en.wikipedia.org/wiki/Python_(programming_language).

Activity 7-7: Writing a Python Script Using GVim

Time Required: 60 minutes

Objective: Write a Python script using GVim.

Description: Security professionals and hackers alike are increasingly using Python. More hacking programs are being written in Python, so any skills you develop in this language will help you in your career. In this activity, you write a basic Python script.

1. Boot your computer into Kali Linux, open a terminal window, and then change the directory to the desktop using the **cd ~/Desktop** command.
2. Type **gvim first.py** and press **Enter**.
3. Select the **Syntax** tab at the top of the GVim window and then select **Automatic** to enable syntax highlighting for your Python project.
4. Press the **i** key to switch to insert mode.
5. On the first line, type **# This is my first Python script program** and press **Enter** to add one of three initial comments.
6. Type **# I should always have comments in my scripts!** and press **Enter** twice.
7. Type **# This code displays 'Hello security testers!' to the screen** and press **Enter**.
8. Type **print('Hello security testers!')** and press **Enter** to have the program display the specified text. Your script should look similar to Figure 7-16.
9. Save the file.
10. In the terminal window, type **python first.py** and press **Enter** to run the program. If you didn't make any errors, your screen should look like Figure 7-17. If you received error messages, read through your file and compare it with the lines of code in this activity's steps. If you correct any errors, save the file and repeat step 10.

Figure 7-16   first.py Python script

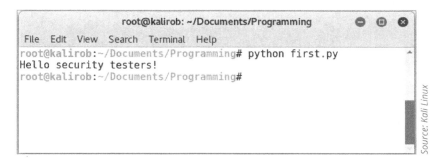

Figure 7-17   Output of the first.py script

Understanding the Basics of Python

Knowing how to get help quickly in any programming language is useful. The `python -h` command lists parameters used with the `python` command (see Figure 7-18).

The website https://python.org/ is an excellent repository of Python information. It has tutorials and frequently asked questions (FAQs) you can access to learn more.

Understanding the BLT of Python

As you learned previously, all programming languages must have a way to branch, loop, and test. The following sections use code examples to show you how Python handles these BLT functions. As you examine the examples, keep the following syntax rules in mind:

- Spacing is important. Python uses spacing to specify blocks of code. Perl uses curly brackets to define blocks of code in if statements and functions; Python does not. You can have a syntax error by not indenting your lines of code correctly.
- When creating a function, insert the `def` keyword in front of the function's name.
- Variables do not begin with any special symbol. Perl uses the $ symbol to indicate a variable, but Python does not.
- There are no special characters at the end of lines of code. Perl uses the semicolon (;) character, but Python does not.
- Comment lines begin with the # symbol.

Branching in Python

To go from one function to another in a Python program, you call the function by entering its name followed by parentheses. In Python, a function must be defined before you can call it; in Perl this didn't matter. For example, the function `name_best_guitarist()` must be inserted in the code before you can call it. In the following

Figure 7-18 Help information from python – h command

Python program, the `name_best_guitarist()` line branches the program to the `name_best_guitarist()` function:

```
# Python program illustrating the branching function
# Documentation is important

# Initialize variables
first_name = "Jimi "
last_name = "Hendrix"

# define the name_best_guitarist function
# a function must be defined before it can be called
def name_best_guitarist():
    print(first_name + last_name + " was the best!")

name_best_guitarist()
```

Many functions take parameters. For example, the function `add_these_numbers()` takes two parameters as input, the numbers to add:

```
def add_these_numbers(x,y):
    z=x+y
    print(z)
```

Functions that don't expect parameters are called with nothing in the parentheses, as when `name_best_guitarist()` was called in the previous example.

Looping in Python

Python has `for` loops and `while` loops just as Perl and C do, although the syntax is different. In this section, you learn about these two looping mechanisms.

The Python `for` loop repeats until it has gone through each item specified in a list of items. It's not an incremental counter loop like those in C and Perl. For example, if you have a list of names and want to use a `for` loop to print each name, you could write the following Python code:

```
names = ["Bob", "Jamal", "Sasha"]
for x in names:
    print(x)
```

If you want to create a `for` loop that counts from a starting number to an ending number, you could use a list of numbers or a function called `range()` to do so:

```
for x in range(6):
    print(x)
```

In the preceding example, the `range(6)` function call creates a sequence of numbers starting at 0 and ending at 5, six numbers in total. If you want to count from 1 to 6, you must modify the code to `print(x+1)` instead of `print(x)`. Keep that in mind when you use the `range()` function in your programming.

The Python `while` loop is similar to the Perl and C `while` loops. The `while` loop repeats a set of code lines as long as a test condition remains true. Remember that Python uses indentation to denote blocks of code, so you do not need brackets in a `while` loop. In the following example, the `while` loop will continue to loop (printing the value of the variable `i` and then incrementing the variable `i` by 1) as long as the variable `i` is less than 6.

```
i = 1
while i < 6:
    print(i)
    i += 1
```

Testing Conditions in Python

Python has operators for comparisons (logical tests) and mathematical calculations. The standard Python operators are identical to Perl operators. Table 7-11 lists the operators you can use in Python.

Table 7-11   Python operators

Operator	Function	Example
+	Addition	`total = sal + commission`
−	Subtraction	`profit = grossSales − costOfGoods`
*	Multiplication	`total = cost * quantity`
/	Division	`GPA = totalPoints / numberOfClasses`
%	Modulus	`x = a % 2`
**	Exponent	`area = 3.14 * (r**2)`
Assignments		
=	Assignment	`lastName = "Rivera"`
+=	Add, then assignment	`a+ = 10 #shorthand for a=a+10`
-=	Subtract, then assignment	`a-=10 #shorthand for a=a-10`
*=	Multiply, then assignment	`a* = 10 #shorthand for a=a*10`

(continues)

Table 7-11   Python operators *(continued)*

Operator	Function	Example
/=	Divide, then assignment	a/ = 10 #shorthand for a=a/10
%=	Modulus, then assignment	a%=10 #shorthand for a=a%10
**=	Exponent and assignment	a**=2 #shorthand for a=a**2
++	Increment	a++ #increment a by 1
—	Decrement	a-- #decrement a by 1
Comparisons		
==	Equal to	a== 1 #compare value of a with 1
!=	Not equal to	a!=1 #a is not equal to 1
>	Greater than	a>10
<	Less than	a<10
>=	Greater than or equal to	a>=10
<=	Less than or equal to	a<=10

If Statements and Logical Operators

The comparison operators listed in Table 7-11 are also known as logical operators. You use logical operators in if statements. An if statement combines logical operators with variables and numbers to create conditional checks. Use an if statement to have your code perform certain operations if a logical conditional check is true, and perhaps perform a different operation if it is not. You can combine an if statement with the keywords else and elseif, and nest if statements to create complex logic checks. Following are some examples of if, else, elif, nested ifs, and condition checks being used to control what code is being executed.

- if—Checks whether a condition is true. Example:

```
if (age < 12)
     print("You must be a know-it-all!")
```

- else—Used when there's only one option to carry out if the condition is not true. Example:

```
if (age > 12)
     print("You must be a know-it-all!")

else
     print("Sorry, but I don't know why the sky is blue.")
```

- elif—Used when there are several conditionals to test. Example:

```
if ( (age > 12) && (age < 20) )
     print("You must be a know-it-all!")
elif (age > 39)
     print("You must lie about your age!")
     else:
          print("To be young...")
```

- You can also include if statements inside other if statements. These are called nested ifs. Example:

```
y = 69
if y > 10:
    print("Greater than ten")
    if y > 20:
        print("Also greater than 20!")
    else:
        print("But not greater than 20")
```

Activity 7-8: Writing a Python Script for Security Testing

Time Required: 30 minutes

Objective: Write a Python script that uses branching, looping, and testing components.

Description: Security professionals often need to automate or create tools to help them conduct security tests. In this activity, you write a Python script that uses the `ping` command and a `for` loop to ping IP numbers for an entire class C network. Your instructor will provide you with the class C network address. If you are not in class, select a class C network of your choice (perhaps your home network). If a ping is successful, it indicates that a computing device has been found at that IP address. You are going to download and install the latest version of Python for Windows and perform this activity in a Windows environment. Remember that incorrect indentation can cause syntax errors in Python, so make sure your indentation matches what is shown in Figure 7-19.

1. Open a web browser and go to **www.python.org/downloads/**. Download and install the latest version of Python for Windows. Make sure to check the box to add Python to PATH.
2. Write down the IP address to be used for the class C network.
3. Start Notepad++ and create a new file called **ping.py**.
4. Type **# This program prompts the user to enter a class C network address** and press **Enter**.
5. Type **# It then uses the ping function to detect active devices at each possible IP address** and press **Enter** twice.
6. Type **# Import modules that you need** and press **Enter**.
7. Type **import subprocess** and press **Enter**.
8. Type **import os** and press **Enter** twice.
9. Type **# Prompt the user to input a network address** and press **Enter**.
10. Type **net_addr = input("Enter a class C network address (ex.192.168.1): ")** and press **Enter** twice.
11. Type **# Create a target to prevent any output from ping processes from being displayed** and press **Enter**.
12. Type **with open(os.devnull, "wb") as bob:** and press **Enter**.
13. Press the **Tab** key once to indent, type **# n will range from 0 to 254 which you will use to create all IP addresses**, and then press **Enter**.
14. Press the **Tab** key once to indent, then type **for n in range(254):** and press **Enter**.
15. Press the **Tab** key twice, then type **# create the next IP address to ping by combining net_addr with the current value of n** and press **Enter**.
16. Press the **Tab** key twice, then type **ip=net_addr+"."+format(n+1)** and press **Enter**.
17. Press the **Tab** key twice, then type **# create a subprocess to ping ip** and press **Enter**.
18. Press the **Tab** key twice, then type **result=subprocess.Popen(["ping", "-n", "1", "-w", "500", ip], stdout=bob, stderr=bob).wait()** and press **Enter**.
19. Press the **Tab** key twice, then type **if result:** and press **Enter**.
20. Press the **Tab** key three times, then type **# if result=0 then nothing is there** and press **Enter**.
21. Press the **Tab** key three times, then type **print(ip, "inactive - no ping response")** and press **Enter**.
22. Press the **Tab** key twice, then type **else:** and press **Enter**.
23. Press the **Tab** key three times, then type **# if result=1 then device detected** and press **Enter**.
24. Press the **Tab** key three times, then type **print(ip, "active - ping responded, device detected")** and press **Enter**.
25. Go through each line of code and make sure the syntax is correct. See Figure 7-19. Note that on line 18, one of the parameters the `ping` command is using is the number one ("1") and not the letter "l". Also make sure your indentation is correct. Notepad++ will auto indent some sections for you, but make sure your indentation matches the indentation shown in Figure 7-19.
26. Save the file to the location of your choice. You will have to navigate to the file from the Windows command prompt, so save it in a memorable location.
27. Open a Windows command prompt and navigate to the folder containing your ping.py file. Run your script by typing **python ping.py** and pressing **Enter**. If you have no errors, your program should begin pinging IP addresses, as shown in Figure 7-20.
28. You can let the program run to completion or, to terminate the Python script, press **Ctrl+C**.

```
# This program prompts the user to enter a class C network address
# It then uses the ping function to detect active devices at each possible IP address

# Import modules that you need
import subprocess
import os

# Prompt the user to input a network address
net_addr = input("Enter a class C network address (ex.192.168.1): ")

# Create a target to prevent any output from ping processes from being displayed
with open(os.devnull, "wb") as bob:
        # n will range from 0 to 254 which you will use to create all IP addresses
        for n in range(254):
                # create the next IP address to ping by combining net_addr with the current value of n
                ip=net_addr+"."+format(n+1)
                # create a subprocess to ping ip
                result=subprocess.Popen(["ping", "-n", "1", "-w", "500", ip],
                        stdout=bob, stderr=bob).wait()
                if result:
                        # if result=0 then nothing is there
                        print(ip, "inactive - no ping response")
                else:
                        # if result=1 then device detected
                        print(ip, "active - ping responded, device detected")
```

Figure 7-19   The ping.py Python script

```
C:\Users\robwi\Documents\PythonPrograms>python ping.py
Enter a class C network address (ex.192.168.1): 192.168.2
192.168.2.1 active - ping responded, device detected
192.168.2.2 inactive - no ping response
192.168.2.3 inactive - no ping response
192.168.2.4 inactive - no ping response
192.168.2.5 inactive - no ping response
192.168.2.6 inactive - no ping response
192.168.2.7 inactive - no ping response
192.168.2.8 inactive - no ping response
192.168.2.9 inactive - no ping response
192.168.2.10 inactive - no ping response
192.168.2.11 inactive - no ping response
192.168.2.12 inactive - no ping response
192.168.2.13 active - ping responded, device detected
192.168.2.14 inactive - no ping response
192.168.2.15 inactive - no ping response
192.168.2.16 inactive - no ping response
192.168.2.17 inactive - no ping response
192.168.2.18 inactive - no ping response
Traceback (most recent call last):
  File "C:\Users\robwi\Documents\PythonPrograms\ping.py", line 18, in <module>
    result=subprocess.Popen(["ping", "-n", "1", "-w", "500", ip],
  File "C:\Users\robwi\AppData\Local\Programs\Python\Python39\lib\subprocess.py", line 1189, in wait
    return self._wait(timeout=timeout)
  File "C:\Users\robwi\AppData\Local\Programs\Python\Python39\lib\subprocess.py", line 1470, in _wait
    result = _winapi.WaitForSingleObject(self._handle,
KeyboardInterrupt
^C
C:\Users\robwi\Documents\PythonPrograms>
```

Figure 7-20   Output of the ping.py Python script

Source: Kali Linux

Python Shell (REPL)

Python also has an interactive shell where you can enter Python commands and have them immediately executed. This shell is also known as the REPL, which stands for Read, Evaluate, Print, Loop. REPL reads a command, evaluates the command, prints the results, and loops back to read more commands. This shell is convenient for performing quick tasks like calculations or performing operations by calling existing functions. You can enter the shell by typing python and pressing Enter in a terminal or command window. Figure 7-21 shows the REPL in action being used to calculate the area of a circle.

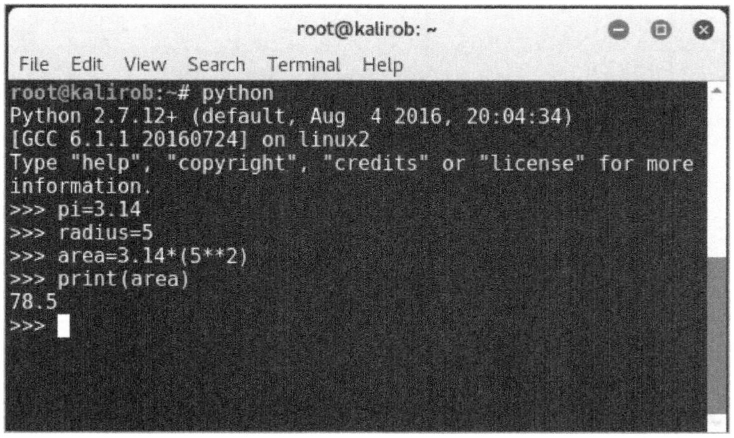

Figure 7-21   The Python REPL shell

Object-Oriented Programming in Python

Python incorporates OOP as well as the functional programming model that you have been using so far. Python supports traditional OOP concepts such as classes, objects, and inheritance. Although a study in OOP is beyond the scope of this book, you can start learning more about using OOP in Python with the tutorial at https://docs.python.org/3/tutorial/classes.html.

Figure 7-22 shows an example of OOP in Python. The program defines a class called Dog and uses it to instantiate and assign attributes to three Dog objects: dog1, dog2, and dog3. It then calls the Dog class member function showInfo() to display the attributes of the Dog objects.

AN OVERVIEW OF RUBY

Another object-oriented language many security testers use is Ruby, which is similar to Perl. Security testers also use Metasploit (www.metasploit.com), a Ruby-based program, to check for vulnerabilities on computer systems. Metasploit contains hundreds of exploits that can be launched on a victim's computer or network, which makes it a useful tool for hackers. Security testers using Metasploit should understand the basics of Ruby and be able to modify Ruby code to suit different environments and targets. For example, security testers might need to modify code for a reverse shell module in Ruby so that it's compatible with the target system where they're conducting vulnerability tests (see Figure 7-23). A reverse shell is a backdoor initiated from inside the target's network that makes it possible to take control of the target even when it's behind a firewall. Search online for "Reverse Shell" to learn more about it.

Figure 7-24 shows some of the many exploits written in Ruby. Note the .rb extension, for Ruby, in program names. In Figure 7-25, the security tester has opened the module for the MS15-020 vulnerability exploit in vim for editing. As you can see, the Ruby syntax is similar to that of object-oriented programming, and the module includes detailed descriptions of the Ruby code.

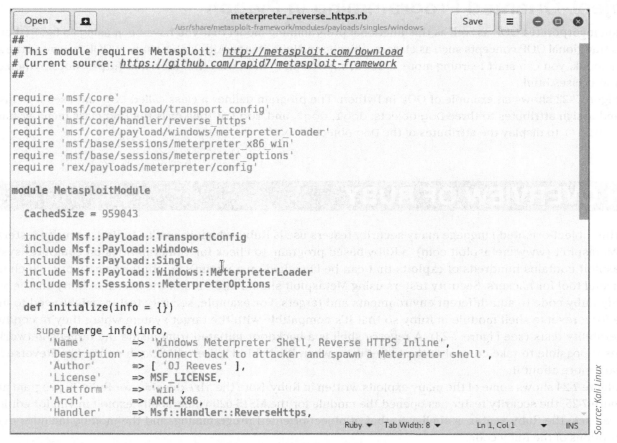

```
C:\Users\robwi\Documents\PythonPrograms\dogOopExample.py - Notepad++                    —  □  ×

File  Edit  Search  View  Encoding  Language  Settings  Tools  Macro  Run  Plugins  Window  ?        X

ping.py ⊠  dogOopExample.py ⊠

 1    # Example program demonstrating Python Object Oriented Programming
 2
 3    # Define class named Dog with attributes breed and gender
 4    # Dog class also has a function showInfo to display attributes
 5
 6   class Dog:
 7     def __init__(DogObject, breed, gender):
 8        DogObject.breed = breed
 9        DogObject.gender = gender
10
11     def showInfo(x):
12        print("Breed is " + x.breed + " and Gender is " + x.gender)
13
14    # create 3 different dog objects using Dog class and assign attributes
15
16    dog1 = Dog("Basset Hound", "Female");
17    dog2 = Dog("Great Dane", "Male");
18    dog3 = Dog("Golden Retriever", "Male");
19
20    # call showInfo function for each dog object to display attributes
21
22    dog1.showInfo()
23    dog2.showInfo()
24    dog3.showInfo()
25

Python file         length : 711  lines : 25    Ln : 24  Col : 1  Pos : 695   Windows (CR LF)  UTF-8   INS
```

Source: Kali Linux

Figure 7-22   Python script dogOopExample.py written in object-oriented code

```
Open  ▼  🗖               meterpreter_reverse_https.rb               Save  ≡  ⊖ ⊙ ⊗
            /usr/share/metasploit-framework/modules/payloads/singles/windows

##
# This module requires Metasploit: http://metasploit.com/download
# Current source: https://github.com/rapid7/metasploit-framework
##

require 'msf/core'
require 'msf/core/payload/transport_config'
require 'msf/core/handler/reverse_https'
require 'msf/core/payload/windows/meterpreter_loader'
require 'msf/base/sessions/meterpreter_x86_win'
require 'msf/base/sessions/meterpreter_options'
require 'rex/payloads/meterpreter/config'

module MetasploitModule

  CachedSize = 959043

  include Msf::Payload::TransportConfig
  include Msf::Payload::Windows
  include Msf::Payload::Single
  include Msf::Payload::Windows::MeterpreterLoader
  include Msf::Sessions::MeterpreterOptions

  def initialize(info = {})

    super(merge_info(info,
      'Name'        => 'Windows Meterpreter Shell, Reverse HTTPS Inline',
      'Description' => 'Connect back to attacker and spawn a Meterpreter shell',
      'Author'      => [ 'OJ Reeves' ],
      'License'     => MSF_LICENSE,
      'Platform'    => 'win',
      'Arch'        => ARCH_X86,
      'Handler'     => Msf::Handler::ReverseHttps,

                                      Ruby ▼  Tab Width: 8 ▼      Ln 1, Col 1    ▼   INS
```

Source: Kali Linux

Figure 7-23   Modifying reverse shell payload code in Ruby

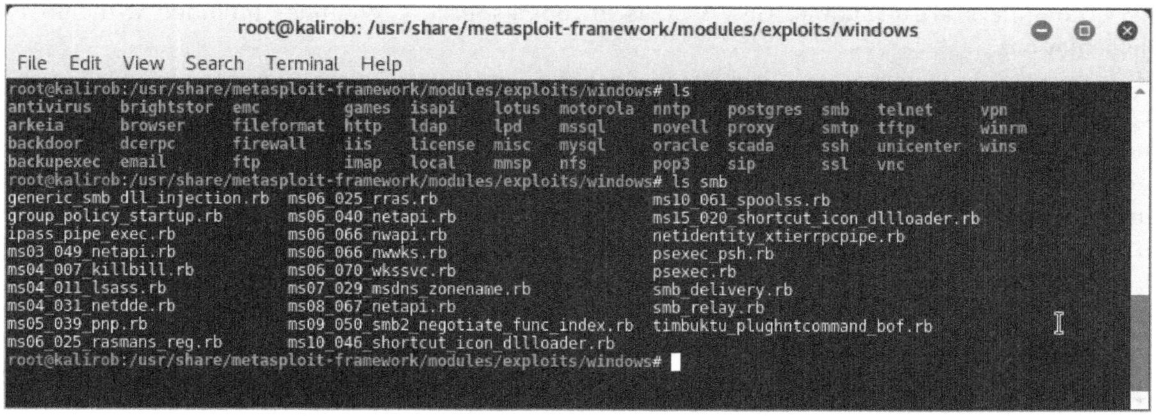

Figure 7-24 Metasploit modules in Ruby

Figure 7-25 Examining the code of a Metasploit module written in Ruby

MODULE SUMMARY

- Writing an algorithm and using pseudocode are good habits to adopt when writing programs.
- Clear documentation of program code is essential.
- C, Perl, and Python are popular programming languages for security professionals and hackers alike.
- Learning the BLT of any programming language can help you master the fundamentals of programming. Branching, looping, and testing are the most important aspects of programming.

- Many C compilers are available. GNU GCC is an open-source C compiler included with most Linux implementations.
- HTML is the primary language used to create webpages. Security professionals need to recognize when something looks suspicious in a webpage, so they should be able to read an HTML file.
- Security professionals should have a basic knowledge of Perl, Python, and C because many security tools are written in these languages. Security professionals who understand these programming languages can modify security tools and create their own customized tools.
- With object-oriented programming, programmers can create classes, which are structures containing both data and functions. Functions in these classes are programs that perform specific tasks.
- WinAPI (formerly called Win32 API) is an interface to the Windows OS that programmers can use to access information about a computer running Windows, such as the computer name, OS name, and so forth.
- Python is a scripting language that supports both the old-school functional paradigm, and the object-oriented programming model. Python uses indentation to denote blocks of code, not brackets or braces as C and Perl do.
- Ruby is a flexible, object-oriented programming language similar to Perl. Security testers and attackers use Metasploit, containing exploit modules written in Ruby, to check for vulnerabilities or to attack systems.

Key Terms

algorithm	compiler	looping
assembly language	conversion specifiers	pseudocode
branching	`do` loop	testing
bug	`for` loop	`while` loop
class	function	

Review Questions

1. A C program must contain which of the following?
   a. Name of the computer programmer
   b. A `main()` function
   c. The `#include<std.h>` header file
   d. A description of the algorithm used

2. An algorithm is defined as which of the following?
   a. A list of possible solutions for solving a problem
   b. A method for automating a manual process
   c. A program written in a high-level language
   d. A set of instructions for solving a specific problem

3. A missing parenthesis or brace might cause a C compiler to return which of the following?
   a. System fault
   b. Interpreter error
   c. Syntax error
   d. Machine-language fault

4. Write a program in C that politely asks the user to enter a string of characters (for example, their name), and then prints that string of characters backwards. Execute the code, and test that your program works.

5. Most programming languages enable programmers to perform which of the following actions? (Choose all that apply.)
   a. Branching
   b. Testing
   c. Faulting
   d. Looping

6. Before writing a program, many programmers outline it first by using which of the following?
   a. Pseudocode
   b. Machine code
   c. Assembly code
   d. Assembler code

7. Which of the following C statements has the highest risk of creating an infinite loop?
   a. `while (a > 10)`
   b. `while (a < 10)`
   c. `for (a = 1; a < 100; ++a)`
   d. `for (;;)`

8. To add comments to a Perl or Python script, you use which of the following symbols?
   a. //
   b. /*
   c. #
   d. <!—<!—

9. Using a Windows computer, write a program in Perl that politely asks the user to enter a string of characters (for example, their name), and then prints that string of characters backwards. Execute the code, and test that your program works.

10. Name two looping mechanisms used in Perl.

11. In C, which looping function performs an action first and then tests to see whether the action should continue to occur?
    a. `for` loop
    b. `while` loop
    c. `do` loop
    d. `unless` loop

12. What is the result of running the following C program?

```
main()
{
   int a = 2; if (a = 1)
         printf("I made a mistake!");
   else
         printf("I did it correctly!");
}
```

   a. "Syntax error: illegal use of ," is displayed.
   b. "I made a mistake!" is displayed.
   c. "Syntax error: variable not declared" is displayed.
   d. "I did it correctly!" is displayed.

13. Using the following Perl code, how many times will "This is easy..." be displayed onscreen?

```
for ($count=1; $count <= 5; $count++)
{
   print "This is easy...";
}
```

   a. 6
   b. 4
   c. None (syntax error)
   d. 5

14. Using a Linux computer, write a program in Perl that politely asks the user to enter a string of characters (for example, their name), and then prints that string of characters backwards. Execute the code, and test that your program works.

15. Which of the following HTML tags is used to create a hyperlink to a remote website?
    a. `<a href=http://URL>`
    b. `<a href="http://URL">`
    c. `<a href="file:///c:/filename>`
    d. `<a href/>`

16. In object-oriented programming, classes are defined as the structures that hold data and functions. True or false?

17. What are the three looping mechanisms in C? (Choose all that apply.)
    a. `for` loop
    b. `while` loop
    c. `if-then-else` loop
    d. `do` loop

18. Which of the following is the Win32 API function for verifying the file system on a Windows computer?
    a. `Filesystem()`
    b. `FsType()`
    c. `System()`
    d. `IsNT()`

19. Using a Windows computer, write a program in Python that politely asks the user to enter a string of characters (for example, their name), and then prints that string of characters backwards. Execute the code, and test that your program works.

20. Which of the following tags enables an HTML programmer to create a loop?
    a. <loop>
    b. <nest>
    c. <while>
    d. HTML doesn't have a looping function or tag.

Case Projects

Case Projects 7-1: Determining Software Engineering Risks for Alexander Rocco

Time Required: 20 minutes

Objective: Analyze some recent code changes and write a memo to the IT security administrator outlining your findings and any recommendations you might have for improving the security of the company's software engineering practices.

Description: After reviewing all the applications Alexander Rocco uses, you notice that many have been modified or changed during the past couple of months. Two of the company's financial applications are written in C and, according to Jose Mendez, the IT security administrator, monitor the company's accounts and financial data. Mr. Mendez discovered that several modifications were made to one program, with no documentation indicating who made the changes or why.

Based on this information, write a memo to Mr. Mendez with your findings and any recommendations you might have for improving the security of the company's software engineering practices. Search the Internet for any information on securing company software. Does the OSSTMM address any of these issues? What improvements should you recommend to better protect this information?

Case Projects 7-2: Developing a Security-Testing Tool

Time Required: 20 minutes

Objective: Write a memo describing the programming language you would use to develop the tool described below, and the method for verifying the information Alexander Rocco management requested.

Description: Your manager at Security Consulting Company has asked you to develop a tool that can gather information from several hundred computers running Windows 10 at Alexander Rocco. The tool needs to verify whether any computers are left running at certain hours in the evening, because management has requested that all computers be turned off no later than 6:00 p.m. Write a memo to your supervisor describing the programming language you would use to develop this tool and the method for verifying the information Alexander Rocco management requested.

DESKTOP AND SERVER OS VULNERABILITIES

After reading this module and completing the exercises, you will be able to:

1 Describe vulnerabilities of the Windows and Linux operating systems

2 Identify specific vulnerabilities and explain ways to fix them

3 Explain techniques to harden Windows and Linux systems

You have learned how to enumerate systems to discover open ports that can be used to access data and resources. After enumerating systems, your job as a security tester is pinpointing potential security problems. You must also be familiar with methods for improving security on tested systems and fixing or minimizing the risks posed by these vulnerabilities. This module examines how to use security testing to analyze an OS for vulnerabilities and correct them. Finally, you explore techniques and best practices for hardening OSs and services.

WINDOWS OS VULNERABILITIES

Many Windows OSs have serious vulnerabilities. In early versions of Windows, including Windows 2000 and earlier, several services and features are unsecured and open for access. To secure these systems, administrators must disable, reconfigure, or uninstall the services and features to lessen their vulnerability to attack. To improve security, later versions of Windows disable most services and features by default. In these environments, administrators must configure necessary services and features to be available, or users can't access the resources they need. In short, security is tighter in these later versions. However, when services aren't available, users often can't do their jobs. An entire module could be devoted to this problem, but for now, keep in mind that a large part of information security in a corporate setting is finding the balance between usability and security.

To find vulnerabilities for any OS, you can check the CVE and CERT vulnerabilities websites (www.cve.mitre.org and www.kb.cert.org/vuls). Table 8-1 briefly describes a few CVEs for Windows Server 2019 and shows how a vulnerability in one OS version can also apply to other versions. (For more detailed explanations of the vulnerabilities listed in this table, visit the CVE website.)

Table 8-1 Windows Server vulnerabilities found at CVE

CVE ID	Description
CVE-2021-34527	Windows 10, Server 2019, Server 2016, Server 2012, Server 2008, Windows 8.1, and Windows 7 have a flaw in the Printer Spooler subsystem that can allow attackers to remotely execute code. This flaw is so severe that Microsoft issued fixes for operating systems that are no longer officially supported (such as Windows 7).
CVE-2021-33740	Windows 10, Server 2019, and Server 2016 have a flaw in the Windows Media subsystem that could allow an attacker to remotely execute code on the vulnerable system.
CVE-2021-33773	Windows 10, Server 2019, Server 2016, Server 2012, and Windows 8.1 have a flaw by which users with remote access connections could elevate their permissions to give them administrative access.
CVE-2021-33756	Windows 10, Server 2019, Server 2016, Server 2012, Server 2008, Windows 8.1, and Windows 7 have a flaw whereby the Windows DNS Snap-in can be exploited to allow Remote Code Execution.

Many of the explanations on the CVE website are complex and might be difficult to understand. However, you should be able to research a vulnerability that's relevant to the security test you're conducting. For example, if the system you're testing uses the Remote Access Connection Manager noted in CVE-2021-33763, you might need to do research on what the Remote Access Connection Manager is (a Windows service that manages virtual private network connections) and whether the version the server in question is running is vulnerable. You might also have to visit the Microsoft website to see whether any patches or security updates are available for this vulnerability. For example, searching for "CVE-2021-33763" on Google reveals several results. If you follow the link to https://msrc.microsoft.com/update-guide/vulnerability/CVE-2021-33763, you'll be taken to the Microsoft Security Update Guide details for that vulnerability, where you can download a list of security updates to patch various Windows OS versions.

Security testers can use information from the CVE site to test a Windows computer and make sure it's been patched with updates from Microsoft that address these known vulnerabilities. Hackers visit websites that offer exploit programs to run against these vulnerabilities, but exploits should only be used in specific cases, and as an ethical hacker, you must have prior approval. In other words, you don't want to dismantle a system to demonstrate the company's security flaws; you want to inform the company when its systems are vulnerable to attack. Many of these known vulnerabilities are found on ports that port-scanning tools can easily detect as open ports. For example, SMB (tcp/139 or tcp/445), SMTP (tcp/25), HTTPS (tcp/443), and RPC (tcp/135) might be vulnerable to attack.

Tools like Nessus and OpenVAS help to automate identifying vulnerabilities for you, but make sure you understand the results that each tool provides by doing further research. When you're conducting research, do more than skim the CVE information. Remember, attention to detail is what separates skillful security testers from the mediocre. Most vulnerabilities are the result of minor errors or omissions in code or configuration settings that can result in major security issues.

Windows File Systems

The purpose of any file system, regardless of the OS, is to store and manage information. A file system organizes information that users create as well as the OS files needed to boot the system, so the file system is the most vital part of any OS. In some cases, this critical component of the OS can be a vulnerability.

File Allocation Table

File Allocation Table (FAT), the original Microsoft file system, is supported by nearly all desktop and server OSs from 1981 to now. Later versions, such as FAT16, FAT32, and Extended FAT (exFAT, developed for Windows Embedded CE), provide for larger file and disk sizes. For example, FAT32 allows a single file to contain up to 4 GB of data and a disk volume to contain up to 8 terabytes (TB). Because of its broad support, FAT32 is also the standard file system for most removable media other than CDs and DVDs. The most serious shortcoming of FAT is that it doesn't support file-level access control lists (ACLs), which are necessary for setting permissions on files. For this reason, using FAT in a multiuser environment results in a critical vulnerability. Microsoft addressed this problem and other shortcomings of FAT when it introduced its first OS for enterprises, Windows NT.

NTFS

New Technology File System (NTFS) was first released as a high-end file system in Windows NT 3.1, and in Windows NT 3.51, it added support for larger files and disk volumes as well as ACL file security. Subsequent Windows versions have included upgrades for compression, disk quotas, journaling, file-level encryption, transactional NTFS, symbolic links, and self-healing. NTFS is used today for Windows 10 systems. Even with strong security features, however, NTFS has some inherent vulnerabilities; some may refer to these vulnerabilities as features. For example, one little-known NTFS feature is alternate data streams (ADSs), written for compatibility with Apple Hierarchical File System (HFS). An ADS can stream (hide) information behind existing files without affecting their function, size, or other information, which makes it possible for system intruders to hide exploitation tools and other malicious files. Several methods can be used to detect ADSs. In Windows Vista and later, a switch has been added to the `dir` command: Enter `dir /r` from the directory you want to analyze to display any ADSs. For previous Windows versions, you need to download a tool such as Streams.exe from https://technet.microsoft.com/en-us/sysinternals/bb897440.aspx. Whatever method you use, you need to determine whether any ADS you detect is supposed to be there. A better and more efficient method of detecting malicious changes to the file system is using host-based file-integrity monitoring tools, such as Tripwire (www.tripwire.com) or Log-Rhythm (www.logrhythm.com). A *nix-based version of Tripwire is also available.

Remote Procedure Call

Remote Procedure Call (RPC) is an interprocess communication mechanism that allows a program running on one host to run code on a remote host. The Conficker worm took advantage of a vulnerability in RPC to run arbitrary code on susceptible hosts. Microsoft Security Bulletin MS08-067, posted October 23, 2008, advised users of this critical vulnerability, which allowed attackers to run their own code, and offered a patch to correct the problem. Even though the vulnerability was published in advisories and a patch was available weeks before the Conficker worm hit on November 21, 2008, millions of computers were affected. Stuxnet, which surfaced in 2010, used the same flaw that Conficker used to spread its infection three years earlier.

Nessus is an excellent tool for determining whether a system is vulnerable due to an RPC-related issue and for many other configuration and patching items as well. In Activity 8-1, you download and install Nessus Essentials on your Windows computer. If you have already installed Nessus Essentials, you can skip this activity.

Activity 8-1: Downloading and Installing Nessus Essentials

Time Required: 30 minutes

Objective: Download and install Nessus Essentials.

Description: In this activity, you download and install Nessus Essentials, a popular vulnerability scanning tool for discovering vulnerabilities in Windows and Linux systems. Nessus Essentials is the free version of Nessus. It has the same functionality as the commercial product Nessus Professional, but restricts the number of IP addresses you can work with.

1. In Windows, start your web browser and go to **www.tenable.com/downloads/nessus**. You need an activation code to install Nessus Essentials, so you can click the link or button on the download page to get one. You also have another opportunity to get an activation code later in the installation steps. The activation code will be sent to the email address you provide.
2. Click the appropriate download link for your operating system. If you are running Windows, you are most likely running a 64-bit version of Windows, so you would choose **Nessus-8.15.0-x64.msi**.
3. After the download is finished, browse to the location of the saved file, and double-click the setup executable file. If you see a warning message, click **Run** or **OK** to continue. The InstallShield Wizard window opens.
4. Close all running Windows applications, and then click **Next**.
5. Follow the prompts and accept license agreements and default settings unless your instructor advises you otherwise.
6. When the installation is finished, your default web browser will open to the Welcome to Nessus Install page. Click the **Connect via SSL** button.
7. On the Welcome to Nessus page, click **Nessus Essentials**, and then click the **Continue** button (see Figure 8-1).

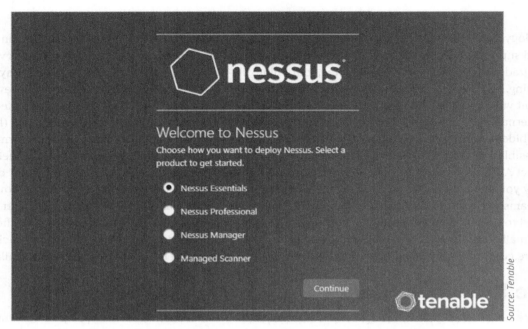

Figure 8-1   Nessus product deployment option screen

8. When you are asked for your activation code, enter the code, and then click the **Continue** button.
   Nessus Essentials finishes the installation and begins to download plugins it needs to perform vulnerability scans.
9. To start Nessus Essentials in the future, open a web browser tab and enter **https://localhost:8834**. You will be
   using Nessus Essentials in an upcoming activity.

NetBIOS

Recall that NetBIOS is software loaded into memory and enables a program to interact with a network resource or device. Network resources are identified with 16-byte NetBIOS names. NetBIOS isn't a protocol; it's the interface to a network protocol that enables a program to access a network resource. It usually works with **NetBIOS Extended User Interface (NetBEUI)**, a fast, efficient protocol that requires little configuration and allows transmitting NetBIOS packets over TCP/IP and various network topologies. NetBIOS over TCP/IP is disabled by default on current versions of Windows but was enabled by default prior to Windows Vista and Server 2008.

Systems running newer Windows OSs can share files and resources without using NetBIOS; however, NetBIOS is still used for backward compatibility, which is important when organizational budgets don't allow upgrading every computer on the network. In addition, customer expectations must be met. For example, customers expect that a document created in Word 2010 can still be read in Word 2019. In fact, they demand it. Therefore, software developers face the challenge of improving OS security while ensuring compatibility with less secure predecessors. As long as newer Windows OSs must work with older NetBIOS-based systems, security will be a challenge.

Server Message Block

In Windows, **Server Message Block (SMB)** is used to share files and usually runs on top of NetBIOS, NetBEUI, or TCP/IP. Several hacking tools that target SMB can still cause damage to Windows networks. Two well-known SMB hacking tools are L0phtcrack's SMB Packet Capture utility and SMBRelay, which intercept SMB traffic and collect usernames and password hashes.

Interestingly, it took Microsoft seven years to patch the vulnerability these hacking tools exploited. Many security researchers point to this situation as another example of the problem caused by ensuring backward compatibility.

By continuing to use a protocol with a known vulnerability (which can also be described as a design flaw), Microsoft exposes its products to attack and exploitation.

Microsoft introduced SMB2 in Windows Vista, SMB3 in Windows 8, and SMB3.1.1 in Windows 10. Each new revision of SMB fixed security issues and often added features and performance improvements. SMB vulnerabilities are a common attack vector exploited by malware. Worms, for example, search for SMB shares and attempt to use vulnerable shares to copy themselves from computer to computer across a network.

Common Internet File System

Common Internet File System (CIFS) is a standardized protocol that replaced SMB in Windows 2000 Server, but to allow backward compatibility, the original SMB was still used.

NOTE

CIFS is now considered obsolete and SMBv3 is normally used instead. However, CIFS might still be used in some legacy systems or as a method of file sharing between Linux/Unix systems and Windows.

CIFS is a remote file system protocol that enables computers to share network resources over the Internet. In other words, files, folders, printers, and other resources can be made available to users throughout a network. For sharing to occur, the network must have an infrastructure that allows placing these resources on the network and a method to control access to resources. CIFS relies on other protocols to handle service announcements notifying users what resources are available on the network and to handle authentication and authorization for accessing these resources. CIFS is also available for many *nix systems.

The Network Neighborhood or My Network Places services use broadcast protocols to announce resources available on a network. Essentially, a computer calls over the network connection "Here I am! My NetBIOS name is Salesmgr, and I have lots of files and folders to share with anyone out there." To share files and folders, CIFS relies on SMB, but it offers many enhancements, including the following:

- Locking features that enable multiple users to access and update a file simultaneously without conflicts
- Caching and read-ahead/write-behind capability
- Support for fault tolerance
- Capability to run more efficiently over slow dial-up lines
- Support for anonymous and authenticated access to files to improve security

To prevent unauthorized access to these files, CIFS relies on SMB's security model. An administrator can select two methods for server security:

- *Share-level security*—A folder on a disk is made available to users for sharing. A password can be configured for the share but isn't required.
- *User-level security*—The resource is made available to network users; however, a username and password are required to access the resource. The SMB server maintains an encrypted version of users' passwords to enhance security.

Newer versions of Windows Server listen on most of the same ports as older versions, which means many old attacks might still work on newer OSs. For example, by recognizing which ports are open on a Windows Server system, a security tester can find vulnerabilities that allow introducing a Trojan or other remote control program for capturing authorized users' passwords and logon names. Most attackers look for servers designated as domain controllers (servers that handle authentication). Windows domain controllers are used to authenticate user accounts, so they contain much of the information attackers want to access. By default, Windows domain controllers listen on the following ports:

- DNS (port 53)
- HTTP (port 80)
- Kerberos (port 88)

- RPC (port 135)
- NetBIOS Name Service (port 137)
- NetBIOS Datagram Service (port 139)
- LDAP (port 389)
- HTTPS (port 443)
- SMB/CIFS (port 445)
- LDAP over SSL (port 636)
- Active Directory global catalog (port 3268)

Windows domain controllers are usually also global catalog (GC) servers. Global catalog servers are used to locate resources in a domain containing thousands or even millions of objects. For example, if a user wants to locate a printer with the word "color" in its description, the domain queries a GC server, which contains attributes such as the resource's name and location and points the user to the network resource.

Null Sessions

Recall that a null session is an anonymous connection established without credentials, such as a username and password. Also called an anonymous logon, a null session can be used to display information about users, groups, shares, and password policies. Null sessions are necessary only if networks need to support older Windows versions. Nonetheless, many organizations still have null sessions enabled, even though all their old Windows systems have been removed from the network. You can use the `Nbtstat`, `Net view`, `Netstat`, `Ping`, `Pathping`, and `Telnet` commands to enumerate NetBIOS vulnerabilities.

Web Services

Older versions of web services and IIS would enable numerous features by default, leaving systems with a large attack surface. Microsoft developed the IIS Lockdown Wizard specifically for locking down IIS versions 4.0 and 5.0. As a security tester, however, you should encourage clients to upgrade any OS and software no longer supported instead of using security workarounds, such as the IIS Lockdown Wizard.

IIS 5.0 is installed by default in Windows 2000 Server, which means that a Windows 2000 server is also a web server using the default configuration, a setup many administrators aren't aware of until a problem occurs. Windows 2000 is a legacy operating system, and the likelihood of coming across an installation still running in an organization is highly unlikely, but the point is not to assume your network has no web server just because you didn't specifically install one.

Although IIS 6.0 (Windows Server 2003) through IIS 10.0.17763 (Windows Server 2019) are installed in a "secure by default" mode, previous versions left crucial holes that made it possible for attackers to sneak into a network. Regardless of the IIS version a system runs, keeping systems patched is important, and system administrators should still be aware of what patches are installed and which services are running on their web servers. Configuring only necessary services and applications is a wise move.

MS SQL Server

Older versions of Microsoft SQL Server have many potential vulnerabilities that can't be covered in detail in this course. The most common critical SQL vulnerability is the null SA password. All versions before SQL Server 2005 have a vulnerability that could allow remote users to gain System Administrator (SA) access through the SA account on the server. During SQL Server 6.5 and 7 installations, the user is prompted—but not required—to set a password on this account. SQL Server 2000 uses Windows Integrated authentication by default, but the user can also select mixed-mode authentication. In this authentication mode, an SA account with a blank password is created, and this account can't be disabled. If attackers find this account, they have administrative access to not only the database, but also potentially the database server. It's unlikely you will come across an installation of SQL Server old enough to have this vulnerability, but servers often use default settings and some of these defaults leave Windows servers vulnerable. Vulnerability scanners such as Nessus and OpenVAS still scan for this SQL Server vulnerability.

Buffer Overflows

Recall that a buffer overflow occurs when data is written to a buffer (temporary memory space) and, because of insufficient bounds checking, corrupts data in memory next to the allocated buffer. Normally, this problem occurs when dangerous functions use input that has not been properly validated. Because of design flaws, several functions don't verify that the numbers or strings they accept fit in the buffer supplied to hold them. If this lack of verification is exploited, it can allow attackers to run shell code. Both C and C++ lack built-in protection against overwriting data in memory, so applications written in these languages are vulnerable to buffer overflow attacks. Because these programming languages are widely used, buffer overflow vulnerabilities are prevalent in many applications and OSs. Buffer overflow attacks don't require an authenticated user and can be carried out remotely. Fortunately, modern software development frameworks include sanitizing routines and other security features to help developers code more securely. However, it's still up to the developer to use these features to create secure code.

Passwords and Authentication

You've already learned that the weakest security link in any network is authorized users. Unfortunately, this link is the most difficult to secure, as it relies on people who might not realize that their actions could expose their organization to a major security breach, resulting in damaged systems, stolen or destroyed information, malware infection, and so forth. There might also be legal issues to deal with after an attack, and a company can lose customers' confidence as a result.

Companies should take steps to address this vulnerability. A comprehensive password policy is critical, as a username and password are often all that stands between an attacker and access. A password policy should include the following:

- Change passwords regularly on system-level accounts.
- Require users to change their passwords quarterly. While this can be a sound practice that many security professionals advocate, some security organizations suggest that frequent password changes make for less secure passwords as users tend to change their passwords in a predictable fashion, such as incrementally changing a number. Also, frequent password changes may encourage users to use the same password for different logons. Therefore, these organizations have suggested removing the password change requirement.
- Require a minimum password length of at least eight characters (and 15 characters for administrative accounts).
- Require complex passwords; in other words, passwords must include both uppercase and lowercase letters, numbers, symbols, and punctuation characters. However, some security organizations suggest that longer passwords are better than complex passwords. Hackers and their automated tools can guess substitutions of $ for S or @ for A, so that type of complexity doesn't enhance security. Because longer passwords take longer to crack, security experts suggest abandoning complexity in favor of length.
- Passwords can't be common words, words found in the dictionary (in any language), or slang, jargon, or dialect.
- Passwords must not be identified with a particular user, such as birthdays, names, or company-related words.
- Never write a password down or store it online or in a file on the user's computer.
- Don't hint at or reveal a password to anyone over the phone, in email, or in person.
- Require users to take caution when logging on to make sure no one sees them entering a password.
- Limit reuse of old passwords.

In addition to these guidelines, administrators can configure domain controllers to enforce password age, length, and complexity. On Windows domain controllers, some aspects of a password policy can be enforced, such as the following:

- *Account lockout threshold*—Set the number of failed attempts before the account is disabled temporarily.
- *Account lockout duration*—Set the period of time the user account is locked out after a specified number of failed logon attempts.

On Windows Server 2008 and newer domain controllers, multiple password policies can be enforced. For example, one password policy might require a complex password of 15 or more characters for administrator accounts, and another password policy might require only eight characters for user accounts with no administrative privileges. Despite the best efforts to promote security by enforcing password policies, a password might still be cracked. The latest tools that incorporate rainbow tables can crack complex passwords surprisingly fast. You explore password cracking in more detail in a later module.

TOOLS FOR IDENTIFYING VULNERABILITIES IN WINDOWS

Many tools are available for discovering Windows vulnerabilities. Using more than one tool for analysis is advisable, so learning a variety of methods and tools is beneficial to your career. Familiarity with several tools also helps you pinpoint problems more accurately. Some tools might report deceptive results, and if these results aren't verified with another method, you might not have an accurate assessment to report. Popular OS vulnerability scanners include Tripwire IP360, Tenable Nessus, Nexpose, and OpenVAS. You were introduced to Nessus and OpenVAS in previous modules. All these products scan both Linux and Windows OSs. In addition, several tools are specifically designed for Windows. In the following section, you explore using Nessus for assessing Windows systems.

Scanning Windows Using Nessus Essentials

Although all computer systems have security problems, many attacks can be avoided with careful system analysis and maintenance, which can include practices from establishing an efficient, regular update scheme to reviewing log files for signs of unusual activity. When Microsoft learns of problems or vulnerabilities in its software, it publishes patches, security updates, service packs, and hotfixes to address them as soon as possible.

Table 8-2 summarizes the types of configuration errors and security issues that can be found on Windows Server.

Table 8-2   Common Windows Server configuration and security issues

Type of issue	Details to check for
Security updates missing	Missing Windows, IIS, and SQL Server security updates
	Missing Exchange Server security updates
	Missing IE security updates
	Missing Windows Media Player and Office security updates
	Missing Microsoft Virtual Machine (VM) and Microsoft Data Access Components (MDAC) security updates
	Missing MSXML and Content Management Server security updates
Windows configuration	Account password expirations left at default settings, not matching company policy (30 days, etc.). This should be changed to match company policy.
	Blank or simple passwords are used for local user accounts. This should be changed to match company password policy.
	File system type on hard drives is insecure. FAT being used when NTFS should be used to provide ACLs. Change to NTFS if possible.
	Auto Logon feature is enabled. Disable if this feature is not required.
	Number of local Administrator accounts should be 1 or 2 at most.
	Is the Guest account enabled? Disable this account if it is not required.
	Restrict Anonymous Registry key setting should be set to not allow anonymous access if not a business requirement.

Type of issue	Details to check for
	List shares on the computer and any unnecessary services running. Make sure shares are credential secured and stop unnecessary services.
	Windows version and whether Windows auditing is enabled. Is the Windows version supported by updates? Auditing creates log entries to track file access. Is this set to meet company policy?
	Firewall status and Automatic Updates status. Is the firewall enabled and configured to match company policy or left at defaults? Are automatic updates configured to match company policy?
IIS (Internet Information Service)	Is the IIS Lockdown tool running? If the server version is older than 2003, IIS Lockdown needs to be running.
	Are IIS sample applications and the IIS Admin virtual folder installed? These are default installation items and should be removed or secured.
	Are IIS parent paths enabled? If enabled, this default setting may need to be evaluated or disabled.
	MSADC and Scripts virtual directories are installed by default and should be removed or disabled.
	IIS logging should be enabled.
	IIS should not be running on a domain controller.
	Does the Administrators group belong in the Sysadmin role? This setting may be a default configuration. If not intended, remove the Administrators group.
	Make sure the CmdExec role is restricted to Sysadmin only.
	SQL Server should not be running on a domain controller.
	The SA account password should not be default or blank, and the Guest account should not have database access.
	Access permissions to SQL Server installation folders should not be left at default settings.
	The Everyone group should not have access to SQL Server Registry keys.
	SQL Server service accounts should not be members of the local Administrators group. If compromised, hackers will have admin access.
	SQL Server accounts should not have blank or simple passwords.
SQL configuration	Check SQL Server authentication mode type to make sure it matches security requirements. The number of Sysadmin role members should be at the minimum.
Desktop application configuration	IE security zone settings for each local user should match company policy.
	Is IE Enhanced Security Configuration enabled for Administrator accounts and is it configured to be secure? Administrator accounts should avoid browsing the Internet, and sessions need to be highly secured.
	Is IE Enhanced Security Configuration enabled for non-Administrator accounts? This setting must be configured to match company policy and not accidentally left at default settings.
	What are the Microsoft Office security zone settings for each local user? These should be set to match company policy and not accidentally left at default settings.

Using Nessus Essentials

In Activity 8-2, you will use Nessus Essentials on a computer running Microsoft Windows. If you have access to a Windows server that you have permission to scan, then use that as your target. You can also scan your own computer to see what vulnerabilities Nessus Essentials might discover.

Activity 8-2: Using Nessus to Scan the Local Computer

Time Required: 30 minutes

Objective: Use Nessus to scan the local computer for vulnerabilities.

Description: In this activity, you scan your computer with Nessus to discover vulnerabilities, including weak or missing passwords. At the end of the activity, submit a summary of your findings to your instructor, along with brief recommendations for correcting the problems you found.

1. Log on to Nessus Essentials. On the My Scans page (see Figure 8-2), click the **New Scan** button.

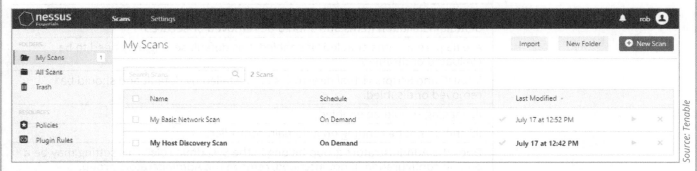

Figure 8-2   Nessus Essentials My Scans page

2. On the Scan Templates page (see Figure 8-3), choose **Basic Network Scan** in the VULNERABILITIES section.

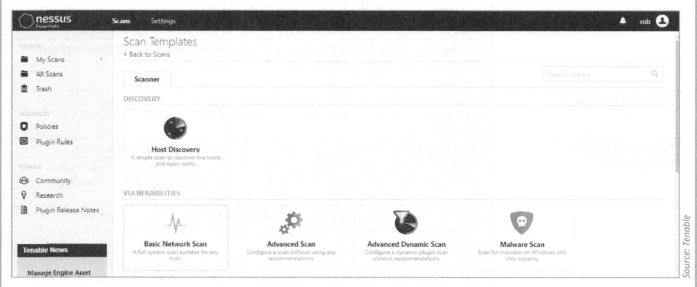

Figure 8-3   Nessus Essentials Scan Templates page

3. On the Settings tab of the New Scan/Basic Network Scan page, enter the name, description, and folder for your scan. For Targets, enter the IP address of the computer you are targeting for your scan. See Figure 8-4. You don't have to provide credentials on the Credentials tab, but if you do, the scan can collect more information. Click **Save**.

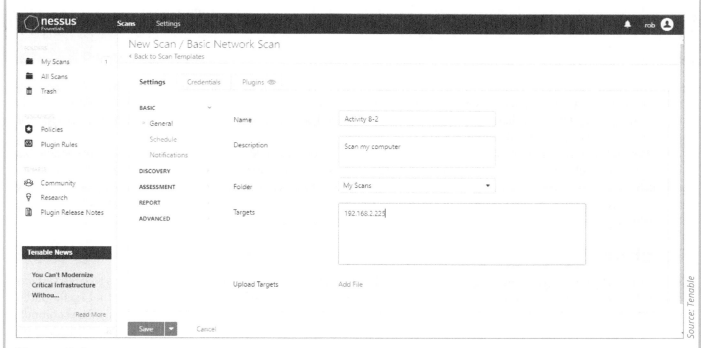

Figure 8-4   Configuring a Nessus Essentials scan

4. On the My Scans page, click the **Launch** button to start your new scan. See Figure 8-5. A green circle icon indicates your scan is in progress.

Figure 8-5   My Scans page with new scan ready to launch

5. When the scan is complete, click its name in the My Scans list to view the results. What problems did Nessus Essentials find? Did it find any password vulnerabilities or other vulnerabilities? Are any results unexpected?

6. Write a brief summary of vulnerability problems that Nessus Essentials found. If time permits, discuss your results with your classmates or instructor. Feel free to conduct more scans.

BEST PRACTICES FOR HARDENING WINDOWS SYSTEMS

As a penetration tester, your job is to find vulnerabilities and report them as defined in your contract. Your responsibility ends there. However, security testers must not only find vulnerabilities; they must be familiar with methods of correcting them. Typically, managers want solutions included with reports of potential problems, particularly for technologies they might not fully understand.

Although the only way to make a system truly secure is to unplug it and lock it away in a vault, this approach defies the purpose of a network. Because you can't lock network computers away to keep them secure, the best option is to be vigilant. A security breach is only one undiscovered vulnerability away, but with careful management, most systems can be secured adequately and still meet users' needs. General practices for making and keeping a network secure are discussed in the following sections.

Patching Systems

The best way to keep systems secure, operating at peak performance, and using the newest features is to *keep systems under your care up to date.* As noted, many attacks have taken advantage of a known vulnerability that has a patch available. There are several methods for obtaining service packs, hotfixes, and patches. If you have only a few computers to maintain (10 or fewer), accessing Windows Update manually from each computer works fine, but this method is still time consuming. Depending on the Windows version, you can configure Automatic Updates on each machine. This option is usually better because it helps ensure that machines are always up to date without the administrator or user's intervention. The downside is that some patches can cause problems, so testing a patch before applying it to a production system is preferable, particularly in large networks.

For a large network, applying updates manually isn't feasible. Configuring Automatic Updates is an option if you have physical access to all computers, though downloading patches to each machine can slow network performance. You have a couple of options for patch management. From 1994 to 2005, Microsoft's **Systems Management Server (SMS)** was the standard for managing Windows security patches on multiple computers in a network. This service assessed machines in a defined domain and could be configured to manage patch deployment. (Although this service had many other capabilities, for the purposes of this module, you only need to know that it can be used for patch management.)

In 2005, **Windows Software Update Services (WSUS)** became available. WSUS is a client/server technology designed to manage patching and updating system software from the network. Instead of downloading updates to each computer, WSUS downloads patches and publishes them internally to servers and desktop systems. Unlike Automatic Updates, which downloads and installs updates automatically, the administrator has control over which updates are deployed. This feature is a major advantage, considering that some updates can cause problems with certain network and application configurations and should be tested before being deployed.

In 2007, Windows **System Center Configuration Manager (SCCM)** became the new standard. SCCM includes a suite of tools to help administrators deploy and manage servers alongside updated patch-management functionality. SCCM even allows for administrators to control mobile devices running Android, iOS, and Windows Mobile OS.

Third-party patch-management solutions are also available from vendors such as BigFix, Tanium, and BladeLogic. Whatever patch-management tools you use, remember that keeping systems up to date is one of the most critical steps in keeping systems secure. As a security tester, you'll often find that patches aren't current on the system you're testing. An effective patch-management scheme might seem like common sense, but administrators can be so busy with other complicated issues that they forget the simple solutions. You must recommend effective patch management to your clients and be able to explain why it's crucial to system security.

Antivirus Solutions

Whether you're working with an enterprise network consisting of thousands of servers and tens of thousands of clients or a small business network of 15 systems and one server, you must use an antivirus solution. For small networks, desktop antivirus tools with automatic updating might be enough, but in a large network, a corporate-level solution is needed. Several excellent products are available and selecting the right one requires some research. An antivirus tool must be planned, installed, and configured correctly to ensure the best protection. An antivirus tool is almost useless if it isn't updated regularly. Ideally, an antivirus tool should automatically download and install updates daily. If your examination of a system reveals that no antivirus tool is running, you should recommend installing one immediately. You must also stress keeping it up to date for the best protection.

Enable Logging and Review Logs Regularly

Logging is a crucial function for monitoring system security. It must be configured carefully to record only useful statistics, because overly verbose logging can easily overwhelm analysts. Review logs regularly for signs of intrusion or other problems on the network. Build prevention and detection by considering what attackers might do if they compromised your network. If you were an attacker and broke into a network you weren't familiar with, you would probably run some Windows administrative commands to understand more about the network. Commands like `ipconfig /all`, `netstat -r`, `net view`, and `gpresult`, especially when grouped together, could be seen as suspicious, given the proper context. If a non-technical user suddenly makes administrative requests, it might be time to investigate further.

Scanning thousands of log entries is time consuming, and missing important entries is likely. A log-monitoring tool is best for this task. Several are available, depending on network needs and budget. Some of these tools even include customizable automation that can give you an edge on an attacker by automating response (e.g., disabling a remote systems network adapter) when the tools detect known malicious activities.

Disable Unused Services and Filtering Ports

Disabling unneeded services and deleting unnecessary applications or scripts make sense because they otherwise give intruders a potential point of entry into a network. For example, if you have a Windows Server 2016 system acting as a file server, you don't need DNS services running on it; doing so leaves port 53 TCP/UDP open and vulnerable to attack. The idea is to open *only* what needs to be open and close everything else—also known as reducing the attack surface. (The attack surface is the amount of code a computer system exposes to unauthenticated outsiders.) With fewer services exposed, an attacker is less likely to find an unpatched vulnerability.

In addition, filtering out unnecessary ports can protect systems from attack. Some ports frequently subject to attack include the following:

- FTP (20 and 21 TCP)
- TFTP (69 UDP)
- Telnet (23 TCP)
- DNS (53 TCP/UDP)
- NTP (123 UDP)
- NetBIOS (135 TCP/UDP, 137 and 138 UDP, 139 TCP)
- SMB (445 TCP/UDP)
- Remote Desktop Protocol (3389 TCP)
- SNMP (161 and 162 TCP/UDP)
- Windows RPC programs (1025 to 1039 TCP/UDP)

The best way to protect a network from SMB attacks is to make sure perimeter routers and firewalls filter out ports 137 to 139 and 445. Blocking ports 139 and 445 has the added benefit of protecting against external null session attacks. Windows Server 2003 doesn't disable SMB on port 445 by default. In fact, if the computer is a domain controller, you need to provide access to SMB. The server's job is to make sure the person attempting to log on to the network is indeed authorized to access network resources. Because you usually want to share resources on a server, closing port 445 could create other problems, such as users not being able to access shared folders and printers.

An attacker can gain entry through many other ports. It isn't possible to close all avenues of attack and still offer the functionality users need, but with careful planning, an administrator can reduce the number of ways into the network. For a complete list of ports and services, consult IANA's Assigned Port Number page at www.iana.org/assignments/port-numbers.

 **CAUTION**   Use caution when disabling services and blocking ports. Make sure that no required services depending on a port or other service are inadvertently disabled.

Other Security Best Practices

In addition to keeping software up to date, running antivirus tools, and disabling services, you can take the following steps to help minimize the risks to a Windows network:

- Minimize the number of users with administrative rights.
- Implement software to prevent sensitive data from leaving the network.
- Use network segmentation to make it more difficult for an attacker to move from computer to computer.
- Restrict the number of applications that are allowed to run on a computer connected to the network.
- Delete unused scripts and sample applications.
- Delete default hidden shares and unnecessary shares.
- Use a different unique naming scheme and passwords for public interfaces.
- Ensure passwords' length and complexity are sufficient.
- Be careful of default permissions, configurations, and passwords.
- Use packet-filtering technologies, such as host-based software firewalls, enterprise-class hardware firewalls, and intrusion detection and prevention systems, that are suited to the environment.
- Use open-source or commercial tools to assess system security.
- Use a file-integrity checker to monitor unauthorized file system modifications and send alerts of these changes.
- Disable the Guest account.
- Disable the local Administrator account.
- Disable accounts of users no longer with the company.
- Make sure no accounts have blank passwords. A robust password policy is crucial.
- Use Windows group policies to enforce security configurations on large networks efficiently and consistently.
- Develop a comprehensive security awareness program for users to reinforce your organization's security policy.
- Keep up with emerging threats. Check with Microsoft, SANS, US-CERT (www.us-cert.gov), and other security organizations for the newest developments.

The security field is changing rapidly, and security professionals must keep up with new developments, threats, and tools. Securing Windows systems can be challenging, but you have access to many tools to pinpoint problems.

LINUX OS VULNERABILITIES

Like any OS, Linux can be made more secure if users are aware of its vulnerabilities and keep current on new releases and fixes. It's assumed you have some experience working with a *nix OS, so the basics of the Linux OS and file system aren't covered in this module. Many Linux versions are available, with differences ranging from slight to major. For example, Red Hat and Fedora Linux use the yum command to update and manage RPM (Red Hat Package Manager) packages, and Ubuntu, Debian, and Kali Linux use the apt-get command to update and manage DEB (Debian) packages. Whatever Linux version you use, you must understand the basics, such as run control and service configuration, directory structure, file system, basic shell commands and scripting, and package management. (If you're unfamiliar with these *nix basics, spend time reviewing them. One of the quickest ways security testers can make a poor impression on clients is to show a lack of knowledge about the systems they're testing.)

A typical Linux distribution has thousands of packages developed by many contributors around the world. With such diverse sources of code, it's inevitable that some code will have flaws that are sometimes discovered only after they have been incorporated in the final product. Too many network administrators believe Windows is easier to attack and view *nix OSs as inherently more secure. Security professionals must understand that making these assumptions can be dangerous because all OSs have vulnerabilities. When conducting a security test on systems running Linux, you should follow the same rules you would for any OS.

Samba

Users expect to share resources over a network, regardless of the OS used, and companies have discovered that users no longer tolerate proprietary systems that can't coexist in a network. To address the issue of interoperability, a group of programmers created Samba (www.samba.org) in 1992 as an open-source implementation of CIFS. With Samba, *nix servers can share resources with Windows clients, and Windows clients can access a *nix resource without realizing that the resource is on a *nix computer. Samba has been ported to non-*nix systems, too, including OpenVMS, NetWare, and AmigaOS. At the time of this writing, security professionals should have a basic knowledge of SMB and Samba because many companies have a mixed environment of Windows and *nix systems.

To access a *nix resource from a Windows computer, CIFS must be enabled on both systems. On networks that require *nix computers to access Windows resources, Samba is often used. It's not a hacking tool; this product was designed to enable *nix computers to "trick" Windows services into believing that *nix resources are Windows resources. A *nix client can connect to a Windows shared printer and vice versa when Samba is configured on the *nix computer. Most new versions of Linux include Samba as an optional package, so you don't need to download, install, and compile it.

Tools for Identifying Linux Vulnerabilities

Visiting the CVE website is a good first step in discovering possible avenues attackers might take to break into a Linux system. Table 8-3 lists a small portion of the CVEs and CANs found when searching on the keyword "Linux." To give you an idea of the multitude of Linux vulnerabilities, more than 500 entries were found. Many of these vulnerabilities can no longer be exploited on systems that have been updated.

Table 8-3   Linux vulnerabilities found at CVE

CVE/CAN	Description
CVE-2021-36148	A buffer overflow in the function dmar_free_irte in the file hypervisor/arch/x86/vtd.c allows the attacker to corrupt memory.
CVE-2021-35039	A vulnerability was found in Linux Kernel up to 5.12.13 affecting the function init_module of the file kernel/module.c. The manipulation with an unknown input leads to a weak authentication vulnerability.
CVE-2019-14896	A heap-based buffer overflow vulnerability was found in the Linux kernel, version kernel-2.6.32, in Marvell WiFi chip driver. A remote attacker could cause a denial of service (system crash) or possibly execute arbitrary code when the lbs_ibss_join_existing function is called after a STA connects to an AP.

You can use CVE information when testing Linux computers for known vulnerabilities. Security testers should review the CVE and CAN information carefully to ensure that a system doesn't have any vulnerabilities listed on the CVE website and has been updated.

You have learned how tools such as OpenVAS (a.k.a. Greenbone Security Assistant) can enumerate multiple OSs. Using enumeration tools, a security tester can do the following:

- Identify a computer on the network by using port scanning and zone transfers.
- Identify the OS the computer is using by conducting port scanning and enumeration.
- Identify, via enumeration, any logon accounts and passwords configured on the computer.
- Learn the names of shared folders by using enumeration.
- Identify services running on the computer.

The following example shows OpenVAS enumerating and finding vulnerabilities on a Linux computer. Figure 8-6 shows the OpenVAS report after a Linux computer with the IP address 192.168.2.144 has been scanned. The figure indicates that OpenVAS discovered a Ubuntu Linux system.

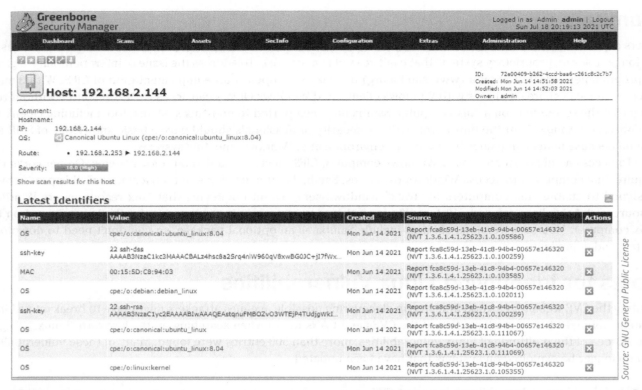

Figure 8-6   OpenVAS has determined the target system is running Ubuntu Linux

In Figure 8-7, note that OpenVAS discovered 39 high-risk vulnerabilities, 73 medium-risk vulnerabilities, and 6 low-risk vulnerabilities. You can tell this machine hasn't been patched in a while.

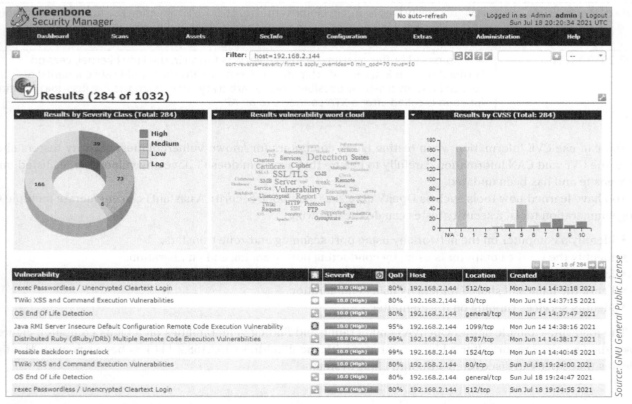

Figure 8-7   Results of OpenVAS scan of 192.168.2.144 showing hundreds of vulnerabilities

You can view individual vulnerabilities by clicking Scans on the navigation bar to display the Results page, as shown in Figure 8-8.

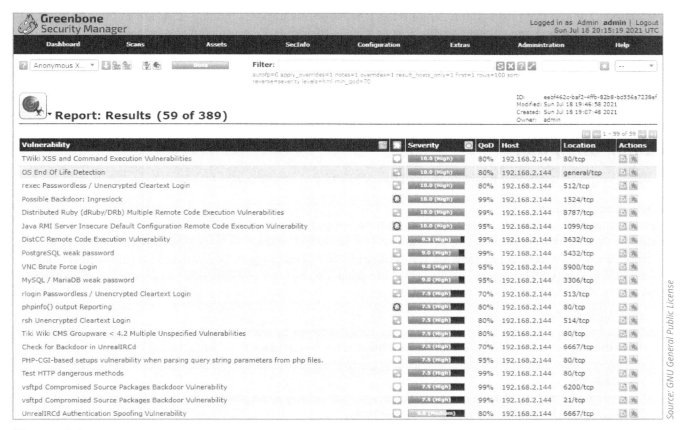

Figure 8-8   Report of OpenVAS scan of 192.168.2.144

With 39 high-risk vulnerabilities, a discussion of the results displayed in Figure 8-8 would require an entire module, but you can see how OpenVAS can be used for security testing. Figure 8-9 shows that OpenVAS discovered a critical "Possible Backdoor: Ingreslock" vulnerability.

Figure 8-9   Possible Backdoor: Ingreslock vulnerability found

A backdoor is a vulnerability where a hacker can secretly connect to an open port on the infected computer and control it. Figure 8-9 shows 1524/tcp under the Location heading, indicating that port 1524 is open. Ingres is a SQL database that is commonly used to support very large commercial government applications. Ingres is designed to have port 1524 open, though this port is often exploited as a backdoor by hackers. Using `netcat` from the command line or a similar tool, attackers can connect to this port and begin their nefarious activities.

If this system is an Internet-facing server, this vulnerability represents a serious risk that external actors can exploit. If this system is not connected to the Internet, it is still vulnerable to internal network threats.

Activity 8-3: Installing and Using OpenVAS to Discover Vulnerabilities on a Linux Computer

Time Required: 45 minutes

Objective: Install and use OpenVAS to discover vulnerabilities on a Linux computer.

Description: OpenVAS is a helpful tool for enumerating an OS. Not only does it warn testers of possible vulnerabilities, but it also recommends how to correct problems it discovers. In this activity, you configure OpenVAS to scan your partner's Linux computer (or if you are working alone, your own Linux computer) and discover any vulnerabilities an attacker might use to gain access.

1. Boot into Kali Linux.
2. Open a Terminal shell and determine your computer's IP address by typing **ifconfig** and pressing **Enter**. Write down the IP address and give it to your partner. Next, start the ssh daemon (sshd) by typing **/etc/init.d/ssh start** and pressing **Enter**. This command allows OpenVAS on your partner's computer to log on and check for vulnerabilities.
3. Type **sudo apt-get install openvas**, press **Enter**, and then press **y** when prompted to download and install the Open VAS package. Wait until this process is complete.
4. Type **sudo gvm-setup** and press **Enter** to start the OpenVAS setup process, which takes a few minutes to complete. (OpenVAS is the scanner component of the Greenbone Vulnerability Manager (GVM), and what used to be openvas-setup is now gvm-setup.) Watch for setup to display the message "User created with password: *<long-random string>*." That long random string is the password for the admin account, so copy it for later. If you don't see this message or need to reset the admin password, use the command **su - _gvm -s /bin/sh -c "gvmd --user=admin --new-password mypasswd; history -c"** and press **Enter**.
5. Type **gvm-check-setup** and press **Enter** to check the setup. If command finds problems, follow each instruction the command provides to correct the problem. Continue running the **gvm-check-setup** command until it reports that setup is okay.
6. OpenVAS uses community feeds (data updates) to keep its databases of CVEs and NVTs (Network Vulnerability Threats) current. Type **sudo gvm-feed-update** and press **Enter** to connect to the feeds and start downloading updates.
7. Type **sudo gvm-start** and press **Enter** to make sure the Open VAS services are running. This command may also automatically open your web browser to the OpenVAS logon page.
8. When OpenVAS is installed and started, you can access it by opening your web browser and browsing to **https://127.0.0.1:9392**. Use **admin** for the username and the long random string you copied in Step 4 for the password. Step 4 also has instructions for resetting this password. Once you authenticate, you'll see a window similar to what is shown in Figure 8-10. If your CVEs or NVTs graphs seem to show no data, you may have to wait until the feeds have updated or try some of the troubleshooting steps listed in the Note at the end of this activity.

Figure 8-10   OpenVAS dashboard

9. Point to the **Configuration** tab and select **Credentials** from the drop-down list. Select the **wand** above the key graphic to add a new credential. Allow your partner to enter his or her system's root credential in the New Credential form, shown in Figure 8-11. Click **Save** and allow OpenVAS a few minutes to process this request.

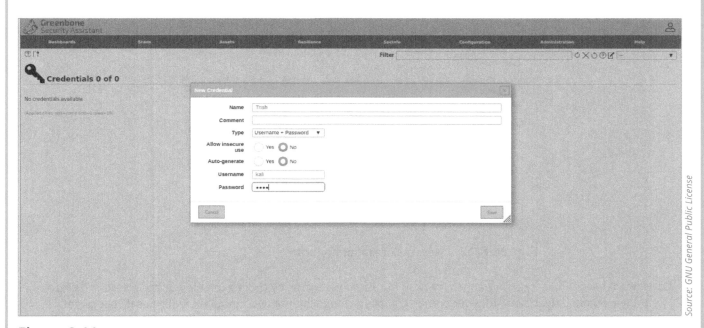

Figure 8-11   OpenVAS credential configuration

10. Point to the **Configuration** tab and select **Targets** from the drop-down list. Select the **light blue icon with the white star** to add a new target. Fill out the New Target form with your partner's system information. Name your task *partner* **computer** (replacing *partner* with your partner's name). Make sure to select the SSH credential you set up, similar to Figure 8-12.

Figure 8-12   OpenVAS new target definition

11. Point to the **Scan Management** tab and select **Tasks** from the drop-down menu. Next to "Tasks (total: 0)," select the **light blue icon with the white star** to add a new scan task. Name your task *partner* **scan** (replacing *partner* with your partner's name). Select your partner's computer in the Scan Targets drop-down list, and then click **Create Task**. Your task details should look similar to Figure 8-13.

Figure 8-13   New task creation for scan

12. Now that everything is set up, launch the scan from the Scans page by clicking the **Play** button (black and white triangle pointing right). Wait for your scan to complete. You might not find many vulnerabilities if your target system is up to date.

13. When the scan is complete, view the results by clicking the **1** next to **Reports**. To dig in deeper, click the date and time of the scan.
14. Using the information OpenVAS discovered, write down the most critical vulnerability on your target system and explain why it is critical. Include the CVE reference ID. What recommendation does OpenVAS make to fix this vulnerability?
15. To exit OpenVAS, close the window. When prompted to save the report, click **No**, and then click **Quit** in the OpenVAS Setup dialog box. Leave Linux running for the next activity.

NOTE

To make sure your OpenVAS CVE and NVT data feeds are updated, you can select CVEs or NVTs from the OpenVAS SecInfo menu. If either show no data, try the following steps:

1. Exit the OpenVAS/GVM interface by closing the browser.
2. Open a Terminal shell, enter the command **gvm-stop**, and then press **Enter**.
3. Type **sudo runuser -u _gvm – greenbone-nvt-sync –rsync** and press **Enter**. This command attempts to synchronize/update the NVT database. (It takes a few minutes to complete.)
4. Type **sudo greenbone-scapdata-sync** and press **Enter**. This command attempts to synchronize/update the SCAP database. (It takes a few minutes to complete.)
5. Type **sudo greenbone-certdata-sync** and press **Enter**. This command attempts to synchronize/update the CERT database. (It takes a few minutes to complete.)
6. Restart Kali Linux by typing **sudo reboot** and pressing **Enter**.
7. Log on to Kali Linux again and in a Terminal shell, type **gvm-start** and press **Enter**.

After attackers discover a vulnerability, they can go to a website describing exploits that take advantage of the vulnerability. In Activity 8-4, you visit another website with information on exploits as well as many articles and tools for security testers.

NOTE

Some software packages in your Kali installation may not be the most recent versions. Even after just a few months of not having patches installed, a Linux system can become a bonanza of vulnerabilities for an attacker. A security tester would probably recommend upgrading the version before spending time looking for vulnerabilities. You can use the `apt-get update && upgrade` command to update your Kali Linux system with the most current patches.

Activity 8-4: Discovering Exploits for Linux Systems

Time Required: 20 minutes
Objective: Research the Internet to discover Linux exploits.
Description: In this activity, you visit a website listing exploits you can use to attack different OSs. As a security tester, you should be aware of the resources available to both security testers and attackers.

1. If necessary, boot your computer into Kali Linux. Start a web browser and go to **www.exploit-db.com**.
2. On the EXPLOITS page, click the **Filters** button and choose **Linux** from the Platform drop-down list. (If you aren't on the EXPLOITS page, click the bug icon in the navigation pane on the left.) Choosing Linux filters the list to show only Linux exploits. In the Search box, enter **wget**. This further reduces the list to show exploits involving the `wget` Linux command.

3. In the Title column, click the **"GNU wget<1.18 – Arbitrary File Upload/ Remote Code Execution"** hyperlink dated 2016-07-06.

4. Read the information on the page for this exploit. It describes the vulnerability and provides Python code that can be used to exploit this vulnerability. (Scroll down to display the Python code.)

5. At the top of the page, click the **2016-4971** hyperlink below the CVE: heading to display the National Vulnerability Database where you can read official information about the vulnerability.

6. To determine the version of wget installed in your Kali Linux environment, open a Terminal shell, and then type **wget -V** and press **Enter**.

7. What version of wget is on your system?

8. Would the wget exploit you found work on your system?

9. Browse **exploit-db.com** for other Linux vulnerabilities.

Checking for Trojans

One method of attacking networks remotely is installing Trojan programs that record keystrokes and other processes without users' knowledge. Trojans can be installed after users click an attachment to an email message, or while users download a file from the Internet thinking it's a patch or a security fix for the OS they're running. Because the web server logs the IP address of all visitors, when users download a file from the Internet, attackers then know the IP address of the person who downloaded the Trojan. When installed on a computer, a Trojan can carry out many actions. Sometimes, it advertises enumerated victim information to a specific port, so the attacker needs to monitor or connect to that port to gather the information. Other times, a Trojan can be programmed to automatically connect back to an attacker machine. Most Trojans perform one or more of the following functions:

- Allow remote administration of the attacked system
- Create a hidden file server on the attacked computer so that files can be uploaded and downloaded without the user's knowledge
- Steal passwords and enumerate installed software from the attacked system and send them to the attacker
- Log all keystrokes a user enters and email the results to the attacker or store them in a hidden file the attacker can access remotely
- Encrypt all of the user's files and hold them ransom
- Destroy all of the data on a victim's system

Linux Trojan programs are sometimes disguised as legitimate programs, such as df or tar, but contain program code that can wipe out file systems on a Linux computer or allow for remote administration. Trojans are more difficult to detect today because programmers develop them to make legitimate calls on outbound ports that an IDS or a firewall wouldn't normally detect. Because the generated traffic looks just like normal network traffic, the Trojan is difficult to detect. For example, a Trojan called Harry makes HTTPS POST requests over port 443. These requests are not unusual on a network. The web server could then be configured to issue commands that are carried out on a Linux computer. The HTTPS traffic appears to be normal network traffic, but the commands sent from the web server could contain other commands requesting that the attacked computer download or copy sensitive files to a remote web server. Some recent Trojans are controlled by encoded, or even encrypted, commands that attackers post on social networking websites. To someone monitoring network traffic coming from these infected systems, the activity might look like a normal user browsing through Facebook or Twitter, for example.

Protecting Linux computers against Trojans that IT professionals have already identified is easier. For example, the Linux.Backdoor.Kaiten Trojan logs on to an Internet Relay Chat (IRC) site automatically and waits for commands from the attacker (controller). Linux antivirus software from McAfee, Sophos, and Symantec can detect this backdoor Trojan.

Even more dangerous are rootkits containing Trojan binary programs ready to be installed by an intruder who has gained root access to a system. Attackers can then hide the tools they use to perform further attacks on the system and have access to backdoor programs. A common Linux rootkit is Linux Rootkit 5 (LRK5), but malware coders create other rootkits almost daily. When a rootkit is installed, legitimate commands are replaced with Trojan programs. For example, if the LRK5 rootkit is installed on a Linux computer, entering the Trojan `killall` command allows the attacker's processes to continue running, even though the Linux administrator thinks all processes were killed. The `ls` command doesn't show files the attacker uses, and the `netstat` command doesn't show suspicious network connections the attacker makes. So everything looks normal to Linux administrators even though they're using Trojan commands.

Activity 8-5: Using Tools to Find Linux Rootkits

Time Required: 15 minutes

Objective: Learn how to find Linux rootkits on the Internet and use a rootkit-checking program.

Description: Attackers can easily locate rootkits for many Linux platforms. In this activity, you visit the www.packetstormsecurity.org website, which has thousands of tools and exploits that attackers or security professionals can use. You also run a rootkit detection program included with Kali Linux to find rootkits running on your system.

1. If necessary, boot your computer into Linux, start a web browser, and go to **www.packetstormsecurity.org**.
2. On the home page, click **Search** in the navigation bar, type **LRK5**, and then press **Enter**. The results list file archives containing code examples that demonstrate the LRK5 exploit.
3. Look through the list for Linux Rootkit 5. The description includes some Linux commands that are hijacked by a Trojan when using this rootkit. List five of these commands.
4. IBM also provides a free service called IBM X-Force Exchange, though you must sign up to use it. IBM X-Force Exchange is a threat intelligence platform where you can look up and share information regarding cybersecurity threats. Go to **https://exchange.xforce.ibmcloud.com/** to sign up, and then do a keyword search for **lojax**. Lojax is another rootkit with a specific claim to fame. What is it about Lojax that makes it unique?
5. Open a Terminal shell, and then type **chkrootkit** and press **Enter** to check for rootkits on your system. Do you recognize any of the Linux commands you wrote down in Step 3?
6. Log off the Linux session but leave your computer running for the case projects at the end of the module.

NOTE

As a security tester, you should check Linux systems periodically for installed rootkits.

More Countermeasures against Linux Attacks

You've learned about some defenses against Linux vulnerabilities, and in this section, you learn about additional countermeasures for protecting a Linux system, especially from remote attacks. The most critical tasks are training users, keeping up on kernel releases and security updates, and configuring systems to improve security. Having a handle on these tasks is an essential start to protecting any network.

User Awareness Training

Making it difficult for social engineers to get information from employees is the best place to start protecting Linux systems from remote attacks. User awareness training should include all employees, from office staff to the CEO. Tell users that no information should be given to outsiders, no matter how harmless the information might seem. Inform them that if attackers know what OS the company is running, they can use that information to conduct network attacks. Make users aware that many exploits can be downloaded from websites and emphasize that knowing which OS is running makes it easier for attackers to select an exploit.

Teach users to be suspicious of people asking questions about the systems they're using and to verify that they're talking to someone claiming to be from the IT Department. Asking for a phone number to call back is a good way to ensure that the person does work for the same company. A 30-minute training session on security procedures can alert users to how easily outsiders can compromise systems and learn proprietary information.

Keeping Current

Software vendors are in a never-ending battle to address vulnerabilities that attackers discover. As soon as a bug or vulnerability is discovered and posted on the Internet, OS vendors usually notify customers of upgrades or patches. Installing these fixes promptly is essential to protect your system.

Most Linux distributions now display warnings to inform users when they're running outdated versions. The warnings in the latest versions of Fedora and Ubuntu Linux are hard to ignore. Figure 8-14 shows the warning displayed when a user logs on to a Ubuntu 20 Linux system that isn't current.

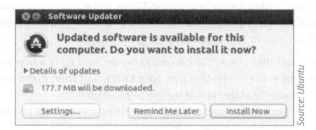

Figure 8-14   Ubuntu Linux Software Updater message

Secure Configuration

Many methods and tools can be used to configure a Linux system to help prevent intrusions. Vulnerability scanners not only detect missing patches, but also help identify when a system is configured poorly. You should use built-in Linux tools, too. Security Enhanced Linux (SELinux), a National Security Agency (NSA) project, is now built into many of the main Linux distributions. SELinux contains several features and modules that use **Mandatory Access Control (MAC)**, an OS security mechanism that enforces access rules based on privileges for interactions between processes, files, and users. If an intrusion happens on a system running SELinux, it's less likely the intruder will be able to take complete control of the system. Classes from enterprise Linux vendors cover use of this tool, and you can find more information at https://en.wikipedia.org/wiki/Security-Enhanced_Linux or by searching for SELinux on any Linux distribution website.

One of the best ways to measure and report objectively on how an OS is secured is to use the free benchmark PDFs and tools provided by the Center for Internet Security (CIS, www.cisecurity.org/cybersecurity-tools/). These benchmarks are available for many versions of *nix and Windows. When you take the time to work through securing a Linux OS by following recommendations in the CIS benchmark, your knowledge of Linux security, and Linux in general, will improve.

Finally, Forcepoint's OS lockdown tool, formerly known as Security Blanket, is now an open-source project called "OS Lockdown."

OS Lockdown is used to harden systems by aligning settings with published STIGs (Security Technical Implementation Guides), custom profiles built from STIGs, or from scratch. OS Lockdown provides the ability to audit systems against variations from those profiles. As an open-source tool, OS Lockdown is free to use. You can install OS Lockdown on Red Hat, CentOS, or Solaris *nix systems to tighten the system's security configuration by using templates. If your client is required to follow certain security policies, OS Lockdown can secure systems quickly and save *nix system administrators from hours of manual configuration work. OS Lockdown can be described as the *nix equivalent of using Windows group policies.

MODULE SUMMARY

- Fresh installations of Windows OSs that don't have their default settings changed present serious vulnerabilities that attackers can exploit. The CVE website is a good place to start when checking for Windows vulnerabilities.
- Vulnerabilities in Windows file systems include lack of ACL support in FAT and risk of malicious ADSs in NTFS.
- Other Windows vulnerabilities involve RPC, an interprocess communication mechanism that allows a program running on one host to run code on a remote host; NetBIOS, which is still used for backward compatibility; and SMB, which is also still used for backward compatibility and contains a vulnerability that enables attackers to intercept SMB traffic and collect usernames and password hashes.
- In Windows, null sessions and default installations can leave passwords blank and resources unprotected, causing major problems.
- Not only can operating systems have vulnerabilities that can be exploited, but applications can be vulnerable, too. For example, older versions of Microsoft SQL Server have a critical SQL vulnerability called a null SA password that enables remote users to gain System Administrator (SA) access through the SA account on the server.
- Buffer overflow attacks can allow attackers to run arbitrary code.
- Users represent a major security vulnerability, so creating a comprehensive password policy and having user awareness training programs are essential.
- Many tools are available for discovering vulnerabilities in Windows systems, such as Nessus. Learning to use more than one tool is essential.
- Steps you can recommend to secure systems include keeping systems updated with the most current patches and updates, running antivirus tools, enabling logging and reviewing logs regularly, disabling unused or unneeded services, and filtering out unnecessary ports.
- Vulnerabilities of the Linux OS can be discovered with security tools, such as OpenVAS, and at the CVE website.
- To address the issue of interoperability, a group of programmers created Samba as an open-source implementation of CIFS.
- Tools such as chkrootkit can detect rootkits installed on Linux systems.
- Built-in Linux tools, such as SELinux, are available for configuring systems securely. In addition, free benchmark tools are available from the Center for Internet Security, and commercial tools with templates can be used to tighten security configurations quickly and easily.

Key Terms

attack surface
Common Internet File System (CIFS)
domain controllers
Mandatory Access Control (MAC)

NetBIOS Extended User Interface (NetBEUI)
Remote Procedure Call (RPC)
Samba
Server Message Block (SMB)

System Center Configuration Manager (SCCM)
Systems Management Server (SMS)
Windows Software Update Services (WSUS)

Review Questions

1. Use Nessus Essentials to perform a web application test scan of the computer where Nessus Essentials is installed. The Nessus Essential interface is a web application, so you are having Nessus test itself. Write a three-paragraph report that details the vulnerabilities found, the CVEs or known exploits they map to, and suggested fixes.

2. In Windows Server 2016, the administrator must enable IIS manually to use it. True or false?
   a. True
   b. False

3. Windows OSs are vulnerable to the Conficker worm because of which of the following?
   a. Arbitrary code
   b. SQL buffer overflow
   c. Blank password
   d. RPC vulnerability

4. Which of the following is a well-known SMB hacking tool? (Choose all that apply.)
   a. SMBRelay
   b. SMBsnag
   c. L0phtcrack's SMB Packet Capture utility
   d. NTPass

5. Which ports should be filtered out to protect a network from SMB attacks?
   a. 134 to 138 and 445
   b. 135, 139, and 443
   c. 137 to 139 and 445
   d. 53 TCP/UDP and 445 UDP

6. For a Windows computer to be able to access a *nix resource, CIFS must be enabled on at least one of the systems. True or false?
   a. True
   b. False

7. Applications written in which programming language are especially vulnerable to buffer overflow attacks? (Choose all that apply.)
   a. C
   b. Perl
   c. C++
   d. Java

8. Which of the following is the most efficient way to determine which OS a company is using?
   a. Run Nmap or other port-scanning programs.
   b. Use the Whois database.
   c. Install a sniffer on the company's network segment.
   d. Call the company and ask.

9. List three measures for protecting systems on any network.

10. Employees should be able to install programs on their company computers as long as the programs aren't copyrighted. True or false?
    a. True
    b. False

11. Which of the following is an OS security mechanism that enforces access rules based on privileges for interactions between processes, files, and users?
    a. MBSA
    b. Mandatory Access Control
    c. Server Message Block
    d. Systems Management Server

12. A good password policy should include which of the following? (Choose all that apply.)
    a. Specifies a minimum password length
    b. Mandates password complexity
    c. States that passwords never expire
    d. Recommends writing down passwords to prevent forgetting them

13. Linux antivirus software can't detect backdoor Trojans. True or false?
    a. True
    b. False

14. Which program can detect rootkits on *nix systems?
    a. chkrootkit
    b. rktdetect
    c. SELinux
    d. Ionx

15. Which organization offers free benchmark information for Windows and Linux?
    a. PacketStorm Security
    b. CVE
    c. Center for Internet Security
    d. Trusted Security Solutions

16. Use OpenVAS to scan a computer running the Windows operating system. Write a three-paragraph report which details the vulnerabilities found, what CVEs or known exploits they map to, and suggested fixes.

17. Use Nessus Essentials to scan a computer running the Linux operating system. Write a three-paragraph report which details the vulnerabilities found, the CVEs or known exploits they map to, and suggested fixes.

Case Projects

Case Project 8-1: Securing an Older Linux OS

After conducting footprinting and using social-engineering techniques on the Alexander Rocco network, you have determined that the company is running several applications on Linux computers. You also discover that the payroll system runs on several Red Hat Enterprise Linux 6.10 (RHEL 6.10) servers. You need to ensure that this version will be supported with patches from the vendor until the new payroll system is installed in 2022. Based on this information, write a brief report stating whether the systems can be secured until they're replaced in 2022, and include recommendations for securing these systems.

Case Project 8-2: Detecting Unauthorized Applications

In conducting a review of the OSs running on the Alexander Rocco network, you detect a program that appears to be unauthorized. No one in the department knows how this program got on the Linux computer. The department manager thinks the program was installed before his start date three years ago. When you review the program's source code, you discover that it contains a buffer overflow vulnerability. Based on this information, write a report to the IT manager stating what course of action should be taken and listing recommendations for management.

Case Project 8-3: Validating Password Strength for Alexander Rocco Corporation

After discovering that most computers and servers at Alexander Rocco run many different versions of Windows, your supervisor has asked you to write a report on the issue of password vulnerabilities. Write a one-page memo to your supervisor describing the password-cracking areas you will test. Your memo should be based on the information you find in Section 11, "Password Cracking," of the OSSTMM.

EMBEDDED OPERATING SYSTEMS: THE HIDDEN THREAT

After reading this module and completing the exercises, you will be able to:

1 Explain what embedded operating systems are and where they're used

2 Describe the Internet of Things (IoT) and other embedded operating systems

3 Identify vulnerabilities of embedded operating systems and best practices for protecting them

Embedded systems include their own operating system, called an "embedded operating system," which is the focus of this module. Many people use a global positioning system (GPS) device or navigation system to find a bank so that they can withdraw cash from an ATM and don't realize that both the GPS device and ATM may be embedded systems that use an embedded operating system (OS). Internet-connected appliances (such as smart TVs) are also embedded systems and are typically referred to as IoT devices. Security professionals should understand that any vulnerability in a PC or server OS might exist for its embedded counterpart. For example, many embedded OSs contain a web server that's potentially vulnerable to attack. If the web server software is required for the device to operate correctly, you might have a problem. In fact, the problem can be worse on an embedded system because of hardware limitations and software compatibility. Software developers often omit many security checks on embedded systems, such as input validation, so that they can "fit" the code on the chip. In addition, pressures to get a product to market as soon as possible may result in less secure code and limited security testing. You can read more about the challenges of developing and securing embedded systems in the following BlackBerry QNX article: https://blackberry.qnx.com/en/embedded-system-security/ultimate-guide/.

When conducting security tests for a company, don't ignore embedded systems. You should not overlook devices because they're small, perform simple tasks, or haven't been exploited in the past. As a security tester, part of your job will be identifying potential security problems, and to do this, you need to think outside the box. With embedded OS vulnerabilities, you might have to start thinking inside the "box," too.

INTRODUCTION TO EMBEDDED OPERATING SYSTEMS

At its most basic, an embedded system is any computer system that isn't a general-purpose PC or server. In addition to GPS devices and some ATMs, embedded systems are found in a wide array of electronic consumer and industrial products: toys, kitchen appliances, printers, industrial control systems, spacecraft, and scientific equipment. An embedded operating system (OS) can be a small program developed specifically for use with embedded systems, or it can be a stripped-down version of an OS commonly used on general-purpose computers. Embedded OSs are usually designed to be small and efficient, so they don't have some functions that general-purpose OSs do, particularly if the specialized applications they run don't use these features. One type of specialized embedded OS is a real-time operating system (RTOS), typically used in devices such as programmable thermostats, appliance controls, and even spacecraft. If you're piloting an F-35 fighter jet, you'll certainly appreciate that the embedded RTOS in your aircraft is designed with an algorithm aimed at multitasking and responding predictably. RTOSs are also found in high-end kitchen ovens, heart pacemakers, and just about every new motor vehicle.

SECURITY BYTES

As you become acquainted with devices that use embedded OSs, you need to think the way attackers do. What system could you attack that could affect hundreds of systems? Thousands of systems? Something as simple as an attack on a company's heating, ventilation, and air-conditioning (HVAC) system—or even a thermostat, for that matter—could do serious harm to the network infrastructure.

With only a cursory survey of a typical corporate building, you can find many embedded systems, including firewalls, switches, routers, web-filtering appliances, network-attached storage (NAS) devices, networked power switches, printers, scanners, copy machines, video projectors, uninterruptible power supply (UPS) consoles, Voice over IP (VoIP) phones and voicemail systems, thermostats, HVAC systems, fire suppression systems, closed-circuit TV systems, elevator management systems, video teleconferencing workstations and consoles, and intercom systems. How many embedded systems can you identify in the building you're in right now?

SECURITY BYTES

Hacking a Model 3 Tesla was the final test in the 2019 Pwn2Own annual hacking event. The White hat hacking team of Amat Cama and Richard Zhu (who go by the team name of Fluoracetate) only needed a few minutes and a few lines of code to hack the Tesla. They exploited a weakness in the browser of the "infotainment" system, and soon their commands were displayed on the Tesla's center console screen. Fluoracetate won most of the challenges they entered and left the competition with $375,000 in prize money and a brand new Tesla. The security flaw was reported to Tesla, and the car company issued a patch to eliminate the vulnerability.

Many dismiss the topic of embedded device security to focus on more popular security issues. Most of the media emphasis is on threats that people can understand and relate to, such as the latest network worm, the most recent Windows attack, or the Colonial Pipeline cyber attack. However, embedded systems are in all networks and perform essential functions, such as routing network traffic and blocking suspicious packets. Many believe that because devices use an embedded OS, no one would bother to attack them or take the time and effort to understand how they work. In fact, the opposite is often the case. For example, three San Francisco hackers purchased several parking meters on eBay to do just that—understand how the devices work. They took apart the parking meters looking for security features and ways to access the internal hardware from the outside, such as an external USB or serial port. They also tried to determine whether someone could jam a card or gum, for example, into the device to disable it and investigated what type of smart card could be inserted, if any. Their goal was to convince the City of San Francisco that a vulnerability study of the parking meter system was worthwhile.

Recently, security researchers were able to reverse-engineer the software on a popular firewall's chipset; software residing on a chip is commonly referred to as firmware. The researchers then inserted modified software to control the firewall's behavior. Hackers who do this could modify a firewall so that they can copy network traffic passing through an interface and give an external IP address full access through the firewall. They can also configure the firewall so that these intrusions would not be detected or generate a single log entry. As the value and quantity of targets with embedded systems increase, attackers will start shifting their focus to embedded systems.

Activity 9-1: Researching Attacks on a Car and a Smart TV

Time Required: 30 minutes

Objective: Learn more about potential attacks on embedded systems.

Descriptions: In 2013, Charlie Miler and Chris Valasek demonstrated they could control the steering wheel and the brakes of a vehicle they were plugged into remotely. In 2015, they proved that, from the comfort of their home, they could hack into a Jeep Cherokee driving on the highway. This remote attack turned a few heads in the industry and, luckily, was responsibly reported by Charlie and Chris before any real damage could be done.

In 2019, hackers took advantage of vulnerable Chromecast and Google Home devices to display messages on consumer TVs promoting the well-known YouTube star PewDiePie. The Swedish-born comedian and video game commentator, whose real name is Felix Kjellberg, was being challenged by T-Series, an Indian music record label and film company, for the top YouTube spot. At the time, both YouTubers' channels had approximately 73 million subscribers.

1. In Windows, start your web browser and go to **www.google.com**.
2. In the search text box, type **Jeep Hack 2015** and press **Enter**.
3. Select the entry from **www.wired.com** and read the article. When you're finished, use the back arrow to return to the search results page.
4. Scroll through the search results and spend time reading two or three other articles about the attack.
5. What attack vector did the hackers use? Do you think the designers could have done something to prevent the attack?
6. Do you think the articles you read gave information others could use to perform similar hacks in the future? Explain your answer.
7. What could the hackers have done if they were malicious?
8. Repeat steps 1–7, but this time search for **Pewdiepie tv hack** and read the https://threatpost.com article.
9. When you're finished, leave the web browser open for the next activity.

As you learned in this activity, the work of only two people could have wreaked havoc on highways nationwide. The work of two other people pranked smart TVs to display an unsolicited message. Your job as a security tester is to try to prevent attacks like these.

WINDOWS AND OTHER EMBEDDED OPERATING SYSTEMS

Recycling common code and reusing technologies are sound software engineering practices. After all, why should you pay a developer to write the same code repeatedly if you can just reuse it? Unfortunately, these practices introduce common points of failure in many products. Many viruses, worms, Trojans, and other attack vectors take advantage of shared code, which increases the impact a single vulnerability can have. You have already learned about vulnerabilities in Windows and Linux. Any vulnerability in these OSs might also exist in the embedded version. For example, the embedded versions of Windows 10 and Windows Server 2012 contain the same software and, with few exceptions, operate the same way as their non-embedded counterparts. Windows XP had a very popular embedded release, which many products continue to use even after extended support expired in January of 2016.

Windows CE was a trimmed-down version of the Windows desktop OS and shouldn't be confused with Windows Embedded 8 or Windows 10 IoT. Some Windows CE source code is available to the public, and much of the rest of it is available to hardware vendors, partners, and developers, based on their licensing level. Windows CE is rare now, but still worth knowing about. Windows Mobile, an old OS based on Windows CE, was designed for use in products such as personal data assistants (PDAs) and smartphones. Now, those legacy devices run a slightly modified version of Windows 10.

Unlike Windows CE, Windows 10 IoT provides the full Windows API and can perform many of the same tasks that the PC version can, although Windows 10 IoT does not have a PC interface. It's designed for use on commodity devices like Raspberry Pi, a small, affordable computer. In addition to commodity devices, Windows 10 IoT can underlie any of the systems mentioned earlier (i.e., GPSs, ATMs, and printers). Windows 10 IoT was designed to make things easy for developers.

As you know, many tools are available for discovering vulnerabilities in Windows systems. You can run some on an embedded OS, and others can be used remotely from the network to discover vulnerabilities in a Windows embedded OS.

Other Proprietary Embedded OSs

VxWorks is a widely used embedded real-time OS developed by Wind River Systems. It's used in many environments and applications and is designed to run efficiently on minimal hardware. In the next activity, you research the variety of systems powered by VxWorks and other embedded OSs. Figure 9-1 shows creating an embedded OS image with VxWorks Workbench, a development toolkit, running on the desktop version of Fedora Linux.

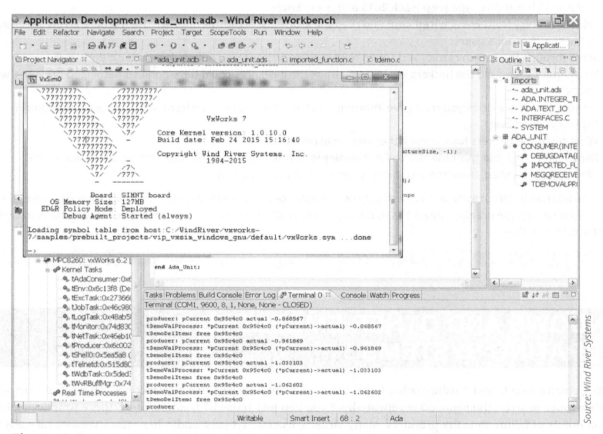

Figure 9-1 Creating an embedded OS image in Wind River's VxWorks Workbench

To give you an idea of the variety of systems using VxWorks, here's a partial list:

- Clementine spacecraft
- Deep Impact space probe
- James Webb Space Telescope (in development)
- Mars exploration rovers *Spirit* and *Opportunity*
- Mars *Perseverance* Lander
- Mars *Phoenix* Lander
- Mars *Reconnaissance* Orbiter

- Radvision 3G communication equipment
- Stardust spacecraft
- SAUVIM (a submersible spacecraft designed for deep-ocean operations)

Green Hill Software also produces a variety of embedded OSs. It designed an embedded OS for the F-35 Joint Strike Fighter as well as an embedded OS certified to run multiple levels of classification (such as unclassified, secret, and top secret) on the same CPU without leakage between levels. This type of OS is called **multiple independent levels of security/safety (MILS)**. The U.S. military uses MILS OSs in high-security environments, and other organizations, such as those controlling nuclear power or municipal sewage plants, use them when separating privileges and functions is crucial. Green Hill also designs embedded OS code used in printers, routers, switches, barcode scanners, and radios. The aforementioned OSs use a microkernel, which sacrifices flexibility for simplicity and fewer hardware resources.

QNX, from QNX Software Systems, is a commercial RTOS used in Cisco's ultrahigh-availability routers and in Logitech universal remotes. Another proprietary embedded OS is Real-Time Executive for Multiprocessor Systems (RTEMS), an open-source embedded OS used in space systems because it supports processors designed specifically to operate in space. It's currently running on the Mars *Reconnaissance* Orbiter along with VxWorks. NASA has improved this spacecraft's survivability by using several small embedded OSs tailored for specific functions instead of a huge monolithic kernel OS that controls every function. However, using multiple embedded OSs also increases the attack surface. Figure 9-2 illustrates the differences in size and resource requirements between monolithic kernel and microkernel OSs.

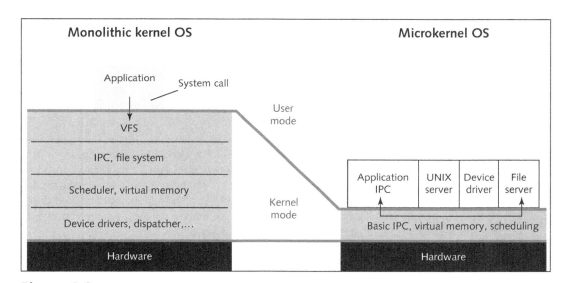

Figure 9-2   Monolithic kernel versus microkernel OSs

*Nix Embedded OSs

Embedded Linux is an example of a monolithic OS used in a multitude of industrial, medical, and consumer items. Embedded versions of Linux and other *nix OSs can be tailored for devices with limited memory or hard drive capacity, such as mobile phones. An advantage of a monolithic kernel is that it can support the widest variety of hardware and allows adding features by using dynamic kernel modules. Other examples of commercial products with *nix embedded OSs are Cisco switches and routers, TomTom and Garmin GPS devices, media players, and medical instruments. Android smartphones and iPhones have a *nix embedded OS at their cores.

In addition to VxWorks, Wind River produces a Linux OS for embedded systems called Wind River Linux. Wind River Linux is a Linux variant RTOS that's suitable for embedded applications requiring a guaranteed response in a mathematically predictable manner.

NOTE

If you want to play around with an RTOS, you can download a copy of FreeRTOS from SourceForge (https://sourceforge.net/projects/freertos/files/FreeRTOS).

Another embedded Linux OS that you can download for use at home is dd-wrt (https://dd-wrt.com/). Initially designed for use on the Linksys WRT54G wireless, this OS can be run on most small office or home routers. Figure 9-3 shows its setup interface.

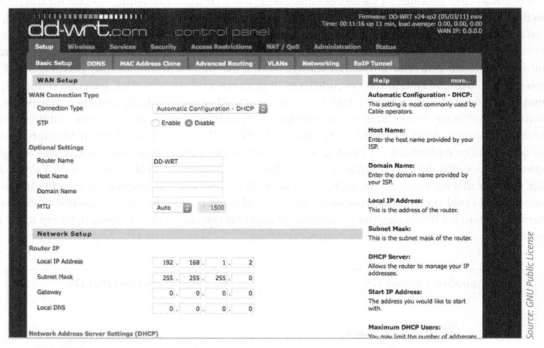

Figure 9-3   Control panel for dd-wrt

 **CAUTION**   Home router embedded systems, such as the Linksys WRT54G, were the target of a large-scale botnet worm attack. Called psyb0t (or the Network Bluepill), this worm spread by exploiting outdated or poorly configured router OSs that contained easy-to-guess passwords. After psyb0t infected tens of thousands of systems, attackers used it to launch distributed denial-of-service (DDoS) or vulnerability exploitation attacks. If you have a wireless router at home, do you know whether it's protected against threats such as psyb0t?

As you have seen, embedded OSs are everywhere on Earth—and beyond, in some cases. As a security tester, you need to know about vulnerabilities in these systems. In the next activity, you research some products using embedded OSs and learn more about their vulnerabilities.

Activity 9-2: Researching Products with Embedded OSs

Time Required: 40 minutes

Objective: Search vulnerability databases to find products using vulnerable embedded OSs.

Description: Until now, most security professionals had little knowledge of the many products that use embedded OSs. In this activity, you search the National Vulnerability Database (NVD) for products using embedded OSs.

1. In Windows, start your web browser, if necessary, and go to **https://nvd.nist.gov**.
2. Click the **NVD MENU** button and then click **SEARCH**.
3. Click the **Vulnerabilities – CVE** button to display the Search Vulnerability Database page.
4. Type **vxworks** in the Keyword Search text box and press **Enter**.
5. Scroll through the search results, and spend some time reading about vulnerabilities of devices that use VxWorks OSs.

6. Continue your research by searching for more terms related to embedded OSs, such as **embedded Linux**, **QNX**, **Netscreen**, **Lexmark**, **Jetdirect**, **Android**, **Canon printers**, **Linksys**, **VOIP**, **dd-wrt**, **iPhone**, **Netgear**, **Foundry**, **Cisco**, and **Nortel**. Write down some examples you find of devices with embedded OSs and describe the vulnerabilities briefly. Spend no more than 20 minutes researching the terms.

7. How many embedded devices and vulnerabilities were you able to find in 20 minutes? Are any of these vulnerable devices likely to be found in a large company or government agency? How about at home?

8. Leave your web browser open for the next activity.

VULNERABILITIES OF EMBEDDED OSs

Some security professionals can remember when computer attacks typically caused damage equivalent to graffiti on a building. Offensive, yes, but not damaging enough to concern most security professionals. However, the impact of attacks has become more serious, and embedded OSs are no exception. In Activity 9-2, you found that many embedded OSs have vulnerabilities. Websites such as www.exploit-db.com and www.packetstormsecurity.org have information on what hackers are doing with these vulnerabilities.

Many hackers today want more than just notoriety, however; they're criminals looking for ways to steal money. One way to profit from hacking is to attack devices where cash is stored and dispensed by a computer: ATMs. ATMs are vulnerable to attacks upon their software performed locally or remotely, or to physical attacks such as using card skimmers or even stealing the machines. At the Black Hat conference in 2010, a security researcher, Barnaby Jack of Juniper Networks, famously demonstrated a vulnerability in a line of popular ATMs that made both local and remote attacks possible. He had two ATMs on stage that he hacked, causing them to spew out dozens of crisp bills. He hacked one machine remotely over a network, and he plugged a USB stick into a port on the other ATM to employ malware. More recently, in 2021, security researchers have sounded the alarm that near field communication readers (NFCs) on ATMs are a vulnerability. NFC is a convenience feature that allows you to tap or wave your bank card on or near a reader device instead of inserting it into the ATM. By using a smartphone with malicious software on it, the NFCs can be exploited to crash the ATM, lock it up in a ransomware attack, hack it to extract credit card data, or jackpot the ATM to have it spew out money. You research ATM vulnerabilities in Activity 9-3.

SECURITY BYTES

As a security tester, you need to remember that sometimes the biggest security threat to an organization is its employees. System administrators, network managers, and technicians often have unfettered, and unmonitored, access to a company's most critical IT components. They're aware of any gaps in existing security processes and know how to cover up illegal activities. Following the "least privileges principle" can help reduce the insider threat, however. This principle specifies giving personnel only the access they need to perform their job duties and revoking access as soon as they no longer need it.

Activity 9-3: Researching ATM Vulnerabilities

Time Required: 20 minutes

Objective: Examine ATM vulnerabilities.

Description: As a security tester, you must be aware of attacks that can occur on systems other than the usual workstations and servers. If a bank contracts you to conduct a security test, and you neglect to research possible attacks on ATMs, you might find yourself in an embarrassing situation if a major attack results in the bank losing millions of dollars. After reading several articles on ATMs, you should have a better awareness of the methods attackers are using to steal money from banks—without needing masks and guns.

1. Start your web browser, if necessary, and go to your favorite search engine. Type **Hacking ATM Machines with just a text** in the search text box, and press **Enter**.

2. An article in *The Hacker News* discusses how attackers can use malware and smartphones to make ATMs dispense cash. What OS is in use? What suggestion did the security company offer to reduce these risks?

3. Continue your search for more current articles on ATM hacking and vulnerabilities. In particular try to find the **wired.com** article about the WinPot ATM malware strain. Based on your research, what OSs do most ATMs use?

4. Leave your web browser open for the next activity.

Embedded OSs Are Everywhere

On the eve of the past millennium, experts warned of an imminent global catastrophe: Billions of embedded systems with the Y2K (for "Year 2000") software flaw would suddenly stop or fail when the clock struck midnight. These embedded systems were located everywhere, including in critical infrastructure controls for power, communications, transportation, and more, so enormous amounts of time and money were spent fixing the embedded systems to prevent potential disaster. Today, there are many more embedded devices to be concerned about than in 2000. These embedded devices don't have the Y2K software flaw, but they're under attack from hackers and terrorists who want to further their financial or political causes. This new threat is why addressing the security of embedded systems early in the design phase—not treating it as an afterthought—is essential.

Embedded OSs Are Networked

For reasons of efficiency and economy, connecting embedded systems to a network has advantages. Being able to manage systems and share services while keeping the amount of human resources and expertise to a minimum helps companies reduce costs. Gaining efficiency and reducing costs have a price, however: Any device added to a network infrastructure increases the potential for security problems. Security testers should address questions such as the following for every machine or device on a network:

- What Peripheral Component Interconnect (PCI) or USB devices are present?
- Where were they manufactured? Is the supply chain trustworthy?
- Which devices have embedded OSs stored in rewriteable (nonvolatile) memory? Rewriteable memory can be flashed (that is, erased and rewritten quickly).
- Which embedded OS is currently loaded on each device?
- Can you make sure the embedded OS hasn't been corrupted or subverted with malicious code? This check is called validating the embedded OS's integrity.

Embedded OSs Are Difficult to Patch

You have learned about the importance of keeping systems patched and antivirus software up to date. With general-purpose PC OSs, it's normal to wait for someone to identify a vulnerability, download and install the patch when it's available, and restart the system, if necessary. This approach doesn't work for many embedded OSs, however, because they must continue operating regardless of the threat, particularly in critical systems, such as power distribution, air traffic control, and medical life support.

Patching on general-purpose computers is usually simple but patching embedded OSs can be a problem. For example, many skilled system administrators know how to patch a web server for Linux, Windows, or Solaris UNIX OSs running on standard Sun or x86 PC hardware, but they might have no clue how to patch a web server running on a tiny chip (called a "16-bit micro-controller") inside a plastic box the size of a deck of cards. Another problem is that buffer overflow attacks might be successful on embedded OSs because few updates are released to correct vulnerabilities. Typically, manufacturers prefer that you upgrade the system rather than the embedded OS, so they might not release updates when vulnerabilities are discovered. Updating the embedded OS on some systems is difficult enough that your clients probably won't do it. Be prepared to explain the best course of action to your clients.

Remember that both general-purpose and embedded OSs use drivers to manage hardware devices. In both types of OSs, drivers are vulnerable to exploitation and occasionally need to be updated or patched. A while back, a vulnerability in drivers for the Intel wireless chipset made it possible to compromise wireless devices remotely. The vulnerability isn't surprising. What is surprising is that few system administrators updated these drivers because they never showed up in the list of "critical" OS patches in Windows Update.

One reason that some vendors of embedded OSs are using open-source software more often is that the cost of developing and patching an OS is shared by the entire open-source community, not just a handful of overworked programmers in a back office. To date, the total cost in programmer hours for developing and patching the Linux kernel is estimated at tens of billions of dollars. Having that much programming expertise available is hard for any company developing embedded systems to turn down. On the other hand, the monolithic Linux kernel was designed to offer the most flexibility and support for sophisticated features; for that reason, it's very large and has many code portions that might need to be patched as vulnerabilities are discovered. For sensitive embedded systems that need only a fraction of the features in the Linux kernel, the risk of having potential vulnerabilities might outweigh the benefits. In this situation, a proprietary kernel might be more suitable.

As a security tester, you might identify minor vulnerabilities in embedded OSs that are extremely expensive to fix. However, the amount of time and expertise an attacker would need to exploit this minor vulnerability is extremely high, too. For these types of vulnerabilities, you must weigh the cost of fixing the vulnerability against the importance of the information the embedded system controls. You might recommend not fixing the vulnerability because it's secure enough for the minor risk involved.

SECURITY BYTES

Heart rate monitors and MRI machines are examples of systems that run embedded Windows OSs. Often these systems can't be patched because they're certified at a specific revision level, or the manufacturer never provided a patch method. This problem was apparent when the Conficker worm infected numerous medical systems around the world. Even in embedded systems that weren't connected directly to the Internet, versions of Conficker spread through removable media. A simple data transfer with USB drives, for example, might be risky.

Embedded OSs Are in Networking Devices

Networking devices, such as routers and switches, usually have software and hardware designed for the tasks of transmitting information across networks. Originally, general-purpose computers were used to perform routing and switching, but high-speed networks now use specialized hardware and embedded OSs. In the past, Cisco mainly used proprietary code in its embedded systems. By using more open-source code, however, Cisco can release new product features more quickly. Cisco uses Linux kernels in its latest VoIP Call Manager appliances and Adaptive Security Appliance (ASA) firewall. Other embedded OSs for networking devices are modified *nix OSs. For example, Juniper and Extreme Networks OSs are based on UNIX.

You might wonder why anyone would bother hacking routers or other networking devices, as they don't contain corporate secrets and don't have lots of storage space or processing capacity that could be stolen. The short answer is that when attackers compromise a host, that's all they might get: a single host. When they compromise a router, they might be able to control every host on the network. From the router, attackers can map the entire network, modify packets to and from hosts, redirect traffic to and from other hosts or networks, attack other networks that are accessible from the compromised router, and make free phone calls with VoIP, if it's configured. In short, controlling a router can give attackers complete access to network resources.

To compromise an entire network through a router, attackers follow the usual methods of footprinting, scanning, and enumerating the target. Embedded OSs in routers are often susceptible to many of the same attacks that plague general-purpose OSs, ranging from simple password guessing to sophisticated buffer overflow attacks. A common vulnerability of routers and other network devices with built-in web management interfaces is the authentication bypass vulnerability. Attackers can take control of a network device or gather sensitive information from it by accessing the device with a specially crafted URL that bypasses the normal authentication mechanism. You might have found examples of authentication bypass vulnerabilities in Activity 9-2. After bypassing authentication, attackers can launch other network attacks by using the access they gained through compromising the router.

Embedded OSs Are in Network Peripherals

Peripheral devices on an organization's network can include printers, scanners, copiers, and networked fax devices. Devices performing more than one of these functions are called multifunction devices (MFDs), multifunction printers (MFPs), or multifunction copiers (MFCs). Usually, the only time system or network administrators think about an MFD is when they're troubleshooting one or adding one to the network. The rest of the time, these network peripherals are forgotten. They're rarely scanned for vulnerabilities or configured for security. MFDs have embedded OSs, however, and a lot of sensitive information is sent to these devices over the network, which makes them attractive targets to hackers. Network and system administrators need to pay attention to vulnerabilities in these devices and take steps to patch or reduce the risks. Information being printed, copied, scanned, and faxed can be susceptible to theft and modification. For example, a compromised MFD can be used to collect information and send it back to the attacker via the systems built-in FTP or email relay system.

Some sophisticated printers run embedded Windows OSs, so they could be infected by common malware, too. MFDs and print servers with hard drives can certainly be used to spread malware if they have network-accessible shares. In 2018, fans of YouTube celebrity PewDiePie hacked printers around the globe and remotely caused the printers to print posters in support of PewDiePie (see Figure 9-4). They later repeated the stunt but included a message urging victims to improve their security.

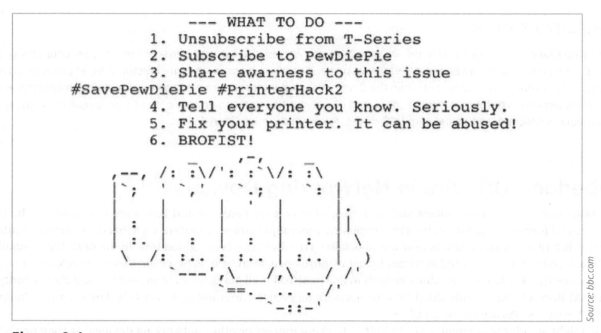

Figure 9-4   PewDiePie Printer Hack Output

In many older printers, all available networking protocols are enabled by default. If a printer is secured via its IP address, attackers could simply connect to it with a different protocol, such as IPX or AppleTalk. Because these printers also have default administrator usernames and passwords, unauthorized users can connect to them as administrators. Today, most printers have only TCP/IP enabled, but unfortunately, default administrator usernames and passwords are still configured. Printers should be reconfigured before connecting them to a network.

Finally, attackers might use social-engineering techniques to masquerade as support technicians so that they can gain physical access to MFDs and replace the printer's hard drive or embedded OS with one containing malicious code. Malicious insiders can also replace the firmware (embedded OS) with specially modified firmware, as shown in Figure 9-5.

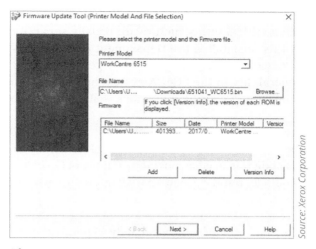

Figure 9-5   Firmware file being uploaded to a networked printer

SECURITY BYTES

Several years ago, a customer working for a large corporation located in Hawaii contacted Xerox Corporation's help desk. His complaint? Print jobs were now taking an inordinate amount of time. After only several minutes of troubleshooting, the technician determined that all print jobs sent to the local printer were also being routed to Eastern Europe.

Activity 9-4: Identifying Printer Vulnerabilities

Time Required: 30 minutes

Objective: Examine printer vulnerabilities.

Description: As security professionals become more competent at hardening computer and network systems, attackers must be creative in finding other weaknesses that give them access to systems. The Internet is a valuable resource for learning about the methods attackers are using now. As a security tester, you'll devote a lot of time to this type of research.

1. Start your web browser, if necessary, and go to your favorite search engine. Type **printer driver exploits** in the search text box, and then press **Enter**.
2. Read the article at the link www.zdnet.com/article/hp-patches-vulnerable-printer-driver-impacting-millions-of-devices. Since this article was written, have there been any improvements to address the risks of embedded OSs?
3. Give a brief description of the vulnerabilities and possible attacks mentioned in the article.
4. Read the article at the link www.darkreading.com/vulnerabilities-threats/significant-vulnerabilities-found-in-6-common-printer-brands. What are some reasons that printers are vulnerable? Which brands had the most vulnerabilities and which had the least? What solutions do the researchers suggest?
5. Exit your web browser.

Supervisory Control and Data Acquisition Systems

Supervisory control and data acquisition (SCADA) systems are used for equipment monitoring in large industries, such as public works and utilities, power generators and dams, transportation systems (such as FAA control towers), manufacturing—anywhere automation is critical. SCADA systems sometimes have many embedded systems as components, which might be vulnerable through the data fed in and out of them or through their embedded OSs.

In any case, it's no exaggeration to say the security of some SCADA systems is a life-or-death proposition. For this reason, SCADA systems controlling critical infrastructure are usually separated from the Internet by an "air gap." Can hackers still get in? To test this possibility, the Department of Homeland Security started Project Aurora to simulate a remote network attack against a large diesel-electric generator used in many U.S. power plants. Project Aurora was able to exploit a vulnerability in the SCADA system and caused the $1 million generator to tear itself apart. Imagine the devastating impact of a coordinated attack that could destroy hundreds of generators at power plants around the world.

In December of 2015, an attack on a Ukrainian power plant left about 700,000 people in the dark for a few hours. It was later uncovered that a piece of malicious code named "Black-Energy" was introduced to infect systems at the power plant. This same malicious code was used against the country of Georgia in 2008. There is still some confusion about how attackers caused the outage, but it's assumed they interacted with a SCADA system to interrupt the flow of power.

In May of 2021, a ransomware cyber attack forced American pipeline operator Colonial Pipeline to temporarily halt all pipeline operations. Colonial Pipeline provides approximately 45 percent of all fuel to the U.S. east coast. The attack led to fuel shortages and a spike in fuel prices. Colonial Pipeline paid a ransom of approximately 5 million dollars to the hackers to have their ransomed systems and data released.

Cell Phones, Smartphones, and Wearable Technology

Tapping a traditional phone line used to require a lot of time, expensive technical equipment, and a warrant. Even then, all you could do was listen to a conversation. Surprisingly, many people have the same security expectations of cell phones and smartphones.

Cell phone vulnerabilities include attackers listening to your phone calls, using your phone as a microphone, and "cloning" your phone's SIM card to make illegal international calls. Using these methods, attackers can find information that's useful for accessing your computer (or your company's network) and might even be able to steal trade or national security secrets.

Smartphones, such as Android devices and iPhones, combine the functions of what was once called a PDA and a cell phone. Security researchers and attackers have created Java-based viruses as well as code that could infect phones running Google Android, Windows Mobile, and the Apple iPhone OS (iOS). With the increasing amount of functionality available in smartphones, the line is blurring between embedded and general-purpose OSs. These OSs, similar to Windows and Red Hat, have vulnerabilities that can compromise your smartphone's security.

Wearable technology, such as smart watches and fitness trackers, also contain embedded operating systems that can be vulnerable to attack. Often wearable technologies interact with smartphones using Bluetooth. This interaction increases the number of ways a smartphone can be attacked (the attack surface), making it more vulnerable.

In 2020, the Blackhat conference revealed a new exploit chain named TiYunZong that can remotely root a wide range of Qualcomm-based Android devices. (To "root" an Android device means to change its operating system using administrator privileges.) In July 2015, the Stagefright Android vulnerabilities were released during the Blackhat conference in Las Vegas. The more serious of these vulnerabilities could be exploited with a malicious Multimedia Messaging Service (MMS) message. A victim phone would automatically download the malicious MMS message, and the attacker could take control of the device. Another vulnerability, also released in 2015, gave attackers a way to gather the fingerprints of exploited victims. While the fingerprint data is stored in a secure location, an attack could read information from the fingerprint sensor itself, exposing personal, biometric information to the attacker.

Trojans have also become a big concern in mobile application stores such as the Google Play Store and Apple App Store. An application can appear to be useful but steal information or processing power from your smartphone. For example, in March of 2021, Google removed 10 apps from the Play Store that contained droppers for financial Trojans. A dropper is malware used to deliver (drop) other malware payloads. Some of the removed applications were Cake VPN, Pacific VPN, BeatPlayer, QR/Barcode Scanner MAX, and QRecorder. These apps avoided Google's standard security protections by pulling malware from GitHub after installation.

If the phone company itself is the attacker, little can be done. In 2009, the national telecommunication company of an Arabian Gulf nation directed all its BlackBerry customers to install an application "to ensure continuous service quality." Customers who didn't comply were threatened with disconnection. Later analysis revealed that this application was a sophisticated spyware program that enabled phone company eavesdroppers to intercept all calls to and from BlackBerrys with this application installed.

Rootkits

Rootkits exist for Windows and *nix OSs, so embedded versions of these OSs are vulnerable to them, too. Rootkits can modify parts of the OS or install themselves as kernel modules, drivers, libraries, and even applications. Rootkit-detection tools and some antivirus software can detect rootkits and prevent them from being installed. However, the problem becomes more difficult if the OS has already been compromised. Installing these tools on an infected system doesn't normally trigger alerts because rootkits can monitor the OS for anti-rootkit tools and neutralize them. Rootkits that pose the biggest threat to any OS (embedded or general-purpose) are those that infect a device's firmware. They're more dangerous because they tend to be extremely small, are loaded in low-level nonvolatile storage that anti-rootkit tools can't access readily, and can persist even after the hard drive has been reformatted. Defenses against low-level rootkits include using Trusted Platform Module (TPM), a cryptographic firmware boot-check processor installed on many recent computer systems. TPM ensures that the OS hasn't been subverted or corrupted, such as with a firmware rootkit. TPM is now the ISO standard ISO/IEC 11889. For more information on this standard, visit www.iso.org.

A computer might have several megabytes of flash ROM on the motherboard and controller cards, such as the Ethernet controller. Firmware rootkits are hard to detect because the code for firmware often isn't checked for possible corruption. Insider hacking is harder to detect with malicious code hidden in a system's flash memory. Disgruntled employees, for example, could install a BIOS-based rootkit in the flash memory of their company computers before they leave the company. They could then use this BIOS rootkit, which would survive having the OS reinstalled, to gain access to the corporate network later.

SECURITY BYTES

For demonstration purposes, Microsoft and University of Michigan researchers developed a BIOS-level rootkit for PCs, called SubVirt, that can survive hard disk replacement and OS reinstallation. SubVirt modifies the boot sequence and loads itself before the OS so that it can operate outside the OS and remain hidden from many rootkit-detection tools. By exploiting hardware virtualization technology from CPU manufacturers, SubVirt can load the original OS as a virtual machine and then intercept the OS's calls to hardware.

What if the system you're using is compromised before it's even purchased? Criminals in Europe have tampered with credit card machines while they're still in the supply chain. The compromised devices continue to function like normal credit card readers with one notable exception: They copy customers' credit card information and transmit it to criminals via a cell phone network. The only way to get rid of these types of infections is to flash (rewrite) the BIOS with a known clean copy, wipe the hard drive, and reload the OS from clean installation media. These tasks can be hugely expensive in both time and money, but at least a method for removing the malware is available.

A popular laptop theft-recovery service, LoJack for Laptops, has some design-level vulnerabilities that rootkits can exploit. Researchers from Core Security Technologies reconfigured LoJack with a custom BIOS rootkit that takes advantage of LoJack's vulnerabilities. Because the infection resides in the computer's BIOS, it persists even after the OS is reinstalled or the hard drive is replaced. Of more concern to security professionals is that the LoJack BIOS agent is stored in a part of the BIOS that isn't overwritten when you flash it. The LoJack BIOS agent periodically "calls home" to a central monitoring authority for instructions in case a laptop is reported stolen. The call-home mechanism allows the monitoring authority to instruct the LoJack BIOS agent to wipe all information as a security measure or to track the stolen system's location. Because so many laptops have this agent installed and it can't be removed, it's an attractive target to attackers.

Activity 9-5: Identifying IoT Device Vulnerabilities

Time Required: 30 minutes

Objective: Scan an IoT device to detect open ports.

Description: IoT devices are more common in homes, but they can also be connected to enterprise networks. Many users remotely connect to their work networks from home, so a compromised IoT device at home can be a threat to a work network. Discovering IoT devices and the ports they have open is a good start in making IoT devices and your network more secure.

1. Determine the IP address for an IoT device on your network (such as a smart TV). You can use Nmap or Zenmap to determine the IP addresses and manufacturers of devices on your network. If you are at work or in the classroom, be sure to request and receive permission to scan the network with Nmap as you may otherwise be detected as an attacker.

2. Once you have found an IoT target, perform an Nmap intense scan on that target IP address only. Do not scan the entire network, especially if you are connected to a school or work network.

3. What ports did you find open? Based on the open ports, what services can you speculate are running on the IoT device? Based on the information you discovered, what kind of attacks might the IoT device be vulnerable to? Briefly document your discoveries and discuss them with a classmate, friend, or family member.

Now that you have a better understanding of embedded OS vulnerabilities, continue reading to learn how you can improve their security.

Best Practices for Protecting Embedded OSs

You've learned that your job as a security tester is to discover and document vulnerabilities and recommend ways to fix them. Now that you know embedded OSs have vulnerabilities similar to those in general-purpose OSs as well as additional security challenges, what can you do?

- Identify all embedded systems in an organization.
- Prioritize the systems or functions that depend on these embedded systems.
- Follow the least privileges principle for access to embedded systems.
- Use data transport encryption, when possible, for embedded system communication.
- Configure embedded systems as securely as possible and follow manufacturers' recommendations.
- When possible, use cryptographic measures, such as TPM, for booting embedded systems, especially when a loss of data or a modification in the system's behavior is a major risk.
- Install patches and updates, when available, to address vulnerabilities. Make sure doing so is possible on the embedded system you're working with, however; some embedded systems can't have any downtime for installing updates and patches.
- Reduce the potential of vulnerabilities by restricting network access to only the IP addresses that need to communicate with embedded systems and reduce the attack surface of embedded systems by disabling or blocking unneeded services.
- Upgrade or replace embedded systems that can't be fixed or pose an unacceptable risk.

MODULE SUMMARY

- An embedded system is any computer system that isn't a general-purpose server or PC. An embedded OS and its hardware are the main components of an embedded system.
- An RTOS is a specialized embedded OS designed with algorithms aimed at multitasking and responding predictably; it is used in devices such as programmable thermostats, appliance controls, planes, and spacecraft.

- Most corporate networks and buildings have numerous embedded systems, such as routers and switches, firewalls, copiers, printers, faxes, digital phones, HVAC systems, intercoms, and fire-suppression systems.
- Microsoft offers several embedded OSs. Windows 10 IoT, the most modern of these offerings, is similar to older versions of Windows Embedded Standard. Windows CE was an embedded OS designed for mobile devices, and Windows Embedded Standard was an example of a Windows PC OS modified for use in embedded systems.
- Microkernel embedded OSs, such as QNX, GreenHills, and VxWorks, trade flexibility for more security and simplicity and are often used when security and safety are crucial.
- *Nix-based embedded OSs are often used for devices in which flexibility and a wide range of feature and hardware support is needed, such as GPSs, PDAs, and iPhones.
- Embedded OSs are more common now than during the worldwide panic caused by the Y2K vulnerability. The fact that they're everywhere emphasizes the importance of incorporating security into the design phase of an embedded OS.
- Embedded OSs are usually networked to increase efficiency. However, they're difficult to patch, which can increase the cost of securing them. Vulnerabilities in embedded OSs are often the same as in general-purpose OSs. Exploiting embedded systems, such as ATMs, can be profitable for criminals.
- Embedded systems are in network devices and peripherals on nearly every network, and compared with general-purpose computing systems, their vulnerabilities are often overlooked.
- SCADA systems are used for critical infrastructure systems, such as power generation and distribution, air traffic and rail control, dams and public works, and heavy industry. Damage to these embedded systems could have catastrophic consequences.
- Smartphones are examples of an ever-evolving embedded system that can be exploited to steal sensitive corporate and personal information.
- Smartphones can be infected with malicious Trojan software and exploited just like Windows and Linux systems.
- Firmware rootkits pose the biggest threat to an embedded OS. Cryptographic boot protection, such as that provided by TPM, can help defend against firmware rootkits.
- Following best practices, such as identifying all embedded systems, patching when possible, following the least privileges principle, and restricting access, are important to ensure the security of embedded systems.

Key Terms

embedded operating system (OS)	multifunction devices (MFDs)	real-time operating system (RTOS)
embedded system	multiple independent levels of	supervisory control and data
firmware	security/safety (MILS)	acquisition (SCADA) systems

Review Questions

1. An embedded OS must be developed specifically for use with embedded systems. True or false?

2. Why are embedded OSs more likely to have unpatched security vulnerabilities than general-purpose OSs do? (Choose all that apply.)
   a. Many security checks are omitted during development to reduce the code size.
   b. Devices with embedded OSs connect to the Internet more frequently.
   c. Manufacturers prefer that you upgrade the system rather than the embedded OS.

   d. Devices with embedded OSs typically can't have any downtime for installing patches.

3. Which of the following describes an RTOS?
   a. An embedded OS capable of multitasking and responding predictably
   b. An embedded OS intended for real-time data manipulation
   c. An embedded OS intended for packet analysis
   d. An embedded OS intended for devices that run multiple OSs

4. Which of the following does not use an embedded OS?
   a. ATM
   b. Workstation running Windows 10
   c. NAS device running Windows Server 2012 for Embedded Systems
   d. Slot machine

5. Provide two reasons rootkits that infect a device's firmware are considered the biggest threat to any OS (embedded or general-purpose).

6. Research the Windows 10 IoT embedded operating system. The following link is a good place to start: https://developer.microsoft.com/en-us/windows/iot/. In a report of three paragraphs, discuss what kinds of products can be built using Windows 10 IoT, describe some of the Windows 10 IoT's security features, and discuss any Windows 10 IoT vulnerabilities that hackers have exploited.

7. VxWorks is which of the following?
   a. Windows embedded OS
   b. Proprietary embedded OS
   c. Linux embedded OS
   d. Windows security validation tool

8. Which of the following is a major challenge of securing embedded OSs?
   a. Training users
   b. Configuration
   c. Patching
   d. Backup and recovery

9. The lack of a familiar interface, such as USB ports, contributes to the difficulty of updating embedded OSs. True or false?

10. Embedded OSs on routers are susceptible to which of the following? (Choose all that apply.)
    a. Authentication bypass attacks
    b. Buffer overflow attacks
    c. Password-guessing attacks
    d. RTOS clock corruption

11. Multifunction devices (MFDs) are rarely:
    a. Targets of network attacks
    b. Installed on Windows networks
    c. Installed on large networks
    d. Scanned for vulnerabilities

12. SCADA systems are used for which of the following?
    a. Monitoring embedded OSs
    b. Monitoring ATM access codes
    c. Monitoring equipment in large-scale industries
    d. Protecting embedded OSs from remote attacks

13. Cell phone vulnerabilities make it possible for attackers to do which of the following? (Choose all that apply.)
    a. Use your phone as a microphone to eavesdrop on meetings or private conversations
    b. Install a BIOS-based rootkit
    c. Clone your phone to make illegal long-distance phone calls
    d. Listen to your phone conversations

14. Pressure to get a product to market as soon as possible sometimes results in embedded systems products having insecure code or poor security testing. True or false?

15. Most printers now have only TCP/IP enabled and don't allow default administrator passwords, so they are inherently more secure. True or false?

16. Research the topic of SCADA attacks. Choose one of the SCADA attacks you discover and in a three-page report, describe the type of embedded system that was attacked, what vulnerability was exploited, and how it was resolved.

17. Take an inventory of your household electronics. Do any of your devices contain an embedded operating system? Choose one of your devices that has an embedded OS and write a three-page report detailing what embedded OS it uses, if hackers have ever exploited this kind of device, and if any security updates are available for your device.

Case Projects

Case Project 9-1: Protecting Embedded OSs on the Alexander Rocco Network

After performing enumeration tests, you discover that the Alexander Rocco network consists of five systems running Windows 10 IoT, two systems running Windows Server 2012 for Embedded Systems, 23 systems running Jetdirect, and five network appliances running embedded Linux.

Based on this information, write a one-page memo to Jawad Safari, the IT manager, outlining some suggestions on possible weaknesses or vulnerabilities in these systems. The memo should include recommendations to reduce the risk of network attacks and cite specific CVE entries (check https://cve.mitre.org).

Case Project 9-2: Identifying Vulnerable Systems That Can't Be Patched

You discover that some devices on the Alexander Rocco network can't be patched against a buffer overflow attack because of FDA certification requirements. What recommendations can you make to reduce the risk these systems pose?

Case Project 9-3: Identifying Vulnerabilities in Mobile Phones

More than five billion mobile phones are in use worldwide, and more people now reach the Internet with mobile phones than they do with PCs. Have you thought about someone hacking your phone? Research your phone model on the Internet to determine what OS it uses and any existing or potential vulnerabilities. For example, could your phone be used as a covert listening device or to send text message spam or perform a DoS attack? Be creative but use real information that you find in your research. Write a one- to two-page report on your findings.

HACKING WEB SERVERS

After reading this module and completing the exercises, you will be able to:

1 Describe web applications

2 Explain web application vulnerabilities

3 Describe the tools used to attack web servers

The Internet has revolutionized commerce and communications. Providing and buying goods and services online is referred to as e-commerce. The lockdowns caused by the COVID-19 pandemic accelerated e-commerce as businesses and consumers went digital. E-commerce's share of global retail trade increased from 14% in 2019 to approximately 17% in 2020. Business communications were also affected by COVID-19 as the amount of remote working and remote conferencing increased dramatically. E-commerce and remote working both require web servers. As the number of web servers and their use increased, so did the hacking of these web servers.

E-commerce and remote working solutions also use web applications and web services. Creating web applications involves using web development platforms, such as Microsoft Active Server Pages (ASP and ASP.NET) and Java Server Pages (JSP).

Normally, a web application is supported by a web server that runs on a general-purpose or embedded OS. Each component (application, server, and OS) has its own set of vulnerabilities, but combining these components increases the risk of a web application compromise affecting a network's overall security. Skilled hackers can often exploit a minor vulnerability in one function, such as a web mail application, and use it as a steppingstone to launch additional attacks against the OS. With the growth in available platforms and e-commerce websites, security vulnerabilities have proliferated. Statistically, the majority of cyber attacks focus on web servers, web applications, and their database infrastructure.

This module gives you an overview of web applications, explains the vulnerabilities of many web components, and describes the tools used to hack web servers.

UNDERSTANDING WEB APPLICATIONS

As you have learned, writing a program without bugs is difficult. The bigger the program, the more bugs or defects are possible, and some defects create security vulnerabilities. The more people who have access to a program, the bigger the risk of security vulnerabilities. The following sections describe web application components and platforms for developing web applications.

Web Application Components

HTML is still the foundation of most web applications and is commonly used for creating static webpages. HTML5 is the latest release in the HTML family. Static webpages display the same information regardless of the time of day or the user who accesses the page. Dynamic webpages can vary the information that's displayed, depending on variables such as current time and date, username, and purchasing history (information collected with cookies or web bugs). For webpages to be dynamic, their code must consist of more than just the basic HTML tags such as `<body>` and `<h1>`. These pages need special components for displaying information that changes depending on user input or information from a back-end server. To do this, dynamic webpages use a variety of tools, including the `<form>` element, Asynchronous JavaScript and XML (AJAX), Common Gateway Interface (CGI), Active Server Pages (ASP.NET), Java Server Pages (JSP), Hypertext Preprocessor (PHP), ColdFusion (CF), JavaScript (JS), and database connector strings, such as Open Database Connector (ODBC). These components are covered in the following sections.

Web Forms

The `<form>` element is used in an HTML document to allow customers to submit information to the web server. You have probably filled out a form when purchasing a product online or registering for an email newsletter, for example. Some forms can be quite long and ask for a lot of information, and some have only a couple of input fields, such as username and password. A web server uses a web application to process information from a form. The following HTML code shows the syntax for a simple form, and Figure 10-1 shows the webpage created with this code.

```
<html>
<body>
<form>
Enter your username:
<input type="text" name="username">
<br>
Enter your password:
<input name="password" type="password">
</form> </body></html>
```

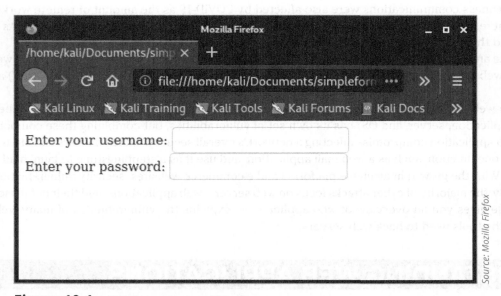

Figure 10-1   HTML webpage with a form

Common Gateway Interface

Another standard that handles moving data from a web server to a web browser is Common Gateway Interface (CGI), which enables web designers to create dynamic HTML web applications. Many dynamic webpages are created with CGI and scripting languages. CGI is the interface that determines how a web server passes data to a web browser. It relies on Perl or another scripting or programming language to create dynamic webpages, which is different from Active Server Pages (covered in a later section). CGI's main role is passing data between a web server and web browser. In fact, the term "gateway" describes this movement of data between the web server and web browser.

CGI programs can be written in many programming and scripting languages, such as C/C++, Perl, UNIX shells, Visual Basic, and Java. Programming languages such as C and C++ require compiling the program before running it. If CGI is implemented with a scripting language, compiling isn't necessary. The following CGI program displays "Hello Security Testers!" in the user's browser. This hello.pl program is written in Perl and would be placed in the cgi-bin directory on the web server:

```
#!/usr/bin/perl
print "Content-type: text/html\n\n";
print "Hello Security Testers!";
```

To check whether the CGI program works, save the program to the cgi-bin directory of your web server, and then enter the URL in your web browser, using the format http://www.myweb.com/cgi-bin/hello.pl. (Substitute the name of your server and the correct path to the cgi-bin directory.)

Third-Party Frameworks and Libraries

Spring, JSF, AngularJS, Yeoman, Sass, and Vaadin are just a few of the hundreds of frameworks designed to make programming easier. Frameworks are typically called on for a specific purpose. For example, the strength of the Spring framework is connecting components, while the Sass framework helps you style your website to enhance user experience. Using libraries saves developers time and means less documentation is required for complex routines of custom code. As third-party libraries grow in popularity, keeping them current and secure becomes more important.

Active Server Pages

Active Server Pages (ASP and ASP.NET) are two other technologies that developers can use to display HTML documents to users on the fly. The original ASP was introduced by Microsoft in 1998 as a server-side interpreted scripting language and is often referred to as Classic ASP. Classic ASP is considered to be a dead language and is no longer used by the mainstream development community. Classic ASP has been succeeded by ASP.NET, which uses a compiled server-side language (such as C#) and the .NET framework. You use ASP and ASP.NET to create dynamic webpages. That is, when a user requests a webpage, one is created at that time. ASP enabled developers to build dynamic, interactive webpages using scripting languages, such as JScript (Microsoft's version of JavaScript) or VBScript. Developers can also use ASP. NET to create dynamic, interactive webpages but as mentioned earlier, it is compiled and commonly written in C#.

Not all web servers support ASP or ASP.NET, so if you want to develop webpages with either one, the server you're using must support this technology. Internet Information Services (IIS) 4.0 and later support ASP, and IIS 5.0 and later support ASP.NET. Keep in mind that the web *server*, not the web browser, must support ASP. In Activities 10-1 and 10-2, you work with IIS to get a better understanding of web applications.

Activity 10-1: Installing Internet Information Services

Time Required: 30 minutes

Objective: Install IIS on your Windows computer.

Description: To host a website, you need to install IIS on your Windows computer. Although IIS is deployed on a server in a production environment, preproduction web development and testing can be done on workstations. IIS 10 is available in Windows 10. Because IIS isn't installed by default, in this activity you install it and use your web browser to check that it was installed correctly. This activity assumes you have never installed IIS on the PC you are using and are installing on a Windows 10 PC.

1. Open Control Panel, and then click **Programs**.
2. In the Programs and Features section, click **Turn Windows features on or off** to open the Windows Features dialog box. If the User Account Control (UAC) message box opens, click **Continue**. Click the **Internet Information Services** check box, and then click the plus symbol to expand the IIS options. Click the **World Wide Web Services** check box. Ensure that the **Application Development Features**, **Common HTTP Features**, and **Security** boxes are checked under World Wide Web Services. Under **Application Development Features**, make sure all ASP and ASP.NET options are selected. Click **Web Management Tools** and ensure that **IIS Management Console** and **IIS Scripts and Tools** are selected under Web Management Tools. When you are finished, your window should look like what is shown in Figure 10-2. Don't clear any options that are already selected.

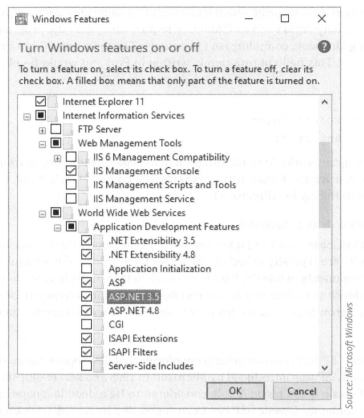

Figure 10-2 Turning Windows features on or off

3. Click **OK** to install IIS. When you see the "Windows completed the requested changes" message, click **Close**.
4. To check that IIS has been installed, click **Start**, type **inetmgr**, and press **Enter** to open the IIS Manager (see Figure 10-3). Click **Help** on the menu bar, and then click **About Internet Information Services**. What version of IIS is installed on your computer?
5. Start a web browser, type the URL **http://localhost**, and then press **Enter** to go to the IIS welcome page. A visitor to your website would see an IIS welcome message because you haven't created a default HTML webpage yet. However, clicking the graphic directs you to Microsoft's official IIS website, where you can learn more about IIS. When you're finished, close the browser window.
6. Next, you need to create a folder on your web server to hold any HTML pages you create. When IIS is installed, a new folder called inetpub is created on the C drive. Open File Explorer. Under the C drive (substitute the correct drive letter if your installation is different), click to expand the **inetpub** folder, and then open the **wwwroot** folder.
7. Right-click the **wwwroot** folder, point to **New**, and then click **Folder**. For the folder name, type *YourFirstName* (substituting your first name), and then press **Enter**.
8. Close any open windows, and leave Windows running for the next activity.

To keep attackers from knowing the directory structure you create on an IIS web server, creating a virtual directory is recommended so that the path a user sees on the web browser isn't the actual path on the web server. A **virtual directory** is a pointer to the physical directory. For example, with virtual directories, a user might see https://www.mycompany.com/jobs/default.aspx instead of https://www.mycompany.com/security/positions/CEH_Cert/default.aspx.

The simpler structure that a virtual directory offers is often easier for users to memorize and navigate. Using this design strategy also enhances security because it helps hide the actual directory structure from attackers.

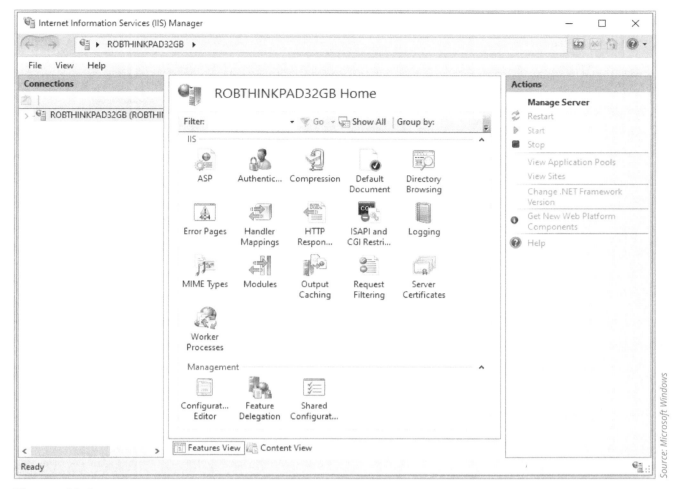

Figure 10-3   The Internet Information Services (IIS) Manager

Activity 10-2: Creating a Virtual Directory

Time Required: 15 minutes
Objective: Learn how to create a virtual directory on an IIS web server.
Description: After IIS is installed and physical directories are created, a web administrator should create virtual directories that prevent site visitors from seeing the physical directory structure. In this activity, you create a virtual directory, using the directory you created in Activity 10-1.

1. Click **Start**, type **inetmgr**, and press **Enter**. In the IIS Manager window, click to expand the computer name, **Sites**, and **Default Web Site** (see Figure 10-4).
2. Right-click the *YourFirstName* folder you created in Activity 10-1 and then click **Add Virtual Directory**.
3. In the Alias text box, type your first name. Type (or browse to) the physical path of the folder you created in Activity 10-1 **(C:\inetpub\wwwroot\YourFirstName)**, and then click **OK** to create a virtual directory that users can access over the web.
4. Close all open windows, and leave Windows running for the next activity.

Figure 10-4   Viewing IIS websites

Previously in this course, you wrote an HTML webpage. In Activity 10-3, you look at a webpage containing ASP.NET statements. The best way to learn ASP.NET is to create a webpage with it. To do this, you need three components: a text editor (e.g., Notepad), a web server (such as an IIS web server), and a web browser (such as Chrome, Microsoft Edge, or Firefox).

Activity 10-3: Creating an ASP.NET Webpage

Time Required: 20 minutes
Objective: Recognize ASP.NET webpages and use ASP.NET to create dynamic webpages.
Description: ASP.NET webpages are created on the web server and enable a developer to create dynamic webpages. In this activity, you create an ASP.NET webpage and use a web browser to view the page.

1. To start Notepad with administrative privileges, click **Start**, type **Notepad**, right-click **Notepad**, and then click **Run as administrator**. (If necessary, click **Yes** in the UAC message box.) In Notepad, type the following code:

```
<html>
<head><title>My First ASP.NET Webpage</title></head>
<body>
<h1>Hello, security professionals</h1>
```

```
The date and time is <%=DateTime.Now %>.
</body>
</html>
```

2. Save the file as **First.aspx** in the C:\inetpub\wwwroot*YourFirstName* folder. Be sure the file is saved with the .aspx extension, not the .txt extension. Exit Notepad.
3. To test the First.aspx webpage, start your web browser, type **http://localhost/*YourFirstName*/First.aspx**, and then press **Enter**. The webpage shows the current date and time of your location, meaning it's dynamic. That is, it changes each time your web browser calls for the webpage. The `<%` and `%>` tags tell the web server to execute the code between the tags and render the result when it loads the page.
4. Right-click the First.aspx webpage in your web browser and select **View page source**. Does the source code show you the ASP.NET commands you entered?
5. Close the web browser and log off Windows for the next activity.

Apache Web Server

As a security tester, you should be aware of Apache, another web server program. As of 2021, Apache Web Server had 31.7% of the web server market share compared to 6.7% for IIS. Familiarity with Apache can be helpful in the security-testing profession. Apache has important advantages over the competition: It works in just about any *nix platform as well as in Windows, and it's free. Installing Apache in Linux is different from installing IIS in Windows, but you don't have to worry about installation because the Apache Web Server daemon (httpd) is installed by default in Kali Linux. Nginx is another free open source web server program and has about the same market share as Apache. Nginx is also installed by default in Kali Linux. In Activity 10-4, you explore the Apache Web Server.

Activity 10-4: Working with Apache Web Server

Time Required: 35 minutes

Objective: Explore basic settings and tasks in Apache Web Server.

Description: Without a doubt, you'll run across Apache Web Server systems when conducting a security test. Because Apache is a sophisticated, modular web server, mastering its features and options can take considerable time. Apache's layout varies, depending on the OS. For example, Apache in Fedora Linux is different from Apache in Ubuntu Linux. In this activity, you explore basic Apache Web Server commands and learn how to find and modify some configuration options (called "Apache directives"). The goal of this activity is to configure a web server with a directory that requires authentication.

1. Boot into Kali Linux. In the following steps, type the command exactly as shown because Linux is case sensitive.
2. Open a Terminal shell. At the command prompt, type **sudo systemctl start apache2** and press **Enter**. If the apache2 service fails to start, it may be because a nginx web server is already running. Stop nginx by entering the command **sudo systemctl stop nginx**, and then enter the command **sudo systemctl start apache2**. Confirm that the apache2 service is running by using the command **systemctl status apache2**, which should show an active (running) status.
3. Start the web browser. In the address bar, type **localhost** and press **Enter**. The website displays instructions on how to manipulate the default apache configuration. Read this page.
4. Open a Terminal shell. At the command prompt, type **sudo systemctl stop apache2** and press **Enter**.
5. To view the default apache configuration files, first type **cd /etc/apache2** and press **Enter** in the Terminal shell to change directories. Type **grep Include apache2.conf** and press **Enter** to list files and directories where the Apache server searches for additional directives at startup (see Figure 10-5). Note the next to last line, IncludeOptional sites-enabled/*.conf. This directory is where Apache checks for website configuration files. You can add a website by adding its configuration file to this directory without having to change the main configuration file apache2.conf.
6. Type **cd /etc/apache2/sites-enabled && ls** and press **Enter**.

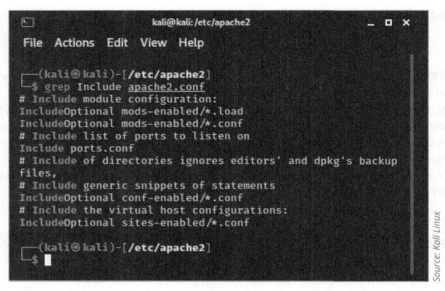

Figure 10-5   Viewing files and directories with an Include statement

7. Open the file in the gedit editor by typing **sudo gedit 000-default.conf** and pressing **Enter**.
8. Enter the following lines at the end of the file, below the </VirtualHost> line:

```
<Directory /var/www/html/restricted>
    Options Indexes FollowSymLinks
    AllowOverride AuthConfig
    Order allow,deny
    allow from all
</Directory>
```

9. Save your changes and exit the gedit editor.
10. In the Terminal shell, create a new directory by typing **sudo mkdir /var/www/html/restricted** and pressing **Enter**.
11. Type **cd /var/www/html/restricted** and press **Enter** to change to the directory you created in Step 10. Type **sudo touch secret.txt** and press **Enter** to create a text file named secret.txt in this directory.
12. Next, you create the .htaccess file in the same directory. This file is the local directory configuration file specified in apache2.conf by the AccessFileName directive. If .htaccess exists in any website directory, Apache checks it first. In this .htaccess file, you point Apache to the location of AuthUserFile (essentially, a password file). Type **sudo vi .htaccess** and press **Enter**. In this case, you need to use vi instead of gedit because gedit will not put the proper Unix (LF) characters at the end of each line, and Apache will fail to read the file properly. Once in vi type **i** to begin inserting the following text:

```
AuthType Basic
AuthName "Password Required"
AuthUserFile /etc/apache2/.htpasswd
Require user tester
```

13. Save your changes and exit the editor by pressing **Esc** and then typing **:wq!** and pressing **Enter**. In the Terminal shell, create a password file by typing **sudo htpasswd -c /etc/apache2/.htpasswd tester** and pressing **Enter**. When prompted, enter a password, confirm it, and then make note of the password. The .htaccess file you created in Step 12 tells Apache to look in the .htpasswd file for the tester user's password. You can run the command **cat /etc/apache2/.htpasswd** to view the password hash for your new user.
14. Restart Apache by typing **sudo systemctl restart apache2** and pressing **Enter**. In the Kali web browser, go to **http://localhost/restricted**, and then enter the username **tester** and the password you created in Step 13. What file is displayed? If you want to be prompted again for a password, you'll have to close and reopen your browser.

15. See whether other computers on your network can access your restricted folder by entering **http://*yourIPaddress*/restricted** in their browsers (replacing *yourIPaddress* with your IP address). If necessary, type **ifconfig eth0** and press **Enter** to find your IP address.
16. Why is entering your credentials on a website not secured with SSL, such as this site, a problem? What is the fix for this problem?
17. Research "Basic authentication security weaknesses" on the Internet. Are there any problems with Basic authentication?
18. Close the Terminal shell, exit the Kali web browser, and log off Kali Linux.

Using Scripting Languages

Webpages can be developed with several scripting languages, such as VBScript and JavaScript. You won't learn how to be a web developer by reviewing the scripting languages covered in this module, but you should be able to recognize when one is being used because many security-testing tools are written with scripting languages. Most macro viruses and all worms that take advantage of cross-site scripting vulnerabilities (discussed later in the module) are based on a scripting language.

PHP Hypertext Processor

Similar to ASP and ASP.NET, PHP Hypertext Processor (PHP) enables web developers to create dynamic webpages. PHP, an open-source server-side scripting language, is embedded in an HTML webpage by using the PHP tags `<?php` and `?>`. Because PHP webpages run on the server, users can't view the source code in their web browsers. PHP was originally used mainly on UNIX systems, but it's used more widely now on many platforms, including Macintosh and Windows. The following excerpt is a code example for a static PHP webpage showing the use of PHP tags:

NOTE

Bolded lines in these code examples show how different scripting languages are indicated.

```
<html>
<head>
<title>My First PHP Program</title>
</head>
<body>
<?php echo "<h1>Hello, Security Testers!</h1>"; ?>
</body>
</html>
```

This page would need to be created on your web server as a .php file, similar to the ASP.NET webpage you created in Activity 10-3. After you have identified that a web server is using PHP, you should use the methods you have learned in this course to investigate further for specific vulnerabilities. For example, several legacy versions of PHP running on Linux can be exploited because of a line in the Php.ini file: The line `file_uploads=on` permits file uploads; however, this setting might allow a remote attacker to run arbitrary code with elevated privileges. The best solution is to upgrade to the latest version of PHP, but if that's not possible, change the line to `file_uploads=off`.

NOTE

You should also be familiar with LAMP (which stands for Linux, Apache, MySQL, and PHP) because it's a collection of open-source software used for many sophisticated, high-traffic web applications. LAMP is known as a solution stack because it stacks several programs into one integrated web application solution. For more information, do an Internet search on the term "LAMP" combined with the Linux version you're using, such as Ubuntu or Fedora. The Windows version of this stack is called WAMP.

ColdFusion

ColdFusion is another server-side scripting language for developing dynamic webpages. Created by Allaire Corporation, it's now owned by Adobe Systems, Inc. ColdFusion integrates web browser, web server, and database technologies. It uses proprietary tags written in ColdFusion Markup Language (CFML). Web applications written in CFML can contain other client-side technologies, such as HTML and JavaScript. The following code is an example of HTML with a CFML tag that redirects the user to a webpage. All CFML tags begin with the letters CF. For example, the column tag is <CFCOL>.

```
<html>
<head>
<title>Using CFML</title>
</head>
<body>
<CFLOCATION URL="www.isecom.org" ADDTOKEN="NO">
</body>
</html>
```

As with the PHP example, security testers should become familiar with vulnerabilities associated with a web server using ColdFusion. A quick search of the Adobe security page (https://helpx.adobe.com/security.html) can narrow your research time, allowing you to focus on the vulnerabilities that affect your organization.

JavaScript

A popular scripting language for creating dynamic webpages, JavaScript also has the power of a programming language. In JavaScript, you can branch, loop, and test (the BLT you learned earlier) and create functions and procedures in HTML webpages. The following code is a simple HTML snippet with JavaScript code added:

```
<html>
<head>
<script type="text/javascript">
function chastise_user()
{
alert ("So, you like breaking rules?")
document.getElementById("cmdButton").focus ()
}
</script>
</head>
<body>
<h3>"If you are a Security Tester, please do not click the command button below!"</h3>
<form>
<input type="button" value="Don't Click!" name="cmdButton"
onClick="chastise_user()" />
</form>
</body>
</html>
```

This code is more complex than the previous examples, but it shows you how scripting languages can include functions and alerts. The third line specifies that JavaScript is the language being used. Next, the chastise_user() function is defined; this function simply displays an alert message. The getElementById() function is a method (a sequence of statements that perform a routine or task) defined by the World Wide Web Consortium (W3C) Document Object Model (DOM). Basically, it returns an object—in this case, a command button you click. The remaining code is fairly self-explanatory. To see how this code works, take a look at the output shown in Figure 10-6.

If the user accepts the security warning and clicks the command button, the alert message box shown in Figure 10-7 is displayed.

Figure 10-6   A command button created with JavaScript

Figure 10-7   An alert message created with JavaScript

JavaScript is widely used, and a variety of vulnerabilities have been exploited in older web browsers. Security testers and administrators should inspect every computer for unpatched or outdated browser versions and keep up with vulnerabilities. For example, Cyber Security Alert AA21-076A, TrickBot Malware (https://us-cert.cisa.gov/ncas/alerts/aa21-076a) describes the TrickBot Trojan. TrickBot uses malicious JavaScript to communicate to the malicious actor's command and control (C2) server to download malware onto the victim's system.

Connecting to Databases

Most webpages that display company information to users are stored on a database server. Webpages that prompt a user for information, such as name, phone number, address, and so on, store the information users enter in a database. The technology used to connect a web application to a database server might vary depending on the OS, but the theory is the same. The following sections discuss some technologies used to connect to a database or an external file system from a web application.

Open Database Connectivity

Open Database Connectivity (ODBC) is a standard database access method developed by the SQL Access Group. The ODBC interface allows an application to access data stored in a database management system (DBMS), such as Microsoft SQL, Oracle, or any system that can recognize and issue ODBC commands. Interoperability between back-end DBMSs is a key feature of the ODBC interface, allowing developers to focus on the application without worrying about a specific DBMS. The ODBC interface accomplishes this interoperability by defining the following:

- A standardized representation for data types
- A library of ODBC function calls that allow an application to connect to a DBMS, run SQL statements, and retrieve the results
- A standard method of connecting to and logging onto a DBMS

Object Linking and Embedding Database

Object Linking and Embedding Database (OLE DB) is a set of interfaces that enable applications to access data stored in a DBMS. Microsoft designed it to be faster, more efficient, and more stable than its predecessor, ODBC. OLE DB relies on connection strings that allow the application to access data stored on an external device. Depending on the data source you're connecting to, you might use a different provider. For example, connecting to an SQL database requires using SQLOLEDB as the provider instead of Microsoft.ACE.

Table 10-1 shows some OLE DB providers available for developers. When conducting a security test on a web server, you should verify how the web server is connecting to a database and, of course, what type of database or resource data is being collected. The following code line is an example of a connection string used to access data in a Microsoft Access database named Personnel:

```
Provider=Microsoft.ACE.OLEDB.12.0;Data Source=C:\Personnel.accdb; User ID=; Password=;
```

Table 10-1   OLE DB Providers

OLE DB provider	Description in connection string
Microsoft Active Directory Service	Provider=ADSDSOOBJECT
Advantage	Provider=Advantage OLE DB Provider
AS/400 (from IBM)	Provider=IBMDA400
AS/400 and VSAM (from Microsoft)	Provider=SNAOLEDB
MS Commerce Server	Provider=Commerce.DSO.1
DB2	Provider=DB2OLEDB
Microsoft Jet	Provider=Microsoft.Jet.OLEDB.4.0
Microsoft.ACE	Provider=Microsoft.ACE.OLEDB.12.0
MS Exchange	Provider=EXOLEDB.DataSource
MySQL	Provider=MySQLProv
Oracle (from Microsoft)	Provider=msdaora
Oracle (from Oracle)	Provider=OraOLEDB.Oracle
MS SQL Server	Provider=SQLOLEDB

ActiveX Data Objects

ActiveX Data Objects (ADO) is a programming interface for connecting a web application to a database. ActiveX defines technologies that allow applications, such as Word or Excel, to interact with the web. ActiveX support has been eliminated from almost every web browser for security reasons. Windows 10 still supports ActiveX but only in the Internet Explorer browser, not in Edge. Microsoft has not completely removed ActiveX support because many businesses still use it. Even though ActiveX is on its way out, it's still useful for demonstrating how to connect to databases. For example, you can insert an Excel spreadsheet in a webpage. To access a database from an ASP webpage, you follow these general steps:

1. Create an ADO connection to the database you want to access.
2. Open the database connection you created in Step 1.
3. Create an ADO recordset, which contains rows from the table you're accessing.
4. Open the recordset.
5. Select the data you need from the recordset, based on particular criteria.
6. Close the recordset.
7. Close the database connection.

Next, take a look at how these steps are performed and what the result looks like in an ASP or ASP.NET webpage. The following code creates and opens the ADO connection:

```
<%
set conn=Server.CreateObject("ADODB.Connection")
conn.Provider="Microsoft.Jet.OLEDB.4.0"
conn.Open "c:\MyDatabase\employee.accdb"
%>
```

Now you need to create a recordset to contain records from a table in your employee.accdb database:

```
<%
set rs=Server.CreateObject("ADODB.recordset")
rs.Open "Select * FROM Employee", conn
…..
rs.close
conn.close
%>
```

You would probably use a loop to print all the records to the webpage, but that's not important here. You want to understand the technology so that you can recognize vulnerabilities when they exist. Now that you have a good foundation on the components of a web application, the following section discusses some of these vulnerabilities.

UNDERSTANDING WEB APPLICATION VULNERABILITIES

Many platforms and programming languages can be used to design a website. Each platform has its advantages and disadvantages. Some are free, and others cost quite a bit; some require only basic skills in creating web applications, and others require an in-depth knowledge of programming. Regardless of the platform, security professionals need to assess the system and examine potential methods for attacking it.

Network security is essential to protect company data and resources from attack. Application security, often referred to as AppSec, was once overlooked by professionals because it is a specialized practice. One reason is that many security professionals have experience in networking but little or no experience in programming. In fact, most network security courses don't cover much programming because the topic can overwhelm students.

No matter how efficient a company's firewalls or intrusion detection systems are, most systems allow the content of HTTPS traffic. Therefore, an attacker can bypass supposed security boundaries as well as any OS hardening that network administrators have done. Simply stated, Network-layer protection doesn't always prevent Application-layer attacks from occurring. An attacker needs only an understanding of some basic programming concepts or scripting languages. To add to the mayhem, attackers usually don't need special tools, and detection of a manual attack on a web application is often difficult. After attackers gain control of a web server, they can use a number of post-exploitation actions, including the following:

- Defacing the website
- Attempting to destroy the application's database or selling its contents
- Attempting to gain control of user accounts
- Launching secondary attacks from the web server or infecting site visitors' systems with malware
- Attempting to gain access to other servers that are part of the network infrastructure

Application Vulnerabilities and Countermeasures

Luckily, there's an organization that helps security professionals understand the vulnerabilities in web applications. Much like ISECOM, Open Web Application Security Project (OWASP) is a not-for-profit foundation dedicated to finding and fighting the causes of web application vulnerabilities. OWASP (www.owasp.org) publishes the

"Ten Most Critical Web Application Security Risks" paper, which has been built into the Payment Card Industry (PCI) Data Security Standard (DSS). The PCI DSS is a requirement for all businesses that sell products online. Visiting the OWASP website to learn more about web application vulnerabilities is recommended. The OWASP paper and its top 10 list are updated every few years. The newest edition has a release date in 2021. As a security tester, you might need to analyze vulnerabilities such as the following in the OWASP top 10 list:

- *A1—Injection vulnerabilities* occur when untrusted data is accepted as input to an application without being properly validated. Any piece of data sent from a web browser to a server could be manipulated and thus represents a potential point of attack. If an attacker can make assumptions about how data might be handled on the server, they can make educated attempts at exploiting the server. Types of injection vulnerabilities include SQL, code, LDAP, and command injection.
- *A2—Authentication flaws and weaknesses* are prevalent when poor session management, weak encryption schemes, or weak logic is used to control or protect the authentication process. Developers often "roll their own" authentication or encryption schemes instead of leveraging existing, vetted libraries. One small oversight by a developer can lead to major weaknesses.
- *A3—Sensitive data exposure* occurs when the proper precautions are not taken to protect application data at rest and in transit. Client-side exposure can include sensitive information that is cached and remains on the user's hard drive after an application is used. This is especially dangerous if users check their bank account balances on a public PC, such as one provided at a library, and cached information contains sensitive banking details that an attacker can use to conduct fraud. Server-side encryption of data-at-rest should be used to protect sensitive data, such as passwords and other customer information. To preserve the secrecy of data-in-transit, encryption must always be forced by the application.
- *A4—XML External Entities (XXE)* are problematic when older or poorly configured XML processors evaluate external entity references within XML documents. External entities can be used to disclose internal files using the file URI handler, internal file shares, internal port scanning, remote code execution, and denial of service attacks.
- *A5—Broken access control* happens when rules are not properly enforced about what authenticated users are allowed to do. Attackers can exploit these flaws to access unauthorized functionality or data, such as find other users' accounts, view sensitive files, modify other users' data, and change access rights.
- *A6—Security misconfigurations* result from poorly configured technologies on top of which a web application runs. These include the operating system, application server, web server, services used for maintenance, and so on. Configuration baselines and checklists can help administrators prevent security misconfigurations.
- *A7—Cross-site scripting (XSS)* vulnerabilities, like injection vulnerabilities, result from a server accepting untrusted, unvalidated input. There are two types of XSS vulnerabilities: stored and reflected. Stored, sometimes referred to as "persistent XSS," is especially harmful because it can be delivered to subsequent users of the application. Reflected XSS relies on social engineering to trick a user into visiting a maliciously crafted link or URL. In either case, the attacker's goal is to execute code on a remote user's computer. To accomplish this, the attacker injects code into a susceptible parameter of the application. The server sends this code to the victim's browser. The user's browser then runs the injected code, causing harmful action on the user's computer.

SECURITY BYTES

The most infamous XSS worm was called "JS.Spacehero" or "Samy," and was spread by hijacking browsers visiting the MySpace website. The worm's creator uploaded a malicious script to his MySpace profile page, and anyone visiting this page was redirected into sending him a friend request. The worm was then embedded in the hijacked user's profile page. In less than 24 hours, more than a million MySpace profile pages were infected, making the JS.Spacehero worm one of the fastest spreading worms ever. MySpace had to shut down the site to clean up the infection, and the worm's creator earned himself a felony conviction. In 2021, Koo, India's homegrown Twitter clone, had to patch an XSS security flaw. This flaw could have allowed hackers to run malicious JavaScript that could steal sensitive data from all of Koo's six million active users.

- *A8—Insecure deserialization* can lead to remote code execution, replay attacks, injection attacks, and privilege escalation attacks. Serialization breaks an object into pieces and expresses those pieces in a different data format that can be restored later. Deserialization puts the serialized pieces back to create the original object. If hackers intercept insecure deserialization information, they may be able to use that information to execute exploits.
- *A9—Using components with known vulnerabilities* cause the web applications using these components to inherit those vulnerabilities. Components, such as libraries, frameworks, and other software modules, run with the same privileges as the application. If a vulnerable component is exploited, such an attack can facilitate serious data loss or server takeover. Applications and APIs using components with known vulnerabilities may undermine application defenses and enable various attacks and impacts.
- *A10—Insufficient logging and monitoring* can allow attackers to go undetected. Coupled with missing or ineffective integration with incident response, this vulnerability allows attackers to further attack systems, maintain persistence, pivot to more systems, and tamper, extract, or destroy data. Most breach studies show the time to detect a breach is more than 200 days, typically detected by external parties rather than internal processes or monitoring.

The OWASP paper on the top 10 vulnerabilities might cover some areas beyond the skills of a beginning security tester, so OWASP offers Broken Web Apps and WebGoat, an online utility that helps beginning security testers understand the web application vulnerabilities covered in this list.

OWASP developed the WebGoat project to help security testers learn how to conduct vulnerability testing on web applications. Experts from all over the world use WebGoat and offer their input. The OWASP developers want to encourage security students to think about how to launch an attack, so solutions aren't given for all exercises. In the following paragraphs, you walk through an example of using WebGoat to learn about some basic web application attacks. You can follow along, if you like, or just review the steps and figures.

Assuming you've booted into Kali Linux, you will need to download the easy-run executable jar version of WebGoat from github. From a terminal, run the following command: **wget https://github.com/WebGoat/WebGoat/releases/download/v8.0.0.M26/webgoat-server-8.0.0.M26.jar**.

Next, browse to where you downloaded the easy-run jar file. Type **java -jar webgoat-server-8.0.0.M26.jar** to run the executable file. WebGoat is updated regularly and a new .jar file is created for new releases. If you choose to download the latest release, or another release, the filename you download and run may be different from the one shown here. You can check the WebGoat Releases page at https://github.com/WebGoat/WebGoat/releases to determine the version number of the current release, which is listed at the top of the page. Scroll down to the Assets section of the page and hover the pointer over the webgoat-server .jar file to display the HTTPS path name to use with the wget command.

Open a browser and go to **http://localhost:8080/WebGoat** to display the WebGoat start page shown in Figure 10-8.

Click the **Register new user** link at the bottom of the Login page to create a username and password. For subsequent visits to the WebGoat login page, you can use these same credentials. Figure 10-9 shows the Register page.

After you register or sign in, you are taken to the introduction module, "What Is WebGoat?" Read through the introduction then click the **General** link in the navigation pane on the left and select **HTTP Basics** to display the page shown in Figure 10-10.

Read the information on the first page, which outlines the Concept, Goals, and how HTTP works. Use the navigation arrows and icons to go to the next page, where you enter a name. The server accepts the HTTP request and reverses the input. For example, entering the name "student" returns the value "tneduts." Navigate to the last page to take a short quiz on HTTP basics.

The exercises become more complex after the first one, so you probably won't be able to do them quickly. For example, the SQL Injection (intro) security exercise teaches you the basics of SQL and SQL injection, and has dynamic sections where you can try SQL injection exploits for yourself. See Figure 10-11.

SQL stands for Structured Query Language, a popular language used by websites to access databases. SQL injection is an exploit where the malicious actor enters SQL commands into input fields of a website in an attempt to circumvent security and access data. (SQL injection is discussed in greater detail later in this module.)

Other exercises show different aspects of web security. For example, one exercise requires setting up a client/server configuration so that you can sniff traffic containing credentials to a website; another involves using vulnerable components such as functions from open source GitHub code repositories that have known security flaws. The last set of exercises, called challenges (see Figure 10-12), take beginning students to a higher level, challenging them to break authentication schemes, force an administrator password reset, and vote in a poll without logging on.

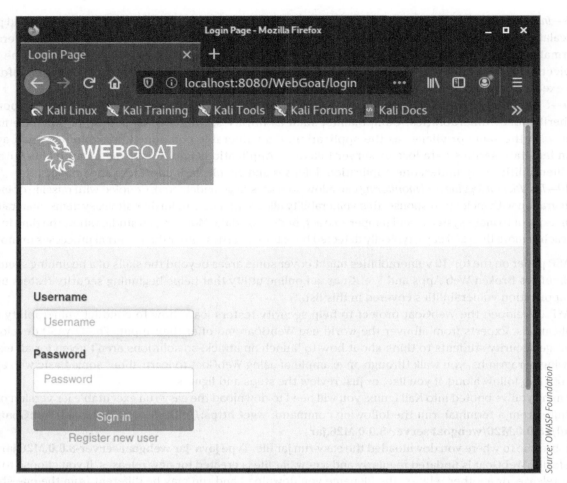

Source: OWASP Foundation

Figure 10-8   WebGoat start page

Web Application Test Execution

An application can be tested using two main techniques: **Static Application Security Testing (SAST)** and **Dynamic Application Security Testing (DAST)**. SAST is analyzing an application's source code for vulnerabilities and is, therefore, only possible when the source code of an application is available. SAST is a reliable way to enumerate most application vulnerabilities that result from coding errors. SAST is also known as "white box testing." DAST is analyzing a running application for vulnerabilities. It can also be used alongside SAST to prioritize SAST findings. If source code is not available to testers, DAST is all they can perform. DAST is also known as "black box testing." Another application testing technique called **Interactive Application Security Testing (IAST)** combines elements of both SAST and DAST and uses an agent inside the application to perform its analysis in real-time at any point in the development process. IAST is also known as "gray box testing." This section focuses largely on the execution of DAST.

Several security-testing checklists and guides walk a security tester through dynamic testing of each component of a web application, ensuring full coverage. The following sections are based on the "OWASP Web Application Penetration Testing Guide" (www.owasp.org/index.php/Web_Application_Penetration_Testing), which has been developed and vetted by experts from around the world.

Information Gathering and Architecture Mapping

Depending on the tester's experience level and amount of training in securing web infrastructures, it might be difficult to understand the nuances of web application development. Remember that, most of the time, teams are used when performing a security test. If you have only a little experience with web applications, you might want to consider adding a team member who has expertise in this subject. Each area covered in the following sections might require specialized knowledge. Questions to consider during this phase include: Does the application have a database? Does the

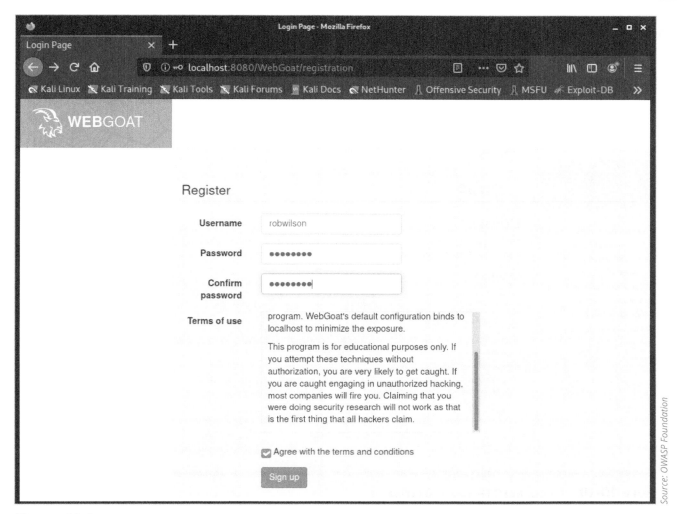

Figure 10-9   WebGoat Register page

application require authentication? Does the application have static or dynamic pages? What languages and platforms does the application use? Are there devices between your web browser and the application designed to stop attacks from occurring? How does data flow in the application?

Platform Security and Configuration

With so many platforms available for web developers, it's no wonder that so many vulnerabilities exist. Knowing whether a web application was developed on an IIS server with ASP.NET and SQL Server or on a Linux Apache Web Server system using PHP and MySQL gives both attackers and security testers the ammunition to do their jobs. Remember that you conduct footprinting to discover what OS and DBMS the attacked system is using. The more you know about the system, the easier it is to gather information about its vulnerabilities and common misconfigurations. Questions to consider during this phase include: Do the underlying platforms and components contain known vulnerabilities? Is the web server configured to protect the confidentiality of the users who connect to it? Are there administrative interfaces to the infrastructure components and the applications being tested?

Authentication and Session Testing

Many web applications require that a server other than the web server authenticate users. For example, a web application might require using a Windows Server 2019 server running Active Directory Services for authentication. In this case, you should examine how authentication information is passed between the two servers. Is an encrypted channel used, or is data passed in cleartext that can be retrieved easily? Is the server used for authentication properly configured and patched? Are logon and password information stored in a secured location, or is it possible for an intruder

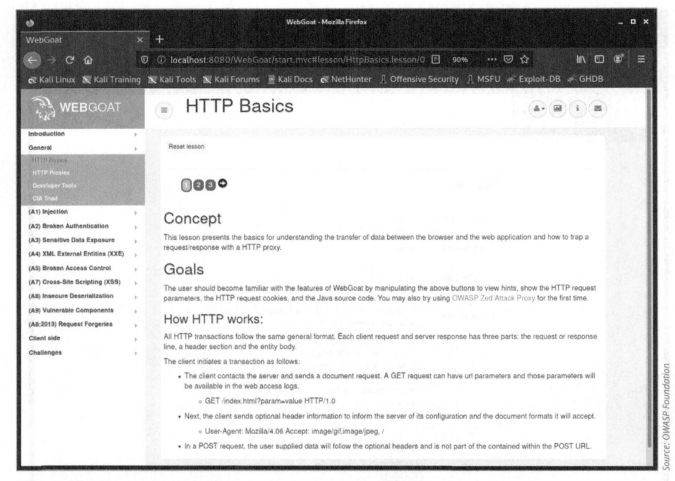

Figure 10-10   WebGoat HTTP Basics exercise

to access and retrieve the information? Other questions to consider during this phase include: Does the user's session time out adequately? Does the application use cookies, and are they kept securely? Does the site allow a user to log out, and does that log-out function expire the session?

Authorization Testing

Authorization is the act of checking a user's privileges to allow or deny access to a page, field, resource, or action in an application. Application developers commonly use hidden fields in tables and obscured URLs to enforce their access control instead of checking users' privileges before processing a request. If low-privilege users know what URLs to request, they can escalate their privileges in a poorly designed application. Insecure direct object references, described earlier, are discovered during authorization testing. Authorization testing can reveal major areas of concern and is an important part of any application test.

Input Validation

Input validation is the act of filtering, rejecting, or sanitizing a user's untrusted input before the application processes it. Input validation problems can lead to data disclosure, alteration, and destruction. When applications accept untrusted input, an attacker can often craft malicious requests that cause the application to perform an unexpected action. This is where the injection vulnerability arises. An attacker can cause a server to run code, overfill a buffer, perform database queries, reflect malicious content back to users, and many other destructive actions.

One example of input validation gone wrong is SQL injection. Web applications that prompt users for information or display available inventory to users usually have a back-end database server storing all this information. The inventory

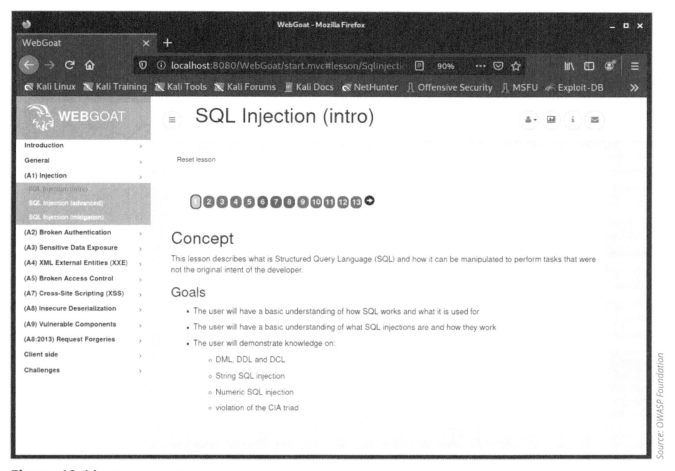

Figure 10-11   WebGoat SQL Injection (intro) exercise

database has tables containing the information to display to customers, and a customer database usually stores data about users that might include credit card information. In this case, database security is of paramount importance. Who has access to the tables? What database software and version are used—for example, Oracle 19c, Microsoft SQL Server 2019, or MySQL? Is there a possibility of SQL injection being used to attack the system? In **SQL injection (SQLi)**, the attacker supplies SQL commands when prompted to fill in a web application field.

Following is a basic SQL statement to select records (rows) in a table named books:

```
SELECT * FROM books WHERE lname ="Leno";
```

In an SQL injection, attackers insert ("inject") their own SQL statements within this statement.

Remember the logon form created with HTML in the "Web Application Components" section? To demonstrate SQL injection vulnerabilities, you can use an ASP webpage that is similar to that logon form. Whether the webpage is based on ASP or ASP.NET based is not important. The SQL injection vulnerability comes from the webpage using a SQL database and not performing input validation. Proper input validation could prevent users from entering SQL statements into the "Enter your username:" or "Enter your password:" input prompts in the ASP webpage input form below.

```
<form name="Validate" action="validate.asp" method="post">
Enter your username: <input type="text" name="username">
Enter your password: <input type="text" name="password">
<input type="submit">
</form>
```

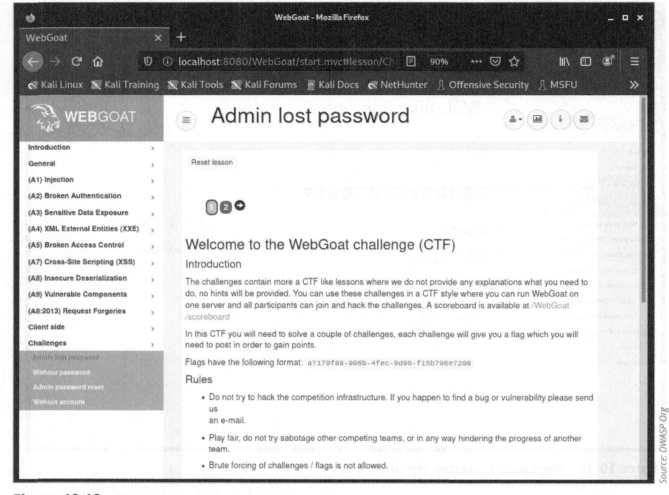

Figure 10-12 WebGoat Challenges page

The contents of the username and password parameters are passed to the ASP page, validate.asp. To verify that the username and password are correct, many web applications have a secured database of valid usernames and passwords. The validate.asp page could look something like the following:

```
<%
```

1. `Dim username, password, sql_statement`
2. `Dim conn, rs`
3. `username = Request.Form("username")`
4. `password = Request.Form("password")`
5. `set conn = server.createObject("ADODB.Connection")`
6. `set rs = server.createObject("ADODB.Recordset")`
7. `sql_statement ="SELECT * FROM customer`
   `WHERE tblusername ='" & username & "' AND`
   `tblpassword '" & password & "'"`
   `conn.Open "Provider=SQLOLEDB; Data Source=(local);`
8. `Initial Catalog=CustomerDB; User Id=sa; Password="`
9. `rs.activeConnection = conn`
10. `rs.open sql_statement`
11. `if not rs.eof then`

```
12. response.write "Welcome!"
13. else
14. response.write "Please reenter your username and password"
15. end if
%>
```

The line numbers are for reference only and are not used in an actual ASP web application. Lines 1 and 2 declare the variables used in the rest of the code: username, password, sql_statement, conn (for the connection), and rs (for the recordset). Dim stands for dimension, which was used in the days of BASIC programming to declare variables.

Lines 3 and 4 define the username and password variables. In Lines 5 and 6, the set conn and set rs commands create the connection string object and recordset objects that will be used. In Line 7, the sql_statement variable holds the SQL statement used to query the database.

Lines 8 and 9 show that SQLOLEDB, the OLE DB provider for SQL Server, is used to connect to the database server. In this case, a database named CustomerDB is accessed, as shown in the Catalog statement.

Line 10 shows that by storing the SQL statement in a variable, you can run it later with rs.open sql_statement. Line 11 checks for the end-of-file (EOF) marker. If no records are found that match what the customer entered (username, password), the web browser displays the message to reenter the username and password information. If a match is found, the SELECT statement lists all the records in the customer table. So what's the problem, you ask?

Take a look at the customer table that was created and the command for inserting four records in it:

```
CREATE TABLE customer
(
tblCustomerID CHAR (10);
tblusername VARCHAR(25);
tblpassword VARCHAR(25);
/
INSERT INTO customer (tblusername, tblpassword)
VALUES ("bob", "password");
INSERT INTO customer (tblusername, tblpassword)
VALUES ("ted", "pa$$w0rd");
INSERT INTO customer (tblusername, tblpassword)
VALUES ("alice", "G0uLd");
INSERT INTO customer (tblusername, tblpassword)
VALUES ("carol", "n@tw00d");
```

If Bob logs on with his credentials, the SELECT statement is as follows:

```
SELECT * FROM customer
WHERE tblusername = 'bob>' AND tblpassword ='password'
```

Suppose Bob enters the following when prompted for his username:

```
' OR 1=1--
```

The SQL statement is then the following:

```
SELECT * FROM customer
WHERE tblusername = ' OR 1=1-- AND tblpassword = ' '
```

Because 1 = 1 is always true, the query is carried out successfully. Double hyphens (--) are used in SQL to indicate a comment.

Are there more tricks to hacking into a database? Take a look at a couple of other things an attacker could have entered when prompted for a username and password:

```
Please enter username: ' OR 1=1--
Please enter password: ' OR 1=1--
```

The SQL statement is then as follows:

```
SELECT * FROM customer
WHERE tblusername = ' OR 1=1-- AND tblpassword = ' OR 1=1--
```

Instead of the SQL statement comparing values, the user enters with values in the customer table, it compares a quotation mark to another quotation mark, which of course returns a true condition. Hence, all rows are returned. It's surprising that many systems connected to the Internet have this vulnerability. You shouldn't test for this vulnerability by attempting SQL injections on websites because this attack is considered intrusive and is subject to criminal prosecution. However, you should test any web applications when you're performing a security test and are authorized in writing to do so. Basic testing should look for the following:

- Whether you can enter text containing punctuation marks of any kind
- Whether you can enter a single quotation mark followed by any SQL keywords, such as WHERE, SELECT, INSERT, UNION, and so on
- Whether you get any sort of database error when attempting to inject SQL statements (meaning SQL injection is possible)

Sometimes, a web application will give a tester no indication that a SQL statement was run. OWASP calls this "Blind SQL injection," which has its own set of tests that are required for detection. An attacker can inject a waitfor delay '00:00:10'- command to MSSQL. If the SQL statement is successfully processed, it will instruct the server to wait for 10 seconds before responding. If not successful, the server responds without delay. This, and other tricks, can be used to detect Blind SQL injection.

SECURITY BYTES

When students apply for graduate school, waiting for an acceptance letter can be painful, but a hacker offered them a way of getting an answer quickly. The hacker gained access to internal admissions records for Harvard, Stanford, MIT, and other top business schools by exploiting vulnerabilities discovered in a web application called ApplyYourself. The hacker then posted hacking hints on *Business Week*'s online forum. To read more, visit www.thecrimson.com/article/2005/3/3/hacker-tips-off-b-school-applicants-tipped/. Applicants, regardless of their hacking background, could now find out whether they had been accepted. Harvard Business School identified 119 applicants who hacked the system and stated that it would reject their admissions because of the ethics violation. Some people thought the problem was the lack of security on the ApplyYourself web server, which allowed an attacker to simply modify the web server's displayed URL. The applicants who were caught used their logon names and changed only the URL when connected to the web server. They didn't attempt to hide their tracks or guess passwords. Was what they did unethical? This question might seem difficult to answer, but Harvard had no problem doing just that. Although this incident occurred years ago, it's still a good lesson in poor website security and the repercussions of hacking.

Error Handling

A web application can be configured or written to handle errors in a variety of ways. For example, when an application needs to undergo troubleshooting, developers can enable debugging, which provides rich logging information helpful to diagnose issues. Sometimes, after troubleshooting, the debugging mode might be left on, which provides a valuable source of information for attackers. Developers should minimize the amount of information shared with users when an application encounters an error. Optimally, no information or only a generic message should be displayed to users in these error cases.

Cryptography Testing

Cryptography can be intimidating for junior security testers. Keep in mind that you don't need to understand integer factorization and discrete logarithm functions to find flaws in the implementation of cryptography. Many problems in cryptography are due to simple problems: bad random number generators; a known weak method of encryption; an encryption algorithm with known flaws that allow it to be cracked; an application that doesn't actually enforce the use of secure channels; or a self-signed certificate instead of a purchased certificate. To discover flaws in the actual algorithms, you might need to add a team member who has experience analyzing cryptographic routines. Often, when developers decide to create their own cryptographic schemes instead of using the common crypto frameworks, an experienced tester can find a way to subvert it.

Business Logic Testing

Business logic refers to the procedure a user is expected to follow in an application to accomplish a goal. For example, before conducting a wire transfer, a user must first satisfy the requirement of having at least that amount of money in the transferring account. If the user doesn't have adequate funds, the transfer should be halted. Business logic testing involves using creative ways to bypass these types of checks. Can you somehow trick the application into thinking you have $1,000,000 in your account when you only have $100? What implications might this have for the bank that authorizes a wire transaction for $1,000,000 from an account with $100? These types of flaws can expose a company to legal, financial, and reputational issues and should be a point of focus during application testing.

Client-Side Testing

Client-side issues arise from code executing on the user's machine, typically within the web browser. Often, when developers don't want a field to be changed, they use client-side JavaScript to disable that field. A regular user cannot edit this field, but an attacker or tester can use an intercepting proxy to tamper with it in transit. Client-side controls are insufficient on their own and should be paired with server-side controls that cannot be bypassed. Some other key questions to ask with a client-side test are: Does the application store sensitive information on the client's machine in an insecure manner? Does the application allow for client browser redirection if the server is fed a specially crafted request?

Activity 10-5: Researching SQL Injection Vulnerabilities and Hands-On SQL Injection with WebGoat

Time Required: 30 minutes

Objective: Recognize the many platforms that have SQL injection vulnerabilities, and perform SQL injection using WebGoat.

Description: After determining that a web application is using a back-end database server to store data, a security tester should attempt to test the web application for SQL injection vulnerabilities. In this activity, you visit the Common Vulnerabilities and Exposures (CVE) website to identify some known vulnerabilities.

1. Start your web browser, if necessary, and go to **https://cve.mitre.org**.
2. On the CVE home page, click the **Search CVE List** link on the navigation bar.
3. On the Search CVE List page, type **SQL injection** in the text box and click **Submit**. How many CVE entries are listed?
4. Scroll through the list of vulnerabilities and candidates, reading the descriptions for each entry on the first page. At the end of the list, click the **Back** button on your browser, type **SQL injection phpbb** in the text box, and then click **Submit**. How many entries are listed? Even though the CVEs listed are quite old, many websites might still be vulnerable to phpBB exploits.
5. When an attacker discovers a vulnerability, as you did in this activity, the next step is trying to find out which businesses use the software. To find this information, you can use a search engine. For example, historically websites using the phpBB software add a footnote to home pages stating, "Powered by phpBB." Go to your favorite search engine and search for **"powered by phpbb."** (including the quotation marks). How many websites are listed in the search results? Do you think most sites corrected the vulnerability you discovered?
6. Visiting these websites isn't recommended. Because hackers use the same process to find vulnerable websites to hack, it's likely that some of these websites contain malicious code designed to infect your system. What are the security ramifications of listing the type of software you're running on a website?
7. Exit the web browser.
8. Go to your Kali Linux installation and log on to WebGoat. For some hands-on SQL injection experience, complete the SQL Injection (intro) exercise. If time allows, do the SQL injection advanced and mitigation exercises as well.

As you learned in this activity, some websites use phpBB. After attackers discover a vulnerability, they look for as many targets as possible to attack. As you can see, notifying clients when you discover a vulnerability is crucial—and the faster, the better.

TOOLS FOR WEB ATTACKERS AND SECURITY TESTERS

After vulnerabilities of a web application or an OS platform are discovered, security testers or attackers look for the tools that enable them to test or attack the system. For example, if you learn of a vulnerability in CGI, the next step is discovering whether any systems are using CGI. As you saw in the previous section, all platforms and web application components have vulnerabilities. No matter which platform is used to develop a web application, it probably has a security hole that attackers can exploit to break into the system.

Web Tools

You have already seen that most tools for performing a security test or attacking a network can be found on the Internet and are usually free. Kali Linux is packed with free tools for hacking web applications, which you can find in the Kali Web Application Analysis menu. You can install new tools with the apt-get install *packagename* command. However, other tools might be more suitable for a specific task. The following sections cover some popular tools for hacking web applications. Websites for finding other web application testing tools include www.owasp.org/index.php/Appendix_A:_Testing_Tools and https://packetstormsecurity.org. As a security tester, you should visit these sites before a test to keep track of any new tools and to browse through available exploits. Exploits posted on the Packet Storm website and Exploit Database website (www.exploit-db.com/) are often added to Metasploit plug-ins.

Firefox and Chrome Built-In Developer Tools

Firefox and Chrome each come with a similar set of developer tools that are also useful for an application security tester. These tools allow an attacker to view parameters in requests, examine cookies, and even tamper with and resend requests. These tools can be accessed through the Settings menu in Firefox and Chrome. Figure 10-13 shows the Network tab of Firefox's developer tools in action and the "Edit and Resend" feature.

Burp Suite and Zed Attack Proxy

Burp Suite is included in Kali Linux and offers the tester a number of features for testing web applications and web services. It allows you to intercept traffic between the web browser and the server so you can inspect and manipulate requests before sending them to the server. Burp Suite can also crawl, scan, and use brute force on applications. In fact, it has many similarities to Zed Attack Proxy, which you should be familiar with. Burp Suite Pro and Zed Attack Proxy can often be used interchangeably. Figure 10-14 shows Burp Suite's intercepting proxy functionality, which allows a security tester to inspect request and response details. The left side of Figure 10-14 shows the Burp Suite built in browser being used to navigate to the cbc.ca website. The right side of the figure shows the navigation attempt being intercepted by the Burp Suite proxy. The Burp Suite Community Edition is the free version that comes preinstalled in Kali Linux.

Wapiti

Wapiti is a web application vulnerability scanner that uses a black box approach, meaning it doesn't inspect code. Instead, it inspects a website by searching from the outside for ways to take advantage of XSS, SQL, PHP, JSP, and file-handling vulnerabilities. Although Wapiti can detect common forms that allow uploads or command injection, it uses "fuzzing"—trying to inject data into whatever will accept it. In this way, even new vulnerabilities can be discovered. Other scanners search for known vulnerability signatures only. You can install Wapiti in Kali Linux by using the command **sudo apt-get install wapiti**.

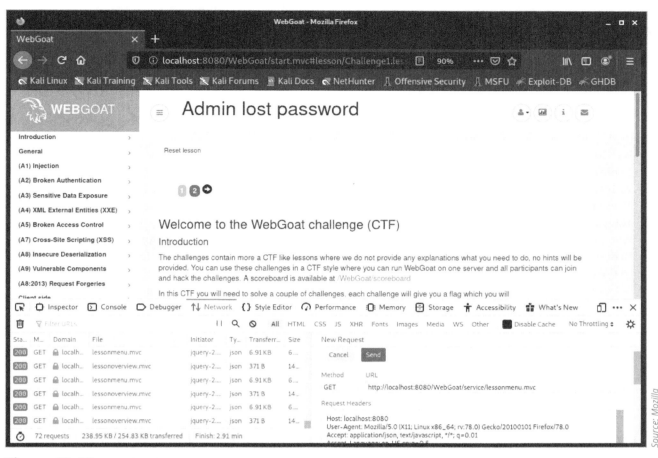

Figure 10-13   Firefox developer tools

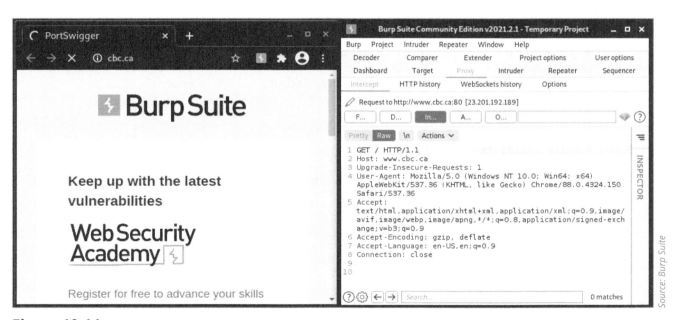

Figure 10-14   Burp Suite intercepting proxy

MODULE SUMMARY

- Web applications can be developed on many platforms. HTML webpages can contain forms, ASP.NET, CGI, and scripting languages, such as VBScript and JavaScript. Note, however, that scripting languages account for more than half of web server attacks.
- Many static webpages have been replaced by dynamic webpages, which are created on the fly when a user calls the page. Dynamic webpages can be created with a variety of techniques, including CGI, ASP.NET, ASP, PHP, ColdFusion, and JavaScript.
- Web forms allow developers to create webpages that visitors can interact with. Care should be taken, however, to ensure that form fields can't be manipulated by attackers.
- Web applications use a variety of technologies to connect to databases, such as ODBC, OLE DB, and ADO. These technologies create a front-end interface, allowing a web application to connect to a back-end database.
- You can install IIS to test your webpages in Windows.
- Web application vulnerabilities can have damaging consequences for a company. An attacker might be able to deface the company website, destroy a critical database, gain access to user accounts, or even gain access to the admin account or root access to other application servers on the network.
- When conducting security tests on web applications, determine whether dynamic webpages were used, whether the web application connects to a back-end database, whether a separate server is used for authenticating users, and what platform was used to develop the web application.
- Web applications that interact with databases might be vulnerable to SQL injection exploits.
- Many tools for testing web application vulnerabilities (and attacking web servers) are available, such as Burp Suite and Wapiti. In addition, OWASP offers open-source software to help security professionals learn about web application vulnerabilities.

Key Terms

Active Server Pages (ASP and
  ASP.NET)
ActiveX Data Objects (ADO)
ColdFusion
Common Gateway Interface (CGI)
Dynamic Application Security
  Testing (DAST)
Dynamic webpages

Interactive Application Security
  Testing (IAST)
Object Linking and Embedding
  Database (OLE DB)
Open Database Connectivity
  (ODBC)
Open Web Application Security
  Project (OWASP)

PHP Hypertext Processor (PHP)
SQL injection (SQLi)
Static Application Security Testing
  (SAST)
Static webpages
virtual directory
WebGoat

Review Questions

1. Using resources discussed in this module and your favorite search engine, search for recent successful SQL injection attacks. In a three-paragraph report, describe the organizations affected by the attack, what operating systems and web server programs were exploited, and details of how the attack was executed.

2. Which of the following can be used to create dynamic webpages? (Choose all that apply.)
   a. ColdFusion
   b. PHP
   c. ASP
   d. MySQL

3. Which of the following can be used to connect a web server to a back-end database server? (Choose all that apply.)
   a. ODBC
   b. OLE DB
   c. ADO
   d. HTML

4. Using resources discussed in this module and your favorite search engine, search for website attacks that had the most impact last year. In a three-paragraph report, describe the organizations affected by the attack, what operating systems and web server programs were exploited, and details of how the attack was executed.

5. What is DAST?
   a. Dynamic Application Static Testing
   b. Dynamic Application Server Takeover
   c. Delivery Application Server Testing
   d. Dynamic Application Security Testing

6. What is authorization testing?
   a. Testing to ensure that an application is properly sanitizing input
   b. Testing an application's access control mechanisms to ensure only authorized users have access to resources
   c. Testing focused on client-side code and the execution of scripts in the user's browser
   d. Testing that is specific to source code, otherwise referred to as Static Application Security Testing (SAST)

7. Entering the value `' OR 1 = 1` in a web application that has an "Enter Your PIN" field is most likely an example of which attack?
   a. SQL injection
   b. Code injection
   c. Buffer overflow
   d. Ethernet flaw

8. HTML webpages containing connection strings are more vulnerable to attack. True or false?

9. The AccessFileName directive in Apache, along with a configuration file (such as .htaccess), can be used to perform which of the following on a website?
   a. Run malicious code in the browser
   b. Protect against XSS worms
   c. Restrict directory access to those with authorized user credentials
   d. Scan for CGI vulnerabilities

10. Which of the following is an open source technology for creating dynamic HTML webpages?
    a. ASP
    b. PHP
    c. Java
    d. Oracle

11. CGI is used in Microsoft ASP pages. True or false?

12. Name three web application vulnerabilities from OWASP's top 10 list.

13. If a web server isn't protected, an attacker can gain access through remote administration interfaces. True or false?

14. Which of the following is used to connect an ASP. NET webpage to an Oracle database? (Choose all that apply.)
    a. ADO
    b. HTML
    c. CGA
    d. OLE DB

15. List an organization with online resources for learning more about web application vulnerabilities.

16. ASP is a legacy web scripting language that was first released in 1996. ASP is discussed in this module because organizations still use it. Perform some Internet research to determine what types of organizations still use ASP, and identify specific organizations by name, if possible. Were any significant web server breaches in the past few years related to ASP issues? Document your findings in a brief report.

17. What tags identify PHP as the scripting language?
    a. `<# #>`
    b. `<% %>`
    c. `<? ?>`
    d. `<! /!>`

18. An HTML webpage containing ASP.NET code must be compiled before running. True or false?

19. Which of the following can be used to detect a new application vulnerability on a website? (Choose all that apply.)
    a. PHP
    b. Nmap
    c. Wapiti
    d. Wfetch

20. IIS is used on more web servers than Apache Web Server. True or false?

Case Projects

Case Project 10-1: Determining Vulnerabilities of Web Servers

After conducting preliminary security testing on the Alexander Rocco Corporation network, you have identified that the company has seven web servers. One is a Windows 2012 R2 Server system running IIS 8.5. Natasha Romanoff, the network administrator, says the web server is used only by sales personnel as a front-end to update inventory data on an Oracle database server. Natasha says this procedure needs to be done remotely, and it's convenient for sales personnel to use a web browser when out of the office. Based on this information, write a one-page report on any possible vulnerabilities in the current configuration of the company's web server. Use the tools and techniques you have learned to search for possible vulnerabilities of IIS 8.5. Your report should include any recommendations that might increase web security.

Case Project 10-2: Discovering Web Application Attack Tools

After discovering that Alexander Rocco Corporation has multiple web servers running on different platforms, you wonder whether your only available security tool, Wapiti, can assess web application vulnerabilities thoroughly.

Based on this information, write a two-page report on other tools for security testers conducting web application vulnerability testing. Use the skills you have gained to search the Internet and explore Kali Linux to find tools for Windows and *nix platforms. The report should state the tool's name, describe the installation method, and include a brief description of what the tool does.

HACKING WIRELESS NETWORKS

After reading this module and completing the exercises, you will be able to:

1 Explain wireless technology

2 Describe wireless networking standards

3 Describe the process of authentication

4 Describe wardriving

5 Describe wireless hacking and tools used by hackers and security professionals

The term "wireless" generally describes equipment and technologies operating in the radio frequency (RF) spectrum between 3 Hz and 300 GHz. Examples of wireless equipment include cell phones, smartphones, AM/FM radios, wireless networking devices, and radar systems. Most wireless networking equipment operates in a smaller portion of the RF spectrum, between 2.4 GHz and 66 GHz. Wireless technology, especially on the Internet of Things (IoT), continues to grow in popularity, which has made securing wireless networks from attackers a primary concern.

This module gives you an overview of wireless networking technology and standards, explains the process of authentication, describes wardriving, and covers some tools attackers use on wireless networks.

UNDERSTANDING WIRELESS TECHNOLOGY

For a wireless network to function, you must have the right hardware and software and use a technology that sends and receives radio waves. At one time, when seeing the comic strip character Dick Tracy talk to his wristwatch, people wondered whether that would ever be possible. The idea that a phone could work without a wire connected to it seemed astounding, even though Alfred J. Gross had invented the walkie-talkie in 1938. In fact, the creator of *Dick Tracy* asked for Gross's permission before using a wireless wristwatch in his comics. (To read more about Al Gross, visit www.retrocom. com.) In 1973, 35 years after the walkie-talkie, Martin Cooper invented the first cell phone, which weighed close to 2 pounds.

Wireless technology is part of your daily life. Here are some wireless devices many people use daily:

- Baby monitors
- Keyless entry systems
- Cell phones
- Smartphones
- Global positioning system (GPS) devices
- Remote controls

- Garage door openers
- Two-way radios
- Bluetooth compatible devices such as smart watches, speakers, and headphones
- Smart TVs
- Smart cars

Components of a Wireless Network

Any network needs certain components to work: communication devices to transmit and receive signals, protocols, and a medium for transmitting data. On a typical LAN, these components are network interface cards (NICs), TCP/IP, and an Ethernet cable (the wire serving as the connection medium). As complex as wireless networks might seem, they too have only a few basic components:

- **Wireless network interface cards (WNICs)**, which transmit and receive wireless signals, and access points (APs), which are the bridges between wired and wireless networks
- Wireless networking protocols, such as Wi-Fi Protected Access (WPA)
- A portion of the RF spectrum, which replaces wire as the connection medium

The following sections explain how an AP and a WNIC function in a wireless network.

Access Points

An **access point (AP)** is a radio transceiver that connects to a network via an Ethernet cable and links a **wireless LAN (WLAN)** to a wired network. Some wireless networks do not connect to a wired network, such as a peer-to-peer networks, but this topology isn't covered because security testers are seldom contracted to secure a peer-to-peer wireless network. Most companies conducting security tests use a WLAN that connects to the company's wired network topology.

RF channels are configured in an AP. Figure 11-1 shows APs detected on channel 11 by Vistumbler (an AP-scanning program covered in "Understanding Wardriving" later in this module). Hackers look for APs as they drive around with an antenna and a laptop computer scanning for access. Channels are explained in more detail later in "The 802.11 Standard." For now, think of a channel as a range or frequency that data travels over, just like a channel on the radio.

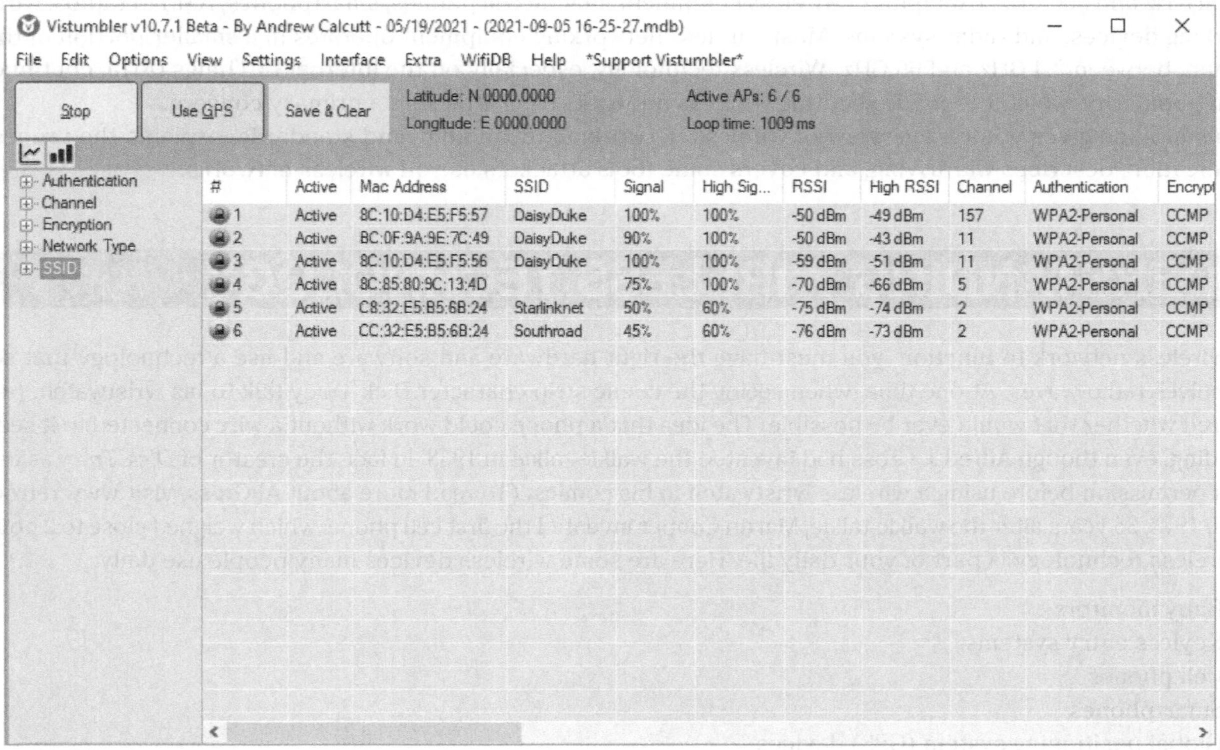

#	Active	Mac Address	SSID	Signal	High Sig...	RSSI	High RSSI	Channel	Authentication	Encrypt
1	Active	8C:10:D4:E5:F5:57	DaisyDuke	100%	100%	-50 dBm	-49 dBm	157	WPA2-Personal	CCMP
2	Active	BC:0F:9A:9E:7C:49	DaisyDuke	90%	100%	-50 dBm	-43 dBm	11	WPA2-Personal	CCMP
3	Active	8C:10:D4:E5:F5:56	DaisyDuke	100%	100%	-59 dBm	-51 dBm	11	WPA2-Personal	CCMP
4	Active	8C:85:80:9C:13:4D		75%	100%	-70 dBm	-66 dBm	5	WPA2-Personal	CCMP
5	Active	C8:32:E5:B5:6B:24	Starlinknet	50%	60%	-75 dBm	-74 dBm	2	WPA2-Personal	CCMP
6	Active	CC:32:E5:B5:6B:24	Southroad	45%	60%	-76 dBm	-73 dBm	2	WPA2-Personal	CCMP

Source: GNU General Public License (GNU GPL)

Figure 11-1   AP channels detected

An AP enables users to connect to a LAN with wireless technology. The AP can be configured to transmit and receive only within a defined area or square footage, depending on the technology. If you're 20 miles away from an AP, you're probably out of range.

Service Set Identifiers

A service set identifier (SSID) is the name used to identify a WLAN, much the same way a VLAN ID is used to identify network VLANs. An SSID is configured on the AP as a unique, 1- to 32-character, case-sensitive alphanumeric name. To access the WLAN the AP connects to, wireless-enabled computers must be configured with the same SSID as the AP. The SSID name, or "code," is attached to each packet to identify it as belonging to that wireless network. The AP usually beacons (broadcasts) the SSID several times a second so that users who have WNICs can see a display of all WLANs within range of the AP's signal. The SSID is broadcast in cleartext (unencrypted text), which can be a security issue. Anyone who detects the SSID of the AP can attempt to connect to it, including hackers. To better secure your AP, you can disable SSID broadcasts so that only people who know (or guess) the SSID can connect to it. In Figure 11-2, the Windows 10 wireless connection manager shows SSIDs advertised by APs within range of the wireless computer. Some WNICs come with built-in wireless connection software that looks different from the Windows utility.

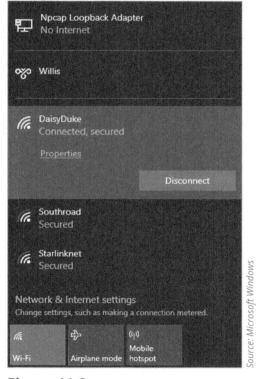

Figure 11-2   SSIDs advertised to a Windows computer

Many vendors have SSIDs set to a default value. For example, Cisco APs previously used the default SSID "tsunami." Typical default SSIDs are single words such as Wireless, Netgear, Linksys, Admin, and Default, though default SSIDs can change often. As a security professional, you must research constantly and gather information to keep abreast of changes in this industry. If an AP is configured to provide its SSID after authentication, wireless hackers can attempt to guess the SSID by using a well-known default SSID. Make sure your client isn't using a default SSID.

Sometimes, a default SSID can tell an attacker that the target AP is old or out of date. If a wireless AP is using the default SSID, it might also be using other defaults such as the default username and password for the administrative login. If hackers wanting to access an AP find a default SSID, they will try the default administrative login credentials first.

Activity 11-1: Finding Vulnerabilities with Default SSIDs

Time Required: 30 minutes

Objective: Learn how recognizing a default SSID can open the door to discovering vulnerabilities.

Description: As you learned earlier, recognizing which OS a customer or client is using is essential before you can detect vulnerabilities in a system or network. This is also true when you're attempting to discover vulnerabilities in an AP. When conducting a security test on a WLAN, you start by looking for SSIDs advertised over the air to determine the type of AP the company is using.

1. If necessary, start your computer in Windows or boot into Kali Linux, and start a web browser. Go to **https://nvd.nist.gov**.

2. In the left pane, click **Search** to go to the Search page.

3. On the Search page, click the **Vulnerabilities – CVE** button to go to the Search Vulnerability Database page.

4. Type **dlink wireless** in the Keyword Search text box, and then click the **Search** button. Review some recent vulnerabilities with a Common Vulnerability Scoring System (CVSS) severity score of 9 or higher.

5. Click the CVE link, and read the vulnerability summary information to learn more about each critical vulnerability. Is an exploit or attack demonstration available?

6. Does the router use a typical default SSID? Because router models (and URLs) change constantly, use your search skills to find the default SSID for the router make and model you selected.

7. What solution would you offer to a client using the router you selected in Step 3?

8. Leave your web browser open for the next activity.

Configuring an Access Point

Configuring an AP varies, depending on the embedded OS supplied by the manufacturer. With most APs, users can access the software through a web browser because the AP has an embedded OS supporting a web server. The following example shows options for dd-wrt, an embedded Linux OS that replaces the embedded OS used on hundreds of routers from Linksys, D-Link, Netgear, Belkin, Microsoft, U.S. Robotics, Dell, Buffalo, and many others. You see how an AP administrator can determine the SSID and channel and configure security (covered later in this module in "Understanding Authentication").

The following example outlines the steps a security professional takes to access and reconfigure a wireless router running dd-wrt with the IP address 192.168.1.1. *Read but do not perform the following steps.*

1. After entering the IP address in a web browser, the user is prompted for a logon name and password. In dd-wrt, the default username is "root," and the default password is "admin." For security reasons, changing these credentials is essential.

2. After a successful logon, you click the Status tab at the top to display the window shown in Figure 11-3. Notice the router model and CPU model listed under Router Information.

3. Click the Wireless tab to display the window shown in Figure 11-4. The user entered "ironman" for the SSID. (*Note:* The default SSID for wireless routers running dd-wrt is "dd-wrt.") The user could have changed the default name to "Cisco" to try to trick attackers into believing the router is a Cisco product; however, picking a name that's not associated with a manufacturer or an OS might be more effective at discouraging attacks. Notice that Channel 6, the default channel for many wireless router OSs, has been selected. To improve security, you might want to disable SSID broadcasts because advertising who you are and whether you're using encryption increases the chance of attack. In dd-wrt, you disable SSID broadcasts by clicking the Disable option button.

4. To configure security, you click the Wireless Security tab. In Figure 11-5, the user has entered a password (called a "WPA shared key" in dd-wrt) that must be supplied by the wireless computer.

NOTE

WNIC manufacturers usually supply connection management software that you can use instead of the built-in Windows utility.

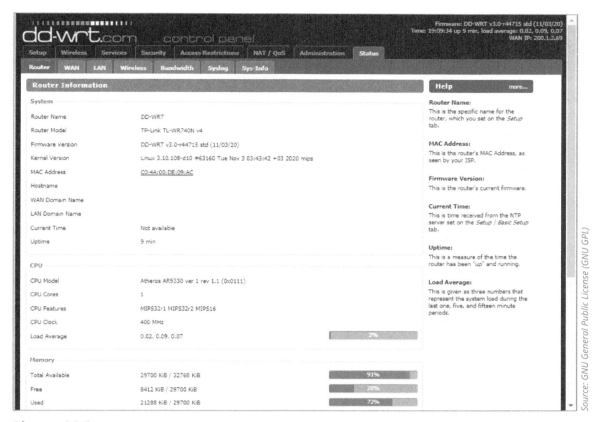

Figure 11-3   Viewing status information in dd-wrt

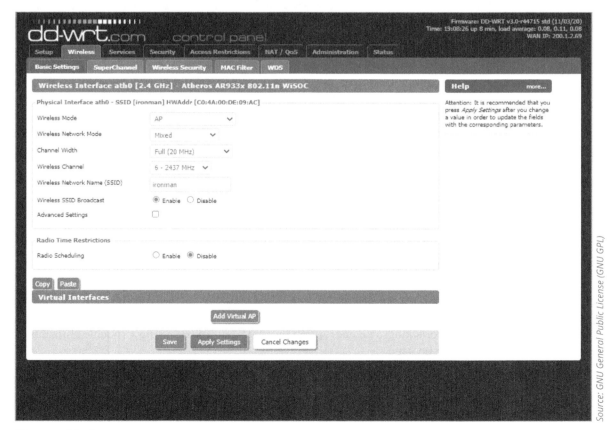

Figure 11-4   Basic wireless configuration in dd-wrt

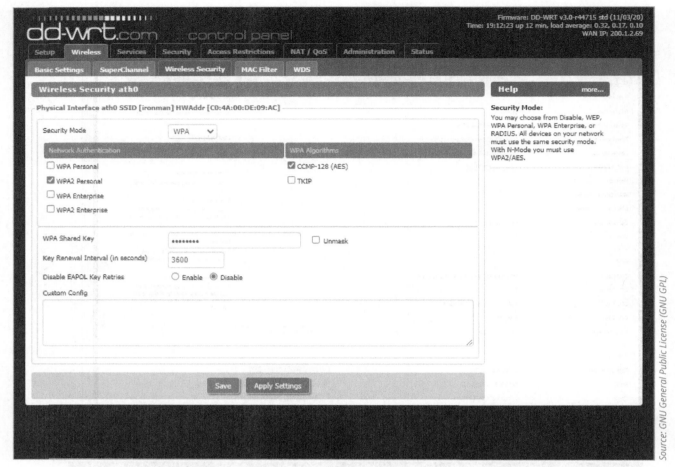

Figure 11-5   Configuring wireless security in dd-wrt

If a company doesn't change its default SSID but decides to disable SSID broadcasts, a determined intruder can use a passive wireless sniffer, such as Kismet (covered later in "Understanding Wardriving"). Kismet can detect SSIDs in WLAN client traffic. If the user didn't assign a WLAN key or change the default administrator password to the AP, you can see how easily an attacker could access the WLAN. As a security tester, you must verify that a WLAN is free of these vulnerabilities. If the WLAN has them, you should recommend that the company close the holes as quickly as possible.

Wireless NICs

To send information over any medium, a computing device must follow the rules for the medium it's traversing, so the correct software and drivers for the NIC must be installed. For example, data traveling over a copper wire must follow rules for how Ethernet signals are sent over that medium. For wireless technology to work, each node or computer must have a WNIC, which converts the radio waves it receives into digital signals the computer understands.

There are many WNICs on the market, but be careful deciding which one to purchase if you're considering using specific tools for detecting APs and decrypting WEP keys or using antennas that can cover a large distance. For instance, AirCrack-ng, a program for cracking WEP encryption on a WLAN, requires using a specific chipset on a WNIC, so only certain brands of WNICs can be used.

UNDERSTANDING WIRELESS NETWORK STANDARDS

A standard is a set of rules formulated by an organization. All industries have standards, and a WLAN is no exception. Just as the Institute of Electrical and Electronics Engineers (IEEE) has standards specifying maximum cable length in an Ethernet network, it sets rules to follow for wireless networks.

Working groups (WGs) of the IEEE are formed to develop new standards. After a WG has reached consensus on a proposal for a standard, the Sponsor Executive Committee must approve the proposal. Finally, after the proposal is recommended by the Standards Review Committee and approved by the IEEE Standards Board, you have a new standard.

IEEE Project 802 was developed to create LAN and WAN standards. (The first meeting was held in February 1980, so the project was given the number 802, with "80" representing the year and "2" representing the month.) WG names are also assigned numbers, such as 11 for the Wireless LAN group, and letters to denote approved projects, such as 802.11a or 802.11b. In this module, you learn about the 802 standards pertaining to wireless networks.

The 802.11 Standard

The first wireless technology standard, 802.11, defined specifications for wireless connectivity as 1 Mbps and 2 Mbps in a LAN. This standard applied to the Physical layer of the OSI model, which deals with wireless connectivity issues of fixed, portable, and moving stations in a local area, and the Media Access Control (MAC) sublayer of the Data Link layer. Often, multiple transmitters are nearby, so radio signals can mix and have the potential to interfere with each other (as signal collision). For this reason, carrier sense multiple access/ collision avoidance (CSMA/CA) is used instead of the CSMA/CD method (collision detection, used in Ethernet).

Many definitions of terms are included in the more than 500 pages of the 802.11 standard. One important distinction is that wireless LANs don't have an address associated with a physical location, as wired LANs do. In 802.11, an addressable unit is called a station (STA). A station is defined as a message destination and might not be a fixed location. Another distinction is made between mobile stations and portable stations. A mobile station is one that accesses the LAN while moving; a portable station is one that can move from location to location but is used only while in a fixed location.

Basic Architecture of 802.11

802.11 uses a basic service set (BSS) as its building block. A BSS is the collection of devices (AP and stations or just stations) that make up a WLAN. A basic service area (BSA) is the coverage area an AP provides. A WLAN running in what's called infrastructure mode always has one or more APs. An independent WLAN without an AP is called an ad-hoc network; independent stations connect in a decentralized fashion. As long as a station is within its BSA, it can communicate with other stations in the BSS. You have probably experienced losing cell phone connectivity when you're out of range of your service area. Similarly, you can lose network connectivity if you aren't in the WLAN's coverage area. To connect two BSSs, 802.11 requires a distribution system (DS) as an intermediate layer. Basically, BSS 1 connects to the DS, which in turn connects to BSS 2. However, how does a station called STA 1 in BSS 1 connect to STA 2 in BSS 2? 802.11 defines an AP as a station providing access to the DS. Data moves between a BSS and the DS through the AP. This process sounds complicated, but Figure 11-6 should clear up any confusion.

The IEEE specifications also define the operating frequency range of 802.11. In the United States, the range is 2.4 to 2.4835 GHz. Think of the frequency as a superhighway in the sky where data travels, and this superhighway encompasses many highways (frequency bands). Each frequency band contains channels, which break up the band into smaller frequency ranges. For example, channel 1 of a frequency band ranging from 2.4 GHz to 2.4835 GHz might use the 2.401 GHz frequency, and channel 2 of this frequency band might use 2.406 GHz. The 802.11 standard defines 11 channels in the 2.4 to 2.462 GHz range. If channels overlap, interference could occur.

Sound travels through the air in waves, and like ocean waves, the length of a sound wave is measured from the peak of one wave to the next. A sound wave's amplitude (height) and frequency (rate at which a sound wave repeats) determine its volume and pitch. Surfers waiting for the next set of waves to ride can accurately determine frequency (the time it takes a set of waves to repeat). Completing a repeating pattern of sound waves is called a cycle. For surfers, a cycle can be minutes. Sound waves, however, repeat at a much faster frequency. For example, a tuning fork vibrates at 440 Hz, or cycles per second. That's 440 waves per second—too fast for a surfer. Different technologies use different frequencies, referred to as bands, to transmit sound. Table 11-1 lists frequency bands.

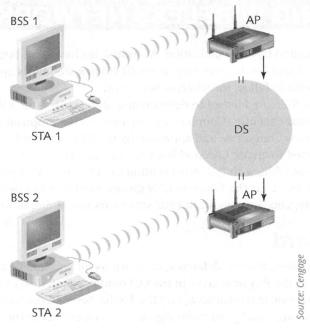

Figure 11-6 Connecting two wireless remote stations

Table 11-1 Frequency Bands

Frequency	Range	Wavelength
Extremely low frequency (ELF)	3–30 Hz	100,000 km–10,000 km
Super low frequency (SLF)	30–300 Hz	10,000 km–1000 km
Voice frequency (VF) or ultra-low frequency (ULF)	300 Hz–3 KHz	1000 km–100 km
Very low frequency (VLF)	3–30 KHz	100 km–10 km
Low frequency (LF)	30–300 KHz	10 km–1 km
Medium frequency (MF)	300 KHz–3 MHz	1 km–100 m
High frequency (HF)	3–30 MHz	100 m–10 m
Very high frequency (VHF)	30–300 MHz	10 m–1 m
Ultra high frequency (UHF)	300 MHz–3 GHz	1 m–10 cm
Super high frequency (SHF)	3–30 GHz	10 cm–1 cm
Extremely high frequency (EHF)	30–300 GHz	1 cm–1 mm

For example, AM radio stations use the medium frequency (MF) band; FM radio stations and search-and-rescue stations use the very high frequency (VHF) band. The distance sound waves need to travel also determines which frequency band to use.

An Overview of Wireless Technologies

Now that you understand the frequencies on which radio waves can travel, take a look at the three technologies WLANs use:

- *Infrared*—Infrared light can't be seen by the human eye. Infrared (IR) technology is restricted to a single room or line of sight because IR light can't penetrate walls, ceilings, or floors.
- *Narrowband*—Narrowband technology uses microwave radio band frequencies to transmit data. The most common uses of this technology are cordless phones and garage door openers.

- *Spread spectrum*—To move over radio waves, data must be modulated on the carrier signal or channel. Modulation defines how data is placed on a carrier signal. For example, spread spectrum modulation means data is spread across a large-frequency bandwidth instead of traveling across just one frequency band. In other words, a group of radio frequencies is selected, and the data is "spread" across this group. Spread spectrum, the most widely used WLAN technology, uses the following methods:

  - *Frequency-hopping spread spectrum* (FHSS): Data hops to other frequencies to avoid interference that might occur over a frequency band. Hopping from one frequency to another occurs at split-second intervals and makes it difficult for an intruder or attacker to jam the communication channel.
  - *Direct sequence spread spectrum* (DSSS): Unlike FHSS, DSSS spreads data packets simultaneously over multiple frequencies instead of hopping to other frequencies. Sub-bits are added to a packet as it travels across the frequency band and are used for recovery, in much the same way RAID-5 uses parity bits to rebuild a hard disk that crashes. Sub-bits are called "chips," and every bit of the original message is represented by multiple bits, called the chipping code.
  - *Orthogonal frequency division multiplexing* (OFDM): The bandwidth is divided into a series of frequencies called tones, which allows a higher throughput (data transfer rate) than FHSS and DSSS do.
  - *Orthogonal frequency division multiplexing Access* (OFDMA): OFDMA is the multiuser extension of single-user OFDM. ODFMA has a throughput three times higher than OFDM for short packets of data or multiple endpoints. OFDMA combines transmissions and sends frames to multiple endpoints simultaneously. It is more efficient with lower latency transmission. This makes OFDMA ideal for IoT devices, video, online gaming, and automation applications.

Additional IEEE 802.11 Projects

The IEEE WG developed additional 802.11 projects, releasing the 802.11a and 802.11b standards in October 1999. 802.11b quickly became the more widely used standard, probably because its hardware was less expensive. Also referred to as Wi-Fi, 802.11b operates in the 2.4 GHz band and increased the throughput to 11 Mbps from the 1 or 2 Mbps of the original 802.11. It allows a total of 11 separate channels to prevent overlapping signals. However, because of each channel's bandwidth requirements, effectively only three channels (1, 6, and 11) can be combined without overlapping and creating interference. This standard also introduced Wired Equivalent Privacy (WEP), which gave many users a false sense of security that data traversing the WLAN was protected. WEP is covered later in "Understanding Authentication."

The 802.11a standard has a different operating frequency range from 802.11 and 802.11b; it operates in three distinct bands in the 5 GHz range. In addition, throughput increases to 54 Mbps, much faster than 802.11b.

The 802.11g standard, released in 2003, operates in the 2.4 GHz band, too. However, because it uses a different modulation, it uses the OFDM method, which increases throughput to 54 Mbps.

The 802.11i standard introduced Wi-Fi Protected Access (WPA) in 2004, which is covered in "Understanding Authentication." For now, note that 802.11i corrected many security vulnerabilities in 802.11b. For security professionals, the 802.11i standard is probably the most important.

The 802.11e standard, released in 2005, has improvements that address the problem of interference. When interference is detected, the signal can jump to another frequency more quickly, providing a better quality of service than 802.11b.

The 802.11n standard, finalized in 2009, operates in the same frequency (2.4 or 5 GHz band) and uses the same encoding as 802.11g. However, by using multiple antennas and wider bandwidth channels, it increases throughput to 600 Mbps.

The 802.11ac standard, released in 2014, uses the 5 GHz band. This standard allows for higher throughput (up to 1 gigabit per second) by multiplying the number of MIMO links and using high-density modulation.

The 802.11ad standard, dubbed "WiGig," allows for transfer rates of up to 7 gigabits per second over the 2.4 GHz, 5 GHz, and 60 GHz bands. In January 2016, TP-Link revealed the first wireless router to support the 802.11ad specification.

The 802.11ah standard, approved in May 2017, targets lower energy consumption, and creates extended-range Wi-Fi networks that can extend beyond typical 2.4 GHz or 5 GHz networks. It is expected to compete with Bluetooth given its lower power needs.

The 802.11aj standard, known as the China Millimeter Wave, is used in China and is basically a rebranding of 802.11ad for use in certain areas of the world. The goal is to maintain backward compatibility with 802.11ad. The technology uses the 45 GHz and 60 GHz spectrums uniquely available in China.

The 802.11x standard, branded as Wi-Fi 6, went live in 2019 and replaces 802.11ac as the de facto wireless standard. Wi-Fi 6 maxes out at 10 Gbps, uses less power, is more reliable in congested environments, and supports better security.

Additional IEEE 802 Standards

The 802.15 standard addresses networking devices in one person's workspace, which is called a wireless personal area network (WPAN). The maximum distance between devices is usually 10 meters. With the Bluetooth telecommunication specification, a fundamental part of the WPAN standard, you can connect portable devices, such as cell phones and computers, without wires. Bluetooth version 2.0 uses the 2.4 GHz band and can transmit data at speeds up to 12 Mbps. It's not compatible with the 802.11 standards. The most recent Bluetooth version, 4.0, was released in 2010 and has moved to the 802.11 band to support speeds of up to 24 Mbps. In 2005, the IEEE began work on using different technologies for the WPAN standard. ZigBee, a current example, is used for automation systems, such as smart lighting systems, temperature controls, and appliances.

The 802.16 standard covers wireless metropolitan area networks (MANs). This standard defines the Wireless MAN Air Interface for wireless MANs and addresses the limited distance available for 802.11b WLANs. The most widely used implementation of wireless MAN technology is called Worldwide Interoperability for Microwave Access (WiMAX). WiMAX was marketed as a viable alternative to so-called last-mile Internet access, which is normally provided by cable and DSL. There are mobile (802.16e) and fixed (802.16d) versions of WiMAX. A typical real-world speed of WiMAX is about 10 Mbps, less than the theoretical 120 Mbps maximum of the 802.16 standard. WiMAX was a failed venture, and efforts ended in 2015. Another MAN standard, 802.20, with a goal similar to mobile WiMAX is called Mobile Broadband Wireless Access (MBWA). It addresses wireless MANs for mobile users in trains, subways, or cars traveling at speeds up to 150 miles per hour. The most common implementation of MBWA, iBurst, is used widely in Asia and Africa.

Table 11-2 summarizes the wireless standards in common use today but doesn't include some wireless standards beyond the scope of this book, such as the licensed 802.11y 3.6 GHz bands, the 4.9 GHz band for U.S. public safety networks, and mobile phone wireless technologies—Evolution Data Optimized (EVDO), Enhanced Data GSM Environment (EDGE), and 3G, 4G/LTE, for example.

Table 11-2 Summary of Approved Wireless Standards

Standard	Frequency	Maximum rate	Modulation method
802.11	2.4 GHz	1 or 2 Mbps	FHSS/DSSS
802.11a	5 GHz	54 Mbps	OFDM
802.11b	2.4 GHz	11 Mbps	DSSS
802.11g	2.4 GHz	54 Mbps	OFDM
802.11n	2.4 GHz & 5 GHz	600 Mbps	OFDM
802.11ac	5 GHz	1 Gbps	OFDM
802.11ad	2.4 GHz, 5 GHz, & 60 GHz	7 Gbps	OFDM
802.11ah	900 MHz	347 Mbps	OFDM
802.11aj	45 GHz & 60 GHz	15 Gbps	OFDM
802.11ax	2.4 GHz & 5 GHz	10 Gbps	OFDMA
802.15	2.4 GHz	2 Mbps	FHSS
802.16 (WiMAX)	10–66 GHz	120 Mbps	OFDM
802.20 (Mobile Wireless Access Working Group)	Below 3.5 GHz	1 Mbps	OFDM
Bluetooth	2.4 GHz	24 Mbps	Gaussian frequency shift keying (GFSK)
HiperLAN/2	5 GHz	54 Mbps	OFDM

Activity 11-2: Visiting the IEEE 802.11 Website

Time Required: 30 minutes

Objective: Learn more about IEEE wireless standards.

Description: You can find a wealth of information at the IEEE website, which makes the standards available for download. In this activity, you visit the IEEE website and research a new and exciting project at IEEE.

1. Start a web browser, if necessary, and go to **http://www.ieee802.org/11/Reports/tgay_update.htm**.
2. Review project goals of the IEEE 802.11ay specification.
3. What is the theoretical throughput of 802.11ay? Looking at Table 11-2, what is the throughput of commonly used protocols 802.11a, b, g, and n?
4. Visit the Wikipedia entry for 802.11 at **https://en.wikipedia.org/wiki/IEEE_802.1**
5. Review the Security section of the Wikipedia article.
6. Explain why a security professional might suggest disabling Wi-Fi Protected Setup (WPS) on a router.
7. Exit your web browser.

UNDERSTANDING AUTHENTICATION

The problem of unauthorized users accessing resources on a network is a major concern for security professionals. An organization that introduces wireless technology to the mix increases the potential for security problems. The 802.1X standard, discussed in the following section, addresses the issue of authentication. Some routers, by default, do not require authentication, which could leave a corporate network at risk.

The 802.1X Standard

Because there must be a method to ensure that others with wireless NICs can't access resources on your wireless network, the 802.1X standard defines the process of authenticating and authorizing users on a network. This standard is especially useful for WLAN security when physical access control is more difficult to enforce than on wired LANs. To understand how authentication takes place on a wireless network, review basic authentication concepts in the following sections.

Point-to-Point Protocol

Many ISPs use Point-to-Point Protocol (PPP) to connect dial-up or DSL users. PPP handles authentication by requiring a user to enter a valid username and password. PPP verifies that users attempting to use the link are indeed who they say they are.

Extensible Authentication Protocol

Extensible Authentication Protocol (EAP), an enhancement to PPP, was designed to allow a company to select its authentication method. For example, a company can use certificates or Kerberos authentication to authenticate a user connecting to an AP. A certificate is a record that authenticates network entities, such as a server or client. It contains X.509 information that identifies the owner, the certification authority (CA), and the owner's public key. You can examine an X.509 certificate by going to www.amazon.ca. This website redirects you to the secure (HTTPS) URL, where you click the padlock icon at the left of the address bar in Chrome, and then click Certificate to see the certificate information shown in Figure 11-7.

The following EAP methods can be used to improve security on a wireless network:

- *Extensible Authentication Protocol-Transport Layer Security* (EAP-TLS)—This method requires assigning the client and server a digital certificate signed by a CA that both parties trust. This CA can be a commercial company that charges a fee, or a server configured by a network administrator to issue certificates. In this way, both the server and client authenticate mutually. In addition to servers requiring that clients prove they are who they say, clients also want servers to verify their identity.
- *Protected EAP*—Protected EAP (PEAP) uses TLS to authenticate the server to the client but not the client to the server. With PEAP, only the server is required to have a digital certificate. (See RFC-2246 for more information on TLS.)

- *Microsoft PEAP*—In Microsoft's implementation of PEAP, a secure channel is created by using TLS as protection against eavesdropping.

802.1X uses the following components to function:

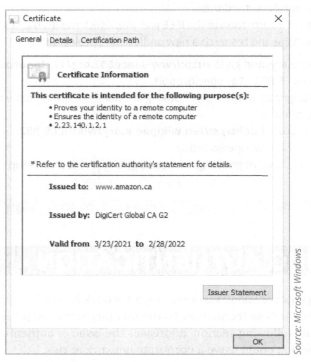

Figure 11-7 Viewing information about an x.509 certificate

- *Supplicant*—A **supplicant** is a wireless user attempting access to a WLAN.
- *Authenticator*—The AP functions as the entity allowing or denying the supplicant's access.
- *Authentication server*—This server, which might be a Remote Access Dial-In User Service (RADIUS) server, is used as a centralized component that authenticates the user and performs accounting functions. For example, an ISP using RADIUS can verify who logged on to the ISP service and how long the user was connected. Most RADIUS servers are *nix based, but the Microsoft implementation of RADIUS is called Internet Authentication Service (IAS) in Windows Server 2000 and Windows Server 2003 and is called Network Policy Server after Windows Server 2008.

Figure 11-8 shows the process of 802.1X, described in the following steps:

1. An unauthenticated client (supplicant) attempts to connect with the AP functioning as the authenticator.
2. The AP responds by enabling a port that passes only EAP packets from the supplicant to the RADIUS server on the wired network.
3. The AP blocks all other traffic until the RADIUS server authenticates the supplicant.
4. After the RADIUS server has authenticated the supplicant, it gives the supplicant access to network resources via the AP.

Until EAP and 802.1X were used on wireless LANs, a device, not a user, was authenticated on the WLAN. Therefore, if a computer was stolen from a company, the thief could connect to resources on the WLAN using the computer for authentication. The following sections describe security features introduced in 802.11b and 802.11i.

Wired Equivalent Privacy

Wired Equivalent Privacy (WEP), part of the 802.11b standard, was developed to encrypt data traversing a wireless network. For some time, it gave many security professionals a false sense of security that wireless technology could be just as safe as wired networks. Unfortunately, WEP has been torn to shreds by security professionals, professors

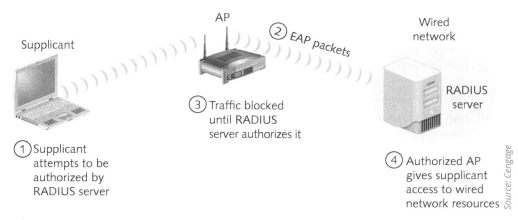

Figure 11-8   A supplicant connecting to an AP and a RADIUS server

from major universities, and hackers who post ways to crack WEP encryption. WEP encryption is easily cracked due to a flaw in its RC4 encryption algorithm. The encryption key used by the algorithm is a 24-bit initialization vector (IV) in combination with a default key. The 24-bit IV is too short and easy to break. Some argue that WEP is still better than no security at all, and when it's combined with the security of a virtual private network (VPN), they claim that WEP works well for home users or small businesses. Still, many saw a need for a better way to protect WLANs.

Wi-Fi Protected Access

Wi-Fi Protected Access (WPA, WPA2, and WPA3), specified in the 802.11i standard, is the replacement for WEP, which is known to have cryptographic weaknesses. WPA improves encryption by using Temporal Key Integrity Protocol (TKIP). TKIP has four enhancements that address encryption vulnerabilities in WEP:

- *Message Integrity Check (MIC)*—MIC, pronounced M-I-C and also called Michael, is a cryptographic message integrity code. Its main purpose is to prevent forgeries, which are packets that attackers create to look like legitimate packets. For example, an MIC uses a secret authentication key, which only the sender and receiver know, and creates a tag (a message integrity code) generated from the key and message sent to the receiver. The sender sends the message and tag to the receiver, who must enter the key, tag, and message in a program that verifies whether the tag created with the three input fields is equal to the tag the program should have created. You don't need to memorize this process but should understand that MIC corrects a known vulnerability in WEP.
- *Extended Initialization Vector (IV) with sequencing rules*—This enhancement was developed to prevent replays. In a replay, an attacker records or captures a packet, saves it, and retransmits the message later. To prevent a replay from occurring, a sequence number is applied to the WEP IV field. If a packet is received with an IV equal to or less than the sequence number received earlier, the packet is discarded.
- *Per-packet key mixing*—This enhancement helps defeat weak key attacks that occurred in WEP. MAC addresses are used to create an intermediate key, which prevents the same key from being used by all links.
- *Rekeying mechanism*—This enhancement provides fresh keys to help prevent attacks that relied on reusing old keys. That is, if the same key is used repeatedly, someone running a program to decipher the key could likely do so after collecting a large number of packets. The same key being used repeatedly was a big problem in WEP.

WPA also added an authentication mechanism using 802.1X and EAP, which weren't available in WEP.

Since the release of WPA, weaknesses have been found in TKIP, which called for a more advanced WPA2. WPA2 replaced WPA in the official Wi-Fi standard. The main difference between WPA and WPA2 is the requirement in WPA2 to use AES encryption instead of TKIP.

WPA3 was released in January 2018. WPA3 officially replaces WPA2 and provides improved security features. For encryption, WPA3 uses AES-256 and SHA-384 in WPA3-Enterprise mode, and still mandates the use of CCMP-128 (AES-128 in CCM Mode) as the minimum encryption algorithm in WPA3-Personal mode. WPA3 replaces pre-shared key (PSK) exchange with Simultaneous Authentication of Equals (SAE) exchange, which results in a more secure initial key exchange.

WPA3 makes it more difficult for hackers to tap into a network using offline password-guessing attacks. WPA2 would allow hackers to capture data from your router and use this data to repeatedly attempt to guess your password, but with WPA3, one incorrect hacking attempt renders this data useless. WPA3 also improves security over public Wi-Fi networks, making it impossible for hackers to recover your data even if they intercept and break an encrypted transmission.

WPA3 is secure but not invulnerable. In particular, it is susceptible to timing attacks during the handshake process. Information gathered from WPA3 from the timing attack can also be used to perform a password partitioning attack, which is similar to a dictionary attack. A dictionary attack is an automated password guessing attack.

Wi-Fi Protected Setup (WPS)

Wi-Fi Protected Setup (WPS) is a wireless authentication standard created to allow users to add devices easily and securely to a wireless network.

WPS makes this process easier by eliminating the need for a user to enter a passphrase. Rather, the user simply presses a button on the router and the WPS-enabled device pairs with the router. Chances are, if you have a modern router at home, it is capable of WPS.

WPS might sound like a great solution, but a major security flaw was discovered in late 2011. This flaw allows an attacker to gain access to a network remotely without knowing the WPA2 password.

UNDERSTANDING WARDRIVING

It's probably no secret that hackers use wardriving—driving around with inexpensive hardware and software that enables them to detect access points that haven't been secured. Surprisingly, some APs have no passwords or security measures, so wardriving can be quite rewarding for hackers. As of this writing, wardriving isn't illegal; using the resources of networks discovered with wardriving is, of course, a different story. Wardriving has now been expanded to include warflying, which involves drones with an antenna and the same software used in wardriving. The testers used Kismet, covered later in this section, which identifies APs that attempt to "cloak" or hide their SSIDs.

How It Works

To conduct wardriving, an attacker or a security tester simply drives around with a Wi-Fi capable smartphone or laptop and software that scans the area for SSIDs. Not all WNICs are compatible with scanning software, so review the software requirements before purchasing the hardware. Antenna prices vary, depending on their quality and the range they can cover. Some are as small as a cell phone's antenna, and some are as large as a bazooka. The larger ones can sometimes return results on networks miles away from the attacker. The smaller ones might require being in close proximity to the AP.

Most scanning software detects the company's SSID, the type of security enabled, and the signal strength, indicating how close the AP is to the attacker. Because attacks against WEP are simple and attacks against WPA are possible, any 802.11 connection not using WPA2 or WPA3 should be considered inadequately secured. The following sections introduce some tools that many wireless hackers and security professionals use.

SECURITY BYTES

An ethical hacker in Houston, previously employed by the county's Technology Department, was accused of breaking into a Texas court's wireless network. While he was conducting scans as part of his job, he noticed a vulnerability in the court's wireless network and was concerned. He demonstrated to a county official and a local reporter how easily he could gain access to the wireless network with just a laptop computer and a WNIC. He was later charged with two counts of unauthorized access of a protected computer system and unauthorized access of a computer system used in justice administration. After a three-day trial and 15 minutes of jury deliberation, he was acquitted. If he had been found guilty of all charges, he would have faced 10 years in prison and a $500,000 fine.

Vistumbler

Vistumbler (www.vistumbler.net) is a freeware tool written for Windows that enables you to detect WLANs using 802.11a, 802.11b, 802.11g, 802.11n, and 802.11ac access points. The tool is easy to install, though not all wireless hardware works with the software, so you must follow the directions carefully and verify that your hardware is compatible. Vistumbler is designed to assist security testers in the following:

- Verifying the WLAN configuration
- Detecting other wireless networks that might be interfering with a WLAN
- Detecting unauthorized APs that might have been placed on a WLAN

NOTE

Vistumbler is also used in wardriving, but remember that in most parts of the world, using someone's network without permission is illegal. This law includes using someone's Internet connection without his or her knowledge or permission.

Another feature of Vistumbler is that it can connect to a GPS, enabling a security tester or hacker to map locations of all WLANs the software detects (see Figure 11-9).

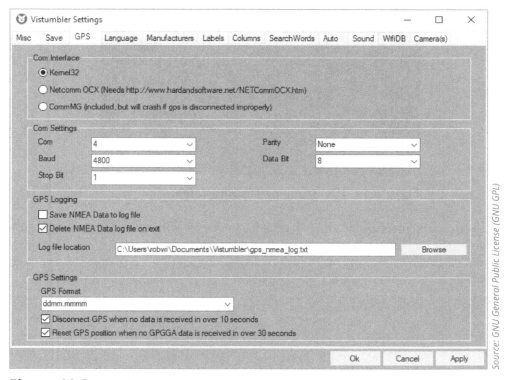

Figure 11-9   Configuring GPS settings in the Vistumbler Settings dialog box

Source: GNU General Public License (GNU GPL)

When Vistumbler identifies an AP signal, it logs the SSID, MAC address, and manufacturer of the AP, the channel on which the signal was heard, the strength of the signal, and whether encryption is enabled (but not a specific encryption type). Attackers can detect APs within a 350-foot radius, though with a good antenna, they can locate APs a couple of miles away. For those with mechanical ability, numerous websites have instructions on building your own antenna with empty bean cans, potato chip cans, and the like. You can also purchase a decent antenna for about $50.

TIP   For directions on building an antenna from a tin can, visit www.wikihow.com/Make-a-Cantenna.

Activity 11-3: Discovering APs with Wifite

Time Required: 15 minutes

Objective: See what information a wireless scanner, such as Wifite, can gather.

Description: When testing a network for vulnerabilities, don't neglect checking for vulnerabilities in any WLANs the company has set up. Wifite is a free Wi-Fi scanner, similar to Vistumbler. Wifite also offers attack features you can use to break insecure wireless networks. For this activity, you examine the scanner functionality of Wifite. You can verify available APs and their SSIDs. If your classroom doesn't have wireless NICs or an AP, you can do the activity later where equipment is available, such as your home or office.

1. If necessary, boot into Kali Linux.
2. Open a Terminal shell and enter **wifite** then press **Enter** to start Wifite. If you're in an area with a few APs, your Wifite terminal window might look like Figure 11-10.

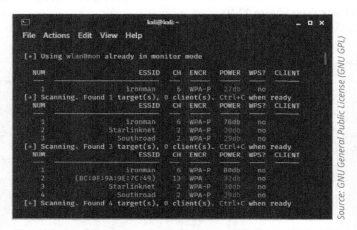

Figure 11-10   Scanning APs with Wifite

3. If SSIDs appear on your screen, examine the CH column. This displays the channel information for each AP. Many systems in Figure 11-10 use channel 6 or channel 2, which could indicate congestion. If you discovered this information during a security test, you might suggest configuring some APs on different channels to your client.
4. Press **Ctrl+C** twice to exit Wifite. Close any open windows.

Kismet

Another common product for conducting wardriving attacks is Kismet (www.kismetwireless.net), written by Mike Kershaw. This product is free and runs on Linux, BSD UNIX, macOS, and even Linux PDAs. The software is advertised as being more than a wireless network detector. Kismet is also a sniffer and an intrusion detection system (IDS) that can sniff 802.11b, 802.11a, 802.11g, 802.11n, 802.11ac, and 802.11ax traffic. It offers the following features:

- Wireshark- and Tcpdump-compatible data logging
- Compatible with AirSnort and AirCrack (covered later in "Tools of the Trade")
- Network IP range detection
- Detection of hidden network SSIDs
- Graphical mapping of networks
- Client/server architecture that allows multiple clients to view a single Kismet server at the same time

- Manufacturer and model identification of APs and clients
- Detection of known default AP configurations
- XML output
- Support for dozens of card types (almost any card that supports monitor mode)

Kismet is a passive scanner, so it can detect even hidden network SSIDs. Kismet can be used to conduct wardriving and to detect rogue APs on a company's network. A rogue AP is a wireless access point installed in an organization without authorization. A rogue AP often has the same SSID as a legimate AP. The bad actor who deployed the rogue hopes that users will connect to it assuming it's the legitimate AP. If users do connect to the rogue AP, hackers can use it to capture their data. This type of rogue AP is often called an evil twin.

If you need GPS support, several tools work with Kismet, such as the GPS daemon (GPSD), GISKismet, and Kisgearth, that can come in handy for accurate AP geopositioning. When Kismet is configured to use GPSD, the output display coordinates pinpointing the location of the AP being scanned. This coordinate data can be fed into Google Earth to create maps.

UNDERSTANDING WIRELESS HACKING

Hacking a wireless network is similar to hacking a wired LAN. Many of the port-scanning and enumeration tools you've learned about can be applied to wireless networks. The following sections describe additional tools that attackers use, which you can use to conduct security tests.

Tools of the Trade

A wireless hacker usually has a laptop computer, a WNIC, an antenna, sniffers (Tcpdump or Wireshark, for example), tools such as Vistumbler or Kismet, and lots of patience. After using Vistumbler or Kismet to determine the network name, SSID, MAC address of the AP, channel, signal strength, type of encryption enabled, and whether WPS is enabled, a security tester is ready to continue testing.

What do attackers or security testers do if WEP or WPA is enabled on the AP? Several tools address this issue. Aircrack-ng, covered in the following sections, is what prompted organizations to replace WEP with the more secure WPA as their authentication method. However, some companies still use 802.11b with WEP enabled, and some even leave their network completely unsecured.

Aircrack-ng

As a security professional, your job is to protect a network and make it difficult for attackers to break in. You might like to believe you can completely *prevent* attackers from breaking in, but unfortunately, this goal is impossible. Aircrack-ng (included in Kali Linux or available free at www.aircrack-ng.org) is the tool most hackers use to access WEP-enabled WLANs. Aircrack-ng replaced AirSnort, a product created by wireless security researchers Jeremy Bruestle and Blake Hegerle, who set out to prove that WEP encryption was faulty and easy to crack. AirSnort was the first widely used WEP-cracking program and woke up nonbelievers who thought WEP was enough protection for a WLAN. Aircrack-ng took up where AirSnort (and the slightly older WEPCrack) left off. It has some useful add-ons, such as a GUI front-end called Fern WIFI Cracker, shown in Figure 11-11 (also included in Kali Linux).

WiFi Pineapple

Wi-Fi hacking enthusiasts Darren Kitchen and Sebastian Kinne created a Swiss-army knife for wireless hacking called the WiFi Pineapple. It can perform scans for wireless access points and set up fake APs to social-engineer users or confuse attackers using airbase-ng. The WiFi Pineapple has another dangerous feature that allows an attacker to emulate any network that a client requests. To understand this, keep in mind that wireless devices are constantly probing for networks they've previously connected to. A feature in the WiFi Pineapple listens for these probes and responds to them as if it were the AP the client had requested. After the client revives the response from the WiFi Pineapple, the client connects to the fake network, leaving any of the client's traffic at risk of being sniffed. You can read more about it on the WiFi Pineapple website (www.wifipineapple.com/). The tool's main page is shown in Figure 11-12.

NOTE

Kali Linux includes a wide range of analysis tools for testing wireless networks.

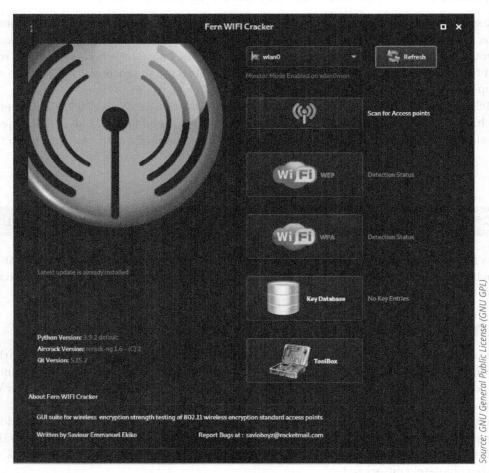

Figure 11-11   Fern WIFI Cracker interface

Figure 11-12   WiFi Pineapple interface

Countermeasures for Wireless Attacks

Protecting a wireless network is a challenge for security professionals because of the inherent design flaws of wireless technology and because, to some extent, engineers are attempting to place a band-aid over a gaping chest wound. Some countermeasure techniques discussed in this section, such as using certificates on all wireless devices, are time consuming and costly.

If you approach securing a wireless LAN as you would a wired LAN, you have a better chance of protecting corporate data and network resources. Would you allow users to have access to network resources simply because they plugged their NICs into the company's switch or hub? Of course not. Then why would you allow users to have access to a wireless LAN simply because they have WNICs and know the company's SSID?

If a company must use wireless technology, your job is to make it as secure as possible. Be sure wireless users are authenticated before being able to access any network resources. Here are some additional guidelines to help secure a wireless network:

- Consider using anti-wardriving software to make it more difficult for attackers to discover your WLAN. Later in this course, you learn about honeypots, which are hosts or networks available to the public that entice hackers to attack them instead of a company's real network. IT personnel can study how an attack is made on the honeypot, which can be useful in securing the company's actual network. To make it more difficult for wardrivers to discover your WLAN, you can use airbase-ng. As its name implies, this program creates fake APs, which keeps wardrivers so busy trying to connect to nonexistent wireless networks that they don't have time to discover your legitimate AP.
- There are measures for preventing radio waves from leaving or entering a building so that wireless technology can be used only by people in the facility. One is using a certain type of paint on the walls, but this method isn't foolproof because some radio waves can leak out if the paint isn't applied correctly.
- Use a router to only allow approved MAC addresses to access your network. Unfortunately, some exploits enable attackers to spoof authorized addresses, but this measure makes exploits more difficult for typical attackers.
- Consider using an authentication server instead of relying on a wireless device to authenticate users. A RADIUS server that can refer all users to a server running Windows Server with Active Directory can be used to authenticate wireless users attempting to access network resources. This method can also prevent an intruder from sending or receiving HTTP, HTTPS, DHCP, SMTP, or any network packets over the network before being authenticated.
- Consider using EAP, which allows using different protocols that enhance security. For example, EAP enables using certificates for authentication, or wireless vendors can implement password-based authentication by using the EAP standard. EAP offers more options for increasing security.
- Consider placing the AP in the demilitarized zone (DMZ) and using a firewall in front of the company's internal network that filters out traffic from unauthorized IP addresses.
- WEP with 104-bit encryption is only marginally better than WEP with 40-bit encryption. If possible, replace WEP with WPA2 or WPA3 for better security, and replace hardware that can't be upgraded to support WPA2 or WPA3. WEP encryption can be cracked easily with just the tools in Kali Linux, and cracking WPA just takes more time.
- Assign static IP addresses to wireless clients instead of using DHCP.
- Disable WPS, which removes the known WPS attack vectors.
- Change the default SSID and disable SSID broadcasts, if possible. If you can't disable SSID broadcasts, rename the default SSID to make it more difficult for attackers to determine the router's manufacturer. For example, leaving the default SSID of Netgear makes it easy for an attacker to determine what router is being used. Changing its SSID to another manufacturer's default SSID or to one not associated with any vendor might deter an attacker.

These methods aren't foolproof. In fact, by the time you read this book, there could be new ways to crack WPA3 and other security methods for protecting wireless LANs. That's what makes the security field fun and dynamic. There are no easy fixes. If there were, these fixes wouldn't last long, unfortunately.

MODULE SUMMARY

- Wireless technology defines how and at what frequency data travels over the radio frequency (RF) spectrum. The term "wireless" generally describes equipment operating in the RF spectrum between 3 Hz and 300 GHz, although most wireless networking equipment operates between 2.4 GHz and 66 GHz.

- The basic components of wireless networks are WNICs, which transmit and receive wireless signals; access points (APs), which are the bridges between wired and wireless networks; wireless networking protocols; and a portion of the RF spectrum that acts as a medium for carrying the signal.

- A service set identifier (SSID) is configured on the AP and used to identify a WLAN. It's a unique, 1- to 32-character, case-sensitive alphanumeric name.

- IEEE's main purpose is to create standards for LANs and WANs. 802.11 is the IEEE standard for wireless networking and includes many additional standards that address security and authentication.

- A BSS is the collection of all devices (APs and stations) that make up a WLAN. A BSA is the wireless coverage area that an AP provides to stations in a WLAN running in infrastructure mode. Although infrastructure mode is the most common in WLANs, independent stations can also establish an ad-hoc decentralized network that doesn't require an AP.

- WLANs use three technologies: infrared, narrowband, and spread spectrum. For data to be moved over radio waves, it must be modulated on the carrier signal or channel. The most common modulation methods for spread spectrum are DSSS and OFDM.

- Bluetooth is the most popular form of WPAN technology (802.15 standard), which usually has a more limited range than a typical WLAN. On the other end of the spectrum is a MAN (802.16 standard), which has a much larger coverage area than a WLAN. LTE is the most common implementation of a wireless MAN.

- WEP, WPA, WPA2, and WPA3 are wireless encryption standards used to protect WLANs from unauthorized access and eavesdropping. WEP is easy to crack, WPA and WPA2 are harder to crack, and WPA3 is the most secure of these three.

- Authentication is usually used with wireless encryption standards to ensure that access to a WLAN is authorized. 802.1X is an example of WLAN authentication and has three components: the supplicant, a wireless user attempting access to a WLAN; the authenticator, the AP that allows or denies a supplicant's access; and the authentication server, such as a RADIUS server.

- Wardriving and warflying involve driving in a car or piloting a drone with a computing device, a WNIC, an antenna, and software that scans for available APs.

- WLANs can be attacked with many of the same tools used for hacking wired LANs. For example, a sniffer such as Wireshark can scan WLANs for logon and password information. Specialized wireless tools include Vistumbler, which can survey APs as part of a wardriving scan, and Kismet, a sophisticated multipurpose wireless tool that can detect hidden network SSIDs.

- Some methods for protecting a wireless network are disabling SSID broadcasts, renaming default SSIDs, using an authentication server, placing the AP in the DMZ, using EAP, upgrading to WPA3, assigning static IP addresses to wireless clients, and using a router to only allow approved MAC addresses to have access to a network.

Key Terms

802.11	Extensible Authentication Protocol	Mobile Broadband Wireless Access
802.1X standard	(EAP)	(MBWA)
access point (AP)	frequency	Modulation
ad-hoc network	Infrared (IR)	Narrowband
amplitude	infrastructure mode	Protected EAP (PEAP)
basic service area (BSA)	Institute of Electrical and	service set identifier (SSID)
basic service set (BSS)	Electronics Engineers (IEEE)	spread spectrum
channels	metropolitan area networks	station (STA)
chipping code	(MANs)	supplicant

wardriving
Wi-Fi Protected Access (WPA, WPA2, and WPA3)
Wi-Fi Protected Setup (WPS)

Wired Equivalent Privacy (WEP)
wireless LAN (WLAN)
wireless network interface cards (WNICs)

wireless personal area network (WPAN)
Worldwide Interoperability for Microwave Access (WiMAX)

Review Questions

1. Which IEEE standard defines authentication and authorization in wireless networks?
   a. 802.11
   b. 802.11a
   c. 802.11b
   d. 802.1X

2. Which EAP method requires installing digital certificates on both the server and client?
   a. EAP-TLS
   b. PEAP
   c. EAP-SSL
   d. EAP-CA

3. Which wireless encryption standard offers the best security?
   a. WPA3
   b. WEP
   c. WPS
   d. WPA

4. Name a tool that can help reduce the risk of a wardriver attacking your WLAN.

5. What protocol was added to 802.11i to address WEP's encryption vulnerability?
   a. MIC
   b. TKIP
   c. TTL
   d. EAP-TLS

6. What IEEE standard defines wireless technology?
   a. 802.3
   b. 802.5
   c. 802.11
   d. All 802 standards

7. What information can be gathered by wardriving? (Choose all that apply.)
   a. SSIDs of wireless networks
   b. Whether encryption is enabled
   c. Whether SSL is enabled
   d. Signal strength

8. Disabling SSID broadcasts must be configured on the computer and the AP. True or false?

9. What TKIP enhancement addressed the WEP vulnerability of forging packets?
   a. Extended Initialization Vector (IV) with sequencing rules
   b. Per-packet key mixing
   c. Rekeying mechanism
   d. Message Integrity Check (MIC)

10. Wi-Fi Protected Access (WPA) was introduced in which IEEE 802 standard?
    a. 802.11a
    b. 802.11b
    c. 802.11i
    d. 802.11

11. Use Vistumbler to scan for APs. Using the information you discover, write a three-paragraph report. In the first paragraph, outline each SSID you have discovered and its configuration information, including what authentication method it is using. In the second paragraph, suggest security improvements for each SSID. In the third paragraph, choose one of the discovered SSIDs and outline what tools you would use to penetration test it.

12. What is a known weakness of wireless network SSIDs?
    a. They're broadcast in cleartext.
    b. They're difficult to configure.
    c. They use large amounts of bandwidth.
    d. They consume an excessive amount of computer memory.

13. Bluetooth technology is more vulnerable to network attacks than WLANs are. True or false?

14. Which of the following channels are available in 802.11b for attempting to prevent overlapping? (Choose all that apply.)
    a. 1
    b. 5
    c. 6
    d. 11

15. Which authentication mechanisms and standards are currently exploitable?
    a. WEP
    b. WPA
    c. WP2
    d. WPS

16. An access point provides which of the following?
    a. Access to the BSS
    b. Access to the DS
    c. Access to a remote station
    d. Access to a secure node

17. WPA3 is the latest and greatest version of the WPA protocol. Security flaws have been discovered in WPA3. Write a three-paragraph report outlining what security flaws have been discovered and what steps have been taken to mitigate these flaws, and then discuss the most critical CVE involving WPA3 that has been reported to date.

18. Perform an analysis of your home Wi-Fi access points. What authentication method are you using? Do you have WPS enabled? Write a three-paragraph report outlining the details of your analysis and suggest changes you can make to improve your home Wi-Fi security.

19. Which of the following typically functions as the 802.1X authenticator, allowing or denying a supplicant's access to a WLAN?
    a. AP
    b. RADIUS server
    c. CA
    d. Public key issuer

20. List three tools for conducting wireless security testing.

Case Projects

Case Project 11-1: Determining Vulnerabilities of Wireless Networks

After conducting a security test on the Alexander Rocco network, you discover that the company has a wireless router configured to issue IP addresses to connecting stations. Vistumbler indicates that channel 6 is active, the SSID is linksys, and WEP is enabled. Based on this information, write a one-page report listing possible vulnerabilities of the WLAN's current configuration. Your report should include recommendations for improving wireless security.

Case Project 11-2: Maintaining Security on Wireless Systems

Jawad Safari, the IT manager at Alexander Rocco, has just purchased a laptop computer. The company has asked you to ensure that privacy and security are maintained on this wireless system. Based on this information, write a one-page report using the information in the OSSTMM, Section E, Wireless Security available at https://www.isecom.org/OSSTMM.3.pdf. Your report should outline guidelines for ensuring the laptop's security.

CRYPTOGRAPHY

After reading this module and completing the exercises, you will be able to:

1 Summarize the history and principles of cryptography

2 Describe symmetric and asymmetric encryption algorithms

3 Explain public key infrastructure (PKI)

4 Describe possible attacks on cryptosystems

5 Compare hashing algorithms and how they ensure data integrity

Protecting data as it traverses the Internet or while it's stored on a computer is one of a network security professional's most important jobs. Companies as well as users don't want others to be able to view confidential documents and files.

In this module, you examine the cryptography technologies that security professionals use to protect a company's data. You see how information can be converted into an unreadable format and how only those with the correct key or "decoder" can read the message. You also look at cryptography attacks and some of the tools used to conduct these attacks.

UNDERSTANDING CRYPTOGRAPHY BASICS

Cryptography is the process of converting plaintext, which is readable text, into ciphertext, which is unreadable or encrypted text. Cryptography can be used on data that people or organizations want to keep private or data that should be accessible to only certain users. In other words, cryptography is used to hide information from unauthorized users. Decryption is the process of converting ciphertext back to plaintext (also called cleartext). As a kid, you might have had a decoder ring from a box of cereal that you could use to write a letter to a friend in secret code. If your friend had the same decoder ring, he or she could decode your letter and read it.

History of Cryptography

Cryptography has been around for thousands of years. For example, some Egyptian hieroglyphics on ancient monuments were encrypted. Parts of the Book of Jeremiah were written using a cipher, or key, known as Atbash. This simple cipher reversed the alphabet— replacing A with Z, for example—and only the person who knew the mapping could decipher (decrypt) the message. This type of cryptography is called a substitution cipher. Julius Caesar developed a similar substitution cipher for encrypting messages by shifting each letter of the alphabet three positions. For example, A was encoded as the letter D. Every culture seems to have used some form of hiding or disguising plaintext. *The Kama Sutra*, written by the Indian scholar

NOTE

You can find an excellent timeline of cryptography in *The Code-breakers: The Comprehensive History of Secret Communication from Ancient Times to the Internet, Revised Edition,* written by David Kahn (Scribner, 1996, ISBN 0684831309).

Vatsyayana almost 2000 years ago, recommends that men and women learn and practice the art of cryptography, which it defines as "the art of understanding writing in cipher and the writing of works in a peculiar way."

As long as people attempt to create encryption algorithms to protect data, others will endeavor to break them. The study of breaking encryption algorithms is called cryptanalysis. It's taught in universities and by government agencies, but hackers also find the challenge of breaking an encryption algorithm intriguing and continue to force developers of encryption algorithms to push the envelope in finding harder-to-break algorithms. When a new encryption algorithm is developed, cryptanalysis is used to ensure that breaking the code is impossible or would take so much time and so many resources that the attempt would be impractical. In other words, if breaking an encryption algorithm requires the processing power of a $500 million supercomputer and 500 years, the algorithm can be considered secure enough for practical purposes.

When cryptanalysis is feasible with a reasonable amount of computing power, however, an attack on the algorithm is deemed "practical," and the algorithm is considered weak.

The War Machines

The most famous encryption device was the Enigma machine, developed by Arthur Scherbius and used by the Germans during World War II. Most books on cryptography discuss this device. How did it work? The operator typed a letter to be encrypted, and the machine displayed the substitution character for the letter. The operator then wrote down this substitution character and turned a rotor or switch. He or she then entered the next letter and again wrote down the substitution character Enigma displayed. When the message was completely encrypted, it was transmitted over the airwaves. Of course, the message could be decrypted only by the Enigma machine at the other end, which knew in what positions to shift the rotors. The code was broken first by a group of Polish cryptographers, and then by the British and Americans. The machine British and American cryptologists used for breaking the code, developed by British mathematician Alan Turing, was called the Bombe.

During World War II, the Japanese developed another notable war machine, called the Purple Machine, that used techniques discovered by Herbert O. Yardley. A team led by William Frederick Friedman, a U.S. Army cryptanalyst known as the Father of U.S. Cryptanalysis, broke the code. The FBI had employed Mr. Friedman and his wife to assist in decrypting radio messages sent by bootleggers and smugglers during the 1930s. These encryption codes proved to be more difficult and complex than those used during wartime.

The main purpose of cryptography is to hide information from others, and there are methods of hiding data that don't use encryption. One is steganography, a way of hiding data in plain view in pictures, graphics, or text. For example, a picture of a man standing in front of the White House might have a hidden message embedded that gives a spy information about troop movements. In 1623, Sir Francis Bacon used a form of steganography by hiding bits of information in variations of the typeface used in books.

Activity 12-1: Creating a Substitution Cipher

Time Required: 30 minutes

Objective: Learn how to create a substitution cipher and encrypt a message.

Description: To better understand cryptography, break into groups of four students. Each group should create a short message no longer than five words in plaintext. Your group encrypts the message with a substitution cipher, and then the other groups (the decrypters) try to decode the message. Each group should create one encrypted message and decrypt each message created by the other groups.

1. The encrypting group writes a five-word message on a blank sheet of paper.
2. Create a substitution cipher to encrypt the message. For example, each character can be shifted three characters so that, for example, the letter A becomes the letter D.
3. Write down the ciphertext message you created with your group's cipher.
4. When instructed to do so, hand your ciphertext messages to the other groups to decrypt.
5. When a group decrypts the message, the group leader should say "Finished!" so that the instructor can see which group completed the task the fastest.
6. After all groups have had a chance to try decrypting messages, discuss the ciphers each group created.

SECURITY BYTES

Did you know that Thomas Jefferson invented a wheel cipher in the 18th century that the Navy redeveloped and used during World War II and named M-138-A? The more things change, the more they remain the same.

UNDERSTANDING SYMMETRIC AND ASYMMETRIC ALGORITHMS

Modern cryptography uses encryption algorithms to encrypt data, banking transactions, other online transactions that use HTTPS, wireless communication (WEP and WPA encryption), and so on. An encryption algorithm is a mathematical function or program that works with a key. The algorithm's strength and the key's secrecy determine how secure the encrypted data is. In most cases, the algorithm isn't a secret; it's known to the public. What is secret is the key. A key is a sequence of random bits generated from a range of allowable values called a keyspace, which is contained in the algorithm. The larger the keyspace, the more keys that can be created. For example, an algorithm with a 256-bit keyspace has 2^{256} possible keys. The more random keys that can be created, the more difficult it is for hackers to guess which key was used to encrypt the data. Of course, using only eight random keys (as shown in Figure 12-1) makes the algorithm too easy to crack and is shown as an example only.

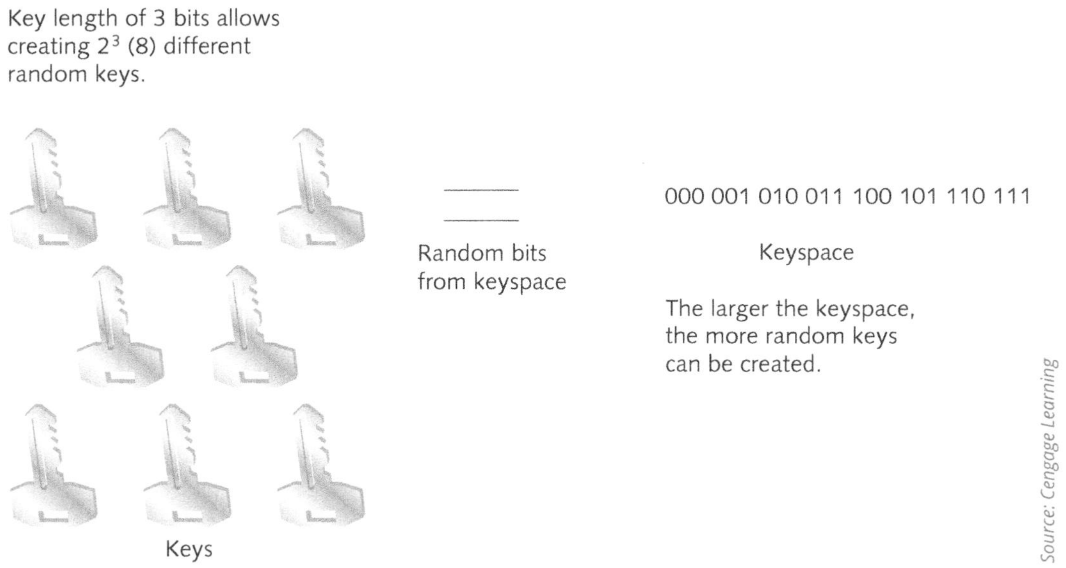

Key length of 3 bits allows
creating 2^3 (8) different
random keys.

Random bits
from keyspace

000 001 010 011 100 101 110 111

Keyspace

The larger the keyspace,
the more random keys
can be created.

Keys

Source: Cengage Learning

Figure 12-1   Selecting random keys from a keyspace

Simply put, a cryptosystem converts between plaintext and ciphertext. Most attempts to break a cryptosystem are related to guessing the key. No matter how strong the algorithm or how large the keyspace, if the key isn't protected, an attacker can decrypt the message. If users share their keys with someone, all bets are off. Table 12-1 summarizes the three types of algorithms.

Having a cryptologist's skills isn't necessary for security testers, but understanding basic cryptology terms is helpful. For example, if you see the description "Blowfish is a block cipher with a key size up to 448 bits," you want to know enough to understand what it means. The following sections examine these algorithm types in more detail and explain some basic terms.

Symmetric Algorithms

Cryptosystems using symmetric algorithms have one key that encrypts and decrypts data. If a user wants to send a message to a colleague, he or she encrypts the message with the secret key, and the colleague, who must have a copy of the same key, decrypts the message. If the user wants to encrypt a different message and send it to another

Table 12-1   Symmetric, asymmetric, and hashing algorithms

Type of algorithm	Description
Symmetric	Uses a single key to encrypt and decrypt data. Both the sender and receiver must agree on the key before data is transmitted. Symmetric algorithms support confidentiality but not authentication and nonrepudiation (covered later in "Asymmetric Algorithms"). However, they're at least 1000 times faster than asymmetric algorithms.
Asymmetric	Uses two keys: one to encrypt data and one to decrypt data. Asymmetric algorithms support authentication and nonrepudiation but are slower than symmetric algorithms. Asymmetric algorithms are also known as public key cryptography.
Hashing	Used for verification. Hashing takes a variable-length input and converts it to a fixed-length output string called a hash value or message digest.

colleague, a different secret key must be used. If hundreds of colleagues are placed in the equation, keeping track of which secret key to use becomes a big problem. To calculate the number of keys needed to support a symmetric system, you use the formula $n(n - 1)/2$. For example, if five users need to use secret keys to transmit data, you need $5(5 - 1)/2$ keys, or 10 keys.

Another problem with secret keys is how to send one to the colleague decrypting your message. Emailing it can be dangerous because the message can be intercepted. You can try putting the secret key on a CD-R or USB drive, but either medium can be misplaced or stolen.

Because two users share the same key in symmetric algorithms, there's no way to know which user sent the message. In other words, symmetric algorithms don't support authentication and nonrepudiation (covered in more detail in "Asymmetric Algorithms").

As you can see, symmetric algorithms have some problems, but as Table 12-1 states, they're fast. They're perfect mechanisms for encrypting large blocks of data quickly and are difficult to break if a large key size is used. The advantages of symmetric algorithms are as follows:

- Much faster than asymmetric algorithms
- Difficult to break if a large key size is used
- Only one key needed to encrypt and decrypt data

Symmetric algorithms have the following disadvantages:

- Require each pair of users to have a unique secret key, making key management a challenge
- Difficult to deliver keys without risk of theft
- Don't provide authentication or nonrepudiation for users

Two types of symmetric algorithms are used currently: stream ciphers and block ciphers. **Stream ciphers** such as A5/1, A5/2, and RC4 operate on plaintext one bit at a time. Messages are treated as a stream of bits, and the stream cipher performs mathematical functions on each bit, which makes these algorithms great candidates for hardware or chip-level encryption devices. **Block ciphers** such as DES, 3DES, AES, and RC5 operate on blocks of bits. These blocks are used as input to mathematical functions that perform substitution and transposition of the bits. Sometimes, when a block cipher separates input into blocks, it must add padding to fill a given block. This padding leaves the cipher susceptible to attack. Publicized attacks include CRIME, BEAST, and Lucky 7, which are all types of Padding Oracle attacks. You can read more detail about Padding Oracle attacks on The Grymoire Blog (https://grymoire.wordpress.com/2014/12/05/cbc-padding-oracle-attacks-simplified-key-concepts-and-pitfalls/).

In the following sections, you take a look at some of the symmetric algorithms that have become standards in the industry. Regardless of the standard, however, symmetric algorithms rely on one and the same key to encrypt and decrypt data.

Activity 12-2: Securing Personal Communication Using Encryption

Time Required: 20 minutes

Objective: Use the Internet to research encrypted personal messaging application.

Description: In this activity, you use the Internet to research encrypted personal messaging applications that can be used to encrypt personal messaging for greater privacy.

1. In Windows, start a web browser, enter the address **www.tomsguide.com/reference/best-encrypted-messaging-apps/**.
2. Read the article to discover some options for encrypting your personal communications. Do you currently use any of these applications? Were you aware that some applications (such as Facebook Messenger) have options for encrypting your communications?
3. Use your web browser to read the article at the following address: **www.wired.com/story/nahoft-iran-messaging-encryption-app/**.
4. What basic type of cryptography does the Nahoft application use?
5. Use your favorite search engine and search for **android steganography apps**.
6. Select a few links to answer the following questions. What is steganography? What are some of the applications that provide this capability? Find a friend and try one of these applications.
7. Exit your web browser and log off Windows for the next activity.

Data Encryption Standard

A discussion of symmetric algorithms must include Data Encryption Standard (DES). The National Institute of Standards and Technology (NIST) wanted a means of protecting sensitive but unclassified data, so in the early 1970s, it invited vendors to submit data encryption algorithms. The best algorithm would become the standard encryption method for government agencies and private-sector companies. IBM had already created a 128-bit algorithm called Lucifer. NIST accepted it as the standard encryption algorithm; however, the National Security Agency (NSA) wanted to make some modifications before allowing it to be used. The NSA decided to reduce the key size from 128 bits to 64 bits and named it Data Encryption Algorithm (DEA). To be clear, DES is the standard, and DEA is the encryption algorithm used for the standard. DEA isn't the most creative name, but the NSA probably thought the name Lucifer didn't have an official government ring to it. The reason the NSA reduced the algorithm's keyspace isn't known. What is known is that 128-bit encryption is far more difficult to crack than 64-bit encryption.

> **NOTE**
>
> Even though DEA uses 64-bit encryption, only 56 bits are effectively used. Eight of the 64 bits are used for parity (error correction).

As with most things, time took its toll on DES. In 1988, NSA thought the standard was at risk of being broken because of its longevity and the increasing power of computers. Any system, no matter how secure, is vulnerable when hackers have years to look for holes. NSA proved to be correct in its assumption. The increased processing power of computers soon made it possible to break DES encryption. In fact, in 1998 a computer system was designed that was able to break the encryption key in only three days. There are also examples of hackers combining the processing power of thousands of computers (without the system owners' knowledge) over the Internet to crack complex encryption algorithms. Many cryptologists are too quick to claim that it would take several Cray supercomputers 200 years to figure out the secret key in their encryption algorithms, when only a few years of improvements in processor speed prove it can be done with just a powerful laptop and access to the Internet.

Triple DES

A new standard was needed because DES was no longer the solution. Triple Data Encryption Standard (3DES) served as a quick fix for the vulnerabilities of DES. To make it more difficult for attackers to crack the encryption code, 3DES performs the original DES computation three times. Keying options can vary for each of the three rounds of DES encryption; however, 3DES is strongest when a unique key is used for each. This more complex computation on data makes 3DES much stronger than DES. This improvement did have a tradeoff in performance, however. 3DES takes longer to encrypt and decrypt data than its predecessor did, but that's a small price to pay for far better security.

Advanced Encryption Standard

Eventually, NIST decided that 3DES was a stop-gap measure for a weak algorithm and a new standard was in order: Advanced Encryption Standard (AES). In 1997, NIST put out another request to the public for a new encryption standard, asking for a symmetric block cipher capable of supporting 128-, 192-, and 256-bit keys. Of the five finalists, NIST chose Rijndael, developed by Joan Daemen and Vincent Rijmen, because of its improvements in security, efficiency, performance, and flexibility. The other four finalists were MARS, RC6, Serpent, and Twofish. (See https://csrc.nist.gov for more details.) AES-256, part of the NSA's Suite B set of cryptographic algorithms, is one of the only commercial algorithms validated as strong enough to protect classified information.

International Data Encryption Algorithm

International Data Encryption Algorithm (IDEA) is a block cipher that operates on 64-bit blocks of plaintext. It uses a 128-bit key and is used in PGP encryption software (covered later in "Asymmetric Algorithms"). IDEA was developed by Xuejia Lai and James Massey to work more efficiently in computers used at home and in businesses. It's free for noncommercial use, but a license must be purchased for commercial use. The final patent for the IDEA block cipher expired in 2012.

Blowfish

Blowfish is another block cipher that operates on 64-bit blocks of plaintext. However, the key length is variable, from 32 bits up to 448 bits. It was developed as a public-domain algorithm by Bruce Schneier, a leading cryptologist and the author of *Applied Cryptography: Protocols, Algorithms, and Source Code in C, Second Edition* (Wiley, 1996, ISBN 0471117099), which is highly recommended for those who want to learn more about the algorithm and view its C source code.

RC4

RC4, the most widely used stream cipher, is used in WEP wireless encryption. It's because of the way RC4 is implemented in WEP that finding the key with air-cracking programs, for example, is so easy. RC4 is considered difficult to break, but it should be avoided for most applications. The algorithm was created by Ronald L. Rivest in 1987 for RSA Security (www.rsa.com).

RC5

RC5 is a block cipher that can operate on different block sizes: 32, 64, or 128 bits. The key size can reach 2048 bits. The algorithm was created by Ronald L. Rivest in 1994 for RSA Security.

Asymmetric Algorithms

Instead of the single key used in symmetric algorithms, asymmetric algorithms use two mathematically related keys, so data encrypted with one key can be decrypted only with the other key. Another name for asymmetric algorithms is public key cryptography; these terms are often used interchangeably. A public key is openly available; in many cases, public keys can be downloaded from websites for the public to use. A private key is the secret key known only by the key owner and should never be shared. Even if people know the public key used to encrypt a message, they can't figure out the key owner's private key. With asymmetric cryptosystems, a public key being intercepted in transmission isn't a concern. In addition, asymmetric algorithms are more scalable than symmetric algorithms because one public key can be used by thousands of users; however, these algorithms require more processor resources, so they're slower.

Before examining some widely used asymmetric algorithms, take a look at a simple example of public key cryptography. There are different ways to encrypt a message with asymmetric algorithms, depending on whether the goal is to provide authentication and nonrepudiation. Authentication verifies that the sender or receiver (or both) is who he or she claims to be. Nonrepudiation ensures that the sender and receiver can't deny sending or receiving the message. These functions aren't supported in symmetric algorithms.

If User A encrypts a message with her private key and sends the message to User B, User B can decrypt the message with User A's public key. A user's private and public keys are mathematically related, meaning a public key can decrypt only a message that has been encrypted with the corresponding private key.

If confidentiality is a major concern for User A, she encrypts the message with the recipient's public key. That way, only the recipient can decrypt the message with his private key. If User A wants to assure User B that she is indeed the person sending the message (authentication), she can encrypt the message with her private key. After all, she's the only person who possesses her private key.

RSA

RSA was published in 1978 by three MIT professors: Ronald L. Rivest, Adi Shamir, and Leonard M. Adleman. It's the first algorithm used for both encryption and digital signing and is still widely used, particularly in e-commerce. The authors offered their findings to anyone who sent them a self-addressed envelope. The NSA took a jaundiced view of this approach and suggested the professors cease and desist. When questioned about the legality of its request, however, NSA didn't respond, and the algorithm was published. You can find more information about RSA and its relationship with the NSA at https://en.wikipedia.org/wiki/RSA_Security.

Many web browsers using the Transport Layer Security (TLS) protocol use the RSA algorithm, which is based on the difficulty of factoring large numbers. To generate a key, RSA uses a one-way function—a mathematical formula that's easy to compute in one direction but difficult or nearly impossible to compute in the opposite direction. For example, multiplying two large prime numbers to determine their product is easy, but when you're given only the product, determining what numbers were used in the calculation is difficult. A simple analogy is making a smoothie. It's easy to blend a banana, strawberries, and ice cubes in a blender, but if you have to reconstruct the banana, strawberries, and ice cubes into their original state after blending them, you might find the task impossible.

Diffie-Hellman

This algorithm was developed in 1976 by Whitfield Diffie and Martin Hellman, originators of the public and private key concept. It doesn't provide encryption but is used to establish one secret key shared between two parties. Although it's often thought of as a key exchange, each party actually generates a shared key based on a mathematical key-agreement relationship. If a key is intercepted during transmission, the network is vulnerable to attack, so key management is an important component of securing data. With a method of sharing a secret key, users can secure their electronic communication without the fear of interception.

Elliptic Curve Cryptography

Elliptic curve cryptography (ECC), developed in 1985, is used for encryption as well as digital signatures and key exchange. ECC is based on complex algebra and calculations on curves. Suffice it to say, it's an efficient algorithm requiring few resources (such as memory, disk space, and bandwidth), so it's a good candidate for wireless devices and cell phones. The NSA has included ECC in its Suite B cryptographic algorithms.

ElGamal

ElGamal is an asymmetric algorithm used to generate keys and digital signatures and encrypt data. Developed by Taher Elgamal in 1985, the algorithm uses discrete logarithms that are complex to solve. Solving a discrete logarithm can take many years and require CPU-intensive operations.

Digital Signatures

Asymmetric algorithms have a useful feature that enables a public key to decrypt a message encrypted with a private key, or vice versa. A public key can only decrypt a message that was encrypted with the corresponding private key. Figure 12-2 shows an unencrypted message signed with a digital signature. The hash calculated from the message content is encrypted with a private key to ensure authentication and nonrepudiation.

Digital Signature Standard

In 1991, NIST established the Digital Signature Standard (DSS) to ensure that digital signatures could be verified. The federal government specified using RSA and Digital Signature Algorithm (DSA) for all digital signatures and using a hashing algorithm to ensure the message's integrity (verifying that the message hasn't been tampered with). NIST requires using Secure Hash Algorithm (SHA), covered later in "Hashing Algorithms." Basically, a digital signature can be created with only a user's private key, and the user's signature can be verified by anyone using this user's public key.

Pretty Good Privacy

Pretty Good Privacy (PGP) was developed by Phil Zimmerman as a free email encryption program that allowed typical users to encrypt email messages. Sounds harmless, but Zimmerman was almost arrested for his innovation. The Justice Department initiated an investigation into whether offering the PGP program to the public was a crime. In the

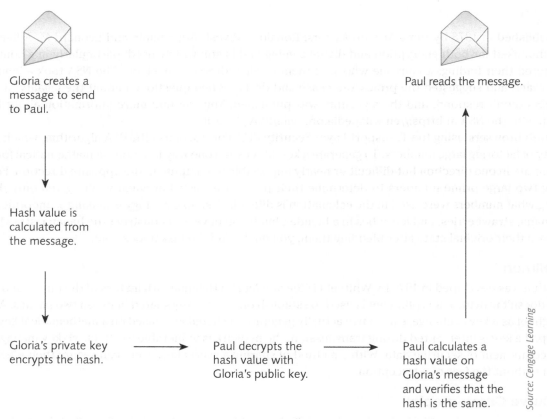

Figure 12-2   Using a digital signature

mid-1990s, any kind of "unbreakable" encryption was considered a weapon and sharing it was compared with selling arms to the enemy.

PGP has evolved considerably since it was created. The Internet standard for PGP messages is now called **OpenPGP**. OpenPGP uses certificates similar to those in PKI, but because a centralized certification authority (CA) isn't used, verification of a CA isn't as efficient as in PKI. OpenPGP can use AES, IDEA, RSA, DSA, and SHA algorithms for managing keys and encrypting, authenticating, and verifying message integrity. The most common free version of OpenPGP is GNU Privacy Guard (GnuPG or GPG; www.gnupg.org). Sometimes, OpenPGP can be used to validate the integrity of open-source Linux distributions and updates when the developers provide a method for verification. If you run any version of Linux, GPG ensures that the software packages and updates you install haven't been tampered with by an intruder or a hacker. GPG is useful for learning how a public key encryption algorithm is used, and best of all, it's free. Although the commercial PGP version (available at www.broadcom.com/products/cyber-security/information-protection/encryption) is compliant with the OpenPGP standard, it's no longer free. However, like many commercial products, PGP provides technical support and has more features, making it suitable for large enterprise networks. OpenPGP is an economical way of sending email with an extra layer of security added. It's not the only technology for sending secure email, however. The following section briefly covers another widely used secure email standard: S/MIME.

Secure Multipurpose Internet Mail Extension

Secure Multipurpose Internet Mail Extension (S/MIME) is another public key encryption standard for encrypting and digitally signing email. It can also encrypt email messages containing attachments and use PKI certificates for authentication. (See RFC-2311 for details on S/MIME version 2, RFC-2633 for information on S/MIME version 3, and RFC-8551 for information on S/MIME version 4.) One reason that S/MIME is widely used for email encryption is that it's built into Microsoft Outlook. Because Outlook is included in the Microsoft Office suite, organizations already using Microsoft Office don't need to install additional software to encrypt email.

Sensitive Data Encryption

As a security tester, you often communicate with clients by email. However, sending test results that reveal vulnerabilities of your client's network via unencrypted email, which is subject to interception, can result in a serious vulnerability. Don't contribute to your client's network security problems by introducing one yourself. Following good security principles increases a client's trust in your work. Therefore, make it a policy to exchange any test results or other sensitive documents in encrypted form. If your client doesn't use encrypted email, you should make doing so one of your first recommendations.

Organizations might also need to encrypt **data at rest**, which means any data not moving through the network or being used by the OS; the term usually refers to data stored on workstations, servers, smartphones, removable drives, backup media, and laptop computers. Many organizations are required by law to encrypt confidential and financial information and report to authorities if this information is unencrypted and has been lost or stolen. Loss of this information usually proves expensive, not only in costs of replacing it but also in bad publicity. Many commercial programs can encrypt data at rest, and free programs, such as VeraCrypt (https://veracrypt.fr/en/Home.html), are available, too. VeraCrypt uses strong encryption algorithms, such as AES-256, which is authorized to protect U.S. government classified information.

Hashing Algorithms

Several hashing algorithms are in use today; Table 12-2 summarizes some of the most common. A **hashing algorithm** is a function that takes a variable-length string or message and produces a fixed-length hash value, also called a **message digest**, used to verify integrity of the data or message. In a sense, it's like a fingerprint of a message. For example, if the message "How are you?" is changed later to "Who are you?" the hash value also changes so that the recipient knows the original message changed during transmission. Two different messages producing the same hash value results in a **collision**. Therefore, a good hashing algorithm is one that's resistant to collisions.

Many legacy systems rely on **Message Digest 5 (MD5)** and **Secure Hash Algorithm 1 (SHA-1)**; however, modern systems are rapidly upgrading to SHA-2 and SHA-3. By the end of 2016, major web browsers no longer supported SHA-1. With a reasonable amount of computing power, MD5 hash collisions can be found in a few days. Attacks on SHA-1, the 160-bit version of SHA, are now considered more practical, and researchers have been publishing attack methods. For example, researchers from Shandong University in eastern China showed that a key hash function in state-of-the-art encryption might be less resistant to attacks than had been thought. Since 2015, experts have recommended not using SHA-1. Federal agencies have been instructed by NIST to remove SHA-1 from future applications and replace it with either SHA-2 or SHA-3. As you can see, security professionals must be vigilant in keeping aware of changes. Banks, e-commerce websites, credit card companies, and the military have used SHA for many years. For this reason, NIST announced a contest, similar to the AES contest discussed previously, to replace SHA instead of just increasing its digest length.

Table 12-2   Hashing algorithms

Algorithm	Description
MD2	Developed by Ronald L. Rivest in 1989, this algorithm was optimized for 8-bit machines.
MD4	Developed by Rivest in 1990. Using a PC, collisions in this version can now be found in less than 1 minute. Microsoft Windows still uses RC4 to store password hashes.
MD5	Developed by Rivest in 1991. It was estimated in 1994 that creating a computer that could find collisions with brute-force attacks would cost $10 million. However, a collision for an MD5 hash can now be found with just a few machines within a few hours.
MD6	Developed by Rivest and his team at MIT in 2008. It uses a Merkle tree-like structure to allow for immense parallel computation of hashes for very long inputs. Speeds in excess of 1 GB/s have been reported as possible for long messages on 16-core CPU architecture. MD6 is not widely used.
SHA-1	SHA-160, commonly known as SHA-1, has been considered broken since 2005 but is now approaching the date when collision attacks will begin to become available. It uses a 160-bit digest and is, at the time this was written, found in many applications in the government and private sector.
SHA-2	A collective designation for the longer digest versions of SHA algorithms: SHA-224, SHA-256, SHA-384, and SHA-512. SHA-2 versions use essentially the same algorithm as SHA-160, but the longer digests make collisions harder to find.
SHA-3	Keccak was selected as the SHA-3 standard by NIST in 2015. Keccak, or SHA-3, can take an input of any size and create an output of any size. SHA-3 is not intended to immediately replace SHA-2 and varies greatly in design from its SHA predecessors. You can read more about the Keccak algorithm on its website (keccak.noekeon.org).

UNDERSTANDING PUBLIC KEY INFRASTRUCTURE

A discussion of public key encryption can't take place without mentioning **public key infrastructure (PKI)**. PKI is not an algorithm; it's a structure consisting of programs, protocols, and security policies for encrypting data and uses public key cryptography to protect data transmitted over the Internet. The topic of PKI can take up an entire book, so this section just gives you an overview of its major components and how PKI is used in creating certificates.

Components of PKI

Another way authentication can take place over a communication channel is with certificates. A **certificate** is a digital document verifying that the two parties exchanging data over the Internet are really who they claim to be. Each certificate contains a unique serial number and must follow the X.509 standard that describes creating a certificate. SSL and S/MIME, for example, are Internet standards that use X.509 certificates.

Public keys are issued by a **certification authority (CA)**. The CA vouches for the company you send your credit card number to when ordering that Harley-Davidson motorcycle online. You probably want to know that the company you're ordering the bike from is valid, not someone who started a bogus website to collect credit card numbers from unsuspecting victims. Think of a CA as a passport agency. When U.S. citizens show their passports to enter a foreign country, the Customs agents viewing the passport don't necessarily trust the passport holders. They do, however, trust the passport agency that issued the passports, so the U.S. citizens are allowed to enter the country.

A certificate that a trusted CA issues binds a public key to the identity of the organization or individual that purchased it. In this way, if you encrypt an email message with the public key of your friend Ye-Jun, you know only she can decrypt the message with her private key that's mathematically related to her public key. You also know that the public key you used is indeed Ye-Jun's public key because you trust the CA that issued it.

Expiring, Revoking, and Suspending Certificates

A certificate issued by a CA is assigned a period of validity, and after that date, the certificate expires. If the keys are still valid and remain uncompromised, the certificate can be renewed with a new expiration date assigned.

At times, a certificate might need to be suspended or revoked before its expiration date, as in the following circumstances:

- A user leaves the company.
- A hardware crash causes a key to be lost.
- A private key is compromised.
- The company that was issued the certificate no longer exists.
- The company supplied false information when requesting the certificate.

The CA compiles a certificate revocation list (CRL) containing all revoked and suspended certificates. A certificate might be suspended when parties fail to honor agreements set forth when the certificate was issued. Instead of the certificate being revoked, it can be suspended so that it's easier to restore if the parties come to an agreement later. If you want to check whether a certificate is still valid, you can download the CRL from the URL specified in the certificate. For CAs that might have a lot of revoked certificates, you can use Online Certificate Status Protocol (OCSP) instead of downloading the CRL. With OCSP, you (or a device) can check a certificate's status without having to download and examine the entire CRL.

HTTP Strict Transport Security

HTTP Strict Transport Security (HSTS) was created in 2012 as a mechanism for web servers to tell clients they require secure communications. HSTS does two things to promote secure client-server communications. First, it forces all traffic between a web browser and a web server to be sent over a secure channel. This is accomplished through a field sent in the header of each web server response, which requires the browser to force HTTPS on all traffic sent to that web server. Figure 12-3 shows the HSTS information stored in a Chrome browser for facebook.com. Second, if the browser cannot validate the web server's certificate, the browser disallows access to the website. While HSTS is not foolproof and attackers could strip the HSTS field from the web server's initial response, it is an important part of a defense-in-depth approach to web security.

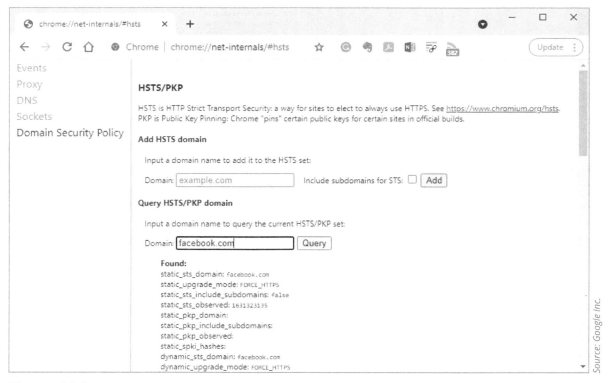

Figure 12-3   Viewing HSTS/PKP information in Google Chrome

Backing Up Keys

Backing up keys is just as important as backing up data. If keys are destroyed and not backed up correctly, encrypted business-critical information might be irretrievable. Companies typically back up their keys and store them offline in a safe or vault. A chain of custody record for keys is often required for companies that process sensitive information or financial transactions.

Microsoft Root CA

Microsoft includes features in its server OSs for configuring a server as a CA instead of using a third-party CA. For example, using the Add Roles and Features Wizard in Windows Server 2019, you as an administrator can select Active Directory Certificate Services, as shown in Figure 12-4. After clicking Next, you can select any features you want to install, including Certificate Authority Management tools.

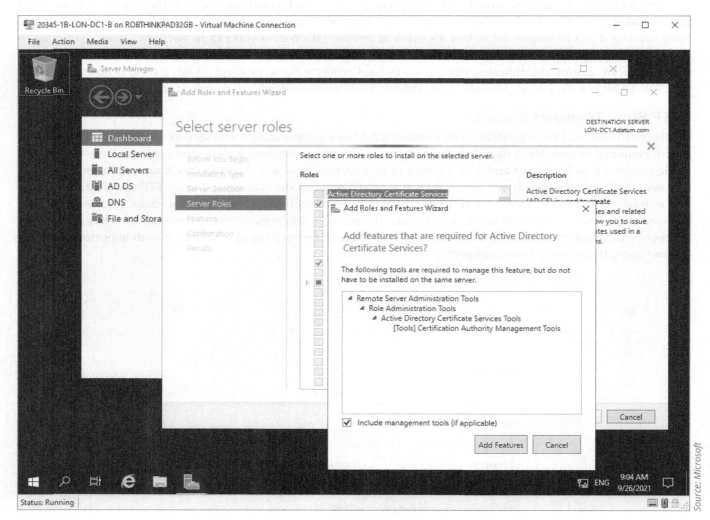

Figure 12-4   Selecting Active Directory Certificate Services

After the server role is installed, you need to configure the CA services by selecting role services, as shown in Figure 12-5. The Certification Authority role is used to issue and manage digital certificates.

Next, you specify the CA type. You can choose an enterprise or a stand-alone CA as the general type, and then select root or subordinate as the specific type (see Figure 12-6). A root CA issues its own certificate, and a subordinate gets its certificate from another CA higher up in the PKI structure.

If you select the root CA type, you must generate a new certificate. You can select three settings for generating certificates: the cryptographic service provider (CSP), the hashing algorithm, and the key length. In Figure 12-7, the default CSP is RSA#Microsoft Software Key Storage Provider, SHA-256 is the hashing algorithm, and the default key

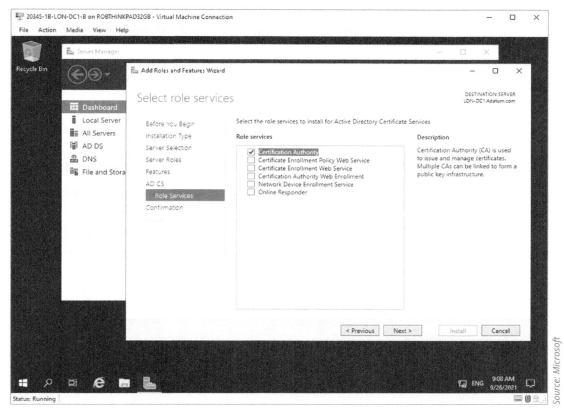

Figure 12-5 Selecting role services to install

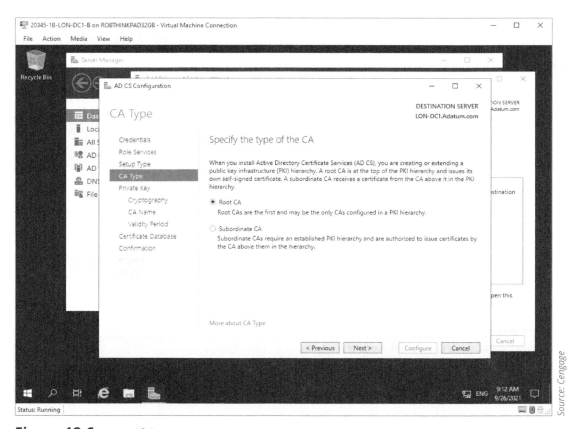

Figure 12-6 Specifying a CA type

length is 2048 bits. Of the CSPs available in Windows Server 2019, many allow weak hashing algorithms, such as SHA-1, MD2, MD4, and MD5. The RSA#Microsoft CSP does allow a digest length up to SHA-512, however.

No matter which CA a company chooses, you should be aware of the type of algorithm used so that you know whether the company is vulnerable to attack if information about the algorithm is compromised. Certificates at risk of being compromised can create a major security flaw for a company and shouldn't be overlooked when conducting a security test.

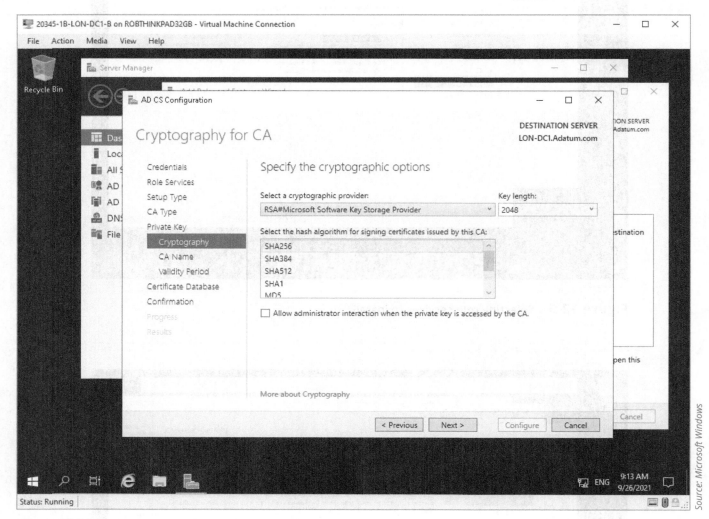

Figure 12-7   Configuring cryptography settings for a CA

Activity 12-3: Creating a Rogue Server Certificate by Breaking a Hashing Algorithm

Time Required: 30 minutes

Objective: Investigate what attackers can do with the results of an MD5 collision.

Description: Collisions for hashing algorithms have historically been a theoretical threat, though recent increases in computing power have made collisions a reality. In 2017, academics from France and Singapore demonstrated a successful SHA-1 collision attack. Collisions in MD5 have been demonstrated for more than a decade. Until recently, even some well-known CAs used MD5 to generate web server SSL certificates. In this activity, you research what's possible when smart researchers decide to call attention to a major security problem on the Internet.

1. Start your web browser in Windows and go to **www.google.com**.
2. Type **creating a rogue ca certificate** and press **Enter**. Click the first link in the search results, which should take you to the Rogue CA research page at the **Phreedom.org** website. (If not, go to **www.phreedom.org** and search for **rogue CA**.)
3. Read the paragraphs summarizing the researchers' findings, and then click the **Slides from the 25c3 presentation** link to download the PowerPoint presentation, which you use to answer the following questions. *Note:* You may have to click through a security warning, depending on the browser you are using.
   - The researchers collected 30,000 website certificates in 2008. How many were signed with MD5?
   - What kind of hardware was used to generate the chosen-prefix collision? How much money did the researchers spend on certificates?
   - What was the impact of generating a rogue CA certificate? What would this certificate allow someone with malicious intentions to do?
   - Which hashing algorithm were CAs forced to use after their signing method was demonstrated as not secure?
   - According to the researchers, what's the only way you can effect change and secure the Internet?
4. Close all open windows.

UNDERSTANDING CRYPTOGRAPHY ATTACKS

Using tools to eavesdrop (such as tcpdump and Wireshark) is considered passive attacking because the attacker is only collecting data sent to and from a cryptosystem. Active attacks attempt to determine the secret key used to encrypt plaintext by actively sending input to a cryptosystem. Remember that if the culprit or the general public know the algorithm, it's usually because companies developing encryption algorithms realize that the public might discover vulnerabilities that the company's programmers missed. Software engineers who develop open-source code products follow this philosophy. Because they release their source code to the public, users can make suggestions and modify or add to the programming code. Ostensibly, making source code available can create a better product. Agencies such as the NSA and CIA don't release information on all the encryption algorithms they're using, however. The following sections describe some common active attacks.

Birthday Attack

You've probably heard the adage that if 23 people are in a room, the probability that two will share the same birthday is about 50 percent. Birthday attacks are used to find the same hash value for two different inputs and reveal any mathematical weaknesses in a hashing algorithm. For example, if an attacker has one hash value and wants to find another message that creates the same hash value, he or she could possibly do so in a couple of hours if the hashing algorithm is weak. SHA-1, discussed previously, uses a 160-bit digest. Theoretically, finding a collision for a different message (the same birthday for a different person, in this analogy) would require 2^{60} computations, which may be possible in the near future.

Mathematical Attack

In a mathematical attack, properties of the algorithm are attacked by using mathematical computations. Attackers perform this type of attack in different ways, depending on the information they can access. There are five main categories for this attack:

- *Ciphertext-only attack*—Attackers have the ciphertext of several messages encrypted with the same encryption algorithm but no access to the plaintext, so they must try to figure out the key used to encrypt the data. Getting a copy of ciphertext is usually easy with a sniffer, such as tcpdump or Wireshark, but this type of attack is by far the most difficult because little or no information is known about the encryption algorithm used.

- *Known-plaintext attack*—Attackers have messages in both encrypted and decrypted forms. This attack is easier than the ciphertext-only attack because patterns in the plaintext can be examined. For example, if a bank's communications to its customers always begin with a particular salutation and end with the familiar "Thanks for your business," attackers can use reverse-engineering techniques to determine the key used to encrypt the data.
- *Chosen-plaintext attack*—Attackers have access to plaintext and ciphertext and can choose which messages to encrypt. Because the whole plaintext message and ciphertext message are available, determining the key is easier. Attackers can get this information by sending an email message to someone stating that the contents aren't to be divulged to anyone except, say, Bob Smith. They would most likely spoof the email message so that the recipient believes the message is from someone known and trusted. When the recipient forwards the message as ciphertext, attackers can then sniff the contents to get both the cleartext they wrote and the ciphertext document the user sent.
- *Chosen-ciphertext attack*—Attackers have access to the ciphertext to be decrypted and the resulting plaintext. They also need access to the cryptosystem to perform this type of attack.
- *Side-channel attack*—This attack, which is completely different from the other categories, relies on the attacker analyzing the hardware used for cryptographic operations. Attackers collect data such as operating temperatures, computation times, electromagnetic emissions, noise, vibrations, and even reflections off a cryptosystem user's eyes to gather information they can use to launch an exploit. Generally, attackers need close proximity to the cryptosystem to collect this information.

Regardless of the type of attack, the attacker builds on the information gained and then conducts another type of attack. Patience and curiosity are usually part of cryptologists' personalities, whether they're working for good or bad purposes.

Brute-Force Attack

Despite its name, this type of attack doesn't require a hammer or martial arts skills; it requires only time and patience. A brute-force attack tries all possible keys in a keyspace.

One example is using a password-cracking program to attempt every possible combination of characters in an effort to break the password hash. Brute-force attacks can be launched on any kind of message digest, such as a certificate request. If you want to find out how long a brute-force attack might take to crack your password, you can download the brute-force time calculator at Mandylion Labs (www.mandylionlabs.com/documents/BFTCalc.xls).

Man-in-the-Middle Attack

In a man-in-the-middle attack, attackers place themselves between the victim computer and another host computer. They can then intercept messages sent from the victim to the host and pretend to be the host computer. This type of attack follows this process:

1. Gloria sends her public key to Bruce, and you, the attacker, intercept the key and send Bruce your public key. Bruce thinks he just received Gloria's public key, but he received yours.
2. Bruce sends Gloria his public key. You intercept this key, too, and send Gloria your public key.
3. Gloria sends a message to Bruce, encrypted in what she thinks is Bruce's public key, but because she's using yours, you can decrypt the message with your private key.
4. You then can reencrypt the message with Bruce's public key and send it to Bruce.
5. Bruce answers Gloria by encrypting his message with what he thinks is Gloria's public key. You intercept the message, decrypt it with your private key, encrypt it with Gloria's real public key, and then send it to Gloria.

You might have to read these steps a few times to understand how this type of attack works. Using index cards with the names of participants written on them might help you get a clearer picture of what's taking place; this technique is used in Activity 12-4.

Activity 12-4: Conducting a Man-in-the-Middle Attack

Time Required: 20 minutes

Objective: Understand how a man-in-the-middle attack works.

Description: Using index cards and breaking into teams of three students, you perform a manual man-in-the-middle attack.

1. Two students should create two index cards. Label one card *FirstName* **PublicKey** and the second card *FirstName* **PrivateKey**. (Substitute your first name for FirstName.)
2. The attacker performing the man-in-the-middle attack should name his or her cards **Attacker PublicKey** and **Attacker PrivateKey**.
3. As the first student hands his or her *FirstName* PublicKey to the second student, the attacker should intercept the transfer and substitute his or her Attacker PublicKey.
4. The student receiving this attacker card is under the impression that he or she received the real public key and would then encrypt a message with this public key and send it back to the sender.
5. The attacker should intercept this card and use his or her private key card to simulate decrypting the message.

SSL/TLS Downgrade Attack

With an **SSL/TLS downgrade attack**, an attacker who intercepts the initial communications between a web server and a web browser can force a vulnerable server to insecurely renegotiate the encryption being used down to a weaker cipher. This works because a web server and a web browser must negotiate which cipher will be used to communicate before they begin. If the client tells the server it can only communicate over weak protocols and the server agrees to use that weak protocol, the ensuing communication could be at risk. For example, in 2014, security researchers released a dangerous downgrade attack in which an attacker could force vulnerable servers to communicate over an extremely weak cipher named "export-grade." The fix for this issue was to make sure all ciphers allowed by a server are secure.

Dictionary Attack

In a **dictionary attack**, after attackers have access to a password file, they can run a password-cracking program that uses a dictionary of known words or passwords as an input file. Most of these input files are available on the Internet and can be downloaded free. Remember that unauthorized password cracking is illegal in most parts of the world, including the United States.

Replay Attack

In a **replay attack**, the attacker captures data and attempts to resubmit the captured data so that the device, which can be a computer or router, thinks a legitimate connection is in effect. If the captured data is logon information, the attacker could gain access to a system and be authenticated. Many systems have countermeasures to prevent these attacks from occurring, such as packets using sequence numbers that detect when a packet is out of order or not in a correct sequence.

UNDERSTANDING PASSWORD CRACKING

As a security professional, you might come across encrypted or password-protected files. Passwords can often be guessed easily, especially when they're names of pets, relatives, or spouses or anniversary and birth dates. A study conducted by the NSA about 30 years ago found that 70 percent of all passwords are written in an area within 4 feet of a user's computer. Also, to paraphrase a social engineer when asked about cracking passwords, "Why spend time trying to decrypt a password when you can just ask for it?"

In most countries, including the United States, cracking someone else's passwords is illegal. (You're allowed to crack your own password if you forget it.) Even an attempt to figure out the encryption method might be illegal in many countries.

If a password uses common words found in a dictionary, most password-cracking programs can use a dictionary file to speed up the process. Brute force is a common method for cracking a password. One way to speed up a brute-force cracking effort is by using a rainbow table. A password-cracking program can use this lookup table of password hash values instead of trying random computations on a password hash's keyspace. For rainbow tables to be effective, however, they need to store a lot of hash values. Also, rainbow tables for passwords that contain more than 10 characters can quickly fill hundreds of terabytes of storage due to the exponential nature of available permutations relative to the length of a password.

A salt, in cryptographic terms, is the use of random data alongside plaintext as an input to a hashing function so that the output is unique. Salts make pre-calculated rainbow tables worthless because the resulting hashes are completely different due to the random data included in the hashing routine. Salts should always be used when storing passwords. In some of the large breaches of websites in recent history, unsalted passwords exposed users' passwords and led to account compromise and additional compromise for users who had the same password across multiple sites.

A graphics processing unit (GPU) greatly exceeds a CPU's capability to process mathematical calculations. A typical GPU has hundreds of cores, whereas a typical CPU has four or eight cores. Each of these cores can process one mathematical calculation per cycle. At the time of this writing, parallel processing across hundreds of cores gives GPUs three to five times greater throughput for hash cracking when compared with CPUs. Programs like Hashcat can be set to leverage the GPU rather than the CPU.

SECURITY BYTES

In 2021, 3.28 billion passwords linked to 2.18 billion unique email addresses were exposed in one of the largest data dumps of breached usernames and passwords. The leaks included 1,502,909 passwords associated with email addresses from government domains across the globe. The passwords are said to have been obtained using techniques such as password hash cracking. The passwords were acquired in a number of ways including files stolen from servers, email phishing attacks, and intercepted insecure plaintext communications.

To conduct password cracking, first you must get the password hash from the system that stores usernames and passwords, which varies based on the OS you're testing. On *nix systems, the password hash is stored in the /etc/shadow file. The Fgdump program extracts files from the Security Accounts Manager (SAM) file, where Windows password hashes are stored. Cracking attacks on passwords can be performed with the following programs:

- *Hashcat*—A fast password-cracking tool built into Kali Linux that can use GPUs for increased efficiency over CPU-based cracking tools
- *John the Ripper*—A lightweight cracking tool available for cracking password files; can use dictionary or simple brute-force methods
- *0phcrack*—The first password hash-cracking program to use rainbow tables
- *EXPECT*—A scripting language for Windows and Linux that performs repetitive tasks, such as password cracking
- *L0phtcrack*—The original password-cracking program now used by many government agencies to test password strength; capable of using rainbow tables
- *Pwdump8*—The latest version of the pwdump program for extracting password hash values of user accounts on a Windows computer

A security tester can use the following steps to gather passwords on a Windows computer.

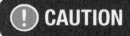 **CAUTION**   Performing these steps on a computer other than your own is illegal in most parts of the world. In fact, using password-cracking software on a computer other than yours can be dangerous.

In the following example, fgdump is used to dump hashes from a Windows 10 computer and John the Ripper is used to crack hashes on a Kali Linux computer:

1. The security tester runs the fgdump program to get hash values of user accounts on the Windows computer (see Figure 12-8). Running Fgdump without options dumps the computer's user accounts to the 127.0.0.1.pwdump file.

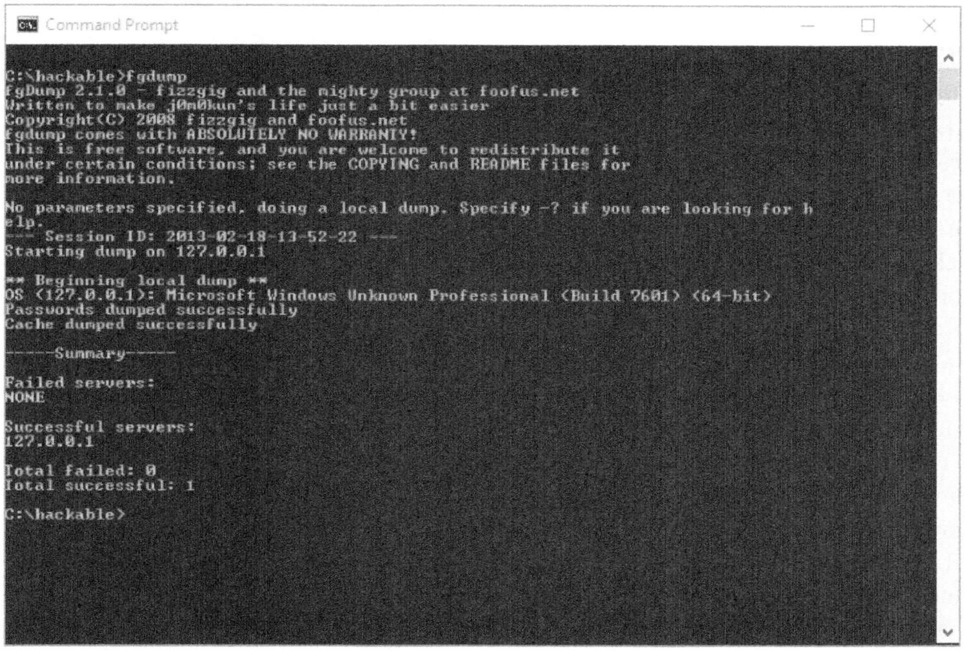

Source: Microsoft Windows

Figure 12-8   Running fgdump

2. Using John the Ripper with 127.0.0.1.pwdump as the input file, the security tester can use the command john -f=NT 127.0.0.1.pwdump to conduct a brute-force attack on the hash values discovered with fgdump. The -f=NT switch is used to specify that passwords are in the NT LAN Manager (NTLM) authentication format. Figure 12-9 shows some command parameters available in John the Ripper. To see a complete list, you can type the command john -h.

Source: GNU General Public License (GNU GPL)

Figure 12-9   Using John the Ripper parameters

This method isn't the fastest way to break a password, but it's effective. Many hackers leave a program such as John the Ripper running for days on a computer devoted to breaking passwords.

MODULE SUMMARY

- Cryptography has been in existence for thousands of years, from Egyptian hieroglyphics to the Enigma machine and on into the 21st century.
- Ciphertext is data that has been encrypted; plaintext, also called cleartext, is data that can be read by anyone.
- Symmetric cryptography uses one key to encrypt and decrypt data. Both sender and receiver must agree on the key before data is transmitted. The two main types of symmetric algorithms are block ciphers and stream ciphers. Block ciphers, such as AES, operate on fixed-length chunks of data, and stream ciphers, such as RC4, operate on one bit of data at a time.
- Asymmetric cryptography, also called public key cryptography, uses two keys: one key to encrypt and another to decrypt data. In public key cryptography, a public key can be downloaded from a website and is mathematically related to a private key known only to the owner. A private key is never shared.
- RSA, ECC, and ElGamal use a one-way function to generate a key that can be used for digital signatures and encryption. They require a key distribution system such as PKI.
- Diffie-Hellman is a key distribution system and is one component that can be used by RSA and other public-key cryptography systems.
- Digital Signature Standard (DSS) ensures that digital signatures can be verified. To create a digital signature, the hash value must be encrypted with the sender's private key.
- OpenPGP is a free public key encryption standard based on the PGP email encryption program. S/MIME is another public key encryption standard, included in Microsoft Outlook, for encrypting email.
- Hashing algorithms are used to verify data integrity. SHA-1 is a widely used hashing algorithm, but because of recently discovered weaknesses, NIST no longer recommends using it for sensitive applications, and federal agencies have been switching to SHA-2 and SHA-3.
- Public key infrastructure (PKI) is a structure made up of several components for encrypting data. PKI includes protocols, programs, and security policies and uses public key cryptography to protect data transmitted over the Internet.
- A digital certificate is a file issued by a certification authority (CA) that binds a public key to information about its owner. A CA is a trusted third party that accepts certificate applications from entities, authenticates applications, issues certificates, and maintains information about certificates.
- In cryptography, an active attack involves sending input to a cryptosystem. Examples of active attacks include brute-force attacks, man-in-the-middle attacks, replay attacks, and dictionary attacks.
- A passive attack on a cryptosystem uses sniffing tools, such as Wireshark and tcpdump, to collect messages from and/or to a given cryptosystem.

Key Terms

Advanced Encryption Standard (AES)
asymmetric algorithms
Authentication
Birthday attacks
Block ciphers
Blowfish
brute-force attack
certificate
certification authority
cipher
ciphertext
cryptanalysis

cryptosystem
data at rest
Data Encryption Algorithm (DEA)
Data Encryption Standard (DES)
dictionary attack
digital signature
encryption algorithm
hashing algorithm
HTTP Strict Transport Security (HSTS)
International Data Encryption Algorithm (IDEA)
key

keyspace
man-in-the-middle attack
mathematical attack
message digest
Message Digest 5 (MD5)
Nonrepudiation
OpenPGP
plaintext
Pretty Good Privacy (PGP)
private key
public key
public key cryptography
public key infrastructure (PKI)

rainbow table
RC4
RC5
replay attack
salt

Secure Hash Algorithm 1 (SHA-1)
Secure Multipurpose Internet Mail
   Extension (S/MIME)
SSL/TLS downgrade attack
steganography

Stream ciphers
substitution cipher
symmetric algorithms
Triple Data Encryption Standard
   (3DES)

Review Questions

1. Digital signatures are used to do which of the following?
   a. Verify that a message was received
   b. Ensure that repudiation is provided
   c. Provide authentication and nonrepudiation
   d. Encrypt sensitive messages

2. What is the standard for PKI certificates?
   a. X.500
   b. X.400
   c. X.509
   d. MySQL.409

3. A man-in-the-middle attack can be performed using a number of hardware and software tools readily available for purchase or download on the Internet. Write a three-paragraph report describing some of these tools. Include information such as where the tools can be acquired, what they cost, and how they are used.

4. A hash value is a fixed-length string used to verify message integrity. True or false?

5. OpenPGP is focused on protecting which of the following?
   a. Web content
   b. Email messages
   c. Database systems
   d. IPSec traffic

6. Intruders can perform which kind of attack if they have possession of a company's password hash file?
   a. Dictionary
   b. Scan
   c. Ciphertext
   d. Buffer overflow

7. Intercepting messages destined for another computer and sending back messages while pretending to be the other computer is an example of what type of attack?
   a. Man-in-the-middle
   b. Smurf
   c. Buffer overflow
   d. Mathematical

8. A certification authority (CA) issues private keys to recipients. True or false?

9. Any cryptography can be cracked given enough time and processing power. The advent of quantum computing has raised concerns about the security of our current encryption algorithms. Perform an Internet search for information and write a three-paragraph report discussing quantum computing and its encryption cracking concerns.

10. Why did the NSA decide to drop support for DES?
    a. The cost was too high.
    b. The encryption algorithm was too slow.
    c. The processing power of computers had increased.
    d. It was too difficult for government agencies to use.

11. Symmetric algorithms can be block ciphers or stream ciphers. True or false?

12. Which of the following describes a chosen-plaintext attack?
    a. The attacker has ciphertext and algorithm.
    b. The attacker has plaintext and algorithm.
    c. The attacker has plaintext, can choose what part of the text gets encrypted, and has access to the ciphertext.
    d. The attacker has plaintext, ciphertext, and the password file.

13. Two different messages producing the same hash value results in which of the following?
    a. Duplicate key
    b. Corrupt key
    c. Collision
    d. Message digest

14. In a replay attack, the attacker captures data and attempts to resubmit the data to circumvent security. Replay attacks are a common strategy in a variety of hacking methods. Write a three-paragraph report that outlines different types of replay attacks. Include information such as what type of system is being replay attacked, what weakness is the attack trying to exploit, and if there is a way to defend from such an attack.

15. Advanced Encryption Standard (AES) replaced DES with which algorithm?
    a. Rijndael
    b. Blowfish
    c. IDEA
    d. Twofish

16. What cryptographic devices were used during World War II? (Choose all that apply.)
    a. Enigma machine
    b. Black Box
    c. Purple Machine
    d. Bombe

17. Asymmetric cryptography systems are which of the following?
    a. Faster than symmetric cryptography systems
    b. Slower than symmetric cryptography systems

    c. The same speed as symmetric cryptography systems
    d. Practical only on systems with multiple processors

18. Diffie-Hellman is used to encrypt email messages. True or false?

19. Hiding data in a photograph is an example of which of the following?
    a. Steganography
    b. Stenography
    c. Ciphertext
    d. Cryptology

20. Which of the following is an asymmetric algorithm?
    a. DES
    b. AES
    c. RSA
    d. Blowfish

Case Projects

Case Project 12-1: Determining Possible Vulnerabilities of Microsoft CA Root Server

In conducting security testing on the Alexander Rocco network, you have found that the company configured one of its Windows Server 2019 computers as an enterprise root CA server. You have also determined that Andrea Lee, the administrator of the CA server, selected MD5 as the hashing algorithm for creating digital signatures. Based on this information, write a one-page report explaining possible vulnerabilities caused by signing certificates with MD5. The report should cite articles about MD5 weaknesses and include recommendations from Microsoft about using MD5 in its software.

Case Project 12-2: Exploring Moral and Legal Issues

After conducting research for Case Project 12-1, you have gathered a lot of background about the release of information on hashing algorithms. Articles on vulnerabilities of SHA-1, MD4, and MD5 abound. The proliferation of programs for breaking encryption codes and the imprisonment of attackers who break encryption have raised many questions about what's moral or legal in releasing information about hashing algorithms. Based on this information, write a one- to two-page report addressing moral and legal issues of releasing software or code for breaking these algorithms. Your paper should also answer these questions:

- Should people who are able to break a hashing algorithm be allowed to post their findings on the Internet?
- Do you think the reporters that report cracking exploits and details are exercising their First Amendment rights when including the source code or procedure for breaking the encryption in an article?
- As a security professional, do you think you have to abide by a higher standard when sharing or disseminating source code that breaks hashing algorithms? Explain.

NETWORK PROTECTION SYSTEMS

After reading this module and completing the exercises, you will be able to:

1. Explain how routers are used as network protection systems

2. Describe firewall technology and tools for configuring firewalls and routers

3. Describe intrusion detection and prevention systems and web-filtering technology

4. Explain the purpose of honeypots

Hackers have many tools at their disposal to attack a network. You have seen how port scanning and enumeration make it possible for attackers to determine the services running on computers and gain access to network resources. In this module, you look at network protection systems that can be used to reduce exposure to these attacks and reduce their occurrence.

Routers, hardware and software firewalls, web filtering, intrusion detection and prevention systems, and honeypots are covered in this module. A network protection system can also include a security incident response team, which is a team of people with the responsibility of protecting a large network.

USING NETWORK PROTECTION SYSTEMS

To protect a network from attack, security professionals must know how to use network protection systems, such as routers, firewalls, intrusion detection and prevention systems, web filtering, and honeypots. For the purposes of this book, a network protection system is simply any device or system designed to protect a network. A Unified Threat Management (UTM) device is a single device that combines many network protection functions, such as those performed by routers, firewalls, intrusion detection and prevention systems, VPNs, web-filtering systems, and malware detection and filtering systems. For instance, modern Cisco routers can perform firewall functions, address translation (Network Address Translation and Port Address Translation), and intrusion prevention in addition to their router function. The term security appliance can describe both UTMs and network protection systems. As hardware technology gets more powerful, security appliances can perform the same functions that once required using several dedicated systems. They also reduce administrative effort because multiple network protection functions are managed via a common interface. In this section, you start learning about network protection systems by seeing how routers are used to reduce network attacks.

Using Routers to Reduce Network Attacks

Routers, which operate at the Network layer of the TCP/IP protocol stack, are hardware devices used to send packets to different network segments. Their main purposes are to reduce broadcast traffic passing over a network and choose the best path for moving packets. For example, if Router A in Spain wants to send a packet to Router B in Iowa, the packet can probably take several paths. Routers use routing protocols in this best-path decision-making process that function in the following ways:

- *Link-state routing protocol*—A router using a link-state routing protocol sends link-state advertisements to other routers; these advertisements identify the network topology and any changes or paths discovered recently on the network. For example, if a new router or path becomes available for a packet, this information is sent to all other routers participating in the network. This method is efficient because only new information is sent over the network. An example of a link-state routing protocol is Open Shortest Path First (OSPF).
- *Distance-vector routing protocol*—If a router is using a distance-vector routing protocol, it passes its routing table (containing all possible paths it has discovered) to neighboring routers on the network. These neighbor routers then forward the routing table to *their* neighbors. Two examples of distance-vector routing protocols are Routing Internet Protocol version 2 (RIPv2) and Enhanced Interior Gateway Routing Protocol (EIGRP).
- *Path-vector routing protocol*—A path-vector routing protocol uses dynamically updated paths or routing tables to transmit packets from one autonomous network to another. It isn't used on LANs because it's used mainly by ISPs and large organizations with multiple Internet connections to other ISPs and organizations. The main path-vector routing protocol is Border Gateway Protocol (BGP), a routing protocol that an ISP uses to transmit packets to their destinations on the Internet.

SECURITY BYTES

BGP does have some security vulnerabilities. For example, attackers might hijack IP space belonging to another ISP by injecting a malicious BGP routing advertisement for a network prefix they don't own. On April Fool's Day 2020, just as the world was coming to grips with the COVID-19 pandemic, Internet traffic that was supposed to flow through more than 200 cloud-based web providers and content delivery networks was redirected through Rostelcom, Russia's state-owned telecommunications provider. Over 8000 Internet traffic routes were affected for approximately two hours, slowing or halting traffic coming from or destined to Amazon, Google, Facebook, and many other sites. For more information about this BGP hijacking incident, visit www.darkreading.com/edge-articles/101-why-bgp-hijacking-just-won-t-die.

 TIP For more information on routing protocols, see *Cisco CCNA Certification: Exam 200-301, 1st Edition* (Todd Lammle, 2020, ISBN 1119677610).

As a security professional, your main concern is confirming that a router filters certain traffic, not designing a router infrastructure and determining the routing protocol an organization uses. The following section explains how a Cisco router is configured to filter traffic.

Configuring Basic Hardware Routers

In this section, Cisco routers are used as an example because they are widely used; millions of Cisco routers are used by companies around the world. Because Cisco has become such a standard among network professionals, vendors offering competitive products often design their configuration interfaces to be similar to Cisco's. So although the information in this section can assist you in performing security tests on companies using Cisco routers in their networks, you won't be completely lost if you see a product from a Cisco competitor, such as Juniper. The principles you learn in this module can be applied to other types of routers. In Activity 13-1, you visit the Cisco website and review some Cisco products. If you've never seen a router or worked with the interfaces discussed in this section, the product photographs on this site can give you an idea of what you'll be working with as a security professional. Recall that a Cisco router is an embedded system that uses Cisco Internetwork Operating System (IOS) to function.

Activity 13-1: Visiting the Cisco Website

Time Required: 30 minutes

Objective: Review Cisco routing products.

Description: Cisco routing products will be an important part of your job as a security professional because many companies use them. In this activity, you visit the company's website and review the type of vulnerability information Cisco makes available to its customers. This information can be helpful if you're performing a security test on a network using Cisco routers.

1. Start a web browser and go to **www.cisco.com**. On the Cisco home page, click Products and Services in the top menu, click Networking in the left pane, and then click Routers.
2. On the Routers page, click Products in the navigation bar. At the time of this writing, the Cisco router page groups its routers into six categories: Branch, WAN aggregation, Service provider, Industrial, Virtual, and Small business. Explore the types of products available. In which category does the main router at your school fall? You might need to ask your instructor which type of router your school uses. If it isn't a Cisco product, who is the vendor?
3. Go to **https://tools.cisco.com/security/center/**. In the Cisco Security search text box, type ios and press Enter to display a list of topics related to IOS vulnerabilities. Examine some recent vulnerabilities in Cisco IOS.
4. Go to **https://nvd.nist.gov**. Click the + (plus sign) next to Vulnerabilities to open the Vulnerabilities menu, and then click **Search & Statistics** to open the Search Vulnerability Database page. In the Keyword Search box, enter **Cisco ios** and press **Enter**. For the remainder of this activity, you use this site and the information returned.
5. Examine the search results. How many records were returned?
6. Click the links beginning with CVE- to read the detailed information for some of the vulnerabilities. Find a CVE with a CVSS Base of at least 7. What does the flaw allow an attacker to do? For software flaws, the NVD website supplies links to the vendor's website to find a patch or workaround. Click the link to the Cisco website and read the information. What does Cisco recommend?
7. Exit your browser and log off Windows for the next activity.

 As you can see from your reading, Cisco IOS has vulnerabilities as does any OS, so security professionals must consider the type of router used when conducting a security test.

SECURITY BYTES

At a Black Hat computer security conference, a 24-year-old researcher named Michael Lynn was instructed by Cisco not to give a presentation on vulnerabilities he found in Cisco's Internet routers. Mr. Lynn claimed the vulnerabilities would allow hackers to take over corporate and government networks. Cisco argued that releasing his findings to the general public was illegal and that Mr. Lynn found the vulnerabilities by reverse-engineering Cisco's product, also illegal in the United States. Most technology companies don't want vulnerabilities in their products to be released to the public until they have the chance to correct the problem themselves or they can control what information is given to the public. The issue of disclosure will be here for quite some time and will most certainly affect security testers.

Cisco Router Components

To help you understand how routers are used as network protection systems, this section describes the components of a Cisco router. Just as a system administrator must understand commands for configuring a server, Cisco router administrators must know commands for configuring a Cisco router. Many components of a Cisco router are similar to those of a computer, so the following components should seem familiar:

- *Random access memory (RAM)*—This component holds the router's running configuration, routing tables, and buffers. If you turn off the router, the contents stored in RAM are erased. Any changes you make to a router's configuration, such as changing the prompt displayed, are stored in RAM and aren't permanent unless you save the configuration.

- *Nonvolatile RAM (NVRAM)*—This component holds the router's configuration file, but the information isn't lost if the router is turned off.
- *Flash memory*—This component holds the IOS the router is using. It's rewriteable memory, so you can upgrade the IOS if Cisco releases a new version or the current IOS version becomes corrupted.
- *Read-only memory (ROM)*—This component contains a minimal version of Cisco IOS that's used to boot the router if flash memory gets corrupted. You can boot the router and then correct any problems with the IOS, possibly installing a new, uncorrupted version.
- *Interfaces*—These components are the hardware connectivity points to the router and the components you're most concerned with. An Ethernet port, for example, is an interface that connects to a LAN and can be configured to restrict traffic from a specific IP address, subnet, or network.

As a security professional, you should know some basic Cisco commands to view information in these components. For example, to see what information is stored in RAM, a Cisco administrator uses this command (with bolded text indicating the actual command):

```
RouterB# show running-config
Here's an example of the abbreviated output of this command for a production router:
Building configuration...
Current configuration : 4422 bytes
! version 12.4
service timestamps debug datetime msec localtime
service timestamps log datetime msec localtime
no service password-encryption
!
hostname R3825_2
!
boot-start-marker
boot-end-marker
!
card type t100
logging buffered 51200 debugging
!
no aaa new-model
!
resource policy
!
clock timezone Hawaii -10
network-clock-participate wic 0
network-clock-select 1 T1 0/0/0
ip subnet-zero
ip cef
!
interface GigabitEthernet0/0
description $ETH-LAN$$ETH-SW-LAUNCH$$INTF-INFO-GE 0/0$
ip address 192.168.10.3 2 55.255.255.0
duplex auto
speed auto
media-type rj45
negotiation auto
h323-gateway voip interface
```

```
h323-gateway voip bind srcaddr 192.168.10.3
!
interface Serial0/0/0:23
no ip address
isdn switch-type primary-ni
isdn incoming-voice voice
isdn bind-l3 ccm-manager
no cdp enable
!
ip classless
ip route 0.0.0.0 0.0.0.0 192.168.10.1
!
ip http server
username netdef privilege 15 secret 5
$1$pod7$ZZWTCxA9O8iBSJbd3tIlL1
!
end
RouterB#
```

Cisco Router Configuration

Two access modes are available on a Cisco router: user mode and privileged mode. In **user mode**, an administrator can perform basic troubleshooting tests and list information stored on the router. In **privileged mode**, an administrator can perform full router configuration tasks. You can see which access mode you're in by looking at the prompt. The router name followed by a > symbol, such as `Router>`, indicates that you're in user mode. A router name followed by a # sign, such as `Router#`, indicates that you're in privileged mode, also called enable mode. When first logging on to a Cisco router, you're in user mode by default. To change to privileged mode, enter the `enable` command, which can be abbreviated as `en`. Usually, you have to enter a password to use this command, unless the Cisco router administrator has little experience and hasn't specified a password.

After you're in privileged mode, you need to enter another command for one of the following modes to configure the router:

- *Global configuration mode*—In this mode, you can configure router settings that affect overall router operation, such as changing the router's displayed banner when a user connects from a remote host via Telnet. The banner might indicate that the router is secured or shouldn't be accessed by unauthorized personnel. To use this mode, enter the `configure terminal` command at the `Router#` prompt. You can also enter an abbreviated command, which the Cisco command interpreter understands, as long as it's not so short that it's ambiguous. Therefore, `config t` works, too. The prompt then changes to `Router (config) #` to indicate global configuration mode. When using a Cisco router or switch, being aware of the prompts is critical.
- *Interface configuration mode*—In this mode, you're configuring an interface on the router, such as a serial or Fast Ethernet port. To use this mode, first enter global configuration mode (with the `config t` command). Next, enter the command for interface configuration mode and the interface name you want to configure, such as `interface fastethernet 0/0`. The prompt then changes to `Router (config-if) #` to indicate interface configuration mode.

Now that you understand the basic modes in which a Cisco router can operate, take a look at Table 13-1, which describes some common commands for viewing a Cisco router's components. If you want to know all the commands available in global configuration mode, type a question mark (?) after the `Router(config)#` prompt.

A Cisco administrator needs to know many other commands that aren't covered in this course. The most critical configuration that security professionals perform is on a router's interfaces. Packets can be filtered or evaluated on a router's interfaces before passing to the next router or the internal network. To control the flow of traffic through a router, access lists are used, as explained in the following section.

Table 13-1   Cisco commands

Mode	Command	Prompt	Description
Privileged or user	`show version`	`Router#` or `Router>`	Displays the router's version information, including the IOS version number
Privileged or user	`show ip route`	`Router#` or `Router>`	Displays the router's routing table
Privileged or user	`show interfaces`	`Router#` or `Router>`	Lists configuration information and statistics for all interfaces on the router
Privileged or user	`show flash`	`Router#` or `Router>`	Shows the contents of flash memory and the amount of memory used and available
Privileged	`show running-config`	`Router#`	Displays the currently running router configuration file
Privileged	`show startup-config`	`Router#`	Displays the contents of NVRAM
Privileged	`copy running-config startup-config`	`Router#`	Copies the running configuration to NVRAM so that changes made are carried out the next time the router is started
Privileged	`copy startup-config running-config`	`Router#`	Copies the startup configuration from NVRAM to memory (RAM)
Global configuration (privileged)	`configure terminal`	`Router (config)#`	Enables you to change configuration settings that affect overall router operation
Interface configuration (privileged)	`interface serial`	`Router (config-if)#`	Enables you to configure the serial interface you identify, such as serial 0
Interface configuration (privileged)	`interface fastethernet`	`Router (config-if)#`	Enables you to configure the Fast Ethernet interface you specify

Using Access Control Lists

Access Control Lists are lists of security rules that analyze incoming and outgoing traffic and determine whether that traffic is going to be rejected or allowed in or out of a specific interface. Each interface of a router can have two unique Access Control Lists, one for analyzing incoming traffic and one for analyzing outgoing traffic. There are several types of access control lists, but this section focuses on IP access lists. IP access lists are lists of IP addresses, subnets, or networks that are allowed or denied access through a router's interface. On a Cisco router, an administrator can create two types of access lists:

- Standard IP access lists
- Extended IP access lists

NOTE

Cisco refers to IP access lists as "access control lists" but refers to the specific file containing the list of commands as an "access list."

Standard IP Access Lists

Standard IP access lists can restrict IP traffic entering or leaving a router's interface based on only one criterion: source IP address. Figure 13-1 shows a network composed of two routers. Network 1 (10.0.0.0) is connected to a Fast Ethernet interface (FE0/0) on Router A. Router A's serial interface (S0/1) is connected to Router B's serial interface (S0/0). Network 2 (192.168.10.0) is connected to Router B's Fast Ethernet interface (FE0/0), and Network 3 (173.110.0.0) is connected to Router B's other Fast Ethernet interface (FE0/1).

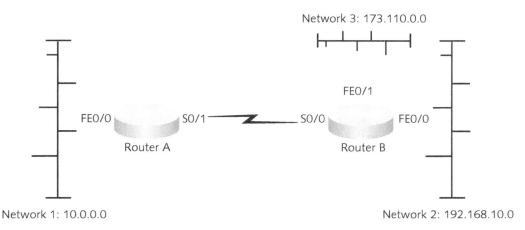

Figure 13-1   Applying access lists to router interfaces

A Cisco administrator who wants to restrict all traffic from Network 3 from entering Network 1 can create a standard IP access list that looks like the following:

```
access-list 1 deny 173.110.0.0 0.0.255.255
access-list permit any
```

Extended IP Access Lists

A standard IP access list is restricted to source IP addresses. So if you want to restrict a user from sending a packet to a specific IP address (destination IP address), you can't use a standard IP access list. Extended IP access lists can restrict IP traffic entering or leaving a router's interface based on the following criteria:

- Source IP address
- Destination IP address
- Protocol type
- Application port number

Configuring an extended IP access list is much the same as configuring a standard IP access list. A network administrator can decide which interface to apply an access list to, based on several variables. For example, a router might have an interface connecting to a OC3 or T4 line. An access list can be applied to only this interface, not to another interface connected to a CAT 6 cable. Access lists are nothing more than lists; they don't become effective until they're applied to interfaces. A detailed discussion of the syntax of access lists is beyond the scope of this course. Because your job might include testing a network with routers, however, you should research access lists in more detail on your own or in another course. If you decide to earn a Cisco Certified Network Associate (CCNA) certification, for example, you need to know how to create, configure, and apply access lists to interfaces. The knowledge you gain from earning this certification is a good addition to your security-testing arsenal.

PROTECTING WITH FIREWALLS

Firewalls can be hardware devices with embedded OSs, or software installed on general-purpose computer systems. Firewalls serve two main purposes: controlling access to traffic entering an internal network and controlling traffic leaving an internal network. Firewalls can be installed on a network to protect a company's internal network from dangers existing on the Internet. On large enterprise networks, firewalls can also protect internal network segments, such as those containing only application servers, from other internal network segments—for example, those containing employee workstations. For instance, a typical enterprise firewall approach is restricting the remote desktop port TCP 3389, used for remote administration of application servers, to only the system administrator network segment and allowing only ports 80 and 443 for web traffic on the network segment containing employee workstations. In this example, clearly, typical employees don't need to administer application servers, so this approach reflects a least-privileges philosophy.

Hardware and software firewalls have advantages and disadvantages. However, instead of making recommendations, this module focuses on how firewalls fit into a security strategy. Briefly, the disadvantage of hardware firewalls is that you're locked into the firewall's hardware, such as the number of interfaces it includes. With a software firewall, you can add NICs easily to the server running the software. A disadvantage of software firewalls is that you might have to worry about configuration problems, such as memory requirements, hard disk space requirements, number of CPUs supported, and so on. Software firewalls also rely on the OS on which they're running. For example, Windows Firewall is available on Windows 10 and Windows Server 2016. Another example is iptables, included with Kali Linux. Hardware firewalls, such as Cisco Adaptive Security Appliance (covered later in this module), are usually faster and can handle a larger throughput than software firewalls can.

As you have seen, a router can also be used to filter traffic entering or leaving its interface. Filtering can be set up with access lists that restrict traffic based on the source IP address, destination IP address, protocol, and port. However, a firewall is specifically designed as a network protection system and has more security features than a router.

Examining Firewall Technology

You have seen numerous methods that attackers use to scan a network and launch exploits. Firewalls can help reduce these attacks by using several technologies:

- Network Address Translation
- Access lists
- Packet filtering
- Stateful packet inspection
- Application layer inspection

Network Address Translation

The most basic security feature of a firewall is **Network Address Translation (NAT)**. One job of a security professional is to hide the internal network from outsiders. With NAT, internal private IP addresses are mapped to public external IP addresses, hiding the internal infrastructure from unauthorized personnel. For example, a user with a private IP address of 10.1.1.15 has her address mapped to an external IP address of 193.145.85.200. The outside world sees only the external IP address and doesn't know the internal IP addresses the company uses.

After hackers know a computer or server's IP address, they scan that system for open or vulnerable ports. Hiding IP addresses from hackers can help prevent these scans from being successful. To accommodate the many addresses that need to be mapped, many organizations use Port Address Translation (PAT), which is derived from NAT. It allows mapping thousands of internal IP addresses to one external IP address.

Access Lists

As discussed in the section on routers, access lists are used to filter traffic based on source IP address, destination IP address, and ports or services. Firewalls also use this technology, as you see later in the section on the Cisco Adaptive Security Appliance firewall. After you understand how to create an access list on a router, creating one on a firewall is a similar process.

Packet Filtering

Another basic security function a firewall performs is packet filtering. Packet filters screen packets based on information in the packet header, such as the following:

- Protocol type
- IP address
- TCP/UDP port

Stateful Packet Inspection

Firewalls usually take the basic filtering a router does a step further by performing stateful packet inspection (SPI). Stateful packet filters record session-specific information about a network connection, including the ports a client uses, in a file called a state table. Table 13-2 is an example of a state table.

Table 13-2   State table example

Source IP	Source port	Destination IP	Destination port	Connection state
10.1.1.100	1022	193.145.85.201	80	Established
10.1.1.102	1040	193.145.85.1	80	Established
10.1.1.110	1035	193.145.85.117	23	Established
192.145.85.20	1080	10.1.1.210	25	Closed

In this state table, several internal hosts using private IP addresses have established connections to external IP addresses. One host has established a Telnet session (port 23), two hosts have established HTTP connections (port 80), and one host has recently closed a connection to an email server (port 25). This state table is a way for the firewall to track the state of connections, based on what kind of traffic is expected in a two-way session. Port scans relying on spoofing or sending packets after a three-way handshake are made ineffective if the firewall uses a state table. If a hacker attempts to send (spoof) a SYN/ACK packet from an IP address not in the state table, the packet is dropped. Recall that a SYN/ACK packet is sent only after a SYN packet has been received.

Stateful packet filters recognize types of anomalies that most routers ignore, such as hundreds or thousands of SYN/ACK packets being sent to a computer, even though the computer hasn't sent out any SYN packets. Because stateless packet filters handle each packet separately, they aren't resistant to spoofing or DoS attacks.

Application Layer Inspection

An application-aware firewall inspects network traffic at a higher level in the OSI model than a traditional stateful packet inspection firewall does. SPI ensures that a packet's source, destination, and port are inspected before forwarding the packet, but a firewall performing application layer inspection also makes sure that the network traffic's application protocol is the type allowed by a rule. For example, many Trojans get past firewalls by launching a reverse shell that originates from the compromised system and connects to a remote system the hacker controls. This reverse shell is the hacker's secure command-and-control tunnel, and it's usually disguised by using a commonly allowed outbound port, such as port 443. The hacker-controlled channel then penetrates from inside the network to outside over the allowed outbound port. Workstations use port 443 outbound for web browsing via the HTTPS protocol. If the reverse shell uses Telnet or SSH protocols on port 443, an application-aware firewall can prevent the reverse shell connecting out on a port reserved for HTTP traffic. Some application-aware firewalls act as a proxy for all connections, thus serving as a safety net for servers or clients (or both), depending on what the firewall is protecting. If an application-aware firewall is protecting a web server, for example, it prevents buffer overflows that target a specific application protocol, such as the ISAPI vulnerability in IIS web server software. An application-aware firewall that is protecting a web application is known as a web application firewall (WAF). Firewalls that have advanced features such as application-awareness and intrusion detection are being marketed as *Next Generation Firewalls* by many security companies. The Cisco FirePOWER Series, the Fortinet FortiGate Series, and the Sophos XG series are examples of Next Generation Firewalls.

Implementing a Firewall

Using a single firewall between a company's internal network and the Internet can be dangerous because if hackers compromise the firewall, they have complete access to the internal network. To reduce this risk, most enterprise firewall topologies use a demilitarized zone, discussed in the following section, to add a layer of defense.

Demilitarized Zone

A demilitarized zone (DMZ) is a small network containing resources that a company wants to make available to Internet users; this setup helps maintain security on the company's internal network. A DMZ sits between the Internet and the internal network and is sometimes referred to as a "perimeter network." Figure 13-2 shows how outside users can access the email and web servers in the DMZ, but the internal network is protected from these outside Internet users.

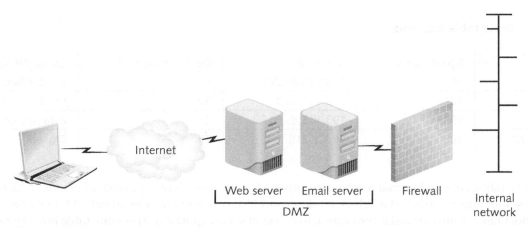

Figure 13-2   A DMZ protecting an internal network

Note that Internet users can access the DMZ without going through the firewall. A better security strategy is placing an additional firewall in the network setup (see Figure 13-3).

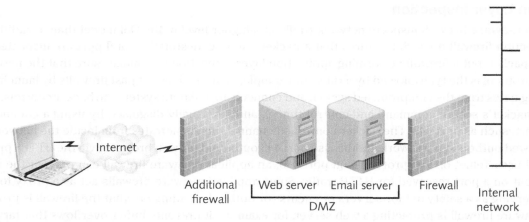

Figure 13-3   An additional firewall used to protect the DMZ

For users to access the internal network from the Internet, they need to pass through two firewalls. This setup is probably the most common design for an enterprise firewall topology.

Examining the Cisco Adaptive Security Appliance Firewall

A good way to learn how a firewall operates is to look at the configuration of one of the most widely used firewalls: the Cisco Adaptive Security Appliance (ASA) firewall. Cisco ASA replaced the Cisco PIX firewall and added advanced modular features, such as intrusion detection and prevention and more sophisticated application layer inspection. In the following sections, you view some configuration commands for an ASA firewall to get an idea of what security professionals need to know. You walk through configuring an ASA to create rules to segment network servers from terminals that only allow traffic on a few ports.

NOTE

Cisco has classes and books on configuring ASA, so the information in this section is just the tip of the iceberg.

Configuring the ASA Firewall

After logging on to an ASA firewall via SSH, you see a logon prompt that's similar to the prompt for logging on to a Cisco router:

```
If you are not authorized to be in this XYZ Hawaii network device, log out immediately!
Username: admin
Password: ********
```

In this example, the administrator created a banner warning that anyone attempting to connect must be authorized before continuing. This banner might seem like a waste of time, but it serves a legal purpose. If the banner had said "Welcome, please log on," intruders might not be prosecuted if they hack into your network. The U.S. legal system has already dropped charges against hackers who entered sites with the word "Welcome" in banners.

After you log on with the correct password, the firewall displays the following information:

```
Type help or '?' for a list of available commands.
ciscoasa>
```

The prompt is the same one you saw when logging on to a Cisco router—the router name followed by a > symbol—so you know you're in user mode. To enter privileged mode, you enter the same enable (en, in this example) command used for a Cisco router and are then prompted to enter a password:

```
ciscoasa> en
Password: ********
```

After entering the correct password, you're placed in privileged mode, indicated by the # prompt. Entering the ? character reveals more commands available in privileged mode. Next, to enter configuration mode in ASA, you use the same command as on a Cisco router: configure terminal or configure t.

Next, look at how the firewall uses access lists to filter traffic. The following access list named PERMITTED_TRAFFIC shows the specific VPN connections to several wiring closets:

```
ciscoasa (config) # show run access-list
access-list PERMITTED_TRAFFIC remark VPN-CONC1 TO TERMINAL CLOSET1B
access-list PERMITTED_TRAFFIC extended permit ip
host 10.13.61.98 host 10.13.61.18
access-list PERMITTED_TRAFFIC remark VPN-CONC2 TO TERMINAL CLOSET1B
access-list PERMITTED_TRAFFIC extended permit ip host 10.13.61.99
host 10.13.61.19
access-list PERMITTED_TRAFFIC remark VPN-CONC3 TO TERMINAL CLOSET1B
access-list PERMITTED_TRAFFIC extended permit ip host 10.13.61.100
host 10.13.61.20
access-list NONE extended deny ip any any log
access-list CAP-ACL extended permit ip any any
```

Next, look at the object group listing in the ASA configuration. An object group is a way to organize hosts, networks, services, protocols, or ICMP types into groups so that a firewall rule can be applied to all objects at once, instead of one at a time. In this example, several hosts are members of the VIRTUAL_TERMINALS object group:

```
ciscoasa# show run object-group
object-group network VIRTUAL_TERMINALS
network-object host 10.11.11.67
network-object host 10.11.11.68
network-object host 10.11.11.69
```

In the following example, notice the object group for networks. It's called AD_SERVERS, a name the firewall administrator chose to represent Active Directory servers. Currently, there's only one host in the group, but the firewall administrator might expand it when more Active Directory servers are added. Next is the object group for services, which is organized as AD_TCP and AD_UDP. Earlier, you learned which ports must be open on a firewall for domain controller Active Directory services to function, so the ports listed in this example should look familiar.

```
object-group network AD_SERVERS
network-object host 10.0.0.25
object-group service AD_TCP tcp
port-object eq domain
port-object eq 88
port-object eq 135
port-object eq ldap
port-object eq 445
port-object eq 1026
object-group service AD_UDP udp
port-object eq domain
port-object eq 88
port-object eq ntp
port-object eq 389
```

Finally, the application services that should be allowed through the firewall are organized in the APP_SERVICES object group. Notice that web (WWW, HTTPS), FTP (FTP, FTP-data), email (POP3, SMTP), and file sharing (port 445) are allowed:

```
object-group service APP_SERVICES tcp
port-object eq ftp-data
port-object eq ftp
port-object eq smtp
port-object eq www
port-object eq pop3
port-object eq https
port-object eq 445
```

Using Configuration and Risk Analysis Tools for Firewalls and Routers

Patching systems is only one part of protecting them from compromise. You must also configure them securely. Fortunately, plenty of resources are available for this task. One of the best websites for finding configuration benchmarks and configuration assessment tools for Cisco routers and firewalls is the Center for Internet Security (CIS, www.cisecurity.org/cis-benchmarks/). A benchmark is an industry consensus of best configuration practices on how (using step-by-step guidance) and why (explaining the reasons for taking these steps) to secure a Cisco router or firewall. For Cisco devices, use the CIS Cisco IOS Benchmark; the most recent version is currently 16.0. Reviewing all the configuration steps in these benchmarks can take quite a bit of time. For this reason, CIS offers a useful tool called Configuration Assessment Tool (CAT) that's faster and easier to use. CAT versions are available for both *nix and Windows systems. If you have time and access to a lab with a Cisco router or firewall, download the CAT tool and run it on your Windows or Kali Linux system.

A commercial tool worth mentioning is RedSeal (redseal.net), a unique network risk analysis and mapping tool. Like the CIS RAT tool, RedSeal can identify configuration vulnerabilities in routers or firewalls, but it also generates professional-looking reports that can be customized with your company logo. In addition to analyzing configuration files from routers and firewalls, RedSeal can analyze IPSs as well as OS vulnerability scans of a network to produce a detailed analysis and mapping. Figure 13-4 shows the network risk map that's generated when you enter Cisco router and firewall configuration files and Nessus scans in RedSeal. It analyzes the configurations of all devices on the network to identify what access is allowed. In considering the architecture to use for network protection, access is determined by combining the rules and ACLs in each device along a network path. To see details of an allowed path, click the corresponding line.

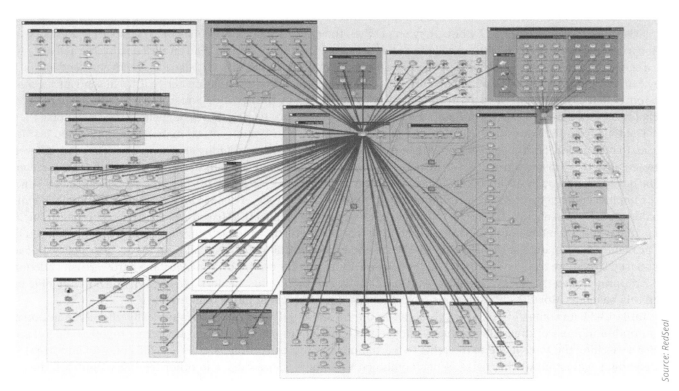

Source: RedSeal

Figure 13-4   The RedSeal network risk map

RedSeal is unique in that it shows a graphical representation of vulnerabilities discovered in the context of the network on which they're found. A RedSeal report and map can be especially useful in conveying information to senior management; the graphical format is easier to understand than pages of wordy reports. (Remember the old adage: A picture is worth a thousand words.) For representing a network's security status, RedSeal is a handy tool.

PROTECTING WITH INTRUSION DETECTION AND PREVENTION SYSTEMS

Intrusion detection systems (IDSs) monitor network devices so that security administrators can identify attacks in progress and stop them. For example, for users to be able to access a web server, a firewall must allow port 80 to be open. Unfortunately, opening this port can also allow a hacker to attack the web server. An IDS examines the traffic traversing the connection to port 80 and compares it with known exploits, similar to virus software using a signature file to identify viruses. If an attacker attempts to exploit a known vulnerability in the web server, the IDS sends an alert of the attack so that the web server administrator can take action. Intrusion prevention systems (IPSs) are similar to IDSs, but they take the additional step of performing some sort of action to prevent the intrusion, instead of just alerting administrators of the attack. The following section describes two types of intrusion detection and prevention systems: network-based and host-based.

Network-Based and Host-Based IDSs and IPSs

Network-based IDSs/IPSs monitor activity on network segments. Essentially, they sniff traffic as it flows over the network and alert a security administrator when something suspicious occurs. Some of these systems can also block traffic. Host-based IDSs/IPSs are most often used to protect a critical network server or database server, although they can also run on workstations. The IDS or IPS software is installed on the system you're attempting to protect, just like installing antivirus software on your desktop system.

IDSs can also be categorized by how they react when they detect suspicious behavior. Systems that don't take any action to stop or prevent an activity are called passive systems. They do, of course, send an alert and log the activity, much like a security guard at a shopping mall witnessing an armed robbery. Active systems also log events and send alerts, but they can also interoperate with routers and firewalls to stop an attack. For example, an active IDS can send an access list to a router that closes an interface to prevent attackers from damaging the network. Some active IDSs send spoofed reset packets that fool the TCP/ IP stacks of both the victim and attacker into tearing down the malicious connection.

The time from the start of an attack to the time it compromises a system can be mere milliseconds, too fast for a human to take action. For this reason, vendors have started focusing their marketing efforts on IPSs. There's a difference between an active IDS and a true IPS. A true network-based IPS is installed inline to the network infrastructure, meaning traffic has to pass through the IPS before going into or out of the network. An active IDS just sniffs traffic and can be turned off or unplugged from the network without affecting network connectivity. Because an IPS is inline, generally it's more capable of stopping malicious traffic than an active IDS is, especially against UDP-based attacks. Many current IDSs include IPS features and often have optional modules, such as malware detection and web filtering. In addition, host-based IPSs are available; they operate at the OS (or kernel) level and intercept traffic that's not allowed by the host policy. Because host-based IPSs share resources with the OS they run on, they can slow down performance if the hardware isn't adequate.

Anomaly-based IDS uses a baseline of normal activity and then sends an alert if the activity deviates significantly from this baseline. Most IDS/IPS solutions have anomaly-detection capabilities built in.

Table 13-3 lists some of the many IDSs and IPSs on the market. IDS manufacturers typically offer IPS functionality as an option in most of their IDS products—hence the tendency to use the IDS and IPS terms together. Spend some time researching the tools listed in the table to learn more about these products. IDSs and IPSs play an important role in defending against network attacks. When combined with routers, firewalls, and other technical controls, they can help you protect the network you've been asked to secure.

Table 13-3   Common intrusion detection and prevention systems

Product	Description
McAfee Network Protection System (www.mcafee.com)	A network-based IDS/IPS with anomaly-detection capabilities
Snort (www.snort.org)	A popular open-source network-based IDS
Cisco Sourcefire (www.cisco.com)	Enterprise Snort-based IDSs and IPSs
FireEye Intrusion Prevention System (www.fireeye.com)	A network-based IDS/IPS which can be deployed as a physical appliance or a cloud-based virtual appliance.

Web Filtering

Attackers commonly target the user workstations that are usually allowed access to the Internet. If they can get an internal user to visit a malicious website or install malicious code from an email attachment, they don't need to break through a firewall. After Trojan code is installed on a user's workstation, attackers can control the Trojan remotely with commands that might seem to be normal traffic. They can take advantage of this compromise to expand through the network by running network scans from the compromised workstation, stealing data accessible on or from the victim system, cracking system passwords, and exploiting vulnerabilities they discover on other systems. Attackers can hide the command-and-control activity inside what appears to be normal HTTP and HTTPS traffic. In this situation, web filtering can be used to detect user's attempts to access known malicious websites and block these attempts, and some web-filtering systems can actually block malicious code before it gets to a user's workstation or before it has a chance to connect to an attacker's control system outside the network. Companies that sell and support these web-filtering devices often categorize domains into different groups. For example, if a user were to visit PNC.com, the web filter would identify that request in the "Financial/Online Banking" category and allow the traffic. However, if a user requested exploit-db.com, the web filter might categorize that request as "Hacking Sites" and deny the request. What about websites that aren't categorized yet? Companies might choose to block access to uncategorized sites to avoid the risk of users visiting an attacker's newly created domain. Blocking access to uncategorized sites is a very effective security practice but could cause inconvenience for users.

Organized cybercriminals often try to hack busy websites that have the best chance of infecting thousands of website visitors with their malicious code. These types of mass compromises are used to initiate drive-by downloads, in which website visitors download malicious code without their knowledge. Usually, the drive-by download exploits a security flaw in the browser or a third-party application, such as Adobe Reader or Microsoft Office. Because malicious websites and code change daily, web-filtering system providers need to update their signatures and databases of malicious websites constantly. Examples of vendors offering web-filtering products on a subscription basis are Fortiguard (www.fortinet.com/support/support-services/fortiguard-security-subscriptions/web-filtering) and Cisco Umbrella (https://umbrella.cisco.com/solutions/web-content-filtering).

Security Operations Center

The IDSs, IPSs, and honeypots (discussed in the next section) that help keep a network secure require administrative expertise to set up, run, and maintain. In smaller companies, when a security event happens, usually administrators have to clean up the mess and then make a report to management or the legal department or work with law enforcement. For large organizations that have sensitive or critical data, normal administrative expertise isn't enough to follow up and do damage assessment, risk remediation, and legal consultation. For these types of organizations, you might need to recommend creating a Security Operations Center (SOC).

Large organizations need a permanent team whose members are responsible solely for security-response functions. Another function of a SOC is monitoring for artifacts left behind by attackers, which indicate that a system or network has been compromised; these are often called indicators of compromise. Security Information and Event Management (SIEM) tools can help the teams identify attacks and indicators of compromise by collecting, aggregating, and correlating log and alert data from routers, firewalls, IDS/IPS, end point logs, web-filtering devices, honeypots, and other security tools. Bringing the alerts together from these devices gives a security-monitoring analyst context to make better-informed decisions. Popular SIEM commercial products include HP ArcSight, RSA EnVision, and IBM QRadar. Open-source SIEM products include AlienVault OSSIM and LOGalyze.

USING HONEYPOTS

A honeypot is a computer placed on the network perimeter that contains information or data intended to lure and then trap hackers. The main goal is to distract hackers from attacking legitimate network resources. A security professional configures the computer to have vulnerabilities so that hackers spend time trying to exploit these vulnerabilities. Another goal of a honeypot is to have hackers connect to the "phony" computer long enough to be detected, as in movies when the FBI wants a criminal to stay on the phone long enough to trace his or her location. In addition, a honeypot can serve as an excellent data collector and early warning system to help characterize new attacks and threats; this information makes it easier for security professionals to defend networks against them.

For more information on honeypots, visit www.honeynet.org. This website offers exercises and challenges that encourage user participation, contains white papers on honeypots, and includes workshop presentations describing the Honeynet Project. If you decide to participate in any exercises, you might want to use a computer lab isolated from any production servers or networks. A test computer should be used because of the possibility of virus infection or data corruption.

How Honeypots Work

If attackers can get to your internal network, they can create havoc. A honeypot appears to have important data or sensitive information stored on it. For example, it could store fake financial data that tempts hackers into attempting to browse through the data. The government and private industry have used honeypots to lure attackers into network areas away from the real data for many years. Basically, the belief is that if hackers discover a vulnerability in a system, they'll spend time exploiting the vulnerability and stop looking for other areas to exploit and access a company's resources.

Honeypots also enable security professionals to collect data on attackers. In this way, the hunter becomes the hunted. Both commercial and open-source honeypots are available, and Tables 13-4 and 13-5 show some products available for security professionals.

Table 13-4 Commercial honeypots

Name	Description
Canary (https://canary.tools)	This honeypot service can be deployed on a network in minutes. Canary devices can be easily configured to look like file servers, routers, Linux, or web servers.
KFSensor (www.keyfocus.net/kfsensor)	This Windows-based honeypot detects the nature of attacks on file shares and Windows services. It also functions as an IDS and can use Snort-compatible signatures.
PacketViper (www.packetviper.com)	A deception-based threat detection, prevention, and response solution that provides a variety of protections including honeypot-like features.

Table 13-5 Open-source honeypots

Name	Description
Cowrie (https://github.com/cowrie/cowrie)	Cowrie is an SSH honeypot designed to catch attackers attempting to brute force or guess SSH credentials. It can send logs into a SIEM for triage.
OpenCanary (opencanary.org)	This honeypot offers multiple configurations that allow it to emulate Linux web servers, Windows servers, MySQL servers, and MS SQL servers. It sends alerts when being attacked and can also send alerts to a SIEM. It is available for download at https://github.com/thinkst/opencanary.
LaBrea Tarpit (labrea.sourceforge.net)	This honeypot answers connection requests in such a way that the attacking machine gets "stuck." It works on FreeBSD, Linux, Solaris, and Windows platforms.
Honeyd (www.honeyd.org)	Written in C for *nix platforms, it can monitor millions of unused IP addresses, simulate hundreds of OSs, and monitor TCP and UDP ports.
Glastopf (https://github.com/mushorg/glastopf)	Glastopf is a honeypot that emulates an extremely vulnerable web application. It's unique in that it replays actual responses to an attacker exploiting a vulnerability. With this design, Glastopf can see secondary and tertiary steps an attacker would take to gain access to a system.
T-Pot (https://github.com/telekom-security/tpotce)	A honeypot platform based on glastopf and other honeypots, with IDS/IPS capabilities based on suricata. It has a graphical interface for displaying and summarizing honeypot activity.

The good news is that creating a honeypot without dedicating a powerful server to the task is possible now. Virtual honeypots are created by using a programming language rather than configuring a physical device. You can download free open-source code and install it on a*nix or Windows computer. In Activity 13-2, you examine some open-source honeypots.

Activity 13-2: Examining an Open-Source Honeypot

Time Required: 30 minutes
Objective: Learn about the open-source honeypot OpenCanary.
Description: As a security professional, you might need to set up a honeypot to delay and detect attackers. In this activity, you look at an open-source honeypot called OpenCanary.

1. Start a web browser, if necessary, and go to **opencanary.org**.
2. Read through the OpenCanary homepage.
3. Under the **Services** section, click the **Linux Web Server** link and review the configuration file.
4. Which ports does the configuration file enable? What software is served from these ports?
5. Go back to the home page and click the following links and review the configurations for each: **Windows Server, MySQL Server, MSSQL Server**.
6. Exit your browser.

If time permits, you might want to download and install OpenCanary. You might also want to set up a lab and get some practice using the honeypots. OpenCanary can trick Nmap (and attackers) into believing it has detected an RDP or SQL server running on a system.

MODULE SUMMARY

- Security professionals can use a variety of network protection systems to protect a network, such as routers, firewalls, intrusion detection and prevention systems, web filters, honeypots, and Unified Threat Management (UTM) devices, which combine multiple network protection functions on one device.
- Routers use access lists to accept or deny traffic through their interfaces. On Cisco routers, access lists can be used to filter traffic entering and leaving a network. Access lists are applied to interfaces on the router.
- Firewalls can be hardware or software and are used to control traffic entering and leaving a network or subnet. Cisco ASA is a popular firewall. Firewalls can be used to create internal network segments and prevent attackers from accessing command-and-control channels from outside a protected network.
- Firewalls use NAT, packet filtering, access control lists, stateful packet inspection, and application layer inspection to filter incoming and outgoing network traffic.
- A DMZ is a small network containing resources that sits between the Internet and the internal network, sometimes referred to as a "perimeter network." It's used when a company wants to make resources available to Internet users yet keep the company's internal network segregated.
- Intrusion detection systems monitor network traffic so that administrators can identify attacks occurring on a network. For example, a computer receiving thousands of SYN packets on different ports over a short period might indicate that an intruder is scanning the network.
- Network-based IDSs monitor activity on network segments, whereas host-based IDSs are used to protect individual endpoints.
- Passive IDSs do not prevent an activity from occurring; they simply alert and log the activity. Active IDSs log and send alerts but also interoperate with routers and firewalls and can close a port or a router interface if they detect possible intrusions.

- Like IDSs, intrusion prevention systems (IPSs) detect malicious activity. However, IPSs are placed inline to the network infrastructure (network-based IPSs) or on the host (host-based IPSs) and can block or prevent malicious activity. IDS vendors typically offer products that can be used as an IDS or IPS.
- Configuring routers and firewalls securely is easier with benchmark tools, such as the free tools available at the CIS website. Commercial tools, such as RedSeal, are helpful in analyzing and mapping network risks.
- Web filtering can block websites containing malicious code, such as those used in drive-by download attacks. Because websites change often, using a subscription service to update web-filtering domain categories and anti-virus signatures is an important protective measure.
- Large organizations might need to form a Security Operations Center (SOC), which is made up of experts with the skills and training to detect and respond to network security incidents.
- Honeypots are computers that emulate servers with bogus information and vulnerabilities, designed to lure hackers away from legitimate network resources and entice them to spend time exploiting the honeypot's vulnerabilities.

Key Terms

Active systems	Intrusion detection systems (IDSs)	security appliance
Anomaly-based IDS	Intrusion prevention systems (IPSs)	Security Information and Event
application-aware firewall	IP access lists	Management (SIEM)
demilitarized zone (DMZ)	link-state routing protocol	Security Operations Center (SOC)
distance-vector routing protocol	Network Address Translation (NAT)	Stateful packet filters
drive-by downloads	Network-based IDSs/IPSs	stateless packet filters
Firewalls	network protection system	state table
honeypot	passive systems	Unified Threat Management (UTM)
Host-based IDSs/IPSs	path-vector routing protocol	user mode
indicators of compromise	privileged mode	web application firewall (WAF)

Review Questions

1. Which type of routing protocol advertises only new paths to other routers on the network?
   a. Link-state routing protocol
   b. Routing table protocol
   c. Path-vector routing protocol
   d. Distance-vector routing protocol

2. A router using a distance-vector routing protocol sends only new information to other routers on the network. True or false?

3. Which of the following Cisco components stores a router's running configuration, routing tables, and buffers?
   a. NVRAM
   b. RAM
   c. ROM
   d. Flash memory

4. If a Cisco router's flash memory becomes corrupted, the router can boot from which of the following components?
   a. ROM
   b. NVRAM

   c. RAM
   d. CD-ROM

5. Network security devices contain software, and often this software has flaws that can be exploited to compromise security. Perform an Internet search to determine what known security flaws have been found in FortiGate products. The Search CVE List section of the cve.mitre.org website is one place you can perform this search. Write a one-page report outlining your discoveries.

6. A standard IP access list can't filter IP packets based on a destination address. True or false?

7. Which of the following describes a tool that collects logs and alerts from multiple devices for security analysis?
   a. Log Management System (LMS)
   b. Security Information and Event Management (SIEM)
   c. Network-based IPS
   d. Honeypot

8. Which of the following describes the main purpose of a firewall? (Choose all that apply.)
   a. Control traffic entering and leaving a network.
   b. Prevent certain applications from running.
   c. Protect internal network segments.
   d. Prevent command-and-control data from being initiated from inside the network.

9. Network security devices contain software, and often this software has flaws that can be exploited to compromise security. Perform an Internet search to determine what known security flaws have been found in Cisco Router products. The Search CVE List section of the cve.mitre.org website is one place you can perform this search. Write a one-page report outlining your discoveries.

10. Firewalls use which of the following to hide the internal network topology from outside users?
    a. Packet filtering
    b. SPI
    c. ACL
    d. NAT

11. A stateful packet inspection firewall keeps track of network connections by using which of the following?
    a. A state table
    b. Fuzzy logic
    c. Least-privileges principle
    d. Autonomous packet flow

12. A firewall that blocks a Telnet session from leaving the network over TCP port 443 uses which of the following?
    a. Stateful inspection
    b. Stateless inspection
    c. Low-level inspection
    d. Application layer inspection

13. Web filters can prevent which type of malicious activity?
    a. DDoS attack
    b. SYN scan
    c. Drive-by download
    d. UDP flood

14. A DMZ is also referred to as which of the following?
    a. Perimeter network
    b. Stateful network
    c. Stateless network
    d. Honeypot

15. Intrusion Prevention Systems contain software, and often this software has flaws that can be exploited to compromise security. Perform an Internet search to determine what known security flaws have been found in Intrusion Prevention products. The Search CVE List section of the cve.mitre.org website is one place you can perform this search. Write a one-page report outlining your discoveries.

16. Which of the following describes a team of professionals whose job is to detect and respond to security incidents?
    a. Computer Emergency Response Team (CERT)
    b. Network Operations Center (NOC)
    c. Data Assurance Group
    d. Security Operations Center (SOC)

17. Which type of IDS can send an access list to a router or firewall when an intrusion is detected on a network?
    a. Active system
    b. Passive system
    c. Firewall system
    d. Host-based system

18. A honeypot might be used in a network for which of the following reasons? (Choose all that apply.)
    a. Lure or entrap hackers so that law enforcement can be informed.
    b. Gather information on new attacks and threats.
    c. Distract hackers from attacking legitimate network resources.
    d. Protect the DMZ from internal attacks.

19. A benchmark is an industry consensus of best practices for writing access lists. True or false?

20. Anomaly detectors use a database of known attack signatures to function. True or false?

Case Projects

Case Project 13-1: Defending the Alexander Rocco Network Against Hacker Threats

After a security breach in which important corporate secrets were lost, the Alexander Rocco Corporation hired you to conduct a security test and offer recommendations for preventing future attacks. Computer forensics specialist Roberto Reyes has informed you that the hackers got in by compromising a website many employees visit; this attack installed Trojan code on users' workstations by using a drive-by download. Because the company's antivirus software didn't detect the code on workstations, attackers were able to launch reverse Telnet command shells and upload confidential documents to hacker-controlled websites. To do this, they used a port that allowed outbound HTTPS traffic through the company firewall.

Based on this information, write a brief report on your recommendations for configuring or revamping the network to defend against these types of threats. The report should give specific examples of how to secure the network, but not rely on a single type of network protection system, and make hardware recommendations, if needed.

Case Project 13-2: Detecting Hackers in the Alexander Rocco Network

You receive a frantic call from the system administrator of the Alexander Rocco network, JW Tabacchi. He tells you he has identified several intrusion attempts from sources over the Internet. You're not sure if the hackers have gained access to the internal network. First, based on the tools described in this module and some of the techniques you've learned in this course, write a one-page report about what you might look for to identify an attacker or a compromised host on your network. Second, make some recommendations on how you might use network protection systems to better detect and prevent compromises in the future.

HANDS-ON ETHICAL HACKING FINAL PROJECT

After reading this module and completing the activities, you will be able to:

1 Set up a penetration testing lab of virtual machines for use in penetration testing activities and practice

2 Perform penetration testing and vulnerability analysis using tools previously discussed in this course

3 Create a penetration testing report document to capture and communicate information regarding the vulnerabilities discovered during your penetration testing

Welcome to the Hands-On Ethical Hacking final project, a.k.a. the Grand Unifying Project (GRUP). The GRUP consists of a series of activities that you will perform to capture the results in a penetration testing report document. In the GRUP activities, you will test for vulnerabilities using some of the tools discussed in other modules. You will perform these tests using a penetration testing lab of virtual computers that you will create. The rest of this module will do the following:

1. Guide you through the process of setting up the penetration testing lab.
2. Guide you to create a penetration testing report document template to capture vulnerabilities and information discovered during your penetration testing.
3. Assign you various activities using different tools to perform penetration testing and gather information to include in your report.

SETTING UP THE PENETRATION TESTING LAB

The penetration testing lab will consist of a number of virtual machines (VMs) running inside of Oracle VirtualBox. You installed VirtualBox in Activity 2-2. You will connect the new VMs using a host-only adapter network in VirtualBox so that your testing environment is isolated from other devices on any real network you are connected to.

You will use the following virtual machines:

1. *Axigen mail server*: Use the Axigen mail server installed in Activity 2-2.
2. *Kali Linux Oracle Virtual Appliance (OVA)*. You may have been using a different Kali Linux installation for previous activities in this book (such as a Kali Live USB boot), but you use the current Kali OVA in the

testing lab. Kali-Linux-2021.2 is the version used in this module. When you are doing these labs, download and install the most current version.

3. *Metasploitable2 OVA*. Metasploitable2 is a VM that has been purposefully constructed to be vulnerable to attack. Metasploitable2 was created to provide penetration testers (pen-testers) with a target containing security flaws that can be used to practice penetration testing (pen-testing).

The computer you use to host the lab environment needs at least 8 GB of memory.

Configuring VirtualBox

You installed VirtualBox and the Axigen Mail Server in Activity 2-2. If you no longer have VirtualBox and Axigen installed, return to Activity 2-2 and follow the instructions. If you have Microsoft Hyper-V virtualization running on your computer, you must disable the Hyper-V service in order for VirtualBox to work. Run the PowerShell command `bcdedit/set hypervisorlaunchtype off` (as an administrator), and then restart your computer to disable Hyper-V.

VirtualBox will host the collection of lab VMs that will serve as targets for your penetration testing. VirtualBox provides the networking option that allows your VMs to communicate with all devices on your network. However, in this module, you don't want to scan everything on the network as this may lead to confusing results or to accessing devices you don't have permission to scan. If you are working on your home network, you can change the networking to a bridged adapter if you want to include your home devices in your pen-testing activities. Another networking option called internal network allows the VMs to connect to each other but not to the host. An internal network isn't appropriate for this module because you will be using Nessus on your host computer to perform scans of the VMs, so you need connectivity between your host computer and the VMs.

For each VM in VirtualBox that is part of the lab environment, you must change the network settings and connect the VM to the host-only adapter network.

To change the network setting of a VM:

1. In the right pane of VirtualBox, right-click the VM.
2. Click **Settings** on the shortcut menu.
3. In the left pane of the Settings window, click **Network**.
4. In the Network form, click the **Attached to** button, and then click **Host-only Adapter**.
5. Click the **Name** button, and then click the name of your host-only adapter network, such as VirtualBox Host-Only Ethernet Adapter, as shown in Figure 14-1.

NOTE

Later in this module, you will perform Nessus scans of various targets. If Nessus scans of the Metasploitable target detect only a few vulnerabilities and not dozens, you can try using the Bridged Adapter setting instead of Host-only for all your VMs and re-run the scans.

In the following sections, you change the network settings as shown for each VM you install and configure.

Configuring Axigen

You installed the Axigen Mail Server in Activity 2-2. If you no longer have Axigen installed, return to Activity 2-2 and follow the instructions.

Change the Axigen network settings so that it connects to the host-only adapter network as shown in Figure 14-2.

Installing and Configuring Kali Linux OVA

You may have been using a different method of running Kali Linux for previous activities in this course, such as using a bootable live USB or a full Linux installation on a computer, but for this module, the Kali Linux instance must be contained in VirtualBox. If you already have Kali Linux installed in VirtualBox, you can use your existing VM as long as you change its network settings to connect it to the Host-only Adapter network.

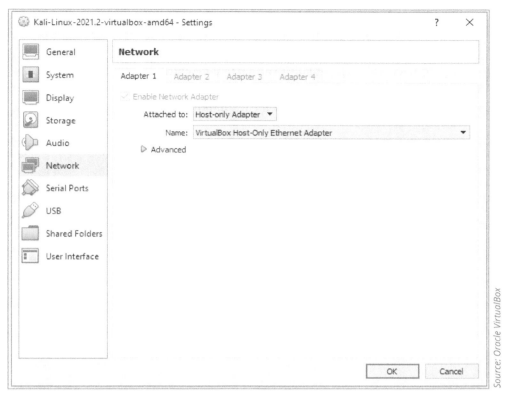

Figure 14-1   Connecting the Kali VM to the Host-only Adapter network

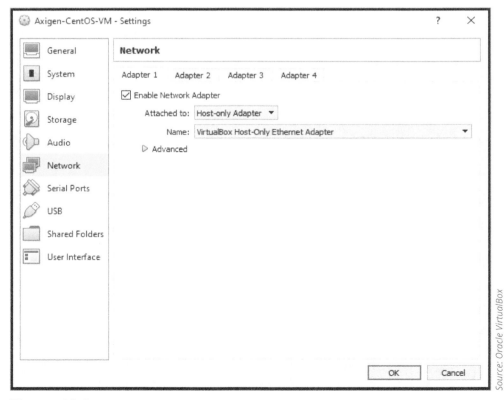

Figure 14-2   Connecting Axigen to the Host-only Adapter Network

OVA stands for Oracle Virtual Appliance. A virtual appliance is a virtual machine that has already been installed on virtual hardware. Importing an OVA is more convenient than building a virtual machine from scratch.

To install the Kali Linux OVA:

1. Use a browser to go to **www.kali.org/get-kali/#kali-virtual-machines**, and then download the OVA file. Choose the VirtualBox 64-bit version.

2. In VirtualBox, click **File** on the menu bar, and then click **Import Appliance** as shown in Figure 14-3.

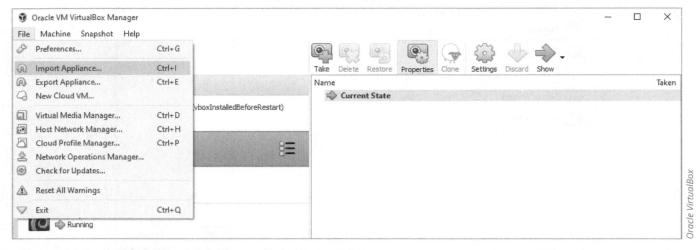

Figure 14-3   Importing a virtual appliance

3. In the Import Virtual Appliance dialog box, click the folder icon to navigate to and select the OVA file you previously downloaded. See Figure 14-4.

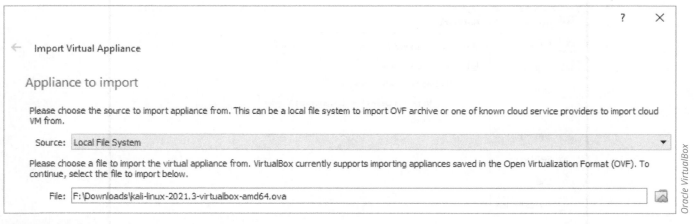

Figure 14-4   Import Virtual Appliance file selection

4. With the OVA file selected, click **Next**.

5. Review the Appliance Settings and then click **Import** to begin the import.

6. When a Software License Agreement window opens, click **Agree** to continue.

7. After the import is complete, right-click the **Kali VM**, click **Settings** on the shortcut menu, and then change the Network Settings so that the Kali VM is on the same network as the other VMs, as shown in Figure 14-2.

Installing and Configuring Metasploitable2

Metasploitable2 has been purposefully constructed to be vulnerable to attack and is designed to provide pen-testers with a target containing security flaws that can be used to practice pen-testing. You download Metasploitable2, provided by Rapid7, in the following steps.

> **NOTE**
>
> You can find detailed installation instructions at www.hacking-tutorial.com/tips-and-trick/install-metasploitable-on-virtual-box/#sthash.2WTSpUIl.dpbs. If the URL no longer works, go to www.hacking-tutorial.com and search for "install metasploitable on virtual box."

Metasploitable is not an OVA. Rapid7 provides all the necessary files to build a new VM in VirtualBox. To create the Metasploitable2 VirtualBox VM:

1. Use a browser to go to **https://information.rapid7.com/download-metasploitable-2017.html**. You will need to register in order to download Metasploitable. Fill in the Download Now form and then click the **SUBMIT** button. After successful registration you will be taken to the download page. Click the **DOWNLOAD METASPLOITABLE NOW** button to download Metasploitable2. If the download doesn't start, right-click the button, copy the link address, open a new tab in your browser, and then paste the address in the address bar. The file download should begin automatically.

2. Use the **Extract All** command to extract the installation files from the compressed file you downloaded. See Figure 14-5 and Figure 14-6.

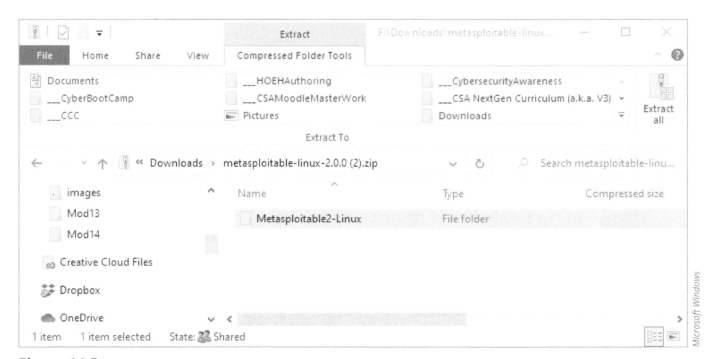

Figure 14-5   Metaspoitable2 compressed file

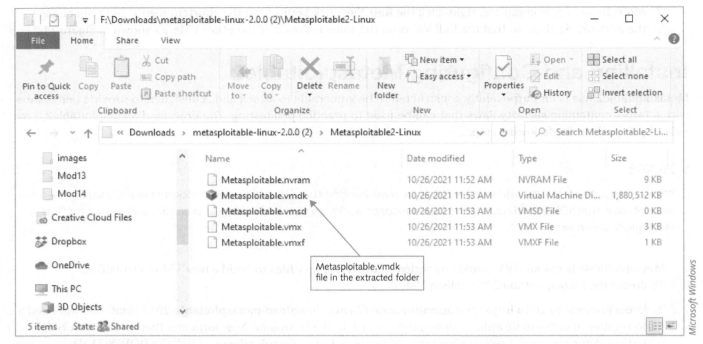

Figure 14-6 Metasploitable extracted files

3. In VirtualBox, click **Machine** on the menu bar, and then click **New**. In the Create Virtual Machine dialog box, enter the Name, Type, Version, and Memory size of the VM as shown in Figure 14-7.

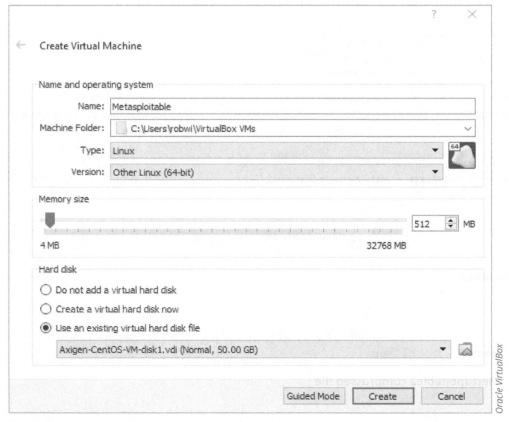

Figure 14-7 Create Virtual Machine dialog box

4. Click the **Use an existing virtual hard disk file** option button if it is not already selected.

5. Click the folder icon in the Hard disk section to open the Hard Disk Selector window. See Figure 14-8.

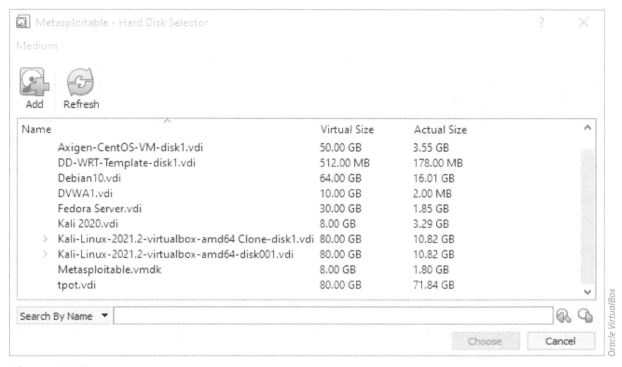

Figure 14-8 Hard Disk Selector window

6. Click the **Add** button and navigate to the extracted folder to find the Metasploitable.vmdk file. You need to add this file to the list of hard disks to use it with the Metasploitable2 VM.

7. Select the **Metasploitable.vmdk** file in the list of hard drives, as shown in Figure 14-9, and then click **Choose**.

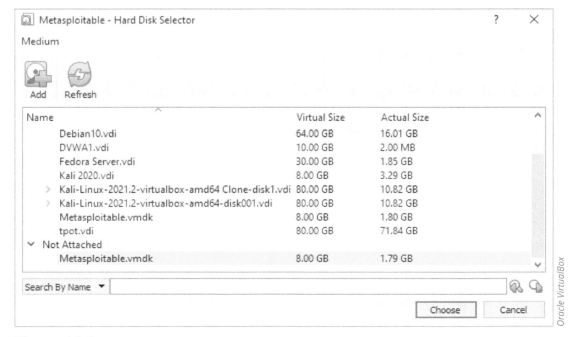

Figure 14-9 Choose the Metasploitable.vmdk file

8. Click the **Create** button shown in Figure 14-10 to create the VM.

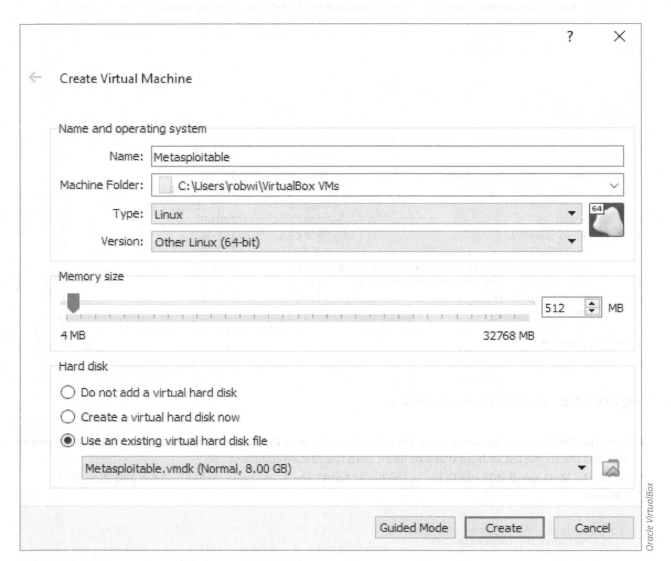

Figure 14-10   Creating the Metasploitable VM

9. In VirtualBox, right-click the **Metasploitable VM** in the right pane, click **Start** on the shortcut menu, and then click **Normal Start** to start the Metasploitable VM.

10. Sign in to the Metasploitable VM using **msfadmin** as the username and **msfadmin** as the password. See Figure 14-11.

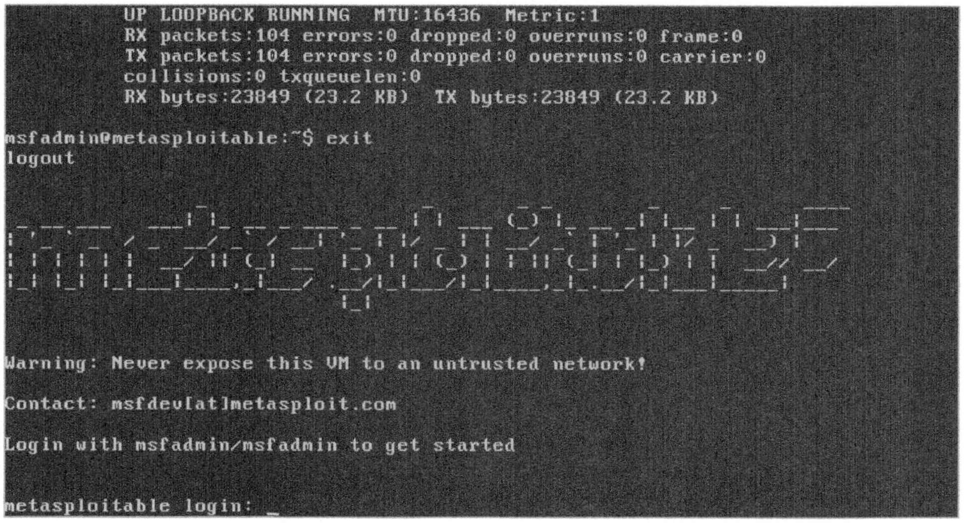
UP LOOPBACK RUNNING MTU:16436 Metric:1
RX packets:104 errors:0 dropped:0 overruns:0 frame:0
TX packets:104 errors:0 dropped:0 overruns:0 carrier:0
collisions:0 txqueuelen:0
RX bytes:23849 (23.2 KB) TX bytes:23849 (23.2 KB)
msfadmin@metasploitable:~$ exit
logout
Warning: Never expose this VM to an untrusted network!
Contact: msfdev[at]metasploit.com
Login with msfadmin/msfadmin to get started
metasploitable login: _

Rapid7 Metasploitable

Figure 14-11 Metasploitable login screen with login info

11. Type **ifconfig** and press **Enter**. Note the IP address of the eth0 interface as shown in Figure 14-12. You use this address to target the VM for pen-testing.

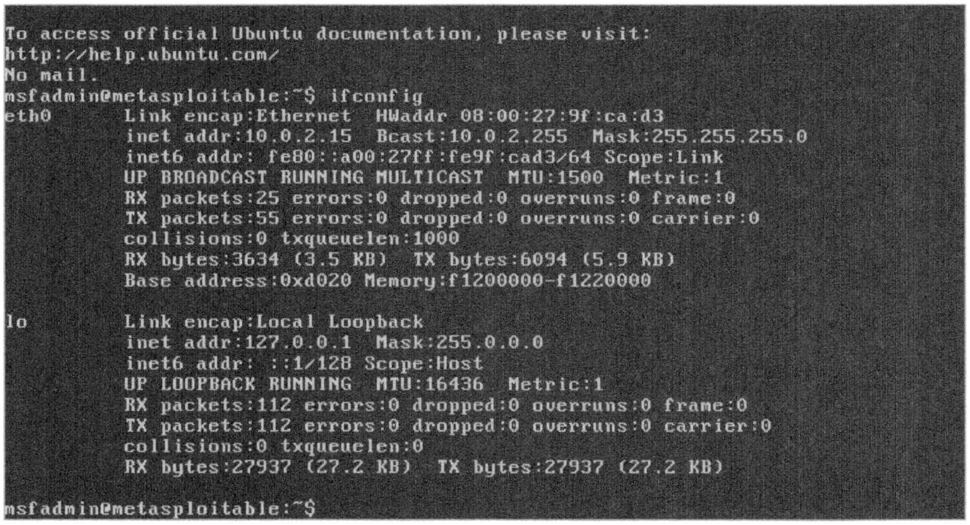
To access official Ubuntu documentation, please visit:
http://help.ubuntu.com/
No mail.
msfadmin@metasploitable:~$ ifconfig
eth0 Link encap:Ethernet HWaddr 08:00:27:9f:ca:d3
inet addr:10.0.2.15 Bcast:10.0.2.255 Mask:255.255.255.0
inet6 addr: fe80::a00:27ff:fe9f:cad3/64 Scope:Link
UP BROADCAST RUNNING MULTICAST MTU:1500 Metric:1
RX packets:25 errors:0 dropped:0 overruns:0 frame:0
TX packets:55 errors:0 dropped:0 overruns:0 carrier:0
collisions:0 txqueuelen:1000
RX bytes:3634 (3.5 KB) TX bytes:6094 (5.9 KB)
Base address:0xd020 Memory:f1200000-f1220000
lo Link encap:Local Loopback
inet addr:127.0.0.1 Mask:255.0.0.0
inet6 addr: ::1/128 Scope:Host
UP LOOPBACK RUNNING MTU:16436 Metric:1
RX packets:112 errors:0 dropped:0 overruns:0 frame:0
TX packets:112 errors:0 dropped:0 overruns:0 carrier:0
collisions:0 txqueuelen:0
RX bytes:27937 (27.2 KB) TX bytes:27937 (27.2 KB)
msfadmin@metasploitable:~$

Rapid7 Metasploitable

Figure 14-12 Using ifconfig to determine the Metasploitable2 VM IP address

CREATING A PENETRATION TESTING REPORT

The ultimate goal of this module is to gather information during your penetration testing activities and then express your findings in a penetration testing report document. The report should contain the following information:

- Details of your findings
- Targets you were penetration testing
- Tests and tools you used
- Summaries to provide the reader with overview information
- Recommendations and conclusions that suggest how to mitigate any security issues found

In this module, you use a specific format to create the penetration testing report, but other formats are available.

NOTE

Search the Internet to find examples of penetration testing reports and templates you can use. For example, see the following site for a sample penetration testing report: www.offensive-security.com/reports/sample-penetration-testing-report.pdf. The SANS Institute also has a whitepaper with guidelines for creating a pen test report at www.sans.org/white-papers/33343/.

For this module, you use a standard technical report format containing information organized as shown in Figure 14-13. You can create your report using Microsoft Word. Your instructor may have access to a Word document template that has already been created for you.

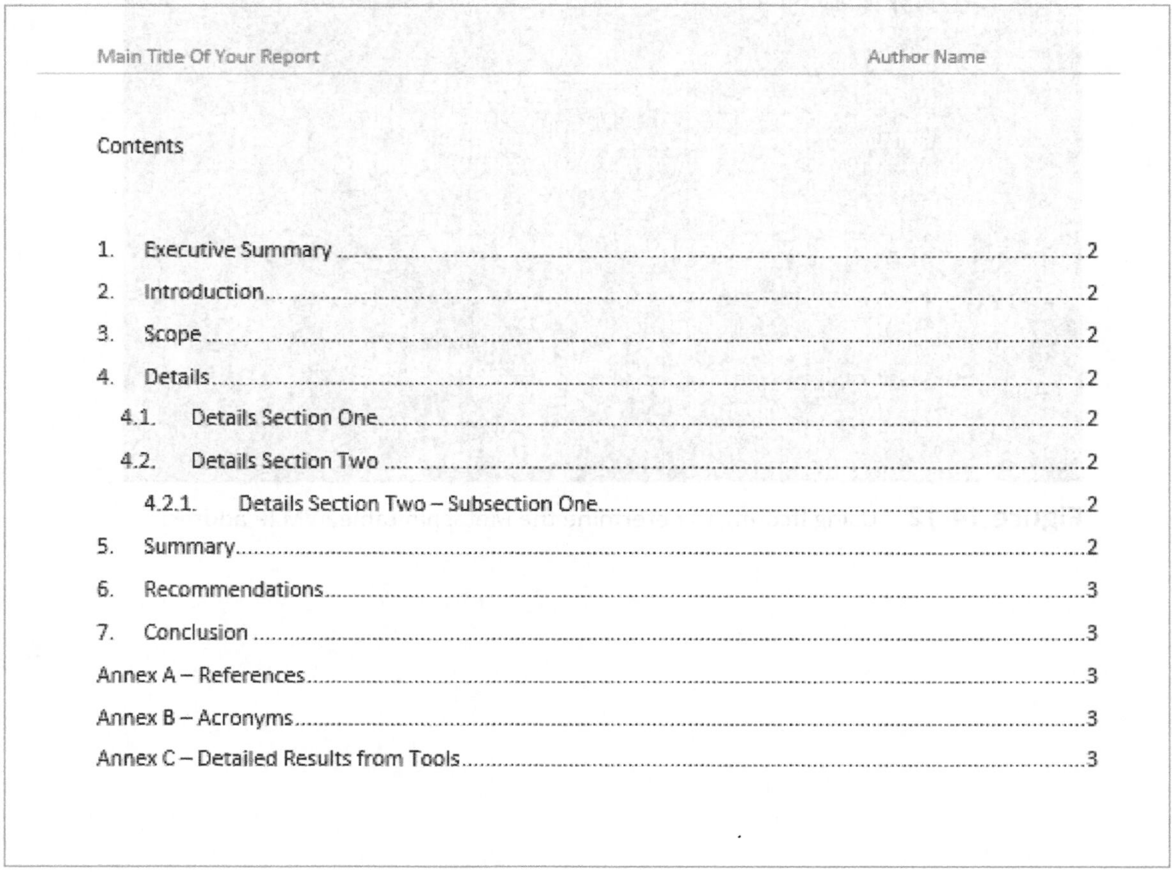

Main Title Of Your Report   Author Name

Contents

1.	Executive Summary	2
2.	Introduction	2
3.	Scope	2
4.	Details	2
	4.1. Details Section One	2
	4.2. Details Section Two	2
	4.2.1. Details Section Two – Subsection One	2
5.	Summary	2
6.	Recommendations	3
7.	Conclusion	3
Annex A – References		3
Annex B – Acronyms		3
Annex C – Detailed Results from Tools		3

Figure 14-13   Penetration testing report table of contents

Include the following sections and content in your report:

1. Executive Summary

   Briefly summarize the scope of your testing and your findings, recommendations, and conclusions in a few short paragraphs. The target audience is executives and managers, so keep technical jargon to a minimum.

2. Introduction

   Introduce the topic of the report and its purpose. Discuss the goal of the penetration testing and how you will achieve and demonstrate the goal. In general, the topic and purpose of the report is to search for vulnerabilities in one or more computing systems. Identify the specific systems you are testing. The purpose is to find vulnerabilities in the systems and the goal is to propose possible solutions for these vulnerabilities.

3. Scope

   If you are targeting only a specific system or set of systems, outline this information in the scope section. For penetration testing, scope details include the targets you are testing and the types of tests you are doing. For example, indicate whether you are performing a full Nessus scan for all vulnerabilities or testing only one web application.

4. Details

   The details section is the longest part of your report where you communicate all your work, discoveries, steps, and results. The convention is to organize and divide the details into multiple sections, subsections, and headings, as follows:

   4.1.   Details Section One

   4.2.   Details Section Two

   4.2.1. Details Section Two – Subsection One

   For penetration testing, you typically have a details section for each system you are testing (such as each computer). In the subsections, outline the details of specific activities or findings (such as the results of a Nessus scan on that system). The contents of these sections are described more fully in the following sections.

   If a single activity impacts many systems, such as an Nmap scan of an entire network, you can capture all those details in one details section and then repeat the results for a specific target in the subsection for that target.

   Each details section should summarize results from the tool you used to gather the information. A complete listing of all the results gathered by a tool is not helpful and may be difficult for the reader to understand. Many tools provide summary reports and tables of findings. Extract this information and include it in the appropriate detail section. Complete listings of all the information found could later be included in an addendum or provided as a supporting file on storage media.

5. Summary

   Summarize your findings and craft an overall message from the information contained in the details section. This is not your conclusion; this section includes a few summary paragraphs. For a penetrating testing report, this section could consist of statements highlighting the systems that urgently need security fixes and identifying the systems found to be well-secured.

6. Recommendations

   Based on your original goal, details, findings, and summary, make an organized set of recommendations. These recommendations should include steps to solve problems, simplify procedures, and improve security. In a penetrating testing report, the recommendations should outline steps to fix any vulnerabilities found during the testing. These typically include applying security patches, upgrading operating systems and software, hardening servers by removing software, and applying best practices.

7. Conclusion

   Wrap up the entire document with a paragraph or two that ties together what your goal, details, discoveries, and recommendations have revealed.

Annex A – References

   Include references to external information sources that you have mentioned in your document, such as websites and books.

Annex B – Acronyms

   If the report uses many acronyms (especially technical jargon), it may be helpful to include a list of acronyms and definitions in a separate section.

Annex C – Detailed Results from Tools

   If you are using tools that gather a lot of data as the basis of your report (for example, network inventory tools or vulnerability assessment tools), you can include that data in a separate section for completeness, perhaps in table format. Providing detailed results allows the reader to check your evidence. In penetration testing, the Nessus tool can generate a report of all its findings in a PDF or HTML format, and you could insert this detailed report here.

Before starting the penetration testing lab work, create the framework of your penetration report document using the structure outlined in this section. In the next section, you perform the pen tests and capture information to include in your report.

SECURITY BYTES

Bug bounties are financial rewards paid by organizations to individuals or groups who discover and report flaws in that organization's software or computer systems. The process used to discover the flaws is essentially penetration testing. In October 2021, Polygon, a blockchain technology company, paid $2 million in bug bounty rewards for a "double spend" vulnerability that could have wreaked havoc across its network. The flaw was discovered by an ethical hacker named Gerhard Wagner. The flaw enabled an attacker to double the amount of cryptocurrency they intended to withdraw up to 233 times.

This flaw could have allowed a malicious actor to deposit only $4,500 and then immediately withdraw $1 million. An attacker with $3.8 million could exploit the flaw to acquire up to $850 million. Apparently, ethical hacking pays. It also appears that crime pays, but ethical hacking is righteous, and crime is not.

PERFORMING THE PENETRATION TESTING

With the penetration testing lab up and running, and your penetration testing report framework in place, you are ready to begin testing for vulnerabilities and capturing your findings. The next sections guide you through a series of penetration activities.

Using the nmap Command

As you have learned, nmap is a useful command-line tool for discovering computing devices and their open ports on a network. You can use the nmap information to target systems with other scanning tools such as Nessus. Remember that the open ports you discover indicate which services are running on a target system, and by extension, what type of system it might be. For example, if you use nmap to scan a system and discover that ports 80 and 443 are open, that's a good indication you have discovered a web server.

Activity 14-1: Performing an Nmap Scan of the Penetration Testing Lab

Time Required: 15 minutes

Objective: Use Nmap to discover targets and open ports in the pen-test lab environment.

Description: The first step in pen-testing your lab environment is to run a nmap scan to discover all targets and any open ports. You will take the results from the nmap scan and add it to your report.

1. Start all virtual machines in your lab environment. Make sure they are connected to the same network.
2. Log on to the Kali Linux VM.
3. Open a terminal session and use the nmap command to scan all the VMs in your testing lab (including the Kali Linux VM). All your lab VMs should be on the same network subnet (perhaps 192.168.56.0), so you can use nmap to scan all the VMs at once by using the network address. You can also scan each VM individually by specifying its IP address in the nmap command. By logging on to each VM, you can determine its IP address by reading the information on the login screen or using the ifconfig command.
4. Capture your nmap output and copy it to your report. Use a screen capture tool such as the Windows Snipping Tool or Snip & Sketch to capture the image.

Using the netcat Command and HTTP Methods

Recall that the netcat (nc) command and HTTP methods are useful command-line tools for extracting information from web servers. The information obtained from the nc command can reveal vulnerabilities and can be used to target systems with other scanning tools such as Nessus. Netcat reveals information such as the web server software the target is running, which may reveal vulnerabilities.

Activity 14-2: Using the `netcat` (`nc`) Command and HTTP Methods to Footprint Target VMs

Time Required: 15 minutes

Objective: Use the `nc` command and HTTP methods to extract information from web servers in the pen-test lab environment.

Description: At least two of the VMs in your lab environment are web servers. Nessus is installed on your host computer along with a web server. The Metasploitable VM is a vulnerable web server. You will use the `netcat` (`nc`) command and HTTP methods to scan each VM to see what kind of web server information you can discover. You will add the results to your report.

1. Start all virtual machines in your lab environment. Make sure they are connected to the same internal network.
2. Log on to the Kali Linux VM.
3. Start a terminal session.
4. Use the `nc` command and HTTP methods on each of the VMs in your lab environment (including the Kali Linux VM) and on your host computer. You will need the IP address of each VM and your host computer to accomplish this task. Once connected to a target with the `nc` command, use HTTP methods such as `GET` and `OPTIONS` to gather information on each VM. Be sure to try the `nc` command and HTTP methods on every VM and the computer hosting Nessus.
5. Capture the results of the tests and copy them to your report. Use a screen capture tool and crop the image to show the command executed and the results.

Using the wget Command

Recall that the `wget` command is a useful command-line tool for extracting information from web servers. The `wget` command allows you to download files from a web server. You can examine those files to find vulnerabilities to target with other pen-testing tools.

Activity 14-3: Using the wget Command on Test Lab VMs and Host Computer Targets

Time Required: 15 minutes

Objective: Use `wget` to attempt to download files from VM targets in the pen-test lab environment.

Description: You can use the `wget` command to download files from a web server, such as the index.html file, which is often the main page of a website. Your nmap activities revealed what ports are open on each lab VM. Any VMs with port 80 or port 443 open are most likely web servers you should target using the `wget` command. Add the results you gathered to your report.

1. Start all virtual machines in your lab environment. Make sure they are connected to the same network.
2. Log on to the Kali Linux VM.
3. Start a terminal session.
4. Start all virtual machines in your lab environment. Make sure they are connected to the same network.
5. Use the `wget` command on each VM in your lab environment and on your host computer. You need the IP address of each VM and your host computer to accomplish this task. Be sure to use `wget` on every VM and on the computer hosting Nessus.
6. Examine the files captured with the `wget` command and place any useful information from the files in your report.

Using the enum4linux Command

Recall that the `enum4linux` command is a useful command-line tool for enumerating Linux systems. You can use the information obtained from this command to target systems with other pen-testing tools such as Nessus.

Activity 14-4: Using the `enum4linux` Command to Enumerate Targets

Time Required: 15 minutes

Objective: Use the `enum4linux` command to enumerate targets in the pen-test lab environment.

Description: The `enum4linux` command is useful for gathering intelligence from Linux-based machines. Your `nmap` activity may have revealed the operating system of your targets if you included that option in your `nmap` scans. Start by targeting suspected Linux-based VMs and then use the `enum4linux` command on all of the VMs and your host computer. Add the results from the `enum4linux` scans to your report.

1. Start all virtual machines in your lab environment. Make sure they are connected to the same network.
2. Log on to the Kali Linux VM.
3. Start a terminal session.
4. Use the `enux4linux` command on each VM in your lab environment and on your host computer. You need the IP address of each VM and your host computer to accomplish this task. Be sure to use `enum4linux` on every VM and on the computer hosting Nessus.
5. Examine the results of the `enum4linux` command and place any useful information in your report.

Using Nessus

You already installed Nessus Essentials on your computer, and in Activity 8-2, you used it to scan a local computer that was running Microsoft Windows. In this section, you use Nessus Essentials to scan all the VMs in your pen-testing lab environment. You can also scan your personal computer where Nessus is installed. Your first step should be to use Nessus to perform a Host Discovery scan on your host-only adapter network and see if it detects all the virtual machines in your pen-test lab environment. Target the host-only adapter network (perhaps 192.168.56.0/24) and not your real network. Your next steps involve scanning each target VM individually for vulnerabilities. Performing a Basic Network scan and possibly a Web Application Test scan of each VM will reveal sufficient information for your report.

To refresh your memory, Figure 14-14 shows where you can find all the vulnerabilities discovered by scan.

Click a discovered vulnerability and then scroll down to discover any CVE numbers for the vulnerability. See Figure 14-15. This information will be useful in Activity 14-6.

Researching Vulnerabilities at the CVE Website

The cve.mitre.org website is useful for researching vulnerabilities. Visit the Search CVE List page (https://cve.mitre.org/cve/search_cve_list.html) to search for vulnerabilities by specific CVE number or with keywords. Use the NIST national vulnerability database search feature at https://nvd.nist.gov/vuln/search to conduct vulnerability research. Nessus vulnerability report information often contain links to CVE information found in the NIST national vulnerability database. In Activity 14-6, you research some CVEs discovered by your Nessus scan. Perform your main research at cve.mitre.org and include a summary of the details in your report. You can also include information from NIST.

Completing the Report

After performing the penetration tests, it is time to finalize your report. Gather all the information you have collected and add the key findings to the details section of the report. You can include all the fine details in an addendum or as a separate data file. Analyze the results of your penetration testing and formulate your summary, conclusions, and recommendations. Since your report contains a lot of information and different sections, create a table of contents so that readers can quickly find what they are looking for. Follow the guidelines given in the "Creating a Penetration Testing Report" section of this module to help you complete each section of the report.

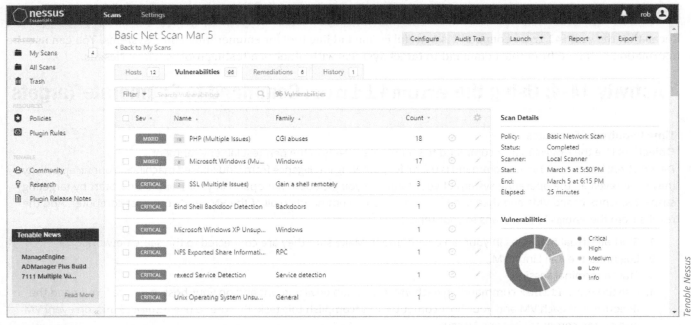

Figure 14-14   Vulnerability information from a Nessus scan

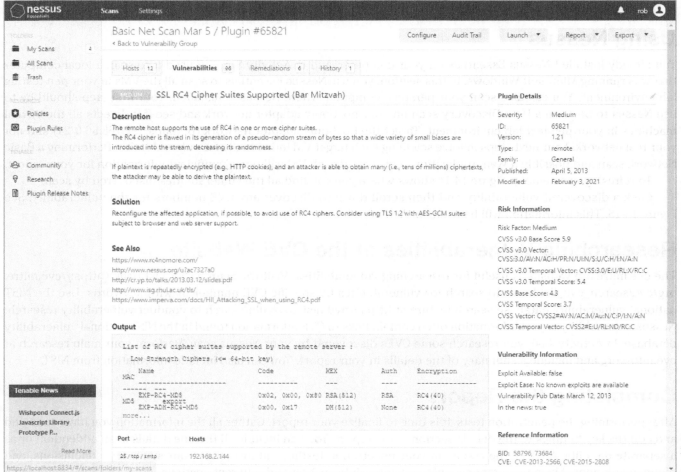

Figure 14-15   CVE information for a vulnerability

Activity 14-5: Using Nessus to Scan the VMs in the Pen-Test Lab

Time Required: 30 minutes

Objective: Use Nessus to scan targets for vulnerabilities.

Description: Nessus is a powerful tool for automatically discovering vulnerabilities in computing devices. You use Nessus to scan all the VMs in your pen-test lab environment and add the results to your report.

1. Start all the virtual machines in your lab environment. Make sure they are connected to the same internal network.
2. Log on to Nessus Essentials on your host computer.
3. Perform a Host Discovery scan on your host-only adapter network and see if it detects all the virtual machines in your pen-test lab environment. Target the host-only adapter network (perhaps 192.168.56.0/24) and not your real network. How do the results compare to your command-line nmap footprinting?
4. Create and execute a Basic Network scan for each VM in your pen-test lab environment.
5. Create and execute a Web App Test scan for each VM in your pen-test lab environment.
6. Extract information from your scans by capturing screens or using the Snipping tool to copy images of tables and charts displayed in Nessus. Include the scan results in your report. You can also use the Report feature in Nessus to create a PDF or HTML report and include all or portions of it in your penetration testing report.
7. Scan your host computer for vulnerabilities, but for your own security, don't include that information in your report.

Activity 14-6: Conducting Research on Discovered Vulnerabilities

Time Required: 30 minutes

Objective: Use the cve.mitre.org website to research the details of several vulnerability CVEs discovered by your Nessus scans.

Description: Many of the vulnerabilities discovered by your Nessus scans may include CVE references. Research several CVEs included in your result. You don't have to research every CVE that Nessus has discovered, but select the most severe CVEs discovered and some of the most interesting ones.

1. From your Nessus scan results, choose several CVE numbers to research.
2. Open a web browser and go to **https://cve.mitre.org/cve/search_cve_list.html**.
3. In the Search CVE List box, enter an exact CVE number and then click **Submit** to start the search.
4. If your search results return any CVEs, click the CVE link to view the details.
5. Include some of the details in your report by copying and pasting the results or using the Snipping Tool to capture images.

HANDS-ON ETHICALLY HACKING REVISITED

The activities in this module use only a few of the tools and methods previously discussed in this course. Now that you have a penetration testing lab environment to experiment with, you may want to try some of the other tools and methodologies and see what they reveal about your lab targets. Feel free to go over each module again, and try the tools and methods described in that module on your penetration testing lab environment.

You have reached the end of the road in this course, but you still have farther to travel. Continue to research the topic of hands-on ethical hacking and gather more intelligence on the matter from different viewpoints. Search the

Internet for examples and demonstrations of the various hacking techniques discussed in this course. While you are searching for hacking techniques, remember to proceed with caution and avoid downloading any unknown tools or executables. Video demonstrations and textual descriptions are relatively safe sources of hacking tutorials. With great power comes great responsibility, so remember to always have your white hat on when exercising some of your newly acquired hands-on ethical hacking abilities.

MODULE SUMMARY

- Oracle VirtualBox is an ideal virtualization manager for hosting a collection of VMs to be used as targets for penetration testing.
- OVA stands for Oracle Virtual Appliance. A virtual appliance is a virtual machine that has already been installed on virtual hardware. Importing an OVA is more convenient than building a virtual machine from scratch.
- Metasploitable2 is a VM that was purposefully constructed to be vulnerable to attack. Metasploitable2 was created by Rapid7 and provides pen-testers with a target containing security flaws that can be used to practice pen-testing.
- A penetration testing report should contain an introduction, details of your findings, details of the targets you are testing, descriptions of tests and tools used, summaries to provide the reader with condensed information, and recommendations and conclusions that suggest how to mitigate any security issues found.
- A complete listing of all the results gathered by a tool is not helpful and may be difficult for the reader to understand if included in the details section of a penetration testing document. Complete listings of all results could be included in an Annex or provided as a supporting file on storage media.
- Bug bounties are financial rewards paid by organizations to individuals or groups who discover and report flaws in that organization's software or computer systems.
- The cve.mitre.org website and the NIST national vulnerability database search feature at https://nvd.nist.gov/vuln/search are excellent for vulnerability research.

Review Questions

1. VirtualBox cannot run VMs unless the Hyper-V service is disabled. True or false?

2. Which type of VirtualBox network adapter allows connectivity between VMs and the host but excludes other devices on the local network?
   a. Bridged adapter
   b. Host-only adapter
   c. NAT
   d. Internal network

3. The Security Bytes section describes a record bug bounty of two million dollars paid by Polygon, a blockchain technology company. Write a four-paragraph report describing two other bug bounties that paid the discoverer large sums of money.

4. Which of the following tools can be used to discover open ports? (Choose two correct answers.)
   a. nc
   b. nmap
   c. Nessus
   d. Wget

5. What color hat should you wear when exercising your hands-on ethical hacking abilities?
   a. black
   b. white
   c. gray
   d. multicolored

LEGAL RESOURCES

Table A-1 Computer crime statutes by state

State	Statute
Alabama	AL Code § 13A-8-112, § 13A-8-113
Alaska	AK Statute § 11.46.740
Arizona	AZ Revised Statute Annotated § 13-2316, 13-2316.01, 13-2316.02
Arkansas	AR Statutes § 5-41 101-206
California	CA Penal Code § 502
Colorado	CO Revised Statute § 18-5.5-101 to 18-5.5-102
Connecticut	CT General Statute § 53a-250 to 53a-261, 53-451
Delaware	DE Code Title 11, § 931-941
Florida	FL Statute Annotated § 815.01 to 815.07, § 668.801 to .805
Georgia	GA Code § 16-9-90 to 16-9-94, § 16-9-150 to 16-9-157
Hawaii	HI Revised Statutes § 708-890 to 708-895.7
Idaho	ID Code § 18-2201 and §18-2202
Illinois	IL Revised Statute Chapter 720, § 5/17-50 to 55
Indiana	IN Code § 35-43-1-4, § 35-43-2-3
Iowa	IA Code § 716.6B
Kansas	KS Statute Annotated § 21-5839
Kentucky	KY Revised Statutes §434.840, 434.845, 434.850, 434.851, 434.853, 434.855, 434.860
Louisiana	LA Revised Statutes Annotated § 14:73.1 to 14:73.8
Maine	ME Revised Statute Annotated Title 17-A, § 431 to 435
Maryland	MD Criminal Code Annotated § 7-302
Massachusetts	MA. General Laws Annotated Chapter 266, § 33A
Michigan	MI Computer Laws § 752.791 to .797
Minnesota	MN Statutes § 609.87 to § 609.893
Mississippi	MS Code Annotated § 97-45-1 to 97-45-33
Missouri	MO Revised Statutes § 537.525, § 569.095, § 569.097, § 569.099
Montana	MT Code Annotated § 45-2-101, § 45-6-310, § 45-6-311
Nebraska	NE Revised Statutes § 28-1341 to § 28-1348

(continues)

Table A-1   Computer crime statutes by state *(continued)*

State	Statute
Nevada	NV Revised Statutes § 205.473 to 205.513
New Hampshire	NH Revised Statutes Annotated § 638:16, 638:17, § 638:18, § 638:19
New Jersey	NJ Revised Statute § 2A:38A-1 to -3, § 2C:20-2, §§ 2C:20-23 to 34
New Mexico	NM Statutes Annotated § 30-45-1 to § 30-45-7
New York	NY Penal Law § 156.00 to 156.50
North Carolina	NC General Statutes § 14-453 to 14-458
North Dakota	ND Century Code § 12.1-06.1-08
Ohio	OH Revised Code Annotated § 2909.01, §2909.04(B), § 2909.07(A)(6), § 2913.01 to .04
Oklahoma	OK Statutes Title 21, § 1951 to § 1959
Oregon	OR Revised Statute § 164.377
Pennsylvania	18 PA Statutes § 5741 to 5749
Rhode Island	RI General Laws § 11-52-1 to 11-52-8
South Carolina	SC Code Annotated § 16-16-10 to 16-16-40
South Dakota	SD Codified Laws Annotated § 43-43B-1 to § 43-43B-8
Tennessee	TN Code Annotated § 39-14-601, -602, -604, and -605
Texas	TX Penal Code Annotated § 33.02
Utah	UT Code Annotated § 76-6-702 to § 76-6-705
Vermont	VT Statute Annotated Title 13, § 4101 to 4107
Virginia	VA Code § 18.2-152.1 to -152.15 and § 19.2-249.2
Washington	WA Revised Code § 9A.52.110, § 9A.52.120, § 9A.52.130, § 9A.48.100, 2016 S.B. 2375, Chap. 164
West Virginia	WV Code § 61-3C-3 to 61-3C-21
Wisconsin	WI Statute § 943.70
Wyoming	WY Statute § 6-3-501 to § 6-3-506 and § 40-25-101

COMPUTER FRAUD AND ABUSE ACT OF 1984

Sec. 1030. Fraud and related activity in connection with computers

(a)   Whoever—

(1)   having knowingly accessed a computer without authorization or exceeding authorized access, and by means of such conduct having obtained information that has been determined by the United States Government pursuant to an Executive order or statute to require protection against unauthorized disclosure for reasons of national defense or foreign relations, or any restricted data, as defined in paragraph y. of section 11 of the Atomic Energy Act of 1954, with reason to believe that such information so obtained could be used to the injury of the United States, or to the advantage of any foreign nation willfully communicates, delivers, transmits, or causes to be communicated, delivered, or transmitted, or attempts to communicate, deliver, transmit or cause to be communicated, delivered, or transmitted the same to any person not entitled to receive it, or willfully retains the same and fails to deliver it to the officer or employee of the United States entitled to receive it;

(2)   intentionally accesses a computer without authorization or exceeds authorized access, and thereby obtains—

• (A) information contained in a financial record of a financial institution, or of a card issuer as defined in section 1602 (n) of title 15, or contained in a file of a consumer reporting agency on a consumer, as such terms are defined in the Fair Credit Reporting Act (15 U.S.C. 1681 et seq.);

- (B) information from any department or agency of the United States; or
- (C) information from any protected computer.

(3) intentionally, without authorization to access any nonpublic computer of a department or agency of the United States, accesses such a computer of that department or agency that is exclusively for the use of the Government of the United States or, in the case of a computer not exclusively for such use, is used by or for the Government of the United States and such conduct affects that use by or for the Government of the United States;

(4) knowingly and with intent to defraud, accesses a protected computer without authorization, or exceeds authorized access, and by means of such conduct furthers the intended fraud and obtains anything of value, unless the object of the fraud and the thing obtained consists only of the use of the computer and the value of such use is not more than $5,000 in any 1-year period;

(5)

- (A) knowingly causes the transmission of a program, information, code, or command, and as a result of such conduct, intentionally causes damage without authorization, to a protected computer;
- (B) intentionally accesses a protected computer without authorization, and as a result of such conduct, recklessly causes damage; or
- (C) intentionally accesses a protected computer without authorization, and as a result of such conduct, causes damage and loss.

(6) knowingly and with intent to defraud traffics (as defined in section 1029) in any password or similar information through which a computer may be accessed without authorization, if—

- (A) such trafficking affects interstate or foreign commerce; or
- (B) such computer is used by or for the Government of the United States.

(7) with intent to extort from any person any money or other thing of value, transmits in interstate or foreign commerce any communication containing any—

- (A) threat to cause damage to a protected computer;
- (B) threat to obtain information from a protected computer without authorization or in excess of authorization or to impair the confidentiality of information obtained from a protected computer without authorization or by exceeding authorized access; or
- (C) demand or request for money or other thing of value in relation to damage to a protected computer, where such damage was caused to facilitate the extortion; shall be punished as provided in subsection (c) of this section.

(b) Whoever conspires to commit or attempts to commit an offense under subsection (a) of this section shall be punished as provided in subsection (c) of this section.

(c) The punishment for an offense under subsection (a) or (b) of this section is—

(1)

- (A) a fine under this title or imprisonment for not more than ten years, or both, in the case of an offense under subsection (a)(1) of this section which does not occur after a conviction for another offense under this section, or an attempt to commit an offense punishable under this subparagraph; and
- (B) a fine under this title or imprisonment for not more than twenty years, or both, in the case of an offense under subsection (a)(1) of this section which occurs after a conviction for another offense under this section, or an attempt to commit an offense punishable under this subparagraph;

(2)

- (A) except as provided in subparagraph (B), a fine under this title or imprisonment for not more than one year, or both, in the case of an offense under subsection (a)(2), (a)(3), or (a)(6) of this section which does not occur after a conviction for another offense under this section, or an attempt to commit an offense punishable under this subparagraph;

- (B) a fine under this title or imprisonment for not more than 5 years, or both, in the case of an offense under subsection (a)(2), or an attempt to commit an offense punishable under this sub-paragraph, if—
  - (i) the offense was committed for purposes of commercial advantage or private financial gain;
  - (ii) the offense was committed in furtherance of any criminal or tortious act in violation of the Constitution or laws of the United States or of any State; or
  - (iii) the value of the information obtained exceeds $5,000; and
- (C) a fine under this title or imprisonment for not more than ten years, or both, in the case of an offense under subsection (a)(2), (a)(3) or (a)(6) of this section which occurs after a conviction for another offense under this section, or an attempt to commit an offense punishable under this subparagraph;

(3)

- (A) a fine under this title or imprisonment for not more than five years, or both, in the case of an offense under subsection (a)(4) or (a)(7) of this section which does not occur after a conviction for another offense under this section, or an attempt to commit an offense punishable under this subparagraph; and
- (B) a fine under this title or imprisonment for not more than ten years, or both, in the case of an offense under subsection (a)(4), or (a)(7) of this section which occurs after a conviction for another offense under this section, or an attempt to commit an offense punishable under this subparagraph;

(4)

- (A) except as provided in subparagraphs (E) and (F), a fine under this title, imprisonment for not more than 5 years, or both, in the case of—
  - (i) an offense under subsection (a)(5)(B), which does not occur after a conviction for another offense under this section, if the offense caused (or, in the case of an attempted offense, would, if completed, have caused)—
    - (I) loss to 1 or more persons during any 1-year period (and, for purposes of an investigation, prosecution, or other proceeding brought by the United States only, loss resulting from a related course of conduct affecting 1 or more other protected computers) aggregating at least $5,000 in value;
    - (II) the modification or impairment, or potential modification or impairment, of the medical examination, diagnosis, treatment, or care of 1 or more individuals;
    - (III) physical injury to any person;
    - (IV) a threat to public health or safety;
    - (V) damage affecting a computer used by or for an entity of the United States Government in furtherance of the administration of justice, national defense, or national security; or
    - (VI) damage affecting 10 or more protected computers during any 1-year period; or
  - (ii) an attempt to commit an offense punishable under this subparagraph;
- (B) except as provided in subparagraphs (E) and (F), a fine under this title, imprisonment for not more than 10 years, or both, in the case of—
  - (i) an offense under subsection (a)(5)(A), which does not occur after a conviction for another offense under this section, if the offense caused (or, in the case of an attempted offense, would, if completed, have caused) a harm provided in subclauses (I) through (VI) of subparagraph (A) (i); or
  - (ii) an attempt to commit an offense punishable under this subparagraph;
- (C) except as provided in subparagraphs (E) and (F), a fine under this title, imprisonment for not more than 20 years, or both, in the case of—

- ○ (i) an offense or an attempt to commit an offense under subparagraphs (A) or (B) of subsection (a)(5) that occurs after a conviction for another offense under this section; or

- ○ (ii) an attempt to commit an offense punishable under this subparagraph;

- (D) a fine under this title, imprisonment for not more than 10 years, or both, in the case of—

- ○ (i) an offense or an attempt to commit an offense under subsection (a)(5)(C) that occurs after a conviction for another offense under this section; or

- ○ (ii) an attempt to commit an offense punishable under this subparagraph;

- (E) if the offender attempts to cause or knowingly or recklessly causes serious bodily injury from conduct in violation of subsection (a)(5)(A), a fine under this title, imprisonment for not more than 20 years, or both;

- (F) if the offender attempts to cause or knowingly or recklessly causes death from conduct in violation of subsection (a)(5)(A), a fine under this title, imprisonment for any term of years or for life, or both; or

- (G) a fine under this title, imprisonment for not more than 1 year, or both, for—

- ○ (i) any other offense under subsection (a)(5); or

- ○ (ii) an attempt to commit an offense punishable under this subparagraph.

(d)

- (1) The United States Secret Service shall, in addition to any other agency having such authority, have the authority to investigate offenses under this section.

- (2) The Federal Bureau of Investigation shall have primary authority to investigate offenses under subsection (a)(1) for any cases involving espionage, foreign counter-intelligence, information protected against unauthorized disclosure for reasons of national defense or foreign relations, or Restricted Data (as that term is defined in section 11y of the Atomic Energy Act of 1954 (42 U.S.C. 2014 (y)), except for offenses affecting the duties of the United States Secret Service pursuant to section 3056 (a) of this title.

- (3) Such authority shall be exercised in accordance with an agreement which shall be entered into by the Secretary of the Treasury and the Attorney General.

(e)   As used in this section—

- (1) the term "computer" means an electronic, magnetic, optical, electrochemical, or other high speed data processing device performing logical, arithmetic, or storage functions, and includes any data storage facility or communications facility directly related to or operating in conjunction with such device, but such term does not include an automated typewriter or typesetter, a portable hand held calculator, or other similar device;

- (2) the term "protected computer" means a computer—

- ○ (A) exclusively for the use of a financial institution or the United States Government, or, in the case of a computer not exclusively for such use, used by or for a financial institution or the United States Government and the conduct constituting the offense affects that use by or for the financial institution or the Government; or

- ○ (B) which is used in or affecting interstate or foreign commerce or communication, including a computer located outside the United States that is used in a manner that affects interstate or foreign commerce or communication of the United States;

- (3) the term "State" includes the District of Columbia, the Commonwealth of Puerto Rico, and any other commonwealth, possession or territory of the United States;

- (4) the term "financial institution" means—

- ○ (A) an institution, with deposits insured by the Federal Deposit Insurance Corporation;

- ○ (B) the Federal Reserve or a member of the Federal Reserve including any Federal Reserve Bank;

- ○ (C) a credit union with accounts insured by the National Credit Union Administration;

- ○ (D) a member of the Federal home loan bank system and any home loan bank;
- ○ (E) any institution of the Farm Credit System under the Farm Credit Act of 1971;
- ○ (F) a broker-dealer registered with the Securities and Exchange Commission pursuant to section 15 of the Securities Exchange Act of 1934;
- ○ (G) the Securities Investor Protection Corporation;
- ○ (H) a branch or agency of a foreign bank (as such terms are defined in paragraphs (1) and (3) of section 1(b) of the International Banking Act of 1978); and
- ○ (I) an organization operating under section 25 or section 25(a) of the Federal Reserve Act;

- (5) the term "financial record" means information derived from any record held by a financial institution pertaining to a customer's relationship with the financial institution;

- (6) the term "exceeds authorized access" means to access a computer with authorization and to use such access to obtain or alter information in the computer that the accesser is not entitled so to obtain or alter;

- (7) the term "department of the United States" means the legislative or judicial branch of the Government or one of the executive departments enumerated in section 101 of title 5;

- (8) the term "damage" means any impairment to the integrity or availability of data, a program, a system, or information;

- (9) the term "government entity" includes the Government of the United States, any State or political subdivision of the United States, any foreign country, and any state, province, municipality, or other political subdivision of a foreign country;

- (10) the term "conviction" shall include a conviction under the law of any State for a crime punishable by imprisonment for more than 1 year, an element of which is unauthorized access, or exceeding authorized access, to a computer;

- (11) the term "loss" means any reasonable cost to any victim, including the cost of responding to an offense, conducting a damage assessment, and restoring the data, program, system, or information to its condition prior to the offense, and any revenue lost, cost incurred, or other consequential damages incurred because of interruption of service; and

- (12) the term "person" means any individual, firm, corporation, educational institution, financial institution, governmental entity, or legal or other entity.

(f) This section does not prohibit any lawfully authorized investigative, protective, or intelligence activity of a law enforcement agency of the United States, a State, or a political subdivision of a State, or of an intelligence agency of the United States.

(g) Any person who suffers damage or loss by reason of a violation of this section may maintain a civil action against the violator to obtain compensatory damages and injunctive relief or other equitable relief. A civil action for a violation of this section may be brought only if the conduct involves 1 of the factors set forth in subclauses (I), (II), (III), (IV), or (V) of subsection (c)(4)(A)(i). Damages for a violation involving only conduct described in subsection (c)(4)(A)(i)(I) are limited to economic damages. No action may be brought under this subsection unless such action is begun within 2 years of the date of the act complained of or the date of the discovery of the damage. No action may be brought under this subsection for the negligent design or manufacture of computer hardware, computer software, or firmware.

(h) The Attorney General and the Secretary of the Treasury shall report to the Congress annually, during the first 3 years following the date of the enactment of this subsection, concerning investigations and prosecutions under subsection (a)(5).

(i)

- (1) The court, in imposing sentence on any person convicted of a violation of this section, or convicted of conspiracy to violate this section, shall order, in addition to any other sentence imposed and irrespective of any provision of State law, that such person forfeit to the United States—

○ (A) such person's interest in any personal property that was used or intended to be used to commit or to facilitate the commission of such violation; and

○ (B) any property, real or personal, constituting or derived from, any proceeds that such person obtained, directly or indirectly, as a result of such violation.

- (2) The criminal forfeiture of property under this subsection, any seizure and disposition thereof, and any judicial proceeding in relation thereto, shall be governed by the provisions of section 413 of the Comprehensive Drug Abuse Prevention and Control Act of 1970 (21 U.S.C. 853), except subsection (d) of that section.

(j) For purposes of subsection (i), the following shall be subject to forfeiture to the United States and no property right shall exist in them:

- (1) Any personal property used or intended to be used to commit or to facilitate the commission of any violation of this section, or a conspiracy to violate this section.

- (2) Any property, real or personal, which constitutes or is derived from proceeds traceable to any violation of this section, or a conspiracy to violate this section.

COMPUTER FRAUD AND ABUSE ACT OF 1986

The Computer Fraud and Abuse Act of 1986 is a United States cybersecurity bill that was enacted in 1986 as an amendment to existing computer fraud law, which had been included in the Comprehensive Crime Control Act of 1984. The law prohibits accessing a computer without authorization, or in excess of authorization.

Criminal offenses under the Act

(a) Whoever—

(1) having knowingly accessed a computer without authorization or exceeding authorized access, and by means of such conduct having obtained information that has been determined by the United States Government pursuant to an Executive order or statute to require protection against unauthorized disclosure for reasons of national defense or foreign relations, or any restricted data, as defined in paragraph y. of section 11 of the Atomic Energy Act of 1954, with reason to believe that such information so obtained could be used to the injury of the United States, or to the advantage of any foreign nation willfully communicates, delivers, transmits, or causes to be communicated, delivered, or transmitted, or attempts to communicate, deliver, transmit or cause to be communicated, delivered, or transmitted the same to any person not entitled to receive it, or willfully retains the same and fails to deliver it to the officer or employee of the United States entitled to receive it;

(2) intentionally accesses a computer without authorization or exceeds authorized access, and thereby obtains—

(A) information contained in a financial record of a financial institution, or of a card issuer as defined in section 1602 (n) [1] of title 15, or contained in a file of a consumer reporting agency on a consumer, as such terms are defined in the Fair Credit Reporting Act (15 U.S.C. 1681 et seq.);

(B) information from any department or agency of the United States; or

(C) information from any protected computer;

(3) intentionally, without authorization to access any nonpublic computer of a department or agency of the United States, accesses such a computer of that department or agency that is exclusively for the use of the Government of the United States or, in the case of a computer not exclusively for such use, is used by or for the Government of the United States and such conduct affects that use by or for the Government of the United States;

(4) knowingly and with intent to defraud, accesses a protected computer without authorization, or exceeds authorized access, and by means of such conduct furthers the intended fraud and obtains anything of value, unless the object of the fraud and the thing obtained consists only of the use of the computer and the value of such use is not more than $5,000 in any 1-year period;

(5)

    (A)   knowingly causes the transmission of a program, information, code, or command, and as a result of such conduct, intentionally causes damage without authorization, to a protected computer;

    (B)   intentionally accesses a protected computer without authorization, and as a result of such conduct, recklessly causes damage; or

    (C)   intentionally accesses a protected computer without authorization, and as a result of such conduct, causes damage and loss.

(6)   knowingly and with intent to defraud traffics (as defined in section 1029) in any password or similar information through which a computer may be accessed without authorization, if—

    (A)   such trafficking affects interstate or foreign commerce; or

    (B)   such computer is used by or for the Government of the United States;

(7)   with intent to extort from any person any money or other thing of value, transmits in interstate or foreign commerce any communication containing any—

    (A)   threat to cause damage to a protected computer;

    (B)   threat to obtain information from a protected computer without authorization or in excess of authorization or to impair the confidentiality of information obtained from a protected computer without authorization or by exceeding authorized access; or

    (C)   demand or request for money or other thing of value in relation to damage to a protected computer, where such damage was caused to facilitate the extortion.

RESOURCES

BOOKS

Module 1

Weiss, Alan. *Getting Started in Consulting.* Wiley, 2019, ISBN 978-111-954215-5.

Weiss, Alan. *The Consulting Bible: Everything You Need to Know to Create and Expand a Seven-Figure Consulting Practice.* Wiley, 2011. ISBN 978-0-470-92808-0.

Module 12

Kahn, David. *The Code Breakers: The Comprehensive History of Secret Communication from Ancient Times to the Internet, Revised Edition.* Scribner, 1996, ISBN 0684831309.

Schneier, Bruce. *Applied Crytopgraphy: Protocols, Algorithms, and Source Code in C, Second Edition.* Wiley, 1996. ISBN 0471117099.

Module 13

Lammle, Todd. Cisco CCNA Certification: Exam 200-301, 1st Edition. Wiley, 2020. ISBN 1119677610.

WEBSITES

Module 1

Professional Certifications, Security Jobs, and Applicable Laws

www.cnbc.com/2019/05/17/cybersecurity-hackers-are-paid-millions-to-use-their-powers-for-good.html

www.comptia.org

www.eccouncil.org

www.forbes.com/sites/daveywinder/2020/05/29/theseincredible-100-million-hackers-could-make-1-billion-by-2025-hackerone-bounty-millionaires/?sh=18c63e477b88

www.giac.org

www.indeed.com

www.isc2.org

www.isecom.org

www.kali.org

www.ncsl.org/research/telecommunications-and-information-technology/computer-hacking-and-unauthorized-access-laws.aspx

www.ncsl.org/research/telecommunications-and-information-technology.aspx

www.offensive-security.com

www.sans.org

toool.us/laws.html

Module 2

Protocols

www.cisco.com/security_services/ciag/documents/v6-v4-threats.pdf

www.iana.org

www.iana.org/assignments/port-numbers

www.ietf.org

www.rapidtables.com/convert/number/ascii-to-hex.htm (ASCII to Hex Converter)

Module 3

Malicious Software (Malware)

www.mcafee.com/enterprise/en-ca/threat-center.html

Searching for Known Vulnerabilities and Exposures

https://docs.microsoft.com/en-us/security-updates/securitybulletins/securitybulletins

www.cve.mitre.org

www.exploit-db.com

www.google.com

www.kb.cert.org/vuls

www.packetstormsecurity.com

www.securityfocus.com

www.us-cert.gov/ncas

Macro Viruses

www.virusbulletin.com/virusbulletin/2014/07/vba-not-dead

Module 4

Footprinting

www.amazon.com

https://archive.org/web

www.arin.net

https://centralops.net/co/domaindossier.aspx

www.elevenpaths.com/labstools/foca/index.html

https://github.com/lanmaster53/recon-ng

https://github.com/laramies/theHarvester

http://gnuwin32.sourceforge.net/packages/wget.htm

https://groups.google.com

www.isc.org/downloads/bind/

www.maltego.com

https://nmap.org/ncat

https://osintframework.com

www.securityfocus.com

https://sitereport.netcraft.com

https://sourceforge.net/projects/metasploitable/files/Metasploitable2

www.spiderfoot.net

https://spyse.com

https://en.wikipedia.org/wiki/web_beacon

www.whitepages.com

https://whois.domaintools.com

Module 5

Port Scanning and Service Mapping

angryip.org

cve.mitre.org

www.fping.org

https://nmap.org/nsedoc/categories/default.html

www.tenable.org

www.tenable.com

www.unicornscan.org

www.us-cert.gov

Module 6

Enumeration

www.kali.org/penetration-testing/openvas-vulnerability-scanning/

https://linuxhint.com/install-openvaskali-linux

www.systemtools.com

www.tenable.com

Module 7

Programming

www.activestate.com/products/perl

https://cve.mitre.org

https://en.wikipedia.org/wiki/Perl

https://en.wikipedia.org/wiki/Python_(programming_language)

www.metasploit.com

https://notepad-plus-plus.org

https://perldoc.perl.org

perldoc.perl.org/Net/Ping.html

www.python.org/downloads

www.w3c.org

Module 8

Desktop and Server OSs

https://en.wikipedia.org/wiki/Security-Enhanced_Linux

https://exchange.xforce.ibmcloud.com

www.exploit-db.com

www.cisecurity.org/cybersecurity-tools

www.cve.mitre.org

www.kb.cert.org/vuls

www.logrhythm.com

https://msrc.microsoft.com/update-guide/vulnerability/CVE-2021-33763

www.packetstormsecurity.com

www.samba.org

https://technet.microsoft.com/en-us/sysinternals/bb897440.aspx

www.tenable.com/downloads/nessus

www.tripwire.com

www.us-cert.gov

Module 9

Embedded OSs

https://blackberry.qnx.com/en/embedded-system-security/ultimate-guide

www.cve.mitre.org

www.darkreading.com/vulnerabilities-threats/significant-vulnerabilities-found-in-6-common-printer-brands

www.dd-wrt.com

exploit-db.com

www.google.com

www.iso.org

https://nvd.nist.gov

www.packetstormsecurity.org

https://sourceforge.net/projects/freertos/files/FreeRTOS

https://threatpost.com

www.wired.com

www.zdnet.com/article/hp-patches-vulnerable-printer-driver-impacting-millions-of-devices

Module 10

Web Server Security

www.cve.mitre.org

www.exploit-db.com/

helpx.adobe.com/security.html

https://github.com/WebGoat/WebGoat/releases/download/v8.0.0.M26/webgoat-server-8.0.0.M26.jar

www.owasp.org

www.owasp.org/index.php/Web_Application_Penetration_Testing

www.owasp.org/index.php/Appendix_A:_Testing_Tools

www.packetstormsecurity.org

www.thecrimson.com/article/2005/3/3/hacker-tips-off-b-school-applicants-tipped

https://us-cert.cisa.gov/ncas/alerts/aa21-076a

Module 11

Wireless Networking

www.aircrack-ng.org

en.wikipedia.org/wiki/IEEE_802.11

www.ieee802.org/11/Reports/tgay_update.htm

www.isecom.org/mirror/OSSTMM.3.pdf

www.kismetwireless.net

nvd.nist.gov

www.retrocom.com

www.vistumbler.net

www.wifipineapple.com

www.wikihow.com/Make-a-Cantenna

Module 12

Cryptography

www.broadcom.com/products/cyber-security/information-protection/encryption

csrc.nist.gov

https://en.wikipedia.org/wiki/RSA_Security

www.gnupg.org

www.google.com

https://grymoire.wordpress.com/2014/12/05/cbc-padding-oracle-attacks-simplified-key-concepts-and-pitfalls

keccak.noekeon.org

www.mandylionlabs.com/documents/BFTCalc.xls

www.phreedom.org

www.tomsguide.com/reference/best-encrypted-messaging-apps

https://veracrypt.fr/en/Home.html

www.rsa.com

https://veracrypt.fr/en/Home.html

www.wired.com/story/nahoft-iran-messaging-encryption-app

Module 13

Network Protection Systems

canary.tools

www.cisco.com

www.cisecurity.org/cis-benchmarks

www.darkreading.com/edge-articles/101-why-bgp-hijacking-just-won-t-die

www.fireeye.com

www.fortinet.com/support/support-services/fortiguard-security-subscriptions/web-filtering)

https://github.com/cowrie/cowrie

https://github.com/mushorg/glastopf

https://github.com/telekom-security/tpotce

www.honeyd.org

www.honeynet.org

www.keyfocus.net/kfsensor

labrea.sourceforge.net

www.mcafee.com

opencanary.org

nvd.nist.gov

www.redseal.net

www.snort.org

tools.cisco.com/security/center

https://umbrella.cisco.com/solutions/web-content-filtering

Module 14

Hands-On Ethical Hacking Final Project

https://cve.mitre.org/cve/search_cve_list.html

https://www.hacking-tutorial.com/tips-and-trick/install-metasploitable-on-virtual-box/#sthash.2WTSpUll.dpbs

https://information.rapid7.com/download-metasploitable-2017.html

https://www.kali.org/get-kali/#kali-virtual-machines

https://nvd.nist.gov/vuln/search

https://www.offensive-security.com/reports/sample-penetration-testing-report.pdf

https://www.sans.org/white-papers/33343/

GLOSSARY

802.11   An IEEE standard that is part of the IEEE 802 set of local area network (LAN) technical standards. It specifies the media access control (MAC) and physical layer (PHY) protocols for implementing wireless local area network (WLAN) computer communication.

802.1X standard   An IEEE standard that defines the process of authenticating and authorizing users on a network before they're allowed to connect.

A

access point (AP)   A radio transceiver that connects to a network via an Ethernet cable and bridges a wireless network with a wired network.

ACK   Acknowledgment; used to signify the receipt of a message; the last part of the SYN, SYN-ACK, ACK three-way TCP handshake.

Active Server Pages (ASP and ASP.NET)   A scripting language for creating dynamic webpages.

active system   An IDS or IPS that logs events, sends out alerts, and can interoperate with routers and firewalls.

ActiveX Data Objects (ADO)   A programming interface for connecting a web application to a database.

ad-hoc network   A wireless network that doesn't rely on an AP for connectivity; instead, independent stations connect to each other in a decentralized fashion.

Advanced Encryption Standard (AES)   A symmetric block cipher standard from NIST that replaced DES. *See also* Data Encryption Standard (DES).

adware   Software that can be installed without a user's knowledge; its main purpose is to determine users' purchasing habits.

algorithm   A set of directions used to solve a problem.

amplitude   The height of a sound wave; determines a sound's volume.

anomaly-based IDS   A type of IDS that sends alerts on network traffic varying from a set baseline.

application-aware firewall   A firewall that inspects network traffic at a higher level in the OSI model than a traditional stateful packet inspection firewall does.

assembly language   A programming language that uses a combination of hexadecimal numbers and expressions to program instructions that are easier to understand than machine-language instructions.

asymmetric algorithm   An encryption methodology using two keys that are mathematically related; also referred to as public key cryptography.

attack   Any attempt by an unauthorized person to access, damage, or use resources of a network or computer system.

attack surface   The amount of code a computer system exposes to unauthenticated outsiders.

authentication   The process of verifying that the sender or receiver (or both) is who they claim to be; this function is available in asymmetric algorithms but not symmetric algorithms.

B

backdoor   A program that an attacker can use to gain access to a computer at a later date. *See also* rootkit.

basic service area (BSA)   The coverage area an access point provides in a wireless network.

basic service set (BSS)   The collection of connected devices in a wireless network.

birthday attack   An attack used to find the same hash value for two different inputs and reveal mathematical weaknesses in a hashing algorithm.

black box model   A penetration testing model in which the testers are not provided with any information such as network architecture diagrams. Testers must rely on publicly available information and gather the rest themselves.

block cipher   A symmetric algorithm that encrypts data in blocks of bits. These blocks are used as input to mathematical functions that perform substitution and transposition of the bits, making it difficult for someone to reverse-engineer the mathematical functions that were used.

Blowfish   A block cipher that operates on 64-bit blocks of plaintext, but its key length can be as large as 448 bits.

botnet   A group of multiple computers, usually thousands, that behave like robots to conduct an attack on a network. The computers are called zombies because their users aren't aware their systems are being controlled by one person. *See also* zombie.

branching   A method that takes you from one area of a program (a function) to another area.

brute-force attack   An attack in which the attacker uses software that attempts every possible combination of characters to guess passwords.

buffer overflow attack   An exploit written by a programmer that finds a vulnerability in poorly written code that doesn't check for a predefined amount of memory space use, and then inserts executable code that fills up the buffer (an area of memory) for the purpose of elevating the attacker's permissions.

bug   A programming error that causes unpredictable results in a program.

C

certificate   A digital document that verifies whether two parties exchanging data over the Internet are really who they claim to be. Each certificate has a unique serial number and must follow the X.509 standard.

certification authority (CA)   A third party, such as VeriSign, that vouches for a company's authenticity and issues a certificate binding a public key to a recipient's private key.

Certified Ethical Hacker (CEH)   A certification from the EC-Council. Passing this certification exam verifies that the tested individual possesses sufficient ethical hacking skills to perform useful vulnerability analyses.

Certified Information Systems Security Professional (CISSP)   A certification from (ISC)². Passing this certification exam verifies that the tested individual possesses sufficient capabilities to effectively design, implement, and manage a best-in-class cybersecurity program.

channel   A specific frequency range within a frequency band in which data is transmitted.

chipping code   Multiple sub-bits representing the original message that can be used for recovery of a corrupted packet traveling across a frequency band.

cipher   A key that maps each letter or number to a different letter or number.

ciphertext   Plaintext (readable text) that has been encrypted.

class   In object-oriented programming, the structure that holds pieces of data and functions.

closed port   A port that is not listening or responding to a packet.

ColdFusion   A server-side scripting language for creating dynamic webpages; supports a wide variety of databases and uses a proprietary markup language known as CFML.

Common Gateway Interface (CGI)   An interface that passes data between a web server and a web browser.

Common Internet File System (CIFS)   A remote file system protocol that enables computers to share network resources over the Internet.

competitive intelligence   A means of gathering information about a business or an industry by using observation, accessing public information, speaking with employees, and so on.

compiler   A program that converts source code into executable or binary code.

computer security   The security of computing devices that aren't part of a network infrastructure.

connectionless   Refers to a communication protocol that is not connection oriented. It does not establish a connection and does not track packets or guarantee delivery. UDP is an example of a connectionless protocol.

connection-oriented protocol   A data communication protocol that uses a handshake to establish a connection between end points; it also tracks packets and guarantees delivery. TCP is an example of a connection-oriented protocol.

conversion specifier   The part of code that tells the compiler how to convert the value indicated in a function.

cookie   A text file containing a message sent from a web server to a user's web browser to be used later when the user revisits the website.

cracker   An individual who breaks into a computer system, often on a network, and bypasses passwords and/or computer program licenses to intentionally breach computer security.

crawling   An automated way to discover pages of a website by following links.

cryptanalysis   A field of study devoted to breaking encryption algorithms.

cryptosystem   A suite of cryptographic algorithms needed to implement a specific security service. A cryptosystem usually consists of three algorithms: one for key generation, one for encryption, and one for decryption.

D

data at rest   Any data not moving through a network or being used by the OS; usually refers to data on storage media.

Data Encryption Algorithm (DEA)   The encryption algorithm used in the DES standard; a symmetric algorithm that uses 56 bits for encryption. *See also* Data Encryption Standard (DES).

Data Encryption Standard (DES)   A NIST standard for protecting sensitive but unclassified data; it was later replaced because the increased processing power of computers made it possible to break DES encryption.

demilitarized zone (DMZ)   A small network containing resources that sits between the Internet and the internal network, sometimes referred to as a "perimeter network." It's used when a company wants to make resources available to Internet users yet keep the company's internal network secure.

denial-of-service (DoS) attack   An attack made to deny legitimate users from accessing network resources.

dictionary attack   An attack in which the attacker runs a password-cracking program that uses a dictionary of known words or passwords as an input file against the attacked system's password file.

digital signature   A method of signing messages by using asymmetric encryption that ensures authentication and nonrepudiation. *See also* authentication *and* nonrepudiation.

distance-vector routing protocol   A routing protocol that passes the routing table (containing all possible paths) to all routers on the network. If a router learns one new path, it sends the entire routing table again, which isn't as efficient as a link-state routing protocol.

distributed denial-of-service (DDoS) attack   An attack made on a host from multiple servers or computers to deny legitimate users from accessing network resources.

do loop   A loop that performs an action and then tests to see whether the action should continue to occur.

domain controller   A Windows server that stores user account information, authenticates domain logons, maintains the master database, and enforces security policies for Windows domains.

drive-by download   A type of attack in which website visitors download and install malicious code or software without their knowledge.

dumpster diving   Gathering information by examining the trash that people discard.

Dynamic Application Security Testing (DAST)   An application testing technique that analyzes a running application for vulnerabilities. DAST is also known as "black box" testing.

dynamic webpage   A webpage that can change on the fly depending on variables, such as the date or time of day.

E

embedded operating system (OS)   An operating system that runs in an embedded system. Designed to be small and efficient, it usually lacks some functions of general-purpose OSs. It can be a small program developed specifically for an embedded system or a stripped-down version of a general-purpose OS.

embedded system   Any computer system that's not a general-purpose PC or server.

encryption algorithm   A mathematical formula or method for converting plaintext into ciphertext.

enum4linux   A command line tool that allows you to enumerate information from Windows, Linux, and Samba systems. It is a wrapper around a number of other utilities, providing a unified, simplified script capable of collecting a significant amount of information.

enumeration   The process of connecting to a system and obtaining information such as logon names, passwords, group memberships, and shared resources.

ethical hacker   A person who breaks into computer systems for the purpose of discovering weaknesses so that they can be mitigated. An ethical hacker uses the same tools that a malicious hacker would but does not have malicious intent.

exploit A program, data, or sequence of commands that takes advantage of a vulnerability in computer software or hardware to cause unintended or unanticipated behavior to occur (such as granting access to unauthorized users).

Extensible Authentication Protocol (EAP) An enhancement to PPP designed to allow an organization to select an authentication method.

F

filtered port A port protected with a network-filtering device, such as a firewall.

firewall A hardware device or software used to control traffic entering and leaving an internal network.

firmware Software residing on a chip.

footprinting Gathering information about a company before performing a security test or launching an attack; sometimes referred to as "reconnaissance."

for loop A loop that initializes a variable, tests a condition, and then increments or decrements the variable.

fping An enhanced Ping utility for pinging multiple targets simultaneously.

frequency The number of sound wave repetitions in a specified time; also referred to as cycles per second.

function A mini program within a main program that performs a particular task.

G

Global Information Assurance Certification (GIAC) An information security certification entity that was founded by the SANS institute.

gray box model A penetration testing model where the tester is given limited information. Often used to determine the level of access a privileged user could gain and the potential damage they could cause.

H

hacker A term that originally was used to describe an advanced computer technology enthusiast but now more commonly refers to an individual who uses technical know-how to break into computer systems.

hacktivist An individual who gains unauthorized access to computer files or networks in order to further social or political ends.

hashing algorithm A function that takes a variable-length string or message and produces a fixed-length hash value, also called a message digest. *See also* message digest.

honeypot A computer placed on the network perimeter that contains information or data intended to lure hackers and distract them from legitimate network resources.

host-based IDS/IPS Software used to protect a critical network server or database server. The software is installed on the system you're attempting to protect, just like installing antivirus software on a desktop system.

hping3 An enhanced Ping utility for crafting TCP and UDP packets to be used in port-scanning activities.

HTTP Strict Transport Security (HSTS) A policy mechanism used to protect websites against man-in-the-middle attacks. HSTS allows webservers to force web browsers to use HTTPS connections instead of HTTP.

I

indicators of compromise Artifacts, left behind by attackers, that indicate that a system or network has been compromised.

infrared (IR) An area in the electromagnetic spectrum with a frequency above microwaves; an infrared signal is restricted to a single room or line of sight because IR light can't penetrate walls, ceilings, or floors. This technology is used for most remote controls.

infrastructure mode The mode a wireless network operates in, whereby centralized connectivity is established with one or more APs. It's the most common type of WLAN and differs from an ad-hoc network, which doesn't require an AP.

initial sequence number (ISN) The unique 32-bit sequence number assigned to each new TCP-based connection. It is used to create unique sequence numbers for packet tracking and delivery guarantee.

Institute for Security and Open Methodologies (ISECOM) An open security research community providing original resources, tools, and certifications in the field of security.

Institute of Electrical and Electronics Engineers (IEEE) An organization that creates standards for the IT industry.

Interactive Application Security Testing (IAST) An application testing technique that combines elements of DAST and SAST and uses an agent inside the application to perform vulnerability analysis in real-time. IAST is also known as "gray box" testing.

International Data Encryption Algorithm (IDEA) A block cipher that operates on 64-bit blocks of plaintext and uses a 128-bit key; used in PGP encryption software.

Internet Assigned Numbers Authority (IANA) A standards organization that oversees global IP address allocation, root zone management in the Domain Name System (DNS), and other Internet Protocol related symbols and Internet numbers.

Internet Control Message Protocol (ICMP) A Transport layer protocol used to communicate information about network connectivity issues. For example, the ping command uses ICMP messages such as destination network unreachable, echo request, and echo reply.

intrusion detection system (IDS) A hardware device or software that monitors network traffic and sends alerts so that security administrators can identify attacks in progress and stop them.

intrusion prevention system (IPS) A network-based or host-based device or software that goes beyond monitoring traffic and sending alerts to block malicious activity they detect.

IP access list A list of IP addresses, subnets, or networks that are allowed or denied access through a router's interface.

K

key A sequence of random bits used in an encryption algorithm to transform plaintext into ciphertext, or vice versa.

keylogger A hardware device or software (spyware) that records keystrokes made on a computer and stores the information for later retrieval.

keyspace The range of all possible key values contained in an encryption algorithm. *See also* key.

L

link-state routing protocol A routing protocol that uses link-state advertisements to send topology changes or new paths to other routers on the network. This method is efficient because only new information is sent, not the entire routing table.

looping The act of repeating a task.

M

macro virus A virus written in a macro programming language, such as Visual Basic for Applications.

malware Malicious software, such as a virus, worm, or Trojan program, used to interfere with the confidentiality, integrity, or access to data, networks, or computer systems.

Mandatory Access Control (MAC) An OS security mechanism that enforces access rules based on privileges for interactions between processes, files, and users; included in SELinux.

man-in-the-middle attack An attack in which attackers place themselves between the victim computer and another host computer, and then intercept messages sent from the victim to the host and pretend to be the host computer.

mathematical attack An attack in which properties of the encryption algorithm are attacked by using mathematical computations. Categories of this attack include ciphertext-only attack, known plaintext attack, chosen-plaintext attack, chosen-ciphertext attack, and side-channel attack.

message digest The fixed-length value that a hashing algorithm produces; used to verify that data or messages haven't been changed.

Message Digest 5 (MD5) A 128-bit cryptographic hash function; still used, even though its weaknesses make finding collisions practical with only moderate computing power. It is most useful for file integrity checking.

metropolitan area network (MAN) The 802.16 standard defines the Wireless MAN Air Interface for wireless MANs and addresses the limited distance available for 802.11b WLANs. The most widely used implementation of wireless MAN technology is WiMAX. *See also* Worldwide Interoperability for Microwave Access (WiMAX).

Mobile Broadband Wireless Access (MBWA) The 802.20 standard, with a goal similar to mobile WiMAX; addresses wireless MANs for mobile users in trains, subways, or cars traveling at speeds up to 150 miles per hour.

modulation A process that defines how data is placed on a carrier signal.

multifunction device (MFD) A peripheral networked device that performs more than one function, such as printing, scanning, and copying. Also known as an MFC (multifunction copier) and MFP (multifunction printer).

multiple independent levels of security/safety (MILS) A type of OS (often embedded) certified to run multiple levels of classification (such as unclassified, secret, and top secret) on the same CPU without leakage between levels; used in the U.S. military for high-security environments and in organizations, such as those controlling nuclear power or municipal sewage plants, for which separating privileges and functions is crucial.

N

narrowband A technology that uses microwave radio band frequencies to transmit data. The most popular uses of this technology are cordless phones and garage door openers.

Nessus Previously, an open-source scanning tool; now licensed by Tenable Network Security. *See* OpenVAS.

NetBIOS Extended User Interface (NetBEUI) A fast, efficient protocol that allows transmitting NetBIOS packets over TCP/IP and various network topologies, such as token ring and Ethernet.

Network Address Translation (NAT) A basic security feature of a firewall used to hide the internal network from outsiders. Internal private IP addresses are mapped to public external IP addresses to hide the internal infrastructure from unauthorized personnel.

Network Basic Input/Output System (NetBIOS) A Windows programming interface that allows computers to communicate across a LAN.

network protection system Any system designed specifically to protect networks or network devices from attacks; includes routers, firewalls, web filters, network-based and host-based IPSs and IDSs, and honeypots.

network security The security of computers or devices that are part of a network infrastructure.

network session hijacking A hacking method in which the attacker takes over a web user's session by stealing the user's session ID and using it to masquerade as the authorized user.

network-based IDS/IPS A device that monitors traffic on network segments and alerts security administrators of suspicious activity.

Nmap A security tool used to identify open ports and detect services and OSs running on network systems.

nonrepudiation The process of ensuring that the sender and receiver can't deny sending or receiving the message; this function is available in asymmetric algorithms but not symmetric algorithms.

null session An unauthenticated connection to a Windows system.

O

Object Linking and Embedding Database (OLE DB) A set of interfaces enabling web applications to access diverse database management systems.

Offensive Security Certified Professional (OSCP) A certification from Offensive Security, an American international company working in information security, penetration testing, and digital forensics. The certification focuses on hands-on offensive information security skills. It consists of two parts: a nearly 24-hour pen testing exam and a documentation report due 24 hours after it.

Open Database Connectivity (ODBC) A standard database access method that allows a web application to interact with a variety of database management systems.

open port A port that responds to ping sweeps and other packets.

Open Source Intelligence (OSINT) Refers to publicly available methods and tools that can be used for footprinting and reconnaissance.

Open Source Security Testing Methodology Manual (OSSTMM) A peer-reviewed methodology for security testing, maintained by the Institute for Security and Open Methodologies (ISECOM).

Open Web Application Security Project (OWASP) A not-for-profit foundation dedicated to finding and fighting web application vulnerabilities.

OpenPGP The Internet public key encryption standard for PGP messages; can use AES, IDEA, RSA, DSA, and SHA algorithms for encrypting, authenticating, verifying message integrity, and managing keys. The most common free version is GNU Privacy Guard (GnuPG or GPG), and a commercial version that's compliant with the OpenPGP standard is available.

OpenVAS A security tool for conducting port scanning, OS identification, and vulnerability assessments.

OSSTMM Open Source Security Testing Methodology Manual

OSSTMM Professional Security Tester (OPST) A technical, skills-based certification designed to accredit professional security analysts.

P

packet monkey An individual (*see* cracker, hacker, *and* script kiddy) who intentionally inundates a website or network with data packets, resulting in a denial-of-service situation for users of the attacked site or network.

passive system An IDS that does not take any action to stop or prevent a security event.

path-vector routing protocol A protocol that uses dynamically updated paths or routing tables to transmit packets from one autonomous network to another.

penetration test An action performed by a penetration tester/ethical hacker used to find security vulnerabilities in computer systems or networks.

PenTest+ A CompTIA certification exam. The certification claims to verify that successful candidates have the knowledge and skills required to plan and scope an assessment, understand legal and compliance requirements, perform vulnerability scanning and penetration testing, analyze data, and effectively report and communicate results.

phishing A type of attack carried out by email; email messages include links to fake websites intended to entice victims into disclosing private information or installing malware.

PHP Hypertext Processor (PHP) An open-source server-side scripting language.

piggybacking A method attackers use to gain access to restricted areas in a company. The attacker follows an employee closely and enters the area with that employee.

Ping of Death attack A crafted ICMP packet larger than the maximum 65,535 bytes; causes the recipient system to crash or freeze.

ping sweep Pinging a range of IP addresses to identify live systems on a network.

plaintext Readable text that hasn't been encrypted; also called cleartext.

port A connection point within a particular device that can be targeted to access a specific process or network service. A port number can be any integer between 0 and 65,535. Some well-known port numbers are reserved for standard services; for example, port 53 is well-known to be used for DNS queries. A port number is combined with the IP address of a device to target the desired service on that device.

port scanning A method of finding out which services a host computer offers.

Pretty Good Privacy (PGP) A free email encryption program that allows typical users to encrypt emails.

private key In a key pair, the secret key used in an asymmetric algorithm that's known only by the key owner and is never shared. Even if the public key that encrypted a message is known, the owner's private key can't be determined.

privileged mode A mode on Cisco routers that allows administrators to perform full router configuration tasks; also called enable mode.

Protected EAP (PEAP) An authentication protocol that uses Transport Layer Security (TLS) to authenticate the server to the client but not the client to the server; only the server is required to have a digital certificate.

protocol A formal description of digital message formats and rules used to exchange messages between computing systems. TCP and UDP are two protocols.

pseudocode An English-like language for outlining the structure of a program.

public key In a key pair, the key that can be known by the public; it works with a private key in asymmetric key cryptography, which is also known as public key cryptography.

public key cryptography Known as asymmetric key cryptography, an asymmetric algorithm that uses two mathematically related keys.

public key infrastructure (PKI) A structure consisting of programs, protocols, and security policies. PKI uses public key cryptography to protect data traversing the Internet.

R

rainbow table A lookup table of password hash values that enables certain programs to crack passwords much faster than with brute-force methods.

ransomware A type of malware that blocks access to a computer system or its data until a sum of money is paid.

RC4 A stream cipher created by Ronald L. Rivest that's used in WEP wireless encryption.

RC5 A block cipher created by Ronald L. Rivest that can operate on different block sizes: 32, 64, and 128 bits. The key size can reach 2048 bits.

real-time operating system (RTOS) A specialized embedded OS designed with algorithms aimed at multitasking and responding predictably; used in devices such as programmable thermostats, appliance controls, planes, and spacecraft.

red team A group that plays the role of an enemy or competitor and provides security feedback from that perspective. Red teams are used in many fields, especially in cybersecurity, airport security, the military, and intelligence agencies.

Remote Procedure Call (RPC) An interprocess communication mechanism that allows a program running on one host to run code on a remote host.

replay attack An attack in which the attacker captures data and attempts to resubmit the data so that a device, such as a workstation or router, thinks a legitimate connection is in effect.

rootkit A program created after an attack for later use by the attacker; it's usually hidden in the OS tools and is difficult to detect. *See also* backdoor.

S

salt In cryptography, random data used as additional input to a one-way cryptographic function. Salts help safeguard passwords in storage.

Samba An open-source implementation of CIFS that allows *nix servers to share resources with Windows clients and vice versa.

sandboxing A security measure where the user can choose to run a program, navigate to a website, or open a file inside of a sandbox application to check if that program, website, or file contains malware. Sandboxie is an example of a free open source sandbox application.

script kiddy An individual who uses existing computer scripts or code to hack into computers, lacking the expertise to write his or her own.

Secure Hash Algorithm (SHA-1) NIST standard hashing algorithm that's much stronger than MD5

but has demonstrated weaknesses. For sensitive applications, NIST recommends not using SHA-1, and federal agencies are replacing it with longer digest versions, collectively called SHA-2.

Secure Multipurpose Internet Mail Extension (S/MIME) A public key encryption standard for encrypting and digitally signing email. It can also encrypt emails containing attachments and use PKI certificates for authentication.

security appliance A device that combines multiple network protection functions, such as those performed by a router, a firewall, and an IPS, on the same piece of hardware.

Security Information and Event Management (SIEM) A class of technology that supports threat detection, compliance, and security incident management through the collection and analysis of security events.

Security Operations Center (SOC) A command center facility for a team of information technology (IT) professionals with expertise in cybersecurity who monitor, analyze, and protect an organization from cyber-attacks.

security test An analysis of an organization's policy and procedures; vulnerabilities are reported to management. This is often done as part of penetration testing.

Server Message Block (SMB) A protocol for sharing files and printers and providing a method for client applications to read, write to, and request services from server programs in a network. SMB has been supported since Windows 95.

service set identifier (SSID) The name of a WLAN; can be broadcast by an AP.

shell An executable piece of programming code that creates an interface to an operating system for executing system commands.

shoulder surfing A technique attackers use; involves looking over the shoulder of an unaware user to observe the keys the user types when entering a password or passcode.

Simple Network Management Protocol (SNMP) An Internet Standard protocol for collecting and organizing information about managed devices on IP networks and for modifying that information to change device behavior.

social engineering Using an understanding of human nature to extract information from people.

spear phishing A type of phishing attack that targets specific people in an organization, using information gathered from previous reconnaissance and footprinting; the goal is to trick recipients into clicking a link or opening an attachment that installs malware.

spidering   An automated way to discover pages of a website by following links.

spread spectrum   A technology that spreads data across a large-frequency bandwidth instead of traveling across one frequency band.

spyware   Software installed on users' computers without their knowledge that records personal information from the source computer and sends it to a destination computer.

SQL injection (SQLi)   A type of exploit that takes advantage of poorly written applications. An attacker can issue SQL statements by using a web browser to retrieve data, change server settings, or possibly gain control of the server.

SSL/TLS downgrade attack   A form of cryptographic attack that attempts to make a system abandon a high-quality mode of operation in favor of an older, lower-quality mode, such as downgrading from an encrypted connection to an unencrypted connection.

state table   A file created by a stateful packet filter that contains information on network connections. *See also* stateful packet filter.

stateful packet filter   A filter on routers that records session-specific information in a file about network connections, including the ports a client uses.

stateless packet filter   A filter on routers that handles each packet separately, so it is not resistant to spoofing or DoS attacks.

Static Application Security Testing (SAST)   An application testing technique that analyzes an application's source code for vulnerabilities. SAST is also known as "white box" testing.

static webpage   A webpage that displays the same information whenever it is accessed.

station (STA)   An addressable unit in a wireless network. A station is defined as a message destination and might not be a fixed location.

steganography   The method of hiding data in plain view in pictures, graphics, or text.

stream cipher   A symmetric algorithm that operates on plaintext one bit at a time.

substitution cipher   A cipher that maps each letter of the alphabet to a different letter. The biblical Book of Jeremiah was written by using a substitution cipher called Atbash.

supervisory control and data acquisition (SCADA) system   A system used for equipment monitoring and automation in large-scale industries and critical infrastructure systems, such as power plants and air traffic control towers; these systems contain components running embedded OSs.

supplicant   A wireless user attempting access to a WLAN.

symmetric algorithm   An encryption algorithm that uses only one key to encrypt and decrypt data. The recipient of a message encrypted with a key must have a copy of the same key to decrypt the message.

SYN   The first third of the TCP three-way handshake (SYN, SYN-ACK, ACK) and used to initiate and establish connections as well as synchronize sequence numbers between devices.

SYN-ACK   The second third of the TCP three-way handshake (SYN, SYN-ACK, ACK) and is used to respond to the SYN connection request. It has two logical parts: SYN and ACK. ACK signifies the response to the sender's SYN request, and SYN signifies what sequence number the sender should start with.

SysAdmin, Audit, Network, Security (SANS) Institute   A private, for-profit company that specializes in information security, cybersecurity training, and selling certificates.

System Center Configuration Manager (SCCM)   A systems management software product developed by Microsoft for managing large groups of computers. SCCM provides remote control, patch management, software distribution, operating system deployment, network access protection, and hardware and software inventory.

Systems Management Server (SMS)   This service includes detailed hardware inventory, software inventory and metering, software distribution and installation, and remote troubleshooting tools.

T

TCP flag   Part of the TCP packet header used to indicate connection state or provide additional information; often used in troubleshooting or hacking.

testing   A process conducted on a variable that returns a value of true or false.

three-way handshake   The exchange of packets used in a TCP/IP network to establish a connection between two devices. The three-way handshake uses the SYN, SYN-ACK, and ACK packets, in that order.

Transmission Control Protocol/Internet Protocol (TCP/IP)   A suite of communication protocols used to interconnect devices on the Internet or on a private computer network.

Triple Data Encryption Standard (3DES)   A standard developed to address the vulnerabilities of DES; it improves security, but encrypting and decrypting data take longer.

Trojan program   A program that disguises itself as a legitimate program or application but has a hidden payload that might send information from the attacked computer to the creator or to a recipient located anywhere in the world.

U

Unified Threat Management (UTM) device   A single device that combines many network protection functions, such as those performed by routers, firewalls, intrusion detection and prevention systems, VPNs, web-filtering systems, and malware detection and filtering systems.

User Datagram Protocol (UDP)   A connectionless communication protocol for establishing low-latency and loss-tolerating connections on an IP network. It is faster than TCP partially because it allows data transfer before an agreement is provided by the receiving party.

user mode   The default method on a Cisco router, used to perform basic troubleshooting tests and list information stored on the router. In this mode, no changes can be made to the router's configuration.

V

virtual directory   A pointer to a physical directory on a web server.

virus   A program that attaches itself to a host program or file.

virus signature file   A file maintained by antivirus software that contains signatures of known viruses; antivirus software checks this file to determine whether a program or file on your computer is infected.

vulnerability   A weakness, flaw, or error in a computing device or its software that allows the device to be accessed or manipulated in an unexpected way (such as allowing unauthorized user to access the device and its data).

vulnerability assessment   The process of identifying, quantifying, and ranking the vulnerabilities in a computer system, application, or network.

W

wardriving   The act of driving around an area with a computing device that has a WNIC, scanning software, and an antenna to discover available SSIDs in the area.

web application firewall (WAF)   An application-awareness firewall that protects web applications by detecting specific threats that target web applications and acting to protect them.

web beacon   A hidden item embedded in webpages for the purpose of tracking user activity and harvesting user information. A web beacon can be a hidden graphic (such as a web bug) or pieces of code in the HTML source.

web bug   A small graphics file referenced in an <IMG> tag, used to collect information about the user. This file is created by a third-party company specializing in data collection.

WebGoat   A web-based application designed to teach security professionals about web application vulnerabilities.

while loop   A loop that repeats an action a certain number of times while a condition is true or false.

white box model   A penetration testing model in which full network and system information is shared with the tester, including network maps and credentials.

white-listing   A security method involving explicitly listing acceptable items, such as programs, IP addresses, or URLs, for an activity; if an item is not on the white-list, its associated activity is denied. For example, a white-list typically contains programs that are allowed to run on a user's computer.

Wi-Fi Protected Access (WPA, WPA2, and WPA3)   An 802.11i standard that addresses WEP security vulnerabilities in 802.11b; improves encryption by using Temporal Key Integrity Protocol (TKIP). *See also* Wired Equivalent Privacy (WEP).

Wi-Fi Protected Setup (WPS)   A network security standard to create a secure wireless home network. WPS enables users who know little about wireless security to add new wireless devices to an existing network without having to enter long passphrases. This is often accomplished by pressing the WPS button on the home wireless router.

Windows Software Update Services (WSUS) A free add-in component that simplifies the process of keeping Windows computers current with the latest critical updates, patches, and service packs. WSUS installs a web-based application that runs on a Windows server.

Wired Equivalent Privacy (WEP) An 802.11b standard developed to encrypt data traversing a wireless network.

wireless LAN (WLAN) A network that relies on wireless technology (radio waves) to operate.

wireless network interface cards (WNICs) Controller cards that send and receive network traffic via radio waves and are required on both APs and wireless-enabled computers to establish a WLAN connection.

wireless personal area network (WPAN) A wireless network specified by the 802.15 standard; usually means Bluetooth technology is used, although newer technologies are being developed. It's for one user only and covers an area of about 10 meters.

Worldwide Interoperability for Microwave Access (WiMAX) The most common implementation of the 802.16 MAN standard. *See also* metropolitan area network (MAN).

worm A program that replicates and propagates without needing a host.

Z

zombie A computer controlled by a hacker to conduct criminal activity without the owners' knowledge; usually part of a botnet. *See also* botnet.

zone transfer A method of transferring records from a DNS server to use in analysis of a network.

INDEX

ISBN-13: 978-0357509760
ISBN-10: 0357509765

90000

9 780357 509760